business 5e

business 5e

O.C. Ferrell
Belmont University

Geoffrey A. Hirt
DePaul University

Linda Ferrell
Belmont University

Mc
Graw
Hill
Education

business

SENIOR VICE PRESIDENT, PRODUCTS & MARKETS: **KURT L. STRAND**

VICE PRESIDENT, GENERAL MANAGER, PRODUCTS & MARKETS: **MICHAEL RYAN**

VICE PRESIDENT, CONTENT DESIGN & DELIVERY: **KIMBERLY MERIWETHER DAVID**

MANAGING DIRECTOR: **SUSAN GOUIJNSTOOK**

DIRECTOR: **MICHAEL ABLASSMEIR**

BRAND MANAGER: **ANKE WEEKES**

DIRECTOR, PRODUCT DEVELOPMENT: **MEGHAN CAMPBELL**

LEAD PRODUCT DEVELOPER: **KELLY DELSO**

PRODUCT DEVELOPER: **GABRIELA G. VELASCO**

MARKETING MANAGER: **MICHAEL GEDATUS**

DIRECTOR, CONTENT DESIGN & DELIVERY: **TERRI SCHIESL**

PROGRAM MANAGER: **MARY CONZACHI**

CONTENT PROJECT MANAGERS: **CHRISTINE VAUGHAN; DANIELLE CLEMENT**

BUYER: **LAURA M. FULLER**

DESIGN: **DEBRA KUBIAK**

CONTENT LICENSING SPECIALISTS: **LORI HANCOCK; DEANNA DAUSENER**

COVER IMAGE: © **PLANET PICTURES/GETTY IMAGES**

COMPOSITOR: **SPi GLOBAL**

TYPEFACE: **10/12 STIX MATHJAX MAIN**

PRINTER: **R.R. DONNELLEY**

M: BUSINESS

Published by McGraw-Hill Education, 2 Penn Plaza, New York, NY 10121. Copyright © 2017 by McGraw-Hill Education. All rights reserved. Printed in the United States of America. Previous edition © 2015, 2013, 2011 and 2009. No part of this publication may be reproduced or distributed in any form or by any means, or stored in a database or retrieval system, without the prior written consent of McGraw-Hill Education, including, but not limited to, in any network or other electronic storage or transmission, or broadcast for distance learning.

Some ancillaries, including electronic and print components, may not be available to customers outside the United States.

This book is printed on acid-free paper.

1 2 3 4 5 6 7 8 9 0 RMN/RMN 1 0 9 8 7 6

ISBN 978-1-259-57814-4
MHID 1-259-57814-3

All credits appearing on page or at the end of the book are considered to be an extension of the copyright page.

Library of Congress Control Number: 2015953389

The Internet addresses listed in the text were accurate at the time of publication. The inclusion of a website does not indicate an endorsement by the authors or McGraw-Hill Education, and McGraw-Hill Education does not guarantee the accuracy of the information presented at these sites.

mheducation.com/highered

brief contents

contents

part two   STARTING AND GROWING A BUSINESS

CHAPTER 4   OPTIONS FOR ORGANIZING BUSINESS 76

CHAPTER 5   SMALL BUSINESS, ENTREPRENEURSHIP, AND FRANCHISING 96

part three   MANAGING FOR QUALITY AND COMPETITIVENESS

CHAPTER 6   THE NATURE OF MANAGEMENT 112

part four   CREATING THE HUMAN RESOURCE ADVANTAGE

part five MARKETING: DEVELOPING RELATIONSHIPS

part SIX   FINANCING THE ENTERPRISE

CHAPTER 14   ACCOUNTING AND FINANCIAL STATEMENTS 266

CHAPTER 15   MONEY AND THE FINANCIAL SYSTEM 290

CHAPTER 16   FINANCIAL MANAGEMENT AND SECURITIES MARKETS 308

TOC images: p. iii, © Jorg Greuel/Getty Images, RF; p. iv (top), © Doug Armand/Getty images, RF; p. iv (bottom), © Comstock Images/Alamy, RF; p. v, © Purestock/Superstock, RF; p. vi, © Ingram Publishing, RF; p. vii, © pictafollo/Getty Images, RF; p. viii, © Stockbyte/PunchStock, RF

changes to the
fifth edition

chapter one

- Expansion of operations management
- Expansion of marketing management
- Reestablishment of relations with Cuba
- New features: "Supply and Demand in Action: Russia's Ban of EU Food Triggers Lower Prices" and "Ben and Jerry's in Conflict with Parent Company"
- New entrepreneurship feature: "Uber Takes on Taxi Industry"
- New Figures: Figure 1.3 "Average Annual Unemployment Rate, Civilian Labor Force 16 Years and Over" and Figure 1.4 "Growth in U.S. Gross Domestic Product"
- New information on deflation
- New Table 1.2 "Economic Indicators of Different Countries"
- New paragraph on standard of living
- New Figure 1.5 "Growth in Social Media Sites"
- Link between diversity and financial performance

chapter two

- New Figure 2.1 "Global Trust in Different Institutions"
- New features: "The NCAA: Should College Athletics Be Paid?" and "Solar Energy Merges Sustainability with Good Business"
- New Tables: Table 2.4 "Least Corrupt Countries;" Table 2.8 "A Selection of the World's Most Ethical Companies;" and Table 2.9 "The Arguments for and Against Social Responsibility"
- European antitrust investigation into Google
- New entrepreneurial feature: "Tankchair: Not Your Average Wheelchair"
- New legal appendix feature: "Sirius XM Faces Complex Copyright Laws"

chapter three

- New features: "Tata Motors Depends on Jaguar and Land Rover" and "Global Warming May Create Economic Independence for Greenland"
- New Figures: Figure 3.1 "U.S. Exports to China (Millions of U.S. Dollars)" and Figure 3.2 "Top Exporting Countries"
- New "Right to Be Forgotten" law in Europe
- New entrepreneurship feature: "Lavender-Laced Teddy Bear Finds Insatiable Demand in China"

chapter four

- New Table 4.2 "Keys to Success in Business Partnerships"
- Definition of a master limited partnership
- New features: "Arizona Tea: The Challenges of Partnerships" and "Companies Use Poison Pill to Maintain Control"
- Description of 501(c)(3) organizations
- New entrepreneurial feature: "OtterBox: From Water Sports Industry to Mobile Technology"

chapter five

- Section on nonstore retailing
- New entrepreneurial feature: "Finding Fortune in a Food Truck"
- New Tables: Table 5.4 "Successful Traits of Young Entrepreneurs" and "Table 5.6 Fastest Growing and Hottest New Franchises"
- Description of micropreneurs
- New features: "New Light Technologies Defies the Odds with Carbon-Based Plastics" and "Warby Parker Does Glasses Its Own Way"
- Description of incubators
- Description of home-based businesses

chapter six

- New features: "Sergio Marchionne Maps Out Strategic Plan for Fiat-Chrysler Merger" and "Business Challenges for GM's First Female CEO"
- New Tables: Table 6.1 "CEO Compensation" and Table 6.4 "Managerial Roles"
- New entrepreneurial feature: Philip Pillsbury: "The Entrepreneur Behind the Billion-Dollar Brand"
- Definition of brainstorming

chapter seven

- New features: "W.L. Gore Succeeds with Informal Organizational Structure" and "Yum! Brands Inc. Develops a Culture of Teambuilding and Employee Recognition"
- New Figures: Figure 7.1 "Most Preferred Company Culture Attributes" and Figure 7.4 "City of Pineapple Paradise Organizational Chart"
- New Table 7.2 "Types of Formal Communication"
- New entrepreneurial feature: "Crisis Management Focused on Communication"
- Example of inappropriate use of e-mail in the workplace

chapter eight

- New Tables: Table 8.1 "Characteristics of Services" and Table 8.3 "2014 Airline Scorecard (Best to Worst)"
- New entrepreneurial feature: "iRobot: Robots for the Real World"
- Paragraph on the use of drones in business operations
- New features: "Food Giants Investing in Sustainability" and "A Manufacturer with Human-Focused Leadership"
- New Figure 8.4 "J.D. Power and Associates Initial Automobile Quality Study"
- Information on ISO 19600

chapter nine

- New features: "New Belgium Brewing—The Exceptional Workplace" and "Clif Bar Ranks as One of the Best Workplaces"
- New entrepreneurial feature: "Radio Flyer Carts in a New Company Culture"
- New Figure 9.2 "Job Aspects Important to Employee Satisfaction"
- New Tables: Table 9.4 "Comparison of Theories X, Y, and Z" and Table 9.5 "Types of Reinforcement"
- New section on goal-setting theory and management by objectives
- Explanation of behavior modification

chapter ten

- New Figures: Figure 10.1 "Recruiting through Social Media;" Figure 10.2 "U.S. Population Employed by Age Group (in Thousands);" Figure 10.3 "How HR Professionals View Performance Evaluations at Their Firms;" and Figure 10.4 "Union Membership Rate by State"
- New features: "Companies Use Charities to Attract Millennials" and "Using Empowered Employees to Help Manage a Changing Work Environment"
- Descriptions of mentoring and exit interview
- New Table 10.7 "Costco versus Walmart"
- New entrepreneurial feature: "Urban Lending Solutions Hires Outside the Box"

chapter eleven

- New entrepreneurial feature: "Blue Bottle Coffee Provides a Quality Experience"
- New features: "Chobani: Marketing Greek Yogurt to America" and "Tesla's Marketing Approach Shocks the Car Industry"
- Section on business-to-business marketing
- Description of mass marketing
- Description of benefit segmentation
- New Table 11.2 "Companies with the Best Customer Service"

chapter twelve

- New features: "Seventh Generation Expands Beyond Household Goods into Water, Tea, Coffee" and "Advertising Regulation Challenges Small Businesses"

- New Tables: Table 12.2 "Common Test-Market Cities;" Table 12.3 "Best-Selling Car Brands in the World;" Table 12.4 "Personal Care and Cleaning Products Customer Satisfaction Ratings;" Table 12.5 "Types of Retailers;" and Table 12.6 "Major Wholesaling Functions"
- Entrepreneurial feature: "Wanelo: 11 Million Users, $100 Million Market Valuation, No Products"
- Definitions of direct marketing and direct selling

chapter thirteen

- New Figures: Figure 13.1 "Top Social Media Platforms for Teenagers" and Figure 13.2 "Percentage of Time Spent Using Different Smartphone Apps"
- New Tables: Table 13.2 "Popular Social and Digital Networks among Users" and Table 13.4 "Best Practices for Digital Marketing Campaigns"
- New entrepreneurial feature: "Lolly Wolly Doodle Company Goes Viral Using Facebook"
- New features: "Should Instagram Try to Make a Profit?" and "The Ethics of Internet Tracking and Behavioral Advertising"
- Updated information on online fraud
- Information on illicit online marketing

chapter fourteen

- New Table 14.1 "Prestige Rankings of Accounting Firms"
- Additional information on Greece and debt
- New features: "Transparency and Sustainability in Financial Disclosure" and "Do 'Bear-Raid' Firms Help Keep Companies Honest?"
- New entrepreneurial feature: "Accounting Firm Keeps Employees Moving"
- Starbucks and McDonald's have been replaced by Microsoft and Google for financial ratio examples

chapter fifteen

- Switzerland and the change in its fixed exchange rate
- Definition of reward cards
- New features: "Dodd-Frank Gives Banks Reason to Stay Smaller" and "The Challenges for Obtaining Small Business Loans"
- New Table 15.4 "Leading Diversified Financial Services Firms"
- New entrepreneurial feature: "Square Inc. Introduces the Square Stand"
- Section on shadow banking

chapter sixteen

- New features: "DuPont Masters Sustainability" and "Increased Disclosure, but Does Anyone Actually Read It?"
- Updated information on Apple financials
- New entrepreneurial feature: "Maveron: A Venture Capital Firm Focused on the Entrepreneur"
- New Figure 16.2 "Recent Performance of Stock Market and Dow Jones Industrial Average (DJIA)"

business 5e

chapter ONE

the dynamics of
business and economics

© narvikk/Getty Images, RF

LEARNING OBJECTIVES

After reading this chapter, you will be able to:

LO 1-1 Define basic concepts such as business, product, and profit.

LO 1-2 Identify the main participants and activities of business and explain why studying business is important.

LO 1-3 Define economics and compare the four types of economic systems.

LO 1-4 Describe the role of supply, demand, and competition in a free-enterprise system.

LO 1-5 Specify why and how the health of the economy is measured.

LO 1-6 Trace the evolution of the American economy and discuss the role of the entrepreneur in the economy.

We begin our study of business in this chapter by examining the fundamentals of business and economics. First, we introduce the nature of business, including its goals, activities, and participants. Next, we describe the basics of economics and apply them to the United States economy. Finally, we establish a framework for studying business in this text. ■

LO 1-1 Define basic concepts such as business, product, and profit.

THE NATURE OF BUSINESS

A **business** tries to earn a profit by providing products that satisfy people's needs and wants. The outcomes of its efforts are **products** that have both tangible and intangible characteristics that provide satisfaction and benefits. When you purchase a product, you are buying the benefits and satisfaction you think the product will provide. A Subway sandwich, for example, may be purchased to satisfy hunger, while a Honda Accord may be purchased to satisfy the need for transportation and the desire to present a certain image.

Most people associate the word *product* with tangible goods—an automobile, smartphone, coat, or some other tangible item. However, a product can also be a service, which occurs when people or machines provide or process something of value to customers. Dry cleaning, a checkup by a doctor, a movie or sports event—these are examples of services. Some services, such as Instagram, an online mobile photo and video sharing service, do not charge a fee for use but obtain revenue from ads on their sites. A product can also be an idea. Accountants and attorneys, for example, generate ideas for solving problems.

The Goal of Business

The primary goal of all businesses is to earn a **profit**, the difference between what it costs to make and sell a product and what a customer pays for it. If a company spends $8 to manufacture, finance, promote, and distribute a product that it sells for $10, the business earns a profit of $2 on each product sold. Businesses have the right to keep and use their profits as they choose—within legal limits—because profit is the reward for the risks they take in providing products. Earning profits contributes to society by creating resources that support our social institutions and government. Businesses that create profits, pay taxes, and create jobs are the foundation of our economy. In addition, profits must be earned in a responsible manner. Not all organizations are businesses, however. **Nonprofit organizations**, such as National Public Radio (NPR), Habitat for Humanity, and other charities and social causes, do not have the fundamental purpose of earning profits, although they may provide goods or services and engage in fundraising. Profits earned by businesses support nonprofit organizations through donations from employees.

To earn a profit, a person or organization needs management skills to plan, organize, and control the activities of the business and to find and develop employees so that it can make products consumers will buy. A business also needs marketing expertise to learn what products consumers need and want and to develop, manufacture, price, promote, and distribute those products. Additionally, a business needs financial resources and skills to fund, maintain, and expand its operations. Other challenges for businesspeople include abiding by laws and government regulations; acting in an ethical and socially responsible manner; and adapting to economic, technological, political, and social changes. Even nonprofit organizations engage in management, marketing, and finance activities to help reach their goals.

To achieve and maintain profitability, businesses have found that they must produce quality products, operate efficiently, and be socially responsible and ethical in dealing with customers, employees, investors, government regulators, and the community. Because these groups have a stake in the success and outcomes of a business, they are sometimes called **stakeholders**. Many businesses, for example, are concerned about how the production and distribution of their products affect the environment. New fuel requirements are forcing automakers to invest in smaller, lightweight cars. During times of low fuel prices, consumers tend to prefer bigger sport-utility vehicles (SUVs) and trucks, putting more of a strain on automakers to meet environmental requirements as well as consumer demands.[1] Others are

business individuals or organizations who try to earn a profit by providing products that satisfy people's needs.

product a good or service with tangible and intangible characteristics that provide satisfaction and benefits.

profit the difference between what it costs to make and sell a product and what a customer pays for it.

nonprofit organizations organizations that may provide goods or services but do not have the fundamental purpose of earning profits.

stakeholders groups that have a stake in the success and outcomes of a business.

Consumers search for organic and locally grown vegetables to support sustainability.
© Jeff Greenough/Getty Images, RF

concerned with promoting science, engineering, and mathematics careers among women. Traditionally these careers have been male-dominated. The Association for Women in Science focuses on helping women reach their full potential in these underrepresented fields.[2] Other companies, such as Home Depot, have a long history of supporting natural disaster victims, relief efforts, and recovery.

LO 1-2 Identify the main participants and activities of business and explain why studying business is important.

The People and Activities of Business

Figure 1.1 shows the people and activities involved in business. At the center of the figure are owners, employees, and customers; the outer circle includes the primary business activities—management, marketing, and finance. Owners have to put up resources—money or credit—to start a business. Employees are responsible for the work that goes on within a business. Owners can manage the business themselves or hire employees to accomplish this task. The president, CEO, and chair of the board of Procter & Gamble, David Taylor, does not own P&G, but is an employee who is responsible for managing all the other employees in a way that earns a profit for investors, who are the real owners. Finally, and most importantly, a business's major role is to satisfy the customers who buy its goods or services. Note also that people and forces beyond an organization's control—such as legal and regulatory forces, the economy, competition, technology, the political environment, and ethical and

social concerns—all have ~~~~~~~~~~~~~~~~ of businesses. You will learn more about these participants in business activities throughout this book. Next, we will examine the major activities of business.

Management Notice that in Figure 1.1 management and employees are in the same segment of the circle. This is because management involves developing plans, coordinating employees' actions to achieve the firm's goals, organizing people to work efficiently, and motivating them to achieve the business's goals. Management involves the functions of planning, organizing, leading, and controlling. Effective managers who are skilled in these functions display effective leadership, decision making, and implementation of work tasks. Management is also concerned with acquiring, developing, and using resources (including people) effectively and efficiently. Amazon enlists workers and suppliers through its Vendor Flex Program to make distribution more efficient.[3]

Operations is another element of management. Managers must oversee the firm's operations to ensure that resources are successfully transformed into goods and services. Although most people associate operations with the development of goods, operations management applies just as strongly to services. Managers at the Ritz-Carlton, for instance, are concerned with transforming resources such as employee actions and hotel amenities into a quality customer service experience. In essence, managers plan, organize, staff, and control the tasks required to carry out the work of the company or nonprofit organization. We take a closer look at management activities in Parts 3 and 4 of this text.

▼ **FIGURE 1.1**
Overview of the Business World

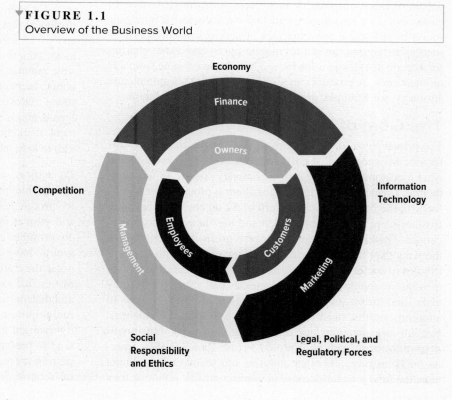

Marketing Marketing and consumers are in the same segment of Figure 1.1 because the focus of all marketing activities is satisfying customers. Marketing includes all the activities designed to provide goods and services that satisfy consumers' needs and wants. Marketers gather information and conduct research to determine what customers want. Using information gathered from marketing research, marketers plan and develop products and make decisions about how much to charge for their products and when and where to make them available. They also analyze the marketing environment to see if products need to be modified. Marketing focuses on the 4 Ps—product, price, place (or distribution), and promotion—also known as the marketing mix. Product management involves such key management decisions as product adoption or deletion, branding, and product positioning. Selecting the right price for the product is essential to the organization as it relates directly to profitability. Distribution is an important management concern because it involves making sure products are available to consumers in the right place at the right time. Marketers use promotion—advertising, personal selling, sales promotion (coupons, games, sweepstakes, movie tie-ins), and publicity—to communicate the benefits and advantages of their products to consumers and increase sales.

Mars, Inc. uses humorous advertising featuring its M&M's® spokescharacters to stimulate interest in M&M's® Chocolate Candies and Starburst® Jellybeans.
© *The Advertising Archives / Alamy*

Nonprofit organizations also use promotion. For example, the National Fluid Milk Processor Promotion Board's "milk mustache" advertising campaign has featured Brooke Shields, Beyoncé Knowles, Sheryl Crow, Elizabeth Hurley, Serena Williams, and even animated "celebrities" such as Garfield.[4] We will examine marketing activities in Part 5 of this text.

Finance Owners and finance are in the same part of Figure 1.1 because, although management and marketing have to deal with financial considerations, it is the primary responsibility of the owners to provide financial resources for the operation of the business. Moreover, the owners have the most to lose if the business fails to make a profit. Finance refers to all activities concerned with obtaining money and using it effectively. People who work as accountants, stockbrokers, investment advisors, or bankers are all part of the financial world. Owners sometimes have to borrow money from banks to get started or attract additional investors who become partners or stockholders. Owners of small businesses in particular often rely on bank loans for funding. Financial management is discussed later in the text.

Why Study Business?

Studying business can help you develop skills and acquire knowledge to prepare for your future career, regardless of whether you plan to work for a multinational Fortune 500 firm, start your own business, work for a government agency, or manage or volunteer at a nonprofit organization. The field of business offers a variety of interesting and challenging career opportunities throughout the world, such as marketing, human resources management, information technology, finance, production and operations, wholesaling and retailing, and many more.

Studying business can also help you better understand the many business activities that are necessary to provide satisfying goods and services—and that these activities carry a price tag. For example, if you buy a DVD or Blu-ray disc, about half of the price goes toward activities related to distribution and the retailer's expenses and profit margins. The production (pressing) of the disc represents about $1, or a small percentage of its price. Most businesses charge a reasonable price for their products to ensure that they cover their production costs, pay their employees, provide their owners with a return on their investment, and perhaps give something back to their local communities and societies. Bill Daniels founded Cablevision, building his first cable TV system in Casper, Wyoming, in 1953, and is now considered "the father of cable television." Prior to Daniels's passing in 2000, he had established a foundation that currently has funding of $1.1 billion and supports a diversity of causes from education to business ethics. During his career, Daniels created the Young Americans Bank, where children could create bank accounts and learn about financial responsibility, and this remains the world's only charter bank for young people. He named the Daniels College of Business through a donation of $20 million to the University of Denver. During his life, he affected many individuals and organizations, and his business success has allowed his legacy to be one of giving and impacting communities throughout the United States.[5] Most of the profits he earned in business continue to support nonprofit organizations and society. Thus, learning about business can help you become a well-informed consumer and member of society.

Business activities help generate the profits that are essential not only to individual businesses and local economies but also to the health of the global economy. Without profits, businesses find it difficult, if not impossible, to buy more raw materials, hire more employees, attract more capital, and create additional products that in turn make more profits and fuel the world economy. Understanding how our free-enterprise economic system allocates resources and provides incentives for industry and the workplace is important to everyone.

LO 1-3 Define economics and compare the four types of economic systems.

The Young Americans Bank in Denver was created by cable magnate Bill Daniels. It is the only chartered bank in the world that makes loans to children.
Courtesy of Young Americans Center for Financial Education

THE ECONOMIC FOUNDATIONS OF BUSINESS

To continue our introduction to business, it is useful to explore the economic environment in which business is conducted. In this section, we examine economic systems, the free-enterprise system, the concepts of supply and demand, and the role of competition. These concepts play important roles in determining how businesses operate in a particular society.

Economics is the study of how resources are distributed for the production of goods and services within a social system. You are already familiar with the types of resources available. Land, forests, minerals, water, and other things that are not made by people are **natural resources**. **Human resources**, or labor, refer to the physical and mental abilities that people use to produce goods and services. **Financial resources**, or **capital**, are the funds used to acquire the natural and human resources needed to provide products. These resources are related to the *factors of production,* consisting of land, labor, capital, and enterprise used to produce goods and services. The firm can also have intangible resources such as a good reputation for quality products or being socially responsible. The goal is to turn the factors of production and intangible resources into a competitive advantage.

Economic Systems

An **economic system** describes how a particular society distributes its resources to produce goods and services. A central issue of economics is how to fulfill an unlimited demand for goods and services in a world with a limited supply of resources. Different economic systems attempt to resolve this central issue in numerous ways, as we shall see.

Although economic systems handle the distribution of resources in different ways, all economic systems must address three important issues:

1. What goods and services, and how much of each, will satisfy consumers' needs?

2. How will goods and services be produced, who will produce them, and with what resources will they be produced?

3. How are the goods and services to be distributed to consumers?

Communism, socialism, and capitalism, the basic economic systems found in the world today (Table 1.1), have fundamental differences in the way they address these issues. The factors of production in command economies are controlled by government planning. In many cases, the government owns or controls the production of goods and services. Communism and socialism are, therefore, considered command economies.

Communism Karl Marx (1818–1883) first described **communism** as a society in which the people, without regard to class, own all the nation's resources. In his ideal political-economic system, everyone contributes according to ability and receives benefits according to need. In a communist economy, the people (through the government) own and operate all businesses and factors of production. Central government planning determines what goods and services satisfy citizens' needs, how the goods and services are produced, and how they are distributed. However, no true communist economy exists today that satisfies Marx's ideal.

On paper, communism appears to be efficient and equitable, producing less of a gap between rich and poor. In practice, however, communist economies have been marked by low standards of living, critical shortages of consumer goods, high prices, corruption, and little freedom. Russia, Poland, Hungary, and other eastern European nations have turned away from communism and toward economic systems governed by supply and demand rather than by central planning. However, their experiments with alternative economic systems have been fraught with difficulty and hardship. Cuba continues to apply communist principles to its economy, but Cuba is also experiencing economic and political change. Countries such as Venezuela have tried to incorporate communist economic principles. However, Venezuela has experienced economic failures even with large oil resources. Other communist countries have encountered similar difficulties. As a result of these economic challenges, communism is declining and its future as an economic system is uncertain. Even Cuba is experiencing changes to its predominately communist system. Massive government layoffs required many Cubans to turn toward the private sector, opening up more opportunities for entrepreneurship. President Obama has called for the reestablishment of relations with Cuba and an end to the embargo. Americans have more opportunities to visit Cuba than they have had for the past 50 years, although they still must apply for licenses and have one of 12 approved reasons for traveling there.[6] Similarly, China has become the first communist country to make strong economic gains by adopting capitalist approaches to business. The Chinese state is the largest shareholder among China's 150 largest companies and influences thousands of other businesses.[7] Economic prosperity has advanced in China with the government claiming to ensure market openness, equality, and fairness through state capitalism.[8]

Socialism **Socialism** is an economic system in which the government owns and operates basic industries—postal service, telephone, utilities, transportation, health care, banking, and some manufacturing—but individuals own most businesses. For example, in France the postal service industry La Poste is fully owned by the French government and makes a profit. Central planning determines what basic goods and services are produced, how they are produced, and how they are distributed. Individuals and small businesses provide other goods and services based on consumer demand and the availability of resources. Citizens are dependent on the government for many goods and services.

Most socialist nations, such as Sweden, India, and Israel, are democratic and recognize basic individual freedoms. Citizens can vote for political offices, but central government planners usually make decisions about what is best for the nation. People are free to go into the occupation of their choice, but they often work in government-operated organizations. Socialists believe their system permits a higher standard of living than other economic systems, but the difference often applies to the nation as a whole rather than to its individual citizens. Socialist economies profess egalitarianism—equal distribution of income and social services. They believe their economies are more stable than those of other nations. Although this may be true, taxes and unemployment are generally higher in socialist countries.

▼ **TABLE 1.1** Comparison of Communism, Socialism, and Capitalism

	Communism	Socialism	Capitalism
Business ownership	Most businesses are owned and operated by the government.	The government owns and operates some major industries; individuals own small businesses.	Individuals own and operate all businesses.
Competition	Government controls competition and regulates the economy.	Restricted in major industries; encouraged in small business.	Encouraged by market forces and government regulations.
Profits	Excess income goes to the government. The government supports economic and political institutions.	Profits earned by small businesses may be reinvested in the business; profits from government-owned industries go to the government.	Individuals and businesses are free to keep profits and use them as they wish after paying taxes.
Product availability and price	Consumers have a limited choice of goods and services; prices are usually high.	Consumers have some choice of goods and services; prices are determined by supply and demand.	Consumers have a wide choice of goods and services; prices are determined by supply and demand.
Employment options	Little choice in choosing a career; most people work for government-owned industries or farms.	More choice of careers; many people work in government jobs.	Unlimited choice of careers.

The Federal Trade Commission enforces anti-trust laws and monitors businesses to ensure fair competition.
© Paul J. Richards/AFP/Getty Images

of the ways in which the United States and Canadian governments regulate business is through laws. Laws such as the Federal Trade Commission Act, which created the Federal Trade Commission to enforce antitrust laws, illustrate the importance of the government's role in the economy. In the last recession, the government provided loans and took ownership positions in banks such as Citigroup, AIG (an insurance company), and General Motors. These actions were thought necessary to keep these firms from going out of business and creating a financial disaster for the economy.

Mixed Economies No country practices a pure form of communism, socialism, or capitalism, although most tend to favor one system over the others. Most nations operate as **mixed economies**, which have elements from more than one economic system. In socialist Sweden, most businesses are owned and operated by private individuals. In capitalist United States, an independent federal agency operates the postal service and another independent agency operates the Tennessee Valley Authority, an electric utility. In Great Britain and Mexico, the governments are attempting to sell many state-run businesses to private individuals and companies. In Germany, the Deutsche Post is privatized and trades on the stock market. In once-communist Russia, Hungary, Poland, and other eastern European nations, capitalist ideas have been implemented, including private ownership of businesses.

Countries such as China and Russia have used state capitalism to advance the economy. State capitalism tries to integrate the powers of the state with the advantages of capitalism. It is led by the government but uses capitalistic tools such as listing state-owned companies on the stock market and embracing globalization.[9] State capitalism includes some of the world's largest companies such as Russia's Gazprom, which is the largest natural gas company. China's ability to make huge investments to the point of creating entirely new industries puts many private industries at a disadvantage.[10] However, economists believe that state-run capitalism can contribute only so much to growth because officials cannot distribute resources as well as the market can.[11]

Perhaps as a result, many socialist countries have also experienced economic difficulties.

Capitalism **Capitalism**, or **free enterprise**, is an economic system in which individuals own and operate the majority of businesses that provide goods and services. Competition, supply, and demand determine which goods and services are produced, how they are produced, and how they are distributed. The United States, Canada, Japan, and Australia are examples of economic systems based on capitalism.

There are two forms of capitalism: pure capitalism and modified capitalism. In pure capitalism, also called a **free-market system**, all economic decisions are made without government intervention. This economic system was first described by Adam Smith in *The Wealth of Nations* (1776). Smith, often called the "father of capitalism," believed that the "invisible hand of competition" best regulates the economy. He argued that competition should determine what goods and services people need. Smith's system is also called *laissez-faire* ("let it be") *capitalism* because the government does not interfere in business.

Modified capitalism differs from pure capitalism in that the government intervenes and regulates business to some extent. One

> **Free enterprise provides an opportunity for a business to succeed or fail on the basis of market demand.**

The Free-Enterprise System

Many economies—including those of the United States, Canada, and Japan—are based on free enterprise, and many communist and socialist countries, such as China and Russia, are applying more principles of free enterprise to their own economic systems. Free enterprise provides an opportunity for a business to succeed or fail on the basis of market demand. In a free-enterprise system, companies that can efficiently manufacture and sell products that consumers desire will probably succeed. Inefficient businesses and those that sell products that do not offer needed benefits will likely fail as consumers take their business to firms that have more competitive products.

A number of basic individual and business rights must exist for free enterprise to work. These rights are the goals of many countries that have recently embraced free enterprise.

1. Individuals must have the right to own property and to pass this property on to their heirs. This right motivates people to work hard and save to buy property.

2. Individuals and businesses must have the right to earn profits and to use the profits as they wish, within the constraints of their society's laws, principles, and values.

3. Individuals and businesses must have the right to make decisions that determine the way the business operates. Although there is government regulation, the philosophy in countries like the United States and Australia is to permit maximum freedom within a set of rules of fairness.

4. Individuals must have the right to choose what career to pursue, where to live, what goods and services to purchase, and more. Businesses must have the right to choose where to locate, what goods and services to produce, what resources to use in the production process, and so on.

Without these rights, businesses cannot function effectively because they are not motivated to succeed. Thus, these rights make possible the open exchange of goods and services. In the countries that favor free enterprise, such as the United States, citizens have the freedom to make many decisions about the employment they choose and create their own productivity systems. Many entrepreneurs are more productive in free-enterprise societies because personal and financial incentives are available that can aid in entrepreneurial success. For many entrepreneurs, their work becomes a part of their system of goals, values, and lifestyle. Consider the panelists ("sharks") on the ABC program *Shark Tank*. Panelists on *Shark Tank* give entrepreneurs a chance to receive funding to realize their dreams by deciding whether to invest in their projects. They include Barbara Corcoran, who built one of New York's largest real estate companies; Mark Cuban, founder of Broadcast.com and MicroSolutions; and Daymond John, founder of clothing company FUBU.[12]

LO 1-4 Describe the role of supply, demand, and competition in a free-enterprise system.

The Forces of Supply and Demand

In the United States and in other free-enterprise systems, the distribution of resources and products is determined by supply and demand. **Demand** is the number of goods and services that

SUPPLY AND DEMAND IN ACTION: RUSSIA'S BAN OF EU FOOD TRIGGERS LOWER PRICES

Conflicts with other countries can impact the equilibrium price of certain products, which in turn can lead to changes in the economic cycle. Many Western powers—including the United States and the European Union (EU)—placed economic sanctions on Russia due to the conflicts in the Ukraine. Russia struck back, imposing a one-year embargo on a number of agricultural imports from any country sanctioning Russia. This had an immediate impact on the EU, where exports to Russia comprise a significant portion of the fruit, vegetable, dairy, and meat markets. Suddenly, a $6.5 billion export market halted.

A visible effect of the embargo included lower food prices across Europe. Considering the perishable nature of agricultural products, many producers have been forced to immediately switch to selling their surplus within the EU. This influx of supply, without any corresponding increase in consumer demand, provided a real-world demonstration of the classic supply and demand chart—prices plummeted. For example, in 2014 the cost of Dutch cucumbers and tomatoes had dropped 80 percent; in the Czech Republic, apple prices were down 70 percent; and Spanish, Italian, and Greek peaches and nectarines were selling at 30–50 percent cheaper.

While these price drops seem wonderful for consumers, producers facing lower prices were unable to turn a profit, which harmed their future viability and the long-term health of major European industries. The EU acknowledged this and called special meetings and provided emergency support measures for the worst-affected markets. This situation demonstrates how major changes in supply and demand brought about by trading conflicts can have an immediate impact on a nation's (or trade bloc's) economy.[13]

Discussion Questions

1. Analyze the EU's food price deflation using the theories of supply and demand, and chart what has happened on a supply and demand graph.

2. How important to business is the surrounding political and regulatory environment? How can businesses best deal with volatile political situations that might end up affecting them?

3. What are some ways the EU and its agricultural producers can deal with their oversupply and deflation issues?

consumers are willing to buy at different prices at a specific time. From your own experience, you probably recognize that consumers are usually willing to buy more of an item as its price falls because they want to save money. Consider hand-made rugs, for example. Consumers may be willing to buy six rugs at $350 each, four at $500 each, but only two at $650 each. The relationship between the price and the number of rugs consumers are willing to buy can be shown graphically with a *demand curve* (see Figure 1.2).

Supply is the number of products that businesses are willing to sell at different prices at a specific time. In general, because the potential for profits is higher, businesses are willing to supply more of a good or service at higher prices. For example, a company that sells rugs may be willing to sell six at $650 each, four at $500 each, but just two at $350 each. The relationship between the price of rugs and the quantity the company is willing to supply can be shown graphically with a *supply curve* (see Figure 1.2).

In Figure 1.2, the supply and demand curves intersect at the point where supply and demand are equal. The price at which the number of products that businesses are willing to supply equals the amount of products that consumers are willing to buy at a specific point in time is the **equilibrium price**. In our rug example, the company is willing to supply four rugs at $500 each, and consumers are willing to buy four rugs at $500 each. Therefore, $500 is the equilibrium price for a rug at that point in time, and most rug companies will price their rugs at $500. As you might imagine, a business that charges more than $500 (or whatever the current equilibrium price is) for its rugs will not sell many and might not earn a profit. On the other hand, a business that charges less than $500 accepts a lower profit per rug than could be made at the equilibrium price.

If the cost of making rugs goes up, businesses will not offer as many at the old price. Changing the price alters the supply curve, and a new equilibrium price results. This is an

> "Demand is the number of goods and services that consumers are willing to buy at different prices at a specific time."

FIGURE 1.2
Equilibrium Price of Handmade Rugs

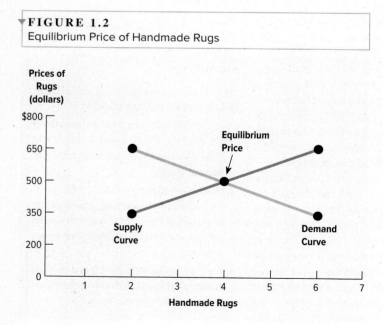

ongoing process, with supply and demand constantly changing in response to changes in economic conditions, availability of resources, and degree of competition. When the supply of oil became greater than demand in 2014–2015, the price per barrel dropped in half within months. The price of oil has fluctuated widely in the past four years, from $80 per barrel in January 2010 to a high of $125 per barrel in March 2012 down to a low of $46 in January 2015.[14] Prices for goods and services vary according to these changes in supply and demand. Supply and demand are the forces that drive the distribution of resources (goods and services, labor, and money) in a free-enterprise economy.

Critics of supply and demand say the system does not distribute resources equally. The forces of supply and demand prevent sellers who have to sell at higher prices (because their costs are high) and buyers who cannot afford to buy goods at the equilibrium price from participating in the market. According to critics, the wealthy can afford to buy more than they need, but the poor may be unable to buy enough of what they need to survive.

This entrepreneur is opening up her own business. Entrepreneurs are more productive in free-enterprise systems.
© *Jim Esposito/Getty Images, RF*

The Nature of Competition

Competition, the rivalry among businesses for consumers' dollars, is another vital element in free enterprise. According to Adam Smith, competition fosters efficiency and low prices by forcing producers to offer the best products at the most reasonable price; those who fail to do so are not able to stay in business. Thus, competition should improve the quality of the goods and services available or reduce prices. Competition allows for open markets and provides opportunities for both individuals and businesses to successfully compete. Entrepreneurs can discover new technology, ways to lower prices, as well as methods for providing better distribution or services. Founder Jeff Bezos of

Amazon.com is a prime example. He created an Internet bookstore at the height of the dot-com era in the 1990s. By avoiding building as well as other brick-and-mortar costs, Amazon was able to offer products at competitive prices and continued to succeed even after the dot-com bubble burst. Today Amazon competes against such retail giants as Walmart in a number of industries, including entertainment, food, and consumer products. Its success in online retail has prompted rivals such as Barnes & Noble to open their own online stores to complement their brick-and-mortar locations.

Within a free-enterprise system, there are four types of competitive environments: pure competition, monopolistic competition, oligopoly, and monopoly.

Pure competition exists when there are many small businesses selling one standardized product, such as agricultural commodities like wheat, corn, and cotton. No one business sells enough of the product to influence the product's price. And, because there is no difference in the products, prices are determined solely by the forces of supply and demand.

Monopolistic competition exists when there are fewer businesses than in a pure-competition environment and the differences among the goods they sell is small. Aspirin, soft drinks, and vacuum cleaners are examples of such goods. These products differ slightly in packaging, warranty, name, and other characteristics, but all satisfy the same consumer need. Businesses have some power over the price they charge in monopolistic competition because they can make consumers aware of product differences through advertising. Jawbone, for example, differentiates its Jambox portable speakers through product design and quality. Consumers value some features more than others and are often willing to pay higher prices for a product

> "Competition, the rivalry among businesses for consumers' dollars, is another vital element in free enterprise."

UBER TAKES ON TAXI INDUSTRY

Thanks to Uber and rivals such as Lyft, taxis are no longer the only way to be driven where you need to go. As a "ride-sharing" service, Uber operates via a mobile phone app that connects drivers—everyday people with cars—with passengers who want to get somewhere. The passenger's credit card is automatically charged, and the driver gets a commission. Since its founding in 2009, Uber has expanded to 92 U.S. and 70 non-U.S. cities. It is valued at over $40 billion.

However, taxi companies and driver unions are fighting back. They argue that the ride-sharing model is a taxi service in disguise and should be held to the same rules as taxies, including strict driver training, licensing, and oversight requirements. Although Uber claims these arguments are the desperate attempts of an outdated industry to protect itself from progress, many governments have begun limiting Uber from operating until they can determine how to regulate it. Uber claims a French law regulating car-service apps is unconstitutional. A rape allegation involving an Uber driver in India also resulted in a temporary nationwide ban on smartphone-enabled taxi services. Uber faces numerous challenges in bringing ride-sharing into the mainstream.[15]

with the features they want. For example, many consumers are willing to pay a higher price for organic fruits and vegetables rather than receive a bargain on nonorganic foods. The same holds true for non-genetically modified foods.

An **oligopoly** exists when there are very few businesses selling a product. In an oligopoly, individual businesses have control over their products' price because each business supplies a large portion of the products sold in the marketplace. Nonetheless, the prices charged by different firms stay fairly close because a price cut or increase by one company will trigger a similar response from another company. In the airline industry, for example, when one airline cuts fares to boost sales, other airlines quickly follow with rate decreases to remain competitive. On the other hand, airlines often raise prices at the same time. Oligopolies exist when it is expensive for new firms to enter the marketplace. Not just anyone can acquire enough financial capital to build an automobile production facility or purchase enough airplanes and related resources to build an airline.

When there is one business providing a product in a given market, a **monopoly** exists. Utility companies that supply electricity, natural gas, and water are monopolies. The government permits such monopolies because the cost of creating the good or supplying the service is so great that new producers cannot compete for sales. Government-granted monopolies are subject to government-regulated prices. Some monopolies exist because of technological developments that are protected by patent laws. Patent laws grant the developer of new technology a period of time (usually 20 years) during which no other producer can use the same technology without the agreement of the original developer. The United States granted its first patent in 1790. Now its patent office receives hundreds of thousands of patent applications a year; Asian countries—including Japan, China, and South Korea—are not far behind.[16] This type of monopoly allows the developer to recover research, development, and production expenses and to earn a reasonable profit. An example of this type of monopoly is the dry-copier process developed by Xerox. Xerox's patents have expired, however, and many imitators have forced market prices to decline.

Economic Cycles and Productivity

Expansion and Contraction Economies are not stagnant; they expand and contract. **Economic expansion** occurs when an economy is growing and people are spending more money. Their purchases stimulate the production of goods and services, which in turn stimulates employment. The standard of living rises because more people are employed and have money to spend. Rapid expansions of the economy, however, may result in **inflation**, a continuing rise in prices. Inflation can be harmful if individuals' incomes do not increase at the same pace as rising prices, reducing their buying power. The worst case of hyperinflation occurred in Hungary in 1946. At one point, prices were doubling every 15.6 hours. One of the most recent cases of hyperinflation occurred in Zimbabwe.[17] Zimbabwe suffered from hyperinflation so severe that its inflation percentage rate rose into the hundreds of millions. With the elimination of the Zimbabwean dollar and certain price controls, the inflation rate began to decrease, but not before the country's economy was virtually decimated.[18]

Economic contraction occurs when spending declines. Businesses cut back on production and lay off workers, and the economy as a whole slows down. Contractions of the economy lead to **recession**—a decline in production, employment, and income. Recessions are often characterized by rising levels of **unemployment**, which is measured as the percentage of the population that wants to work but is unable to find jobs. Figure 1.3 shows the overall unemployment rate in the civilian labor force over the past 80 years. Rising unemployment levels tend to stifle demand for goods and services, which can have the effect of forcing prices downward, a condition known as *deflation*. Deflation poses a serious economic problem because price decreases could result in consumers delaying purchases. If consumers wait for lower prices, the economy could fall into a recession. The European Union faced the dangers of inflation in 2015. France experienced major deflation, an occurrence that spelled trouble for the rest of the Eurozone as France is the union's second largest economy.[19]

The United States has experienced numerous recessions, the most recent ones occurring in 1990–1991, 2002–2003, and 2008–2011. The most recent recession (or economic slowdown) was caused by the collapse in housing prices and consumers' inability to stay current on their mortgage and credit card payments. This caused a crisis in the banking industry, with the government bailing out banks to keep them from failing. This in turn caused a slowdown in spending on consumer goods and an increase in unemployment. Unemployment reached 10 percent of the labor force. Don't forget that personal consumption makes up almost 70 percent of gross domestic product, so consumer behavior is extremely important for economic activity. A severe recession may turn into a **depression**, in which unemployment is very high, consumer spending is low, and business output is sharply reduced, such as what occurred in the United States in the early 1930s. The most recent recession is often called the

recession a decline in production, employment, and income.

unemployment the condition in which a percentage of the population wants to work but is unable to find jobs.

depression a condition of the economy in which unemployment is very high, consumer spending is low, and business output is sharply reduced.

gross domestic product (GDP) the sum of all goods and services produced in a country during a year.

Great Recession because it was the longest and most severe economic decline since the Great Depression.

Economies expand and contract in response to changes in consumer, business, and government spending. War also can affect an economy, sometimes stimulating it (as in the United States during World Wars I and II) and sometimes stifling it (as during the Vietnam, Persian Gulf, and Iraq wars). Although fluctuations in the economy are inevitable and to a certain extent predictable, their effects—inflation, deflation, and unemployment—disrupt lives and thus governments try to minimize them.

LO 1-5 Specify why and how the health of the economy is measured.

Measuring the Economy Countries measure the state of their economies to determine whether they are expanding or contracting and whether corrective action is necessary to minimize the fluctuations. One commonly used measure is **gross domestic product (GDP)**—the sum of all goods and services produced in

FIGURE 1.3
Annual Average Unemployment Rate, Civilian Labor Force 16 Years and Over

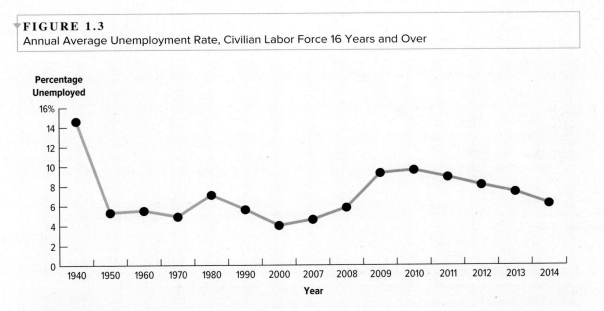

Source: Bureau of Labor Statistics, "Labor Force Statistics from the Current Population Survey," http://data.bls.gov/timeseries/LNS14000000 (accessed January 13, 2015).

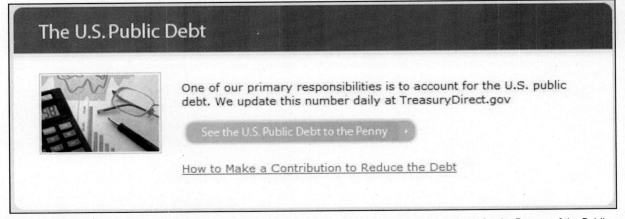

The U.S. Public Debt

One of our primary responsibilities is to account for the U.S. public debt. We update this number daily at TreasuryDirect.gov

See the U.S. Public Debt to the Penny ›

How to Make a Contribution to Reduce the Debt

You can see what the U.S. government currently owes—down to the penny—by going to the website for the Bureau of the Public Debt, https://www.fiscal.treasury.gov/.
Courtesy of the U.S. Department of the Treasury Bureau of the Public Debt

a country during a year. GDP measures only those goods and services made within a country and therefore does not include profits from companies' overseas operations; it does include profits earned by foreign companies within the country being measured. However, it does not take into account the concept of GDP in relation to population (GDP per capita). Figure 1.4 shows the increase in GDP over several years, while Table 1.2 compares a number of economic statistics for a sampling of countries. Note that although the United States has greater GDP than China, when adjusted for cost of living (purchasing power parity), China actually surpasses the United States by $200 billion.[20]

Another important indicator of a nation's economic health is the relationship between its spending and income (from taxes). When a nation spends more than it takes in from taxes, it has a **budget deficit**. In the 1990s, the U.S. government eliminated

---

▼FIGURE 1.4
Growth in U.S. Gross Domestic Product

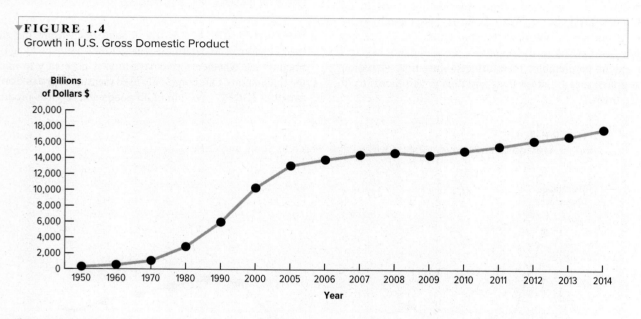

Source: U.S. Department of Commerce Bureau of Economic Analysis, "National Economic Accounts," www.bea.gov/national/index.htm#gdp (accessed February 4, 2015).

▼ TABLE 1.2 Economic Indicators of Different Countries

Country	GDP (in billions of dollars)	GDP per Capita	Unemployment Rate (%)	Inflation Rate (%)
Argentina	$771	$18,600	7.5%	20.8%
Australia	$998.3	$43,000	5.7%	2.4%
Brazil	$2,416	$12,100	5.7%	6.2%
Canada	$1,518	$43,100	7.1%	1.0%
China	$13,390	$9,800	4.1%	2.6%
France	$2,276	$35,700	10.2%	0.9%
Germany	$3,227	$39,500	5.3%	1.6%
India	$4,990	$4,000	8.8%	9.6%
Israel	$273.2	$36,200	5.8%	1.7%
Japan	$4,729	$37,100	4.1%	0.2%
Mexico	$1,845	$15,600	4.9%	4.0%
Russia	$2,553	$18,100	5.8%	6.8%
South Africa	$595.7	$11,500	24.9%	5.8%
United Kingdom	$2,387	$37,300	7.2%	2.0%
United States	$17,711	$52,800	6.2%	1.5%

Sources: Adapted from the CIA, *The World Fact Book*, www.cia.gov/library/publications/the-world-factbook/rankorder/rankorderguide.html (accessed January 13, 2015); U.S. Department of Commerce Bureau of Economic Analysis, "National Economic Accounts," www.bea.gov/national/index.htm#gdp (accessed February 4, 2015).

its long-standing budget deficit by balancing the money spent for social, defense, and other programs with the amount of money taken in from taxes.

In recent years, however, the budget deficit has reemerged and grown to record levels, partly due to defense spending in the aftermath of the terrorist attacks of September 11, 2001. Massive government stimulus spending during the most recent recession also increased the national debt. Because many Americans do not want their taxes increased and Congress has difficulty agreeing on appropriate tax rates, it is difficult to increase taxes and reduce the deficit. Like consumers and businesses, when the government needs money, it borrows from the public, banks, and even foreign investors. In 2014, the national debt (the amount of money the nation owes its lenders) approached a new high at $18 trillion.[21] This figure is especially worrisome because, to reduce the debt to a manageable level, the government either has to increase its revenues (raise taxes) or reduce spending on social, defense, and legal programs, neither of which is politically popular. The size of the national debt and little agreement on how to reduce the deficit caused the credit rating of the U.S. debt to go down. The national debt figure changes daily and can be seen at the Department of the Treasury, Bureau of the Public Debt, website. Table 1.3 describes some of the other ways we evaluate our nation's economy.

LO 1-6 Trace the evolution of the American economy and discuss the role of the entrepreneur in the economy.

THE AMERICAN ECONOMY

As we said previously, the United States is a mixed economy with a foundation based on capitalism and free enterprise. The answers to the three basic economic issues are determined primarily by competition and the forces of supply and demand, although the federal government does intervene in economic decisions to a certain extent. For instance, the federal government exerts oversight over the airline industry to make sure airlines remain economically viable as well as for safety and security purposes. **Standard of living** refers to the level of wealth and material comfort that people have available to them. The United States, Germany, Australia, and Norway all have a high standard of living, meaning that most of their citizens are able to afford basic necessities and some degree of comfort. These nations are often characterized by a high GDP per capita. However, a higher GDP per capita does not automatically translate into a higher standard of living. Costs of goods and services is also a factor. The European Union and Japan, for instance, tend to have higher costs of living than the United States. Higher prices mean that it costs more to obtain a certain level of comfort than it does in other countries. Countries with low standards of living are usually characterized by poverty, higher unemployment, and lower education rates. To understand the current state of the American economy and its effect on business practices, it is helpful to examine its history and the roles of the entrepreneur and the government.

A Brief History of the American Economy

The Early Economy Before the colonization of North America, Native Americans lived as hunter/gatherers and farmers, with some trade among tribes. The colonists who came later operated primarily as an *agricultural economy*. People were self-sufficient and produced everything they needed at home, including food, clothing, and furniture. Abundant natural resources and a moderate climate nourished industries such as farming, fishing, shipping, and fur trading. A few manufactured goods and money for the colonies' burgeoning industries came from England and other countries.

As the nation expanded slowly toward the West, people found natural resources such as coal, copper, and iron ore and used them to produce goods such as horseshoes, farm implements, and kitchen utensils. Farm families who produced surplus goods sold or traded them for things they could not produce

budget deficit the condition in which a nation spends more than it takes in from taxes.

standard of living The level of wealth and material comfort that people have available to them.

▼ **TABLE 1.3** How Do We Evaluate Our Nation's Economy?

Unit of Measure	Description
Trade balance	The difference between our exports and our imports. If the balance is negative, as it has been since the mid-1980s, it is called a trade deficit and is generally viewed as unhealthy for our economy.
Consumer Price Index	Measures changes in prices of goods and services purchased for consumption by typical urban households.
Per capita income	Indicates the income level of "average" Americans. Useful in determining how much "average" consumers spend and how much money Americans are earning.
Unemployment rate	Indicates how many working-age Americans are not working who otherwise want to work.*
Inflation	Monitors price increases in consumer goods and services over specified periods of time. Used to determine if costs of goods and services are exceeding worker compensation over time.
Worker productivity	The amount of goods and services produced for each hour worked.

* Americans who do not work in a traditional sense, such as househusbands/housewives, are not counted as unemployed.

entrepreneur an individual who risks his or her wealth, time, and effort to develop for profit an innovative product or way of doing something.

themselves, such as fine furniture and window glass. Some families also spent time turning raw materials into clothes and household goods. Because these goods were produced at home, this system was called the domestic system.

The Industrial Revolution The 19th century and the Industrial Revolution brought the development of new technology and factories. The factory brought together all the resources needed to make a product—materials, machines, and workers. Work in factories became specialized as workers focused on one or two tasks. As work became more efficient, productivity increased, making more goods available at lower prices. Railroads brought major changes, allowing farmers to send their surplus crops and goods all over the nation for barter or for sale.

Factories began to spring up along the railways to manufacture farm equipment and a variety of other goods to be shipped by rail. Samuel Slater set up the first American textile factory after he memorized the plans for an English factory and emigrated to the United States. Eli Whitney revolutionized the cotton industry with his cotton gin. Francis Cabot Lowell's factory organized all the steps in manufacturing cotton cloth for maximum efficiency and productivity. John Deere's farm equipment increased farm production and reduced the number of farmers required to feed the young nation. Farmers began to move to cities to find jobs in factories and a higher standard of living. Henry Ford developed the assembly-line system to produce automobiles. Workers focused on one part of an automobile and then pushed it to the next stage until it rolled off the assembly line as a finished automobile. Ford's assembly line could manufacture many automobiles efficiently, and the price of his cars was $200, making them affordable to many Americans.

The Manufacturing and Marketing Economies Industrialization brought increased prosperity, and the United States gradually became a *manufacturing economy*—one devoted to manufacturing goods and providing services rather than producing agricultural products. The assembly line was applied to more industries, increasing the variety of goods available to the consumer. Businesses became more concerned with the needs of the consumer and entered the *marketing economy*. Expensive goods such as cars and appliances could be purchased on a time-payment plan. Companies conducted research to find out what products consumers needed and wanted. Advertising made consumers aware of products and important information about features, prices, and other competitive advantages.

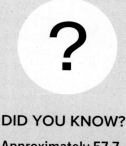

DID YOU KNOW?

Approximately 57.7 percent of adult women are engaged in the workforce.[24]

Because these developments occurred in a free-enterprise system, consumers determined what goods and services were produced. They did this by purchasing the products they liked at prices they were willing to pay. The United States prospered, and American citizens had one of the highest standards of living in the world.

The Service and New Digital Economy After World War II, with the increased standard of living, Americans had more money and more time. They began to pay others to perform services that made their lives easier. Beginning in the 1960s, more and more women entered the workforce. The United States began experiencing major shifts in the population. The U.S. population grew 9.7 percent in the past decade to about 316 million. This is the slowest pace of growth since the Great Depression, with the South leading the population gains. The United States is undergoing a baby bust, with record lows in the country's fertility rate.[22] While the birthrate in the United States is declining, new immigrants help with population gains.[23] The profile of the family is also changing: Today there are more single-parent families and individuals living alone, and in two-parent families, both parents often work.

One result of this trend is that time-pressed Americans are increasingly paying others to do tasks they used to do at home, like cooking, laundry, landscaping, and child care. These trends have gradually changed the United States to a *service economy*—one devoted to the production of services that make life easier for busy consumers. Businesses increased their demand for services, especially in the areas of finance and information technology. Service industries such as restaurants, banking, health care, child care, auto repair, leisure-related industries, and even education are growing rapidly and may account for as much as 80 percent of the U.S. economy. These trends continue with advanced technology contributing to new service products based on technology and digital media that provide smartphones, social networking, and virtual worlds. This has led to the growth of e-commerce, or transactions involving goods and services over the Internet. E-commerce has led to firms that would have been unheard of a few decades ago, such as eBay, Facebook, and Amazon.com. Figure 1.5 shows the growth in social media usage among adults over a three-year period. More about the digital world, business, and new online social media can be found in Chapter 13.

The Role of the Entrepreneur

An **entrepreneur** is an individual who risks his or her wealth, time, and effort to develop for profit an innovative product or

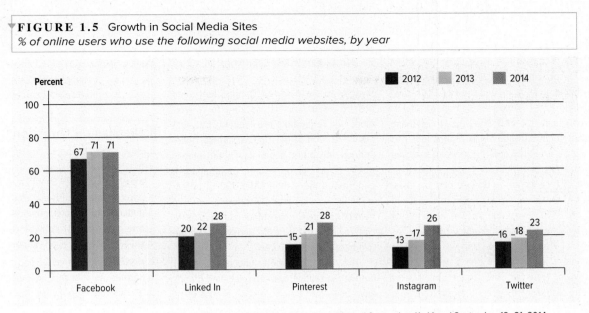

FIGURE 1.5 Growth in Social Media Sites
% of online users who use the following social media websites, by year

Percent

Legend: ■ 2012 ■ 2013 ■ 2014

Facebook: 67, 71, 71
Linked In: 20, 22, 28
Pinterest: 15, 21, 28
Instagram: 13, 17, 26
Twitter: 16, 18, 23

Source: Pew Research Center's Internet Project Surveys, 2012–2014. 2014 data collected September 11–14 and September 18–21, 2014. *N* = 1,597 Internet users ages 18+, www.pewinternet.org/2015/01/09/social-mediaupdate-2014/.

way of doing something. Stephen Gordon is a true American entrepreneur. Gordon opened a hardware store from his house that sold hardware intended for use in renovation. Calling it Restoration Hardware, Gordon faced many obstacles and was saved from bankruptcy with a family loan. However, through word-of-mouth marketing and smart business decisions, today the $1.6 billion company has expanded into 85 stores.[25]

The free-enterprise system provides the conditions necessary for entrepreneurs to succeed. In the past, entrepreneurs were often inventors who brought all the factors of production together to produce a new product. Thomas Edison, whose inventions include the record player and lightbulb, was an early American entrepreneur. Henry Ford was one of the first persons to develop mass assembly methods in the automobile industry. Other entrepreneurs, so-called captains of industry, invested in the country's growth. John D. Rockefeller built Standard Oil out of the fledgling oil industry, and Andrew Carnegie invested in railroads and founded the United States Steel Corporation. Andrew Mellon built the Aluminum Company of America and Gulf Oil. J.P. Morgan started financial institutions to fund the business activities of other entrepreneurs. Although these entrepreneurs were born in another century, their legacy to the American economy lives on in the companies they started, many of which still operate today. Colonel Eli Lilly in Indianapolis, Indiana, was continually frustrated with the quality of pharmaceutical products sold at the time. As a pharmaceutical chemist, he decided to start his own firm that would offer the highest-quality medicines. His firm, Eli Lilly and Company, would go on to make landmark achievements, including being one

of the first pharmaceutical firms to mass-produce penicillin. Today, Eli Lilly is the 10th largest pharmaceutical firm in the world.[26]

Entrepreneurs are constantly changing American business practices with new technology and innovative management techniques. Bill Gates, for example, built Microsoft, a software company whose products include Word and Windows, into a multibillion-dollar enterprise. Frederick Smith had an idea to deliver packages overnight, and now his FedEx Company plays an important role in getting documents and packages delivered all over the world for businesses and individuals. Steve Jobs co-founded Apple and turned the company into a successful consumer electronics firm that revolutionized many different industries, with products such as the iPod, iPhone, Mac computers, and iPad. The company went from near bankruptcy in the 1990s to become one of the most valuable brands in the entire world. Entrepreneurs have been associated with such uniquely American concepts as Dell Computers, Ben & Jerry's, Levi's, McDonald's, Dr Pepper, Apple, Google, Facebook, and Walmart. Walmart, founded by entrepreneur Sam Walton, was the first retailer to reach $100 billion in sales in one year and now routinely passes that mark, with more than $473 billion.[27] We will examine the importance of entrepreneurship further in Chapter 5.

The Role of Government in the American Economy

The American economic system is best described as modified capitalism because the government regulates business

Ben & Jerry's has a reputation for social responsibility and social activism. For example, in 1996 it sued the city of Chicago and the state of Illinois for the right to label its products as free of rBGH (a growth hormone given to cows to boost milk production), and in 2005 it helped create the world's largest Baked Alaska (a type of frozen dessert) as part of a campaign to oppose opening Alaska's Arctic National Wildlife Refuge to drilling.

In 2000, Ben & Jerry's was acquired by Unilever, a large multiproduct company. As part of the acquisition, Unilever agreed to remain hands-off about Ben & Jerry's social activism. However, this agreement is now being tested over a recent hot-button issue: the fight to pass laws requiring labeling of products containing genetically modified organisms (GMOs).

Ben & Jerry's has been vocal about its support for GMO labeling. It is working to switch entirely to non-GMO ingredients, and has provided financial backing for a Vermont law requiring GMO labeling (the first law of its kind in the United States). Unilever, on the other hand, has been equally public about its opposition to labeling; it contributed more than $450,000 to defeat a similar labeling law in California and is a member of the Grocery Manufacturers Association suing to block the Vermont law from taking effect.

The conflict has been uncomfortable for both organizations. Some pro-labeling groups have boycotted Ben & Jerry's because of its ties to Unilever. For its part, Unilever has kept to the agreement and declined to pressure Ben & Jerry's, but both companies' reputations may be damaged by their tie to each other. If the conflict continues to deepen, a resolution or even compromise will be needed.[28]

Discussion Questions

1. How involved should the relationship be between a large parent company and its many subsidiaries? Should the parent company require its subsidiaries to adhere to a unified set of values, practices, and corporate culture, or are differences and diversity allowable (or even valuable)?

2. How should companies tied together in a business relationship deal with fundamental differences between their values and practices?

3. What should Ben & Jerry's do in this situation? What should Unilever do?

Google Wallet is a mobile payments system that allows users to store their credit card or debit card information. When checking out at stores, users can bring up the app and use the information to pay for their purchases.
© PC Plus Magazine/Future/Getty Images

Many companies engage in socially responsible behavior to give back to their communities. Home Depot partners with Habitat for Humanity to build homes for disadvantaged families.
© Ariel Skelley/Blend Images/the Agency Collection/Getty Images, RF

to preserve competition and protect consumers and employees. Federal, state, and local governments intervene in the economy with laws and regulations designed to promote competition and to protect consumers, employees, and the environment. Many of these laws are discussed in the Chapter 2 Appendix.

> # BUSINESS ETHICS GENERALLY REFERS TO THE STANDARDS AND PRINCIPLES TO DEFINE APPROPRIATE AND INAPPROPRIATE CONDUCT IN THE WORKPLACE.

Additionally, government agencies such as the U.S. Department of Commerce measure the health of the economy (GDP, productivity, etc.) and, when necessary, take steps to minimize the disruptive effects of economic fluctuations and reduce unemployment. When the economy is contracting and unemployment is rising, the federal government through the Federal Reserve Board (see Chapter 15) tries to spur growth so that consumers will spend more money and businesses will hire more employees. To accomplish this, it may reduce interest rates or increase its own spending for goods and services. When the economy expands so fast that inflation results, the government may intervene to reduce inflation by slowing down economic growth. This can be accomplished by raising interest rates to discourage spending by businesses and consumers. Techniques used to control the economy are discussed in Chapter 15.

The Role of Ethics and Social Responsibility in Business

In the past few years, you may have read about a number of scandals at a number of well-known corporations, including General Motors, Honda, and Walmart, and even leading banks such as Bank of America and Citigroup. In many cases, misconduct by individuals within these firms had an adverse effect on current and retired employees, investors, and others associated with these firms. In some cases, individuals went to jail for their actions. These scandals undermined public confidence in corporate America and sparked a new debate about ethics in business. Business ethics generally refers to the standards and principles to define appropriate and inappropriate conduct in the workplace. In many cases, these standards have been codified as laws prohibiting actions deemed unacceptable.

Society is increasingly demanding that businesspeople behave socially responsibly toward their stakeholders, including customers, and also their employees, investors, government regulators, communities, and the natural environment. Diversity in the workforce is not only socially responsible but also highly beneficial to the financial performance of companies. According to a McKinsey consulting firm study, organizations that have diverse leadership are more likely to report higher financial returns. This study defined diversity as women and minorities. Diversity creates increased employee satisfaction and improved decision making.[29]

While one view is that ethics and social responsibility are a good supplement to business activities, there is an alternative viewpoint. Research has shown that ethical behavior can not only enhance a company's reputation but can also drive profits.[30] The ethical and socially responsible conduct of companies such as Whole Foods, Starbucks, and the hotel chain Marriott provides evidence that good ethics is good business. There is growing recognition that the long-term value of conducting business in an ethical and socially responsible manner that considers the interests of all stakeholders creates superior financial performance.[31]

To promote socially responsible and ethical behavior while achieving organizational goals, businesses can monitor changes and trends in society's values. Businesses should determine what society wants and attempt to predict the long-term effects of their decisions. While it requires an effort to address the interests of all stakeholders, businesses can prioritize and attempt to balance conflicting demands. The goal is to develop a solid reputation of trust, avoid misconduct, and develop effective workplace ethics.

CAN YOU LEARN BUSINESS IN A CLASSROOM?

Obviously, the answer is yes, or there would be no purpose for this textbook! To be successful in business, you need knowledge, skills, experience, and good judgment. The topics covered in this chapter and throughout this book provide some of the knowledge you need to understand the world of business. The boxed features and examples within each chapter describe experiences to help you develop good business judgment. However, good judgment is based on knowledge and experience plus personal insight and understanding. Therefore, you need more courses in business, along with some practical experience in the business

> **TEAM EXERCISE**
>
> Major economic systems, including capitalism, socialism, and communism, as well as mixed economies, were discussed in this chapter. Assuming that you want an economic system that is best for the majority, not just a few members, of society, defend one of the economic systems as the best system. Form groups and try to reach agreement on one economic system. Defend why you support the system that you advance.

world, to help you develop the special insight necessary to put your personal stamp on knowledge as you apply it. The challenge in business is in the area of judgment, and judgment does not develop from memorizing an introductory business textbook. If you are observant in your daily experiences as an employee, as a student, and as a consumer, you will improve your ability to make good business judgments.

Whether you choose to work at an organization or become an entrepreneur, you will be required to know the basic concepts and principles in this book. It should be exciting to think about your opportunities and the challenges of creating a successful career. Our society needs a strong economic foundation to help people develop a desired standard of living. Our world economy is becoming more digital and competitive, requiring new skills and job positions. Individuals like you can become leaders in business, nonprofits, and government to create a better life.

Figure 1.6 is an overview of how the chapters in this book are linked together and how the chapters relate to the participants, the activities, and the environmental factors found in the business world. The topics presented in the chapters that follow are those that will give you the best opportunity to begin the process of understanding the world of business. ■

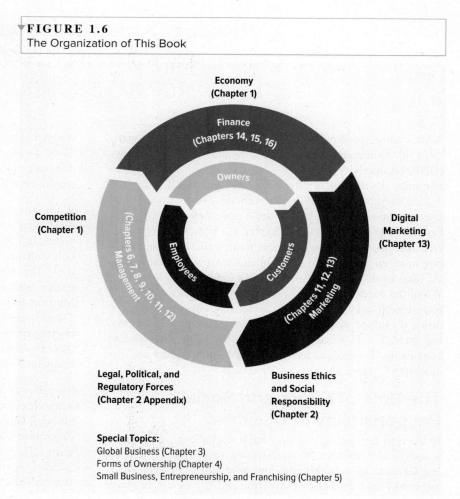

FIGURE 1.6
The Organization of This Book

Special Topics:
Global Business (Chapter 3)
Forms of Ownership (Chapter 4)
Small Business, Entrepreneurship, and Franchising (Chapter 5)

SO YOU WANT A JOB // in the Business World /

When most people think of a career in business, they see themselves entering the door to large companies and multinationals that they read about in the news and that are discussed in class. In a national survey, students indicated they would like to work for Google, Walt Disney, Apple, and Ernst & Young. In fact, most jobs are not with large corporations, but are in small companies, nonprofit organizations, government, and even self-employed individuals. There are nearly 22 million individuals who own their own businesses and have no employees. With more than 75 percent of the economy based on services, there are jobs available in many industries, such as health care, finance, education, hospitality, entertainment, and transportation. The world is changing quickly and large corporations replace

the equivalent of their entire workforce every four years.

The fast pace of technology today means that you have to be prepared to take advantage of emerging job opportunities and markets. You must also become adaptive and recognize that business is becoming more global, with job opportunities around the world. If you want to obtain such a job, you shouldn't miss a chance to spend some time overseas. To get you started on the path to thinking about job opportunities, consider all of the changes in business today that might affect your possible long-term track and that could bring you lots of success. You may want to stay completely out of large organizations and corporations and put yourself in a position for an entrepreneurial role as a self-employed contractor or small-business owner. However, there are many who

feel that experience in larger businesses is helpful to your success later as an entrepreneur.

You're on the road to learning the key knowledge, skills, and trends that you can use to be a star in business. Business's impact on our society, especially in the area of sustainability and improvement of the environment, is a growing challenge and opportunity. Green businesses and green jobs in the business world are provided to give you a glimpse at the possibilities. Along the way, we will introduce you to some specific careers and offer advice on developing your own job opportunities. Research indicates that you won't be that happy with your job unless you enjoy your work and feel that it has a purpose. Since you spend most of your waking hours every day at work, you need to seriously think about what is important to you in a job.[32]

two

business ethics and
social responsibility

© Robert Churchill/Getty Images, RF

LEARNING OBJECTIVES

After reading this chapter, you will be able to:

LO 2-1 Define business ethics and social responsibility and examine their importance.

LO 2-2 Detect some of the ethical issues that may arise in business.

LO 2-3 Specify how businesses can promote ethical behavior.

LO 2-4 Explain the four dimensions of social responsibility.

LO 2-5 Debate an organization's social responsibilities to owners, employees, consumers, the environment, and the community.

Any organization, including nonprofits, has to manage the ethical behavior of employees and participants in the overall operations of the organization. Firms that are highly ethical tend to be more profitable with more satisfied employees and customers.[1] Therefore, there are no conflicts between profits and ethics—in fact, unethical conduct is more likely to lower profits than raise them. Wrongdoing by some businesses has focused public attention and government involvement on encouraging more acceptable business conduct. Any organizational decision may be judged as right or wrong, ethical or unethical, legal or illegal.

In this chapter, we take a look at the role of ethics and social responsibility in business decision making. First we define business ethics and examine why it is important to understand ethics' role in business. Next we explore a number of business ethics issues to help you learn to recognize such issues when they arise. Finally, we consider steps businesses can take to improve ethical behavior in their organizations. The second half of the chapter focuses on social responsibility and unemployment. We survey some important issues and detail how companies have responded to them. ■

BUSINESS ETHICS AND SOCIAL RESPONSIBILITY

In this chapter, we define **business ethics** as the principles and standards that determine acceptable conduct in business organizations. Personal ethics, on the other hand, relates to an individual's values, principles, and standards of conduct. The acceptability of behavior in business is determined by not only the organization but also stakeholders such as customers, competitors, government regulators, interest groups, and the public, as well as each individual's personal principles and values. The publicity and debate surrounding highly visible legal and ethical issues at a number of well-known firms, including General Motors, Target, and JPMorgan Chase, highlight the need for businesses to integrate ethics and responsibility into all business decisions. For instance, Target was criticized for not having appropriate internal controls in place to prevent the theft of millions of their customers' credit and debit card accounts. High-risk trading at JPMorgan Chase led to massive losses that affected the company's reputation and resulted in fines. Most unethical activities within organizations are supported by an organizational culture that encourages employees to bend the rules. On the other hand, trust in business is the glue that holds relationships together. In Figure 2.1, you can see that trust in banks is lower than in other industries, except for media and government.

Organizations that exhibit a high ethical culture encourage employees to act with integrity and adhere to business values. Many experts agree that ethical leadership, ethical values, and compliance are important in creating good business ethics. To truly create an ethical culture, however, managers must

business ethics
principles and standards that determine acceptable conduct in business.

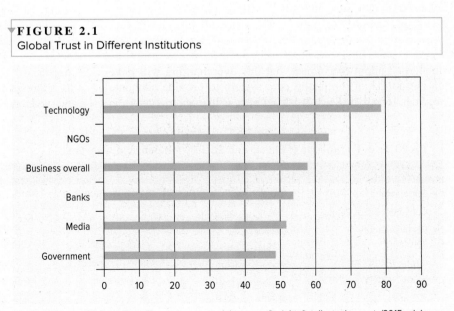

▼**FIGURE 2.1**
Global Trust in Different Institutions

Source: Edelman, *Edelman Trust Barometer*, www.edelman.com/insights/intellectualproperty/2015-edelman-trust-barometer/ (accessed February 5, 2015).

show a strong commitment to ethics and compliance. This "tone at the top" requires top managers to acknowledge their own role in supporting ethics and compliance, create strong relationships with the general counsel and the ethics and compliance department, clearly communicate company expectations for ethical behavior to all employees, educate all managers and supervisors in the business about the company's ethics policies, and train managers and employees on what to do if an ethics crisis occurs.[2]

Businesses should not only make a profit but also consider the social implications of their activities. However, profits permit businesses to contribute to society. The firms that are more well known for their strong social contributions tend to be those that are more profitable. We define **social responsibility** as a business's obligation to maximize its positive impact and

warranted. For instance, one task force charged 90 people—several of them doctors—with filing false Medicare claims costing $260 million.[3]

The most basic ethical and social responsibility concerns have been codified by laws and regulations that encourage businesses to conform to society's standards, values, and attitudes. For example, after accounting scandals at a number of well-known firms in the early 2000s shook public confidence in the integrity of corporate America, the reputations of every U.S. company suffered regardless of their association with the scandals.[4] To help restore confidence in corporations and markets, Congress passed the Sarbanes-Oxley Act, which criminalized securities fraud and stiffened penalties for corporate fraud. After the financial crisis occurred in the most recent recession, the Dodd-Frank Act was passed to reform the financial industry and offer consumers protection against complex and/or deceptive financial products. At a minimum, managers are expected to obey all laws and regulations. Most legal issues

[**"Businesses should not only make a profit but also consider the social implications of their activities."**]

minimize its negative impact on society. Although many people use the terms *social responsibility* and *ethics* interchangeably, they do not mean the same thing. Business ethics relates to an *individual's* or a *work group's* decisions that society evaluates as right or wrong, whereas social responsibility is a broader concept that concerns the impact of the *entire business's* activities on society. From an ethical perspective, for example, we may be concerned about a health care organization overcharging the government for Medicare services. From a social responsibility perspective, we might be concerned about the impact that this overcharging will have on the ability of the health care system to provide adequate services for all citizens. It would appear that such concern is

arise as choices that society deems unethical, irresponsible, or otherwise unacceptable. However, all actions deemed unethical by society are not necessarily illegal, and both legal and ethical concerns change over time (see Table 2.1). Business law refers to the laws and regulations that govern the conduct of business. Many problems and conflicts in business could be avoided if owners, managers, and employees knew more about business law and the legal system. Business ethics, social responsibility, and laws together act as a compliance system, requiring that businesses and employees act responsibly in society. In this chapter, we explore ethics and social responsibility; the appendix addresses business law, including the Sarbanes-Oxley Act and the Dodd-Frank Act.

▼ **TABLE 2.1** Timeline of Ethical and Socially Responsible Activities

1960s	1970s	1980s	1990s	2000s
• Social issues	• Business ethics	• Standards for ethical conduct	• Corporate ethics programs	• Transparency in financial markets
• Consumer Bill of Rights	• Social responsibility	• Financial misconduct	• Regulation to support business ethics	• Corporate misconduct
• Disadvantaged consumer	• Diversity	• Self-regulation	• Health issues	• Intellectual property
• Environmental issues	• Bribery	• Codes of conduct	• Safe working conditions	• Regulation of accounting and finance
• Product safety	• Discrimination	• Ethics training	• Detecting misconduct	• Executive compensation
	• Identifying ethical issues			

THE ROLE OF ETHICS IN BUSINESS

You have only to pick up *The Wall Street Journal* or *USA Today* to see examples of the growing concern about legal and ethical issues in business. For example, the nation's largest truck-stop chain, Pilot Flying J, paid $92 million to settle claims for allegedly failing to manage its employees for appropriate conduct. According to the federal government, Pilot Flying J employees were skimping on rebates owed to their customers.[5] Regardless of what an individual believes about a particular action, if society judges it to be unethical or wrong, whether correctly or not, that judgment directly affects the organization's ability to achieve its business goals.[6]

Well-publicized incidents of unethical and illegal activity—ranging from accounting fraud to using the Internet to steal another person's credit card number, from deceptive advertising of food and diet products to unfair competitive practices in the computer software industry—strengthen the public's perceptions that ethical standards and the level of trust in business need to be raised. On the other hand, it is worth noting that the mass media frequently report about firms that engage in misconduct related to bribery, fraud, and unsafe products. However, the good ethical conduct of the vast majority of firms is not reported as often. Therefore,

the public often gets the impression that misconduct is more widespread than it is in reality.

Often, misconduct charges start as ethical conflicts but evolve into legal disputes when cooperative conflict resolution cannot be accomplished. Headline-grabbing scandals like those associated with executive compensation and benefits packages create ethical concerns. The average CEO earns 331 times as much as the average employee and 774 times as much as minimum-wage workers.[7] Public outrage over executive compensation is prompting companies to begin reevaluating how they compensate their CEOs relative to corporate performance. Cisco's CEO saw a 22 percent decrease in compensation because of failing to meet targets for revenue and operating income.[8]

However, it is important to understand that business ethics goes beyond legal issues. Ethical conduct builds trust among individuals and in business relationships, which validates and promotes confidence in business relationships. Establishing trust and confidence is much more difficult in organizations that have reputations for acting unethically. If you were to discover, for example, that a manager had misled you about company benefits when you were hired, your trust and confidence in that company would probably diminish. And if you learned that a colleague had lied to you about something, you probably would not trust or rely on that person in the future.

Ethical issues are not limited to for-profit organizations either. Ethical issues include all areas of organizational activities, including nonprofits and government. In government, several politicians and some high-ranking officials have faced disciplinary actions over ethical indiscretions. For instance, former Virginia governor Bob McDonnell was found guilty of accepting bribes worth $177,000 in exchange for assisting a wealthy donor's organization. He was sentenced to two years in prison.[9] Even sports can be subject to ethical lapses. The National Football League was harshly criticized for its lax handling of domestic abuse. After a Baltimore Ravens running back was seen on camera abusing his fiancée, the public was infuriated when the NFL initially suspended him for only two games. As a result, the NFL has changed its policies on how it handles domestic abuse incidents.[10] Thus, whether made in science, politics, sports, or business, most decisions are judged as right or wrong, ethical or unethical. Negative judgments can affect an organization's ability to build relationships with customers and suppliers, attract investors, and retain employees.[11]

Although we will not tell you in this chapter what you ought to do, others—your superiors, co-workers, and family—will make judgments about the ethics of your actions and decisions. Learning how to recognize and resolve ethical issues is a key step in evaluating ethical decisions in business.

This reusable bag was made with 100% recycled plastic bottles. Many consumers are buying products made from recyclable materials due to increasing concern for the environment.
© Mark Boulton/Alamy

Recognizing Ethical Issues in Business

Recognizing ethical issues is the most important step in understanding business ethics. An **ethical issue** is an identifiable problem, situation, or opportunity that requires a person to choose from among several actions that may be evaluated as right or wrong, ethical or unethical. Learning how to choose from alternatives and make a decision requires not only good personal values but also knowledge and competence in the business area of concern. Employees also need to know when to comment on their organizations' business policies and codes of ethics or have discussions with co-workers or managers on appropriate conduct. Ethical decision making is not always easy because there are gray areas that create dilemmas, no matter how decisions are made. For instance, should an employee report a co-worker for time theft? Should a salesperson omit facts about a product's safety record in his presentation to a customer? Such questions require the decision maker to evaluate the ethics of his or her choice and decide whether to ask for guidance.

Ralph Lauren reported that its subsidiary had bribed government officials in Argentina. Because it took quick action to address the misconduct, the company did not face charges.
© NC1 WENN Photos/Newscom

Many business issues seem straightforward and easy to resolve on the surface, but are in reality very complex. A person often needs several years of experience in business to understand what is acceptable or ethical. For example, it is considered improper to

> "Many business issues seem straightforward and easy to resolve on the surface, but are in reality very complex."

THE NCAA: SHOULD COLLEGE ATHLETES BE PAID?

The National Collegiate Athletic Association (NCAA) was founded in 1905 to serve as a national regulator and organizer of college football in the United States. It has around 1,100 member schools and regulates a wide variety of intercollegiate sports.

Since its founding over a century ago, the NCAA has refused to allow student athletes in its sports to be paid other than through academic scholarships. This is true even though the organization and its member colleges make millions of dollars off licensing top players' names, images, and likenesses for use in television, videogames, and other media. The NCAA's continuing stance has been that college athletes are "amateurs," and to pay them would destroy the pure competitive spirit and nonprofessional nature of college sports.

In August 2014, a California federal district court judge struck down this long-standing practice, finding it violated federal antitrust laws. The judge ruled that starting July 2016, the NCAA must allow member colleges to create trust funds for student athletes where a portion of their licensing revenue can be deposited and later accessed by them after graduation. The NCAA may cap the amount each student makes at $5,000 per year, but that still adds up to hundreds of millions in revenue potentially redirected back to the players.

The NCAA is in the process of appealing the decision and may also seek a special congressional exemption from antitrust laws (Major League Baseball enjoys a similar exemption). If the decision stands, however, only time will tell how the ruling will affect the NCAA and the atmosphere of college sports in general.[12]

Discussion Questions

1. Why has this issue become such a controversial topic?

2. Who are the various stakeholders of the NCAA? How will each of them be affected by this decision?

3. Are there potential negative impacts of this decision on college athletes? If so, what does this illustrate about the subtleties and difficulties of ethical decision making?

give or accept **bribes**, which are payments, gifts, or special favors intended to influence the outcome of a decision. A bribe benefits an individual or a company at the expense of other stakeholders. Companies that do business overseas should be aware that bribes are a significant ethical issue and are, in fact, illegal in many countries. In the United States, the Foreign Corrupt Practices Act imposes heavy penalties on companies found guilty of bribery. After bribery was discovered among its Mexican branch, Walmart underwent a lengthy Justice Department investigation. Its own internal probe into the matter cost the company $439 million.[13]

Ethics is also related to the culture in which a business operates. In the United States, for example, it would be inappropriate for a businessperson to bring an elaborately wrapped gift to a prospective client on their first meeting—the gift could be viewed as a bribe. In Japan, however, it is considered impolite *not* to bring a gift. Experience with the culture in which a business operates is critical to understanding what is ethical or unethical. On the other hand, firms must also abide by the values and policies of global business.

To help you understand ethical issues that perplex business-people today, we will take a brief look at some of them in this section. Ethical issues can be more complex now than in the past. The vast number of news-format investigative programs

or watching YouTube. In this case, the employee is misusing not only time but also company resources by using the company's computer and Internet access for personal use.[15] Time theft costs can be difficult to measure but are estimated to cost companies hundreds of billions of dollars annually. It is widely believed that the average employee steals 4.5 hours a week with late arrivals, leaving early, long lunch breaks, inappropriate sick days, excessive socializing, and engaging in personal activities such as online shopping and watching sports while on the job. All of these activities add up to lost productivity and profits for the employer—and relate to ethical issues in the area of time theft.

Abusive and Intimidating Behavior Abusive or intimidating behavior is another common ethical problem for employees. These concepts can mean anything from physical threats, false accusations, profanity, insults, yelling, harshness, and unreasonableness to ignoring someone or simply being annoying; and the meaning of these words can differ by person—you

ethical issue an identifiable problem, situation, or opportunity that requires a person to choose from among several actions that may be evaluated as right or wrong, ethical or unethical.

bribes payments, gifts, or special favors intended to influence the outcome of a decision.

> ## One of the principal causes of unethical behavior in organizations is rewards for overly aggressive financial or business objectives.

has increased consumer and employee awareness of organizational misconduct. In addition, the multitude of cable channels and Internet resources has improved the awareness of ethical problems among the general public.

One of the principal causes of unethical behavior in organizations is rewards for overly aggressive financial or business objectives. It is not possible to discuss every issue, of course. However, a discussion of a few issues can help you begin to recognize the ethical problems with which businesspersons must deal. Many ethical issues in business can be categorized in the context of their relation with abusive and intimidating behavior, conflicts of interest, fairness and honesty, communications, misuse of company resources, and business associations. The National Business Ethics Survey (NBES) found that workers witness many instances of ethical misconduct in their organizations (see Table 2.2).

Misuse of Company Time Theft of time is a major area of misconduct observed in the workplace.[14] One example of misusing time in the workplace is by engaging in activities that are not necessary for the job. For instance, many employees spend an average of one hour each day using social networking sites

probably have some ideas of your own. Abusive behavior can be placed on a continuum from a minor distraction to a disruption of the workplace. For example, what one person may define as

▼ **TABLE 2.2** Percentage of U.S. Workforce Observing Specific Forms of Misconduct

	2011 (%)	2013 (%)
Overall	45%	41%
Abusive behavior	21%	18%
Lying to employees	20%	17%
Conflict of interest	15%	12%
Violating company Internet use policies	16%	12%
Discrimination against employees	15%	12%
Violations of health or safety regulations	13%	10%
Lying to customers, vendors, the public	12%	10%
Retaliation against reporters of misconduct		10%
Falsifying time reports/hours worked	12%	10%
Stealing or theft	12%	9%

Source: Ethics Resource Center, *2013 National Business Ethics Survey® of the U.S. Workforce* (Arlington, VA: Ethics Resource Center, 2014), pp. 41–42.

Misuse of company time through the use of personal social media is very costly to businesses.
© Jane Williams/Alamy

▼ **TABLE 2.3** Actions Associated with Bullies

1. Spreading rumors to damage others
2. Blocking others' communication in the workplace
3. Flaunting status or authority to take advantage of others
4. Discrediting others' ideas and opinions
5. Use of e-mails to demean others
6. Failing to communicate or return communication
7. Insults, yelling, and shouting
8. Using terminology to discriminate by gender, race, or age
9. Using eye or body language to hurt others or their reputation
10. Taking credit for others' work or ideas

Source: © O.C. Ferrell, 2016.

yelling might be another's definition of normal speech. Civility in our society is a concern, and the workplace is no exception. The productivity level of many organizations has been diminished by the time spent unraveling abusive relationships.

Abusive behavior is difficult to assess and manage because of diversity in culture and lifestyle. What does it mean to speak profanely? Is profanity only related to specific words or other such terms that are common in today's business world? If you are using words that are normal in your language but that others consider to be profanity, have you just insulted, abused, or disrespected them?

Within the concept of abusive behavior, intent should be a consideration. If the employee was trying to convey a compliment but the comment was considered abusive, then it was probably a mistake. The way a word is said (voice inflection) can be important. Add to this the fact that we now live in a multicultural environment—doing business and working with many cultural groups—and the businessperson soon realizes the depth of the ethical and legal issues that may arise. There are problems of word meanings by age and within cultures. For example, an expression such as "Did you guys hook up last night?" can have various meanings, including some that could be considered offensive in a work environment.

Bullying is associated with a hostile workplace when a person or group is targeted and is threatened, harassed, belittled, verbally abused, or overly criticized. Bullying may create what some consider a hostile environment, a term generally associated with sexual harassment. Although sexual harassment has legal recourse, bullying has little legal recourse at this time. Bullying is a widespread problem in the United States, and can cause psychological damage that can result in health-endangering consequences to the target. Surveys reveal that bullying in the workplace is on the rise.[16] As Table 2.3 indicates, bullying can use a mix of verbal, nonverbal, and manipulative threatening expressions to damage workplace productivity. One may wonder why workers tolerate such activities. The problem is that 72 percent of bullies outrank their victims.[17] Additionally, bullying can occur in any type of business. A bullying scandal at the Miami Dolphins involved a player who abruptly left the team after a hazing incident. The player claimed he had been bullied mercilessly by three starters on the Dolphins' offensive line, which harmed his mental well-being.[18]

Misuse of Company Resources Misuse of company resources has been identified by the Ethics Resource Center as a leading issue in observed misconduct in organizations. Issues might include spending an excessive amount of time on personal e-mails, submitting personal expenses on company expense reports, or using the company copier for personal use. Part of the reason that American Apparel founder and CEO Dov Charney was fired was because an investigation discovered that he had allegedly misused company funds.[19] While serious resource abuse can result in firing, some abuse can have legal repercussions. An Amtrak employee was found guilty of padding his expense report by over $3,300 for meals that did not occur. The employee was arrested, dismissed from Amtrak, and forced to make restitution.[20]

The most common way that employees abuse resources is by using company computers for personal use. Typical examples of using a computer for personal use include shopping on the Internet, downloading music, doing personal banking, surfing the Internet for entertainment purposes, or visiting Facebook. Some companies have chosen to block certain sites such as YouTube or Pandora from employees. However, other companies choose to take a more flexible approach. For example, many have instituted policies that allow for some personal computer use as long as the use does not detract significantly from the workday.

No matter what approach a business chooses to take, it must have policies in place to prevent company resource abuse. Because misuse of company resources is such a widespread problem, many companies, like Coca-Cola, have implemented official policies delineating acceptable use of company resources. Coca-Cola's policy states that company assets should not be used for personal benefit but does allow employees some freedom in this area. The policy specifies that it is acceptable for employees to make the occasional personal phone call or e-mail, but they should use common sense to know when these activities become excessive. This kind of policy is in line with that of many companies, particularly large ones that can easily lose millions of dollars and thousands of hours of productivity to these activities.[21]

Conflict of Interest

A conflict of interest, one of the most common ethical issues identified by employees, exists when a person must choose whether to advance his or her own personal interests or those of others. For example, a manager in a corporation is supposed to ensure that the company is profitable so that its stockholder-owners receive a return on their investment. In other words, the manager has a responsibility to investors. If she instead makes decisions that give her more power or money but do not help the company, then she has a conflict of interest—she is acting to benefit herself at the expense of her company and is not fulfilling her responsibilities as an employee. To avoid conflicts of interest, employees must be able to separate their personal financial interests from their business dealings. In the wake of the 2008 meltdown on Wall Street, stakeholders and legislators pushed for reform of the credit rating industry. Many cited rampant conflicts of interest between financial firms and the companies that rate them as part of the reason no one recognized the impending financial disaster. Conflict of interest has long been a serious problem in the financial industry because the financial companies pay the credit raters money to be rated. Because different rating companies exist, financial firms can also shop around for the best rating. There is no third-party mediator who oversees the financial industry and how firms are rated.[22]

Insider trading is an example of a conflict of interest. Insider trading is the buying or selling of stocks by insiders who possess material that is still not public. The Justice Department has taken an aggressive stance toward insider trading. An ex-trader at SAC Capital received a nine-year prison sentence. SAC paid $1.2 billion in fines and penalties.[23] However, a decision by the federal appeals court ruled that to be convicted an insider trader must gain a tangible reward for using nonpublic company information. This might potentially make it more difficult for prosecutors to make insider trading convictions in the future.[24] Bribery can also be a conflict of interest. While bribery is an increasing issue in many countries, it is more prevalent in some countries than in others. Transparency International has developed a Corruption Perceptions Index (Table 2.4). There are 16 countries perceived as less corrupt than the United States.[25]

Fairness and Honesty

Fairness and honesty are at the heart of business ethics and relate to the general values of decision makers. At a minimum, businesspersons are expected to follow all applicable laws and regulations. But beyond obeying the law, they are expected not to harm customers, employees, clients, or competitors knowingly through deception, misrepresentation, coercion, or discrimination. Honesty and fairness can relate to how the employees use the resources of the organization. In contrast, dishonesty is usually associated with a lack of integrity, lack of disclosure, and lying. One common example of dishonesty is theft of office supplies. Although the majority of office supply thefts involve small things such as pencils or Post-it Notes,

▼ **TABLE 2.4** Least Corrupt Countries

Rank	Country	CPI Score*
1	Denmark	92
2	New Zealand	91
3	Finland	89
4	Sweden	87
5	Norway/Switzerland	86
7	Singapore	84
8	Netherlands	83
9	Luxembourg	82
10	Canada	81
11	Australia	80

*Corruption Perceptions Index (CPI) score relates to perceptions of the degree of public sector corruption as seen by businesspeople and country analysts and ranges between 0 (highly corrupt) and 10 (very clean).

Source: Corruption Perceptions Index 2014, Copyright Transparency International 2014, http://www.transparency.org/cpi2014/results (accessed January 14, 2015).

some workers admit to stealing more expensive items or equipment such as computers or software. Employees should be aware of policies on stealing items and recognize how these decisions relate to ethical behavior.

One aspect of fairness relates to competition. Although numerous laws have been passed to foster competition and make monopolistic practices illegal, companies sometimes gain control over markets by using questionable practices that harm competition. For instance, the European Commission started an antitrust investigation into Google's practices to determine whether it was engaging in anticompetitive behavior. Several companies including Microsoft claimed that Google promoted its own search results over those of competitors in spite of their relevance. Because Google holds 90 percent of the search engine market in Europe, the controversy over how it is using its dominant position to remain ahead of competitors is not likely to die down. The European Union's Parliament has called for the breakup of Google to separate its search engine business from its other services.[26] In many cases, the alleged misconduct not only can have monetary and legal implications but can also threaten reputation, investor confidence, and customer loyalty. In the case of Pool Corporation, the company had allegedly bullied pool manufacturers by threatening to refuse to distribute their products if they did business with other pool distributors. Such behavior is unacceptable. At the minimum, a business found guilty of anticompetitive practices will be forced to stop such conduct. However, many companies end up paying millions in penalties to settle allegations.[27]

Another aspect of fairness and honesty relates to disclosure of potential harm caused by product use. For instance, the Food and Drug Administration (FDA) has become increasingly concerned about the calorie content of food sold in restaurants. It is concerned that consumers are unaware of just how many calories they are consuming, which is leading to health concerns

Being honest and truthful in communications is important for business success.
© Minerva Studio/Getty Images, RF

well as deceptive personal-selling tactics, anger consumers and can lead to the failure of a business. Truthfulness about product safety and quality is also important to consumers. General Motors, Toyota, and Honda all faced fines for product quality issues and for not issuing recalls in a timely manner. In many of these situations, the companies were found to be slow on issuing recalls or making them well known, which resulted in accidents in some cases.

Some companies fail to provide enough information for consumers about differences or similarities between products. For example, driven by high prices for medicines, many consumers are turning to Canadian, Mexican, and overseas Internet sources for drugs to treat a variety of illnesses and conditions. However, research suggests that a significant percentage of these imported pharmaceuticals may not actually contain the labeled drug, and the counterfeit drugs could even be harmful to those who take them.[31]

Another important aspect of communications that may raise ethical concerns relates to product labeling. This becomes an even greater concern with potentially harmful products like cigarettes. In Europe, the European Parliament revised the EU Tobacco Products Directive so that picture and health warnings would have to cover 65 percent of the front and back and 50 percent of the sides of cigarette packages.[32] The United Kingdom wants to go further by eliminating branding on cigarette packaging. A proposed regulation would mandate that cigarette packages contain the manufacturer's name as well as health warnings and pictures but no distinctive colors or logos.[33] However, labeling of other products raises ethical

as consumers are increasingly turning toward prepared foods. To make consumers more aware, the FDA is requiring chain restaurants, vending machines, takeout counters, amusement parks, and theaters to list calorie information on menu boards.[28]

Dishonesty has become a significant problem in the United States. Approximately 64 students from Dartmouth College faced discipline after they were caught in a cheating scandal—for a class that involved ethics. Attendance and participation for the class was largely measured by students using handheld clickers to answer questions or participate. An investigation revealed that numerous students were not attending class, instead giving their clickers to fellow classmates to use in class to hide their absences.[29] If today's students are tomorrow's leaders, there is likely to be a correlation between acceptable behavior today and tomorrow. This adds to the argument that the leaders of today must be prepared for the ethical risks associated with this downward trend.

Even military officers have felt the pressure to cheat. At one Air Force base in Montana, nearly half of the Air Force officers at the base cheated on a proficiency exam. Another investigation was launched shortly afterward to determine whether senior Navy enlistees in South Carolina cheated on an exam containing classified information. Another 800 soldiers in the army were placed under criminal investigation for being involved in kickbacks to soldiers who recruited friends. As a result of these scandals, the military is increasing its ethics training.[30]

Communications Communications is another area in which ethical concerns may arise. False and misleading advertising, as

turnitin

Features   Resources   Customers   Training   Support   About

Overview   Originality Check   Online Grading   Peer Review   iPad   Integrations   What's New   Demos   FAQs   Get a Quote

Reduce Plagiarism

Check students' work for improper citation or potential plagiarism by comparing it against the world's largest academic database.

⊙ Demo

Turnitin is an Internet service that allows teachers to determine if their students have plagiarized content.
© Studio Works/Alamy

Pom Wonderful pomegranate juice was found to have unsupported health claims about its products in its advertising.
© KAREN BLEIER/Getty Images

puts the employee and the company at legal risk, but employees may feel pressured to do so by their superior's authority. The NBES found that employees who feel pressured to compromise ethical standards view top and middle managers as the greatest source of such pressure.[34]

It is the responsibility of managers to create a work environment that helps the organization achieve its objectives and fulfill its responsibilities. However, the methods that managers use to enforce these responsibilities should not compromise employee rights. Organizational pressures may encourage a person to engage in activities that he or she might otherwise view as unethical, such as invading others' privacy or stealing a competitor's secrets. The firm may provide only vague or lax supervision on ethical issues, creating the opportunity for misconduct. Managers who offer no ethical direction to employees create many opportunities for manipulation, dishonesty, and conflicts of interest.

Plagiarism—presenting someone else's work as your own without mentioning the source—is another ethical issue. As a student, you may be familiar with plagiarism in school—for example copying someone else's term paper or quoting from a published work or Internet source without acknowledging it. In business, an ethical issue arises when an employee copies reports or presents the work or ideas of others as his or her own. A manager attempting to take credit for a subordinate's ideas is engaging in another type of plagiarism.

Making Decisions about Ethical Issues

It can be difficult to recognize specific ethical issues in practice. Managers, for example, tend to be more concerned about issues that affect those close to them, as well as issues that have immediate rather than long-term consequences. Thus, the perceived importance of an ethical issue substantially affects choices. However, only a few issues receive scrutiny, and most receive no attention at all.[35] Managers make intuitive decisions sometimes without recognizing the embedded ethical issue.

Table 2.5 lists some questions you may want to ask yourself and others when trying to determine whether an action is ethical.

▼ **TABLE 2.5** Questions to Consider in Determining Whether an Action Is Ethical

Are there any potential legal restrictions or violations that could result from the action?
Does your company have a specific code of ethics or policy on the action?
Is this activity customary in your industry? Are there any industry trade groups that provide guidelines or codes of conduct that address this issue?
Would this activity be accepted by your co-workers? Will your decision or action withstand open discussion with co-workers and managers and survive untarnished?
How does this activity fit with your own beliefs and values?

questions when it threatens basic rights, such as freedom of speech and expression. This is the heart of the controversy surrounding the movement to require warning labels on movies and videogames, rating their content, language, and appropriate audience age. Although people in the entertainment industry claim that such labeling violates their First Amendment right to freedom of expression, other consumers—particularly parents—believe that labeling is needed to protect children from harmful influences. Similarly, alcoholic beverage and cigarette manufacturers have argued that a total ban on cigarette and alcohol advertisements violates the First Amendment. Internet regulation, particularly that designed to protect children and the elderly, is on the forefront in consumer protection legislation. Because of the debate surrounding the acceptability of these business activities, they remain major ethical issues.

Business Relationships
The behavior of businesspersons toward customers, suppliers, and others in their workplace may also generate ethical concerns. Ethical behavior within a business involves keeping company secrets, meeting obligations and responsibilities, and avoiding undue pressure that may force others to act unethically.

Managers in particular, because of the authority of their position, have the opportunity to influence employees' actions. For example, a manager might influence employees to use pirated computer software to save costs. The use of illegal software

codes of ethics
formalized rules and
standards that describe
what a company
expects of its
employees.

whistleblowing
the act of an employee
exposing an employer's
wrongdoing to outsiders,
such as the media or
government regulatory
agencies.

Open discussion of ethical issues does not eliminate ethical problems, but it does promote both trust and learning in an organization.[36] When people feel that they cannot discuss what they are doing with their co-workers or superiors, there is a good chance that an ethical issue exists. Once a person has recognized an ethical issue and can openly discuss it with others, he or she has begun the process of resolving that issue.

LO 2-3 Specify how businesses can promote ethical behavior.

Improving Ethical Behavior in Business

Understanding how people make ethical choices and what prompts a person to act unethically may result in better ethical decisions. Ethical decisions in an organization are influenced by three key factors: individual moral standards and values, the influence of managers and co-workers, and the opportunity to engage in misconduct (Figure 2.2). While you have great control over your personal ethics outside the workplace, your co-workers and superiors exert significant control over your choices at work through authority and example. In fact, the activities and examples set by co-workers, along with rules and policies established by the firm, are critical in gaining consistent ethical compliance in an organization. If the company fails to provide good examples and direction for appropriate conduct, confusion and conflict will develop and result in the opportunity for misconduct. If your boss or co-workers leave work early, you may be tempted to do so as well. If you see co-workers engaged in personal activities such as shopping online or ignoring misconduct, then

> **Many employees use different ethical standards at work than they do at home.**

you may be more likely to do so also. Having sound personal values is important because you will be responsible for your own conduct.

Because ethical issues often emerge from conflict, it is useful to examine the causes of ethical conflict. Business managers and employees often experience some tension between their own ethical beliefs and their obligations to the organizations in which they work. Many employees use different ethical standards at work than they do at home. This conflict increases when employees feel that their company is encouraging unethical conduct or exerting pressure on them to engage in it.

It is difficult for employees to determine what conduct is acceptable within a company if the firm does not have established ethics policies and standards. And without such policies and standards, employees may base decisions on how their peers and superiors behave. Professional **codes of ethics** are formalized rules and standards that describe what the company expects of its employees. Codes of ethics do not have to be so detailed that they take into account every situation, but they should provide guidelines and principles that can help employees achieve organizational objectives and address risks in an acceptable and ethical way. Eaton's code of ethics, for instance, provides examples, questions, and other aids to help its employees across the globe understand the firm's ethical standards. The development of a code of ethics should include not only a firm's executives and board of directors, but also legal staff and employees from all areas of a firm.[37] Table 2.6 lists some key things to consider when developing a code of ethics.

Codes of ethics, policies on ethics, and ethics training programs advance ethical behavior because they prescribe which activities are acceptable and which are not, and they limit the opportunity for misconduct by providing punishments for violations of the rules and standards. This creates compliance requirements to establish uniform behavior among all employees. Codes and policies on ethics encourage the creation of an ethical culture in the company. According to the NBES, employees in organizations that have written codes of conduct and ethics training, ethics offices or hotlines, and systems for reporting are more likely to report misconduct when they observe it. The survey found that a company's ethical culture is the greatest determinant of future misconduct.[38]

The enforcement of ethical codes and policies through rewards and punishments increases the acceptance of ethical standards by employees. For example, employees at Granite Construction are highly encouraged

▼**FIGURE 2.2**
Three Factors That Influence Business Ethics

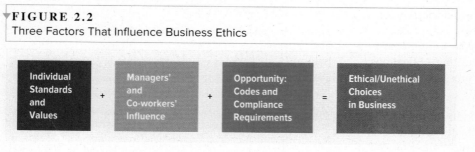

| Individual Standards and Values | + | Managers' and Co-workers' Influence | + | Opportunity: Codes and Compliance Requirements | = | Ethical/Unethical Choices in Business |

▼ TABLE 2.6 Key Things to Consider in Developing a Code of Ethics

- Create a team to assist with the process of developing the code (include management and nonmanagement employees from across departments and functions).
- Solicit input from employees from different departments, functions, and regions to compile a list of common questions and answers to include in the code document.
- Make certain that the headings of the code sections can be easily understood by all employees.
- Avoid referencing specific U.S. laws and regulations or those of specific countries, particularly for codes that will be distributed to employees in multiple regions.
- Hold employee group meetings on a complete draft version (including graphics and pictures) of the text, using language that everyone can understand.
- Inform employees that they will receive a copy of the code during an introduction session.
- Let all employees know that they will receive future ethics training that will, in part, cover the important information contained in the code document.

Source: Adapted from William Miller, "Implementing an Organizational Code of Ethics," *International Business Ethics Review* 7 (Winter 2004), pp. 1, 6–10.

> **The current trend is to move away from legally based ethical initiatives in organizations to cultural- or integrity-based initiatives that make ethics a part of core organizational values.**

to engage in ethical behavior. Granite Construction holds six mandatory training sessions to manage risks, offers computer-based training for employees, provides ethics training for board members, and uses Field Compliance Officers to monitor compliance throughout the company. Granite's strong ethics inspired the creation of the Construction Industry Ethics and Compliance Initiative, consisting of a network of construction firms dedicated to supporting ethics throughout the industry.[39]

One of the most important components of an ethics program is a means through which employees can report observed misconduct anonymously. Although the risk of retaliation is still a major factor in whether an employee will report illegal conduct, the NBES found that whistleblowing has increased in the past few years. Approximately 65 percent of respondents said they reported misconduct when they observed it.[40] **Whistleblowing** occurs when an employee exposes an employer's wrongdoing to outsiders, such as the media or government regulatory agencies. However, more companies are establishing programs to encourage employees to report illegal or unethical practices internally so that they can take steps to remedy problems before they result in legal action or generate negative publicity. Unfortunately, whistleblowers are often treated negatively in organizations. The government therefore tries to encourage employees to report observed misconduct. Congress has also taken steps to close a legislative loophole in whistleblowing legislation that has

led to the dismissal of many whistleblowers. In 2010, Congress passed the Dodd-Frank Act, which includes a "whistleblower bounty program." The Securities and Exchange Commission can now award whistleblowers between 10 and 30 percent of monetary sanctions over $1 million. The hope is that incentives will encourage more people to come forward with information regarding corporate misconduct. The largest whistleblower reward to date has been $30 million. The SEC felt that the fraud would have gone undetected if not for the whistleblower and is hoping this reward incentivizes other employees to step forward when they observe fraud.[41]

The current trend is to move away from legally based ethical initiatives in organizations to cultural- or integrity-based initiatives that make ethics a part of core organizational values. Organizations recognize that effective business ethics programs are good for business performance. Firms that develop higher levels of trust function more efficiently and effectively and avoid damaged company reputations and product images. Organizational ethics initiatives have been supportive of many positive and diverse organizational objectives, such as profitability, hiring, employee satisfaction, and customer loyalty.[42] Conversely, lack of organizational ethics initiatives and the absence of workplace values such as honesty, trust, and integrity can have a negative impact on organizational objectives and employee retention. According to one study, three of the most common factors that

corporate citizenship
the extent to which businesses meet the legal, ethical, economic, and voluntary responsibilities placed on them by their stakeholders.

executives give for why turnover increases are employee loss of trust in the company, a lack of transparency among company leaders, and unfair employee treatment.[43]

LO 2-4 Explain the four dimensions of social responsibility.

THE NATURE OF SOCIAL RESPONSIBILITY

For our purposes, we classify four stages of social responsibility: financial, legal compliance, ethics, and philanthropy (Table 2.7). Another way of categorizing these four dimensions of social responsibility is by economic, legal, ethical, and voluntary (including philanthropic).[44] Earning profits is the economic foundation, and complying with the law is the next step. However, a business whose *sole* objective is to maximize profits is not likely to consider its social responsibility, although its activities will probably be legal. (We looked at ethical responsibilities in the first half of this chapter.) Finally, voluntary responsibilities are additional activities that may not be required but that promote human welfare or goodwill. Legal and economic concerns have long been acknowledged in business, and voluntary and ethical issues are being addressed by most firms.

Corporate citizenship is the extent to which businesses meet the legal, ethical, economic, and voluntary responsibilities placed on them by their various stakeholders. It involves the activities and organizational processes adopted by businesses to meet their social responsibilities. A commitment to corporate citizenship by a firm indicates a strategic focus on fulfilling the social responsibilities expected of it by its stakeholders. For example, CVS is attempting to demonstrate corporate citizenship by eliminating tobacco products from its pharmacies. Although this will cost the firm $2 billion in sales, CVS believes it is contradictory to market itself as a health

care services business while still selling a dangerous product.[45] Corporate citizenship involves action and measurement of the extent to which a firm embraces the corporate citizenship philosophy and then follows through by implementing citizenship and social responsibility initiatives. One of the major corporate citizenship issues is the focus on preserving the environment. The majority of people agree that climate change is a global emergency, but there is no agreement on how to solve the problem.[46] Another example of a corporate citizenship issue might be animal rights—an issue that is important to many stakeholders. As the organic and local foods movements grow and become more profitable, more and more stakeholders are calling for more humane practices in factory farms as well.[47] Large factory farms are where most Americans get their meat, but some businesses are looking at more animal-friendly options in response to public outcry.

Part of the answer to the climate change crisis is alternative energy such as solar, wind, biofuels, and hydro applications. The drive for alternative fuels such as ethanol from corn has added new issues such as food price increases and food shortages. More than 2 billion consumers earn less than $2 a day in wages. Sharply increased food costs have led to riots and government policies to restrict trade in basic commodities such as rice, corn, and soybeans.[48]

To respond to these developments, most companies are introducing eco-friendly products and marketing efforts. Universal Lubricants is a company on a mission to change the future of oil. The company produces its products from recycled oil collected from petrochemical companies. The oil is sold to other manufacturers to be used in transportation, agricultural, and other industries.[49] However, although 69 percent of consumers say it is all right for a firm not to be environmentally perfect as long as it is honest, 78 percent claim that they will boycott firms caught making misleading environmental claims.[50] This is because many businesses are promoting themselves as green-conscious and concerned about the environment without actually making the necessary commitments to environmental health.

The Ethisphere Institute selects an annual list of the world's most ethical companies based on the following criteria: corporate citizenship and responsibility; corporate governance; innovation that contributes to the public well-being; industry leadership; executive leadership and tone from the top; legal, regulatory, and reputation track record; and internal systems and ethics/compliance program.[51] Table 2.8 shows 26 from that list.

Although the concept of social responsibility is receiving more and more attention, it is still not universally accepted. Table 2.9 lists some of the arguments for and against social responsibility.

▼ **TABLE 2.7** Social Responsibility Requirements

Stage	Example
Stage 1: Financial Viability	Starbucks offers investors a healthy return on investment, including paying dividends.
Stage 2: Compliance with Legal and Regulatory Requirements	Starbucks specifies in its code of conduct that payments made to foreign government officials must be lawful according to the laws of the United States and the foreign country.
Stage 3: Ethics, Principles, and Values	Starbucks offers health care benefits to part-time employees and supports coffee growers by offering them fair prices.
Stage 4: Philanthropic Activities	Starbucks created the Starbucks Foundation to award grants to eligible nonprofits and to give back to their communities.

▼ **TABLE 2.8** A Selection of the World's Most Ethical Companies

L'OREAL	Allstate Insurance Company
Starbucks Coffee Company	Hospital Corporation of America (HCA)
Marks and Spencer	Xerox Corporation
General Electric Company	U.S. Bank
T-Mobile USA Inc.	Cummins
PepsiCo	Ford Motor Company
ManpowerGroup	Google Inc.
Colgate-Palmolive Company	Gap, Inc.
International Paper	Texas Instruments Incorporated
Adobe Systems Incorporated	Waste Management
UPS	Kellogg Company
Accenture	Aflac Incorporated
Marriott International	Levi Strauss & Co.

Source: "2015 World's Most Ethical Companies—Honorees," *Ethisphere,* http://ethisphere.com/worlds-most-ethical/wme-honorees/ (accessed July 30, 2015).

▼ **TABLE 2.9** The Arguments for and against Social Responsibility

For:

1. Social responsibility rests on stakeholder engagement and results in benefits to society and improved firm performance.

2. Businesses are responsible because they have the financial and technical resources to address sustainability, health, and education.

3. As members of society, businesses and their employees should support society through taxes and contributions to social causes.

4. Socially responsible decision making by businesses can prevent increased government regulation.

5. Social responsibility is necessary to ensure economic survival: If businesses want educated and healthy employees, customers with money to spend, and suppliers with quality goods and services in years to come, they must take steps to help solve the social and environmental problems that exist today.

Against:

1. It sidetracks managers from the primary goal of business—earning profits. The responsibility of business to society is to earn profits and create jobs.

2. Participation in social programs gives businesses greater power, perhaps at the expense of concerned stakeholders.

3. Does business have the expertise needed to assess and make decisions about social and economic issues?

4. Social problems are the responsibility of the government agencies and officials, who can be held accountable by voters.

5. Creation of nonprofits and contributions to them are the best ways to implement social responsibility.

LO 2-5 Debate an organization's social responsibilities to owners, employees, consumers, the environment, and the community.

Social Responsibility Issues

As with ethics, managers consider social responsibility on a daily basis. Among the many social issues that managers must consider are their firms' relations with owners and stockholders, employees, consumers, regulators, stakeholders including the community, and environmental advocates. For example, Denise Morrison, CEO of Campbell Soup, believes that businesses must take seriously their leadership roles and commitment to social responsibility.[52]

Social responsibility is a dynamic area with issues changing constantly in response to society's demands. There is much evidence that social responsibility is associated with improved business performance. Consumers are refusing to buy from businesses that receive publicity about misconduct. A number of studies have found a direct relationship between social responsibility and profitability as well as a link that exists between employee commitment and customer loyalty—two major concerns of any firm trying to increase profits.[53] This section highlights a few of the many social responsibility issues that managers face; as managers become aware of and work toward the solution of current social problems, new ones will certainly emerge.

Relations with Owners and Stockholders Businesses must first be responsible to their owners, who are primarily concerned with earning a profit or a return on their investment in a company. In a small business, this responsibility is fairly easy to fulfill because the owner (or owners) personally manages the business or knows the managers well. In larger businesses, particularly corporations owned by thousands of stockholders, ensuring responsibility becomes a more difficult task.

A business's obligations to its owners and investors, as well as to the financial community at large, include maintaining proper accounting procedures, providing all relevant information to investors about the current and projected performance of the firm, and protecting the owners' rights and investments. In short, the business must maximize the owners' investments in the firm.

Employee Relations Another issue of importance to a business is its responsibilities to employees. Without employees, a business cannot carry out its goals. Employees expect businesses to provide a safe workplace, pay them adequately for their work, and keep them informed of what is happening in their company. They want employers to listen to their grievances and treat them fairly. Even Berkshire Hathaway, known for its well-paid managers and ethical conduct, has experienced challenges in employee relations. Employees from Berkshire Hathaway business NetJets, acquired in 1998, protested what they believed were unfair cost cuts even though demand for the company's services had increased. At one point NetJets pilots picketed outside a Las Vegas resort where Warren Buffett was located.[54]

Congress has passed several laws regulating safety in the workplace, many of which are enforced by the Occupational Safety and Health Administration (OSHA). Labor unions have also made significant contributions to achieving safety in the workplace

consumerism the activities that independent individuals, groups, and organizations undertake to protect their rights as consumers.

and improving wages and benefits. Most organizations now recognize that the safety and satisfaction of their employees are critical ingredients in their success, and many strive to go beyond what is legally expected of them. Healthy, satisfied employees also supply more than just labor to their employers. Employers are beginning to realize the importance of obtaining input from even the lowest-level employees to help the company reach its objectives.

A major social responsibility for business is providing equal opportunities for all employees regardless of their sex, age, race, religion, or nationality. Diversity is also helpful to a firm financially. Firms with gender-diverse leadership are 15 percent more likely to report financial returns higher than the industry average, while those with ethnic-diverse leadership are 35 percent more likely.[55] Despite these benefits, women and minorities have been slighted in the past in terms of education, employment, and advancement opportunities; additionally, many of their needs have not been addressed by business. Discrimination still occurs in business. The Equal Employment Opportunity Commission (EEOC) filed a lawsuit against a Popeye's Chicken franchisee for $25,000 to settle allegations that it denied an applicant employment due to his HIV positive status.[56] Women, who continue to bear most child-rearing responsibilities, often experience conflict between those responsibilities and their duties as employees. Consequently, day care has become a major employment issue for women, and more companies are providing day care facilities as part of their effort to recruit and advance women in the workforce. In addition, companies are considering alternative scheduling such as flex-time and job sharing to accommodate employee concerns. Telecommuting has grown significantly over the past 5 to 10 years as well. Many Americans today believe business has a social obligation to provide special opportunities for women and minorities to improve their standing in society.

Consumer Relations A critical issue in business today is business's responsibility to customers, who look to business to provide them with satisfying, safe products and to respect their rights as consumers. The activities that independent individuals, groups, and organizations undertake to protect their rights as consumers are known as **consumerism**. To achieve their objectives, consumers and their advocates write letters to companies, lobby government agencies, make public service announcements, and boycott companies whose activities they deem irresponsible.

Many of the desires of those involved in the consumer movement have a foundation in John F. Kennedy's 1962 consumer bill of rights, which highlighted four rights. The *right to safety* means that a business must not knowingly sell anything that could result in personal injury or harm to consumers. Defective or dangerous products erode public confidence in the ability of business to serve society. They also result in expensive litigation that ultimately increases the cost of products for all consumers. The right to safety also means businesses must provide a safe place for consumers to shop.

The *right to be informed* gives consumers the freedom to review complete information about a product before they buy it. This means that detailed information about ingredients, risks, and instructions for use are to be printed on labels and packages. When companies mislead consumers about the benefits of their products, then they infringe on consumers' rights to be informed. Ticketmaster paid $400 million in credit to buyers for fees deemed to be misleading. The company charged order processing and delivery fees that were not entirely spent in these two areas. This violated consumers' rights to be informed about what they were paying for.[57] The *right to choose* ensures that consumers have access to a variety of goods and services at competitive prices. The assurance of both satisfactory quality and service at a fair price is also a part of the consumer's right to choose. The *right to be heard* assures consumers that their interests will receive full and sympathetic consideration when the government

TANKCHAIR: NOT YOUR AVERAGE WHEELCHAIR

Brad Soden was enjoying life until a bad car crash left his wife-to-be paralyzed from the waist down. Her distress at being limited in joining the family on nature trips motivated Soden, a self-taught tinkerer, to take action. The result was the Tankchair, a heavy-duty wheelchair whose treads-instead-of-wheels allow an ATV-like level of terrain mobility, powered by an electric motor capable of speeds of up to 30 mph. Not only did the invention give Soden's wife back her freedom, but it has also developed into a company that is now Soden's full-time job.

Each Tankchair is customized for its user, from head controls for neck-down paralysis, to fishing reels and cigarette lighters, to a police car–style chair decked out with lights, sirens, and a megaphone for a former officer (after receiving the chair, he was rehired as an investigator). At $12,000 or more, the devices are expensive, and they do not fit the regulatory definition "wheelchair" so that Medicare will cover them. However, with over 200 customers so far—and many organizations helping to pay—Tankchair seems poised to continue changing lives.[58]

formulates policy. It also ensures the fair treatment of consumers who voice complaints about a purchased product.

The role of the Federal Trade Commission's Bureau of Consumer Protection exists to protect consumers against unfair, deceptive, or fraudulent practices. The bureau, which enforces a variety of consumer protection laws, is divided into five divisions. The Division of Enforcement monitors legal compliance and investigates violations of laws, including unfulfilled holiday delivery promises by online shopping sites, employment opportunities fraud, scholarship scams, misleading advertising for health care products, and more.

Sustainability Issues Most people probably associate the term *environment* with nature, including wildlife, trees, oceans, and mountains. Until the 20th century, people generally thought of the environment solely in terms of how these resources could be harnessed to satisfy their needs for food, shelter, transportation, and recreation. As the earth's population swelled throughout the 20th century, however, humans began to use more and more of these resources and, with technological advancements, to do so with ever-greater efficiency. Although these conditions have resulted in a much-improved standard of living, they come with a cost. Plant and animal species, along with wildlife habitats, are disappearing at an accelerated rate, while pollution has rendered the atmosphere of some cities a gloomy haze. How to deal with these issues has become a major concern for business and society in the 21st century.

Although the scope of the word *sustainability* is broad, in this book we discuss the term from a strategic business perspective. Thus, we define **sustainability** as conducting activities in such a way as to provide for the long-term well-being of the natural environment, including all biological entities. Sustainability involves the interaction among nature and individuals, organizations, and business strategies and includes the assessment and improvement of business strategies, economic sectors, work practices, technologies, and lifestyles so that they

maintain the health of the natural environment. In recent years, business has played a significant role in adapting, using, and maintaining the quality of sustainability.

Environmental protection emerged as a major issue in the 20th century in the face of increasing evidence that pollution, uncontrolled use of natural resources, and population growth were putting increasing pressure on the long-term sustainability of these resources. Governments around the globe responded with environmental protection laws during the 1970s. In recent years, companies have been increasingly incorporating these issues into their overall business strategies. Some nonprofit organizations have stepped forward to provide leadership in gaining the cooperation of diverse groups in responsible environmental activities. For example, the Coalition for Environmentally Responsible Economies (CERES)—a union of businesses, consumer groups, environmentalists, and other stakeholders—has established a set of goals for environmental performance.

In the following sections, we examine some of the most significant sustainability and environmental health issues facing business and society today, including pollution and alternative energy.

Pollution A major issue in the area of environmental responsibility is pollution. Water pollution results from dumping toxic chemicals and raw sewage into rivers and oceans, oil spills, and the burial of industrial waste in the ground where it may filter into underground water supplies. Fertilizers and insecticides used in farming and grounds maintenance also run off into water supplies with each rainfall. Water pollution problems are especially notable in heavily industrialized areas. Medical waste—such as used syringes, vials of blood, and HIV-contaminated materials—has turned up on beaches in New York, New Jersey, and Massachusetts as well as other places. Society is demanding that water supplies be clean and healthful to reduce the potential danger from these substances.

Air pollution is usually the result of smoke and other pollutants emitted by manufacturing facilities, as well as carbon monoxide and hydrocarbons emitted by motor vehicles. In addition to the health risks posed by air pollution, when some chemical compounds emitted by manufacturing facilities react with air and rain, acid rain results. Acid rain has contributed to the deaths of many forests and lakes in North America as well as in Europe. Air pollution may also contribute to global warming; as carbon dioxide collects in the earth's atmosphere, it traps the sun's heat and prevents the earth's surface from cooling. It is indisputable that the global surface temperature has been increasing over the past 35 years. Worldwide passenger vehicle ownership has been growing due to rapid industrialization and consumer purchasing power in China, India, and other developing countries with large

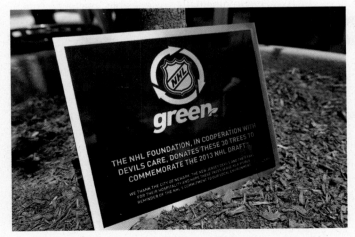

The National Hockey League's NHL Green initiative partners with organizations to contribute toward improving the environment
© Dave Sandford/National Hockey League/Getty Images

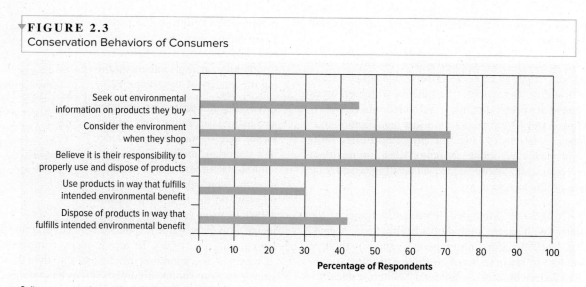

Online survey conducted March 7–10, 2013, by ORC International among a demographically representative sample of 1,068 adults, comprising 552 men and 516 women 18 years of age and older. The margin of error associated with a sample of this size is ±3% at a 95% level of confidence.

Source: Cone Communications, "Cone Releases 2013 Cone Communications Green Gap Trend Tracker," April 2, 2013, www.conecomm. com/2013-green-gap-trend-tracker-1 (accessed January 15, 2015).

populations. The most important way to contain climate change is to control carbon emissions. The move to green buildings, higher-mileage cars, and other emissions reductions resulting from better efficiency have the potential to generate up to 50 percent of the reductions needed to keep warming at no more than 82.4°F (28°C) above present temperatures—considered the "safe" level.[59] The 2007 U.S. Federal Energy bill raised corporate average fuel economy (CAFE) standards to 35 mpg for cars by 2020, while Europe has the goal of a 40-mpg standard by the same deadline. This becomes problematic when gas prices decrease because consumer demand for SUVs and trucks tends to rise significantly. Because buildings create half of U.S. greenhouse emissions, there is tremendous opportunity to develop conservation measures. For example, some utilities charge more for electricity in peak demand periods, which encourages behavioral changes that reduce consumption. More and more consumers are recognizing the need to protect the planet. Figure 2.3 shows the conservation habits of consumers when they purchase, use, and dispose of products. Although most consumers admit that sustainable products are important and that they bear responsibility for properly using and disposing of the product, many admit that they fail to do this.

Land pollution is tied directly to water pollution because many of the chemicals and toxic wastes that are dumped on the land eventually work their way into the water supply. A study conducted by the Environmental Protection Agency found residues of prescription drugs, soaps, and other contaminants in virtually every waterway in the United States. Effects of these pollutants on humans and wildlife are uncertain, but there is some evidence to suggest that fish and other water-dwellers are starting to suffer serious effects.[61] Land pollution results from the dumping of residential and industrial waste, strip mining, forest fires, and poor forest conservation. In Brazil and other South American countries, rain forests are being destroyed—to make way for farms and ranches, at a cost of the extinction of the many animals and plants (some endangered species) that call the rain forest home. For example, annual deforestation in the Brazilian rain forest encompasses an area about the size of Delaware. The good news is that deforestation rates in Brazil may be decreasing due to new laws against illegal logging.[62] Large-scale deforestation also depletes the oxygen supply available to humans and other animals.

DID YOU KNOW?

About 50 million tons of electronic waste is generated each year, including discarded laptops, mobile phones, and televisions.[60]

Related to the problem of land pollution is the larger issue of how to dispose of waste in an environmentally responsible manner. Americans use approximately 100 billion plastic bags per year.[63] Hawaii and the city of Los Angeles have banned plastic bag use, and the rest of California, Delaware, New York, Illinois, Maine, and Rhode Island have adopted reuse, relabel, or recycling programs for plastic bags.[64] Under the new law, shoppers will have to bring their own reusable bags or pay 10 cents for each paper bag. Los Angeles is the biggest city in the United States to ban plastic bag usage so far.[65]

Alternative Energy With ongoing plans to reduce global carbon emissions, countries and companies alike are looking toward alternative energy sources. Traditional fossil fuels are problematic because of their emissions but also because stores have been greatly depleted.

SOLAR ENERGY MERGES SUSTAINABILITY WITH GOOD BUSINESS

The current understanding of solar energy seems inextricably linked with concepts like sustainability, environmentalism, and "going green." There have been ups and downs in the solar business. Starting around 2005, the solar energy industry experienced a boom. The public desire to move toward sustainable energy sources fueled government subsidies, investment in research and development, and other favorable forces. New companies formed and grew rapidly, and the future looked bright. Unfortunately, the boom did not last. When the global economic recession hit, governments and investors were forced to pare back on solar subsidies and investment. Other market forces, such as an influx of Chinese firms oversupplying solar panels at extremely low prices, contributed to a crash in profitability and demand. Many companies went out of business, and those that survived had to reestablish investor confidence and reevaluate their approach.

In the past few years, the solar industry seems to have rebounded once more, with solar panel prices again increasing and companies returning to profitability. Supporters tend to view solar power as an ethical solution to the energy crisis because it has the potential to significantly decrease the negative environmental impact of traditional fossil fuels. However, some industry leaders and analysts argue that for the solar industry to truly mature and prosper, it must be founded on solid economic competitiveness, not just ethical and environmental ideals. They say that rather than relying on subsidies and the "sustainability" image, solar companies need to learn how to better utilize standard strategic advantages such as economies of scale and practical product development. If they are right, then perhaps a day will come when solar is no longer a "green" solution, but simply a good solution.[67]

Discussion Questions

1. What kind of image does the solar industry currently have in terms of sustainability and business ethics? Why does it have this image?

2. Can it truly be potentially detrimental to be known for sustainability?

3. Does the solar power industry have to move away from its "green" label to become stable, or is there another solution?

Foreign fossil fuels are often imported from politically and economically unstable regions, often making it unsafe to conduct business there. However, the United States is becoming an energy powerhouse with its ability to drill for natural gas in large shale reserves. This is allowing the United States to move forward on its goals to reach energy independence. On the other hand, concerns over how these drilling methods are affecting the environment make this a controversial topic.

The U.S. government has begun to recognize the need to look toward alternative forms of energy as a source of fuel and electricity. There have been many different ideas as to which form of alternative energy would best suit the United States' energy needs. These sources include wind power, solar power, nuclear power, biofuels, electric cars, and hydro- and geothermal power.

Tesla uses electric charging as an alternative to traditional gasoline.
© P Cox/Alamy

As of yet, no "best" form of alternative fuel has been selected to replace gasoline. Additionally, there are numerous challenges with the economic viability of alternative energy sources. For instance, wind and solar power cost significantly more than traditional energy; watts from wind power are estimated to be 290 percent higher than from natural gas; and the costs of solar photovoltaic is estimated to be 230 percent more expensive. Alternative energy will likely require government subsidies to make any significant strides. However, the news for solar power might be getting brighter. Solar companies in the United States are beginning to rebound. Electric cars are also gaining importance. Most automobile companies such as BMW, General Motors, Nissan, and Toyota are introducing electric cars to help with sustainability.

Response to Environmental Issues Partly in response to federal legislation such as the National Environmental Policy Act of 1969 and partly due to consumer concerns, businesses are responding to environmental issues. Many small and large companies, including Walt Disney Company, Chevron, and Scott Paper, have created an executive position—a vice president of environmental affairs—to help them achieve their business goals in an environmentally responsible manner. Some companies are finding that environmental consciousness can save them money. For example, one San Diego hotel saved more than $40,000 by changing how it uses energy and adopting more energy-saving devices.[66]

Many firms are trying to eliminate wasteful practices, the emission of pollutants, and/or the use of harmful chemicals from their manufacturing processes. Other companies are seeking ways to improve their products. Utility providers, for example, are increasingly supplementing their services with alternative energy sources, including solar, wind, and geothermal power. Environmentalists are concerned that some companies are merely

> **"Environmentalists are concerned that some companies are merely *greenwashing,* or 'creating a positive association with environmental issues for an unsuitable product, service, or practice.'"**

greenwashing, or 'creating a positive association with environmental issues for an unsuitable product, service, or practice.'

In many places, local utility customers can even elect to purchase electricity from green sources—primarily wind power—for a few extra dollars a month. Austin Energy of Austin, Texas, has an award-winning GreenChoice program that includes many small and large businesses among its customers.[68] Indeed, a growing number of businesses and consumers are choosing green power sources where available. New Belgium Brewing Company, the third-largest craft brewer in the United States, is the first all-wind-powered brewery in the country. Many businesses have turned to *recycling,* the reprocessing of materials—aluminum, paper, glass, and some plastic—for reuse. Such efforts to make products, packaging, and processes more environmentally friendly have been labeled "green" business or marketing by the public and media. New Belgium, for instance, started selling aluminum cans of its beers because aluminum is easily recyclable and creates less waste. Lumber products at The Home Depot may carry a seal from the Forest Stewardship Council to indicate that they were harvested from sustainable forests using environmentally friendly methods.[69] Likewise, most Chiquita bananas are certified through the Better Banana Project as having been grown with more environmentally and labor-friendly practices.[70]

It is important to recognize that, with current technology, environmental responsibility requires trade-offs. Society must weigh the huge costs of limiting or eliminating pollution against the health threat posed by pollution. Environmental responsibility imposes costs on both business and the public. Although people certainly do not want oil fouling beautiful waterways and killing wildlife, they insist on low-cost, readily available gasoline and heating oil. People do not want to contribute to the growing garbage-disposal problem, but they often refuse to pay more for "green" products packaged in an environmentally friendly manner, to recycle as much of their own waste as possible, or to permit the building of additional waste-disposal facilities (the "not in my backyard," or NIMBY, syndrome). Managers must coordinate environmental goals with other social and economic ones.

Community Relations A final, yet very significant, issue for businesses concerns their responsibilities to the general welfare of the communities and societies in which they operate. Many businesses simply want to make their communities better places for everyone to live and work. The most common way that businesses exercise their community responsibility is through donations to local and national charitable organizations. For example, General Electric employees hold fundraising efforts to raise money for the United Way. Additionally, GE donates 2 percent of its appliance sales from its online GE Appliance Outlet Store to the United Way.[71] Small businesses also give back to their communities. Chattanooga-based coffee retailer Blue Smoke Coffee donates 10 percent of its sales to environmental and humanitarian causes.[72] Even small companies participate in philanthropy through donations and volunteer support of local causes and national charities, such as the Red Cross and the United Way.

UNEMPLOYMENT

After realizing that the current pool of prospective employees lacks many basic skills necessary to work, many companies have become concerned about the quality of education in the United States. Unemployment has become a significant problem since the onset of the financial crisis in 2008. In the years following, unemployment reached as high as 10 percent in the United States. Although it has fallen to about 6 percent since then, many consumers remain unemployed.[73]

Most would argue that unemployment is an economic issue, but it also carries ethical implications. Protests often occur in areas where unemployment is high, particularly when there seems to be a large gap between rich and poor. In Milan, Italy, high rates of unemployment caused consumers to protest as top leaders from the European Union attended a conference. Italian protestors were opposed to the hiring and firing rules being proposed by Italy's prime minister. They called for laws that would provide more protection for workers terminated without cause.[74]

Factory closures are another ethical issue because factories usually employ hundreds of workers. Sometimes it is necessary to close a plant due to economic reasons. However, factory closures

Unemployed individuals face much competition in securing a good job.
© Steve Debenport/Getty Images, RF

not only affect individual employees, but their communities as well. When an Electrolux factory moved from Webster City, Iowa, to Juarez, Mexico, the city of 8,000 people lost its main employer. This is having repercussions on other businesses in the area because more unemployed people mean fewer sales.[75]

Another criticism levied against companies involves hiring standards. Studies appear to show that while there are plenty of people unemployed, approximately 35 percent of companies cite employees' lack of experience as to why there are so many unfilled positions. Yet only about 28 percent are investing in more training and development for new hires. While it is important for employees to have certain skills, many feel that businesses must be willing to train employees if they want to fill their vacancies and decrease the unemployment rate.[76]

On the other hand, several businesses are working to reduce unemployment. After becoming frustrated with high unemployment

---

TEAM EXERCISE

Sam Walton, founder of Walmart, had an early strategy for growing his business related to pricing. The "Opening Price Point" strategy used by Walton involved offering the introductory product in a product line at the lowest point in the market. For example, a minimally equipped microwave oven would sell for less than anyone else in town could sell the same unit. The strategy was that if consumers saw a product, such as the microwave, and saw it as a good value, they would assume that all of the microwaves were good values. Walton also noted that most people don't buy the entry-level product; they want more features and capabilities and often trade up.

Form teams and assign the role of defending this strategy or casting this strategy as an unethical act. Present your thoughts on either side of the issue.

---

rates, Cincinnati-based Fifth Third Bancorp partnered with Oregon-based NextJob to try to get unemployed bank customers reemployed. The two organizations collaborated on a website that featured job seekers who needed employment and provided one-on-one coaching. More recently they have taken this endeavor a step further by featuring the stories of three job seekers and engaging the public to use their social networks to connect each job seeker with a potential employer.[77]

Additionally, businesses are beginning to take more responsibility for the hard-core unemployed. These are people who have never had a job or who have been unemployed for a long period of time. Some have mental or physical disabilities; some are homeless. Organizations such as the National Alliance of Businessmen fund programs to train the hard-core unemployed so that they can find jobs and support themselves. Such commitment enhances self-esteem and helps people become productive members of society.

SO YOU WANT A JOB // in Business Ethics and Social Responsibility /

In the words of Kermit the Frog, "It's not easy being green." It may not be easy, but green business opportunities abound. A popular catchphrase, "Green is the new black," indicates how fashionable green business is becoming. Consumers are more in tune with and concerned about green products, policies, and behaviors by companies than ever before. Companies are looking for new hires to help them see their business creatively and bring insights to all aspects of business operations. The American Solar Energy Society estimates that the number of green jobs could rise to 40 million in the United States by 2030. Green business strategies not only give a firm a commercial advantage in the marketplace, but also help lead the way toward a greener world. The fight to reduce our carbon footprint in an attempt against climate change has opened up opportunities for renewable energy, recycling, conservation, and increasing overall efficiency in the way resources are used. New businesses that focus on hydro, wind, and solar power are on the rise and will need talented business-people to lead them. Carbon emissions trading is gaining popularity as large corporations and individuals alike seek to lower their footprints. A job in this growing field could be similar to that of a stock trader, or you could lead the search for carbon-efficient companies in which to invest.

In the ethics arena, current trends in business governance strongly support the development of ethics and compliance departments to help guide organizational integrity. This alone is a billion-dollar business, and there are jobs in developing organizational ethics programs, developing company policies, and training employees and management. An entry-level position might be as a communication specialist or trainer for programs in a business ethics department. Eventually, there's an opportunity to become an ethics officer that would have typical responsibilities of meeting with employees, the board of directors, and top management to discuss and provide advice about ethics issues in the industry, developing and distributing a code of ethics, creating and maintaining an anonymous, confidential service to answer questions about ethical issues, taking actions on possible ethics code violations, and reviewing and modifying the code of ethics of the organization.

There are also opportunities to promote initiatives to help companies relate social responsibility to stakeholder interests and needs. These jobs could involve coordinating and implementing philanthropic programs that give back to others important to the organization or developing a community volunteering program for employees. In addition to the human relations function, most companies develop programs to assist employees and their families to improve their quality of life. Companies have found that the healthier and happier employees are, the more productive they will be in the workforce.

Social responsibility, ethics, and sustainable business practices are not a trend; they are good for business and the bottom line. New industries are being created and old ones are adapting to the new market demands, opening up many varied job opportunities that will lead not only to a paycheck but also to the satisfaction of making the world a better place.[78]

appendix

the legal and regulatory environment

Business law refers to the rules and regulations that govern the conduct of business. Problems in this area come from the failure to keep promises, misunderstandings, disagreements about expectations, or, in some cases, attempts to take advantage of others. The regulatory environment offers a framework and enforcement system to provide a fair playing field for all businesses. The regulatory environment is created based on inputs from competitors, customers, employees, special interest groups, and the public's elected representatives. Lobbying by pressure groups who try to influence legislation often shapes the legal and regulatory environment.

SOURCES OF LAW

Laws are classified as either criminal or civil. *Criminal law* not only prohibits a specific kind of action, such as unfair competition or mail fraud, but also imposes a fine or imprisonment as punishment for violating the law. A violation of a criminal law is thus called a crime. *Civil law* defines all the laws not classified as criminal, and it specifies the rights and duties of individuals and organizations (including businesses). Violations of civil law may result in fines but not imprisonment. The primary difference between criminal and civil law is that criminal laws are enforced by the state or nation, whereas civil laws are enforced through the court system by individuals or organizations.

Criminal and civil laws are derived from four sources: the Constitution (constitutional law), precedents established by judges (common law), federal and state statutes (statutory law), and federal and state administrative agencies (administrative law). Federal administrative agencies established by Congress control and influence business by enforcing laws and regulations to encourage competition and protect consumers, workers, and the environment. The Supreme Court is the ultimate authority on legal and regulatory decisions for appropriate conduct in business.

COURTS AND THE RESOLUTION OF DISPUTES

The primary method of resolving conflicts and business disputes is through **lawsuits**, where one individual or organization takes another to court using civil laws. The legal system, therefore, provides a forum for businesspeople to resolve disputes based on our legal foundations. The courts may decide when harm or damage results from the actions of others.

> "The primary method of resolving conflicts and business disputes is through lawsuits, where one individual or organization takes another to court using civil laws."

These fast-food workers are on strike in an attempt to convince restaurants to raise the minimum wage paid to employees.
© epa european pressphoto agency b.v./Alamy

Because lawsuits are so frequent in the world of business, it is important to understand more about the court system where such disputes are resolved. Both financial restitution and specific actions to undo wrongdoing can result from going before a court to resolve a conflict. All decisions made in the courts are based on criminal and civil laws derived from the legal and regulatory system.

A businessperson may win a lawsuit in court and receive a judgment, or court order, requiring the loser of the suit to pay monetary damages. However, this does not guarantee the victor will be able to collect those damages. If the loser of the suit lacks the financial resources to pay the judgment—for example, if the loser is a bankrupt business—the winner of the suit may not be able to collect the award. Most business lawsuits involve a request for a sum of money, but some lawsuits request that a court specifically order a person or organization to do or to refrain from doing a certain act, such as slamming telephone customers.

The Court System

Jurisdiction is the legal power of a court, through a judge, to interpret and apply the law and make a binding decision in a particular case. In some instances, other courts will not enforce the decision of a prior court because it lacked jurisdiction. Federal courts are granted jurisdiction by the Constitution or by Congress. State legislatures and constitutions determine which state courts hear certain types of cases. Courts of general jurisdiction hear all types of cases; those of limited jurisdiction hear only specific types of cases. The Federal Bankruptcy Court, for example, hears only cases involving bankruptcy. There is some combination of limited and general jurisdiction courts in every state.

In a **trial court** (whether in a court of general or limited jurisdiction and whether in the state or the federal system), two tasks must be completed. First, the court (acting through the judge or a jury) must determine the facts of the case. In other words, if there is conflicting evidence, the judge or jury must decide whom to believe. Second, the judge must decide which law or set of laws is pertinent to the case and must then apply those laws to resolve the dispute.

An **appellate court**, on the other hand, deals solely with appeals relating to the interpretation of law. Thus, when you hear about a case being appealed, it is not retried but rather reevaluated. Appellate judges do not hear witnesses but instead base their decisions on a written transcript of the original trial. Moreover, appellate courts do not draw factual conclusions; the appellate judge is limited to deciding whether the trial judge made a mistake in interpreting the law that probably affected the outcome of the trial. If the trial judge made no mistake (or if mistakes would not have changed the result of the trial), the appellate court will let the trial court's decision stand. If the appellate court finds a mistake, it usually sends the case back to the trial court so that the mistake can be corrected. Correction may involve the granting of a new trial. On occasion, appellate courts modify the verdict of the trial court without sending the case back to the trial court.

Alternative Dispute Resolution Methods

Although the main remedy for business disputes is a lawsuit, other dispute resolution methods are becoming popular. The schedules of state and federal trial courts are often crowded; long delays between the filing of a case and the trial date are common. Further, complex cases can become quite expensive to pursue. As a result, many businesspeople are turning to alternative methods of resolving business arguments: mediation and arbitration, the mini-trial, and litigation in a private court.

Mediation is a form of negotiation to resolve a dispute by bringing in one or more third-party mediators, usually chosen by the disputing parties, to help reach a settlement. The mediator suggests different ways to resolve a dispute between the parties. The mediator's resolution is nonbinding—that is, the parties do not have to accept the mediator's suggestions; they are strictly voluntary.

Arbitration involves submission of a dispute to one or more third-party arbitrators, usually chosen by the disputing parties, whose decision usually is final. Arbitration differs from mediation in that an arbitrator's decision must be followed, whereas a mediator merely offers suggestions and facilitates negotiations. Cases may be submitted to arbitration because a contract—such as a labor contract—requires it or because the parties agree to do so. Some consumers are barred from taking claims to court by agreements drafted by banks, brokers, health plans, and others. Instead, they are required to take complaints to mandatory arbitration. Arbitration can be an attractive alternative to a lawsuit because it is often cheaper and quicker, and the parties frequently can choose arbitrators who are knowledgeable about the particular area of business at issue.

A method of dispute resolution that may become increasingly important in settling complex disputes is the **mini-trial**, in which both parties agree to present a summarized version of their case to an independent third party. That person then advises them of his or her impression of the probable outcome if the case were to be tried. Representatives of both sides then attempt to negotiate a settlement based on the advisor's recommendations. For example, employees in a large corporation who believe they have muscular or skeletal stress injuries caused by the strain of repetitive motion in using a computer could agree to a mini-trial to address a dispute related to damages. Although the mini-trial itself does not resolve the dispute, it can help the parties resolve the case before going to court. Because the mini-trial is not subject to formal court rules, it can save companies a great deal of money, allowing them to recognize the weaknesses in a particular case.

In some areas of the country, disputes can be submitted to a private nongovernmental court for resolution. In a sense, a **private court system** is similar to arbitration in that an independent third party resolves the case after hearing both sides of the story. Trials in private courts may be either informal or highly formal, depending on the people involved. Businesses typically agree to have their disputes decided in private courts to save time and money.

REGULATORY ADMINISTRATIVE AGENCIES

Federal and state administrative agencies (listed in Table A.1) also have some judicial powers. Many administrative agencies, such as the Federal Trade Commission, decide disputes that involve their regulations. In such disputes, the resolution process is usually called a hearing rather than a trial. In these cases, an administrative law judge decides all issues.

Federal regulatory agencies influence many business activities and cover product liability, safety, and the regulation or deregulation of public utilities. Usually, these bodies have the power to enforce specific laws, such as the Federal Trade Commission Act, and have some discretion in establishing operating rules and regulations to guide certain types of industry practices. Because of this discretion and overlapping areas of responsibility, confusion or conflict regarding which agencies have jurisdiction over which activities is common.

Of all the federal regulatory units, the **Federal Trade Commission (FTC)** most influences business activities related to questionable practices that create disputes between businesses and their customers. Although the FTC regulates a variety of business practices, it allocates a large portion of resources to

▼ **TABLE A.1** The Major Regulatory Agencies

Agency	Major Areas of Responsibility
Federal Trade Commission (FTC)	Enforces laws and guidelines regarding business practices; takes action to stop false and deceptive advertising and labeling.
Food and Drug Administration (FDA)	Enforces laws and regulations to prevent distribution of adulterated or misbranded foods, drugs, medical devices, cosmetics, veterinary products, and particularly hazardous consumer products.
Consumer Product Safety Commission (CPSC)	Ensures compliance with the Consumer Product Safety Act; protects the public from unreasonable risk of injury from any consumer product not covered by other regulatory agencies.
Interstate Commerce Commission (ICC)	Regulates franchises, rates, and finances of interstate rail, bus, truck, and water carriers.
Federal Communications Commission (FCC)	Regulates communication by wire, radio, and television in interstate and foreign commerce.
Environmental Protection Agency (EPA)	Develops and enforces environmental protection standards and conducts research into the adverse effects of pollution.
Federal Energy Regulatory Commission (FERC)	Regulates rates and sales of natural gas products, thereby affecting the supply and price of gas available to consumers; also regulates wholesale rates for electricity and gas, pipeline construction, and U.S. imports and exports of natural gas and electricity.
Equal Employment Opportunity Commission (EEOC)	Investigates and resolves discrimination in employment practices.
Federal Aviation Administration (FAA)	Oversees the policies and regulations of the airline industry.
Federal Highway Administration (FHA)	Regulates vehicle safety requirements.
Occupational Safety and Health Administration (OSHA)	Develops policy to promote worker safety and health and investigates infractions.
Securities and Exchange Commission (SEC)	Regulates corporate securities trading and develops protection from fraud and other abuses; provides an accounting oversight board.
Consumer Financial Protection Bureau	Regulates financial products and institutions to ensure consumer protection.

> OF ALL THE FEDERAL REGULATORY UNITS, THE FEDERAL TRADE COMMISSION (FTC) MOST INFLUENCES BUSINESS ACTIVITIES RELATED TO QUESTIONABLE PRACTICES THAT CREATE DISPUTES BETWEEN BUSINESSES AND THEIR CUSTOMERS.

curbing false advertising, misleading pricing, and deceptive packaging and labeling. When it receives a complaint or otherwise has reason to believe that a firm is violating a law, the FTC issues a complaint stating that the business is in violation.

If a company continues the questionable practice, the FTC can issue a cease-and-desist order, which is an order for the business to stop doing whatever has caused the complaint. In such cases, the charged firm can appeal to the federal courts to have the order rescinded. However, the FTC can seek civil penalties in court—up to a maximum penalty of $10,000 a day for each infraction—if a cease-and-desist order is violated. In its battle against unfair pricing, the FTC has issued consent decrees alleging that corporate attempts to engage in price fixing or invitations to competitors to collude are violations even when the competitors in question refuse the invitations. The commission can also require companies to run corrective advertising in response to previous ads considered misleading.

The FTC also assists businesses in complying with laws. New marketing methods are evaluated every year. When general sets of guidelines are needed to improve business practices in a particular industry, the FTC sometimes encourages firms within that industry to establish a set of trade practices voluntarily. The FTC may even sponsor a conference bringing together industry leaders and consumers for the purpose of establishing acceptable trade practices.

Unlike the FTC, other regulatory units are limited to dealing with specific goods, services, or business activities. The Food and Drug Administration (FDA) enforces regulations prohibiting the sale and distribution of adulterated, misbranded, or hazardous food and drug products. For example, the FDA outlawed the sale and distribution of most over-the-counter hairloss remedies after research indicated that few of the products were effective in restoring hair growth.

The Environmental Protection Agency (EPA) develops and enforces environmental protection standards and conducts research into the adverse effects of pollution. The Consumer Product Safety Commission recalls about 300 products a year, ranging from small, inexpensive toys to major appliances. The Consumer Product Safety Commission's website provides details regarding current recalls.

The Consumer Product Safety Commission has fallen under increasing scrutiny in the wake of a number of product safety scandals involving children's toys. The most notable of these issues was lead paint discovered in toys produced in China. Some items are not even targeted to children but can be dangerous because children think they are food. Magnetic desk toys and Tide Pods have both been mistaken as candy by children.

IMPORTANT ELEMENTS OF BUSINESS LAW

To avoid violating criminal and civil laws, as well as discouraging lawsuits from consumers, employees, suppliers, and others, businesspeople need to be familiar with laws that address business practices.

The Uniform Commercial Code

At one time, states had their own specific laws governing various business practices, and transacting business across state lines was difficult because of the variation in the laws from state to state. To simplify commerce, every state—except Louisiana—has enacted the Uniform Commercial Code (Louisiana has enacted portions of the code). The **Uniform Commercial Code (UCC)** is a set of statutory laws covering several business law topics. Article II of the Uniform Commercial Code, which is discussed in the following paragraphs, has a significant impact on business.

Sales Agreements Article II of the Uniform Commercial Code covers sales agreements for goods and services such as installation but does not cover the sale of stocks and bonds, personal services, or real estate. Among its many provisions, Article II stipulates that a sales agreement can be enforced even though it does not specify the selling price or the time or place of delivery. It also requires that a buyer pay a reasonable price for goods at the time of delivery if the buyer and seller have not reached an agreement on price. Specifically, Article II addresses the rights of buyers and sellers, transfers of ownership, warranties, and the legal placement of risk during manufacture and delivery.

Article II also deals with express and implied warranties. An **express warranty** stipulates the specific terms the seller will honor. Many automobile manufacturers, for example, provide three-year or 36,000-mile warranties on their vehicles, during which period they will fix any and all defects specified in the warranty. An **implied warranty** is imposed on the producer or seller by law, although it may not be a written document provided at the time of sale. Under Article II, a consumer may assume that the product for sale has a clear title (in other words, that it is not stolen) and that the product will serve the purpose for which it was made and sold as well as function as advertised.

The Law of Torts and Fraud

A **tort** is a private or civil wrong other than breach of contract. For example, a tort can result if the driver of a Domino's Pizza delivery car loses control of the vehicle and damages property or injures a person. In the case of the delivery car accident, the injured persons might sue the driver and the owner of the company—Domino's in this case—for damages resulting from the accident.

Fraud is a purposefully unlawful act to deceive or manipulate to damage others. Thus, in some cases, a tort may also represent a violation of criminal law. Health care fraud has become a major issue in the courts.

An important aspect of tort law involves **product liability**—businesses' legal responsibility for any negligence in the design, production, sale, and consumption of products. Product liability laws have evolved from both common and statutory law. Some states have expanded the concept of product liability to include injuries by products whether or not the producer is proven negligent. Under this strict product liability, a consumer who files suit because of an injury has to prove only that the product was defective, that the defect caused the injury, and that the defect made the product unreasonably dangerous. For example, a carving knife is expected to be sharp and is not considered defective if you cut your finger using it. But an electric knife could be considered defective and unreasonably dangerous if it continued to operate after being switched off.

Reforming tort law, particularly in regard to product liability, has become a hot political issue as businesses look for relief from huge judgments in lawsuits. Although many lawsuits are warranted—few would disagree that a wrong has occurred when a patient dies because of negligence during a medical procedure or when a child is seriously injured by a defective toy, and that the families deserve some compensation—many suits are not. Because of multimillion-dollar judgments, companies are trying to minimize their liability, and sometimes they pass on the costs of the damage awards to their customers in the form of higher prices. Some states have passed laws limiting damage awards and some tort reform is occurring at the federal level. Table A.2 lists the state court systems the U.S. Chamber of Commerce's Institute for Legal Reform has identified as being "friendliest" and "least friendly" to business in terms of juries' fairness, judges' competence and impartiality, and other factors.

▼ **TABLE A.2** State Court Systems' Reputations for Supporting Business

Most Friendly to Business	Least Friendly to Business
Delaware	Mississippi
Nebraska	West Virginia
Virginia	Alabama
Iowa	Louisiana
Idaho	California
Utah	Texas
New Hampshire	Illinois
Minnesota	Montana
Kansas	Arkansas
Wisconsin	Missouri

Source: U.S. Chamber of Commerce Institute for Legal Reform, "States," www.instituteforlegalreform.com/states (accessed January 14, 2015).

The Law of Contracts

Virtually every business transaction is carried out by means of a **contract**, a mutual agreement between two or more parties that can be enforced in a court if one party chooses not to comply with the terms of the contract. If you rent an apartment or house, for example, your lease is a contract. If you have borrowed money under a student loan program, you have a contractual agreement to repay the money. Many aspects of contract law are covered under the Uniform Commercial Code.

A "handshake deal" is in most cases as fully and completely binding as a written, signed contract agreement. Indeed, many oil-drilling and construction contractors have for years agreed to take on projects on the basis of such handshake deals. However, individual states require that some contracts be in writing to be enforceable. Most states require that at least some of the following contracts be in writing:

- Contracts involving the sale of land or an interest in land
- Contracts to pay somebody else's debt
- Contracts that cannot be fulfilled within one year
- Contracts for the sale of goods that cost more than $500 (required by the Uniform Commercial Code)

Only those contracts that meet certain requirements—called *elements*—are enforceable by the courts. A person or business seeking to enforce a contract must show that it contains the following elements: voluntary agreement, consideration, contractual capacity of the parties, and legality.

For any agreement to be considered a legal contract, all persons involved must agree to be bound by the terms of the contract. *Voluntary agreement* typically comes about when one party makes an offer and the other accepts. If both the offer and the acceptance are freely, voluntarily, and knowingly made, the acceptance forms the basis for the contract. If, however, either the offer or the acceptance is the result of fraud or force, the individual or organization subject to the fraud or force can void, or invalidate, the resulting agreement or receive compensation for damages.

The second requirement for enforcement of a contract is that it must be supported by *consideration*—that is, money or something of value must be given in return for fulfilling a contract. As a general rule, a person cannot be forced to abide by the terms of a promise unless that person receives a consideration. The something of value could be money, goods, services, or even a promise to do or not to do something.

Contractual capacity is the legal ability to enter into a contract. As a general rule, a court cannot enforce a contract if either party to the agreement lacks contractual capacity. A person's contractual capacity may be limited or nonexistent if he or she is a minor (under the age of 18), mentally unstable, retarded, insane, or intoxicated.

Legality is the state or condition of being lawful. For an otherwise binding contract to be enforceable, both the purpose of and the consideration for the contract must be legal. A contract in which a bank loans money at a rate of interest prohibited by law, a practice known as usury, would be an illegal contract, for example. The fact that one of the parties may commit an illegal act while performing a contract does not render the contract itself illegal, however.

Breach of contract is the failure or refusal of a party to a contract to live up to his or her promises. In the case of an apartment lease, failure to pay rent would be considered breach of contract. The breaching party—the one who fails to comply—may be liable for monetary damages that he or she causes the other person.

The Law of Agency

An **agency** is a common business relationship created when one person acts on behalf of another and under that person's control. Two parties are involved in an agency relationship: The **principal** is the one who wishes to have a specific task accomplished; the **agent** is the one who acts on behalf of the principal to accomplish the task. Authors, movie stars, and athletes often employ agents to help them obtain the best contract terms.

An agency relationship is created by the mutual agreement of the principal and the agent. It is usually not necessary that such an agreement be in writing, although putting it in writing is certainly advisable. An agency relationship continues as long as both the principal and the agent so desire. It can be terminated by mutual agreement, by fulfillment of the purpose of the agency, by the refusal of either party to continue in

the relationship, or by the death of either the principal or the agent. In most cases, a principal grants authority to the agent through a formal *power of attorney,* which is a legal document authorizing a person to act as someone else's agent. The power of attorney can be used for any agency relationship, and its use is not limited to lawyers. For instance, in real estate transactions, often a lawyer or real estate agent is given power of attorney with the authority to purchase real estate for the buyer. Accounting firms often give employees agency relationships in making financial transactions.

Both officers and directors of corporations are fiduciaries, or people of trust, who use due care and loyalty as an agent in making decisions on behalf of the organization. This relationship creates a duty of care, also called duty of diligence, to make informed decisions. These agents of the corporation are not held responsible for negative outcomes if they are informed and diligent in their decisions. The duty of loyalty means that all decisions should be in the interests of the corporation and its stakeholders. Many people believe that executives at financial firms such as Countrywide Financial, Lehman Brothers, and Merrill Lynch failed to carry out their fiduciary duties. Lawsuits from shareholders called for the officers and directors to pay large sums of money from their own pockets.

The Law of Property

Property law is extremely broad in scope because it covers the ownership and transfer of all kinds of real, personal, and intellectual property. **Real property** consists of real estate and everything permanently attached to it; **personal property** basically is everything else. Personal property can be further subdivided into tangible and intangible property. *Tangible property* refers to items that have a physical existence, such as automobiles, business inventory, and clothing. *Intangible property* consists of rights and duties; its existence may be represented by a document or by some other tangible item. For example, accounts receivable, stock in a corporation, goodwill, and trademarks are all examples of intangible personal property. **Intellectual property** refers to property, such as musical works, artwork, books, and computer software, that is generated by a person's creative activities.

Copyrights, patents, and trademarks provide protection to the owners of property by giving them the exclusive right to use it. *Copyrights* protect the ownership rights on material (often intellectual property) such as books, music, videos, photos, and computer software. The creators of such works, or their heirs, generally have exclusive rights to the published or unpublished works for the creator's lifetime plus 70 years. *Patents* give inventors exclusive rights to their invention for 20 years. The most intense competition

> "An agency is a common business relationship created when one person acts on behalf of another and under that person's control."

for patents is in the pharmaceutical industry. Most patents take a minimum of 18 months to secure.

A *trademark* is a brand (name, mark, or symbol) that is registered with the U.S. Patent and Trademark Office and is thus legally protected from use by any other firm. Among the symbols that have been so protected are McDonald's golden arches and Coca-Cola's distinctive bottle shape. It is estimated that large multinational firms may have as many as 15,000 conflicts related to trademarks. Companies are diligent about protecting their trademarks both to avoid confusion in consumers' minds and because a term that becomes part of everyday language can no longer be trademarked. The names *aspirin* and *nylon,* for example, were once the exclusive property of their creators but became so widely used as product names (rather than brand names) that now anyone can use them.

As the trend toward globalization of trade continues, and more and more businesses trade across national boundaries, protecting property rights, particularly intellectual property such as computer software, has become an increasing challenge. Although a company may be able to register as a trademark a brand name or symbol in its home country, it may not be able to secure that protection abroad. Some countries have copyright and patent laws that are less strict than those of the United States; some countries will not enforce U.S. laws. China, for example, has often been criticized for permitting U.S. goods to be counterfeited there. Such counterfeiting harms not only the sales of U.S. companies but also their reputations if the knock-offs are of poor quality. Thus, businesses engaging in foreign trade may have to take extra steps to protect their property because local laws may be insufficient to protect them.

The Law of Bankruptcy

Although few businesses and individuals intentionally fail to repay (or default on) their debts, sometimes they cannot fulfill their financial obligations. Individuals may charge goods and services beyond their ability to pay for them. Businesses may take on too much debt to finance growth, or business events such as an increase in the cost of commodities can bankrupt a company. An option of last resort in these cases is bankruptcy, or legal insolvency. Some well-known companies that have declared bankruptcy include Hostess, American Airlines, and Blockbuster.

Individuals or companies may ask a bankruptcy court to declare them unable to pay their debts and thus release them from the obligation of repaying those debts. The debtor's assets may then be sold to pay off as much of the debt as possible. In the case of a personal bankruptcy, although the individual is released from repaying debts and can start over with a clean slate, obtaining credit after bankruptcy proceedings is very difficult. About 2 million households in the United States filed for bankruptcy in 2005, the most ever. However, a new, more restrictive law went into effect in late 2005, allowing fewer consumers to use bankruptcy to eliminate their debts. The law makes it harder for consumers to prove that they should be allowed to clear their debts for what is called a "fresh start" or Chapter 7 bankruptcy. Although the person or company in debt usually initiates bankruptcy proceedings, creditors may also initiate them. The subprime mortgage crisis of early 2008 caused a string of bankruptcies among individuals and Chapter 7 and 11 bankruptcies among banks and other businesses as well. Tougher bankruptcy laws and a slowing economy converged on the subprime crisis to create a situation in which bankruptcy filings skyrocketed. Table A.3 describes the various levels of bankruptcy protection a business or individual may seek.

LAWS AFFECTING BUSINESS PRACTICES

One of the government's many roles is to act as a watchdog to ensure that businesses behave in accordance with the wishes of society. Congress has enacted a number of laws that affect business practices; some of the most important of these are summarized in Table A.4. Many state legislatures have enacted similar laws governing business within specific states.

The **Sherman Antitrust Act**, passed in 1890 to prevent businesses from restraining trade and monopolizing markets, condemns "every contract, combination, or conspiracy in restraint of trade." For example, a request that a competitor agree to fix prices or divide markets would, if accepted, result in a violation of the Sherman Act. AT&T faced serious resistance from the U.S. Justice Department after it announced its bid to acquire T-Mobile. Because there are only a few dominant cell phone

▼ **TABLE A.3** Types of Bankruptcy

Chapter 7	Requires that the business be dissolved and its assets liquidated, or sold, to pay off the debts. Individuals declaring Chapter 7 retain a limited amount of exempt assets, the amount of which may be determined by state or federal law, at the debtor's option. Although the type and value of exempt assets varies from state to state, most states' laws allow a bankrupt individual to keep an automobile, some household goods, clothing, furnishings, and at least some of the value of the debtor's residence. All nonexempt assets must be sold to pay debts.
Chapter 11	Temporarily frees a business from its financial obligations while it reorganizes and works out a payment plan with its creditors. The indebted company continues to operate its business during bankruptcy proceedings. Often, the business sells off assets and less-profitable subsidiaries to raise cash to pay off its immediate obligations.
Chapter 13	Similar to Chapter 11 but limited to individuals. This proceeding allows an individual to establish a three- to five-year plan for repaying his or her debt. Under this plan, an individual ultimately may repay as little as 10 percent of his or her debt.

▼ **TABLE A.4** Major Federal Laws Affecting Business Practices

Act (Date Enacted)	Purpose
Sherman Antitrust Act (1890)	Prohibits contracts, combinations, or conspiracies to restrain trade; establishes as a misdemeanor monopolizing or attempting to monopolize.
Clayton Act (1914)	Prohibits specific practices such as price discrimination, exclusive dealer arrangements, and stock acquisitions in which the effect may notably lessen competition or tend to create a monopoly.
Federal Trade Commission Act (1914)	Created the Federal Trade Commission; also gives the FTC investigatory powers to be used in preventing unfair methods of competition.
Robinson-Patman Act (1936)	Prohibits price discrimination that lessens competition among wholesalers or retailers; prohibits producers from giving disproportionate services of facilities to large buyers.
Wheeler-Lea Act (1938)	Prohibits unfair and deceptive acts and practices regardless of whether competition is injured; places advertising of foods and drugs under the jurisdiction of the FTC.
Lanham Act (1946)	Provides protections and regulation of brand names, brand marks, trade names, and trademarks.
Celler-Kefauver Act (1950)	Prohibits any corporation engaged in commerce from acquiring the whole or any part of the stock or other share of the capital assets of another corporation when the effect substantially lessens competition or tends to create a monopoly.
Fair Packaging and Labeling Act (1966)	Makes illegal the unfair or deceptive packaging or labeling of consumer products.
Magnuson-Moss Warranty (FTC) Act (1975)	Provides for minimum disclosure standards for written consumer product warranties; defines minimum consent standards for written warranties; allows the FTC to prescribe interpretive rules in policy statements regarding unfair or deceptive practices.
Consumer Goods Pricing Act (1975)	Prohibits the use of price maintenance agreements among manufacturers and resellers in interstate commerce.
Antitrust Improvements Act (1976)	Requires large corporations to inform federal regulators of prospective mergers or acquisitions so that they can be studied for any possible violations of the law.
Trademark Counterfeiting Act (1980)	Provides civil and criminal penalties against those who deal in counterfeit consumer goods or any counterfeit goods that can threaten health or safety.
Trademark Law Revision Act (1988)	Amends the Lanham Act to allow brands not yet introduced to be protected through registration with the Patent and Trademark Office.
Nutrition Labeling and Education Act (1990)	Prohibits exaggerated health claims and requires all processed foods to contain labels with nutritional information.
Telephone Consumer Protection Act (1991)	Establishes procedures to avoid unwanted telephone solicitations; prohibits marketers from using automated telephone dialing system or an artificial or prerecorded voice to certain telephone lines.
Federal Trademark Dilution Act (1995)	Provides trademark owners the right to protect trademarks and requires relinquishment of names that match or parallel existing trademarks.
Digital Millennium Copyright Act (1998)	Refined copyright laws to protect digital versions of copyrighted materials, including music and movies.
Children's Online Privacy Protection Act (2000)	Regulates the collection of personally identifiable information (name, address, e-mail address, hobbies, interests, or information collected through cookies) online from children under age 13.
Sarbanes-Oxley Act (2002)	Made securities fraud a criminal offense; stiffened penalties for corporate fraud; created an accounting oversight board; and instituted numerous other provisions designed to increase corporate transparency and compliance.
Do Not Call Implementation Act (2003)	Directs FCC and FTC to coordinate so their rules are consistent regarding telemarketing call practices, including the Do Not Call Registry.
Dodd-Frank Wall Street Reform and Consumer Protection Act (2010)	Increases accountability and transparency in the financial industry, protects consumers from deceptive financial practices, and establishes the Consumer Financial Protection Bureau.

carriers in the market, the Justice Department believed that the merger would make AT&T too powerful. Critics feared that the merger would lead to higher prices for consumers. Due to increased pressure from the Justice Department, AT&T dropped its bid to acquire T-Mobile—a move that cost it a $4 billion charge.[79] The Sherman Antitrust Act, still highly relevant 100 years after its passage, is being copied throughout the world as the basis for regulating fair competition.

Because the provisions of the Sherman Antitrust Act are rather vague, courts have not always interpreted it as its creators intended. The Clayton Act was passed in 1914 to limit specific activities that can reduce competition. The **Clayton Act** prohibits price discrimination, tying and exclusive agreements, and the acquisition of stock in another corporation when the effect may be to substantially lessen competition or tend to create a monopoly. In addition, the Clayton Act prohibits members of one company's board of directors from holding seats on the boards of competing corporations. The act also exempts farm cooperatives and labor organizations from antitrust laws.

In spite of these laws regulating business practices, there are still many questions about the regulation of business. For instance, it is difficult to determine what constitutes an acceptable degree of competition and whether a monopoly is harmful to a particular market. Many mergers were permitted that resulted in less competition in the banking, publishing, and automobile industries. In some industries, such as utilities, it is not cost effective to have too many competitors. For this reason, the government permits utility monopolies, although recently, the telephone, electricity, and communications industries have been deregulated. Furthermore, the antitrust laws are often rather vague and require interpretation, which may vary from judge to judge and court to court. Thus, what one judge defines as a monopoly or trust today may be permitted by another judge a few years from now. Businesspeople need to understand what the law says on these issues and try to conduct their affairs within the bounds of these laws.

THE INTERNET: LEGAL AND REGULATORY ISSUES

Our use and dependence on the Internet is increasingly creating a potential legal problem for businesses. With this growing use come questions of maintaining an acceptable level of privacy for consumers and proper competitive use of the medium. Some might consider that tracking individuals who visit or hit their website by attaching a cookie (identifying you as a website visitor for potential recontact and tracking your movement throughout the site) is an improper use of the Internet for business purposes. Others may find such practices acceptable and similar to the practices of non-Internet retailers who copy information from checks or ask customers for their name, address, or phone number before they will process a transaction. There are few specific laws that regulate business on the Internet, but the standards for acceptable behavior that are reflected in the basic laws and regulations designed for traditional businesses can be applied to business on the Internet as well. One law aimed specifically at advertising on the Internet is the CAN-SPAM Act of 2004. The law restricts unsolicited e-mail advertisements by requiring the consent of the recipient. Furthermore, the CAN-SPAM Act follows the opt-out model wherein recipients can elect to not receive further e-mails from a sender simply by clicking a link.[80]

Whether you like it or not, Google, like Yahoo! and AOL, tracks people's web browsing patterns. By tracking the sites you visit, the companies' advertisers can aim ads targeted closer to your interests.
© JGI/Tom Grill/Blend Images, RF

The central focus for future legislation of business conducted on the Internet is the protection of personal privacy. The present basis of personal privacy protection is the U.S. Constitution, various Supreme Court rulings, and laws such as the 1971 Fair Credit Reporting Act, the 1978 Right to Financial Privacy Act, and the 1974 Privacy Act, which deals with the release of government records. With few regulations on the use of information by businesses, companies legally buy and sell information on customers to gain competitive advantage. Sometimes existing laws are not enough to protect people, and the ease with which information on customers can be obtained becomes a problem. For example, identity theft has increased due to the proliferation of the use of the Internet. In one survey performed by regulators, more than half of U.S. brokerage firms claim they have experienced attempts from cybercriminals to trick them into wiring client funds. This often occurs when cybercriminals hack into the clients' e-mail accounts to steal the clients' identities. They then use the accounts to trick the brokers into thinking they are the clients. A former trader at Morgan Stanley Smith Barney was tricked into wiring a total of $521,500 as a result of fraudulent requests.[81] It has been suggested that the treatment of personal data as property will ensure privacy rights by recognizing that customers have a right to control the use of their personal data.

Internet use is different from traditional interaction with businesses in that it is readily accessible, and most online businesses can develop databases of information on customers. Congress has restricted the development of databases on children using the Internet. The Children's Online Privacy Protection Act of 2000 prohibits website and Internet providers from seeking personal information from children under age 13 without parental consent. Companies are still running afoul of COPPA. The Federal Trade Commission charged Yelp and TinyCo with using apps to collect information from children. TinyCo, which markets apps specifically toward children, was forced to pay a $300,000 fine.[83]

The Internet has also created a copyright dilemma for some organizations that have found that the web addresses of other online firms either match or are very similar to their company trademark. "Cybersquatters" attempt to sell back the registration of these matching sites to the trademark owner. Companies such as Taco Bell, MTV, and KFC have paid thousands of dollars to gain control of domain names that match or parallel company trademarks. The Federal Trademark Dilution Act of 1995 helps companies address this conflict. The act provides trademark owners the right to protect trademarks, prevents the use of trademark-protected entities, and requires the relinquishment of names that match or closely parallel company trademarks. The reduction of geographic barriers, speed of response, and memory capability of the Internet will continue to create new challenges for the legal and regulatory environment in the future.

LEGAL PRESSURE FOR RESPONSIBLE BUSINESS CONDUCT

To ensure greater compliance with society's desires, both federal and state governments are moving toward increased organizational accountability for misconduct. Before 1991, laws mainly punished those employees directly responsible for an offense. Under new guidelines established by the Federal Sentencing Guidelines for Organizations (FSGO), however, both the responsible employees and the firms that employ them are held accountable for violations of federal law. Thus, the government now places responsibility for controlling and preventing misconduct squarely on the shoulders of top management. The main objectives of the federal guidelines are to train employees, self-monitor and supervise employee conduct, deter unethical acts, and punish those organizational members who engage in illegal acts.

A 2004 amendment to the FSGO requires that a business's governing authority be well informed about its ethics program with respect to content, implementation, and effectiveness. This

"To ensure greater compliance with society's desires, both federal and state governments are moving toward increased organizational accountability for misconduct."

places the responsibility squarely on the shoulders of the firm's leadership, usually the board of directors. The board must ensure that a high-ranking manager is accountable for the day-to-day operational oversight of the ethics program. The board must provide for adequate authority, resources, and access to the board or an appropriate subcommittee of the board. The board must ensure that confidential mechanisms are available so that the organization's employees and agents may report or seek guidance about potential or actual misconduct without fear of retaliation. Finally, the board is required to oversee the discovery of risks and to design, implement, and modify approaches to deal with those risks.

If an organization's culture and policies reward or provide opportunities to engage in misconduct through lack of managerial concern or failure to comply with the seven minimum requirements of the FSGO (provided in Table A.5), then the organization may incur not only penalties but also the loss of customer trust, public confidence, and other intangible assets. For this reason, organizations cannot succeed solely through a legalistic approach to compliance with the sentencing guidelines; top management must cultivate high ethical standards that will serve as barriers to illegal conduct. The organization must want to be a good citizen and recognize the importance of compliance to successful workplace activities and relationships. In fact, the top concern of corporate lawyers is ethics and compliance. Implementing ethics and compliance ranks higher than any other concern, possibly due to the pressures placed on companies by the passage of Sarbanes-Oxley, the Dodd-Frank Act, and the Federal Sentencing Guidelines.[84]

The federal guidelines also require businesses to develop programs that can detect—and that will deter employees from engaging in—misconduct. To be considered effective, such compliance programs must include disclosure of any wrongdoing, cooperation with the government, and acceptance of responsibility for the misconduct. Codes of ethics, employee ethics training, hotlines (direct 800 phone numbers), compliance directors, newsletters,

brochures, and other communication methods are typical components of a compliance program. The ethics component, discussed in Chapter 2, acts as a buffer, keeping firms away from the thin line that separates unethical and illegal conduct.

Despite the existing legislation, a number of ethics scandals in the early 2000s led Congress to pass—almost unanimously—the **Sarbanes-Oxley Act**, which criminalized securities fraud and strengthened penalties for corporate fraud. It also created an accounting oversight board that requires corporations to establish codes of ethics for financial reporting and to develop greater transparency in financial reports to investors and other interested parties. Additionally, the law requires top corporate executives to sign off on their firms' financial reports, and they risk fines and jail sentences if they misrepresent their companies' financial position. Table A.6 summarizes the major provisions of the Sarbanes-Oxley Act.

The Sarbanes-Oxley Act has created a number of concerns and is considered burdensome and expensive to corporations. Large corporations report spending more than $4 million each year to comply with the act, according to Financial Executives International. The act has caused more than 500 public companies a year to report problems in their accounting systems. Additionally, Sarbanes-Oxley failed to prevent and detect the widespread misconduct of financial institutions that led to the financial crisis.

On the other hand, there are many benefits, including greater accountability of top managers and boards of directors, that improve investor confidence and protect employees, especially their retirement plans. It is believed that the law has more benefits than drawbacks—with the greatest benefit being that boards of directors and top managers are better informed. Some companies such as Cisco and Pitney Bowes report improved efficiency and cost savings from better financial information.

In spite of the benefits Sarbanes-Oxley offers, it did not prevent widespread corporate corruption from leading to the most recent recession. The resulting financial

> "In spite of the benefits Sarbanes-Oxley offers, it did not prevent widespread corporate corruption from leading to the most recent recession."

▼ **TABLE A.5** Seven Steps to Compliance

1. Develop standards and procedures to reduce the propensity for criminal conduct.
2. Designate a high-level compliance manager or ethics officer to oversee the compliance program.
3. Avoid delegating authority to people known to have a propensity to engage in misconduct.
4. Communicate standards and procedures to employees, other agents, and independent contractors through training programs and publications.
5. Establish systems to monitor and audit misconduct and to allow employees and agents to report criminal activity.
6. Enforce standards and punishments consistently across all employees in the organization.
7. Respond immediately to misconduct and take reasonable steps to prevent further criminal conduct.

Source: United States Sentencing Commission, *Federal Sentencing Guidelines for Organizations,* 1991.

crisis prompted the Obama administration to create new regulation to reform Wall Street and the financial industry. In 2010, the Dodd-Frank Wall Street Reform and Consumer Protection Act was passed. In addition to new regulations for financial institutions, the legislation created a Consumer Financial Protection Bureau (CFPB) to protect consumers from complex or deceptive financial products. Table A.7 highlights some of the major provisions of the Dodd-Frank Act.

The Dodd-Frank Act contains 16 titles meant to increase consumer protection, enhance transparency and accountability in the financial sector, and create new financial agencies. In some

▼ **TABLE A.6** Major Provisions of the Sarbanes-Oxley Act

1. Requires the establishment of a Public Company Accounting Oversight Board in charge of regulations administered by the Securities and Exchange Commission.
2. Requires CEOs and CFOs to certify that their companies' financial statements are true and without misleading statements.
3. Requires that corporate boards of directors' audit committees consist of independent members who have no material interests in the company.
4. Prohibits corporations from making or offering loans to officers and board members.
5. Requires codes of ethics for senior financial officers; code must be registered with the SEC.
6. Prohibits accounting firms from providing both auditing and consulting services to the same client without the approval of the client firm's audit committee.
7. Requires company attorneys to report wrongdoing to top managers and, if necessary, to the board of directors; if managers and directors fail to respond to reports of wrongdoing, the attorney should stop representing the company.
8. Mandates whistleblower protection for persons who disclose wrongdoing to authorities.
9. Requires financial securities analysts to certify that their recommendations are based on objective reports.
10. Requires mutual fund managers to disclose how they vote shareholder proxies, giving investors information about how their shares influence decisions.
11. Establishes a 10-year penalty for mail/wire fraud.
12. Prohibits the two senior auditors from working on a corporation's account for more than five years; other auditors are prohibited from working on an account for more than seven years. In other words, accounting firms must rotate individual auditors from one account to another from time to time.

Source: Pub. L. 107-204, 116 Stat. 745 (2002).

▼ **TABLE A.7** Major Provisions of the Dodd-Frank Wall Street Reform and Consumer Protection Act

1. Enhances stability of the finance industry through the creation of two new financial agencies, the Financial Oversight Stability Council and the Office of Financial Research.
2. Institutes an orderly liquidation procedure for the Federal Deposit Insurance Corporation to liquidate failing companies.
3. Eliminates the Office of Thrift Supervision and transfers its powers to the Comptroller of the Currency.
4. Creates stronger regulation and greater oversight of hedge funds.
5. Establishes the Federal Insurance Agency to gather information and oversee the insurance industry for risks.
6. Requires regulators to have regulations in place for banks. Also prohibits and/or limits proprietary trading, hedge fund sponsorship and private equity funds, and relationships with hedge funds and private equity funds.
7. Regulates derivatives and complex financial instruments by limiting where they can be traded and ensuring that traders have the financial resources to meet their responsibilities.
8. Provides a framework for creating risk-management standards for financial market utilities and the payment, clearing, and settlement activities performed by institutions.
9. Improves investor protection through acts such as creating a whistleblower bounty program and increasing consumer access to their credit scores.
10. Institutes the Consumer Financial Protection Bureau to educate consumers and protect them from deceptive financial products.
11. Attempts to reform the Federal Reserve in ways that include limiting the Federal Reserve's lending authority, reevaluating methods for Federal Reserve regulations and the appointment of Federal Reserve Bank directors, and instituting additional disclosure requirements.
12. Reforms mortgage activities with new provisions that include increasing the lender's responsibility to ensure the borrower can pay back the loan, prohibiting unfair lending practices, requiring additional disclosure in the mortgage loan process, and imposing penalties against those found guilty of noncompliance with the new standards.

Source: *Brief Summary of the Dodd-Frank Wall Street Reform and Consumer Protection Act,* www.banking.senate.gov/public/_files/070110_Dodd_Frank_Wall_Street_Reform_comprehensive_summary_Final.pdf (accessed February 5, 2015).

ways, Dodd-Frank is attempting to improve upon provisions laid out in the Sarbanes-Oxley Act. For instance, Dodd-Frank takes whistleblower protection a step further by offering additional incentives to whistleblowers for reporting misconduct. If whistleblowers report misconduct that results in penalties of more than $1 million, the whistleblower will be entitled to a percentage of the settlement.[85] Additionally, complex financial instruments must now be made more transparent so that consumers will have a better understanding of what these instruments involve.

The act also created three new agencies: the Consumer Financial Protection Bureau (CFPB), the Office of Financial Research, and the Financial Stability Oversight Council. Although the CFPB was created to protect consumers, the other two agencies work to maintain stability in the financial industry so such a crisis will not recur in the future.[86] Although it is too early to tell whether these regulations will serve to create widescale positive financial reform, the Dodd-Frank Act is certainly leading to major changes on Wall Street and in the financial sector. ■

chapter three

business in a
borderless world

© Robert Churchill/Getty Images, RF

LEARNING OBJECTIVES

After reading this chapter, you will be able to:

LO 3-1 Explore some of the factors within the international trade environment that influence business.

LO 3-2 Investigate some of the economic, legal, political, social, cultural, and technological barriers to international business.

LO 3-3 Specify some of the agreements, alliances, and organizations that may encourage trade across international boundaries.

LO 3-4 Summarize the different levels of organizational involvement in international trade.

LO 3-5 Contrast two basic strategies used in international business.

onsumers around the world can drink Coca-Cola and Pepsi; eat at McDonald's and Pizza Hut; buy an Apple phone made in China; and watch CNN and MTV on Samsung televisions. It may surprise you that German automaker BMW has manufacturing facilities in Mexico and South Africa that export many cars to the United States. In fact, one-third of all 3 Series models sold in the United States are built in South Africa.[1] The products you consume today are just as likely to have been made in China, India, or Germany as in the United States.[3] Likewise, consumers in other countries buy Western electrical equipment, clothing, rock music, cosmetics, and toiletries, as well as computers, robots, and household goods.

?

Many U.S. firms are finding that international markets provide tremendous opportunities for growth. Accessing these markets can promote innovation while intensifying global competition, thereby spurring companies to market better and less expensive products. Today, the more than 7 billion people that inhabit the earth comprise one tremendous marketplace.

In this chapter, we explore business in this exciting global marketplace. First, we look at the nature of international business, including barriers and promoters of trade across international boundaries. Next, we consider the levels of organizational involvement in international business. Finally, we briefly discuss strategies for trading across national borders. ■

LO 3-1 Explore some of the factors within the international trade environment that influence business.

THE ROLE OF INTERNATIONAL BUSINESS

International business refers to the buying, selling, and trading of goods and services across national boundaries. Falling political barriers and new technology are making it possible for more and more companies to sell their products overseas as well as at home. And, as differences among nations continue to narrow, the trend toward the globalization of business is becoming increasingly important. Starbucks serves millions of global customers at 21,000 locations in over 65 countries.[4] The Internet and the ease by which mobile applications can be developed provide many companies with easier entry to access global markets than opening brick-and-mortar stores.[5] Amazon.com, an online retailer, has distribution centers from Nevada to Germany that fill millions of orders a day and ship them to customers in every corner of the world. More than 70 percent of revenues from Apple stores comes from outside the United States.[6] Caterpillar also derives more than half of its sales from outside the United States.[7] Indeed, most of the world's population and two-thirds of its total purchasing power are outside the United States.

international business tthe buying, selling, and trading of goods and services across national boundaries.

> "Falling political barriers and new technology are making it possible for more and more companies to sell their products overseas as well as at home."

When McDonald's sells a Big Mac in Moscow, Sony sells a television in Detroit, or a small Swiss medical supply company sells a shipment of orthopedic devices to a hospital in Monterrey, Mexico, the sale affects the economies of the countries involved. The U.S. market, with 316 million consumers, makes up only 5 percent of the more than 7 billion people elsewhere in the world to whom global companies must consider marketing.[9] Global marketing requires balancing your global brand with the needs of local consumers.[10] To begin our study of international business, we must first consider some economic issues: why nations trade, exporting and importing, and the balance of trade.

Why Nations Trade

Nations and businesses engage in international trade to obtain raw materials and goods that are otherwise unavailable to them or are available elsewhere at a lower price than that at which they themselves can produce. A nation, or individuals and organizations from a nation, sell surplus materials and goods to acquire funds to buy the goods, services, and ideas its people need. Poland, for example, began trading with Western nations in order to acquire new technology and techniques. Poland has taken these lessons and revitalized its formerly communist economy.[11] It was the only European Union (EU) country to avoid an economic recession during the financial crisis.[12] Which goods and services a nation sells depends on what resources it has available.

Some nations have a monopoly on the production of a particular resource or product. Such a monopoly, or **absolute advantage**, exists when a country is the only source of an item,

American companies such as McDonald's have become widely popular in China. This restaurant in Beijing features elements from the Chinese culture as well as from American culture.
© China/Alamy

TATA MOTORS DEPENDS ON JAGUAR AND LAND ROVER

Although operating internationally can create a strategic advantage, it can also result in increased costs and fierce competition. This is something that Indian automotive manufacturer Tata Motors knows all too well. Despite operating two successful luxury car brands—Jaguar and Land Rover—the Indian carmaker has struggled to introduce a successful vehicle into its home market.

In 2008, the company introduced the $1,600 Tata Nano, a small vehicle marketed to budget-conscious consumers. Although the low price tag was supposed to position the stripped-down car as an alternative to inexpensive motorcycles, consumers quickly labeled the car as cheap, unsafe, and unfashionable. During the same period, Tata's international competitors introduced "new" car models in India that they currently

sold in other countries. Unlike its competitors, Tata did not have a vast variety of car models that could be quickly rebranded or used as a template for future designs. This left one option for Tata to improve its competitive position—spend years completely designing a new car.

Five years after the introduction of the Nano, Tata finally launched the Zest, a compact sedan that costs around $10,000. While its introduction is a step in the right direction, Tata Motors knows that it will need to continue designing new cars if it wants to be globally competitive. The Bolt is the newest car in Tata's pipeline and was introduced in 2015. Both the Bolt and Zest feature the same engine, but the Bolt is a hatchback model that is marketed more as a compact sports-utility vehicle. Tata Motors's global sales in

passenger vehicles was down 1.11 percent from a year earlier, while sales of its luxury brand, Jaguar, rose 2.44 percent during the same time period. According to a *Forbes* estimate, the company's premium Jaguar Land Rover division accounts for 95 percent of its current valuation or sales.[8]

Discussion Questions

1. How did Tata Motors become the largest Indian carmaker when its domestic division experienced declining profits?

2. If Tata abandoned its domestic car strategy and focused on the premium segment, how would this affect international sales?

3. If Tata increases or decreases its domestic market share, how will this affect its international strategy?

Many companies choose to outsource manufacturing to factories in Asia due to lower costs of labor.
© Qilai Shen/Bloomberg/Getty Images

the only producer of an item, or the most efficient producer of an item. An example would be an African mining company that possesses the only mine where a specialty diamond can be found. Russia has an absolute advantage in yuksporite, a rare and useful mineral that can be found only in Russia.

to countries where labor and supplies are less expensive. Outsourcing has become a controversial practice in the United States because many jobs have moved overseas where those tasks can be accomplished for lower costs. For years, call-center jobs have been outsourced to countries such as India and the Philippines. However, changes in technology and increased costs of doing business overseas are leading some companies to bring call-center jobs back to the United States.[14]

Trade between Countries

To obtain needed goods and services and the funds to pay for them, nations trade by exporting and importing. **Exporting** is the sale of goods and services to foreign markets. The United States exports more than $2.3 trillion in goods and services.[15] In China, Tesla Motors Inc. is working to implement charging stations for electric vehicles (EVs) for its exports as well as for use by Chinese-made EVs. U.S. companies that view China as both a growth market for exports and a market for lower-cost labor for imports can strategically integrate these into their operations. Successful integration can lead to significantly higher profits than companies that only focus on one of the opportunities. Apple, for example, designed a less expensive version of the iPhone for the Chinese smartphone market, while also utilizing

> "Outsourcing has become a controversial practice in the United States because many jobs have moved overseas where those tasks can be accomplished for lower costs."

Most international trade is based on **comparative advantage**, which occurs when a country specializes in products that it can supply more efficiently or at a lower cost than it can produce other items. Hawaii has a comparative advantage in producing pineapples and Kona coffee because of the climate. France has a comparative advantage in making wine because of its agricultural capabilities, reputation, and the experience of its vintners. The United States, having adopted new technological methods in hydraulic fracturing, has created a comparative advantage in the mining and exporting of natural gas.[13] Other countries, particularly India and Ireland, are also gaining a comparative advantage over the United States in the provision of some services, such as call-center operations, engineering, and software programming. As a result, U.S. companies are increasingly **outsourcing**, or transferring manufacturing and other tasks

Chinese resources for manufacturing.[16] U.S. businesses export many goods and services, particularly agricultural, entertainment (movies, television shows, etc.), and technological products. **Importing** is the purchase of goods and services from foreign sources. Many of the goods you buy in the United States are likely to be imports or to have some imported components. Sometimes you may not even realize they are imports. The United States imports more than $2.9 trillion in goods and services.[17]

Balance of Trade

You have probably read or heard about the fact that the United States has a trade deficit, but what is a trade deficit? A nation's **balance of trade** is the difference in value between its exports and imports. Because the United States (and some other nations as well) imports more products than it exports, it has a negative

trade deficit a nation's negative balance of trade, which exists when that country imports more products than it exports.

balance of payments the difference between the flow of money into and out of a country.

balance of trade, or **trade deficit**. Table 3.1 shows the trade deficit for the United States. The United States has a trade deficit of $505 billion.[18] The trade deficit fluctuates according to such factors as the health of the United States and other economies, productivity, perceived quality, and exchange rates. As Figure 3.1 indicates, U.S. exports to China have been rapidly increasing but not fast enough to offset the imports from China. Trade deficits are harmful because they can mean the failure of businesses, the loss of jobs, and a lowered standard of living.

Of course when a nation exports more goods than it imports, it has a favorable balance of trade, or trade surplus. Until about 1970, the United States had a trade surplus due to an abundance of natural resources and the relative efficiency of its manufacturing systems. Table 3.2 shows the top 10 countries

▼ **TABLE 3.2** Top 10 Countries with Which the United States Has Trade Deficits/Surpluses

Trade Deficit	Trade Surplus
1. China	Hong Kong
2. Japan	United Arab Emirates
3. Germany	Netherlands
4. Mexico	Switzerland
5. Saudi Arabia	Belgium
6. Canada	Brazil
7. India	Australia
8. Ireland	Panama
9. South Korea	Singapore
10. Italy	Argentina

Sources: "Top Ten Countries with Which the U.S. Has a Trade Deficit," April 2013, www.census.gov/foreign-trade/top/dst/current/deficit.html (accessed February 9, 2015); "Top Ten Countries with Which the U.S. Has a Trade Surplus," April 2013, www.census.gov/foreign-trade/top/dst/current/surplus.html (accessed February 9, 2015).

▼ **TABLE 3.1** U.S. Trade Deficit, 1990–2014 (in billions of dollars)

	2000	2008	2009	2010	2011	2012	2013	2014
Exports	$1,075.3	$1,841.6	$1,583.1	$1,853.6	$2,127.0	$2,216.0	$2,280.2	$2,345.4
Imports	1,447.8	2,550.3	1,966.8	2,348.3	2,675.6	2,754.1	2,756.6	2,850.5
Trade surplus/deficit	−372.5	−708.7	−383.8	−494.7	−548.6	−537.6	−476.4	−505.1

Sources: U.S. Bureau of the Census, Foreign Trade Division, *U.S. Trade in Goods and Services—Balance of Payments (BOP) Basis,* February 6, 2014, www.census.gov/foreign-trade/statistics/historical/gands.pdf (accessed February 9, 2015).

▼**FIGURE 3.1**
U.S. Exports to China (millions of U.S. dollars)

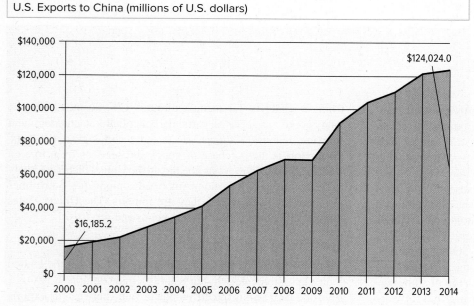

Source: "Trade in Goods (Imports, Exports and Trade Balance) with China," U.S. Bureau of the Census, Foreign Trade Statistics, www.census.gov/foreign-trade/balance/c5700.html (accessed February 9, 2015).

with which the United States has a trade deficit and a trade surplus.

The difference between the flow of money into and out of a country is called its **balance of payments**. A country's balance of trade, foreign investments, foreign aid, loans, military expenditures, and money spent by tourists comprise its balance of payments. As you might expect, a country with a trade surplus generally has a favorable balance of payments because it is receiving more money from trade with foreign countries than it is paying out. When a country has a trade deficit, more money flows out of the country than into it. If more money flows out of the country than into it from tourism and other sources, the country may experience declining production and higher unemployment, because there is less money available for spending.

INTERNATIONAL TRADE BARRIERS

Completely free trade seldom exists. When a company decides to do business outside its own country, it will encounter a number of barriers to international trade. Any firm considering international business must research the other country's economic, legal, political, social, cultural, and technological background. Such research will help the company choose an appropriate level of involvement and operating strategies, as we will see later in this chapter.

> **LO 3-2** Investigate some of the economic, legal, political, social, cultural, and technological barriers to international business.

Economic Barriers

When looking at doing business in another country, managers must consider a number of basic economic factors, such as economic development, infrastructure, and exchange rates.

Economic Development When considering doing business abroad, U.S. businesspeople need to recognize that they cannot take for granted that other countries offer the same things as are found in *industrialized nations*—economically advanced countries such as the United States, Japan, Great Britain, and Canada. Many countries in Africa, Asia, and South America, for example, are in general poorer and less economically advanced than those in North America and Europe; they are often called *less-developed countries* (LDCs). LDCs are characterized by low per-capita income (income generated by the nation's production of goods and services divided by the population), which means that consumers are less likely to purchase nonessential products. Nonetheless, LDCs represent a potentially huge and profitable market for many businesses because they may be buying technology to improve their infrastructures, and much of the population may desire consumer products. For example, automobile manufacturers are looking toward LDCs as a way to expand their customer base. The rising middle class has caused many consumers in India and China to desire their own vehicles. The automobile market in China is now larger than the market in the United States.

A country's level of development is determined in part by its **infrastructure**, the physical facilities that support its economic activities, such as railroads, highways, ports, airfields, utilities and power plants, schools, hospitals, communication systems, and commercial distribution systems. When doing business in LDCs, for example, a business may need to compensate for rudimentary distribution and communication systems, or even a lack of technology.

Exchange Rates The ratio at which one nation's currency can be exchanged for another nation's currency is the **exchange rate**. Exchange rates vary daily and can be found in newspapers and through many sites on the Internet. Familiarity with exchange rates is important because they affect the cost of imports and exports. When the value of the U.S. dollar declines relative to other currencies, such as the euro, the price of imports becomes relatively expensive for U.S. consumers. On the other hand, U.S. exports become relatively cheap for international markets—in this example, the EU. The U.S. dollar is most frequently used in international trade, with 81 percent of trade finance conducted in U.S. dollars.[19]

Occasionally, a government may intentionally alter the value of its currency through fiscal policy. Devaluation decreases the value of currency in relation to other currencies. If the U.S. government were to devalue the dollar, it would lower the cost of American goods abroad and make trips to the United States less expensive for foreign tourists. Thus, devaluation encourages the sale of domestic goods and tourism. On the other hand, when Switzerland's central bank let the value of the Swiss franc rise by 30 percent against the euro in 2015, it resulted in increasing the costs of exports. This made everything exported from Switzerland more expensive, including tourism. However, Swiss brands including expensive watches were offered at large discounts if bought using Swiss francs.[20] Revaluation, as in the Swiss example, increases the value of a currency in relation to other currencies, but occurs rarely.

> " Devaluation decreases the value of currency in relation to other currencies. "

Ethical, Legal, and Political Barriers

A company that decides to enter the international marketplace must contend with potentially complex relationships among the different laws of its own nation, international laws, and the laws of the nation with which it will be trading; various trade restrictions imposed on international trade; changing political climates; and different ethical values. Legal and ethical requirements for successful business are increasing globally. For instance, India has strict limitations on foreign retailers that want to operate within the country. Many sectors do not allow foreign companies to have a 100 percent ownership stake, requiring them to partner with domestic firms to do business in

infrastructure the physical facilities that support a country's economic activities, such as railroads, highways, ports, airfields, utilities and power plants, schools, hospitals, communication systems, and commercial distribution systems.

exchange rate the ratio at which one nation's currency can be exchanged for another nation's currency.

India. Additionally, online retailers such as Walmart.com and Amazon.com were not permitted to sell products they themselves sourced but could sell only products sourced from third-party suppliers. Yet this ban is expected to be lifted in order to boost consumption and benefit domestic firms in India. India is not the only country that is hesitant about foreign companies operating through the Internet.[22] Internet legislation in other countries is causing some companies to pause out of concern. Brazil has passed a law dictating that Internet companies that offer services in the country, such as Google and Yahoo!, abide by strong privacy rules and limitations on how they can store and share user information. This could result in significant extra costs that could serve as a deterrent to foreign investment.[23]

Laws and Regulations The United States has a number of laws and regulations that govern the activities of U.S. firms engaged in international trade. For example, the Webb-Pomerene Export Trade Act of 1918 exempts American firms from antitrust laws if those firms are acting together to enter international trade. This law allows selected U.S. firms to form monopolies to compete with foreign monopolistic organizations, although they are not allowed to limit free trade and competition within the United States or to use unfair methods of competition in international trade. The United States also has a variety of friendship, commerce, and navigation treaties with other nations. These treaties allow business to be transacted between citizens of the specified countries. Ireland is an up-and-coming example of a country that attracts American foreign investment. Corporate tax rates that are among the lowest in Europe, low wages, and sufficient infrastructure are just a few of the reasons investors are attracted to Ireland.

This has led many U.S. firms—including Eaton and Burger King—to undergo tax inversions, which occur when companies relocate their headquarters to countries with a lower tax rate. For instance, Caterpillar avoided $2.4 billion in U.S. taxes by diverting its profits to Switzerland. Tax inversions have been heavily criticized by U.S. lawmakers, who see

Counterfeit products such as these fake luxury handbags are major challenges for international firms.
© Bloomberg/Getty Images

these companies as using tax loopholes to avoid taxes. Ireland is passing legislation closing certain loopholes in their own tax systems, a change that could put a damper on corporate tax inversions.[24]

Once outside U.S. borders, businesspeople are likely to find that the laws of other nations differ from those of the United States. Many of the legal rights that Americans take for granted do not exist in other countries, and a firm doing business abroad must understand and obey the laws of the host country. Some countries have strict laws limiting the amount of local currency that can be taken out of the country and the amount of currency that can be brought in; others limit how foreign companies can operate within the country.

In Mexico, for example, foreigners cannot directly own property in what is known as the "Restricted Zone." The Restricted Zone includes land within 100 kilometers of Mexico's international borders along with land within 50 kilometers of Mexico's oceans and beaches.[25]

Some countries have copyright and patent laws that are less strict than those of the United States, and some countries fail to honor U.S. laws. Because copying is a tradition in China and Vietnam and laws protecting copyrights and intellectual property are weak and minimally enforced, those countries are flooded with counterfeit videos, movies, CDs, computer software, furniture, and clothing. Companies are angry because the counterfeits harm not only their sales, but also their reputations if the knockoffs are of poor quality. Such counterfeiting is not limited to China or Vietnam. It is estimated that nearly half of all software installed on personal computers worldwide is illegally pirated or copied.[26] In countries where these activities occur, laws against them may not be sufficiently enforced if counterfeiting is deemed illegal. Thus, businesses engaging in foreign trade may have to take extra steps to protect their products because local laws may be insufficient to do so.

Tariffs and Trade Restrictions

Tariffs and other trade restrictions are part of a country's legal structure but may be established or removed for political reasons. An **import tariff** is a tax levied by a nation on goods imported into the country. A *fixed tariff* is a specific amount of money levied on each unit of a product brought into the country, while an *ad valorem tariff* is based on the value of the item. Most countries allow citizens traveling abroad to bring home a certain amount of merchandise without paying an import tariff. A U.S. citizen may bring $200 worth of merchandise into the United States duty free. After that, U.S. citizens must pay an ad valorem tariff based on the cost of the item and the country of origin. Thus, identical items purchased in different countries might have different tariffs.

Countries sometimes levy tariffs for political reasons, as when they impose sanctions against other countries to protest their actions. However, import tariffs are more commonly imposed to protect domestic products by raising the price of imported ones. Such protective tariffs have become controversial, as

Americans become increasingly concerned over the U.S. trade deficit. Protective tariffs allow more expensive domestic goods to compete with foreign ones. For example, the United States has imposed tariffs on steel imported into the United States because imports have caused many local steelworks to crash.[27] Other markets can produce steel more cheaply than the United States. Many people and special interest groups in the United States, such as unions, would like to see tariffs placed on Chinese steel, which is significantly less expensive, in order to protect remaining U.S. steel production. The United States has also imposed tariffs on imported sugar for almost two centuries. The EU levies tariffs on many products, including some seafood imports.

Critics of protective tariffs argue that their use inhibits free trade and competition. Supporters of protective tariffs say they insulate domestic industries, particularly new ones, against well-established foreign competitors. Once an industry matures, however, its advocates may be reluctant to let go of the tariff that protected it. Tariffs also help when, because of low labor costs and other advantages, foreign competitors can afford to sell their products at prices lower than those charged by domestic companies. Some Americans argue that tariffs should be used to keep domestic wages high and unemployment low.

Exchange controls restrict the amount of currency that can be bought or sold. Some countries control their foreign trade by forcing businesspeople to buy and sell foreign products through a central bank. If John Deere, for example, receives payments for its tractors in a foreign currency, it may be required to sell

While there is a still a trade embargo, relations between Cuba and the United States are improving with more opportunities for travel and cultural exchanges.
© Dave Moyer, RF

quota a restriction on the number of units of a particular product that can be imported into a country.

embargo a prohibition on trade in a particular product.

dumping the act of a country or business selling products at less than what it costs to produce them.

cartel a group of firms or nations that agrees to act as a monopoly and not compete with each other, in order to generate a competitive advantage in world markets.

as the European Union tried to do against Argentina and Indonesia for allegedly dumping biodiesel imports.

the currency to that nation's central bank. When foreign currency is in short supply, as it is in many LDCs, the government uses foreign currency to purchase necessities and capital goods and produces other products locally, thus limiting its need for foreign imports.

A **quota** limits the number of units of a particular product that can be imported into a country. A quota may be established by voluntary agreement or by government decree. The United States imposes quotas on certain goods, such as garments produced in Vietnam and China. Quotas are designed to protect the industries and jobs of the country imposing the quota.

An **embargo** prohibits trade in a particular product. Embargoes are generally directed at specific goods or countries and may be established for political, economic, health, or religious reasons. While the United States currently maintains a trade embargo with Cuba, European hotel chains are engaged in a building boom on the Caribbean island, where tourism is the number-one industry. U.S. hotel chains are eager to build in Cuba but have no opportunity until the embargo is lifted. Until recently, U.S. tourists were forbidden by the U.S. government to vacation in Cuba because of the embargo. However, the government has begun to allow more Americans to visit Cuba with certain restrictions, and President Obama established diplomatic relations and opened the U.S. embassy. It is much easier to travel to Cuba, and U.S. citizens can bring back $100 worth of Cuban cigars and rum.[28] U.S. farmers export hundreds of millions of dollars' worth of commodities to Cuba each year, based on a 2000 law that provided permission for some trade to the embargoed country.[29] Health embargoes prevent the importing of various pharmaceuticals, animals, plants, and agricultural products. Muslim nations forbid the importation of alcoholic beverages on religious grounds.

One common reason for setting quotas or tariffs is to prohibit **dumping**, which occurs when a country or business sells products at less than what it costs to produce them. The European Union claimed that Argentina and Indonesia were dumping biodiesel imports into their countries. They responded by instituting antidumping fees on biodiesel imports from these two countries.[30] A company may dump its products for several reasons. Dumping permits quick entry into a market. Sometimes dumping occurs when the domestic market for a firm's product is too small to support an efficient level of production. In other cases, technologically obsolete products that are no longer salable in the country of origin are dumped overseas. Dumping is relatively difficult to prove, but even the suspicion of dumping can lead to the imposition of quotas or tariffs,

Political Barriers Unlike legal issues, political considerations are seldom written down and often change rapidly. Nations that have been subject to economic sanctions for political reasons in recent years include Cuba, Iran, Syria, and North Korea. While these were dramatic events, political considerations affect international business daily as governments enact tariffs, embargoes, or other types of trade restrictions in response to political events.

Businesses engaged in international trade must consider the relative instability of countries such as Iraq, Ukraine, and Venezuela. Political unrest in countries such as Pakistan, Somalia, and the Democratic Republic of the Congo may create a hostile or even dangerous environment for foreign businesses. Natural disasters, like typhoons in the Philippines or the massive mudslide in Afghanistan, can cripple a country's government, making the region even more unstable. Even a developed country such as Japan had its social, economic, and political institutions stressed by the 2011 earthquake and tsunamis. Finally, a sudden change in power can result in a regime that is hostile to foreign investment. Some businesses have been forced out of a country altogether, as when Hugo Chávez created a socialist revolution in Venezuela that forced out or took over American oil companies. Whether they like it or not, companies are often involved directly or indirectly in international politics.

Political concerns may lead a group of nations to form a **cartel**, a group of firms or nations that agrees to act as a monopoly and not compete with each other, to generate a competitive advantage in world markets. Probably the most famous

Two honey suppliers were charged with dumping violations involving honey imports from China.
© Anastasy Yarmolovich/Getty Images, RF

cartel is the Organization of the Petroleum Exporting Countries (OPEC), founded in the 1960s to increase the price of petroleum throughout the world and to maintain high prices. By working to ensure stable oil prices, OPEC hopes to enhance the economies of its member nations. For example, oil prices dropped in 2015. OPEC did not cut back on supply but instead focused on gaining market share.

Social and Cultural Barriers

Most businesspeople engaged in international trade underestimate the importance of social and cultural differences; but these differences can derail an important transaction. Burger King formed a joint venture with Everstone Group to begin opening locations in India. The fast-food chain can take lessons from already established competitors that learned the necessity of adapting their menus to reflect the religious and social customs of the region. Within a year the partners announced plans to open up 12 Burger King outlets.[31] Additionally, Tiffany & Co. learned that more attentive customer service was necessary in order to succeed in Japan, and bold marketing and advertising served as the recipe for success in China.[32] And in Europe, Starbucks took the unprecedented step of allowing its locations to be franchised in order to reach smaller markets that are unfamiliar. This way Starbucks reduced some of the cultural and social risks involved in entering such markets.[33] Unfortunately, cultural norms are rarely written down, and what is written down may well be inaccurate.

Cultural differences include differences in spoken and written language. Although it is certainly possible to translate words from one language to another, the true meaning is sometimes misinterpreted or lost. Consider some translations that went awry in foreign markets:

- Scandinavian vacuum manufacturer Electrolux used the following in an American campaign: "Nothing sucks like an Electrolux."

- The Coca-Cola name in China was first read as "Ke-kou-ke-la," meaning "bite the wax tadpole."

- In Italy, a campaign for Schweppes Tonic Water translated the name into Schweppes Toilet Water.[34]

Translators cannot just translate slogans, advertising campaigns, and website language; they must know the cultural differences that could affect a company's success.

Differences in body language and personal space also affect international trade. Body language is nonverbal, usually unconscious communication through gestures, posture, and facial expression. Personal space is the distance at which one person feels comfortable talking to another. Americans tend to stand a moderate distance away from the person with whom they are speaking. Arab businessmen tend to stand face-to-face with the object of their conversation. Additionally, gestures vary from culture to culture, and gestures considered

▼ **TABLE 3.3** Cultural Behavioral Differences

Region	Gestures Viewed as Rude or Unacceptable
Japan, Hong Kong, Middle East	Summoning with index finger
Middle and Far East	Pointing with index finger
Thailand, Japan, France	Sitting with soles of shoes showing
Brazil, Germany	Forming a circle with fingers (the "OK" sign in the United States)
Japan	Winking to mean "I love you"
Buddhist countries	Patting someone on the head

Source: Adapted from Judie Haynes, "Communicating with Gestures," *EverythingESL* (n.d.), www.everythingesl.net/inservices/body_language.php (accessed January 15, 2015).

acceptable in American society—pointing, for example—may be considered rude in others. Table 3.3 shows some of the behaviors considered rude or unacceptable in other countries. Such cultural differences may generate uncomfortable feelings or misunderstandings when businesspeople of different countries negotiate with each other.

Family roles also influence marketing activities. Many countries do not allow children to be used in advertising, for example. Advertising that features people in nontraditional social roles may or may not be successful either. Fine Indian jeweler Tanishq was criticized for an advertisement aired in its native country. The advertisement depicted a marriage ceremony between a single mother and a man who was obviously not the father of the child. Critics claimed the ad disregarded Indian values and morals because widowed and divorced women are often shunned from their communities. Remarriage and premarital relations, under any circumstances, are not appropriate in Indian culture. Others saw the ad as starting a conversation about women's rights.[35]

The people of other nations quite often have a different perception of time as well. Americans value promptness; a business meeting scheduled for a specific time seldom starts more than a few minutes late. In Mexico and Spain, however, it is not unusual for a meeting to be delayed half an hour or more. Such a late start might produce resentment in an American negotiating in Spain for the first time.

Companies engaged in foreign trade must observe the national and religious holidays and local customs of the host country. In many Islamic countries, for example, workers expect to take a break at certain times of the day to observe religious rites. Companies also must monitor their advertising to guard against offending customers. In Thailand and many other countries, public displays of affection between the sexes are unacceptable in advertising messages; in many Middle Eastern nations, it is unacceptable to show the soles of one's feet.[36] In Russia, smiling is considered appropriate only in private settings, not in business.

With the exception of the United States, most nations use the metric system. This lack of uniformity creates problems for both buyers and sellers in the international marketplace. American

General Agreement on Tariffs and Trade (GATT) a trade agreement, originally signed by 23 nations in 1947, that provided a forum for tariff negotiations and a place where international trade problems could be discussed and resolved.

World Trade Organization (WTO) international organization dealing with the rules of trade between nations.

sellers, for instance, must package goods destined for foreign markets in liters or meters, and Japanese sellers must convert to the English system if they plan to sell a product in the United States. Tools also must be calibrated in the correct system if they are to function correctly. Hyundai and Honda service technicians need metric tools to make repairs on those cars.

The literature dealing with international business is filled with accounts of sometimes humorous but often costly mistakes that occurred because of a lack of understanding of the social and cultural differences between buyers and sellers. Such problems cannot always be avoided, but they can be minimized through research on the cultural and social differences of the host country.

Technological Barriers

Many countries lack the technological infrastructure found in the United States, and some marketers are viewing such barriers as opportunities. For instance, marketers are targeting many countries such as India and China and some African countries where there are few private phone lines. Citizens of these countries are turning instead to wireless communication through cell phones. Technological advances are creating additional global marketing opportunities. Along with opportunities, changing technologies also create new challenges and competition. The U.S. market share of the personal computer market is dropping as new competitors emerge that are challenging U.S. PC makers. Out of the top six global PC companies—Lenovo, Hewlett-Packard, Dell, Acer, Asus, and Apple—three are from Asian countries.[37]

Cell phone services are growing rapidly in the Middle East and Africa. They offer a viable alternative to landlines, which require infrastructure not always available in rural areas.
© Terry Vine/Getty Images, RF

LO 3-3 Specify some of the agreements, alliances, and organizations that may encourage trade across international boundaries.

TRADE AGREEMENTS, ALLIANCES, AND ORGANIZATIONS

Although these economic, political, legal, and sociocultural issues may seem like daunting barriers to international trade, there are also organizations and agreements—such as the General Agreement on Tariffs and Trade, the World Bank, and the International Monetary Fund—that foster international trade and can help companies get involved in and succeed in global markets. Various regional trade agreements, such as the North American Free Trade Agreement and the EU, also promote trade among member nations by eliminating tariffs and trade restrictions. In this section, we'll look briefly at these agreements and organizations.

General Agreement on Tariffs and Trade

During the Great Depression of the 1930s, nations established so many protective tariffs covering so many products that international trade became virtually impossible. By the end of World War II, there was considerable international momentum to liberalize trade and minimize the effects of tariffs. The **General Agreement on Tariffs and Trade (GATT)**, originally signed by 23 nations in 1947, provided a forum for tariff negotiations and a place where international trade problems could be discussed and resolved. More than 100 nations abided by its rules. GATT sponsored rounds of negotiations aimed at reducing trade restrictions. The most recent round, the Uruguay Round (1988–1994), further reduced trade barriers for most products and provided new rules to prevent dumping.

The **World Trade Organization (WTO)**, an international organization dealing with the rules of trade between nations, was created in 1995 by the Uruguay Round. Key to the World Trade Organization are the WTO agreements, which are the legal ground rules for international commerce. The agreements were negotiated and signed by most of the world's trading nations and ratified by their parliaments. The goal is to help producers of goods and services and exporters and importers conduct their business. In addition to administering the WTO trade agreements, the WTO presents a forum for trade negotiations, monitors national trade policies, provides technical assistance and training for developing countries, and cooperates with other international organizations. Based in Geneva, Switzerland, the WTO has also adopted a leadership role in negotiating trade disputes among nations.[38] For example, when Indonesia and Argentina wanted to contest the EU's tariffs against their biodiesel imports, they filed their dispute with the WTO.[39]

The North American Free Trade Agreement

The **North American Free Trade Agreement (NAFTA)**, which went into effect on January 1, 1994, effectively merged Canada, the United States, and Mexico into one market of nearly 470 million consumers. NAFTA virtually eliminated all tariffs on goods produced and traded among Canada, Mexico, and the United States to create a free trade area. NAFTA makes it easier for U.S. businesses to invest in Mexico and Canada; provides protection for intellectual property (of special interest to high-technology and entertainment industries); expands trade by requiring equal treatment of U.S. firms in both countries; and simplifies country-of-origin rules, hindering Japan's use of Mexico as a staging ground for further penetration into U.S. markets.

Canada's nearly 35 million consumers are relatively affluent, with a per-capita GDP of $43,100.[40] Trade in goods between the United States and Canada totals approximately $682 billion.[41] In fact, Canada is the single largest trading partner of the United States.[42]

With a per-capita GDP of $15,600, Mexico's more than 120 million consumers are less affluent than Canadian consumers.[43] However, trade with the United States and Mexico has tripled since NAFTA was initiated. Trade between the United States and Mexico totals more than $530 billion.[44] Millions of Americans cite their heritage as Mexican, making them the most populous Hispanic group in the country. These individuals often have close ties to relatives in Mexico and assist in Mexican–U.S. economic development and trade. Mexico is on a course of a market economy, rule of law, respect for human rights, and responsible public policies. There is also a commitment to the environment and sustainable human development. Many U.S. companies have taken advantage of Mexico's low labor costs and proximity to the United States to set up production facilities, sometimes called *maquiladoras*. Mexico is also attracting major technological industries, including electronics, software, and aerospace. Investors see many growth opportunities in Mexico, particularly in light of recent reforms. For instance, Mexico passed legislation to open up its state-controlled oil reserves to foreign companies. Additionally, if the United States does well economically, Mexico—its biggest customer—is also likely to do well.[45]

However, there is great disparity within Mexico. The country's southern states cannot seem to catch up with the more affluent northern states on almost any socioeconomic indicator. The disparities are growing, as can be seen comparing the south to the northern industrial capital of Monterrey, which is beginning to seem like south Texas.[46] Drug gang wars threaten the economic stability of Mexico, especially in the northern states close to the U.S. border. On the other hand, this situation is improving as the economy is growing and violence is decreasing.

North American Free Trade Agreement (NAFTA) agreement that eliminates most tariffs and trade restrictions on agricultural and manufactured products to encourage trade among Canada, the United States, and Mexico.

Despite its benefits, NAFTA has been controversial, and disputes continue to arise over the implementation of the trade agreement. While many Americans feared the agreement would erase jobs in the United States, Mexicans have been disappointed that the agreement failed to create more jobs. Moreover, Mexico's rising standard of living has increased the cost of doing business there; many hundreds of *maquiladoras* have closed their doors and transferred work to China and other nations where labor costs are cheaper. Indeed, China has become the United States' second largest importer.[47] On the other hand, high transportation costs, intellectual property theft, quality failures, and the difficulty management often incurs in controlling a business so far away and under a communist regime are now causing some manufacturers to reconsider opting for Mexican factories over China, even going so far as to relocate from China back to Mexico.[48]

Although NAFTA has been controversial, it has become a positive factor for U.S. firms wishing to engage in international marketing. Because licensing requirements have been relaxed under the pact, smaller businesses that previously could not afford to invest in Mexico and Canada will be able to do business in those markets without having to locate there. NAFTA's long phase-in period provided time for adjustment by those firms affected by reduced tariffs on imports.

NAFTA, which went into effect on January 1, 1994, has increased trade among Mexico, the United States, and Canada.
© *scibak/Getty Images, RF*

Furthermore, increased competition should lead to a more efficient market, and the long-term prospects of including most countries in the Western Hemisphere in the alliance promise additional opportunities for U.S. marketers.

The European Union

The **European Union (EU)**, also called the *European Community* or *Common Market,* was established in 1958 to promote trade among its members, which initially included Belgium, France, Italy, West Germany, Luxembourg, and the Netherlands. East and West Germany united in 1991, and by 1995 the United Kingdom, Spain, Denmark, Greece, Portugal, Ireland, Austria, Finland, and Sweden had joined as well. The Czech Republic, Estonia, Hungary, Latvia, Lithuania, Poland, Slovakia, and Slovenia joined in 2004. In 2007, Bulgaria and Romania also became members, Cyprus and Malta joined in 2008, and Croatia joined in 2013, which brought total membership to 28. Macedonia, Iceland, and Turkey are candidate countries that hope to join the EU in the near future.[49] Until 1993, each nation functioned as a separate market, but at that time members officially unified into one of the largest single world markets, which today has nearly half a billion consumers with a GDP of more than $15.8 trillion.[50]

To facilitate free trade among members, the EU is working toward standardization of business regulations and requirements, import duties, and value-added taxes; the elimination of customs checks; and the creation of a standardized currency for use by all members. Many European nations (Austria, Belgium, Finland, France, Germany, Greece, Ireland, Italy, Luxembourg, the Netherlands, Portugal, Spain, and Slovenia) link their exchange rates to a common currency, the *euro;* however, some EU members such as the United Kingdom have rejected use of the euro in their countries. Although the common currency requires many marketers to modify their pricing strategies and will subject them to increased competition, the use of a single currency frees companies that sell goods among European countries from the nuisance of dealing with complex exchange rates.[51] The long-term goals are to eliminate all trade barriers within the EU, improve the economic efficiency of the EU nations, and stimulate economic growth, thus making the union's economy more competitive in global markets, particularly against Japan and other Pacific Rim nations, and North America. However, several disputes and debates still divide the member nations, and many barriers to completely free trade remain. Consequently, it may take many years before the EU is truly one deregulated market.

The EU has also enacted some of the world's strictest laws concerning antitrust issues, which have had unexpected consequences for some non-European firms. For instance, the European Union passed a law that established for Internet users the "right to be forgotten." Under the law, Internet users in the EU can request that Internet search engines such as Google and Bing remove links involving personal information that does not hold a public interest. This is the first time such a rule has been implemented, and supporters believe this ruling should be applied worldwide. The European Parliament is also encouraging the breakup of Google's search engine business from its other businesses.[52]

The prosperity of the EU has suffered in recent years. EU members experienced a severe economic crisis in 2010 that required steep bailouts from the International Monetary Fund (IMF). The first country to come to the forefront was Greece, which had so much debt that it risked default. With an increase in Greek bond yields and credit risks—along with a severe deficit and other negative economic factors—the country's economy plummeted. Because Greece uses the euro as its currency, the massive downturn decreased the euro's value. This had a profound effect on other countries in the euro zone. (The euro zone refers collectively to European member countries that have adopted the euro as their form of currency.) Ireland and Portugal were particularly vulnerable because they had some of the region's largest deficits.[53] Ireland began experiencing problems similar to Greece, including a debt crisis, failing economic health, and rising bond yields.[54] Both Ireland and Portugal required bailout packages. Spain and Cyprus also requested bailouts.

Greece continues to struggle even after the initial bailout because it did not have enough funds to repay its bondholders. Greece was forced to default. A default by one nation in the EU negatively affects the rest of the members by making them appear riskier as well.[55] Greece has discussed withdrawing from the eurozone in an attempt to reduce debt. Such a move would lead to more bank busts in Greece, unemployment over 25 percent, and the likely exit of Greece from the EU. It is feared that an exit would prompt other governments in southern Europe to contemplate doing the same, potentially reducing the ability of the euro to survive as a single currency.[56] Germany, on the other hand, has largely avoided the economic woes plaguing other countries. Germany has many exporting companies and has a smaller budget deficit and smaller household debt, which has enabled it to weather the crisis better than other EU members.[57]

Asia-Pacific Economic Cooperation

The **Asia-Pacific Economic Cooperation (APEC)**, established in 1989, promotes open trade and economic and technical cooperation among member economies, which initially included Australia, Brunei Darussalam, Canada, Indonesia, Japan, Korea, Malaysia, New Zealand, the Philippines, Singapore, Thailand, and the United States. Since then, the alliance has grown to include Chile; China; Hong Kong, Mexico; Papua New Guinea; Peru; Russia; Chinese Taipei; and Vietnam. The 21-member alliance represents approximately 40 percent of the world's population, 44 percent of world trade, and 55 percent of world GDP. In comparison, the United States holds 22 percent of global GDP.[58] APEC differs from other international trade alliances in its commitment to facilitating business and its practice of allowing the business/private sector to participate in a wide range of APEC activities.[59]

APEC companies have become increasingly competitive and sophisticated in global business in the past three decades. The Japanese and South Koreans in particular have made tremendous inroads on world markets for automobiles, cameras, and audio and video equipment. Products from Samsung, Sony, Canon, Toyota, Daewoo, Mitsubishi, Suzuki, and Lenovo are sold all over the world and have set standards of quality by which other products are often judged. The People's Republic of China, a country of more than 1.3 billion people, has launched a program of economic reform to stimulate its economy by privatizing many industries, restructuring its banking system, and increasing public spending on infrastructure (including railways and telecommunications). As a result, China has become a hub for manufacturing, although growth has slowed in recent years to less than 7.5 percent.[60] China's export market has consistently outpaced its import growth in recent years and its GDP is the world's second largest economy, behind the United States. In fact, China has overtaken the United States as the world's largest trader.[61]

This is the ASEAN flag. The symbol for the ASEAN trading bloc is in the middle.
© Zoonar GmbH / Alamy, RF

Increased industrialization has also caused China to become the world's largest emitter of greenhouse gases. China has overtaken the United States to become the world's largest oil importer.[62] On the other hand, China has also begun a quest to become a world leader in green initiatives and renewable energy. This is an increasingly important quest as the country becomes more polluted.

Another risk area for China is the fact that the government owns or has stakes in so many enterprises. On the one hand, China's system of state-directed capitalism has benefited the country because reforms and

> " APEC companies have become increasingly competitive and sophisticated in global business in the past three decades. "

decisions can be made more quickly. On the other hand, state-backed companies lack many of the competitors that private industries have. Remember that competition often spurs innovation and lowers costs. If China's firms lack sufficient competition, their costs may very likely increase.[64] China's growing debt liabilities have also caused concern among foreign investors.[65]

Less visible Pacific Rim regions, such as Thailand, Singapore, Taiwan, Vietnam, and Hong Kong, have also become major manufacturing and financial centers. Vietnam,

LAVENDER-LACED TEDDY BEAR FINDS INSATIABLE DEMAND IN CHINA

In 2007, Robert Ravens retired and, with his wife, bought a lavender farm in Tasmania, Australia. They soon came up with the idea of stuffing teddy bears with a mixture of dried lavender and wheat; the lavender would impart a lovely scent, and the wheat would allow the bear to stay pleasantly warm after being heated in a microwave. The Ravens called their invention "Bobbie Bear" and sold

the cute purple bears at a premium price, using the popular item to drive tourism to their farm.

Their retirement was turned upside down, however, when several popular Chinese celebrities took a liking to Bobbie Bear and promoted it on popular social media sites. Demand exploded. The Ravens went from selling 3,500 bears in 2011 to 30,000 in

2013 and, despite raising the bear's price at least five times, still cannot produce enough Bobbie Bears to meet demand. The global economy and social media reach have thus unexpectedly provided the Ravens with a dream market position and customer base, and there is still no end in sight to the success of their unique product idea.[63]

5 percent growth rate in GDP. Combined GDP is at $2.5 trillion, but analysts estimate it will grow to $4.7 trillion by 2020.[68] ASEAN's goals include the promotion of free trade, peace, and collaboration between its members.[69] In 1993, ASEAN began to reduce or phase out tariffs among countries and eliminate nontariff trade barriers.[70] This elimination of tariffs will encourage additional trade among countries and could be beneficial to businesses that want to export to other countries in the trading bloc.

with one of the world's most open economies, has bypassed its communist government with private firms moving ahead despite bureaucracy, corruption, and poor infrastructure. In a country of 88 million, Vietnamese firms now compete internationally with an agricultural miracle, making the country one of the world's main providers of farm produce. Starbucks is expanding into Vietnam, with its first store in Ho Chi Minh City.[66]

Association of Southeast Asian Nations

The **Association of Southeast Asian Nations (ASEAN)**, established in 1967, promotes trade and economic integration among member nations in Southeast Asia, including Malaysia, the Philippines, Singapore, Thailand, Brunei Darussalam, Vietnam, Laos, Indonesia, Myanmar, and Cambodia.[67] The 10-member alliance represents 600 million people and has a

However, ASEAN is facing challenges in becoming a unified trade bloc. Unlike members of the EU, the economic systems of ASEAN members are quite different, with political systems including dictatorships (Myanmar), democracies (Philippines and Malaysia), constitutional monarchies (Cambodia), and communism (Vietnam).[71] In Thailand the military staged a coup and placed the country under martial law, a change that impacted not only Thailand, but also ASEAN as a whole.[72] Major conflicts have also occurred between member-nations.

Despite these challenges, ASEAN plans to increase economic integration in 2015, but unlike the EU, it will not have a common currency or fully free labor flows between member-nations. In this way, ASEAN plans to avoid some of the pitfalls that occurred among nations in the EU during the latest worldwide recession.[73]

World Bank

The **World Bank**, more formally known as the International Bank for Reconstruction and Development, was established by the industrialized nations, including the United States, in 1946 to loan money to underdeveloped and developing countries.

It loans its own funds or borrows funds from member countries to finance projects ranging from road and factory construction to the building of medical and educational facilities. The World Bank and other multilateral development banks (banks with international support that provide loans to developing countries) are the largest source of advice and assistance for developing nations. The International Development Association and the International Finance Corporation are associated with the World Bank and provide loans to private businesses and member countries.

International Monetary Fund

The **International Monetary Fund (IMF)** was established in 1947 to promote trade among member nations by eliminating trade barriers and fostering financial cooperation. It also makes short-term loans to member countries that have balance-of-payment deficits and provides foreign currencies to member nations. The IMF tries to avoid financial crises and panics by alerting the international community about countries that will

Coffee is an important export for Panama.
© Philip Scalia/Alamy

not be able to repay their debts. The IMF's Internet site provides additional information about the organization, including news releases, frequently asked questions, and members.

The IMF is the closest thing the world has to an international central bank. If countries get into financial trouble, they can borrow from the World Bank. However, the global economic crisis created many challenges for the IMF as it was forced to significantly increase its loans to both emerging economies and more developed nations. The usefulness of the IMF for developed countries is limited because these countries use private markets as a major source of capital.[74] Yet the European debt crisis changed this somewhat. Portugal, Ireland, Greece, and Spain (often referred to with the acronym PIGS) required billions of dollars in bailouts from the IMF to keep their economies afloat.

> **The IMF is the closest thing the world has to an international central bank.**

LO 3-4 Summarize the different levels of organizational involvement in international trade.

GETTING INVOLVED IN INTERNATIONAL BUSINESS

Businesses may get involved in international trade at many levels—from a small Kenyan firm that occasionally exports African crafts to a huge multinational corporation such as Shell Oil that sells products around the globe. The degree of commitment of resources and effort required increases according to the level at which a business involves itself in international trade. This section examines exporting and importing, trading companies, licensing and franchising, contract manufacturing, outsourcing and offshoring, joint ventures and alliances, direct investment, and multinational corporations.

Exporting and Importing

Many companies first get involved in international trade when they import goods from other countries for resale in their own businesses. For example, a grocery store chain may import bananas from Honduras and coffee from Colombia. A business may get involved in exporting when it is called upon to supply a foreign company with a particular product. Such exporting enables enterprises of

countertrade agreements foreign trade agreements that involve bartering products for other products instead of for currency.

all sizes to participate in international business. Exporting to other countries becomes a necessity for established countries that seek to grow continually. Products often have higher sales growth potential in foreign countries than they have in the parent country. For instance, General Motors and Yum! Brands sell more of their products in China than in the United States. Walmart experienced sales growth in international markets. Figure 3.2 shows some of the world's largest exporting countries.

Exporting sometimes takes place through **countertrade agreements**, which involve bartering products for other products instead of for currency. Such arrangements are fairly common in international trade, especially between Western companies and eastern European nations. An estimated 40 percent or more of all international trade agreements contain countertrade provisions.

Although a company may export its wares overseas directly or import goods directly from their manufacturer, many choose to deal with an intermediary, commonly called an *export agent*. Export agents seldom produce goods themselves; instead, they usually handle international transactions for other firms. Export agents either purchase products outright or take them on consignment. If they purchase them outright, they generally mark up the price they have paid and attempt to sell the product in the

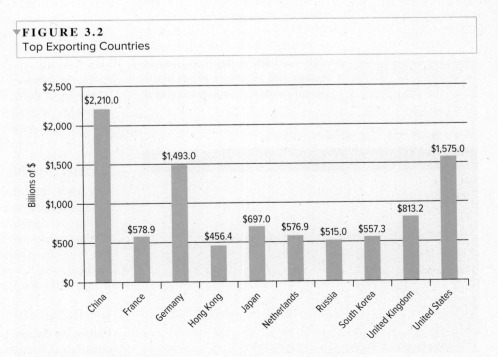

▼**FIGURE 3.2**
Top Exporting Countries

Billions of $

- China: $2,210.0
- France: $578.9
- Germany: $1,493.0
- Hong Kong: $456.4
- Japan: $697.0
- Netherlands: $576.9
- Russia: $515.0
- South Korea: $557.3
- United Kingdom: $813.2
- United States: $1,575.0

Source: "Country Comparison: Exports," The CIA *World Factbook*, www.cia.gov/library/publications/the-world-factbook/rankorder/2078rank.html (accessed February 9, 2015).

trading company a firm that buys goods in one country and sells them to buyers in another country.

licensing a trade agreement in which one company—the licensor—allows another company—the licensee—to use its company name, products, patents, brands, trademarks, raw materials, and/or production processes in exchange for a fee or royalty.

franchising a form of licensing in which a company—the franchiser—agrees to provide a franchisee a name, logo, methods of operation, advertising, products, and other elements associated with a franchiser's business in return for a financial commitment and the agreement to conduct business in accordance with the franchiser's standard of operations.

contract manufacturing the hiring of a foreign company to produce a specified volume of the initiating company's product to specification; the final product carries the domestic firm's name.

international marketplace. They are also responsible for storage and transportation.

An advantage of trading through an agent instead of directly is that the company does not have to deal with foreign currencies or the red tape (paying tariffs and handling paperwork) of international business. A major disadvantage is that, because the export agent must make a profit, either the price of the product must be increased or the domestic company must provide a larger discount than it would in a domestic transaction.

Trading Companies

A **trading company** buys goods in one country and sells them to buyers in another country. Trading companies handle all activities required to move products from one country to another, including consulting, marketing research, advertising, insurance, product research and design, warehousing, and foreign exchange services to companies interested in selling their products in foreign markets. Trading companies are similar to export agents, but their role in international trade is larger. By linking sellers and buyers of goods in different countries, trading companies

promote international trade. WTSC Industrial Group is a trading company that offers a 24-hour-per-day online world trade system connecting 20 million companies in 245 countries.[75]

Licensing and Franchising

Licensing is a trade arrangement in which one company—the licensor—allows another company—the licensee—to use its company name, products, patents, brands, trademarks, raw materials, and/or production processes in exchange for a fee or royalty. The Coca-Cola Company and PepsiCo frequently use licensing as a means to market their soft drinks, apparel, and other merchandise in other countries. Licensing is an attractive alternative to direct investment when the political stability of a foreign country is in doubt or when resources are unavailable for direct investment. Licensing is especially advantageous for small manufacturers wanting to launch a well-known brand internationally. Yoplait is a French yogurt that is licensed for production in the United States.

Franchising is a form of licensing in which a company—the franchiser—agrees to provide a franchisee the name, logo, methods of operation, advertising, products, and other elements associated with the franchiser's business, in return for a financial commitment and the agreement to conduct business in accordance with the franchiser's standard of operations. Wendy's, McDonald's, H&R Block, and Holiday Inn are well-known franchisers with international visibility. Table 3.4 lists some of the top global franchises.

Licensing and franchising enable a company to enter the international marketplace without spending large sums of money abroad or hiring or transferring personnel to handle overseas affairs. They also minimize problems associated with shipping costs, tariffs, and trade restrictions, and they allow the firm to establish goodwill for its products in a foreign market, which will help the company if it decides to produce or market its products directly in the foreign country at some future date. However, if the licensee (or franchisee) does not maintain high standards of quality, the product's image may be hurt; therefore, it is important for the licensor to monitor its products overseas and to enforce its quality standards.

Contract Manufacturing

Contract manufacturing occurs when a company hires a foreign company to produce a specified volume of the firm's product or component of a product to specification; the final product carries the domestic firm's name. Spalding, for example, relies on contract manufacturing for its sports equipment; Reebok uses Korean contract manufacturers to manufacture many of its athletic shoes.

Outsourcing

Earlier, we defined outsourcing as transferring manufacturing or other tasks (such as information technology operations) to companies in countries where labor and supplies are less expensive. Many U.S. firms have outsourced tasks to India, Ireland, Mexico,

▼ **TABLE 3.4** Top Global Franchises

Franchise	Country	Ranking
Subway	United States	1
McDonald's	United States	2
DIA	Spain	10
InterContinental Hotels Group	United Kingdom	15
Groupe Casino	France	29
Tim Hortons	Canada	32
Kumon North America Inc.	Japan	43
Husse	Sweden	61
Cartridge World	Australia	79
Five Guys Burgers and Fries	United States	99

Source: "Top 100 Global Franchises—Rankings," *Franchise Direct*, www.franchisedirect.com/top100globalfranchises/rankings/ (accessed February 9, 2015).

and the Philippines, where there are many well-educated workers and significantly lower labor costs. Services, such as taxes or customer service, can also be outsourced.

Although outsourcing has become politically controversial in recent years amid concerns over jobs lost to overseas workers, foreign companies transfer tasks and jobs to U.S. companies—sometimes called *insourcing*—far more often than U.S. companies outsource tasks and jobs abroad.[76] However, some firms are bringing their outsourced jobs back after concerns that foreign workers were not adding enough value. Companies such as General Electric and Caterpillar are returning to the United States due to increasing labor costs in places such as China, the expense of shipping products across the ocean, and fears of fraud or intellectual property theft. Companies from other countries have also been moving some of their production to the United States; Chinese computer-maker Lenovo is opening a production facility in the United States. Apple also announced it would start building a line of Mac computers in America.[77]

Offshoring

Offshoring is the relocation of a business process by a company, or a subsidiary, to another country. Offshoring is different than outsourcing: the company retains control of the process because it is not subcontracting to a different company. Companies may choose to offshore for a number of reasons, ranging from lower wages, skilled labor, or taking advantage of time zone differences in order to offer services around the clock. Some banks have chosen not to outsource because of concerns about data security in other countries. These institutions may instead engage in offshoring, which allows a company more control over international operations because the offshore office is an extension of the company. Barclays Bank, for instance, has an international offshore banking unit called Barclays Wealth International. This branch helps the company better serve wealthy clients with international banking needs.[78]

Joint Ventures and Alliances

Many countries, particularly LDCs, do not permit direct investment by foreign companies or individuals. A company may also lack sufficient resources or expertise to operate in another country. In such cases, a company that wants to do business in another country may set up a **joint venture** by finding a local partner (occasionally, the host nation itself) to share the costs and operation of the business. General Motors has been able to break into the Chinese market by partnering with local companies. During the 1990s, GM formed a joint venture with state-owned SAIC Motor to form Shanghai General Motors Company. It currently operates 10 joint ventures and two wholly owned foreign enterprises in China.[79]

In some industries, such as automobiles and computers, strategic alliances are becoming the predominant means of competing. A **strategic alliance** is a partnership formed to create competitive advantage on a worldwide basis. In such industries, international competition is so fierce and the costs of competing on a global basis are so high that few firms have the resources to go it alone, so they collaborate with other companies. An example of a strategic alliance is the partnership between Avon and Greek skincare brand KORRES to sell KORRES products in Latin America. KORRES benefits because it is able to tap into Avon's large market presence in Latin America. In turn, Avon gets to develop, manufacture, and sell KORRES products and also has the opportunity to purchase KORRES intellectual property rights for products sold in the region.[80]

Direct Investment

Companies that want more control and are willing to invest considerable resources in international business may consider **direct investment**, the ownership of overseas facilities. Direct investment may involve the development and operation of new facilities—such as when Starbucks opens a new coffee shop in Japan—or the purchase of all or part of an existing operation in a foreign country. The Walgreen Co. purchased its remaining ownership stake in the Swiss company Alliance Boots, which runs pharmacy and beauty shops in several European countries. This significantly increases Walgreen's reach into Europe.[81]

There are several Starbucks coffee locations in Dubai, United Arab Emirates, including in its malls and airport.
© imageBROKER / Alamy

offshoring the relocation of business processes by a company or subsidiary to another country. Offshoring is different than outsourcing because the company retains control of the offshored processes.

joint venture a partnership established for a specific project or for a limited time.

strategic alliance a partnership formed to create competitive advantage on a worldwide basis.

direct investment the ownership of overseas facilities.

Walmart has chosen to invest directly in China. However, it must still make adjustments to fit with the local culture. For instance, Walmart was pressured to allow Chinese employees to unionize.
© Li Jian Xinhua News Agency/Newscom

INTERNATIONAL BUSINESS STRATEGIES

Planning in a global economy requires businesspeople to understand the economic, legal, political, and sociocultural realities of the countries in which they will operate. These factors will affect the strategy a business chooses to use outside its own borders.

Developing Strategies

Companies doing business internationally have traditionally used a **multinational strategy**, customizing their products, promotion, and distribution according to cultural, technological, regional, and national differences. Domino's has achieved extreme success in India, which has become its largest market outside the United States. The company reinvented itself in India to balance its Western brand image with local tastes and preferences. This has led to toppings unique to India including the use of Indian spices and a spicy raw-banana pizza in southern India.[84] Many soap and detergent manufacturers have adapted their products to local water conditions, washing equipment, and washing habits. For customers in some LDCs, Colgate-Palmolive Co. has developed an inexpensive, plastic, hand-powered washing machine for use in households that have no electricity. Even when products are standardized, advertising often has to be modified to adapt to language and cultural differences. Also, celebrities used in advertising in the United States may be unfamiliar to foreign consumers and thus would not be effective in advertising products in other countries.

More and more companies are moving from this customization strategy to a **global strategy (globalization)**, which involves standardizing products (and, as much as possible, their promotion and distribution) for the whole world, as if it were a single entity. Examples of globalized products are American clothing, movies, music, and cosmetics. As it has become a global brand, Starbucks has standardized its products and stores. Starbucks was ranked as one of the world's most engaged brands in terms of online activities, even surpassing Coca-Cola, which is another global brand.

Before moving outside their own borders, companies must conduct environmental analyses to evaluate the potential of and problems associated with

The highest level of international business involvement is the **multinational corporation (MNC)**, a corporation, such as IBM or ExxonMobil, that operates on a worldwide scale, without significant ties to any one nation or region. Table 3.5 lists 10 well-known multinational corporations. MNCs are more than simple corporations. They often have greater assets than some of the countries in which they do business. Nestlé, with headquarters in Switzerland, operates more than 400 factories around the world and receives revenues from Europe; North, Central, and South America; Africa; and Asia.[82] The Royal Dutch/Shell Group, one of the world's major oil producers, is another MNC. Its main offices are located in The Hague and London. Other MNCs include BASF, BP, Matsushita, Mitsubishi, Siemens, Texaco, Toyota, and Unilever. Many MNCs have been targeted by antiglobalization activists at global business forums, and some protests have turned violent. The activists contend that MNCs increase the gap between rich and poor nations, misuse and misallocate scarce resources, exploit the labor markets in LDCs, and harm their natural environments.[83]

▼ **TABLE 3.5** Large Multinational Companies

Company	Country	Description
Royal Dutch Shell	Netherlands	Oil and gas; largest company in the world in terms of revenue
Toyota	Japan	Largest automobile manufacturer in the world
Walmart	United States	Largest retailer in the world; largest private employer in the world
Siemens	Germany	Engineering and electronics; largest engineering company in Europe
Nestlé	Switzerland	Nutritional, snack-food, and health-related consumer goods
Samsung	South Korea	Subsidiaries specializing in electronics, electronic components, telecommunications equipment, medical equipment, and more
Unilever	United Kingdom	Consumer goods including cleaning and personal care, foods, beverages
Boeing	United States	Aerospace and defense; largest U.S. exporter
Lenovo	China	Computer technology; highest share of PC market
Subway	United States	Largest fast-food chain; fastest growing franchises in 105 countries

various markets and to determine what strategy is best for doing business in those markets. Failure to do so may result in losses and even negative publicity. Some companies rely on local managers to gain greater insights and faster response to changes within a country. Astute businesspeople today "think globally, act locally." That is, while constantly being aware of the total picture, they adjust their firms' strategies to conform to local needs and tastes.

Managing the Challenges of Global Business

As we've pointed out in this chapter, many past political barriers to trade have fallen or been minimized, expanding and opening new market opportunities. Managers who can meet the challenges of creating and implementing effective and sensitive business strategies for the global marketplace can help lead their companies to success. For example, the Commercial Service is the global business solutions unit of the U.S. Department of Commerce that offers U.S. firms wide and deep practical knowledge of international markets and industries, a unique global network, inventive use of information technology, and a

multinational corporation (MNC) a corporation that operates on a worldwide scale, without significant ties to any one nation or region.

multinational strategy a plan, used by international companies that involves customizing products, promotion, and distribution according to cultural, technological, regional, and national differences.

global strategy (globalization) a strategy that involves standardizing products (and, as much as possible, their promotion and distribution) for the whole world, as if it were a single entity.

TEAM EXERCISE

Visit Transparency International's Country Corruption Index website: www.transparency.org/cpi2014/results. Form groups and select two countries. Research some of the economic, ethical, legal, regulatory, and political barriers that would have an impact on international trade. Be sure to pair a fairly ethical country with a fairly unethical country (Sweden with Myanmar, Australia with Haiti). Report your findings.

focus on small and midsized businesses. Another example is the benchmarking of best international practices that benefits U.S. firms, which is conducted by the network of CIBERs (Centers for International Business Education and Research) at leading business schools in the United States. These CIBERs are funded by the U.S. government to help U.S. firms become more competitive globally. A major element of the assistance that these governmental organizations can provide firms (especially for small and medium-sized firms) is knowledge of the internationalization process.[85] Small businesses, too, can succeed in foreign markets when their managers have carefully studied those markets and prepared and implemented appropriate strategies. Being globally aware is therefore an important quality for today's managers and will become a critical attribute for managers of the 21st century. ■

SO YOU WANT A JOB // in Global Business /

Have you always dreamt of traveling the world? Whether backpacking your way through Central America or sipping espressos at five-star European restaurants is your style, the increasing globalization of business might just give you your chance to see what the world has to offer. Most new jobs will have at least some global component, even if located within the United States, so being globally aware and keeping an open mind to different cultures is vital in today's business world. Think about the 1.3 billion consumers in China that have already purchased 500 million mobile phones. In the future, some of the largest markets will be in Asia.

Many jobs discussed in chapters throughout this book tend to have strong international components. For example, product management and distribution management are discussed as

marketing careers in Chapter 12. As more and more companies sell products around the globe, their function, design, packaging, and promotions need to be culturally relevant to many different people in many different places. Products very often cross multiple borders before reaching the final consumer, both in their distribution and through the supply chain to produce the products.

Jobs exist in export and import management, product and pricing management, distribution and transportation, and advertising. Many "born global" companies such as Google operate virtually and consider all countries their market. Many companies sell their products through eBay and other Internet sites and never leave the United States. Today communication and transportation facilitates selling and buying products worldwide with delivery in a few days. You may have

sold or purchased a product on eBay outside the United States without thinking about how easy and accessible international markets are to business. If you have, welcome to the world of global business.

To be successful you must have an idea not only of differing regulations from country to country, but of different languages, ethics, and communication styles and varying needs and wants of international markets. From a regulatory side, you may need to be aware of laws related to intellectual property, copyrights, antitrust, advertising, and pricing in every country. Translating is never only about translating the language. Perhaps even more important is ensuring that your message gets through. Whether on a product label or in advertising or promotional materials, the use of images and words varies widely across the globe.

four

options for
organizing business

© Chris Ryan/age fotostock, RF

The legal form of ownership taken by a business is seldom of great concern to you as a customer. When you eat at a restaurant, you probably don't care whether the restaurant is owned by one person (a sole proprietorship), has two or more owners who share the business (a partnership), or is an entity owned by many stockholders (a corporation); all you want is good food. If you buy a foreign car, you probably don't care whether the company that made it has laws governing its form of organization that are different from those for businesses in the United States. All businesses must select a form of organization that is most appropriate for their owners and the scope of their business. A business's legal form of ownership affects how it operates, how much taxes it pays, and how much control its owners have.

This chapter examines three primary forms of business ownership—sole proprietorship, partnership, and corporation—and weighs the advantages and disadvantages of each. These forms are the most often used whether the business is a traditional bricks-and-mortar company, an online-only one, or a combination of both. We take a look at S corporations, limited liability companies, and cooperatives and discuss some trends in business ownership. We also touch on one of the most common forms of organization for nonprofits. You may wish to refer to Table 4.1 to compare the various forms of business ownership mentioned in the chapter. ■

LO 4-1   Define and examine the advantages and disadvantages of the sole properietorship form of organization.

SOLE PROPRIETORSHIPS

Sole proprietorships, businesses owned and operated by one individual, are the most common form of business organization in the United States. Common examples include many retailers such as restaurants, hair salons, flower shops, dog kennels, and independent grocery stores. Sole proprietors also include independent contractors who complete projects for different organizations but are not employees. Many sole proprietors focus on services—small retail stores, financial counseling, automobile repair, child care, and the like—rather than on the manufacture of goods, which often requires large sums of money not available to most small businesses. As you can see in Figure 4.1, proprietorships far outnumber corporations, but they net far fewer sales and less income.

Sole proprietorships are typically small businesses employing fewer than 50 people. (We'll look at small businesses in greater detail in Chapter 5.) Sole proprietorships constitute approximately three-fourths of all businesses in the United States. It is interesting to note that women business owners are less likely to

sole proprietorships
businesses owned and operated by one individual; the most common form of business organization in the United States.

[**"Sole proprietorships constitute approximately three-fourths of all businesses in the United States."**]

▼ **TABLE 4.1** Various Forms of Business Ownership

Structure	Ownership	Taxation	Liability	Use
Sole Proprietorship	One owner	Individual income taxed	Unlimited	Owned by a single individual and is the easiest way to conduct business
Partnership	Two or more owners	Individual owners' income taxed	Somewhat limited	Easy way for two individuals to conduct business
Corporation	Any number of shareholders	Corporate and shareholder taxed	Limited	A legal entity with shareholders or stockholders
S Corporation	Up to 100 shareholders	Taxed as a partnership	Limited	A legal entity with tax advantages for restricted number of shareholders
Limited Liability Company	Unlimited number of shareholders	Taxed as a partnership	Limited	Avoid personal lawsuits

FIGURE 4.1
Comparison of Sole Proprietorships, Partnerships, and Corporations

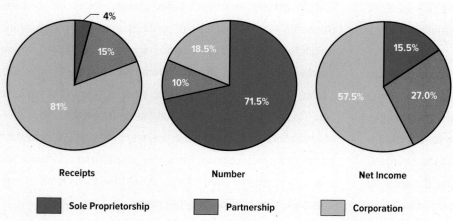

Receipts

4%
15%
81%

Number

18.5%
10%
71.5%

Net Income

15.5%
27.0%
57.5%

■ Sole Proprietorship   ■ Partnership   ■ Corporation

Source: U.S. Bureau of the Census, *The 2012 Statistical Abstract*, www.census.gov/compendia/statab/2012/tables/12s0744.pdf (accessed January 30, 2015).

get access to credit than their male counterparts.[1] In many areas, small businesses make up the vast majority of the economy.

Advantages of Sole Proprietorships

Sole proprietorships are generally managed by their owners. Because of this simple management structure, the owner/manager can make decisions quickly. This is just one of many advantages of the sole proprietorship form of business.

Ease and Cost of Formation Forming a sole proprietorship is relatively easy and inexpensive. In some states, creating a sole proprietorship involves merely announcing the new business in the local newspaper. Other proprietorships, such as barber shops and restaurants, may require state and local licenses and permits because of the nature of the business. The cost of these permits may run from $25 to $100. Lawyers are not usually needed to create such enterprises, and the owner can usually take care of the required paperwork without much outside assistance.

Of course, an entrepreneur starting a new sole proprietorship must find a suitable site from which to operate the business even if it is an online business. Some sole proprietors look no farther than their garage or a spare bedroom when seeking a workshop or office. Among the more famous businesses that sprang to life in their founders' homes are Google, Walt Disney, Dell, eBay, Hewlett-Packard, Apple, and Mattel.[2] Computers, personal copiers, scanners, and websites have been a boon for home-based businesses, permitting them to interact quickly with customers, suppliers, and others. Many independent salespersons and contractors can perform their work using a smartphone or tablet computer as they travel. E-mail and social networks have made it possible for many proprietorships to develop in the services area. Internet connections also allow small businesses to establish websites to promote their products and even to make low-cost long-distance phone calls with voice-over Internet protocol (VoIP) technology. One of the most famous services using VoIP is Skype, which allows people to make free calls over the Internet.

Secrecy Sole proprietorships make possible the greatest degree of secrecy. The proprietor, unlike the owners of a partnership or corporation, does not have to discuss publicly his or her operating plans, minimizing the possibility that competitors can obtain trade secrets. Financial reports need not be disclosed, as do the financial reports of publicly owned corporations.

Distribution and Use of Profits All profits from a sole proprietorship belong exclusively to the owner. He or she does not have to share them with any partners or stockholders. The owner decides how to use the funds—for expansion of the business, or salary increases, for travel to purchase additional inventory, or to find new customers.

Flexibility and Control of the Business The sole proprietor has complete control over the business and can make decisions on the spot without anyone else's approval. This control allows the owner to respond quickly to competitive business conditions or to changes in the economy. The ability to quickly change prices or products can provide a competitive advantage for the business.

Many local cafés are sole proprietorships.
© *Alex Treadway/Getty Images*

Government Regulation Sole proprietorships have the most freedom from government regulation. Many government regulations—federal, state, and local—apply only to businesses that have a certain number of employees, and securities laws apply only to corporations that issue stock. Nonetheless, sole proprietors must ensure that they follow all laws that do apply to their business. For example, sole proprietorships must be careful to obey employee and consumer protection regulation.

Taxation Profits from sole proprietorships are considered personal income and are taxed at individual tax rates. The owner, therefore, pays one income tax that includes the business and individual income. Another tax benefit is that a sole proprietor is allowed to establish a tax-exempt retirement account or a tax-exempt profit-sharing account. Such accounts are exempt from current income tax, but payments taken after retirement are taxed when they are received.

Closing the Business A sole proprietorship can be dissolved easily. No approval of co-owners or partners is necessary. The only legal condition is that all financial obligations must be paid or resolved. If a proprietor does a going-out-of-business sale, most states require that the business actually close.

Disadvantages of Sole Proprietorships

What may be seen as an advantage by one person may turn out to be a disadvantage to another. For profitable businesses managed by capable owners, many of the following factors do not cause problems. On the other hand, proprietors starting out with little management experience and little money are likely to encounter many of the disadvantages.

Unlimited Liability The sole proprietor has unlimited liability in meeting the debts of the business. In other words, if the business cannot pay its creditors, the owner may be forced to use personal, nonbusiness holdings such as a car or a home to pay off the debts. There are only a few states in which houses and homesteads cannot be taken by creditors, even if the proprietor declares bankruptcy. The more wealth an individual has, the greater is the disadvantage of unlimited liability.

Limited Sources of Funds Among the relatively few sources of money available to the sole proprietorship are banks, friends, family, the Small Business Administration, or his or her own funds. The owner's personal financial condition determines his or her credit standing. Additionally, sole proprietorships may have to pay higher interest rates on funds borrowed from banks than do large corporations because they are considered greater risks. More proprietors are using nonbank

financial institutions for transactions that charge higher interest rates than banks. Often, the only way a sole proprietor can borrow for business purposes is to pledge a car, a house, other real estate, or other personal assets to guarantee the loan. If the business fails, the owner may lose the personal assets as well as the business. Publicly owned corporations, in contrast, can not only obtain funds from commercial banks but can sell stocks and bonds to the public to raise money. If a public company goes out of business, the owners do not lose personal assets. However, they will lose the value of their stocks or bonds.

> **Sole proprietorships have the most freedom from government regulation.**

Limited Skills The sole proprietor must be able to perform many functions and possess skills in diverse fields such as management, marketing, finance, accounting, bookkeeping, and personnel management. Specialized professionals, such as accountants or attorneys, can be hired by businesses for help or advice. Sometimes, sole proprietors need assistance with certain business functions. For instance, Network Solutions

Sole proprietorships often have greater difficulty attracting talented employees because of competition from larger companies.
© *PhotoDisc/PhotoLink/Getty Images, RF*

offers web services for small and medium-sized businesses that want to grow their online presence. The company offers website hosting, or storage space and access for web-sites, as well as tools to help build a website and online marketing services.[3] Many businesses take advantage of these kinds of services to gain a competitive advantage. In the end, however, it is up to the business owner to make the final decision in all areas of the business.

Lack of Continuity The life expectancy of a sole proprietorship is directly linked to that of the owner and his or her ability to work. The serious illness of the owner could result in failure of the business if competent help cannot be found.

It is difficult to arrange for the sale of a proprietorship and at the same time assure customers that the business will continue to meet their needs. For instance, how does one sell a veterinary practice? A veterinarian's major asset is patients. If the vet dies suddenly, the equipment can be sold, but the patients will not necessarily remain loyal to the office. On the other hand, a veterinarian who wants to retire could take in a younger partner and sell the practice to the partner over time. One advantage to the partnership is that some of the customers are likely to stay with the business, even if ownership changes.

Lack of Qualified Employees It is sometimes difficult for a small sole proprietorship to match the wages and benefits offered by a large competing corporation because the proprietorship's profits may not be as high. In addition, there may be less room for advancement within a sole proprietorship, so the owner may have difficulty attracting and retaining qualified employees. On the other hand, the trend of large corporations downsizing and outsourcing tasks has created renewed opportunities for small businesses to acquire well-trained employees.

Taxation Although we listed taxation as an advantage for sole proprietorships, it can also be a disadvantage, depending on the proprietor's income. Under current tax rates, sole proprietors pay a higher marginal tax rate than do small corporations on income of less than $75,000. However, sole proprietorships avoid the double taxation of corporate and personal taxes that occurs with corporations. The tax effect often determines whether a sole proprietor chooses to incorporate his or her business.

LO 4-2 Identify two types of partnership and evaluate the advantages and disadvantages of the partnership form of organization.

PARTNERSHIPS

One way to minimize the disadvantages of a sole proprietorship and maximize its advantages is to have more than one owner. Most states have a model law governing partnerships based on the Uniform Partnership Act. This law defines a **partnership** as "an association of two or more persons who carry on as co-owners of a business for profit." Partnerships are the least used form of business (see Figure 4.1). They are typically larger than sole proprietorships but smaller than corporations.

Partnerships can be a fruitful form of business, as long as you follow some basic keys to success, which are outlined in Table 4.2.

Types of Partnership

There are two basic types of partnership: general partnership and limited partnership. A **general partnership** involves a complete sharing in the management of a business. In a general partnership, each partner has unlimited liability for the debts of the business. For example, Webco, a military retail service provider, is a general partnership that has four locations in the United States. These four locations are strategic business units that focus on many product categories at once. This strategy has allowed the company to become a leader in

▼ **TABLE 4.2** Keys to Success in Business Partnerships

1. Keep profit sharing equitable based on contributions.
2. Partners should have different skill sets or resource contributions.
3. Ethics and compliance are required.
4. Maintain effective communication skills.
5. Maintain transparency with stakeholders.
6. Be realistic in resource and financial management.
7. Previous experience related to business is helpful.
8. Maintain life balance in time spent on business.
9. Focus on customer satisfaction and product quality.
10. Maintain resources in line with sales and growth expectations and planning.

It is sometimes difficult for a small sole proprietorship to match the wages and benefits offered by a large competing corporation because the proprietorship's profits may not be as high.

▼ TABLE 4.3 Issues and Provisions in Articles of Partnership

1. Name, purpose, location
2. Duration of the agreement
3. Authority and responsibility of each partner
4. Character of partners (i.e., general or limited, active or silent)
5. Amount of contribution from each partner
6. Division of profits or losses
7. Salaries of each partner
8. How much each partner is allowed to withdraw
9. Death of partner
10. Sale of partnership interest
11. Arbitration of disputes
12. Required and prohibited actions
13. Absence and disability
14. Restrictive covenants
15. Buying and selling agreements

category management in the military retail market, sustaining its business for more than 50 years.[4] Professionals such as lawyers, accountants, and architects often join together in general partnerships.

A **limited partnership** has at least one general partner, who assumes unlimited liability, and at least one limited partner, whose liability is limited to his or her investment in the business. Limited partnerships exist for risky investment projects where the chance of loss is great. The general partners accept the risk of loss; the limited partners' losses are limited to their

initial investment. Limited partners do not participate in the management of the business but share in the profits in accordance with the terms of a partnership agreement. Usually the general partner receives a larger share of the profits after the limited partners have received their initial investment back. A *master limited partnership (MLP)* is a limited partnership traded on securities exchanges. MLPs have the tax benefits of a limited partnership but the liquidity (ability to convert assets into cash) of a corporation. Popular examples of MLPs include oil and gas companies and pipeline operators.[5]

Articles of Partnership

Articles of partnership are legal documents that set forth the basic agreement between partners. Most states require articles of partnership, but even if they are not required, it makes good sense for partners to draw them up. Articles of partnership usually list the money or assets that each partner has contributed (called *partnership capital*), state each partner's individual management role or duty, specify how the profits and losses of the partnership will be divided among the partners, and describe how a partner may leave the partnership as well as any other restrictions that might apply to the agreement. Table 4.3 lists some of the issues and provisions that should be included in articles of partnership.

limited partnership a business organization that has at least one general partner, who assumes unlimited liability, and at least one limited partner, whose liability is limited to his or her investment in the business.

articles of partnership legal documents that set forth the basic agreement between partners.

ARIZONA TEA: THE CHALLENGES OF PARTNERSHIPS

Partnerships have their share of legal and business-related advantages and disadvantages. One important concern that is often ignored, however, is the personal element: What happens if partners later develop irreconcilable differences?

In the early 1990s, John Ferolito and Don Vultaggio were close friends and had already been business partners for over two decades, distributing beer and malt liquor in New York. Seeking a more lucrative opportunity, and noting Snapple's success in the bottled tea and fruit juice industry, the pair founded AriZona Iced Tea in 1992. Their unique, affordable 24-ounce cans of tea were a hit, and the company grew to become the market leader in the sector.

By 1997, however, the long-time partners' relationship had fallen apart. This was especially problematic because, with each partner holding a 50 percent share, both had equal voting power. Ferolito prevented an "inevitable deadlock" by agreeing to withdraw from involvement in day-to-day operations. However, when he later sought in 2005 to sell his share of the company, he was blocked by a provision of their agreement preventing the sale of either partner's share without both partners' consent. Vultaggio eventually agreed to buy Ferolito's share and take full control. Yet instead of fixing the problem, this sparked a drawn-out legal battle over the valuation of the company (and how much Vultaggio should pay Ferolito), which continued

for more than six years. The partnership challenges faced by the owners of AriZona demonstrate how important it is for partners to plan for potential future disagreements in their articles of partnership.[6]

● Discussion Questions

1. What could the AriZona Iced Tea founders have done to avoid this drawn-out conflict from occurring?

2. Why do partners often fail to consider, and plan for, the possibility of later personal fallout?

3. What are some ways that the partnership agreement could be structured to avoid major disadvantages that often come with this organizational form?

> ## WHEN A BUSINESS HAS SEVERAL PARTNERS, IT HAS THE BENEFIT OF A COMBINATION OF TALENTS AND SKILLS AND POOLED FINANCIAL RESOURCES. 99

Advantages of Partnerships

Law firms, accounting firms, and investment firms with several hundred partners have partnership agreements that are quite complicated in comparison with the partnership agreement among two or three people owning a computer repair shop. The advantages must be compared with those offered by other forms of business organization, and not all apply to every partnership.

Ease of Organization Starting a partnership requires little more than drawing up articles of partnership. No legal charters have to be granted, but the name of the business should be registered with the state.

Availability of Capital and Credit When a business has several partners, it has the benefit of a combination of talents and skills and pooled financial resources. Partnerships tend to be larger than sole proprietorships and therefore have greater earning power and better credit ratings. Because many limited partnerships have been formed for tax purposes rather than for economic profits, the combined income of all U.S. partnerships is quite low, as shown in Figure 4.1. Nevertheless, the professional partnerships of many lawyers, accountants, and banking firms make quite large profits. For instance, the 725 partners in the international law firm Morgan, Lewis & Bockius take home an average of nearly $1 billion a year.[7]

Combined Knowledge and Skills Partners in the most successful partnerships acknowledge each other's talents and avoid confusion and conflict by specializing in a particular area of

Biz Stone, Evan Williams, and Jack Dorsey (not pictured) co-founded Twitter in 2006.
© Lynn Goldsmith/Corbis News Premium/Corbis

expertise such as marketing, production, accounting, or service. The diversity of skills in a partnership makes it possible for the business to be run by a management team of specialists instead of by a generalist sole proprietor. Co-founders Justin Wetherill, Edward Trujillo, and David Reiff credit diversity as being a key component to the success of their company uBreakiFix, an iPhone repair service. In just eight years, the startup has grown to 58 stores in 21 markets, generating more than $17 million in revenue. It has also embarked on a franchising strategy, which is sure to spur further growth.[8] Service-oriented partnerships in fields such as law, financial planning, and accounting may attract customers because clients may think that the service offered by a diverse team is of higher quality than that provided by one person. Larger law firms, for example, often have individual partners who specialize in certain areas of the law—such as family, bankruptcy, corporate, entertainment, and criminal law.

Decision Making Small partnerships can react more quickly to changes in the business environment than can large partnerships and corporations. Such fast reactions are possible because the partners are involved in day-to-day operations and can make decisions quickly after consultation. Large partnerships with hundreds of partners in many states are not common. In those that do exist, decision making is likely to be slow. However, some partnerships have been successful despite their large size. The accounting firm PricewaterhouseCoopers LLP (PwC) is the third largest accounting and advisory firm in the United States with more than 10,000 partners and principals and more than 195,000 personnel. The company has gross revenues of more than $34 billion. Some have attributed PwC's success to its strong diversification techniques and the ability to operate in different market niches.[9]

Regulatory Controls Like a sole proprietorship, a partnership has fewer regulatory controls affecting its activities than does a corporation. A partnership does not have to file public financial statements with government agencies or send out quarterly financial statements to several thousand owners, as do corporations such as Apple and Ford Motor Co. A partnership does, however, have to abide by all laws relevant to the industry or profession in which it operates as well as state and federal laws relating to financial reports, employees, consumer protection, environmental regulations, and so on, just as the sole proprietorship does.

Disadvantages of Partnerships

Partnerships have many advantages compared to sole proprietorships and corporations, but they also have some disadvantages.

Limited partners have no voice in the management of the partnership, and they may bear most of the risk of the business while the general partner reaps a larger share of the benefits. There may be a change in the goals and objectives of one partner but not the other, particularly when the partners are multinational organizations. This can cause friction, giving rise to an enterprise that fails to satisfy both parties or even forcing an end to the partnership. Many partnership disputes wind up in court or require outside mediation. A partnership can be jeopardized when two business partners cannot resolve disputes. For instance, two co-founders of photo sharing mobile application Snapchat reached a financial settlement with their former fraternity brother, who sued the co-founders because the business was based around his idea.[10] In some cases, the ultimate solution may be dissolving the partnership. Major disadvantages of partnerships include the following.

Unlimited Liability

In general partnerships, the general partners have unlimited liability for the debts incurred by the business, just as the sole proprietor has unlimited liability for his or her business. Such unlimited liability can be a distinct disadvantage to one partner if his or her personal financial resources are greater than those of the others. A potential partner should check to make sure that all partners have comparable resources to help the business in time of trouble. This disadvantage is eliminated for limited partners, who can lose only their initial investment.

Business Responsibility

All partners are responsible for the business actions of all others. Partners may have the ability to commit the partnership to a contract without approval of the other partners. A bad decision by one partner may put the other partners' personal resources in jeopardy. Personal problems such as a divorce can eliminate a significant portion of one partner's financial resources and weaken the financial structure of the whole partnership.

Life of the Partnership

A partnership is terminated when a partner dies or withdraws. In a two-person partnership, if one partner withdraws, the firm's liabilities would be paid off and the assets divided between the partners. Obviously, the partner who wishes to continue in the business would be at a serious disadvantage. The business could be disrupted, financing would be reduced, and the management skills of the departing partner would be lost. The remaining partner would have to find another or reorganize the business as a sole proprietorship. In very large partnerships such as those found in law firms and investment banks, the continuation of the partnership may be provided for in the articles of partnership. The provision may simply state the terms for a new partnership agreement among the remaining partners. In such cases, the disadvantage to the other partners is minimal.

> " All partners are responsible for the business actions of all others. "

Selling a partnership interest has the same effect as the death or withdrawal of a partner. It is difficult to place a value on a partner's share of the partnership. No public value is placed on the partnership, as there is on publicly owned corporations. What is a law firm worth? What is the local hardware store worth? Coming up with a fair value that all partners can agree to is not easy. Selling a partnership interest is easier if the articles of partnership specify a method of valuation. Even if there is not a procedure for selling one partner's interest, the old partnership must still be dissolved and a new one created. In contrast, in the corporate form of business, the departure of owners has little effect on the financial resources of the business, and the loss of managers does not cause long-term changes in the structure of the organization.

Distribution of Profits

Profits earned by the partnership are distributed to the partners in the proportions specified in the articles of partnership. This may be a disadvantage if the division of the profits does not reflect the work each partner puts into the business. You may have encountered this disadvantage while working on a student group project: You may have felt that you did most of the work and that the other students in the group received grades based on your efforts. Even the perception of an unfair profit-sharing agreement may cause tension between the partners, and unhappy partners can have a negative effect on the profitability of the business.

Limited Sources of Funds

As with a sole proprietorship, the sources of funds available to a partnership are limited. Because no public value is placed on the business (such as the current trading price of a corporation's stock), potential partners do not always know what one partnership share is worth, although third parties can access the value. Moreover, because partnership shares cannot be bought and sold easily in public markets, potential owners may not want to tie up their money in assets that cannot be readily sold on short notice. Accumulating enough funds to operate a national business, especially a business requiring intensive investments in facilities and equipment, can be difficult. Partnerships also may have to pay higher interest rates on funds borrowed from banks than do large corporations because partnerships may be considered greater risks.

Taxation of Partnerships

Partnerships are quasi-taxable organizations. This means that partnerships do not pay taxes when submitting the partnership tax return to the Internal Revenue Service. The tax return simply provides information about the profitability of the organization and the distribution of profits among the partners. Partners must report their share of profits on their individual tax returns and pay taxes at the income tax rate for individuals. Master limited partnerships require financial reports similar to corporations, which are discussed in the next section.

corporation a legal entity, created by the state, whose assets and liabilities are separate from its owners.

stock shares of a corporation that may be bought or sold.

dividends profits of a corporation that are distributed in the form of cash payments to stockholders.

corporate charter a legal document that the state issues to a company based on information the company provides in the articles of incorporation.

CORPORATIONS

When you think of a business, you probably think of a huge corporation such as General Electric, Procter & Gamble, or Sony because a large portion of your consumer dollars goes to such corporations. A **corporation** is a legal entity, created by the state, whose assets and liabilities are separate from its owners. As a legal entity, a corporation has many of the rights, duties, and powers of a person, such as the right to receive, own, and transfer property. Corporations can enter into contracts with individuals or with other legal entities, and they can sue and be sued in court.

Corporations account for the majority of all U.S. sales and income. Thus, most of the dollars you spend as a consumer probably go to incorporated businesses (see Figure 4.1). Most corporations are not mega-companies like General Mills or Ford Motor Co.; even small businesses can incorporate. As we shall see later in the chapter, many smaller firms elect to incorporate as "S corporations," which operate under slightly different rules and have greater flexibility than do traditional "C corporations" like General Mills.

Corporations are typically owned by many individuals and organizations who own shares of the business, called **stock** (thus, corporate owners are often called *shareholders* or *stockholders*). Stockholders can buy, sell, give or receive as gifts, or inherit their shares of stock. As owners, the stockholders are entitled to all profits that are left after all the corporation's other obligations have been paid. These profits may be distributed in the form of cash payments called **dividends**. For example, if a corporation earns $100 million after expenses and taxes and decides to pay the owners $40 million in dividends, the stockholders receive 40 percent of the profits in cash dividends. However, not all after-tax profits are paid to stockholders in dividends. Some corporations may retain profits to expand the business. For example, Google retains its earnings and does not pay out dividends. The company claims it needs cash on hand to remain flexible and competitive. However, with its cash earning only 1 percent a year, investors have begun placing pressure on the firm to provide a return to stockholders through dividends or by repurchasing some of its shares. Corporations do have to pay taxes on all profits, just like individuals.[11]

Creating a Corporation

A corporation is created, or incorporated, under the laws of the state in which it incorporates. The individuals creating the corporation are known as *incorporators*. Each state has a specific procedure, sometimes called *chartering the corporation,* for incorporating a business. Most states require a minimum of three incorporators; thus, many small businesses can be and are incorporated. Another requirement is that the new corporation's name cannot be similar to that of another business. In most states, a corporation's name must end in "company," "corporation," "incorporated," or "limited" to show that the owners have limited liability. (In this text, however, the word *company* means any organization engaged in a commercial enterprise and can refer to a sole proprietorship, a partnership, or a corporation.)

The incorporators must file legal documents generally referred to as *articles of incorporation* with the appropriate state office (often the secretary of state). The articles of incorporation contain basic information about the business. The following 10 items are found in the Model Business Corporation Act, issued by the American Bar Association, which is followed by most states:

1. Name and address of the corporation.

2. Objectives of the corporation.

3. Classes of stock (common, preferred, voting, nonvoting) and the number of shares for each class of stock to be issued.

4. Expected life of the corporation (corporations are usually created to last forever).

5. Financial capital required at the time of incorporation.

6. Provisions for transferring shares of stock between owners.

7. Provisions for the regulation of internal corporate affairs.

8. Address of the business office registered with the state of incorporation.

9. Names and addresses of the initial board of directors.

10. Names and addresses of the incorporators.

Based on the information in the articles of incorporation, the state issues a **corporate charter** to the company. After securing this charter, the owners hold an organizational meeting at which they establish the corporation's bylaws and elect a board of directors. The bylaws might set up committees of the board of directors and describe the rules and procedures for their operation.

Types of Corporations

If the corporation does business in the state in which it is chartered, it is known as a *domestic corporation.* In other states where the corporation does business, it is known as a *foreign corporation.* If a corporation does business outside the nation in which it is incorporated, it is called an *alien corporation*. A corporation may be privately or publicly owned.

A **private corporation** is owned by just one or a few people who are closely involved in managing the business. These people, often a family, own all the corporation's stock, and no stock is sold to the public. Many corporations are quite large, yet remain private, including Publix Super Markets. It is the nation's eighth largest privately held corporation with annual revenues of nearly $29 billion. Founded in 1930, today the company is run by the founder's grandson, who is the fourth family member to lead the company.[12] The fifth largest privately held company in the United States is Mars, founded by Frank C. Mars, who spent time in Switzerland learning to create chocolate confectionaries. The company grew significantly through the acquisition of the Wm. Wrigley Jr. Company. Founded in Tacoma, Washington, in 1911, Mars is now the world's leading confectionary company and a leader in pet care products with Pedigree and Whiskas.[13] The business was successful early on because it paid employees three times the normal wage for the time. The company remains successful to this day largely because of its established brands, such as M&M's, and healthy snack lines for kids, like Generation Max.[14] Other well-known privately held companies include HJ Heinz, Cargill, Toys 'R' Us, and Amway.[15] Privately owned corporations are not required to disclose financial information publicly, but they must, of course, pay taxes.

A **public corporation** is one whose stock anyone may buy, sell, or trade. Table 4.4 lists 10 U.S. corporations with more than half of their revenue coming from outside of the United States. Despite its high revenue, Amazon has negative profits.[16] Thousands of smaller public corporations in the United States have sales under $10 million. In large public corporations such as AT&T, the stockholders are often far removed from the management of the company. In other public corporations, the managers are often the founders and the major shareholders. Moelis & Co., for example, became a public corporation under the terms that the founder, chair, and CEO would remain in his position and control more than 50 percent of the company.[17] *Forbes*'s Global 2000 companies generate around $38 trillion in revenues, $3 trillion in profits, and $161 trillion in assets. They are worth $44 trillion in market value.[18] Asia-Pacific companies account for the majority of the Global 2000 companies, but other nations are catching up. The rankings of the Global 2000 span across 62 countries.[19] Publicly owned corporations must disclose financial information to the public under specific laws that regulate the trade of stocks and other securities.

A private corporation that needs more money to expand or to take advantage of opportunities may have to obtain financing by

private corporation a corporation owned by just one or a few people who are closely involved in managing the business.

public corporation a corporation whose stock anyone may buy, sell, or trade.

> "Privately owned corporations are not required to disclose financial information publicly, but they must, of course, pay taxes."

▼ **TABLE 4.4** American Companies with More Than Half of Their Revenues from Outside the United States

Company	Description
Caterpillar Inc.	Designs, manufactures, markets, and sells machinery, engines, and financial products
Dow Chemical	Manufactures chemicals, with products including plastics, oil, and crop technology
General Electric	Operates in the technology infrastructure, energy, capital finance, and consumer and industrial fields, with products including appliances, locomotives, weapons, lighting, and gas
General Motors	Sells automobiles with brands including Chevrolet, Buick, Cadillac, and Isuzu
IBM	Conducts technological research, develops intellectual property including software and hardware, and offers consulting services
Intel	Manufactures and develops semiconductor chips and microprocessors
McDonald's	Operates second largest chain of fast-food restaurants worldwide after Subway
Nike	Designs, develops, markets, and sells athletic shoes and clothing
Procter & Gamble	Sells consumer goods with brands including Tide, Bounty, Crest, and Iams
Yum! Brands	Operates and licenses restaurants including Taco Bell, Kentucky Fried Chicken, and Pizza Hut

"going public" through an **initial public offering (IPO)**, that is, becoming a public corporation by selling stock so that it can be traded in public markets. Digital media companies are leading a surge in initial public offerings. Chinese e-commerce company Alibaba released the largest IPO globally at $25 billon.[20]

Also, privately owned firms are occasionally forced to go public with stock offerings when a major owner dies and the heirs have large estate taxes to pay. The tax payment may only be possible with the proceeds of the sale of stock. This happened to the brewer Adolph Coors Inc. After Adolph Coors died, the business went public and his family sold shares of stock to the public in order to pay the estate taxes.

not owned by a government entity. Organizations such as the Sesame Workshop, the Elks Clubs, the American Lung Association, the American Red Cross, museums, and private schools provide services without a profit motive. To fund their operations and services, nonprofit organizations solicit donations from individuals and companies and grants from the government and other charitable foundations. Nonprofits do not have shareholders, and most are organized as 501(c)(3) organizations. A 501(c)(3) organization receives certain tax exemptions, and donors contributing to these organizations may reduce their tax deductibility for their donations. Organizations that have 501(c)(3) status include public charities (e.g., the Leukemia & Lymphoma Society), private foundations (e.g., the Daniels Fund), and private operating foundations that sponsor and fund their own programs (e.g., day camp for underprivileged children).[22]

> ## Taking a corporation private is also one technique for avoiding a takeover by another corporation.

On the other hand, public corporations can be "taken private" when one or a few individuals (perhaps the management of the firm) purchase all the firm's stock so that it can no longer be sold publicly. Taking a corporation private may be desirable when owners want to exert more control over the firm or they want the flexibility to make decisions for restructuring operations. For example, Michael Dell took his company private in order to set a new direction as PC sales continue to decline. Becoming a private company again allows Dell to focus on the needs of the company more fully than having to worry about the stock price for investors.[21] Taking a corporation private is also one technique for avoiding a takeover by another corporation.

Quasi-public corporations and nonprofits are two types of public corporations. **Quasi-public corporations** are owned and operated by the federal, state, or local government. The focus of these entities is to provide a service to citizens, such as mail delivery, rather than earning a profit. Indeed, many quasi-public corporations operate at a loss. Examples of quasi-public corporations include the National Aeronautics and Space Administration (NASA) and the U.S. Postal Service.

Like quasi-public corporations, **nonprofit corporations** focus on providing a service rather than earning a profit, but they are

Elements of a Corporation

The Board of Directors
A **board of directors**, elected by the stockholders to oversee the general operation of the corporation, sets the long-range objectives of the corporation. It is the board's responsibility to ensure that the objectives are achieved on schedule. Board members have a duty of care and loyalty to oversee the management of the firm or for any misuse of funds. An important duty of the board of directors is to hire corporate officers, such as the president and the chief executive officer (CEO), who are responsible to the directors for the management and daily operations of the firm. The role and expectations of the board of directors took on greater significance after the accounting scandals of the early 2000s and the passage of the Sarbanes-Oxley Act.[23] As a result, most corporations have restructured how they compensate board directors for their time and expertise.

However, some experts now speculate that Sarbanes-Oxley did little to motivate directors to increase company oversight. Seven board members stepped down after American Apparel CEO Dov Charney was ousted after years of alleged misconduct.[24] At the same time, the pay rate of directors is rising. On average, corporate directors are paid around $250,000 in the largest corporations. Over the past several years, the trend of increasing directors' pay continues to reach higher and higher limits. Although such pay is meant to attract top-quality directors, concerns exist over whether excessive pay will have unintended consequences. Some believe that this trend is contributing to the declining effectiveness in corporate governance.[25]

Directors can be employees of the company *(inside directors)* or people unaffiliated with the company *(outside directors)*. Inside directors are usually the officers responsible for running the company. Outside directors are often top executives from other companies, lawyers, bankers, even professors. Directors today are increasingly chosen for their expertise, competence, and ability to bring diverse perspectives to strategic discussions. Outside directors are also thought to bring more independence to the monitoring function because they are not bound by past allegiances, friendships, a current role in the company, or some other issue that may create a conflict of interest. Many of the corporate scandals uncovered in recent years might have been prevented if each of the companies' boards of directors had been better qualified, more knowledgeable, and more independent.

There is a growing shortage of available and qualified board members. Boards are increasingly telling their own CEOs that they should be focused on serving their company, not serving on outside boards. Because of this, the average CEO sits on less than one outside board. This represents a decline from a decade ago when the average was two. Because many CEOs are turning down outside positions, many companies have taken steps to ensure that boards have experienced directors. They have increased the mandatory retirement age to 72 or older, and some have raised it to 75 or even older. Minimizing the amount of overlap between directors sitting on different boards helps to limit conflicts of interest and provides for independence in decision making.

Stock Ownership Corporations issue two types of stock: preferred and common. Owners of **preferred stock** are a special class of owners because, although they generally do not have any say in running the company, they have a claim to profits before any other stockholders do. Other stockholders do not receive any dividends unless the preferred stockholders have already been paid. Dividend payments on preferred stock are usually a fixed percentage of the initial issuing price (set by the board of directors). For example, if a share of preferred stock originally cost $100 and the dividend rate was stated at 7.5 percent, the

dividend payment will be $7.50 per share per year. Dividends are usually paid quarterly. Most preferred stock carries a cumulative claim to dividends. This means that if the company does not pay preferred-stock dividends in one year because of losses, the dividends accumulate to the next year. Such dividends unpaid from previous years must also be paid to preferred stockholders before other stockholders can receive any dividends.

Although owners of **common stock** do not get such preferential treatment with regard to dividends, they do get some say in the operation of the corporation. Their ownership gives them the right to vote for members of the board of directors and on other important issues. Common stock dividends may vary according to the profitability of the business, and some corporations do not issue dividends at all, but instead plow their profits back into the company to fund expansion.

Common stockholders are the voting owners of a corporation. They are usually entitled to one vote per share of common stock. During an annual stockholders' meeting, common stockholders elect a board of directors. Some boards find it easier than others to attract high profile individuals. For example, the board of Procter & Gamble consists of Ernesto Zedillo, former president of Mexico; Kenneth I. Chenault, CEO

> ## Common stockholders are the voting owners of a corporation.

Owners of common stock do not get preferential treatment regarding dividends, but do get the ability to vote on board members and other important issues.
© Tupungato/Getty Images, RF

of the American Express Company; Scott D. Cook, founder of Intuit Inc.; Patricia A. Woertz, board chair of Archer Daniels Midland; W. James McNerney Jr., CEO of Boeing; Margaret C. Whitman, CEO of Hewlett-Packard; and others.[26] Because they can choose the board of directors, common stockholders have some say in how the company will operate. Common stockholders may vote by *proxy,* which is a written authorization by which stockholders assign their voting privilege to someone else, who then votes for his or her choice at the stockholders' meeting. It is a normal practice for management to request proxy statements from shareholders who are not planning to attend the annual meeting. Most owners do not attend annual meetings of the very large companies, such as Westinghouse or Boeing, unless they live in the city where the meeting is held.

Common stockholders have another advantage over preferred shareholders. In most states, when the corporation decides to sell new shares of common stock in the marketplace, common stockholders have the first right, called a *preemptive right,* to purchase new shares of the stock from the corporation. A preemptive right is often included in the articles of incorporation. This right is important because it allows stockholders to purchase new shares to maintain their original positions. For example, if a stockholder owns 10 percent of a corporation that decides to issue new shares, that stockholder has the right to buy enough of the new shares to retain the 10 percent ownership.

Advantages of Corporations

Because a corporation is a separate legal entity, it has some very specific advantages over other forms of ownership. The biggest advantage may be the limited liability of the owners.

Limited Liability
Because the corporation's assets (money and resources) and liabilities (debts and other obligations) are separate from its owners', in most cases the stockholders are not held responsible for the firm's debts if it fails. Their liability or potential loss is limited to the amount of their original investment. Although a creditor can sue a corporation for not paying its debts, even forcing the corporation into bankruptcy, it cannot make the stockholders pay the corporation's debts out of their personal assets. Occasionally, the owners of a private corporation may pledge personal assets to secure a loan for the corporation; this would be most unusual for a public corporation.

Ease of Transfer of Ownership
Stockholders can sell or trade shares of stock to other people without causing the termination of the corporation, and they can do this without the prior approval of other shareholders in public corporations. The transfer of ownership (unless it is a majority position) does not affect the daily or long-term operations of the corporation.

Perpetual Life
A corporation usually is chartered to last forever unless its articles of incorporation stipulate otherwise. The existence of the corporation is unaffected by the death or withdrawal of any of its stockholders. It survives until the owners sell it or liquidate its assets. However, in some cases, bankruptcy ends a corporation's life. Bankruptcies occur when companies are unable to operate and earn profits. Eventually, uncompetitive businesses must close or seek protection from creditors in bankruptcy court while the business tries to reorganize.

External Sources of Funds
Of all the forms of business organization, the public corporation finds it easiest to raise money. When a large or public corporation needs to raise more money, it can sell more stock shares or issue bonds (corporate "IOUs," which pledge to repay debt), attracting funds from anywhere in the United States and even overseas. The larger a corporation becomes, the more sources of financing are available to it. We take a closer look at some of these in Chapter 15.

Expansion Potential
Because large public corporations can find long-term financing readily, they can easily expand into national and international markets. And, as a legal entity, a corporation can enter into contracts without as much difficulty as a partnership. For instance, Apple expanded its securities with a sale of $6.5 billion in bonds, while Microsoft's bond sale eclipsed Apple's at $10.75 billion.[27]

Disadvantages of Corporations

Corporations have some distinct disadvantages resulting from tax laws and government regulation.

Double Taxation
As a legal entity, the corporation must pay taxes on its income just like you do. The United States has one of the highest corporate tax rates in the world, at an average rate of 35 percent.[28] When after-tax corporate profits are paid

Volkswagen is one of the largest corporations in the world.
© *Jim West/Alamy*

out as dividends to the stockholders, the dividends are taxed a second time as part of the individual owner's income. This process creates double taxation for the stockholders of dividend paying corporations. Double taxation does not occur with the other forms of business organization.

Forming a Corporation The formation of a corporation can be costly. A charter must be obtained, and this usually requires the services of an attorney and payment of legal fees. Filing fees ranging from $25 to $150 must be paid to the state that awards the corporate charter, and certain states require that an annual fee be paid to maintain the charter. Today, a number of Internet services such as LegalZoom.com and Business.com make it easier, quicker, and less costly to form a corporation. However, in making it easier for people to form businesses without expert consultation, these services have increased the risk that people will not choose the kind of organizational form that is right for them. Sometimes, one form works better than another. The business's founders may fail to take into account disadvantages, such as double taxation with corporations.

Disclosure of Information Corporations must make information available to their owners, usually through an annual report to shareholders. The annual report contains financial information about the firm's profits, sales, facilities and equipment, and debts, as well as descriptions of the company's operations, products, and plans for the future. Public corporations must also file reports with the Securities and Exchange Commission (SEC), the government regulatory agency that regulates securities such as stocks and bonds. The larger the firm, the more data the SEC requires. Because all reports filed with the SEC are available to the public, competitors can access them. Additionally, complying with securities laws takes time.

Employee–Owner Separation Many employees are not stockholders of the company for which they work. This separation of owners and employees may cause employees to feel that their work benefits only the owners. Employees without an ownership stake do not always see how they fit into the corporate picture and may not understand the importance of profits to the health of the organization. If managers are part owners but other employees are not, management–labor relations take on a different, sometimes difficult, aspect from those in partnerships and sole proprietorships. However, this situation is changing as more corporations establish employee stock ownership plans (ESOPs), which give shares of the company's stock to its employees. Such plans build a partnership between employee and employer and can boost productivity because they motivate employees to work harder so that they can earn dividends from their hard work as well as from their regular wages.

DID YOU KNOW?

The first corporation with a net income of more than $1 billion in one year was General Motors, with a net income in 1955 of $1,189,477,082.[29]

OTHER TYPES OF OWNERSHIP

In this section we take a brief look at joint ventures, S corporations, limited liability companies, and cooperatives—businesses formed for special purposes.

Joint Ventures

A **joint venture** is a partnership established for a specific project or for a limited time. The partners in a joint venture may be individuals or organizations, as in the case of the international joint ventures discussed in Chapter 3. Control of a joint venture may be shared equally, or one partner may control decision making. Joint ventures are especially popular in situations that call for large investments, such as extraction of natural resources and the development of new products, and can even take place between businesses and governments. They offer companies the chance to use their mutual talents to pursue opportunities that would have been more difficult to achieve operating alone. For example, Raytheon and General Dynamics launched a joint venture called Range Generation Next (RGNext) to pursue an opportunity to operate, maintain, and sustain the U.S. Air Force Space and Missile Systems Center's Launch and Test Range System.[30]

S Corporations

An **S corporation** is a form of business ownership that is taxed as though it were a partnership. Net profits or losses of the corporation pass to the owners, thus eliminating double taxation. The benefit of limited liability is retained. Formally known as Subchapter S Corporations, they have become a popular form of business ownership for entrepreneurs and represent almost half of all corporate filings.[31] The owners of an S corporation get the benefits of tax advantages and limited liability. Advantages of S corporations include the simple method of taxation, the limited liability of shareholders, perpetual life, and the ability to shift income and appreciation to others. Disadvantages include restrictions on the number (100) and types (individuals, estates, and certain trusts) of shareholders and the difficulty of formation and operation.

Limited Liability Companies

A **limited liability company (LLC)** is a form of business ownership that provides limited liability, as in a corporation, but is taxed like a partnership. Although relatively new in the United States, LLCs have existed for many years abroad. Professionals such as lawyers, doctors, and engineers often use the LLC form of ownership. Many consider the LLC a blend of the best characteristics of corporations, partnerships, and sole proprietorships. One of the major reasons for the LLC form of ownership is to protect the members' personal assets in case of lawsuits. LLCs are flexible, simple to run, and do not require the members to hold meetings, keep minutes, or make resolutions, all of which are necessary in corporations. Mrs. Fields Famous Brands, LLC—known for its cookies and brownies—is an example of a limited liability company.[32]

Cooperatives

Another form of organization in business is the **cooperative** or **co-op**, an organization composed of individuals or small businesses that have banded together to reap the benefits of belonging to a larger organization. Berkshire Co-op Market, for example, is a grocery store cooperative based in Massachusetts.[33] Ocean Spray is a cooperative of cranberry farmers. REI operates a bit differently because it is owned by consumers rather than farmers or small businesses. A co-op is set up not to make money as an entity. It exists so that its members can become more profitable or save money. Co-ops are generally expected to operate without profit or to create only enough profit to maintain the co-op organization.

Many cooperatives exist in small farming communities. The co-op stores and markets grain; orders large quantities of fertilizer, seed, and other supplies at discounted prices; and reduces costs and increases efficiency with good management. A co-op can purchase supplies in large quantities and pass on the savings to its members. It also can help distribute the products of its members more efficiently than each could on an individual basis. A cooperative can advertise its members' products and thus generate demand. Ace Hardware, a cooperative of independent hardware store owners, allows its members to share in the savings that result from buying supplies in large quantities; it also provides advertising, which individual members might not be able to afford on their own.

REI is organized as a consumer cooperative.
© Cal Cam/Alamy

OTTERBOX: FROM WATER SPORTS INDUSTRY TO MOBILE TECHNOLOGY

In 1998 Curt Richardson created OtterBox, a limited liability company (LLC) that sold a waterproof case he had developed in his Fort Collins, Colorado, garage. It was targeted toward the water sports market as a way for surfers and scuba divers to protect their electronics. As an LLC, Richardson had limited liability and was taxed as a partnership with fewer restrictions. This form of organization had the advantage of being able to adapt quickly to market changes, which came in handy when the iPhone was launched in 2001. OtterBox decided to transition into the mobile technology industry and focused on selling to retailers and wireless carriers, who would then sell to end consumers.

OtterBox cases were a hit. Customers valued the cases for their high-quality design and protection capabilities. Today, OtterBox has annual revenues of $575 million and is looking for additional expansion opportunities, such as the business-to-business market. OtterBox is also building iPad cases to target the education industry. OtterBox's ability to recognize key opportunities will be a major factor in its continued success.[34]

LO 4-4 Define and debate the advantages and disadvantages of mergers, acquisitions, and leveraged buyouts.

TRENDS IN BUSINESS OWNERSHIP: MERGERS AND ACQUISITIONS

Companies large and small achieve growth and improve profitability by expanding their operations, often by developing and selling new products or selling current products to new groups of customers in different geographic areas. Such growth, when carefully planned and controlled, is usually beneficial to the firm and ultimately helps it reach its goal of enhanced profitability. But companies also grow by merging with or purchasing other companies.

A **merger** occurs when two companies (usually corporations) combine to form a new company. An **acquisition** occurs when one company purchases another, generally by buying most of its stock. The acquired company may become a subsidiary of the buyer, or its operations and assets may be merged with those of the buyer. The government sometimes scrutinizes mergers and acquisitions in an attempt to protect customers from monopolistic practices. For example, the decision to authorize American Airlines' acquisition of U.S. Airways was carefully analyzed, as was the merger of Sirius and XM Satellite Radio. Google paid $3.2 billion for "smart home" company Nest Labs.[35] The company was just one of many that Google has acquired. While these acquisitions have the potential to diversify Google's service offerings and benefit it financially, some believe that Google might be investing in companies of which it has little knowledge. In these cases, acquisitions could end up harming the acquiring company.[36] Acquisitions sometimes involve the purchase of a division or some other part of a company rather than the entire company. The late 1990s saw a merger and acquisition frenzy, which is slowing in the 21st century (see Table 4.5).

> COMPANIES LARGE AND SMALL ACHIEVE GROWTH AND IMPROVE PROFITABILITY BY EXPANDING THEIR OPERATIONS, OFTEN BY DEVELOPING AND SELLING NEW PRODUCTS OR SELLING CURRENT PRODUCTS TO NEW GROUPS OF CUSTOMERS IN DIFFERENT GEOGRAPHIC AREAS.

▼ **TABLE 4.5** Major Mergers and Acquisitions Worldwide 2000–2015

Rank	Year	Acquirer	Target	Transaction Value (in millions of U.S. dollars)
1	2000	America Online Inc. (AOL) (*Merger*)	Time Warner	$164,747
2	2000	Glaxo Wellcome Plc.	SmithKline Beecham Plc.	75,961
3	2004	Royal Dutch Petroleum Co.	Shell Transport & Trading Co.	74,559
4	2006	AT&T Inc.	BellSouth Corporation	72,671
5	2001	Comcast Corporation	AT&T Broadband & Internet Svcs.	72,041
6	2004	JP Morgan Chase & Co.	Bank One Corporation	58,761
7	2013	American Airlines	U.S. Airways	11,000
8	2015	Albertsons	Safeway	9,400
9	2008	Bank of America	Countrywide	4,000
10	2008	JP Morgan Chase & Co.	Bear Stearns Companies Inc.	1,100

Unless noted, deal was an acquisition.

Sources: Institute of Mergers, Acquisitions and Alliances Research, *Thomson Financial*, www.imaa-institute.org/en/publications+mergers+acquisitions+m&a.php#Reports (accessed March 16, 2010); "JPMorgan Chase Completes Bear Stearns Acquisition," JPMorganChase News Release, May 31, 2008, www.bearstearns.com/includes/pdfs/PressRelease_BSC_31May08.pdf (accessed March 1, 2010); Michael Calia, "Safeway Sales Rise as Albertsons Merger Nears," *The Wall Street Journal*, October 15, 2014, www.wsj.com/articles/safeway-sales-rise-as-albertsons-merger-nears-1413371091 (accessed January 30, 2015).

The name "poison pill" carries negative connotations. Poison pills in the securities markets occur when a company adopts rules mandating that if an investor gains a certain percentage of shares in the firm, then the company will issue more stock to existing shareholders to dilute the investor's share. The more shares the company releases, the harder it is for any one investor to gather enough shares to make a sizable difference in decision making. This has traditionally been used to avoid takeover bids by other companies. However, today poison pills are increasingly being used to keep activist investors from gaining control and forcing strategic changes.

Poison pills are controversial. Some see the use of poison pills as a way for the board of directors and management to maintain control in spite of objections of investors. Because of their questionable nature, poison pills are prohibited in the United Kingdom. However, they have been legally upheld in the United States.

Companies that have adopted poison pills include American Apparel, Allergan, Family Dollar, News Corp., Hertz, and Sotheby's. Sotheby's had adopted a rule that capped the trigger for activist investors at 10 percent—anything more would trigger the poison pill. However, it capped the limit of a passive investor at 20 percent. It is estimated that 15 percent of companies have adopted poison pills that have different trigger limits for active and passive investors.

Hertz also adopted a poison pill that capped investor shares at 10 percent after activist investor Carl Icahn showed interest in waging a proxy battle to force changes. However, after negotiations Hertz agreed to cap the trigger at 20 percent and allow Icahn to assign three of his own nominees as independent board members. Therefore, the poison pill can be used to force investors to negotiate and balance control over decisions.[37]

Discussion Questions

1. Why do public companies adopt poison pill plans?
2. Do poison pills seem to stop active investors from pursuing company changes? Why or why not?
3. Do you think poison pill plans are ethical? Why or why not?

When firms that make and sell similar products to the same customers merge, it is known as a *horizontal merger,* as when Martin Marietta and Lockheed, both defense contractors, merged to form Lockheed Martin. Horizontal mergers, however, reduce the number of corporations competing within an industry, and for this reason they are usually reviewed carefully by federal regulators before the merger is allowed to proceed.

When companies operating at different but related levels of an industry merge, it is known as a *vertical merger.* In many instances, a vertical merger results when one corporation merges with one of its customers or suppliers. For example, if Burger King were to purchase a large Idaho potato farm—to ensure a ready supply of potatoes for its french fries—a vertical merger would result.

A *conglomerate merger* results when two firms in unrelated industries merge. For example, the purchase of Sterling Drug, a pharmaceutical firm, by Eastman Kodak, best-known for its films and cameras, represents a conglomerate merger because the two companies are of different industries. (Kodak later sold Sterling Drug to a pharmaceutical company.)

When a company (or an individual), sometimes called a *corporate raider,* wants to acquire or take over another company, it first offers to buy some or all of the other company's stock at a premium over its current price in a *tender offer.* Most such offers are "friendly," with both groups agreeing to the proposed deal, but some are "hostile," when the second company does not want to be taken over. Global animal health company Zoetis adopted a poison pill after activist investor William

Eli Lilly purchased Novartis's animal health unit for $5.4 billion.
© Konrad Fiedle/Bloomberg/Getty Images

Ackman's hedge fund acquired an 8.5 percent stake in the company. Zoetis's poison pill is set to go off if an outside investor purchases 15 percent or more of the stock.[38]

To head off a hostile takeover attempt, a threatened company's managers may use one or more of several techniques. They may ask stockholders not to sell to the raider; file a lawsuit in an effort to abort the takeover; institute a *poison pill* (in which the firm allows stockholders to buy more shares of stock at prices lower than the current market value) or *shark repellant* (in which management requires a large majority of stockholders to approve the takeover); or seek a *white knight* (a more acceptable firm that is willing to acquire the threatened company). In some cases, management may take the company private or even take on more debt so that the heavy debt obligation will "scare off" the raider.

In a **leveraged buyout (LBO)**, a group of investors borrows money from banks and other institutions to acquire a company (or a division of one), using the assets of the purchased company to guarantee repayment of the loan. In some LBOs, as much as 95 percent of the buyout price is paid with borrowed money, which eventually must be repaid.

Because of the explosion of mergers, acquisitions, and leveraged buyouts in the 1980s and 1990s, financial journalists coined the term *merger mania.* Many companies joined the merger mania simply to enhance their own operations by consolidating them with the operations

of other firms. Mergers and acquisitions enabled these companies to gain a larger market share in their industries, acquire valuable assets such as new products or plants and equipment, and lower their costs. Mergers also represent a means of making profits quickly, as was the case during the 1980s when many companies' stock was undervalued. Quite simply, such companies represent a bargain to other companies that can afford to buy them. Additionally, deregulation of some industries has permitted consolidation of firms within those industries for the first time, as is the case in the banking and airline industries.

leveraged buyout (LBO) a purchase in which a group of investors borrows money from banks and other institutions to acquire a company (or a division of one), using the assets of the purchased company to guarantee repayment of the loan.

SO YOU'D LIKE TO // Start a Business /

If you have a good idea and want to turn it into a business, you are not alone. Small businesses are popping up all over the United States, and the concept of entrepreneurship is hot. Entrepreneurs seek opportunities and creative ways to make profits. Business emerges in a number of different organizational forms, each with its own advantages and disadvantages. Sole proprietorships are the most common form of business organization in the United States. They tend to be small businesses and can take pretty much any form—anything from a hair salon to a scuba shop, from an organic produce provider to a financial advisor. Proprietorships are everywhere serving consumers' wants and needs. Proprietorships have a big advantage in that they tend to be simple to manage—decisions get made quickly when the owner and the manager are the same person and they are fairly simple and inexpensive to set up. Rules vary by state, but at most all you will need is a license from the state.

Many people have been part of a partnership at some point in their life. Group work in school is an example of a partnership. If you ever worked as a DJ on the weekend with your friend and split

the profits, then you have experienced a partnership. Partnerships can be either general or limited. General partners have unlimited liability and share completely in the management, debts, and profits of the business. Limited partners, on the other hand, consist of at least one general partner and one or more limited partners who do not participate in the management of the company but share in the profits. This form of partnership is used more often in risky investments where the limited partner stands only to lose his or her initial investment. Real estate limited partnerships are an example of how investors can minimize their financial exposure, given the poor performance of the real estate market in recent years. Although it has its advantages, partnership is the least utilized form of business. Part of the reason is that all partners are responsible for the actions and decisions of all other partners, whether or not all of the partners were involved. Usually, partners will have to write up an Articles of Partnership that outlines respective responsibilities in the business. Even in states where it is not required, it is a good idea to draw up this

document as a way to cement each partner's role and hopefully minimize conflict. Unlike a corporation, proprietorships and partnerships both expire upon the death of one or more of those involved.

Corporations tend to be larger businesses, but do not need to be. A corporation can consist of nothing more than a small group of family members. In order to become a corporation, you will have to file in the state under which you wish to incorporate. Each state has its own procedure for incorporation, meaning there are no general guidelines to follow. You can make your corporation private or public, meaning the company issues stocks, and shareholders are the owners. While incorporating is a popular form of organization because it gives the company an unlimited lifespan and limited liability (meaning that if your business fails, you cannot lose personal funds to make up for losses), there is a downside. You will be taxed as a corporation and as an individual, resulting in double taxation. No matter what form of organization suits your business idea best, there is a world of options out there for you if you want to be or experiment with being an entrepreneur.

Some people view mergers and acquisitions favorably, pointing out that they boost corporations' stock prices and market value, to the benefit of their stockholders. In many instances, mergers enhance a company's ability to meet foreign competition in an increasingly global marketplace. Additionally, companies that are victims of hostile takeovers generally streamline their operations, reduce unnecessary staff, cut costs, and otherwise become more efficient with their operations, which benefits their stockholders whether or not the takeover succeeds.

Critics, however, argue that mergers hurt companies because they force managers to focus their efforts on avoiding takeovers rather than managing effectively and profitably. Some

companies have taken on a heavy debt burden to stave off a takeover, later to be forced into bankruptcy when economic downturns left them unable to handle the debt. Mergers and acquisitions also can damage employee morale and productivity, as well as the quality of the companies' products.

Many mergers have been beneficial for all involved; others have had damaging effects for the companies, their employees, and customers. No one can say whether mergers will slow or increase, but many experts say the utilities, telecommunications, financial services, natural resources, computer hardware and software, gaming, managed health care, and technology industries are likely targets. ∎

small business, entrepreneurship, and franchising

© Vikki Grant/SuperStock, RF

LEARNING OBJECTIVES

After reading this chapter, you will be able to:

LO 5-1 Define entrepreneurship and small business.

LO 5-2 Investigate the importance of small business in the U.S. economy and why certain fields attract small business.

LO 5-3 Specify the advantages of small-business ownership.

LO 5-4 Summarize the disadvantages of small-business ownership, and analyze why many small businesses fail.

LO 5-5 Describe how you go about starting a small business and what resources are needed.

LO 5-6 Evaluate the demographic, technological, and economic trends that are affecting the future of small business.

LO 5-7 Explain why many large businesses are trying to "think small."

Although many business students go to work for large corporations upon graduation, others may choose to start their own business or to find employment opportunities in small organizations with 500 or fewer employees. Small businesses employ about half of all private-sector employees.[1] Each small business represents the vision of its owners to succeed through providing new or better products. Small businesses are the heart of the U.S. economic and social system because they offer opportunities and demonstrate the freedom of people to make their own destinies. Today, the entrepreneurial spirit is growing around the world, from Russia and China to India, Germany, Brazil, and Mexico. For instance, within eastern Europe, approximately 24 percent of the population is engaged in entrepreneurial activities. Within the BRIC countries (Brazil, Russia, India, and China), the average is only slightly less at 21 percent.[2]

This chapter surveys the world of entrepreneurship and small business. First we define entrepreneurship and small business and examine the role of small business in the American economy. Then we explore the advantages and disadvantages of small-business ownership and analyze why small businesses succeed or fail. Next, we discuss how an entrepreneur goes about starting a business and the challenges facing small businesses today. Finally, we look at entrepreneurship in larger organizations. ■

LO 5-1 Define entrepreneurship and small business.

THE NATURE OF ENTREPRENEURSHIP AND SMALL BUSINESS

In Chapter 1, we defined an entrepreneur as a person who risks his or her wealth, time, and effort to develop for profit an innovative product or way of doing something. **Entrepreneurship** is the process of creating and managing a business to achieve desired objectives. Many large businesses you may recognize (Levi Strauss and Co., Procter & Gamble, McDonald's, Dell Computers, Microsoft, and Google) all began as small businesses based on the visions of their founders. Some entrepreneurs who start small businesses have the ability to see emerging trends; in response, they create a company to provide a product that serves customer needs. For example, rather than inventing a major new technology, an innovative company may take advantage of technology to create new markets, such as Amazon.com. Or they may offer a familiar product that has been improved or placed in a unique retail environment, such as Starbucks and its coffee shops. A company may innovate by focusing on a particular market segment and delivering a combination of features that consumers in that segment could not find anywhere else. Porch.com was founded as a way to connect homeowners with contractors. Founder Matt Ehrlichman conceived of the idea after becoming frustrated with problems in building his own house. Porch.com's software provides a more transparent way to link homeowners with licensed professionals. Approximately $1.5 trillion worth of home remodeling projects have been featured through the site. The software is so effective that home improvement store Lowe's installed it in 1,700 retail locations.[3]

entrepreneurship the process of creating and managing a business to achieve desired objectives.

Of course, smaller businesses do not have to evolve into highly visible companies to be successful, but those entrepreneurial efforts that result in rapidly growing businesses gain visibility along with success. Entrepreneurs who have achieved success, like Michael Dell (Dell Computers), Bill Gates (Microsoft), Larry Page and Sergey Brin (Google), and the late Steve Jobs (Apple) are some of the most well known. Table 5.1 lists some of the greatest entrepreneurs of the past few decades.

▼ **TABLE 5.1** Great Entrepreneurs of Innovative Companies

Company	Entrepreneurs
Hewlett-Packard	Bill Hewlett, David Packard
Walt Disney Productions	Walt Disney
Starbucks	Howard Schultz
Amazon.com	Jeff Bezos
Dell	Michael Dell
Microsoft	Bill Gates
Apple	Steve Jobs
Walmart	Sam Walton
Google	Larry Page, Sergey Brin
Ben & Jerry's	Ben Cohen, Jerry Greenfield
Ford	Henry Ford
General Electric	Thomas Edison

social entrepreneurs individuals who use entrepreneurship to address social problems.

small business any independently owned and operated business that is not dominant in its competitive area and does not employ more than 500 people.

Small Business Administration (SBA) an independent agency of the federal government that offers managerial and financial assistance to small businesses.

The entrepreneurship movement is accelerating, and many new, smaller businesses are emerging. Technology once available only to the largest firms can now be obtained by a small business. Websites, podcasts, online videos, social media, cellular phones, and even expedited delivery services enable small businesses to be more competitive with today's giant corporations. Small businesses can also form alliances with other companies to produce and sell products in domestic and global markets.

Another growing trend among small businesses is social entrepreneurship. **Social entrepreneurs** are individuals who use entrepreneurship to address social problems. They operate by the same principles as other entrepreneurs but view their organizations as vehicles to create social change. Although these entrepreneurs often start their own nonprofit organizations, they can also operate for-profit organizations committed to solving social issues. CEO of Toms Blake Mycoskie is an example of a social entrepreneur who founded the firm with the purpose of donating one pair of shoes to a child in need for every pair of shoes sold to consumers. Since its founding, Toms has given away 35 million pairs of shoes and has now expanded its social entrepreneurship model to coffee. For every bag of Toms coffee sold, the company provides 140 liters of clean water to those in need.[4] Muhammad Yunus, founder of micro-lending organization Grameen Bank, is another example of a social entrepreneur. Yunus seeks to combat poverty by providing small loans to low-income individuals to start their own businesses.

What Is a Small Business?

This question is difficult to answer because smallness is relative. In this book, we will define a **small business** as any independently owned and operated business that is not dominant in its competitive area and does not employ more than 500 people. A local Mexican restaurant may be the most patronized Mexican restaurant in your community, but because it does not dominate the restaurant industry as a whole, the restaurant can be considered a small business. This definition is similar to the one used by the **Small Business Administration (SBA)**, an independent agency of the federal government that offers managerial and financial assistance to small businesses. On its website, the SBA outlines the first steps in starting a small business and offers a wealth of information to current and potential small-business owners.

The Role of Small Business in the American Economy

No matter how you define a small business, one fact is clear: They are vital to the American economy. As you can see in Table 5.2, more than 99 percent of all U.S. firms are classified as small businesses, and they employ about half of private workers. Small firms are also important as exporters, representing 98 percent of U.S. exporters of goods and contributing 31 percent of the value of exported goods.[5] In addition, small businesses are largely responsible for fueling job creation and innovation. Small businesses also provide opportunities for minorities and women to succeed in business. Women own more than 10 million businesses nationwide, with great success in the professional services, retail, communication, and administrative services areas.[6] Minority-owned businesses have been growing faster than other classifiable firms as well, representing almost 15 percent of all small businesses.[7] For example, Mexican-born José de Jesús Legaspi went into the real estate business and focused his market niche on inner-city areas with a high percentage of Hispanic consumers. When Legaspi decided to begin investing in struggling malls, he refashioned the malls he acquired as cultural centers appealing to Hispanic consumers of all generations. One of his malls, renamed La Gran Plaza, went from being 20 percent occupied to 80 percent.[8]

Job Creation The energy, creativity, and innovative abilities of small-business owners have resulted in jobs for many people. About 65 percent of net new jobs annually were created by small businesses.[9] Table 5.3 indicates that 99.7 percent of all businesses employ fewer than 500 people. Businesses employing 19 or fewer people account for 89.6 percent of all businesses.[10]

▼ **TABLE 5.2** Importance of Small Businesses to Our Economy

Small firms represent 99.7 percent of all employer firms.
Small firms have generated 63 percent of net new jobs.
Small firms hire approximately 37 percent of high-tech workers (such as scientists, engineers, computer programmers, and others).
Small firms produce 16 times more patents per employee than large patenting firms.
Small firms employ nearly half of all private-sector employees.
Small firms pay 42 percent of the total U.S. private payroll.

Source: Small Business Administration Department of Advocacy, "Frequently Asked Questions," March 2014, www.sba.gov/sites/default/files/FAQ_March_2014_0.pdf (accessed February 13, 2015).

▼ **TABLE 5.3** Number of Firms by Employment Size

Firm Size	Number of Firms	Percentage of All Firms
0–19 employees	5,130,348	89.6%
20–99 employees	494,170	8.6
100–499 employees	83,423	1.5
500+ employees	18,219	0.3

Source: "Statistics of U.S. Businesses (SUSB)," *Statistics of U.S. Businesses,* www.census.gov/econ/susb/index.html (accessed February 13, 2015).

Many small businesses today are being started because of encouragement from larger ones. Many new jobs are also created by big-company–small-company alliances. Whether through formal joint ventures, supplier relationships, or product or marketing cooperative projects, the rewards of collaborative relationships are creating many jobs for small-business owners and their employees. In India, many small information technology (IT) firms provide IT services to global markets. Because of lower costs, international companies often can find Indian businesses to provide their information processing solutions.[11]

Innovation Perhaps one of the most significant strengths of small businesses is their ability to innovate and to bring significant benefits to customers. Small firms produce more than half of all innovations. Among the important 20th-century innovations by U.S. small firms are the airplane, the audio tape recorder, fiber-optic examining equipment, the heart valve, the optical scanner, the pacemaker, the personal computer, soft contact lenses, the Internet, and the zipper. For instance, the founder and CEO of the small firm UniKey, Phil Dumas, invented a new way for consumers to keep their doors locked. Dumas invented Kevo, a motorized deadbolt lock that links to users' iPhones. With just the touch of a finger, consumers can lock and unlock their doors from remote locations. UniKey distributes products in major retailers such as Lowe's and Home Depot. This is just one example of a small company with the ability to innovate and contribute to the benefit of customers.[12]

The innovation of successful firms takes many forms. For instance, franchises make up approximately 2 percent of small businesses. Many of today's largest businesses started off as small firms that used innovation to achieve success.[13] Small-business owner Ray Kroc found a new way to sell hamburgers and turned his ideas into one of the most successful fast-food franchises in the world—McDonald's. Small businesses have become an integral part of our lives. Travis Kalanick co-launched the successful company Uber, an app-based car service company rapidly growing in demand. Much like Ray Kroc, Kalanick's innovative concept has the potential to change its industry. Its low cost and convenience is making it a major player in transportation rivaling traditional cab companies, drawing the ire of the taxi companies and governments that believe Uber should be regulated more like the taxi industry. Some drivers for Uber work full time, but many work part time to supplement their income. They are true entrepreneurs who use their own cars and manage their own businesses.[14] Entrepreneurs provide fresh ideas and usually have greater flexibility to change than do large companies.

Allegiant Travel is a publicly traded company that operates scheduled and chartered flights. It has been listed among Forbes's top 20 small workplaces in America.
© ZUMA Press, Inc/Alamy

LO 5-2 Investigate the importance of small business in the U.S. economy and why certain fields attract small business.

Industries That Attract Small Business

Small businesses are found in nearly every industry, but retailing and wholesaling, services, manufacturing, and high technology are especially attractive to entrepreneurs. These fields are relatively easy to enter and require low initial financing. Small-business owners in these industries also find it easier to focus on specific groups of consumers; new firms in these industries initially suffer less from heavy competition than do established firms.

Retailing Retailers acquire goods from producers or wholesalers and sell them to consumers. Main streets and shopping centers and malls are generally lined with independent music stores, sporting-goods stores, dry cleaners, boutiques, drugstores, restaurants, caterers, service stations, and hardware stores that sell directly to consumers. Retailing attracts entrepreneurs because gaining experience and exposure in retailing is relatively easy. Additionally, an entrepreneur opening a new retail store or establishing a website does not have to spend the large sums of money for the equipment and distribution systems that a manufacturing business requires. All that a new retailer needs is the ability to understand a market and provide a product that satisfies a need. However, it is important for entrepreneurs to anticipate the costs of opening a retail or wholesale business beforehand. When Patrick Leon Esquerré decided to open up a French bakery, he invested $100,000 into the bakery—all the money he

The retailing industry is particularly attractive to entrepreneurs. Pike's Perk Coffee & Tea House is a small locally owned coffee shop in Colorado Springs, Colorado.
© Richard Cummins/Alamy

Direct selling involves the marketing of products to ultimate consumers through face-to-face sales presentations at home, in the workplace, and in party environments. Well-known direct selling companies include Amway, Avon, Herbalife, and Mary Kay. The cost of getting involved in direct selling is low and often involves buying enough inventory to get started. Many people view direct selling as a part-time business opportunity. Often those who become independent contractors for direct selling companies are enthusiastic about the product and have the opportunity to recruit other distributors and receive commissions on their sales.

Wholesalers provide both goods and services to producers and retailers. They can assist their customers with almost every business function. Wholesalers supply products to industrial, retail, and institutional users for resale or for use in making other products. Wholesaling activities range from planning and negotiating for supplies, promoting, and distributing (warehousing and transporting) to providing management and merchandising assistance to clients. Wholesalers are extremely important for many products, especially consumer goods, because of the marketing activities they perform. Although it is true that wholesalers themselves can be eliminated, their functions must be passed on to some other organization such as the producer, or another intermediary, often a small business. Frequently, small businesses are closer to the final customers and know what it takes to keep them satisfied. Some smaller businesses start out manufacturing, but find their real niche as a supplier or distributor of larger firms' products. Sysco is a full-service wholesaler for food products that serves restaurants and other institutions.

had. He was able to raise more money from friends in France and Texas and opened up his first bakery, La Madeleine. After guests started asking for food, Esquerré used his mother's recipes to expand the menu. Eventually, the company began selling its products through stores such as Sam's Club. Esquerré's initial $100,000 investment has led to 63 restaurant locations today.[15]

Many opportunities exist for nonstore retailing as well. Nonstore retailing involves selling products outside a retail facility. There are two types of nonstore retailing: direct marketing—which uses the telephone, catalogs, and other media to give consumers an opportunity to place orders by mail, telephone, or the Internet—and direct selling. Nonstore retailing is an area that provides great opportunities for entrepreneurs because of a lower cost of entry. JCPenney also found that it significantly impacts sales. The organization decided to engage in more direct marketing by resurrecting its catalog—which it had discontinued in 2010—based on market research findings suggesting that catalog users are more inspired to purchase items online.[16] Smaller businesses can engage in a form of direct marketing by featuring their products on eBay, Amazon, or Etsy.

> **The service sector includes businesses that do not actually produce tangible goods.**

Services The service sector includes businesses that do not actually produce tangible goods. Services include intangible products that involve a performance, inauguration, or any effort to provide something of value that cannot be physically possessed. Services can also be part of the wholesale market and involve any product that is intangible and therefore cannot be touched. The service sector accounts for 80 percent of U.S. jobs, excluding farmworkers. Real estate, insurance and personnel agencies, barbershops, banks, television and computer repair shops, copy centers, dry cleaners, and accounting firms are all service businesses. Services also attract individuals—such as hairstylists and barbers, morticians, jewelers, doctors, and veterinarians—whose skills are not usually required by large firms. Many of these service providers are retailers who provide their services to ultimate consumers. An example of a growing service sector is home sourcing, where individuals are involved in customer contact jobs such as call centers.

Manufacturing Manufacturing goods can provide unique opportunities for small businesses. Consider Nashville-based specialty chocolate company Olive & Sinclair. Within four

A few years ago, four Wharton business students bonded over the high price of stylish prescription glasses (up to $700 or more each). When they discovered it was a single company's near-monopoly over the optical industry that led to steep prices, the idea for Warby Parker was born. The startup's premise is simple: By designing and manufacturing glasses in-house, and doing without the traditionally high profit margins of the industry, Warby Parker can sell designer-style prescription eyeglasses for $95 each. It offers online customers a try-before-you-buy option—five pairs for five days at no cost. Additionally, for every pair bought, another is distributed to developing nations. By 2014, Warby Parker announced it had donated over 1 million pairs of eyeglasses, and the company has been valued at over $300 million.

Some analysts attribute Warby Parker's success to its unique culture and branding approach; it goes beyond simply selling eyeglasses to incorporate quirky and subtle counterculture elements into everything it does. Others find the company to be an example of "good old-fashioned amazing execution." From customer approach to employee treatment, the company is doing good business.

However, others are voicing concerns. The company is still in the entrepreneurial growth stage, meaning it survives on investment capital and has not yet reached self-sufficient profitability. Is Warby Parker's idealistic vision truly viable? Another concern is the possibility of acquisition, an option often sought by entrepreneurial investors who want a quick return on their money. Will Warby Parker end up being bought out by the same high-priced company it set out to challenge initially? These questions will define the company's future as it transitions into a more mature stage of growth.[17]

Discussion Questions

1. Why has Warby Parker been successful?

2. Does Warby Parker exhibit any of the classic strengths, or weaknesses, of an entrepreneurial startup?

3. What are some challenges that Warby Parker will likely face as it matures as a company?

---

years of its founding, the company was selling chocolates in the United States, London, Singapore, and Japan. The manufacturing of the chocolate is distinctively "southern" in nature. Its varieties include two ingredients—buttermilk and brown sugar—commonly associated with the South and a grinding process used to make southern-style grits. This association appeals to global consumers. Today, Olive & Sinclair manufactures 1,500 chocolate bars each day.[18] Small businesses sometimes have an advantage over large firms because they can customize products to meet specific customer needs and wants. Such products include custom artwork, jewelry, clothing, and furniture.

High Technology *High technology* is a broad term used to describe businesses that depend heavily on advanced scientific and engineering knowledge. People who were able to innovate or identify new markets in the fields of computers, biotechnology, genetic engineering, robotics, and other markets have become today's high-tech giants. One innovative technology was developed by a teenager interested in virtual reality. Only a few years ago, virtual reality was considered a dead technology past its prime. However, when 19-year-old Palmer Luckey developed a virtual gaming headset, it caught the attention of programmer John Carmack. Together, they brought virtual reality to a new level for gamers. The company, Oculus Rift, was sold to Facebook for $2 billion.[20] In general, high-tech businesses require greater capital and have higher initial startup costs than do other small businesses. Many of the biggest, nonetheless, started out in garages, basements, kitchens, and dorm rooms.

LO 5-3 Specify the advantages of small-business ownership.

?

DID YOU KNOW?

Small businesses hire 37 percent of high-tech workers in the United States.[19]

ADVANTAGES OF SMALL-BUSINESS OWNERSHIP

There are many advantages to establishing and running a small business. These can be categorized into personal advantages and business advantages. Table 5.4 lists some of the traits that can help entrepreneurs succeed.

Independence

Independence is probably one of the leading reasons that entrepreneurs choose to go into business for themselves. Being a small-business owner means being your own boss. Many people start their own businesses because they believe they will do better for themselves than they could do by remaining with their current employer or by changing jobs. They may feel stuck on the corporate ladder and that no business would take them seriously enough to fund their ideas. Sometimes people who venture forth to start their own small business are those who simply cannot work for someone else. Such people may say that they just do not fit the "corporate mold."

More often, small-business owners just want the freedom to choose whom they work with, the flexibility to pick where and when to work, and the option of working in a family setting. The

TABLE 5.4 Successful Traits of Young Entrepreneurs

Trait	Definition	Trait	Definition
Intuitive	Using one's intuition to derive what's true without conscious reasoning	Innovative	Being able to come up with new and creative ideas
Productive	Being able to produce large amounts of something during a specific time period	Risk-taker	Having the ability to pursue risky endeavors despite the possibility of failure
Resourceful	Understanding how to use and spend resources wisely	Persistent	Continuing in a certain action in spite of obstacles
Charismatic	Having the ability to inspire others behind a central vision	Friendly	Being able to have mutually beneficial interactions with people

availability of the computer, copy machine, fax, and Internet has permitted many people to work at home. In the past, most of them would have needed the support that an office provides.

Costs

As already mentioned, small businesses often require less money to start and maintain than do large ones. Obviously, a firm with just 25 people in a small factory spends less money on wages and salaries, rent, utilities, and other expenses than does a firm employing tens of thousands of people in several large facilities. Rather than maintain the expense of keeping separate departments for accounting, advertising, and legal counseling, small businesses often hire other firms (sometimes small businesses themselves) to supply these services as they are needed. Additionally, small-business owners can sometimes rely on friends and family members to help them save money by volunteering to work on a difficult project.

Flexibility

With small size comes the flexibility to adapt to changing market demands. Small businesses usually have only one layer of management—the owners. Decisions therefore can be made and executed quickly. In larger firms, decisions about even routine matters can take weeks because they must pass through multiple levels of management before action is authorized. When Taco Bell introduces a new product, for example, it must first research what consumers want, then develop the product and test it before introducing it nationwide—a process that sometimes takes years. An independent snack shop, however, can develop and introduce a new product (perhaps to meet a customer's request) in a much shorter time.

Focus

Small firms can focus their efforts on a precisely defined market niche—that is, a specific group of customers. Many large corporations must compete in the mass market or for large market segments. Smaller firms can develop products for particular groups of customers or to satisfy a need that other companies have not addressed. For example, Hampton Creek, based in San Francisco, focuses on using technology to produce sustainable protein products. The company developed a new type of egg substitute made from plant materials. This concept is likely to attract vegetarians and consumers concerned with sustainability, but founder and CEO Josh Tetrick has bigger plans. His concept is not to focus solely on a niche industry; he believes the solutions discovered at Hampton Creek will eventually help solve food shortages through alternatives that do not place a strain on the environment.[21] By targeting small niches or product needs, businesses can sometimes avoid competition from larger firms, helping them grow into stronger companies.

Reputation

Reputation, or how a firm is perceived by its various stakeholders, is highly significant to an organization's success. Small firms, because of their capacity to focus on narrow niches, can develop enviable reputations for quality and service. A good example of a small business with a formidable reputation is W. Atlee Burpee and Co., which has the country's premier bulb and seed catalog. Burpee has an unqualified returns policy (complete satisfaction or your money back) that demonstrates a strong commitment to customer satisfaction.

> **LO 5-4** Summarize the disadvantages of small-business ownership, and analyze why many small businesses fail.

DISADVANTAGES OF SMALL-BUSINESS OWNERSHIP

The rewards associated with running a small business are so enticing that it's no wonder many people dream of it. However, as with any undertaking, small-business ownership has its disadvantages.

High Stress Level

A small business is likely to provide a living for its owner, but not much more (although there are exceptions as some examples in this chapter have shown). There are ongoing worries about competition, employee problems, new equipment, expanding inventory, rent increases, or changing market demand. In addition to other stresses, small-business owners tend to be victims of physical and psychological stress. The small-business person is often the owner, manager,

Small firms can focus on narrow niche markets such as pastries and gain a reputation for quality and service.
© Claudia Dewald/Getty Images, RF

sales force, shipping and receiving clerk, bookkeeper, and custodian. Having to multitask can result in long hours for most small-business owners. Many creative persons fail, not because of their business concepts, but rather because of difficulties in managing their business.

High Failure Rate

Despite the importance of small businesses to our economy, there is no guarantee of success. Half of all new employer firms fail within the first five years.[22] Restaurants are a case in point. Look around your own neighborhood, and you can probably spot the locations of several restaurants that are no longer in business.

Entrepreneurs experience a great deal of independence but also a great deal of stress. Many fail.
© WendellandCarolyn/E+/Getty Images, RF

Small businesses fail for many reasons (see Table 5.5). A poor business concept—such as insecticides for garbage cans (research found that consumers are not concerned with insects in their garbage)—will produce disaster nearly every time. Expanding a hobby into a business may work if a genuine market niche exists, but all too often people start such a business without identifying a real need for the goods or services. Other notable causes of small-business failure include the burdens imposed by government regulation, insufficient funds to withstand slow sales, and vulnerability to competition from larger companies. However, three major causes of small-business failure deserve a close look: undercapitalization, managerial inexperience or incompetence, and inability to cope with growth.

Undercapitalization The shortest path to failure in business is **undercapitalization**, the lack of funds to operate a business normally. Too many entrepreneurs think that all they need is enough money to get started, that the business can survive on cash generated from sales soon thereafter. But almost all businesses suffer from seasonal variations in sales, which make cash tight, and few businesses make money from the start. Many small rural operations cannot obtain financing within their own communities because small rural banks often lack the necessary financing expertise or assets sizable enough to counter the risks involved with small-business loans. Without sufficient funds, the best small-business idea in the world will fail.

Managerial Inexperience or Incompetence Poor management is the cause of many business failures. Just because an entrepreneur has a brilliant vision for a small business does not mean he or she has the knowledge or experience to manage a growing business effectively. A person who is good at creating great product ideas and marketing them may lack the skills and experience to make good management decisions in hiring, negotiating, finance, and control. Moreover, entrepreneurs may neglect those areas of management they know little about or find tedious, at the expense of the business's success.

▼ **TABLE 5.5** Challenges in Starting a New Business

1. Underfunded (not providing adequate startup capital)
2. Not understanding your competitive niche
3. Lack of effective utilization of websites and social media
4. Lack of a marketing and business plan
5. If operating a retail store, poor site selection
6. Pricing mistakes—too high or too low
7. Underestimating the time commitment for success
8. Not finding complementary partners to bring in additional experience
9. Not hiring the right employees and/or not training them properly
10. Not understanding legal and ethical responsibilities

Inability to Cope with Growth Sometimes the very factors that are advantages for a small business turn into serious disadvantages when the time comes to grow. Growth often requires the owner to give up a certain amount of direct authority, and it is frequently hard for someone who has called all the shots to give up control. It has often been said that the greatest impediment to the success of a business is the entrepreneur. Similarly, growth requires specialized management skills in areas such as credit analysis and promotion—skills that the founder may lack or not have time to apply. The founders of many small businesses, including Dell Computers, found that they needed to bring in more experienced managers to help manage their companies through growing pains.

Poorly managed growth probably affects a company's reputation more than anything else, at least initially. And products that do not arrive on time or goods that are poorly made can quickly reverse a success. The principal immediate threats to small and midsized businesses include rising inflation, energy and other supply shortages or cost escalations, and excessive household and/or corporate debt. For this reason, some small-business owners choose to stay small and are not interested in widescale growth. These business owners, called *micropreneurs,* operate small-scale businesses with no more than five employees. It is estimated that 95 percent of small businesses are microbusinesses.[23]

> **LO 5-5**   Describe how you go about starting a small business and what resources are needed.

STARTING A SMALL BUSINESS

We've told you how important small businesses are, and why they succeed and fail, but *how do you go about* starting your own business in the first place? To start any business, large or small, you must have some kind of general idea. Sam Walton, founder of Walmart stores, had a vision of a discount retailing enterprise that spawned the world's largest retailing empire and changed the way companies look at business. Next, you need to devise a strategy to guide planning and development in the business. Finally, you must make decisions about form of ownership, the financial resources needed, and whether to acquire an existing business, start a new one, or buy a franchise.

The Business Plan

A key element of business success is a **business plan**—a precise statement of the rationale for the business and a step-by-step explanation of how it will achieve its goals. The business plan should include an explanation of the business, an analysis of the competition, estimates of income and expenses, and other information. It should also establish a strategy for acquiring sufficient funds to keep the business going. Many financial institutions decide whether to loan a small business money based on its business plan. A good business plan should act as a guide and reference document—not a shackle that limits the business's flexibility and decision-making ability. The business plan must be revised periodically to ensure that the firm's goals and strategies adapt to changes in the environment. Business plans allow companies to assess market potential, determine price and manufacturing requirements, identify optimal distribution channels, and refine product selection. Three co-founders, one of them a college student, created a business plan for their startup company Project Wedge. Project Wedge is hardware that can turn a smartphone, laptop, or tablet computer into a projector. The team won first place in Pacific Lutheran University's business plan competition, which included $7,500. The company has also raised funds on Kickstarter.[24] The SBA website provides an overview of a plan for small businesses to use to gain financing.

Forms of Business Ownership

After developing a business plan, the entrepreneur has to decide on an appropriate legal form of business ownership—whether it is best to operate as a sole proprietorship, partnership, or corporation—and to examine the many factors that affect that decision, which we explored in Chapter 4.

Financial Resources

The expression "it takes money to make money" holds especially true in developing a business enterprise. To make money from a small business, the owner must first provide or obtain money (capital) to get started and to keep it running smoothly. Even a small retail store will probably need at least $50,000 in initial financing to rent space, purchase or lease necessary equipment and furnishings, buy the initial inventory, and provide working capital. Often, the small-business owner has to put up a significant percentage of the necessary capital. Few new business owners have a large amount of their own capital and must look to other sources for additional financing.

Equity Financing The most important source of funds for any new business is the owner. Many owners include among their

> "The most important source of funds for any new business is the owner."

Small-business owners often use debt financing from banks or the Small Business Administration to start their own organization.
© Ariel Skelley/Blend Images LLC, RF

personal resources ownership of a home, the accumulated value in a life-insurance policy, or a savings account. A new business owner may sell or borrow against the value of such assets to obtain funds to operate a business. Additionally, the owner may bring useful personal assets—such as a computer, desks and other furniture, a car or truck—as part of his or her ownership interest in the firm. Such financing is referred to as *equity financing* because the owner uses real personal assets rather than borrowing funds from outside sources to get started in a new business. The owner can also provide working capital by reinvesting profits into the business or simply by not drawing a full salary.

Small businesses can also obtain equity financing by finding investors for their operations. They may sell stock in the business to family members, friends, employees, or other investors. For example, Harvard alumnus Katrina Lake created a website called Stitch Fix that uses algorithms and personal stylists to develop sets, or "fixes," of clothes based upon the consumer's individual tastes. The fixes are mailed to the consumer, who pays for what she wants to keep and mails the rest back. Stitch Fix is meant to appeal to consumers who want to keep shopping simple and are turned off by the large number of choices on websites such as Amazon.com. Despite high shipping costs, Stitch Fix received $12 million from a venture-capital firm. These investors believe Stitch Fix has significant potential to expand and be successful.[25] **Venture capitalists** are persons or organizations that agree to provide some funds for a new business in exchange for an ownership interest or stock. Venture capitalists hope to purchase the stock of a small business at a low price and then sell the stock for a profit after the business has grown successful. Although these forms of equity financing have helped many small businesses, they require that the small-business owner share the profits of the business—and sometimes control, as well—with the investors.

Debt Financing
New businesses sometimes borrow more than half of their financial resources. Banks are the main suppliers of external financing to small businesses. On the federal level, the SBA offers financial assistance to qualifying businesses. They can also look to family and friends as sources for long-term loans or other assets, such as computers or an automobile, that are exchanged for an ownership interest in a business. In such cases, the business owner can usually structure a favorable repayment schedule and sometimes negotiate an interest rate below current bank rates. If the business goes bad, however, the emotional losses for all concerned may greatly exceed the money involved. Anyone lending a friend or family member money for a venture should state the agreement clearly in writing before any money changes hands.

The amount a bank or other institution is willing to loan depends on its assessment of the venture's likelihood of success and of the entrepreneur's ability to repay the loan. The bank will often require the entrepreneur to put up *collateral,* a financial interest in the property or fixtures of the business, to guarantee payment of the debt. Additionally, the small-business owner may have to provide personal property as collateral, such as his or her home, in which case the loan is called a *mortgage.* If the small business fails to repay the loan, the lending institution may eventually claim and sell the collateral or mortgage to recover its loss.

Banks and other financial institutions can also grant a small business a *line of credit*—an agreement by which a financial institution promises to lend a business a predetermined sum on demand. A line of credit permits an entrepreneur to take quick

Some of the advantages of small businesses include flexibility, lower startup costs, and perhaps most desirable, the ability to be your own boss.
© DreamPictures/Blend Images/Corbis, RF

franchise a license to sell another's products or to use another's name in business, or both.

franchiser the company that sells a franchise.

franchisee the purchaser of a franchise.

advantage of opportunities that require external funding. Small businesses may obtain funding from their suppliers in the form of a *trade credit*—that is, suppliers allow the business to take possession of the needed goods and services and pay for them at a later date or in installments. Occasionally, small businesses engage in *bartering*—trading their own products for the goods and services offered by other businesses. For example, an accountant may offer accounting services to an office supply firm in exchange for office supplies and equipment.

Additionally, some community groups sponsor loan funds to encourage the development of particular types of businesses. State and local agencies may guarantee loans, especially to minority businesspeople or for development in certain areas.

Approaches to Starting a Small Business

Starting from Scratch versus Buying an Existing Business Although entrepreneurs often start new small businesses from scratch much the way we have discussed in this section, they may elect instead to buy an existing business. This has the advantage of providing a built-in network of customers, suppliers, and distributors and reducing some of the guesswork inherent in starting a new business from the ground up.

> " Many small-business owners find entry into the business world through franchising. "

However, an entrepreneur who buys an existing business also takes on any problems the business already has.

Franchising Many small-business owners find entry into the business world through franchising. A license to sell another's products or to use another's name in business, or both, is a **franchise**. The company that sells a franchise is the **franchiser**. Dunkin' Donuts, Subway, and Jiffy Lube are well-known franchisers with national visibility. The purchaser of a franchise is called a **franchisee**.

The franchisee acquires the rights to a name, logo, methods of operation, national advertising, products, and other elements associated with the franchiser's business in return for a financial commitment and the agreement to conduct business in accordance with the franchiser's standard of operations. The initial fee to join a franchise varies greatly. In addition, franchisees buy equipment, pay for training, and obtain a mortgage or lease. The franchisee also pays the franchiser a monthly or annual fee based on a percentage of sales or profits. In return, the franchisee often receives building specifications and designs, site recommendations, management and accounting support, and perhaps most importantly, immediate name recognition. Visit the website of the International Franchise Association to learn more on this topic.

The practice of franchising first began in the United States in the 19th century when Singer used it to sell sewing machines. The method of goods distribution soon became commonplace in the automobile, gasoline, soft drink, and hotel industries. The concept of franchising grew especially rapidly during the 1960s, when it expanded to diverse industries. Table 5.6 shows the 10 fastest growing franchises and the top 10 new franchises.

FINDING FORTUNE IN A FOOD TRUCK

Just three years into his career as a lawyer, Eric Silverstein decided it wasn't for him and spent the final year developing a business plan for a restaurant. However, no bank would lend him the seed money he needed. Finally, he got the idea for a food truck, which he could launch for only $40,000 raised mostly from family and friends. In 2010 he founded The Peached Tortilla, serving Austin,

Texas, with a fusion style menu that includes Japanese, Chinese, Malaysian, and southern U.S. influences.

Silverstein spent $12,000 of his $40,000 on initial setup costs, and the rest went to covering the losses of the first three months. He survived on $30,000 of personal savings, and otherwise lived and breathed his business. However, his hard work paid off. The

Peached Tortilla has won awards, reached almost $1 million in revenue, and is in the process of opening its first brick-and-mortar location. Silverstein's story fits with the classic entrepreneurial success: a good idea, a quality product, and lots of hard work.[26]

▼ TABLE 5.6 Fastest Growing and Hottest New Franchises

Top 10 Fastest Growing Franchises	Top 10 Hottest New Franchises
Subway	Mac Tools
7-Eleven Inc.	Bricks 4 Kidz
Mac Tools	Orange Leaf Frozen Yogurt
Jan-Pro Franchising Int'l. Inc.	Sears Hometown & Outlet Stores
Dunkin' Donuts	Fitness Revolution
Cruise Planners	The Ground Guys LLC
Vanguard Cleaning Systems	Paul Davis Emergency Services
Jimmy John's Gourmet Sandwiches	Doc Popcorn
Great Clips	Title Boxing Club
Pizza Hut Inc.	Fuzzy's Taco Shop

Sources: "2014 Fastest-Growing Franchise Rankings," *Entrepreneur,* www.entrepreneur.com/franchises/rankings/fastestgrowing-115162/2014,-1.html (accessed February 13, 2015); "2014 New Franchise Rankings," www.entrepreneur.com/franchises/rankings/topnew-115520/2014,-1.html (accessed February 13, 2015).

The entrepreneur will find that franchising has both advantages and disadvantages. Franchising allows a franchisee the opportunity to set up a small business relatively quickly, and because of its association with an established brand, a franchise outlet often reaches the break-even point faster than an independent business would. Franchisees commonly report the following advantages:

- Management training and support.
- Brand-name appeal.
- Standardized quality of goods and services.
- National and local advertising programs.
- Financial assistance.
- Proven products and business formats.
- Centralized buying power.
- Site selection and territorial protection.
- Greater chance for success.[27]

However, the franchisee must sacrifice some freedom to the franchiser. Some shortcomings experienced by franchisees include:

- Franchise fees and profit sharing with the franchiser.
- Strict adherence to standardized operations.
- Restrictions on purchasing.
- Limited product line.
- Possible market saturation.
- Less freedom in business decisions.[28]

Strict uniformity is the rule rather than the exception. Entrepreneurs who want to be their own bosses are often frustrated with the restrictions of a franchise. In these cases, direct selling might be a better option because entrepreneurs are involved with well-known brands and have the ability to run their businesses as they see fit.

Help for Small-Business Managers

Because of the crucial role that small business and entrepreneurs play in the U.S. economy, a number of organizations offer programs to improve the small-business owner's ability to compete. These include entrepreneurial training programs and programs sponsored by the SBA. Such programs provide small-business owners with invaluable assistance in managing their businesses, often at little or no cost to the owner.

Entrepreneurs can learn critical marketing, management, and finance skills in seminars and college courses. In addition, knowledge, experience, and judgment are necessary for success in a new business. While knowledge can be communicated and some experiences can be simulated in the classroom, good judgment must be developed by the entrepreneur. Local chambers of commerce and the U.S. Department of Commerce offer information and assistance helpful in operating a small business. National publications such as *Inc.* and *Entrepreneur* share statistics, advice, tips, and success/failure stories. Additionally, most urban areas have weekly business journals/newspapers that provide stories on local businesses as well as on business techniques that a manager or small business can use.

The SBA offers many types of management assistance to small businesses, including counseling for firms in difficulty, consulting on improving operations, and training for owner/managers and their employees. Among its many programs, the SBA funds Small Business Development Centers (SBDCs). These are business clinics, usually located on college campuses, that provide counseling at no charge and training at only a nominal charge. SBDCs are often the SBA's principal means of providing direct management assistance.

The Service Corps of Retired Executives (SCORE) and the Active Corps of Executives (ACE) are volunteer agencies funded by the SBA to provide advice for owners of small firms. Both are staffed by experienced managers whose talents and experience the small firms could not ordinarily afford. SCORE has more than 11,000 volunteers in 320 chapters in the United States and has served nearly 10 million small businesses.[29] The SBA also has organized Small Business Institutes (SBIs) on almost 500 university and college campuses in the United States. Seniors, graduate students, and faculty at each SBI provide onsite management counseling.

Finally, the small-business owner can obtain advice from other small-business owners, suppliers, and even customers.

> # COMMUNICATING WITH OTHER BUSINESS OWNERS IS A GREAT WAY TO FIND IDEAS FOR DEALING WITH EMPLOYEES AND GOVERNMENT REGULATION, IMPROVING PROCESSES, OR SOLVING PROBLEMS.

A customer may approach a small business it frequents with a request for a new product, for example, or a supplier may offer suggestions for improving a manufacturing process. Networking—building relationships and sharing information with colleagues—is vital for any businessperson, whether you work for a huge corporation or run your own small business. Incubators, or organizations created to accelerate the development and success of startup organizations, often provide network opportunities and potential capital to jumpstart a business.[30] Communicating with other business owners is a great way to find ideas for dealing with employees and government regulation, improving processes, or solving problems. New technology is making it easier to network. For example, some states are establishing social networking sites for the use of their businesses to network and share ideas.

The Latino population is the biggest and fastest growing minority segment in the United States—and a lucrative market for businesses looking for ways to meet the segment's many needs.
© moodboard/Getty Images, RF

> **LO 5-6** Evaluate the demographic, technological, and economic trends that are affecting the future of small business.

THE FUTURE FOR SMALL BUSINESS[31]

Although small businesses are crucial to the economy, their size and limited resources can make them more vulnerable to turbulence and change in the marketplace than large businesses. Next, we take a brief look at the demographic, technological, and economic trends that will have the most impact on small business in the future.

Demographic Trends

America's baby boom started in 1946 and ended in 1964. Many boomers are over 50, and in the next few years, millions more will pass that mark. The baby boomer generation represents 24 percent of Americans.[32] This segment of the population is wealthy, but many small businesses do not actively pursue it. Some exceptions, however, include Gold Violin, which sells designer canes and other products online and through a catalog, and LifeSpring Nutrition, which delivers nutritional meals and snacks directly to the customer. Industries such as travel, financial planning, and health care will continue to grow as boomers age. Many experts believe that the boomer demographic is the market of the future.

Another market with huge potential for small business is the echo boomers, also called millennials or Generation Y. Millennials number around 75 million and possess a number of unique characteristics. Born between the early 1980s and the early 2000s, this cohort is not solely concerned about money. Those who fall into this group are also concerned with advancement, recognition, and improved capabilities. They need direct, timely feedback and frequent encouragement and recognition. Millennials do well when training sessions combine entertainment with learning. Working remotely is more acceptable to this group than previous generations, and virtual communication may become as important as face-to-face meetings.[33]

Yet another trend is the growing number of immigrants living in the United States, who now represent about 13 percent of the population. If this trend continues, by 2050 nearly one in five Americans will be classified as immigrants. The Latino population, the nation's largest minority group, is expected to triple in size by 2050 and comprise at least 29 percent of the population.[34]

This vast group provides still another greatly untapped market for small businesses. Retailers who specialize in ethnic products, and service providers who offer bi- or multilingual employees, will find a large amount of business potential in this market. Table 5.7 ranks top cities in the United States for small businesses and startups.

Technological and Economic Trends

Advances in technology have opened up many new markets to small businesses. Undoubtedly, the Internet will continue to provide new opportunities for small businesses. Imgur is a photo-sharing hub filled with trivial and humorous photos. It has become popular as a meme site. The company generates income by posting display advertisements from movie studios and videogame publishers. Users do not have to register to show approval or disapproval of a photo. The company's users upload 1.5 million images every day and is becoming one of the most traveled to sites in the world.[35] Technology has also enabled the substantial growth of entrepreneurs working out of their houses, known as *home-based businesses.* Many of today's largest businesses started from out of their homes, including Mary Kay, Ford, and Apple. Approximately

▼ **TABLE 5.7** Most Business-Friendly Cities

1. Austin, Texas
2. Virginia Beach, Virginia
3. Houston, Texas
4. Colorado Springs, Colorado
5. San Antonio, Texas
6. Nashville, Tennessee
7. Dallas-Fort Worth, Texas
8. Raleigh-Durham, North Carolina

Source: "8 Most Business-Friendly Cities," *CNN Money,* 2013, http://money.cnn.com/gallery/smallbusiness/2013/06/18/best-places-launch-cities/index.html (accessed February 13, 2015).

52 percent of all small businesses are based out of the home. Technological advancements have increased the ability of home-based businesses to interact with customers and operate effectively.[36]

Technological advances and an increase in service exports have created new opportunities for small companies to expand their operations abroad. Changes in communications and technology can allow small companies to customize their services quickly for international customers. Also, free trade agreements and trade alliances are helping to create an environment in which small businesses have fewer regulatory and legal barriers.

In recent years, economic turbulence has provided both opportunities and threats for small businesses. As large information technology companies such as Cisco, Oracle, and Sun Microsystems had to recover from an economic slowdown and an

NEWLIGHT TECHNOLOGIES DEFIES THE ODDS WITH CARBON-NEGATIVE PLASTIC

Mark Herrema and Kenton Kimmel were two entrepreneurs with an idea they knew would succeed—despite the skepticism of naysayers. Herrema observed how nature had the ability to capture carbon from the air. As concerns over global warming continued to grow, Herrema believed it was possible to imitate nature by capturing this carbon and using it to create plastic. Experts in the industry thought they were crazy. The entrepreneurs were told time and again that their idea would be too costly to implement. Despite the doubts, the men were confident they could develop the right technology to make it work. They worked 14- to 16-hour days as a bellhop

and valet to generate money to test their ideas. California-based Newlight Technologies was founded in 2003.

Against what seemed like impossible odds, the company has succeeded in finding a way to turn methane captured from dairy farms into plastic. Called AirCarbon, it is being used to create chairs, food containers, and cell phone cases. Newlight Technologies has raised $19 million in funding to expand production of its carbon-negative plastic so it can compete with traditional oil-based plastics. The company is working with *Fortune* 500 companies to turn plastic into products for different industries. However, perhaps

the greatest advantage is that unlike traditional plastics, AirCarbon takes carbon emissions *out* of the air instead of emitting them. Herrema believes widescale use of this invention will have the ability to reduce the effects of global warming.[37]

Discussion Questions

1. What did it take for the two entrepreneurs to succeed with their idea?

2. What was the biggest objection to the idea of developing carbon-negative plastic?

3. Why is AirCarbon an innovative invention that could potentially change the industry?

intrapreneurs

individuals in large firms who take responsibility for the development of innovations within the organizations.

oversupply of Internet infrastructure products, some smaller firms found new niche markets. Smaller companies can react quickly to change and can stay close to their customers. While well-funded dot-coms were failing, many small businesses were learning how to use the Internet to promote themselves and sell products online. For example, arts and crafts dealers and makers of specialty products found they could sell their wares on existing websites, such as eBay. Service providers related to tourism, real estate, and construction also found they could reach customers through their own or existing websites.

Deregulation of the energy market and interest in alternative fuels and in fuel conservation have spawned many small businesses. Southwest Windpower Inc. manufactures and markets small wind turbines for producing electric power for homes, sailboats, and telecommunications. Solar Attic Inc. has developed a process to recover heat from home attics to use in heating water or swimming pools. As entrepreneurs begin to realize that worldwide energy markets are valued in the hundreds of billions of dollars, the number of innovative companies entering this market will increase. In addition, many small businesses have the desire and employee commitment to purchase such environmentally friendly products. New Belgium Brewing Company received the U.S. Environmental Protection Agency and Department of Energy Award for leadership in conservation for making a 10-year commitment to purchase wind energy. The company's employees unanimously agreed to cover the increased costs of wind-generated electricity from the employee profit-sharing program.

The future for small business remains promising. The opportunities to apply creativity and entrepreneurship to serve customers are unlimited. While large organizations such as Walmart, which has more than 2.2 million employees, typically must adapt to change slowly, a small business can adapt immediately to customer

TEAM EXERCISE

Explore successful global franchises. Go to the companies' websites and find the requirements for applying for three franchises. The chapter provides examples of successful franchises. What do the companies provide, and what is expected to be provided by the franchiser? Compare and contrast each group's findings for the franchises researched. For example, at Subway the franchisee is responsible for paying the initial franchise fee, finding locations, making leasehold improvements and purchasing equipment, hiring employees and operating restaurants, and paying an 8 percent royalty to the company and a fee into the advertising fund. The company provides access to formulas and operational systems, store design and equipment ordering guidance, a training program, an operations manual, a representative on-site during opening, periodic evaluations and ongoing support, and informative publications.

and community needs and changing trends. This flexibility provides small businesses with a definite advantage over large companies.

> **LO 5-7** Explain why many large businesses are trying to "think small."

MAKING BIG BUSINESSES ACT "SMALL"

The continuing success and competitiveness of small businesses through rapidly changing conditions in the business world have led many large corporations to take a closer look at what makes their smaller rivals tick. More and more firms are emulating small businesses in an effort to improve their own bottom line. Beginning in the 1980s and continuing through the present, the buzzword in business has been to *downsize* or *right-size* to reduce management layers, corporate staff, and work tasks in order to make the firm more flexible, resourceful, and innovative. Many well-known U.S. companies, including IBM, Ford, Apple, General Electric, Xerox, and 3M, have downsized to improve their competitiveness, as have German, British, and Japanese firms. Other firms have sought to make their businesses "smaller" by making their operating units function more like independent small businesses, each responsible for its profits, losses, and resources. Of course, some large corporations, such as Southwest Airlines, have acted like small businesses from their inception, with great success.

Trying to capitalize on small-business success in introducing innovative new products, more and more companies are attempting to instill a spirit of entrepreneurship into even the largest firms. In major corporations, **intrapreneurs**, like entrepreneurs, take responsibility for, or "champion," the development of innovations of any kind *within* the larger organization.[38] Often, they use company resources and time to develop a new product for the company. ∎

SO YOU WANT TO BE AN // Entrepreneur or Small-Business Owner

In times when jobs are scarce, many people turn to entrepreneurship as a way to find employment. As long as there are unfulfilled needs from consumers, there will be a demand for entrepreneurs and small businesses. Entrepreneurs and small-business owners have been, and will continue to be, a vital part of the U.S. economy, whether in retailing, wholesaling, manufacturing, technology, or services. Creating a business around your idea has a lot of advantages. For many people, independence is the biggest advantage of forming their own small business, especially for those who do not work well in a corporate setting and like to call their own shots. Smaller businesses are also cheaper to start up than large ones in terms of salaries, infrastructure, and equipment. Smallness also provides a lot of flexibility to change with the times. If consumers suddenly start demanding new and different products, a small business is more likely to deliver quickly.

Starting your own business is not easy, especially in slow economic times. Even in a good economy, taking an idea and turning it into a business has a very high failure rate. The possibility of failure can increase even more when money is tight. Reduced revenues and expensive materials can hurt a small business more than a large one because small businesses have fewer resources. When people are feeling the pinch from rising food and fuel prices, they tend to cut back on other expenditures—which could potentially harm your small business. The increased cost of materials will also affect your bottom line. However, several techniques can help your company survive:

- Set clear payment schedules for all clients. Small businesses tend to be worse about collecting payments than large ones, especially if the clients are acquaintances. However, you need to keep cash flowing into the company in order to keep business going.

- Take the time to learn about tax breaks. A lot of people do not realize all of the deductions they can claim on items such as equipment and health insurance.

- Focus on your current customers, and don't spend a lot of time looking for new ones. It is far less expensive for a company to keep its existing customers happy.

- Although entrepreneurs and small-business owners are more likely to be friends with their customers, do not let this be a temptation to give things away for free. Make it clear to your customers what the basic price is for what you are selling and charge for extra features, extra services, etc.

- Make sure the office has the conveniences employees need—like a good coffee maker and other drinks and snacks. This will not only make your employees happy, but it will also help maintain productivity by keeping employees closer to their desks.

- Use your actions to set an example. If money is tight, show your commitment to cutting costs and making the business work by doing simple things like taking the bus to work or bringing a sack lunch every day.

- Don't forget to increase productivity in addition to cutting costs. Try not to focus so much attention on cost cutting that you don't try to increase sales.

In unsure economic times, these measures should help new entrepreneurs and small-business owners sustain their businesses. Learning how to run a business on a shoestring is a great opportunity to cut the fat and to establish lean, efficient operations.[39]

the nature
of management

© Naypong/iStock /Getty Images, RF

LEARNING OBJECTIVES

After reading this chapter, you will be able to:

LO 6-1 Define management, and explain its role in the achievement of organizational objectives.

LO 6-2 Describe the major functions of management.

LO 6-3 Distinguish among three levels of management and the concerns of managers at each level.

LO 6-4 Specify the skills managers need in order to be successful.

LO 6-5 Summarize the systematic approach to decision making used by many business managers.

For any organization—small or large, for profit or nonprofit—to achieve its objectives, it must have resources to support operations to create products to market, employees to make and sell the products, and financial resources to purchase additional goods and services, pay employees, and generally operate the business. To accomplish this, it must also have one or more managers to plan, organize, staff, direct, and control the work that goes on.

This chapter introduces the field of management. It examines and surveys the various functions, levels, and areas of management in business. The skills that managers need for success and the steps that lead to effective decision making are also discussed. ■

LO 6-1 Define management, and explain its role in the achievement of organizational objectives.

THE IMPORTANCE OF MANAGEMENT

Management is a process designed to achieve an organization's objectives by using its resources effectively and efficiently in a changing environment. *Effectively* means having the intended result; *efficiently* means accomplishing the objectives with a minimum of resources. **Managers** make decisions about the use of the organization's resources and are concerned with planning, organizing, staffing, directing, and controlling the organization's activities so as to reach its objectives. The decision to introduce new products in order to reach objectives is often a key management duty. For instance, Samsung managers were involved in the decision to introduce their new line of curved televisions with Ultra High Definition to rejuvenate sales. The curved screen increases the clarity of viewing from all angles and has proportions similar to movie theater screens, making this an attractive alternative to going to movie theaters.[1] Management is universal. It takes place not only in business, but also in government, the military, labor unions, hospitals, schools, and religious groups—any organization requiring the coordination of resources.

Every organization must acquire resources (people, services, raw materials and equipment, financial, and information) to effectively pursue its objectives and coordinate their use to turn out a final good or service. Employees are one of the most important resources in helping a business attain its objectives. Successful companies recruit, train, compensate, and provide benefits (such as shares of stock and health insurance) to foster employee loyalty. Acquiring suppliers is another important part of managing resources and ensuring that products are made available to customers. As firms reach global markets, companies such as Walmart, Corning, and Charles Schwab enlist hundreds of diverse suppliers that provide goods and services to support operations. A good supplier maximizes efficiencies and provides creative solutions to help the company reduce expenses and reach its objectives. Finally, the manager needs adequate financial resources to pay for essential activities. Primary funding comes from owners and shareholders, as well as banks and other financial institutions. All these resources and activities must be coordinated and controlled if the company is to earn a profit. Organizations must also have adequate supplies of resources of all types, and managers must carefully coordinate their use if they are to achieve the organization's objectives.

management
a process designed to achieve an organization's objectives by using its resources effectively and efficiently in a changing environment.

managers those individuals in organizations who make decisions about the use of resources and who are concerned with planning, organizing, staffing, directing, and controlling the organization's activities to reach its objectives.

Mary Barra, the CEO of General Motors, must lead the company through a recall crisis involving faulty ignition switches.
© Bill Pugliano/Getty Images News/Getty Images

LO 6-2 Describe the major functions of management.

MANAGEMENT FUNCTIONS

To harmonize the use of resources so that the business can develop, produce, and sell products, managers engage in a series of activities: planning, organizing, staffing, directing, and controlling (Figure 6.1). Although this book discusses each of the five functions separately, they are interrelated; managers may perform two or more of them at the same time.

Planning

Planning, the process of determining the organization's objectives and deciding how to accomplish them, is the first function of management. Planning is a crucial activity, for it designs the map that lays the groundwork for the other functions. It involves forecasting events and determining the best course of action from a set of options or choices. The plan itself specifies what should be done, by whom, where, when, and how. For some managers, one major decision that requires extensive planning is selecting the right type of automation for warehouses and distribution facilities. Data gathering is a major phase of the planning process to determine what the facilities need and which automation can maximize order efficiency. Potential pitfalls in this process that managers should plan for include being swayed by advanced technology that is not needed, underautomating the facility, or overautomating the facility.[2] All businesses—from the smallest restaurant to the largest multinational corporation—need to develop plans for achieving success. But before an organization can plan a course of action, it must first determine what it wants to achieve.

Mission A **mission**, or mission statement, is a declaration of an organization's fundamental purpose and basic philosophy.

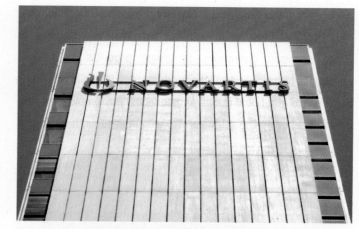

Novartis made the strategic plan to acquire some of GlaxoSmithKline's businesses and intellectual property rights for $16 billion.
© vario images GmbH & Co.KG / Alamy

It seeks to answer the question: "What business are we in?" Good mission statements are clear and concise statements that explain the organization's reason for existence. A well-developed mission statement, no matter what the industry or size of business, will answer five basic questions:

1. Who are we?

2. Who are our customers?

3. What is our operating philosophy (basic beliefs, values, ethics, etc.)?

4. What are our core competencies and competitive advantages?

5. What are our responsibilities with respect to being a good steward of environmental, financial, and human resources?

A mission statement that delivers a clear answer to these questions provides the foundation for the development of a strong organizational culture, a good marketing plan, and a coherent business strategy. Sustainable cleaning products company Seventh Generation states that its mission is to "inspire a revolution that nurtures the health of the next seven generations."[3]

Goals A goal is the result that a firm wishes to achieve. A company almost always has multiple goals, which illustrates the complex nature of business. A goal has three key components: an attribute sought, such as profits, customer satisfaction, or product quality; a target to be achieved, such as the volume of sales or extent of management training to be achieved; and a time frame, which is the time period in which the goal is to be achieved. CVS Health, under CEO Larry J. Merlo, set the goal of becoming a health care provider. As a result, the organization announced it would stop selling cigarettes because it

▼**FIGURE 6.1**
The Functions of Management

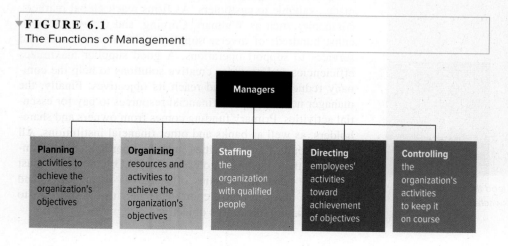

fundamentally conflicted with the company's goal. Electronic cigarettes are also not sold at CVS because the harm they may cause consumers is still to be determined. To be successful, company goals should be specific. This allows for better decision making in organizations.[4] To be successful at achieving goals, it is necessary to know what is to be achieved, how much, when, and how succeeding at a goal is to be determined.

Objectives Objectives, the ends or results desired by an organization, derive from the organization's mission. A business's objectives may be elaborate or simple. Common objectives relate to profit, competitive advantage, efficiency, and growth. The principal difference between goals and objectives is that objectives are generally stated in such a way that they are measurable. Organizations with profit as an objective want to have money and assets left over after paying off business

and using brick-and-mortar locations for testing new products.[5] Objectives provide direction for all managerial decisions; additionally, they establish criteria by which performance can be evaluated.

Plans There are three general types of plans for meeting objectives— strategic, tactical, and operational. A firm's highest managers develop its **strategic plans**, which establish the long-range objectives and overall strategy or course of action by which the firm fulfills its mission. Strategic plans generally cover periods ranging from one year or longer. They include plans to add products, purchase companies, sell unprofitable

> ## "Objectives, the ends or results desired by an organization, derive from the organization's mission."

expenses. Objectives regarding competitive advantage are generally stated in terms of percentage of sales increase and market share, with the goal of increasing those figures. Efficiency objectives involve making the best use of the organization's resources. Dalhousie University has developed energy calculators for small and medium-sized businesses to help them become more aware of their energy usage and to reduce their energy expenditure. Growth objectives relate to an organization's ability to adapt and to get new products to the marketplace in a timely fashion. One of the most important objectives for businesses is sales. Nike, for example, set its sales objectives for 2017 to reach $36 billion. In order to do this, it is putting effort into direct-to-consumer sales channels

Herbalife does business in 90 countries, and contingency plans must often be made for fluctuating exchange rates.
© Patrick Fallon/Bloomberg/Getty Images

segments of the business, issue stock, and move into international markets. For example, Sony decided to sell its unprofitable personal computer unit in order to mitigate projected losses of up to $1.1 billion. Companies have been known to close U.S. plants and move manufacturing activities overseas when faced with stiff competition, rising costs, and slowing sales. However, many companies, including General Electric, Ford, and Whirlpool, are moving these activities back to the United States (an activity known as reshoring) as transportation costs and wages in Asian countries rise.[6] Strategic plans must take into account the organization's capabilities and resources, the changing business environment, and organizational objectives. Plans should be market-driven, matching customers' desire for value with operational capabilities, processes, and human resources.[7]

Tactical plans are short range and designed to implement the activities and objectives specified in the strategic plan. These plans, which usually cover a period of one year or less, help keep the organization on the course established in the strategic plan. Because tactical plans allow the organization to react to changes in the environment while continuing to focus on the company's overall strategy, management must periodically review and update them. Declining performance or failure to meet objectives set out in tactical plans may be one reason for revising them. The Michigan Department of Natural Resources Fisheries division developed a strategic plan to run through 2017. To implement this strategic plan, the department constructed a tactical plan with about 100 tasks to complete. For instance, a major goal of the tactical plan is to prevent the introduction of aquatic invasive species.[8] The differences between the two types of planning result in different activities in the short term versus the long term. For instance, a strategic plan might include

and communicating with the public, employees, and officials about the nature of and the company's response to the problem. Communication is especially important to minimize panic and damaging rumors; it also demonstrates that the company is aware of the problem and plans to respond.

the use of social media to reach consumers. A tactical plan could involve finding ways to increase traffic to the site or promoting premium content to those who visit the site. A fast-paced and ever-changing market requires companies to develop short-run or tactical plans to deal with the changing environment.

A retailing organization with a five-year strategic plan to invest $5 billion in 500 new retail stores may develop five tactical plans (each covering one year) specifying how much to spend to set up each new store, where to locate, and when to open each new store. Tactical plans are designed to execute the overall strategic plan. Because of their short-term nature, they are easier to adjust or abandon if changes in the environment or the company's performance so warrant.

Operational plans are very short term and specify what actions specific individuals, work groups, or departments need to accomplish in order to achieve the tactical plan and ultimately the strategic plan. They apply to details in executing activities in one month, week, or even day. For example, a work group may be assigned a weekly production quota to ensure there are sufficient products available to elevate market share (tactical goal) and ultimately help the firm be number one in its product category (strategic goal). Returning to our retail store example, operational plans may specify the schedule for opening one new store, hiring and training new employees, obtaining merchandise, and opening for actual business.

Another element of planning is **crisis management** or **contingency planning**, which deals with potential disasters such as product tampering, oil spills, fire, earthquake, computer viruses, or even a reputation crisis due to unethical or illegal conduct by one or more employees. Unfortunately, many businesses do not have updated contingency plans to handle the types of crises that their companies might encounter. Approximately 51 percent of companies have outdated disaster recovery and business continuity plans.[9] Businesses that have correct and well-thought-out contingency plans tend to respond more effectively when problems occur than do businesses that lack such planning.

Many companies, including Ashland Oil, H. J. Heinz, and Johnson & Johnson, have crisis management teams to deal specifically with problems, permitting other managers to continue to focus on their regular duties. Some companies even hold periodic disaster drills to ensure that their employees know how to respond when a crisis does occur. After the horrific earthquake in Japan, many companies in U.S. earthquake zones reevaluated their crisis management plans. Crisis management plans generally cover maintaining business operations throughout a crisis

Sometimes disasters occur that no one can anticipate, but companies can still plan for how to react to a disaster. Seats Inc.—a Wisconsin-based manufacturer of quality seating for highway driving, school buses, locomotive operations, and more—is one company that displayed exemplary disaster recovery planning. When a fire destroyed the facility used to mold the foam used for its chairs, the company immediately sprang into action. Partnering with another foam manufacturer, Seats Inc. retooled some of its equipment and sent its employees to the other facility to restore operations. Because of its quick action, the company was back in operation within a month after the fire.[10] Incidents such as this highlight the importance of planning for crises and the need to respond publicly and quickly when a disaster occurs.

Organizing

Rarely are individuals in an organization able to achieve common goals without some form of structure. **Organizing** is the structuring of resources and activities to accomplish objectives in an efficient and effective manner. Managers organize by reviewing plans and determining what activities are necessary to implement them; then they divide the work into small units and assign it to specific individuals, groups, or departments. As companies reorganize for greater efficiency, more often than not, they are organizing work into teams to handle core processes such as new product development instead of organizing around traditional departments such as marketing and production. Organizing occurs continuously because change is inevitable.

Organizing is important for several reasons. It helps create synergy, whereby the effect of a whole system equals more than that of its parts. It also establishes lines of authority, improves communication, helps avoid duplication of resources, and can improve competitiveness by speeding up decision making. When Crocs Inc. decided to reorganize its business after overexpansion, it decided to exit 75 to 100 leases of stores, downsize its employees, and reduce the number of styles it sells. Although these were difficult moves to make, Crocs believes these measures are necessary to restore the company to profitability after overextending its reach into other product categories.[11] Because organizing is so important, we'll take a closer look at it in Chapter 7.

Staffing

Once managers have determined what work is to be done and how it is to be organized, they must ensure that the organization has enough employees with appropriate skills to do the work. Hiring people to carry out the work of the organization is known as **staffing**. Beyond recruiting people for positions within the firm, managers must determine what skills are needed for specific jobs, how to motivate and train employees, how much to pay, what benefits to provide, and how to prepare employees for higher-level jobs in the firm at a later date. These elements of staffing will be explored in detail in Chapters 9 and 10.

Another aspect of staffing is **downsizing**, the elimination of significant numbers of employees from an organization, which has been a pervasive and much-talked-about trend. Staffing can be outsourced to companies that focus on hiring and managing employees. For instance, Collabera provides IT staffing and a range of services to both Fortune 500 companies and midsized companies across the globe. The company has also been named "Best Staffing Firm to Work For" for three consecutive years, citing excellence in teamwork, trust, effectiveness, and compensation and benefits.[12] Many firms downsize by outsourcing production, sales, and technical positions to companies in other countries with lower labor costs. Downsizing has helped numerous firms reduce costs quickly and become more profitable (or become profitable after lengthy losses) in a short period of time. Whether it is called downsizing, rightsizing, trimming the fat, or the new reality in business, the implications of downsizing have been dramatic. During the last economic recession, many companies laid off workers to cut costs. The nationwide unemployment rate climbed above 10 percent, but after the recovery, unemployment dropped significantly.[13]

Downsizing and outsourcing, however, have painful consequences. Obviously, the biggest casualty is those who lose their jobs, along with their incomes, insurance, and pensions. Some find new jobs quickly; others do not. Another victim is the morale of the remaining employees at downsized firms. Those left behind often feel insecure, angry, and sad, and their productivity may decline as a result, the opposite of the effect sought. Studies have found that firms that lay off more than 10 percent of their surviving workforce can expect to see turnover increase to 15.5 percent versus 10.4 percent at firms that do not have layoffs.[14]

After a downsizing event, an effective manager will promote optimism and positive thinking and minimize criticism and fault-finding. Management should also build teamwork and encourage positive group discussions. Honest communication is important during a time of change and will lead to trust. In reality, when departments are downsized, the remaining employees end up working harder to fill the gaps left by layoffs. Truthfulness about what has happened and about future expectations is essential.

Directing

Once the organization has been staffed, management must direct the employees. **Directing** is motivating and leading employees to achieve organizational objectives. Good directing involves telling employees what to do and when to do it through the implementation of deadlines, and then encouraging them to do their work. For example, as a sales manager, you would need to learn how to motivate salespersons; provide leadership; teach sales teams to be responsive to customer needs; and manage organizational issues as well as evaluate sales results. Finally, directing also involves determining and administering appropriate rewards and recognition. All managers are involved in directing, but it is especially important for lower-level managers who interact daily with the employees operating the organization. For example, an assembly-line supervisor for Frito-Lay must ensure that her workers know how to use their equipment properly and have the resources needed to carry out their jobs safely and efficiently, and she must motivate her workers to achieve their expected output of packaged snacks.

Managers may motivate employees by providing incentives—such as the promise of a raise or promotion—for them to do a good job. But most workers want more than money from their jobs: They need to know that their employer values their ideas and input. Managers should give younger employees some decision-making authority as soon as possible. Smart managers, therefore, ask workers to contribute ideas for reducing costs, making equipment more efficient, improving customer service, or even developing new products. For example, Rackspace, an IT hosting company, has made employee engagement

Some companies choose to recruit people to hire through online job websites such as Monster.com. Monster.com is one of the world's largest employment websites. Using websites like Monster.com falls under the staffing function of management.
© Mark Dierker/McGraw-Hill Education

a top priority to bring customer service to the highest level.[15] This participation makes workers feel important, and the company benefits. Recognition and appreciation are often the best motivators. Employees who understand more about their effect on the financial success of the company may be induced to work harder for that success, and managers who understand the needs and desires of workers can encourage their employees to work harder and more productively. The motivation of employees is discussed in detail in Chapter 9.

Controlling

Planning, organizing, staffing, and directing are all important to the success of an organization, whether its objective is earning a profit or something else. But what happens when a firm fails to reach its goals despite a strong planning effort? **Controlling** is the process of evaluating and correcting activities to keep the organization on course. Control involves five activities: (1) measuring performance, (2) comparing present performance with standards or objectives, (3) identifying deviations from the standards, (4) investigating the causes of deviations, and (5) taking corrective action when necessary.

Controlling and planning are closely linked. Planning establishes goals and standards. By monitoring performance and comparing it with standards, managers can determine whether performance is on target. When performance is substandard, management must determine why and take appropriate actions to get the firm back on course. In short, the control function helps managers assess the success of their plans. You might relate this to your performance in this class. If you did not perform as well on early projects or exams, you must take corrective action such as increasing studying or using website resources to achieve your overall objective of getting an A or B in the course. When the outcomes of plans do not meet expectations, the control process facilitates revision of the plans. Control can take many forms such as visual inspections, testing, and statistical modeling processes. The basic idea is to ensure that operations meet requirements and are satisfactory to reach objectives.

The control process also helps managers deal with problems arising outside the firm. For example, if a firm is the subject of negative publicity, management should use the control process to determine why and to guide the firm's response.

> **This participation makes workers feel important, and the company benefits.**

SERGIO MARCHIONNE MAPS OUT STRATEGIC PLAN FOR FIAT–CHRYSLER MERGER

Sergio Marchionne, CEO of Fiat Chrysler Automobiles (FCA), has developed a five-year plan for the merged company. In 2014 Italian carmaker Fiat spent $4.35 billion to buy out Chrysler's minority shareholder and assume full ownership of the company. This merger makes FCA the seventh largest automaker in the world. If Marchionne has his way, FCA will successfully compete against global giants such as General Motors and Toyota.

FCA has adopted the five-year strategic plan to increase the company's global presence. The plan calls for FCA to increase its world sales of automobiles from 4.4 to 7 million by 2018. Within the next five years FCA wants to quadruple sales of Maseratis,

sell 150,000 Alfa Romeo automobiles in the United States, and increase American vehicle sales from 1 to 3.1 million. This large-scale strategic plan involves a number of other actions as well. For instance, the company plans to find a new design and production site for the Chrysler minivan, collaborate with a Chinese partner to begin building Jeeps in Asia, and create a marketing strategy to increase sales of the Alfa Romeo automobile in the United States. Marchionne also plans to integrate the Ferrari brand with the Fiat brand more closely.

FCA has already taken a number of steps toward achievement of its goals. For instance, it launched its Alfa 4C Roadster in the United States over the summer and discontinued the

midsized Avenger Sedan. While these plans seem ambitious, Marchionne has proven that he is more than capable of handling the challenge. To ensure the company will set out on the right path, he plans to continue leading FCA for another three years.[16]

Discussion Questions

1. Describe some ways in which FCA plans to use strategic plans.

2. How does Sergio Marchionne demonstrate strong leadership?

3. What are some of the steps FCA is planning on taking to achieve its five-year strategic goals?

top managers the president and other top executives of a business, such as the chief executive officer (CEO), chief financial officer (CFO), and chief operations officer (COO), who have overall responsibility for the organization.

LO 6-3 Distinguish among three levels of management and the concerns of managers at each level.

TYPES OF MANAGEMENT

All managers—whether the sole proprietor of a jewelry store or the hundreds of managers of a large company such as Paramount Pictures—perform the five functions just discussed. In the case of the jewelry store, the owner handles all the functions, but in a large company with more than one manager, responsibilities must be divided and delegated. This division of responsibility is generally achieved by establishing levels of management and areas of specialization—finance, marketing, and so on.

Levels of Management

As we have hinted, many organizations have multiple levels of management—top management, middle management, and first-line, or supervisory management. These levels form a pyramid, as shown in Figure 6.2. As the pyramid shape implies, there are generally more middle managers than top managers, and still more first-line managers. Very small organizations may have only one manager (typically, the owner), who assumes the responsibilities of all three levels. Large businesses have many managers at each level to coordinate the use of the organization's resources. Managers at all three levels perform all five management functions, but the amount of time they spend on each function varies, as we shall see (Figure 6.3).

Top Management In businesses, **top managers** include the president and other top executives, such as the chief executive officer (CEO), chief financial officer (CFO), and chief operations officer (COO), who have overall responsibility for the organization. For example, Mark Zuckerberg, CEO and founder of Facebook, manages the overall strategic direction of the company and plays a key role in representing the company to stakeholders. Sheryl Sandberg, Facebook's chief operating officer, is responsible for the daily operation of the company. The COO reports to the CEO and is often considered to be number two in command. In public corporations, even chief executive officers have a boss—the firm's board of directors. With technological advances accelerating and privacy concerns increasing, some companies are adding a new top management position—chief privacy officer (CPO). The position of privacy officer has grown so widespread that the International Association of Privacy Professionals boasts 21,000 members in 83 countries.[17]

FIGURE 6.2
Levels of Management

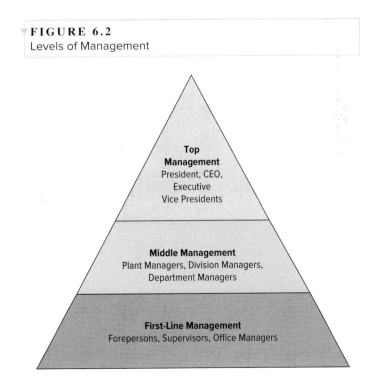

Top Management
President, CEO, Executive Vice Presidents

Middle Management
Plant Managers, Division Managers, Department Managers

First-Line Management
Forepersons, Supervisors, Office Managers

John Hammergren, CEO of McKesson, is the highest-paid CEO at $131.2 million.
© David Maxwell/Bloomberg/Getty Images

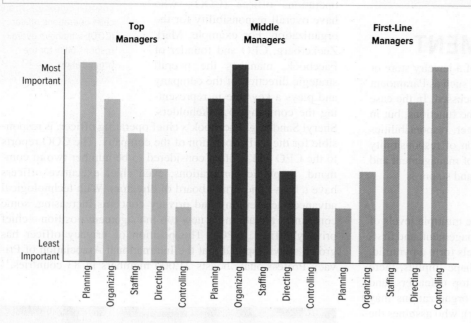

In government, top management refers to the president, a governor, or a mayor or city manager; in education, a chancellor of a university or a superintendent of education.

Top-level managers spend most of their time planning. They make the organization's strategic decisions, decisions that focus on an overall scheme or key idea for using resources to take advantage of opportunities. They decide whether to add products, acquire companies, sell unprofitable business segments, and move into foreign markets. Top managers also represent their company to the public and to government regulators.

Given the importance and range of top managements' decisions, top managers generally have many years of varied experience and command top salaries. In addition to salaries, top managers' compensation packages typically include bonuses, long-term incentive awards, stock, and stock options. Table 6.1 lists the compensation packages of different CEOs. Top management may also get perks and special treatment that is criticized by stakeholders.

Compensation committees are increasingly working with boards of directors and CEOs to attempt to keep pay in line with performance in order to benefit stockholders and key stakeholders. The majority of major companies cite their concern about attracting capable leadership for the CEO and other top executive positions in their organizations. However, many firms are trying to curb criticism of excessive executive compensation

?

DID YOU KNOW?

Only 4.6 percent of *Fortune* 500 CEOs are women.[18]

by trying to align CEO compensation with performance. In other words, if the company performs poorly, the CEO will not be paid as well.[19] Successful management translates into happy stockholders who are willing to compensate their top executives fairly and in line with performance.

Workforce diversity is an important issue in today's corporations. Effective managers at enlightened corporations have found that diversity is good for workers and for the bottom line. Putting together different kinds of people to solve problems often results in better solutions. Sodexo Inc. has frequently made DiversityInc's list of most diverse companies. Its consistent nomination to the list is due to its corporate culture of inclusion and diversity and their priority as a part of the company's overall strategy.[20] A diverse workforce is better at making decisions regarding issues related to consumer diversity. Public relations agencies are working toward making their workforces more diverse with the help of special interest groups such as the Public Relations Society of America, PRSA Foundation, and the Council of Public Relations Firms. Reaching fast growing demographic groups such as Hispanics, African Americans, Asian Americans, and others will be beneficial to large companies as they begin to target these markets.[21] Managers from companies devoted to workforce diversity devised five rules that make diversity recruiting work (see Table 6.2). Diversity is explored in greater detail in Chapter 10.

▼ **TABLE 6.1** CEO Compensation

CEO	Company	Compensation
Leslie Moonves	CBS Corp.	$65.4 million
Richard Adkerson	Freeport-McMoRan Copper & Gold	38.9 million
Philippe Dauman	Viacom	36.8 million
Jeffrey Bewkes	Time Warner Inc.	32.4 million
James Cracchiolo	Ameriprise Financial Inc.	20.7 million
Virginia Rometty	IBM	13.2 million
Fred Smith	FedEx	10.9 million
Frank Blake	Home Depot	10.8 million
Ursula Burns	Xerox	10.2 million
Martin Craighead	Baker Hughes	9.9 million

Source: From an analysis of proxy statements by *The Wall Street Journal* and Hays Group.

Middle Management Rather than making strategic decisions about the whole organization, **middle managers** are responsible for tactical planning that will implement the general guidelines established by top management. Thus, their responsibility is more narrowly focused than that of top managers. Middle managers are involved in the specific operations of the organization and spend more time organizing than other managers. In business, plant managers, division managers, and department managers make up middle management. The product manager for laundry detergent at a consumer products manufacturer, the department chairperson in a university, and the head of a human resources department for a nonprofit are all middle managers. The ranks of middle managers have been shrinking as more and more companies downsize to be more productive.

First-Line Management Most people get their first managerial experience as **first-line managers**, those who supervise workers and the daily operations of the organization. They are responsible for

middle managers
those members of an organization responsible for the tactical planning that implements the general guidelines established by top management.

first-line managers
those who supervise both workers and the daily operations of an organization.

> "Most people get their first managerial experience as first-line managers, those who supervise workers and the daily operations of the organization."

▼ **TABLE 6.2** Five Rules of Successful Diversity Recruiting

Rule	Action
1. Get everyone involved.	Educate all employees on the tangible benefits of diversity recruiting to garner support and enthusiasm for those initiatives.
2. Showcase your diversity.	Prospective employees are not likely to become excited about joining your company just because you say that your company is diversity-friendly; they need to see it.
3. Work with diversity groups within your community.	By supporting community-based diversity organizations, your company will generate the priceless word-of-mouth publicity that will lead qualified diversity candidates to your company.
4. Spend money.	If you are serious about diversity recruiting, you will need to spend some money getting your message out to the right places.
5. Sell, sell, sell—and measure your return on investment.	Employers need to sell their company to prospective diversity employees and present them with a convincing case as to why their company is a good fit for the diversity candidate.

Source: Adapted from Juan Rodriguez, "The Five Rules of Successful Diversity Recruiting," Diversityjobs.com, www.diversityjobs.com/Rules-of-Successful-Diversity-Recruiting (accessed February 25, 2010).

PHILIP PILLSBURY: THE ENTREPRENEUR BEHIND THE BILLION-DOLLAR BRAND

Although Charles Pillsbury co-founded the successful Pillsbury Company, it was his grandson who led the company toward its status as a billion-dollar brand. In 1940 Philip Pillsbury became president of his grandfather's flour milling company. He had worked as a miller early in life and knew the industry. As the markets changed, Pillsbury's entrepreneurial instinct and management skills allowed him to transform the company's direction from commodities to consumer products.

Pillsbury was a visionary with strong conceptual skills who recognized growing opportunities in the consumer market. He targeted this market by investing in product research and development, resulting in product lines such as cake mixes and refrigerated rolls, biscuits, and cookies. He also infused the company's marketing with the Grand National Recipe & Baking Contest, which later became known as the annual Pillsbury Bake-Off. Influential judges including Eleanor Roosevelt drew the attention of 700,000 new customers. International expansion was also part of Pillsbury's strategy, and he implemented it with global acquisitions. By 1974 Pillsbury had increased the company's sales by seven times the 1940 level to $315 million. Eventually the Pillsbury Company became so successful that it was purchased by General Mills in 2001 for $10.5 billion.[22]

financial managers those who focus on obtaining needed funds for the successful operation of an organization and using those funds to further organizational goals.

production and operations managers those who develop and administer the activities involved in transforming resources into goods, services, and ideas ready for the marketplace.

human resources managers those who handle the staffing function and deal with employees in a formalized manner.

marketing managers those who are responsible for planning, pricing, and promoting products and making them available to customers.

information technology (IT) managers those who are responsible for implementing, maintaining, and controlling technology applications in business, such as computer networks.

implementing the plans established by middle management and directing workers' daily performance on the job. They spend most of their time directing and controlling. Common titles for first-line managers are foreperson, supervisor, and office service manager.

Areas of Management

At each level, there are managers who specialize in the basic functional areas of business: finance, production and operations, human resources (personnel), marketing, and administration.

Each of these management areas is important to a business's success. For instance, a firm cannot survive without someone obtaining needed financial resources (financial managers) or staff (human resources managers). While larger firms will most likely have all of these managers, and even more depending upon that particular firm's needs, in smaller firms these important tasks may fall onto the owner or a few employees. Yet whether or not companies have managers for specific areas, every company must have someone responsible for obtaining financial resources, transforming resources into finished products for the marketplace, hiring and/or dealing with staff, marketing goods and services, handling the firm's information technology resources, and managing a business segment or the overall business. These different types of managers are described in Table 6.3.

> **LO 6-4** Specify the skills managers need in order to be successful.

SKILLS NEEDED BY MANAGERS

Managers are typically evaluated using the metrics of how effective and efficient they are. Managing effectively and efficiently requires certain skills—technical expertise, conceptual skills, analytical skills, human relations skills, and leadership. Table 6.4 describes some of the roles managers may fulfill.

Technical Expertise

Managers need **technical expertise**, the specialized knowledge and training required to perform jobs related to their area of management. Accounting managers need to be able to perform accounting jobs, and production managers need to be able to perform production jobs. Although a production manager may not actually perform a job, he or she needs technical expertise to train employees, answer questions, provide guidance, and solve problems. Technical skills are most needed by first-line managers and are least critical to top-level managers.

Conceptual Skills

Conceptual skills, the ability to think in abstract terms, and to see how parts fit together to form the whole, are needed by all managers, but particularly top-level managers. Top management must be able to evaluate continually where the company will be in the future. Conceptual skills also involve the ability

▼ **TABLE 6.3** Areas of Management

Manager	Function
Financial manager	Focuses on obtaining the money needed for the successful operation of the organization and using that money in accordance with organizational goals.
Production and operations manager	Develops and administers the activities involved in transforming resources into goods, services, and ideas ready for the marketplace.
Human resources manager	Handles the staffing function and deals with employees in a formalized manner.
Marketing manager	Responsible for planning, pricing, and promoting products and making them available to customers through distribution.
Information technology (IT) manager	Responsible for implementing, maintaining, and controlling technology applications in business, such as computer networks.
Administrative manager	Manages an entire business or a major segment of a business; does not specialize in a particular function.

▼ **TABLE 6.4** Managerial Roles

General Role Category	Specific Role	Example Activity
Interpersonal	Figure	Attending award banquet
	Liaison	Coordinating production schedule with supply manager
	Leadership	Conducting performance appraisal for subordinates
Informational	Monitor	Contacting government regulatory agencies
	Disseminator	Conducting meetings with subordinates to pass along policy changes
	Spokesperson	Meeting with consumer group to discuss product safety
Decisional	Entrepreneur	Changing work process
	Disturbance handler	Deciding which unit moves into new facilities
	Resource allocator	Deciding who receives new computer equipment
	Negotiator	Settling union grievance

Source: Roles developed by management professor Henry Mintzberg.

to think creatively. Recent scientific research has revealed that creative thinking, which is behind the development of many innovative products and ideas, including fiber optics and compact disks, can be learned. As a result, IBM, AT&T, GE, Hewlett-Packard, Intel, and other top U.S. firms hire creative consultants to teach their managers how to think creatively.

This financial manager of a city hedge fund analyzes data from financial charts. Financial managers are responsible for obtaining the necessary funding for organizations to succeed, both in the short term and in the long term.
© *NAN104/Getty Images, RF*

Analytical Skills

Analytical skills refer to the ability to identify relevant issues and recognize their importance, understand the relationships between them, and perceive the underlying causes of a situation. When managers have identified critical factors and causes, they can take appropriate action. All managers need to think logically, but this skill is probably most important to the success of top-level managers. To be analytical, it is necessary to think about a broad range of issues and to weigh different options before taking action. Because analytical skills are so important, questions that require analytical skills are often a part of job interviews. Questions such as "Tell me how you would resolve a problem at work if you had access to a large amount of data?" may be part of the interview process. The answer would require the interviewee to try to explain how to sort data to find relevant facts that could resolve the issue. Analytical thinking is required in complex or difficult situations where the solution is often not clear. Resolving ethical issues often requires analytical skills.

Human Relations Skills

People skills, or **human relations skills**, are the ability to deal with people, both inside and outside the organization. Those who can relate to others, communicate well with others, understand

"When managers have identified critical factors and causes, they can take appropriate action."

the needs of others, and show a true appreciation for others are generally more successful than managers who lack such skills. People skills are especially important in hospitals, airline companies, banks, and other organizations that provide services. For example, Southwest Airlines places great value on its employees. New hires go through extensive training to teach employees about the airline and its reputation for impeccable customer service. All employees in management positions at Southwest take mandatory leadership classes that address skills related to listening, staying in touch with employees, and handling change without compromising values.

LEADERSHIP

Leadership is the ability to influence employees to work toward organizational goals. Strong leaders manage and pay attention to the culture of their organizations and the needs of their customers. Table 6.5 offers some tips for successful leadership.

> " Strong leaders manage and pay attention to the culture of their organizations and the needs of their customers. "

Managers often can be classified into three types based on their leadership style. *Autocratic leaders* make all the decisions and then tell employees what must be done and how to do it. They generally use their authority and economic rewards to get employees to comply with their directions. Martha Stewart is an example of an autocratic leader. She built up her media empire by paying close attention to every detail.[23] *Democratic leaders* involve their employees in decisions. The manager presents a situation and encourages his or her subordinates to express opinions and contribute ideas. The manager then considers the employees' points of view and makes the decision. Herb Kelleher, co-founder of Southwest Airlines, had a democratic leadership style. Under his leadership, employees were encouraged to discuss concerns and provide input.[24] *Free-rein leaders* let their employees work without much interference. The manager sets performance standards and allows employees to find their own ways to meet them. For this style to be effective, employees must know what the standards are, and they must be motivated to attain them. The free-rein style of leadership can be a powerful motivator because it demonstrates a great deal of trust and confidence in the employee. Warren Buffett, CEO of Berkshire Hathaway, exhibits free-rein leadership among the managers who run the company's various businesses.

The effectiveness of the autocratic, democratic, and free-rein styles depends on several factors. One consideration is the type of employees. An autocratic style of leadership is generally best for stimulating unskilled, unmotivated employees; highly skilled, trained, and motivated employees may respond better to democratic or free-rein leadership styles. Employees who have been involved in decision making generally require less supervision than those not similarly involved. Other considerations are the manager's abilities and the situation itself. When a situation requires quick decisions, an autocratic style of leadership may be best because the manager does not have to consider input from a lot of people. If a special task force must be set up to solve a quality-control problem, a normally democratic manager may give free rein to the task force.

Ursula Burns, CEO of Xerox, has great human relations skills and leadership abilities, as demonstrated by her ability to relate to others. Under her leadership, Xerox has restructured to focus more on business services.
© ERIC PIERMONT/AFP/Getty Images

▼ **TABLE 6.5** Requirements for Successful Leadership

1. Communicate objectives and expectations.
2. Gain the respect and trust of stakeholders.
3. Develop shared values.
4. Acquire and share knowledge.
5. Empower employees to make decisions.
6. Be a role model for appropriate behavior.
7. Provide rewards and take corrective action to achieve goals.

Many managers, however, are unable to use more than one style of leadership. Some are incapable of allowing their subordinates to participate in decision making, let alone make any decisions. Thus, what leadership style is "best" depends on specific circumstances, and effective managers will strive to adapt their leadership style as circumstances warrant. Many organizations offer programs to develop good leadership skills. When plans fail, very often leaders are held responsible for what goes wrong. For example, Hertz Global Holdings Inc. terminated its CEO after disappointing company performance and accounting problems. Whereas executives used to be let go gently, the age of activist investors is prompting many boards who fire executives to do so without trying to sugarcoat the reasons behind it.[25]

Another type of leadership style that has been gaining in popularity is *authentic leadership*. Authentic leadership is a bit different from the other three leadership styles because it is not exclusive. Both democratic and free-rein leaders could qualify as authentic leaders depending upon how they conduct themselves among stakeholders. Authentic leaders are passionate about the goals and mission of the company, display corporate values in the workplace, and form long-term relationships with stakeholders.[26] Kim Jordan of New Belgium Brewing is an authentic leader. As co-founder of the company, she helped develop the firm's core values and has ensured that everything New Belgium does aligns with these values.

Employee Empowerment

employee empowerment when employees are provided with the ability to take on responsibilities and make decisions about their jobs.

Businesses are increasingly realizing the benefits of participative corporate cultures characterized by employee empowerment. **Employee empowerment** occurs when employees are provided with the ability to take on responsibilities and make decisions about their jobs. Employee empowerment does not mean that managers are not needed. Managers are important for guiding employees, setting goals, making major decisions, and other responsibilities emphasized throughout this chapter. However, companies that have a participative corporate culture have found it to be beneficial because employees feel like they are taking an active role in the firm's success.

Leaders who wish to empower employees adopt systems that support an employee's ability to provide input and feedback on company decisions. Participative decision making, a type of decision making that involves both manager and employee input, supports employee empowerment within the organization. One of the best ways to encourage participative decision making is through employee and managerial training. As mentioned earlier, employees should be trained in leadership skills, including teamwork, conflict resolution, and decision making. Managers should also be trained in ways to empower

> ## Employees who have been involved in decision making generally require less supervision than those not similarly involved.

While leaders might incorporate different leadership styles depending on the business and the situation, all leaders must be able to align employees behind a common vision to be effective.[27] Strong leaders also realize the value that employees can provide by participating in the firm's corporate culture. It is important that companies develop leadership training programs for employees. Because managers cannot oversee everything that goes on in the company, empowering employees to take more responsibility for their decisions can aid in organizational growth and productivity. Leadership training also enables a smooth transition when an executive or manager leaves the organization. For instance, when Bristol-Myers Squibb CEO Lamberto Andreotti stepped down, the company made sure his successor was up to the task. Bristol-Myers already had a succession plan in place and gave the position to the company's chief operating officer due to his experience and leadership expertise.[28]

employees to make decisions while also guiding employees in challenging situations in which the right decision might not be so clear.[29]

A section on leadership would not be complete without a discussion of leadership in teams. In today's business world, decisions made by teams are becoming the norm. Employees at Zappos, for instance, often work in teams and are encouraged to make decisions that they believe will reinforce the company's mission and values. Teamwork has often been an effective way for encouraging employee empowerment. Although decision making in teams is collective, the most effective teams are those in which all employees are encouraged to contribute their ideas and recommendations. Because each employee can bring in his or her own unique insights, teams often result in innovative ideas or decisions that would not have been reached by only one or two people. However, truly empowering employees in team decision making can be difficult. It is quite common for more outspoken employees to dominate the team and engage in groupthink, in which team members go with the majority rather than what they think is the right decision. Training employees how to listen to one another and provide relevant feedback can help prevent these common challenges. Another way is to rotate the team leader so that no one person can assume dominancy.[30]

> **LO 6-5** Summarize the systematic approach to decision making used by many business managers.

DECISION MAKING

Managers make many different kinds of decisions, such as the hours in a workday, which employees to hire, what products to introduce, and what price to charge for a product. Decision making is important in all management functions and at all levels, whether the decisions are on a strategic, tactical, or operational level. A systematic approach using the following six steps usually leads to more effective decision making: (1) recognizing and defining the decision situation, (2) developing options to resolve the situation, (3) analyzing the options, (4) selecting the best option, (5) implementing the decision, and (6) monitoring the consequences of the decision (Figure 6.4).

Recognizing and Defining the Decision Situation

The first step in decision making is recognizing and defining the situation. The situation may be negative (e.g., huge losses on a particular product) or positive (e.g., an opportunity to increase sales).

> After developing a list of possible courses of action, management should analyze the practicality and appropriateness of each option.

Situations calling for small-scale decisions often occur without warning. Situations requiring large-scale decisions, however, generally occur after some warning signs. Effective managers pay attention to such signals. Declining profits, small-scale losses in previous years, inventory buildup, and retailers' unwillingness to stock a product are signals that may foreshadow huge losses to come. If managers pay attention to such signals, problems can be contained.

Once a situation has been recognized, management must define it. Losses reveal a problem—for example, a failing product. One manager may define the situation as a product quality problem; another may define it as a change in consumer preference. These two viewpoints may lead to vastly different solutions. The first manager may seek new sources of raw materials of better quality. The second manager may believe that the product has reached the end of its lifespan and decide to discontinue it. This example emphasizes the importance of carefully defining the problem rather than jumping to conclusions.

Developing Options

Once the decision situation has been recognized and defined, the next step is to develop a list of possible courses of action. The best lists include both standard and creative plans.

Brainstorming, a technique in which group members spontaneously suggest ideas to solve a problem, is an effective way to encourage creativity and explore a variety of options. As a general rule, more time and expertise are devoted to the development stage of decision making when the decision is of major importance. When the decision is of less importance, less time and expertise will be spent on this stage. Options may be developed individually, by teams, or through analysis of similar situations in comparable organizations. Creativity is a very important part of selecting the most viable option. Creativity depends on new and useful ideas, regardless of where they originate or the method used to create them. The best option can range from a required solution to an identified problem, to a volunteered solution to an observed problem by an outside work group member.[31]

Analyzing Options

After developing a list of possible courses of action, management should analyze the practicality and appropriateness of each option. An option may be deemed impractical because of a lack of financial resources, legal restrictions, ethical and social responsibility considerations,

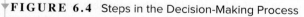

▼FIGURE 6.4 Steps in the Decision-Making Process

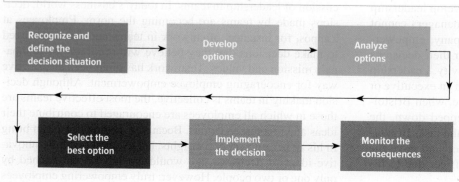

When Mary Barra took the helm as CEO of General Motors, it made her GM's first-ever female CEO and the first female to lead any major global automobile company. As CEO, Barra is responsible for setting the vision and direction of the huge international firm and guiding GM from its troubled past into a profitable future. To do so, she is applying the management and leadership lessons she learned on her journey to the top.

Barra spent her entire career at GM, starting in 1980 as an engineering intern. She later became an assistant to then-CEO Jack Smith, and subsequently moved into leadership—first as the manager of an assembly plant, and eventually into various top-management roles. Throughout these roles, Barra has achieved leadership success in eliminating complexity and encouraging innovation. For example, as HR chief, she reduced the company's 10-page dress code down to two words: "Dress appropriately." She is also known for her ability to organize and streamline, bringing "order to chaos" in the huge and complicated global product development department.

These talents served her well as she tackled GM's business issues. Although GM has returned to profitability since its bankruptcy, its market share in the United States is at a historic low, profit margins are weaker than competitors, and some of its brands such as Opel in Europe are losing money. The scandal with the faulty ignition switches forced Barra to testify to Congress about GM's knowledge about product defects. Barra had to bring all her experience to bear to maintain GM's current strengths and enable it to go forward toward continued success.[32]

Discussion Questions

1. How will Mary Barra's experiences as a leader of various departments help her now as CEO? Are there different skills she might have learned that will now be useful?

2. What types of management traits and skills has Barra exhibited in her leadership style?

3. Are there any potential downsides to hiring a CEO who has spent her entire career at the company?

---

authority constraints, technological constraints, economic limitations, or simply a lack of information and expertise. For example, a small computer manufacturer may recognize an opportunity to introduce a new type of computer but lack the financial resources to do so. Other options may be more practical for the computer company: It may consider selling its technology to another computer company that has adequate resources, or it may allow itself to be purchased by a larger company that can introduce the new technology.

When assessing appropriateness, the decision maker should consider whether the proposed option adequately addresses the situation. When analyzing the consequences of an option, managers should consider its impact on the situation and on the organization as a whole. For example, when considering a price cut to boost sales, management must think about the consequences of the action on the organization's cash flow and consumers' reaction to the price change.

Selecting the Best Option

When all courses of action have been analyzed, management must select the best one. Selection is often a subjective procedure because many situations do not lend themselves to quantitative analysis. Of course, it is not always necessary to select only one option and reject all others; it may be possible to select and use a combination of several options. William Wrigley Jr. made a decision to sell his firm to Mars for $23 billion. The firm was founded by his great-grandfather in 1891, but hard times forced Wrigley to take what was considered to be the best option. This option was to create the Mars-Wrigley firm, currently the world's largest confectionary company with a distribution network in 180 countries.[33] A different set of choices would have been available to the company had it been able to purchase Hershey for $12 billion a few years earlier.

Implementing the Decision

To deal with the situation at hand, the selected option or options must be put into action. Implementation can be fairly simple or very complex, depending on the nature of the decision. Effective implementation of a decision to abandon a product, close a plant, purchase a new business, or something similar requires planning. For example, when a product is dropped, managers must decide how to handle distributors and customers and what to do with the idle production facility. Additionally, they should anticipate resistance from people within the organization. (People tend to resist change because they fear the unknown.) Finally, management should be ready to deal with the unexpected consequences. No matter how well planned

Technology can help managers maintain an agenda, analyze options, and make decisions.
© Mutlu Kurtbas/iStock/Getty Images Plus/Getty Images, RF

implementation is, unforseen problems will arise. Management must be ready to address these situations when they occur.

Monitoring the Consequences

After managers have implemented the decision, they must determine whether it has accomplished the desired result. Without proper monitoring, the consequences of decisions may not be known quickly enough to make efficient changes. If the desired result is achieved, management can reasonably conclude that it made a good choice. If the desired result is not achieved, further analysis is warranted. Was the decision simply wrong, or did the situation change? Should some other option have been implemented?

If the desired result is not achieved, management may discover that the situation was incorrectly defined from the beginning. That may require starting the decision-making process all over again. Finally, management may determine that the decision was good even though the desired results have not yet shown up, or it may determine a flaw in the decision's implementation. In the latter case, management would not change the decision but would change the way in which it is implemented.

MANAGEMENT IN PRACTICE

Management is not a cut-and-dried process. There is no mathematical formula for managing an organization and achieving organizational goals, although many managers passionately wish for one! Managers plan, organize, staff, direct, and control, but management expert John P. Kotter says even these functions can be boiled down to two basic activities:

1. Figuring out what to do despite uncertainty, great diversity, and an enormous amount of potentially relevant information, and

2. Getting things done through a large and diverse set of people despite having little direct control over most of them.[34]

Managers spend as much as 75 percent of their time working with others—not only with subordinates but with bosses, people outside their hierarchy at work, and people outside the organization itself. In these interactions, they discuss anything and everything remotely connected with their business.

Managers spend a lot of time establishing and updating an agenda of goals and plans for carrying out their responsibilities.

TEAM EXERCISE

Form groups and assign the responsibility of locating examples of crisis management implementation for companies dealing with natural disasters (explosions, fires, earthquakes, etc.), technology disasters (viruses, plane crashes, compromised customer data, etc.), or ethical or legal disasters. How did these companies communicate with key stakeholders? What measures did the company take to provide support to those involved in the crisis? Report your findings to the class.

An **agenda** contains both specific and vague items, covering short-term goals and long-term objectives. Like a calendar, an agenda helps the manager figure out what must be done and how to get it done to meet the objectives set by the organization. Technology tools such as smartphones can help managers manage their agendas, contacts, communications, and time.

Managers also spend a lot of time **networking**—building relationships and sharing information with colleagues who can help them achieve the items on their agendas. Managers spend much of their time communicating with a variety of people and participating in activities that on the surface do not seem to have much to do with the goals of their organization. Nevertheless, these activities are crucial to getting the job done. Networks are not limited to immediate subordinates and bosses; they include other people in the company as well as customers, suppliers, and friends. These contacts provide managers with information and advice on diverse topics. Managers ask, persuade, and even intimidate members of their network in order to get information and to get things done.

Networking helps managers carry out their responsibilities. Social media sites have increased the ability of both managers and subordinates to network. Internal social networks such as Yammer allow employees to connect with one another, while social networks such as Facebook or Twitter enable managers to connect with customers. Sales managers are even using social networks to communicate with their distributors. LinkedIn has been used for job networking and is gaining in popularity among the younger generation as an alternative to traditional job hunting. Some speculate that social networks might eventually replace traditional résumés and job boards.[35]

Websites like LinkedIn are helping managers and employees network with one another to achieve their professional goals.
© Ingvar Björk/Alamy

SO YOU WANT TO BE A MANAGER // What Kind of Manager Do You Want to Be? /

Managers are needed in a wide variety of organizations. Experts suggest that employment will increase by millions of jobs by 2016. But the requirements for the jobs become more demanding with every passing year—with the speed of technology and communication increasing by the day, and the stress of global commerce increasing pressures to perform. However, if you like a challenge and if you have the right kind of personality, management remains a viable field. Even as companies are forced to restructure, management remains a vital role in business. In fact, the Bureau of Labor Statistics predicts that management positions in public relations, marketing, and advertising are set to increase around 12 percent overall between 2006 and 2016.

Financial managers will be in even more demand, with jobs increasing 13 percent in the same time period. Computer and IT managers will continue to be in strong demand, with the number of jobs increasing 16 percent between 2006 and 2016.[36]

Salaries for managerial positions remain strong overall. While pay can vary significantly depending on your level of experience, the firm where you work, and the region of the country where you live, below is a list of the nationwide average incomes for a variety of different managers:

Chief executive: $178,400

Computer and information systems manager: $132,570

Marketing manager: $133,700

Financial manager: $126,660

General and operations manager: $116,090

Medical/health services manager: $101,340

Administrative services manager: $90,190

Human resources manager: $111,180

Sales manager: $123,150[37]

In short, if you want to be a manager, there are opportunities in almost every field. There may be fewer middle management positions available in firms, but managers remain a vital part of most industries and will continue to be long into the future—especially as navigating global business becomes ever more complex.

Finally, managers spend a great deal of time confronting the complex and difficult challenges of the business world today. Some of these challenges relate to rapidly changing technology (especially in production and information processing), increased scrutiny of individual and corporate ethics and social responsibility, the impact of social media, the changing nature of the workforce, new laws and regulations, increased global competition and more challenging foreign markets, declining educational standards (which may limit the skills and knowledge of the future labor and customer pool), and time itself—that is, making the best use of it. But such diverse issues cannot simply be plugged into a computer program that supplies correct, easy-to-apply solutions. It is only through creativity and imagination that managers can make effective decisions that benefit their organizations. ■

organization, teamwork, and communication

© Brand X Pictures/Superstock, RF

LEARNING OBJECTIVES

After reading this chapter, you will be able to:

LO 7-1 Explain the importance of organizational culture.

LO 7-2 Define organizational structure, and relate how organizational structures develop.

LO 7-3 Describe how specialization and departmentalization help an organization achieve its goals.

LO 7-4 Determine how organizations assign responsibility for tasks and delegate authority.

LO 7-5 Compare and contrast some common forms of organizational structure.

LO 7-6 Distinguish between groups and teams, and identify the types of groups that exist in organizations.

LO 7-7 Describe how communication occurs in organizations.

An organization's structure determines how well it makes decisions and responds to problems, and it influences employees' attitudes toward their work. A suitable structure can minimize a business's costs and maximize its efficiency. Even companies that operate within the same industry may utilize different organizational structures. For example, in the consumer electronics industry, Samsung is organized as a conglomerate with separate business units or divisions. Samsung is largely decentralized. Apple, under CEO Tim Cook, has moved from a hierarchical structure to a more collaborative approach between divisions.[1]

Because a business's structure can so profoundly affect its success, this chapter will examine organizational structure in detail. First, we discuss how an organization's culture affects its operations. Then we consider the development of structure, including how tasks and responsibilities are organized through specialization and departmentalization. Next, we explore some of the forms organizational structure may take. Finally, we consider communications within business. ■

LO 7-1 Explain the importance of organizational culture.

ORGANIZATIONAL CULTURE

One of the most important aspects of organizing a business is determining its **organizational culture**, a firm's shared values, beliefs, traditions, philosophies, rules, and role models for behavior. Also called corporate culture, an organizational culture exists in every organization, regardless of size, organizational type, product, or profit objective. Sometimes behaviors, programs, and policies enhance and support the organizational culture. Netflix, for example, established a "freedom and responsibility culture," which has become a culture code many Silicon Valley companies have used as a template for establishing their organizational cultures. One way Netflix expresses

extracurricular activities, and stories. Employees often learn the accepted standards through discussions with co-workers.

The organizational culture at the Four Seasons hotel chain is service oriented with its adoption of the universal rule: treat others the way you would like to be treated. To encourage employees to be dedicated to service, the Four Seasons offers unique perks such as the ability to request transfers among its 90 properties around the world.[3] Disneyland/DisneyWorld and McDonald's have organizational cultures focused on cleanliness, value, and service. The company Zappos.com created a culture of "fun and a little weirdness." The company has a flexible work environment with very few rules, and employees are encouraged to socialize and engage in unique activities (such as ringing cowbells when

organizational culture a firm's shared values, beliefs, traditions, philosophies, rules, and role models for behavior.

> ## Also called corporate culture, an organizational culture exists in every organization, regardless of size, organizational type, product, or profit objective.

this culture is by not having a vacation policy. Employees are expected to be responsible and disciplined while working, and in exchange, they are allowed the freedom to take vacation when they like and for as long as they like.[2] A firm's culture may be expressed formally through its mission statement, codes of ethics, memos, manuals, and ceremonies, but it is more commonly expressed informally. Examples of informal expressions of culture include dress codes (or the lack thereof), work habits,

visitors arrive). Zappos's goal is to make both employees and customers feel good. Customer service is such a must at Zappos that new hires must work for one month at a call center, even if the new employees are not going to be interacting with customers normally.[4] When such values and philosophies are shared by all members of an organization, they will be expressed in its relationships with stakeholders. However, organizational cultures that lack such positive values may result in employees who are

structure the arrangement or relationship of positions within an organization.

unproductive and indifferent and have poor attitudes, which will be reflected externally to customers. The corporate culture may have contributed to the misconduct at a number of well-known companies. A survey found that executives in financial and technology companies are mostly cut-throat in collecting intelligence about competition, creating a corporate culture in which unethical acts might be tolerated if it means beating the competition.[6]

Organizational culture helps ensure that all members of a company share values and suggests rules for how to behave and deal with problems within the organization. Figure 7.1 illustrates the importance of honesty, transparency, and a relaxed work environment in an organizational culture. The key to success in any organization is satisfying stakeholders, especially customers. Establishing a positive organizational culture sets the tone for all other decisions, including building an efficient organizational structure.

Southwest Airlines has developed a culture where employees have fun and provide quality service to passengers.
© Kayte Deioma / PhotoEdit

LO 7-2 Define organizational structure, and relate how organizational structures develop.

DEVELOPING ORGANIZATIONAL STRUCTURE

Structure is the arrangement or relationship of positions within an organization. Rarely is an organization, or any group of individuals working together, able to achieve common objectives without some form of structure, whether that structure is explicitly defined or only implied. A professional

W. L. GORE SUCCEEDS WITH INFORMAL ORGANIZATIONAL STRUCTURE

W. L. Gore & Associates, the chemical and manufacturing company best known for Gore-Tex fabric, is a fascinating success story. It has over 10,000 employees at offices in over 50 countries, is ranked 22nd on *Fortune*'s 2014 "100 Best Companies to Work For" list, and—from its founding in 1958—has never posted an operating loss. During this time, it has held to a unique management structure: almost no formalized bosses, no structured hierarchy, and no set chains of command. In doing so, it has proven that a structure antithetical to a traditional hierarchical management structure can work well if done correctly.

Gore uses what it calls a "team-based, flat lattice" organizational structure. The company is built around self-creating, multidisciplinary teams, which form in response to problems, opportunities, or shared skills and interests. Employees can choose their own projects but in return hold themselves, and each other, strictly accountable to deliver results. As CEO Terri Kelly puts it, "There are two sides to the coin: freedom to decide and a commitment to deliver on your promises." Leaders emerge naturally from these teams and gain management power not by formalized titles or privileges but by the demonstrated willingness of others to follow them. Compensation is determined by a detailed peer review process meant to award employees who have contributed most to the company with the highest salaries.

Gore does not pretend that it has overcome the need for company organization, strong leadership, employee accountability, and high performance needed for all organizations. Instead, it simply claims to have found alternative ways to achieve them, such as a strong focus on exemplifying company values and a powerful peer-review and accountability system. Whatever analysts might say about the company's unusual approach, it has been successful.[5]

Discussion Questions

1. Why does W. L. Gore's unique management structure work?

2. What trade-offs does W. L. Gore make by using the flat lattice structure? In other words, are there certain disadvantages that W. L. Gore has chosen to accept in return for other benefits?

3. Would you like to work in a flat lattice–style organization? Why or why not?

132 PART 3 | Managing for Quality and Competitiveness

FIGURE 7.1
Most Preferred Company Culture Attributes

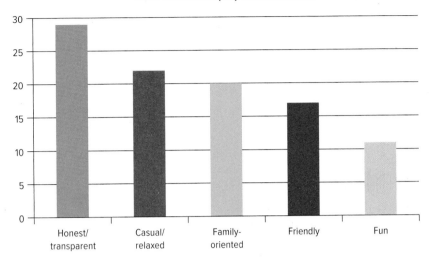

Most Preferred Company Culture Attributes

Source: Software Advice survey of 886 U.S. adults, 2014.

baseball team such as the Colorado Rockies is a business organization with an explicit formal structure that guides the team's activities so that it can increase game attendance, win games, and sell souvenirs such as T-shirts. But even an informal group playing softball for fun has an organization that specifies who will pitch, catch, bat, coach, and so on. Governments and nonprofit organizations also have formal organizational structures to facilitate the achievement of their objectives. Getting people to work together efficiently and coordinating the skills of diverse individuals require careful planning. Developing appropriate organizational structures is

therefore a major challenge for managers in both large and small organizations.

An organization's structure develops when managers assign work tasks and activities to specific individuals or work groups and coordinate the diverse activities required to reach the firm's objectives. When Macy's, for example, has a sale, the store manager must work with the advertising department to make the public aware of the sale, with department managers to ensure that extra salespeople are scheduled to handle the increased customer traffic, and with merchandise buyers to ensure that enough sale merchandise is available to meet expected consumer demand. All the people occupying these positions must work together to achieve the store's objectives.

The best way to begin to understand how organizational structure develops is to consider the evolution of a new business such as a clothing store. At first, the business is a sole proprietorship in which the owner does everything—buys, prices, and displays the merchandise; does the accounting and tax records; and assists customers. As the business grows, the owner hires a salesperson and perhaps a merchandise buyer to help run the store. As the business continues to grow, the owner hires more salespeople. The growth and success of the business now require the owner to be away from the store frequently, meeting with suppliers, engaging in public relations, and attending trade shows. Thus, the owner must designate someone to manage the salespeople and maintain the accounting, payroll, and tax functions. If the owner decides to expand by opening more stores, still more managers will be needed. Figure 7.2 shows these stages of growth

FIGURE 7.2
The Evolution of a Clothing Store, Phases 1, 2, and 3

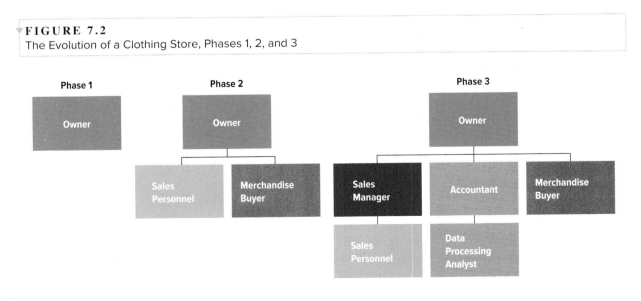

with three **organizational charts** (visual displays of organizational structure, chain of command, and other relationships).

Growth requires organizing—the structuring of human, physical, and financial resources to achieve objectives in an effective and efficient manner. Growth necessitates hiring people who have specialized skills. With more people and greater specialization, the organization needs to develop a formal structure to function efficiently. Imagine the various organizational changes that Nokia has undergone. It was founded in 1865 as a paper mill in Finland

Specialization

After identifying all activities that must be accomplished, managers then break these activities down into specific tasks that can be handled by individual employees. This division of labor into small, specific tasks and the assignment of employees to do a single task is called **specialization**.

The rationale for specialization is efficiency. People can perform more efficiently if they master just one task rather than all tasks. In *The Wealth of Nations,* 18th-century economist Adam Smith discussed specialization, using the manufacture of straight pins as an example. Individually, workers could produce 20 pins a day when each employee produced complete pins. Thus, 10 employees working independently of each other could produce 200 pins a day. However, when one worker drew the wire, another straightened it, a third cut it, and a fourth

> "Growth requires organizing—the structuring of human, physical, and financial resources to achieve objectives in an effective and efficient manner."

and has become a global telecommunications company serving more than 1 billion customers. During its history, the company has transformed itself various times—including as a rubber company, television maker, and a cable company—each time changing the organizational structure to accommodate its business.[7] As we shall see, structuring an organization requires that management assign work tasks to specific individuals and departments and assign responsibility for the achievement of specific organizational objectives.

LO 7-3 Describe how specialization and departmentalization help an organization achieve its goals.

ASSIGNING TASKS

For a business to earn profits from the sale of its products, its managers must first determine what activities are required to achieve its objectives. At Celestial Seasonings, for example, employees must purchase herbs from suppliers, dry the herbs and place them in tea bags, package and label the tea, and then ship the packages to grocery stores around the country. Other necessary activities include negotiating with supermarkets and other retailers for display space, developing new products, planning advertising, managing finances, and managing employees. All these activities must be coordinated, assigned to work groups, and controlled. Two important aspects of assigning these work activities are specialization and departmentalization.

ground the point, 10 workers could produce 48,000 pins per day.[8] To save money and achieve the benefits of specialization, some companies outsource and hire temporary workers to provide key skills. Many highly skilled, diverse, experienced workers are available through temp agencies.

Specialization means workers do not waste time shifting from one job to another, and training is easier. However, efficiency is not the only motivation for specialization. Specialization also occurs when the activities that must be performed within an organization are too numerous for one person to handle.

Job specialization is common in automobile manufacturing. By dividing work into smaller specialized tasks, employees can perform their work more quickly and efficiently.
© Ulrich Baumgarten/Getty Images

departmentalization
the grouping of jobs into working units usually called departments, units, groups, or divisions.

functional departmentalization
the grouping of jobs that perform similar functional activities, such as finance, manufacturing, marketing, and human resources.

product departmentalization
the organization of jobs in relation to the products of the firm.

geographic departmentalization
the grouping of jobs according to geographic location, such as state, region, country, or continent.

Recall the example of the clothing store. When the business was young and small, the owner could do everything; but when the business grew, the owner needed help waiting on customers, keeping the books, and managing other business activities.

Overspecialization can have negative consequences. Employees may become bored and dissatisfied with their jobs, and the result of their unhappiness is likely to be poor quality work, more injuries, and high employee turnover. In extreme cases, employees in crowded specialized electronic plants are unable to form working relationships with one another. In some factories in Asia, workers are cramped together and overworked. Fourteen global vehicle manufacturers pledged to increase their oversight of the factories in their supply chain to ensure human rights and healthy working conditions. However, the task is monumental for these global companies because their supply chains encompass many different countries with different labor practices, and it can be difficult to oversee the operations of dozens of suppliers and subcontractors.[9] This is why some manufacturing firms allow job rotation so that employees do not become dissatisfied and leave. Although some degree of specialization is necessary for efficiency, because of differences in skills, abilities, and interests, all people are not equally suited for all jobs. We examine some strategies to overcome these issues in Chapter 9.

Departmentalization

After assigning specialized tasks to individuals, managers next organize workers doing similar jobs into groups to make them easier to manage. **Departmentalization** is the grouping of jobs into working units usually called departments, units, groups, or divisions. As we shall see, departments are commonly organized by function, product, geographic region, or customer (Figure 7.3). Most companies use more than one departmentalization plan to enhance productivity. For instance, many consumer goods manufacturers have departments for specific product lines (beverages, frozen dinners, canned goods, and so on) as well as departments dealing with legal, purchasing, finance, human resources, and other business functions. For smaller companies, accounting can be set up online, almost as an automated department. Accounting software can handle electronic transfers so you never have to worry about a late bill. Many city governments also have departments for specific services (e.g., police, fire, waste disposal) as well as departments for legal, human resources, and other business functions.

> **Specialization means workers do not waste time shifting from one job to another, and training is easier.**

Figure 7.4 depicts the organizational chart for the fictional city of Pineapple Paradise, showing these departments.

Functional Departmentalization **Functional departmentalization** groups jobs that perform similar functional activities, such as finance, manufacturing, marketing, and human resources. Each of these functions is managed by an expert in the work done by the department—an engineer supervises the production department; a financial executive supervises the finance department. This approach is common in small organizations. Green Mountain Coffee is departmentalized into six functions: sales and marketing, operations, human resources, finance, information systems, and social responsibility. A weakness of functional departmentalization is that, because it tends to emphasize departmental units rather than the organization as a whole, decision making that involves more than one department may be slow, and it requires greater coordination. Thus, as businesses grow, they tend to adopt other approaches to organizing jobs.

Product Departmentalization **Product departmentalization**, as you might guess, organizes jobs around the products of the firm. Unilever has global units, including personal care, foods, refreshment, and home care.[10] Each division develops and implements its own product plans, monitors the results, and takes corrective action as necessary. Functional activities—production, finance, marketing, and others—are located within each product division. Consequently, organizing by products duplicates functions and resources and emphasizes the product rather than achievement of the organization's overall objectives. However, it simplifies decision making and helps coordinate all activities related to a product or product group. PepsiCo Inc. is organized into six business units: (1) PepsiCo Americas Beverages; (2) Frito-Lay North America; (3) Quaker Foods North America; (4) Latin America Foods; (5) PepsiCo Europe; and (6) PepsiCo Asia, Middle East and Africa. PepsiCo has actually adopted a combination of two types of departmentalization. While it clearly uses product departmentalization in North America, the company chooses to divide its segments into geographic regions—a type of geographic departmentalization.[11]

Geographic Departmentalization **Geographic departmentalization** groups jobs according to geographic location,

customer departmentalization
the arrangement of jobs around the needs of various types of customers.

such as a state, region, country, or continent. Diageo, the premium beverage company known for brands such as Johnny Walker and Tanqueray, is organized into five geographic regions, allowing the company to get closer to its customers and respond more quickly and efficiently to regional competitors.[12] Multinational corporations often use a geographic approach because of vast differences between different regions. Coca-Cola, General Motors, and Caterpillar are organized by region. However, organizing by region requires a large administrative staff and control system to coordinate operations, and tasks are duplicated among the different regions.

Customer Departmentalization Customer departmentalization arranges jobs around the needs of various types of customers. Procter & Gamble, for example, recently restructured its business divisions according to types of customers: global baby, feminine and family care; global beauty, hair and personal care; global health and grooming; and global fabric and home care. This allows the company to address the unique

FIGURE 7.3
Departmentalization

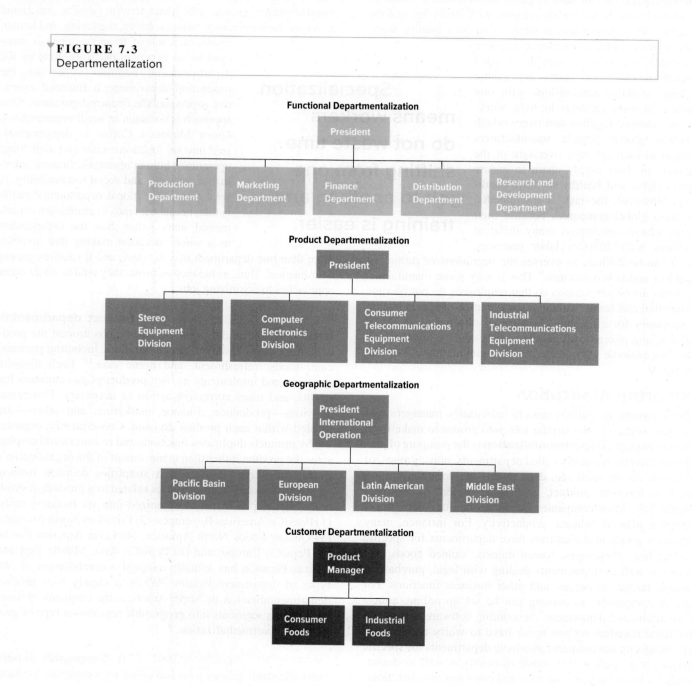

Functional Departmentalization

President
- Production Department
- Marketing Department
- Finance Department
- Distribution Department
- Research and Development Department

Product Departmentalization

President
- Stereo Equipment Division
- Computer Electronics Division
- Consumer Telecommunications Equipment Division
- Industrial Telecommunications Equipment Division

Geographic Departmentalization

President International Operation
- Pacific Basin Division
- European Division
- Latin American Division
- Middle East Division

Customer Departmentalization

Product Manager
- Consumer Foods
- Industrial Foods

FIGURE 7.4
City of Pineapple Paradise Organizational Chart

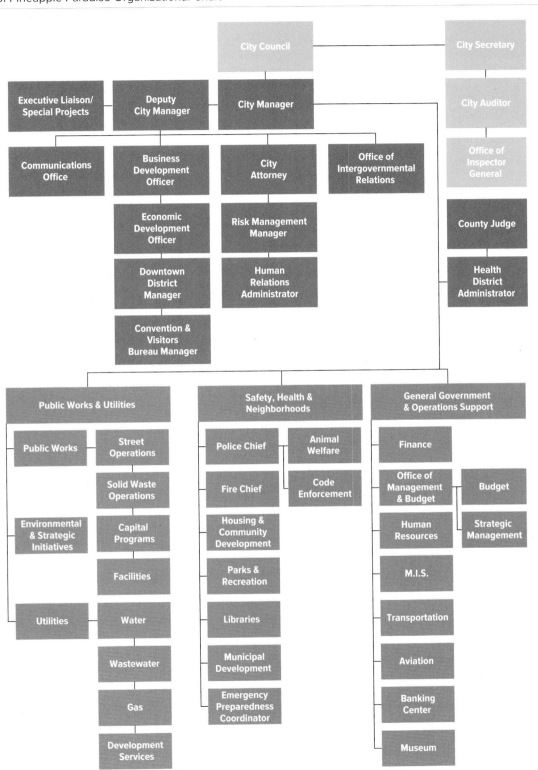

delegation of authority giving employees not only tasks, but also the power to make commitments, use resources, and take whatever actions are necessary to carry out those tasks.

responsibility the obligation, placed on employees through delegation, to perform assigned tasks satisfactorily and be held accountable for the proper execution of work.

accountability the principle that employees who accept an assignment and the authority to carry it out are answerable to a superior for the outcome.

requirements of each group.[13] Airlines, such as British Airways and Delta, provide prices and services customized for either business/frequent travelers or infrequent/vacationing customers. Customer departmentalization, like geographic departmentalization, does not focus on the organization as a whole and therefore requires a large administrative staff to coordinate the operations of the various groups.

> **LO 7-4** Determine how organizations assign responsibility for tasks and delegate authority.

ASSIGNING RESPONSIBILITY

After all workers and work groups have been assigned their tasks, they must be given the responsibility to carry them out. Management must determine to what extent it will delegate responsibility throughout the organization and how many employees will report to each manager.

Delegation of Authority

Delegation of authority means not only giving tasks to employees but also empowering them to make commitments, use resources, and take whatever actions are necessary to carry out those tasks. Let's say a marketing manager at Nestlé has

Managers can delegate authority, giving tasks and empowering employees to use resources to accomplish objectives.
© skynesher/Getty Images, RF

assigned an employee to design a new package that is less wasteful (more environmentally responsible) than the current package for one of the company's frozen dinner lines. To carry out the assignment, the employee needs access to information and the authority to make certain decisions on packaging materials, costs, and so on. Without the authority to carry out the assigned task, the employee would have to get the approval of others for every decision and every request for materials.

As a business grows, so do the number and complexity of decisions that must be made; no one manager can handle them all. Nordstrom delegates authority to its customer service personnel by telling them to use their best judgment when dealing with customers. This allows employees to offer the best tailored service to each individual customer and is one reason the retailer is known for its superior customer service.[14] Delegation of authority frees a manager to concentrate on larger issues, such as planning or dealing with problems and opportunities.

Delegation also gives a **responsibility**, or obligation, to employees to carry out assigned tasks satisfactorily and holds them accountable for the proper execution of their assigned work. The principle of **accountability** means that employees who accept an assignment and the authority to carry it out are answerable to a superior for the outcome. Returning to the Nestlé example, if the packaging design prepared by the employee is unacceptable or late, the employee must accept the blame. If the new design is innovative, attractive, and cost-efficient, as well as environmentally responsible, or is completed ahead of schedule, the employee will accept the credit.

The process of delegating authority establishes a pattern of relationships and accountability between a superior and his or her subordinates. The president of a firm delegates responsibility for all marketing activities to the vice president of marketing. The vice president accepts this responsibility and has the authority to obtain all relevant information, make certain decisions, and delegate any or all activities to his or her subordinates. The vice president, in turn, delegates all advertising activities to the advertising manager, all sales activities to the sales manager, and so on. These managers then delegate specific tasks to their subordinates. However, the act of delegating authority to a subordinate does not relieve the superior of accountability for the delegated job. Even though the vice president of marketing delegates work to subordinates, he or she is still ultimately accountable to the president for all marketing activities.

Degree of Centralization

The extent to which authority is delegated throughout an organization determines its degree of centralization.

Centralized Organizations

In a **centralized organization**, authority is concentrated at the top, and very little decision-making authority is delegated to lower levels. Although decision-making authority in centralized organizations rests with top levels of management, a vast amount of responsibility for carrying out daily and routine procedures is delegated to even the lowest levels of the organization. Many government organizations, including the U.S. Army, the Postal Service, and the IRS, are centralized.

Businesses tend to be more centralized when the decisions to be made are risky and when low-level managers are not highly skilled in decision making. In the banking industry, for example, authority to make routine car loans is given to all loan managers, while the authority to make high-risk loans, such as for a large residential development, may be restricted to upper-level loan officers.

Overcentralization can cause serious problems for a company, in part because it may take longer for the organization as a whole to implement decisions and to respond to changes and problems on a regional scale. McDonald's, for example, was one of the last chains to introduce a chicken sandwich because of the amount of research, development, test marketing, and layers of approval the product had to go through.

Decentralized Organizations

A **decentralized organization** is one in which decision-making authority is delegated as far down the chain of command as possible. Decentralization is characteristic of organizations that operate in complex, unpredictable environments. Businesses that face intense competition often decentralize to improve responsiveness and enhance creativity. Lower-level managers who interact with the external environment often develop a good understanding of it and thus are able to react quickly to changes. Johnson & Johnson has a very decentralized, flat organizational structure.

Delegating authority to lower levels of managers may increase the organization's productivity. Decentralization requires that lower-level managers have strong decision-making skills. In recent years, the trend has been toward more decentralized organizations, and some of the largest and most successful companies, including GE, IBM, Google, and Nike, have decentralized decision-making authority. McDonald's, Taco Bell, and Pizza Hut have established themselves in the growing Indian market by decentralizing operations by varying products in specific markets to better meet customer demands. McDonald's, for example, has implemented spicy and vegetarian menu options in India to appeal to native tastes. Becoming decentralized can be difficult for a fast-food restaurant that relies on standardized processes and core products. Burger King's core offering, the Whopper, will not likely be well accepted in India because beef is rarely eaten. Some suggest the chain should offer vegetarian pizza since it is popular in India. Diversity and decentralization are the keys to being better, not just bigger.[15] Nonprofit organizations benefit from decentralization as well.

Span of Management

How many subordinates should a manager manage? There is no simple answer. Experts generally agree, however, that top managers should not directly supervise more than four to eight people, while lower-level managers who supervise routine tasks are capable of managing a much larger number of subordinates. For example, the manager of the finance department may supervise 25 employees, whereas the vice president of finance may supervise only five managers. **Span of management** refers to the number of subordinates who report to a particular manager. A *wide span of management* exists when a manager directly supervises a very large number of employees. A *narrow span of management* exists when a manager directly supervises only a few subordinates (Figure 7.5). At Whole Foods, the best employees are recruited and placed in small teams. Employees are empowered to discount, give away, and sample products, as well as to assist in creating a respectful workplace where goals are achieved, individual employees succeed, and customers are core in business decisions. Whole Foods teams get to vote on new employee hires as well. This approach allows Whole Foods to offer unique and "local market" experiences in each of its stores. This level of customization is in contrast to more centralized national supermarket chains such as Kroger, Safeway, and Publix.[16]

centralized organization a structure in which authority is concentrated at the top, and very little decision-making authority is delegated to lower levels.

decentralized organization an organization in which decision-making authority is delegated as far down the chain of command as possible.

span of management the number of subordinates who report to a particular manager.

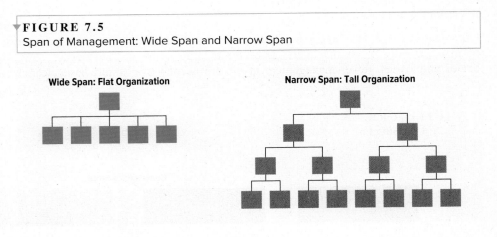

▼**FIGURE 7.5**
Span of Management: Wide Span and Narrow Span

Wide Span: Flat Organization

Narrow Span: Tall Organization

Should the span of management be wide or narrow? To answer this question, several factors need to be considered. A narrow span of management is appropriate when superiors and subordinates are not in close proximity, the manager has many responsibilities in addition to the supervision, the interaction between superiors and subordinates is frequent, and problems are common. However, when superiors and subordinates are located close to one another, the manager has few responsibilities other than supervision, the level of interaction between superiors and subordinates is low, few problems arise, subordinates are highly competent, and a set of specific operating procedures governs the activities of managers and their subordinates, a wide span of management will be more appropriate. Narrow spans of management are typical in centralized organizations, while wide spans of management are more common in decentralized firms.

Organizational Layers

Complementing the concept of span of management is **organizational layers**, the levels of management in an organization. A company with many layers of managers is considered tall; in a tall organization, the span of management is narrow (see Figure 7.5). Because each manager supervises only a few subordinates, many layers of management are necessary to carry out the operations of the business. McDonald's, for example, has a tall organization with many layers, including store managers, district managers, regional managers, and functional managers (finance, marketing, and so on), as well as a chief executive officer and many vice presidents. Because there are more managers in tall organizations than in flat organizations, administrative costs are usually higher. Communication is slower because information must pass through many layers.

Organizations with few layers are flat and have wide spans of management. When managers supervise a large number of employees, fewer management layers are needed to conduct the organization's activities. Managers in flat organizations typically perform more administrative duties than managers in tall organizations because there are fewer of them. They also spend more time supervising and working with subordinates.

Many of the companies that have decentralized also flattened their structures and widened their spans of management, often by eliminating layers of middle management. As mentioned earlier in this chapter, Johnson & Johnson has both a decentralized and flat organizational structure. Other corporations, including Avon, AT&T, and Ford Motor Company, embraced a more decentralized structure to reduce costs, speed up decision making, and boost overall productivity.

LO 7-5 Compare and contrast some common forms of organizational structure.

FORMS OF ORGANIZATIONAL STRUCTURE

Along with assigning tasks and the responsibility for carrying them out, managers must consider how to structure their authority relationships—that is, what structure the organization itself will have and how it will appear on the organizational chart. Common forms of organization include line structure, line-and-staff structure, multidivisional structure, and matrix structure.

> " *Organizations with few layers are flat and have wide spans of management.* "

Line Structure

The simplest organizational structure, **line structure**, has direct lines of authority that extend from the top manager to employees at the lowest level of the organization. For example, a convenience store employee at 7-Eleven may report to an assistant manager, who reports to the store manager, who reports to a regional manager, or, in an independent store, directly to the owner (Figure 7.6). This structure has a clear chain of command, which enables managers to

▼**FIGURE 7.6**
Line Structure

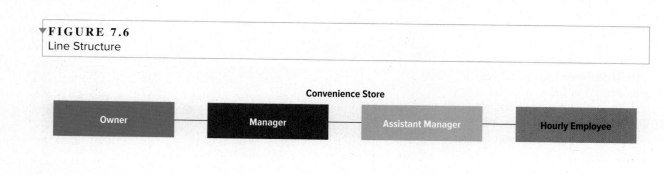

Convenience Store

| Owner | Manager | Assistant Manager | Hourly Employee |

make decisions quickly. A mid-level manager facing a decision must consult only one person, his or her immediate supervisor. However, this structure requires that managers possess a wide range of knowledge and skills. They are responsible for a variety of activities and must be knowledgeable about them all. Line structures are most common in small businesses.

Line-and-Staff Structure

The **line-and-staff structure** has a traditional line relationship between superiors and subordinates, and specialized managers—called staff managers—are available to assist line managers (Figure 7.7). Line managers can focus on their area of expertise in the operation of the business, while staff managers provide advice and support to line departments on specialized matters such as finance, engineering, human resources, and the law. In the city of Pineapple Paradise (refer back for Figure 7.4), for example, assistant city managers are line managers who oversee groups of related departments. However, the city attorney and business development manager are effectively staff managers who report directly to the city manager (the city equivalent of a business chief executive officer). Staff managers do not have direct authority over line managers or over the line manager's subordinates, but they do have direct authority over subordinates in their own departments. However, line-and-staff organizations may experience problems with overstaffing and ambiguous lines of communication. Additionally, employees may become frustrated because they lack the authority to carry out certain decisions.

Multidivisional Structure

As companies grow and diversify, traditional line structures become difficult to coordinate, making communication difficult and decision making slow. When the weaknesses of the structure—the "turf wars," miscommunication, and working at cross-purposes—exceed the benefits, growing firms tend to **restructure**, or change the basic structure of an organization. Growing firms tend to restructure into the divisionalized form. A **multidivisional structure** organizes departments into larger groups called divisions. Just as departments might be formed on the basis of geography, customer, product, or a combination of these, so too divisions can be formed based on any of these methods of organizing. Within each of these divisions, departments may be organized by product, geographic region, function, or some combination of all three. Indra Nooyi, CEO of PepsiCo, rearranged the company's organizational structure. Prior to her tenure, PepsiCo was organized geographically. She created new units that spanned international boundaries and made it easier for employees in different geographic regions to share business practices.[17]

Multidivisional structures permit delegation of decision-making authority, allowing divisional and department managers to specialize. They allow those closest to the action to make the decisions that will affect them. Delegation of authority and divisionalized work also mean that better decisions are made faster, and they tend to be more innovative. Most important, by focusing each division on a common region, product, or customer, each is more likely to provide products that meet the needs of its particular customers. However, the divisional structure inevitably creates work duplication, which makes it more difficult to realize the economies of scale that result from grouping functions together.

line-and-staff structure a structure having a traditional line relationship between superiors and subordinates and also specialized managers—called staff managers—who are available to assist line managers.

restructure to change the basic structure of an organization

multidivisional structure a structure that organizes departments into larger groups called divisions.

FIGURE 7.7
Line-and-Staff Structure

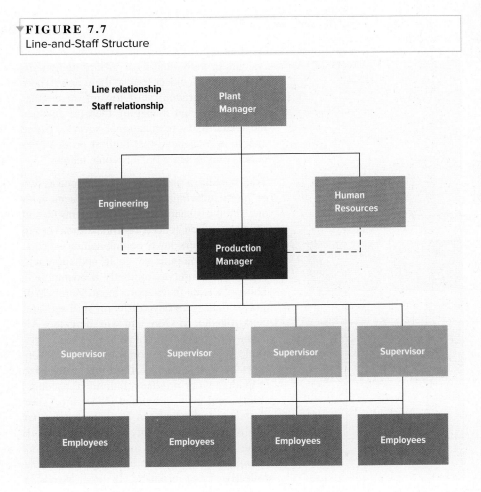

— Line relationship
- - - Staff relationship

Plant Manager

Engineering

Human Resources

Production Manager

Supervisor | Supervisor | Supervisor | Supervisor

Employees | Employees | Employees | Employees

Matrix Structure

Another structure that attempts to address issues that arise with growth, diversification, productivity, and competitiveness is the matrix. A **matrix structure**, also called a project management structure, sets up teams from different departments, thereby creating two or more intersecting lines of authority (Figure 7.8). One of the first organizations to design and implement a matrix structure was the National Aeronautics and Space Administration (NASA) for the space program because it needed to coordinate different projects at the same time. The matrix structure superimposes project-based departments on the more traditional, function-based departments. Project teams bring together specialists from a variety of areas to work together on a single project, such as developing a new fighter jet. In this arrangement, employees are responsible to two managers—functional managers and project managers. Matrix structures are usually temporary: Team members typically go back to their functional or line department after a project is finished. However, more firms are becoming permanent matrix structures, creating and dissolving project teams as needed to meet customer needs. The aerospace industry was one of the first to apply the matrix structure, but today it is used by universities and schools, accounting firms, banks, and organizations in other industries.

Matrix structures provide flexibility, enhanced cooperation, and creativity, and they enable the company to respond quickly to changes in the environment by giving special attention to specific projects or problems. However, they are generally expensive and quite complex, and employees may be confused as to whose authority has priority—the project manager's or the immediate supervisor's.

LO 7-6 Distinguish between groups and teams, and identify the types of groups that exist in organizations.

THE ROLE OF GROUPS AND TEAMS IN ORGANIZATIONS

Regardless of how they are organized, most of the essential work of business occurs in individual work groups and teams, so we'll take a closer look at them now. There has been a gradual shift toward an emphasis on teams and managing them to enhance individual and organizational success. Some experts now believe that highest productivity results only when groups become teams.[18]

Traditionally, a **group** has been defined as two or more individuals who communicate with one another, share a common identity, and have a common goal. A **team** is a small group whose members have complementary skills; have a common purpose, goals, and approach; and hold themselves mutually accountable.[19] Think of a team like a sports team. Members of a basketball team have different skill sets and work together to score and win the game. All teams are groups, but not all groups are teams. Table 7.1 points out some important differences between them. Work groups emphasize individual work products, individual accountability, and even individual leadership. Your class is a group that can be separated further into teams of two or three classmates. Work teams share leadership roles, have both individual and mutual accountability, and create collective work products. In other words, a

FIGURE 7.8
Matrix Structure

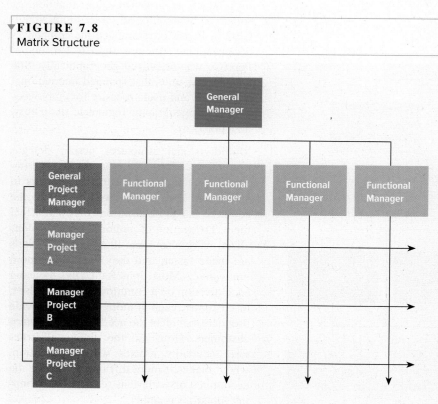

▼ **TABLE 7.1** Differences between Groups and Teams

Working Group	Team
Has strong, clearly focused leader	Has shared leadership roles
Has individual accountability	Has individual and group accountability
Has the same purpose as the broader organizational mission	Has a specific purpose that the team itself delivers
Creates individual work products	Creates collective work products
Runs efficient meetings	Encourages open-ended discussion and active problem-solving meetings
Measures its effectiveness indirectly by its effects on others (e.g., financial performance of the business)	Measures performance directly by assessing collective work products
Discusses, decides, and delegates	Discusses, decides, and does real work together

Source: Robert Gatewood, Robert Taylor, and O. C. Ferrell, *Management: Comprehension Analysis and Application,* 1995, p. 427. Copyright © 1995 Richard D. Irwin, a Times Mirror Higher Education Group, Inc., company. Reproduced with permission of McGraw-Hill Education.

work group's performance depends on what its members do as individuals, while a team's performance is based on creating a knowledge center and a competency to work together to accomplish a goal. On the other hand, it is also important for team members to retain their individuality and avoid becoming just "another face in the crowd." The purpose of teams should be toward collaboration versus collectivism. Although the team is working toward a common goal, it is important that all team members actively contribute their ideas and work together to achieve this common goal.[20]

The type of groups an organization establishes depends on the tasks it needs to accomplish and the situation it faces. Some specific kinds of groups and teams include committees, task forces, project teams, product-development teams, quality-assurance teams, and self-directed work teams. All of these can be *virtual teams*—employees in different locations who rely on e-mail, audio conferencing, fax, Internet, videoconferencing, or other technological tools to accomplish their goals. Virtual teams are becoming a part of everyday business, with the number of employees working remotely from their employer increasing more than 80 percent in the last several years.[21] Virtual teams have also opened up opportunities for different companies. For instance, inside salespeople use virtual technology such as e-mail and social media to connect with prospects and clients.[22]

Committees

A **committee** is usually a permanent, formal group that does some specific task. For example, many firms have a compensation or finance committee to examine the effectiveness of these areas of operation as well as the need for possible changes. Ethics committees are formed to develop and revise codes of ethics, suggest methods for implementing ethical standards, and review specific issues and concerns.

Task Forces

A **task force** is a temporary group of employees responsible for bringing about a particular change. A task force typically comes from across all departments and levels of an organization. Task force membership is usually based on expertise rather than organizational position. Occasionally, a task force may be formed from individuals outside a company. Coca-Cola has often used task forces to address problems and provide recommendations for improving company practices or products. While some task forces might last a few months, others last for years. When Coca-Cola faced lawsuits alleging discrimination practices in hiring and promotion, it developed a five-year task force to examine pay and promotion practices among minority employees. Its experiences helped Coca-Cola realize the advantages of having a cross-functional task force made up of employees from different departments, and it continued to use task forces to tackle major company issues. Other companies that have also recognized the benefits of task forces include IBM, Prudential, and General Electric.[23]

Teams

Teams are becoming far more common in the U.S. workplace as businesses strive to enhance productivity and global competitiveness. In general, teams have the benefit of being able to pool members' knowledge and skills and make greater use of them than can individuals working alone. Team building is becoming increasingly popular in organizations, with around half of executives indicating their companies have team-building training. Teams require harmony, cooperation, synchronized effort,

project teams groups similar to task forces that normally run their operation and have total control of a specific work project.

product-development teams a specific type of project team formed to devise, design, and implement a new product.

and flexibility to maximize their contribution.[24] Teams can also create more solutions to problems than can individuals. Furthermore, team participation enhances employee acceptance of, understanding of, and commitment to team goals. Teams motivate workers by providing internal rewards in the form of an enhanced sense of accomplishment for employees as they achieve more, and external rewards in the form of praise and certain perks. Consequently, they can help get workers more involved. They help companies be more innovative, and they can boost productivity and cut costs.

According to psychologist Ivan Steiner, team productivity peaks at about five team members. People become less motivated and group coordination becomes more difficult after this size. Jeff Bezos, Amazon.com CEO, says that he has a "two-pizza rule": If a team cannot be fed by two pizzas, it is too large. Keep teams small enough where everyone gets a piece of the action.[25]

Project Teams
Project teams are similar to task forces, but normally they run their operation and have total control of a specific work project. Like task forces, their membership is likely to cut across the firm's hierarchy and be composed of people from different functional areas. They are almost always temporary, although a large project, such as designing and building a new airplane at Boeing Corporation, may last for years.

At Google, small teams work on research and engineering projects that often last 6–12 months.
© Stuart Isett/Polaris/Newscom

Product-development teams are a special type of project team formed to devise, design, and implement a new product. Sometimes product-development teams exist within a functional area—research and development—but now they more frequently include people from numerous functional areas and may even include customers to help ensure that the end product meets the customers' needs. Intel informs its product-development process through indirect input from customers. It has a social scientist on staff who leads a research team on how customers actually use products. This is done mainly by observation and

YUM! BRANDS INC. DEVELOPS A CULTURE OF TEAM BUILDING AND EMPLOYEE RECOGNITION

Yum! Brands—the global fast food company behind KFC, Pizza Hut, and Taco Bell—has had a successful decade. Since being spun off from PepsiCo in 1997, it has provided its stockholders a return on investment over four times higher than the S&P 500 index and has become the world's largest restaurant company by number of stores (over 39,000 locations). What is the secret to its success? Analysts believe the company's unique culture consistently produces high-performing business teams.

The best-known feature of Yum! Brands' culture is a quirky but effective employee recognition system. According to CEO David Novak, recognizing and thanking teams for good work is extremely important, but most

company recognition efforts fail because they are not personalized, genuine, and timely. In Novak's view, a simple but heartfelt and immediate acknowledgement of a job well done is far more effective than an expensive but impersonal award, such as a ceremonial dinner or fancy trophy, given weeks later.

Novak puts his theory into an extreme form of practice. Before becoming CEO, as president of KFC, his award of choice was the classic rubber chicken. Now, he uses a teeth-on-legs toy known as the "Walk the Talk Award." The magic is in the recognition process itself; the award is given immediately after an employee or team impresses him, always with a personalized message written on the item and meant as a genuine acknowledgment of their value.

This practice is widespread throughout the company, with every Yum! Brands leader using his or her own unique award—from plastic hogs to roof tiles. Yum! Brands shows the benefits a company can experience with a unique corporate culture recognizing teamwork and employee efforts.[26]

Discussion Questions

1. Why would effective employee recognition lead to higher business team performance?

2. Why has Yum! Brands' unique recognition system succeeded where so many others fail?

3. Can you think of ways other companies could use Yum! Brands' award method?

asking questions. Once enough information is gathered, it is relayed to the product-development team and incorporated into the designs.[27]

Quality-Assurance Teams

Quality-assurance teams, sometimes called **quality circles**, are fairly small groups of workers brought together from throughout the organization to solve specific quality, productivity, or service problems. Although the *quality circle* term is not as popular as it once was, the concern about quality is stronger than ever. Companies such as IBM and Xerox as well as companies in the automobile industry have used quality circles to shift the organization to a more participative culture. The use of teams to address quality issues will no doubt continue to increase throughout the business world.

Self-directed Work Teams

A **self-directed work team (SDWT)** is a group of employees responsible for an entire work process or segment that delivers a product to an internal or external customer.[28] SDWTs permit the flexibility to change rapidly to meet the competition or respond to customer needs. The defining characteristic of an SDWT is the extent to which it is empowered or given authority to make and implement work decisions. Thus, SDWTs are designed to give employees a feeling of "ownership" of a whole job. Employees at 3M as well as an increasing number of companies encourage employees to be active to perform a function or operational task. With shared team responsibility for work outcomes, team members often have broader job assignments and cross-train to master other jobs, thus permitting greater team flexibility.

DID YOU KNOW?

A survey of employees revealed that approximately 65 percent consider how their employers communicate with them to be a key factor in their job satisfaction.[29]

employees. Intranets increase communication across different departments and levels of management and help with the flow of everyday business activities. Another innovative approach is cloud computing. Rather than using physical products, companies using cloud computing technology can access computing resources and information over a network. Cloud computing allows companies to have more control over computing resources and can be less expensive than hardware or software. Salesforce.com uses cloud computing in its customer relationship management solutions.[30] Companies can even integrate aspects of social media into their intranets, allowing employees to post comments and pictures, participate in polls, and create group calendars. However, increased access to the Internet at work has also created many problems, including employee abuse of company e-mail and Internet access.[31] The increasing use of e-mail as a communication tool also inundates employees and managers with e-mails, making it easier to overlook individual communications. For this reason, it is advised that employees place a specific subject in the subject line, keep e-mails brief, and avoid using e-mail if a problem would be better solved through face-to-face interaction.[32]

quality-assurance teams (or quality circles) small groups of workers brought together from throughout the organization to solve specific quality, productivity, or service problems.

self-directed work team (SDWT) a group of employees responsible for an entire work process or segment that delivers a product to an internal or external customer.

LO 7-7 Describe how communication occurs in organizations.

COMMUNICATING IN ORGANIZATIONS

Communication within an organization can flow in a variety of directions and from a number of sources, each using both oral and written forms of communication. The success of communication systems within the organization has a tremendous effect on the overall success of the firm. Communication mistakes can lower productivity and morale.

Alternatives to face-to-face communications—such as meetings—are growing, thanks to technology such as voice-mail, e-mail, social media, and online newsletters. Many companies use internal networks called intranets to share information with

Yammer is a social network that companies can use to connect employees with one another.
© *NetPhotos/Alamy*

Formal and Informal Communication

Formal channels of communication are intentionally defined and designed by the organization. They represent the flow of communication within the formal organizational structure, as shown on organizational charts. Table 7.2 describes the different forms of formal communication. Traditionally, formal communication patterns were classified as vertical and horizontal, but with the increased use of teams and matrix structures, formal communication may occur in a number of patterns (Figure 7.9).

Along with the formal channels of communication shown on an organizational chart, all firms communicate informally as well. Communication between friends, for instance, cuts across department, division, and even management–subordinate boundaries. Such friendships and other nonwork social relationships comprise the *informal organization* of a firm, and their impact can be great.

The most significant informal communication occurs through the **grapevine**, an informal channel of communication, separate from management's formal, official communication channels. Grapevines exist in all organizations. Information passed along the grapevine may relate to the job or organization, or it may be gossip and rumors unrelated to either. The accuracy of grapevine information has been of great concern to managers.

Managers can turn the grapevine to their advantage. Using it as a "sounding device" for possible new policies is one example. Managers can obtain valuable information from the grapevine that could improve decision making. Some

organizations use the grapevine to their advantage by floating ideas, soliciting feedback, and reacting accordingly. People love to gossip, and managers need to be aware that grapevines exist in every organization. Managers who understand how the grapevine works also can use it to their advantage by feeding it facts to squelch rumors and incorrect information. For instance, rather than confronting employees about gossip and placing them on the defense, some employers ask employees—especially those who are the spreaders of gossip—for assistance in squelching the untrue rumors. This tactic turns employees into advocates for sharing truthful information.[33]

Monitoring Communications

Technological advances and the increased use of electronic communication in the workplace have made monitoring its use necessary for most companies. Failing to monitor employees'

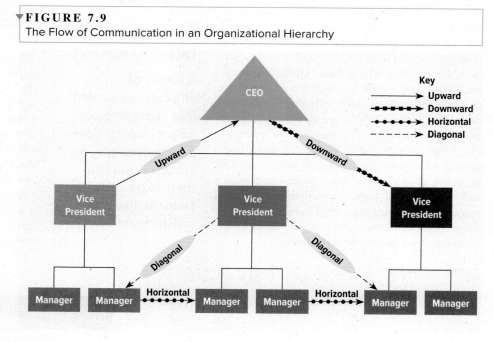

▼FIGURE 7.9
The Flow of Communication in an Organizational Hierarchy

▼ TABLE 7.2 Types of Formal Communication

Type	Definition	Examples
Upward	Flows from lower to higher levels of the organization	Progress reports, suggestions for improvement, inquiries, grievances
Downward	Traditional flow of communication from upper organizational levels to lower organizational levels	Directions, assignments of tasks and responsibilities, performance feedback, details about strategies and goals, speeches, employee handbooks, job descriptions
Horizontal	Exchange of information among colleagues and peers on the same organizational level, such as across or within departments, to inform, support, and coordinate activities both within the department and between other departments	Task forces, project teams, communication from the finance department to the marketing department concerning budget requirements
Diagonal	When individuals from different levels and different departments communicate	A manager from the finance department communicates with a lower-level manager from the marketing department

CRISIS MANAGEMENT FOCUSED ON COMMUNICATION

Founder and CEO of New Hampshire–based Rustic Crust Pizza, Brad Sterl, was out of town when he learned that the factory of his 18-year-old frozen pizza company had burned to the ground. This placed the livelihood of his more than 100 employees into jeopardy. The next day he contacted customers and brokers to reassure them the company would recover. In less than a week Sterl had gathered his employees together and formally communicated that they would continue to receive paychecks during the crisis. He made their objectives for recovery clear, and informed employees that the company would be running 24/7 for the next several months at a temporary facility. Sterl credits this employee communication as being the essential component to recovery.

He expanded his team by 30 individuals and—due to their strong relationship with the community—was able to quickly secure permits, receive backing for construction, and begin rebuilding. Even during this time period, Rustic Crust Pizza continued to pursue sales deals successfully, such as a securing a deal to supply 1,400 Safeway stores with its all-natural frozen pizza crusts.[35]

---

use of e-mail, social media, and the Internet can be costly. Many companies require that employees sign and follow a policy on appropriate Internet use. These agreements often require that employees will use corporate computers only for work-related activities. Additionally, several companies use software programs to monitor employee computer usage. Instituting practices that show respect for employee privacy but do not abdicate employer responsibility are increasingly necessary in today's workplace. Merck, for instance, has a section on employee privacy in its code of conduct that reassures both current and former employees that their information will be protected and used only for legitimate business purposes.[34]

Improving Communication Effectiveness

Without effective communication, the activities and overall productivity of projects, groups, teams, and individuals will be diminished. Communication is an important area for a firm to address at all levels of management. Apple supplier Foxconn is one example of how essential communication is to a firm. Despite criticisms of unfair labor conditions, the Fair Labor Association determined that Foxconn had formal procedures in place at its factories to prevent many major accidents. However, it concluded that the firm had a communication problem. These procedures were not being communicated to the factory workers, contributing to unsafe practices and two tragic explosions.[36]

One of the major issues of effective communication is obtaining feedback. If feedback is not provided, then communication will be ineffective and can drag down overall performance. Managers should always encourage feedback, including concerns and challenges about issues. Most employees listen much more than they actively communicate to others. It is interesting to note that employees list a failure to listen to their concerns as a top complaint in the workplace.[37] What this suggests is lack of feedback. Therefore, managers should encourage employees to provide feedback—even if it is negative. Employees often notice issues that managers overlook, and employee feedback can alert managers to these issues. This will allow the organization to identify strengths and weaknesses and make adjustments when needed. At the same time, strong feedback mechanisms help empower employees as they feel that their voices are being heard.

At the interpersonal level, interruptions can be a serious threat to effective communication. Various activities can interrupt the message. For example, interjecting a remark can create discontinuance in the communication process or disrupt the uniformity of the message. Even small interruptions can be a problem if the messenger cannot adequately understand or interpret the communicator's message. One suggestion is to give the communicator space or time to make another statement rather than quickly responding or making your own comment.

Strong and effective communication channels are a requirement for companies to distribute information to different levels of the company. Businesses have several channels for communication, including face-to-face, e-mail, phone, and written communication (for example, memos). Each channel has advantages and disadvantages, and some are more appropriate to use than others. For instance, a small task requiring little instruction might be communicated through a short memo or e-mail. An in-depth task would most likely require a phone conversation or face-to-face contact. E-mail has become especially helpful for businesses, and both employees and managers are increasingly using e-mail rather than memos or phone conversations. However, it is important that employees use e-mail correctly. Inappropriate use of e-mail can include forwarding sexually explicit or otherwise offensive material. Additionally,

> ### TEAM EXERCISE
> Assign the responsibility of providing the organizational structure for a company one of your team members has worked for. Was your organization centralized or decentralized in terms of decision making? Would you consider the span of control to be wide or narrow? Were any types of teams, committees, or task forces utilized in the organization? Report your work to the class.

SO YOU WANT A JOB // in Managing Organizational Culture, Teamwork, and Communication /

Jobs dealing with organizational culture and structure are usually at the top of the organization. If you want to be a CEO or high-level manager, you will help shape these areas of business. On the other hand, if you are an entrepreneur or small-business person, you will need to make decisions about assigning tasks, departmentalization, and assigning responsibility. Even managers in small organizations have to make decisions about decentralization, span of management, and forms of organizational structure. While these decisions may be part of your job, there are usually no job titles dealing with these specific areas. Specific jobs that attempt to improve organizational culture could include ethics and compliance positions as well as those who are in charge of communicating memos, manuals, and policies that help establish the culture. These positions will be in communications, human resources, and positions that assist top organizational managers.

Teams are becoming more common in the workplace, and it is possible to become a member of a product-development group or quality assurance team. There are also human resources positions that encourage teamwork through training activities. The area of corporate communications provides lots of opportunities for specific jobs that facilitate communication systems. Thanks to technology, there are job positions to help disseminate information through online newsletters, intranets, or internal computer networks to increase collaboration. In addition to the many advances using electronic communications, there are technology concerns that create new job opportunities. Monitoring workplace communications such as the use of e-mail and the Internet has created new industries. There have to be internal controls in the organization to make sure that the organization does not engage in any copyright infringement. If this is an area of interest, there are specific jobs that provide an opportunity to use your technological skills to assist in maintaining appropriate standards in communicating and using technology.

If you go to work for a large company with many divisions, you can expect a number of positions dealing with the tasks discussed here. If you go to work for a small company, you will probably engage in most of these tasks as a part of your position. Organizational flexibility requires individual flexibility, and those employees willing to take on new domains and challenges will be the employees who survive and prosper in the future.

many employees have used work e-mail accounts to send personal information. This may be against company policy. It is important for employees to remember that e-mail sent from corporate accounts is the property of the firm, so they should exert caution in making sure their e-mail messages contain appropriate content. It is therefore important for companies to communicate their e-mail policies throughout the organization. Communicators using e-mail, whether managers or employees, must exert caution before pushing that "Send" button.

Communication is necessary in helping every organizational member understand what is expected of him or her. Many business problems can be avoided if clear communication exists within the company. Even the best business strategies are of little use if those who will oversee them cannot understand what is intended. Communication might not seem to be as big of a concern to management as finances, human resources, and marketing, but in reality it can make the difference between successful implementation of business activities or failure. ■

chapter eight

managing service and
manufacturing operations

© Small_frog/Vetta/Getty Images, RF

All organizations create products—goods, services, or ideas—for customers. Thus, organizations as diverse as Toyota, Campbell Soup, UPS, and a public hospital share a number of similarities relating to how they transform resources into the products we consume. Most hospitals use similar admission procedures, while online social media companies, like Facebook and Twitter, use their technology and operating systems to create social networking opportunities and sell advertising. Such similarities are to be expected. But even organizations in unrelated industries take similar steps in creating goods or services. The check-in procedures of hotels and commercial airlines are comparable, for example. The way Subway assembles a sandwich and the way GMC assembles a truck are similar (both use automation and an assembly line). These similarities are the result of operations management, the focus of this chapter.

Here, we discuss the role of production or operations management in acquiring and managing the resources necessary to create goods and services. Production and operations management involves planning and designing the processes that will transform those resources into finished products, managing the movement of those resources through the transformation process, and ensuring that the products are of the quality expected by customers. ■

THE NATURE OF OPERATIONS MANAGEMENT

Operations management (OM), the development and administration of the activities involved in transforming resources into goods and services, is of critical importance. Operations managers oversee the transformation process and the planning and designing of operations systems, managing logistics, quality, and productivity. Quality and productivity have become fundamental aspects of operations management because a company that cannot make products of the quality desired by consumers, using resources efficiently and effectively, will not be able to remain in business. OM is the "core" of most organizations because it is responsible for the creation of the organization's goods and services. Some organizations like General Motors produce tangible products, but service is an important part of the total product for the customer.

Historically, operations management has been called "production" or "manufacturing" primarily because of the view that it was limited to the manufacture of physical goods. Its focus was on methods and techniques required to operate a factory efficiently. The change from "production" to "operations" recognizes the increasing importance of organizations that provide services and ideas. Additionally, the term *operations* represents an interest in viewing the operations function as a whole rather than simply as an analysis of inputs and outputs.

Today, OM includes a wide range of organizational activities and situations outside of manufacturing, such as health care, food service, banking, entertainment, education, transportation, and charity. Thus, we use the terms **manufacturing** and **production** interchangeably to represent the activities and processes used in making *tangible* products, whereas we use the broader term **operations** to describe those processes used in the making of *both tangible and intangible products*. Manufacturing provides tangible products such as Hewlett-Packard's latest printer, and operations provides intangibles such as a stay at Wyndham Hotels and Resorts.

The Transformation Process

At the heart of operations management is the transformation process through which **inputs** (resources such as labor, money, materials, and energy) are converted into **outputs** (goods, services, and ideas). The transformation process combines inputs in predetermined ways using different equipment, administrative procedures, and technology to create a product (Figure 8.1). To ensure that this process generates quality products efficiently, operations managers control the process by taking measurements (feedback)

operations management (OM) the development and administration of the activities involved in transforming resources into goods and services.

manufacturing the activities and processes used in making tangible products; also called production.

production the activities and processes used in making tangible products; also called manufacturing.

operations the activities and processes used in making both tangible and intangible products.

inputs the resources—such as labor, money, materials, and energy—that are converted into outputs.

outputs the goods, services, and ideas that result from the conversion of inputs.

at various points in the transformation process and comparing them to previously established standards. For example, if an airline has a standard of 90 percent of its flights departing on time but only 80 percent depart on time, a 10 percent negative deviation exists. If there is any deviation between the actual and desired outputs, the manager may take some sort of corrective action. All adjustments made to create a satisfying product are a part of the transformation process.

Transformation may take place through one or more processes. In a business that manufactures oak furniture, for example, inputs pass through several processes before being turned into the final outputs—furniture that has been designed to meet the desires of customers (Figure 8.2). The furniture maker must first strip the oak trees of their bark and saw them into appropriate sizes—one step in the transformation process. Next, the firm dries the strips of oak lumber, a second form of transformation. Third, the dried wood is routed into its appropriate shape and made smooth. Fourth, workers assemble and treat the wood pieces, then stain or varnish the piece of assembled furniture. Finally, the completed piece of furniture is stored

until it can be shipped to customers at the appropriate time. Of course, many businesses choose to eliminate some of these stages by purchasing already processed materials—lumber, for example—or outsourcing some tasks to third-party firms with greater expertise.

LO 8-2 Explain how operations management differs in manufacturing and service firms.

Operations Management in Service Businesses

Different types of transformation processes take place in organizations that provide services, such as airlines, colleges, and most nonprofit organizations. An airline transforms inputs such as employees, time, money, and equipment through processes such as booking flights, flying airplanes, maintaining equipment, and training crews. The output of these processes is flying passengers and/or packages to their destinations. In a nonprofit organization like Habitat for Humanity, inputs such as money, materials, information, and volunteer time and labor are used to transform raw materials into homes for needy families. In this setting, transformation processes include fund-raising and promoting the cause in order to gain new volunteers and donations of supplies, as well as pouring concrete, raising walls, and setting roofs. Transformation processes occur in all organizations, regardless of what they produce or their objectives. For most organizations, the ultimate objective is for the produced outputs to be worth more than the combined costs of the inputs.

Unlike tangible goods, services are effectively actions or performances that must be directed toward the consumers who use them. Thus, there is a significant customer-contact component to most services. Examples of high-contact services include health care, real estate, tax preparation, and food service. At the Inn at Little Washington in Washington, Virginia, for example, food servers are critical to delivering the perfect dining experience expected by the most discriminating diners. Wait staff are expected not only to be courteous, but also to demonstrate a detailed knowledge of the restaurant's offerings, and

FIGURE 8.1
The Transformation Process of Operations Management

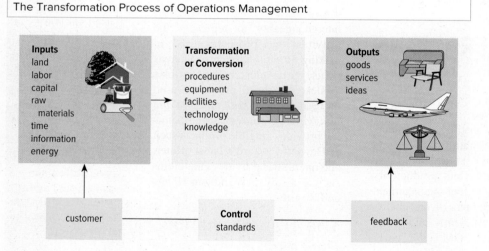

FIGURE 8.2
Inputs, Outputs, and Transformation Processes in the Manufacture of Oak Furniture

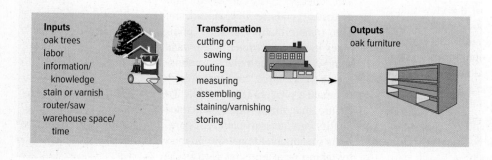

▼ **TABLE 8.1** Characteristics of Services

Service Characteristic	Examples
Intangibility	Going to a concert or sports event such as baseball, basketball, or football
Inseparability of production and consumption	Going to a chiropractor; air travel; veterinary services
Perishability	Seats at a speaker's presentation
Customization	Haircut; legal services
Customer contact	Restaurants; direct selling such as Tupperware parties

Sources: Adapted from Valerie A. Zeithaml, A. Parasuraman, and Leonard L. Berry, *Delivering Quality Service: Balancing Customer Perceptions and Expectations* (New York: Free Press, 1990); K. Douglas Hoffman and John E.G. Bateson, *Essentials of Services Marketing* (Mason, OH: Cengage Learning, 2001); Ian P. McCarthy, Leyland Pitt, and Pierre Berthon, "Service Customization through Dramaturgy," *Mass Customization*, 2011, pp. 45–65.

Businesses that manufacture tangible goods and those that provide services or ideas are similar yet different. For example, both types of organizations must make design and operating decisions. Most goods are manufactured prior to purchase, but most services are performed after purchase. Flight attendants at Southwest Airlines, hotel service personnel, and even the New York Giants football team engage in performances that are a part of the total product. Though manufacturers and service providers often perform similar activities, they also differ in several respects. We can classify these differences in five basic ways.

even to assess the mood of guests in order to respond to diners appropriately.[1] Low-contact services, such as online auction services like eBay, often have a strong high-tech component. Table 8.1 shows common characteristics of services.

Regardless of the level of customer contact, service businesses strive to provide a standardized process, and technology offers an interface that creates an automatic and structured response. The ideal service provider will be high tech and high touch.

Nature and Consumption of Output

First, manufacturers and service providers differ in the nature and consumption of their output. For example, the term *manufacturer* implies a firm that makes tangible products. A service provider, on the other hand, produces more intangible outputs such as U.S. Postal Service delivery of priority mail or a business stay in a Hyatt hotel. As mentioned earlier, the very nature of the service provider's product requires a higher degree of customer

> "Businesses that manufacture tangible goods and those that provide services or ideas are similar yet different."

JetBlue, for example, strives to maintain an excellent website; friendly, helpful customer contact; and satellite TV service at every seat on each plane. Thus, service organizations must build their operations around good execution, which comes from hiring and training excellent employees, developing flexible systems, customizing services, and maintaining adjustable capacity to deal with fluctuating demand.[2]

Another challenge related to service operations is that the output is generally intangible and even perishable. Few services can be saved, stored, resold, or returned.[3] A seat on an airline or a table in a restaurant, for example, cannot be sold or used at a later date. Because of the perishability of services, it can be extremely difficult for service providers to accurately estimate the demand in order to match the right supply of a service. If an airline overestimates demand, it will still have to fly each plane even with empty seats. The flight costs the same regardless of whether it is 50 percent full or 100 percent full, but the former will result in much higher costs per passenger. If the airline underestimates demand, the result can be long lines of annoyed customers or even the necessity of bumping some customers off of an overbooked flight.

contact. Moreover, the actual performance of the service typically occurs at the point of consumption. At the Hyatt, the business traveler may evaluate in-room communications and the restaurant. Automakers, on the other hand, can separate the production of a car from its actual use, but the service dimension requires closer contact with the consumer. Manufacturing, then, can occur in an isolated environment, away from the customer. However, service providers, because of their need for customer contact, are often more limited than manufacturers in selecting work methods, assigning jobs, scheduling work, and exercising control over operations. For this reason, Freddie Mac implemented the Quality Control Information Manager (QCIM) system, a secure, web-based system that allows lenders access to the status of quality control loan file requests. The system makes it easier to control this important aspect of lending.[4] The quality of the service experience is often controlled by a service contact employee. However, some hospitals are studying the manufacturing processes and quality control mechanisms applied in the automotive industry in an effort to improve their service quality. By analyzing work processes to find unnecessary steps to eliminate and using teams to identify and address problems as soon as they occur, these hospitals are

Subway's inputs are sandwich components such as bread, tomatoes, and lettuce, while its outputs are customized sandwiches.
© RosaIreneBetancourt 8/Alamy

slashing patient waiting times, decreasing inventories of wheel-chairs, readying operating rooms sooner, and generally moving patients through their hospital visit more quickly, with fewer errors, and at a lower cost.[5]

Uniformity of Inputs

A second way to classify differences between manufacturers and service providers has to do with the uniformity of inputs. Manufacturers typically have more control over the amount of variability of the resources they use than do service providers. For example, each customer calling Fidelity Investments is likely to require different services due to differing needs, whereas many of the tasks required to manu-facture a Ford Focus are the same across each unit of output. Consequently, the products of service organizations tend to be more "customized" than those of their manufacturing coun-terparts. Consider a haircut versus a bottle of shampoo. The haircut is much more likely to incorporate your specific desires (customization) than is the bottle of shampoo.

Uniformity of Output

Manufacturers and service providers also differ in the uniformity of their output, the final product. Because of the human element inherent in providing services, each service tends to be performed differently. Not all grocery checkers, for example, wait on customers in the same way. If a barber or stylist performs 15 haircuts in a day, it is unlikely that any two of them will be exactly the same. Consequently, human and technological elements associated with a service can result in a different day-to-day or even hour-to-hour perfor-mance of that service. The service experience can even vary at McDonald's or Burger King despite the fact that the two chains employ very similar procedures and processes. Moreover, no two customers are exactly alike in their perception of the ser-vice experience. Health care offers another excellent example

of this challenge. Every diagnosis, treatment, and surgery varies because every individual is differ-ent. In manufacturing, the high degree of automa-tion available allows manufacturers to generate uniform outputs and, thus, the operations are more effective and efficient. For example, we would expect every TAG Heuer or Rolex watch to maintain very high standards of quality and performance.

Labor Required

A fourth point of differ-ence is the amount of labor required to produce an output. Service providers are generally more labor-intensive (require more labor) because of the high level of customer contact, perishability of the output (must be consumed immediately), and high degree of variation of inputs and outputs (customization). For example, Adecco provides temporary support personnel. Each temporary worker's performance determines Adecco's prod-uct quality. A manufacturer, on the other hand, is likely to be more capital-intensive because of the machinery and technology used in the mass production of highly similar goods. For instance, it would take a considerable investment for Ford to make an electric car that has batteries with a longer life.

Measurement of Productivity

The final distinction between service providers and manufacturers involves the measurement of productivity for each output produced. For manufacturers, measuring productivity is fairly straightforward because of the tangibility of the output and its high degree of uniformity. For the service provider, variations in demand (for example, higher demand for air travel in some seasons than in others), variations in service requirements from job to job, and the intangibility of the product make productivity measurement more difficult. Consider, for example, how much easier it is to measure the productivity of employees involved in the pro-duction of Intel computer processors as opposed to serving the needs of Prudential Securities' clients.

It is convenient and simple to think of organizations as being either manufacturers or service providers as in the preceding discussion. In reality, however, most organizations are a com-bination of the two, with both tangible and intangible qualities embodied in what they produce. For example, Porsche pro-vides customer services such as toll-free hotlines and warranty protection, while banks may sell checks and other tangible products that complement their primarily intangible product offering. Thus, we consider "products" to include both tan-gible physical goods and intangible service offerings. It is the level of tangibility of its principal product that tends to clas-sify a company as either a manufacturer or a service provider. From an OM standpoint, this level of tangibility greatly influ-ences the nature of the company's operational processes and procedures.

standardization
the making of identical interchangeable components or products.

modular design
the creation of an item in self-contained units, or modules, that can be combined or interchanged to create different products.

PLANNING AND DESIGNING OPERATIONS SYSTEMS

Before a company can produce any product, it must first decide what it will produce and for what group of customers. It must then determine what processes it will use to make these products as well as the facilities it needs to produce them. These decisions comprise operations planning. Although planning was once the sole realm of the production and operations department, today's successful companies involve all departments within an organization, particularly marketing and research and development, in these decisions.

Planning the Product

Before making any product, a company first must determine what consumers want and then design a product to satisfy that want. Most companies use marketing research (discussed in Chapter 11) to determine the kinds of goods and services to provide and the features they must possess. Twitter and Facebook provide new opportunities for businesses to discover what consumers want, then design the product accordingly. Approximately 39 percent of retailers use social media to facilitate planning in the product-development process. Social media is an important tool for developing customer relationships, and 33 percent of retailers claim that they use customer relationship management to enhance business intelligence.[6] Marketing research can also help gauge the demand for a product and how much consumers are willing to pay for it. But when a market's environment changes, firms have to be flexible.

Developing a product can be a lengthy, expensive process. For example, in the automobile industry, developing the new technology for night vision, parking assist systems, and a satellite service that locates and analyzes car problems has been a lengthy, expensive process. Most companies work to reduce development time and costs. Intel and Micron created a joint venture to reduce development time and pool their resources in developing cutting-edge NAND Flash technology. NAND Flash technology is memory often used in smartphones and tablets. The two companies are continuing to partner together to create 3D NAND technology, which they hope will become the industry leader.[7] Once management has developed an idea for a product that customers will buy, it must then plan how to produce the product.

Within a company, the engineering or research and development department is charged with turning a product idea into a workable design that can be produced economically. In smaller companies, a single individual (perhaps the owner) may be solely responsible for this crucial activity. Regardless of who is responsible for product design, planning does not stop with a blueprint for a product or a description of a service; it must also work out efficient production of the product to ensure that enough is available to satisfy consumer demand. How does a lawn mower company transform steel, aluminum, and other materials into a mower design that satisfies consumer and environmental requirements? Operations managers must plan for the types and quantities of materials needed to produce the product, the skills and quantity of people needed to make the product, and the actual processes through which the inputs must pass in their transformation to outputs.

Designing the Operations Processes

Before a firm can begin production, it must first determine the appropriate method of transforming resources into the desired product. Often, consumers' specific needs and desires dictate a process. Customer needs, for example, require that all 3/4-inch bolts have the same basic thread size, function, and quality; if they did not, engineers and builders could not rely on 3/4-inch bolts in their construction projects. A bolt manufacturer, then, will likely use a standardized process so that every 3/4-inch bolt produced is like every other one. On the other hand, a bridge often must be customized so that it is appropriate for the site and expected load; furthermore, the bridge must be constructed on site rather than in a factory. Typically, products are designed to be manufactured by one of three processes: standardization, modular design, or customization.

Standardization Most firms that manufacture products in large quantities for many customers have found that they can make them cheaper and faster by standardizing designs. **Standardization** is making identical, interchangeable components or even complete products. With standardization, a customer may not get exactly what he or she wants, but the product generally costs less than a custom-designed product. Television sets, ballpoint pens, and tortilla chips are standardized products; most are manufactured on an assembly line. Standardization speeds up production and quality control and reduces production costs. And, as in the example of the 3/4-inch bolts, standardization provides consistency so that customers who need certain products to function uniformly all the time will get a product that meets their expectations. Standardization becomes more complex on a global scale because different countries have different standards for quality. To help solve this problem, the International Organization for Standardization (ISO) has developed a list of global standards that companies can adopt to assure stakeholders that they are complying with the highest quality, environmental, and managerial guidelines.

Modular Design **Modular design** involves building an item in self-contained units, or modules, that can be combined or interchanged to create different products. IKEA furniture, for

customization making products to meet a particular customer's needs or wants.

capacity the maximum load that an organizational unit can carry or operate.

fixed-position layout a layout that brings all resources required to create the product to a central location.

example, embodies a modular design with several components. This allows for customers to mix and match components for customized design. Because many modular components are produced as integrated units, the failure of any portion of a modular component usually means replacing the entire component. Modular design allows products to be repaired quickly, thus reducing the cost of labor, but the component itself is expensive, raising the cost of repair materials. Many automobile manufacturers use modular design in the production process. Manufactured homes are built on a modular design and often cost about one-fourth the cost of a conventionally built house.

Customization

Customization is making products to meet a particular customer's needs or wants. Products produced in this way are generally unique. Such products include repair services, photocopy services, custom artwork, jewelry, and furniture, as well as large-scale products such as bridges, ships, and computer software. For instance, bicycles are popular products to customize. A company called Breadwinner Cycles designs eight models of bicycles in such a way that riders can customize various features and sizes to fit their specific needs.[8] Mass customization relates to making products that meet the needs or wants of a large number of individual customers. The customer can select the model, size, color, style, or design of the product. Dell can customize a computer with the exact configuration that fits a customer's needs. Services such as fitness programs and travel packages can also be custom designed for a large number of individual customers. For both goods and services, customers get to make choices and have options to determine the final product.

Planning Capacity

Planning the operational processes for the organization involves two important areas: capacity planning and facilities planning. The term **capacity** basically refers to the maximum load that an organizational unit can carry or operate. The unit of measurement may be a worker or machine, a department, a branch, or even an entire plant. Maximum capacity can be stated in terms of the inputs or outputs provided. For example, an electric plant might state plant capacity in terms of the maximum number of kilowatt-hours that can be produced without causing a power outage, while a restaurant might state capacity in terms of the maximum

DID YOU KNOW?

Hershey's has the production capacity to make more than 80 million chocolate kisses per day.[9]

number of customers who can be effectively—comfortably and courteously—served at any one particular time.

Efficiently planning the organization's capacity needs is an important process for the operations manager. Capacity levels that fall short can result in unmet demand, and consequently, lost customers. On the other hand, when there is more capacity available than needed, operating costs are driven up needlessly due to unused and often expensive resources. To avoid such situations, organizations must accurately forecast demand and then plan capacity based on these forecasts. Another reason for the importance of efficient capacity planning has to do with long-term commitment of resources. Often, once a capacity decision—such as factory size—has been implemented, it is very difficult to change the decision without incurring substantial costs. Large companies have come to realize that although change can be expensive, not adjusting to future demand and stakeholder desires will be more expensive in the long run. For this reason, Toyota and its subsidiaries have acquired ISO 14001 certification at many of its locations worldwide.[10] These systems help firms monitor their impact on the environment.

Planning Facilities

Once a company knows what process it will use to create its products, it then can design and build an appropriate facility in which to make them. Many products are manufactured in factories, but others are produced in stores, at home, or where the product ultimately will be used. Companies must decide where to locate their operations facilities, what layout is best for producing their particular product, and even what technology to apply to the transformation process.

Many firms are developing both a traditional organization for customer contact and a virtual organization. Charles Schwab Corporation, a securities brokerage and investment company, maintains traditional offices and has developed complete telephone and Internet services for customers. Through its website, investors can obtain personal investment information and trade securities over the Internet without leaving their home or office.

Facility Location Where to locate a firm's facilities is a significant question because, once the decision has been made and implemented, the firm must live with it due to the high costs involved. When a company decides to relocate or open a facility at a new location, it must pay careful attention to factors such as proximity to market, availability of raw materials, availability of transportation, availability of power, climatic influences, availability of labor, community

Apple stores are designed to make the most efficient use of space. The layout of the stores allows customers to test its products before purchasing.
© *Mark Lennihan/AP Images*

characteristics (quality of life), and taxes and inducements. Inducements and tax reductions have become an increasingly important criterion in recent years. Nevada offered tax breaks to Tesla so that the company would locate its $5 billion battery factory within the state. The tax breaks exempt the company from paying property taxes for 10 years, as well as sales, local sales, and excise taxes for 25 years.[11] Apple has followed the lead of other major companies by locating its manufacturing facilities in Asia to take advantage of lower labor and production costs. The facility-location decision is complex because it involves the evaluation of many factors, some of which cannot be measured with precision. Because of the long-term impact of the decision, however, it is one that cannot be taken lightly.

Facility Layout Arranging the physical layout of a facility is a complex, highly technical task. Some industrial architects specialize in the design and layout of certain types of businesses. There are three basic layouts: fixed-position, process, and product.

A company using a **fixed-position layout** brings all resources required to create the product to a central location. The product—perhaps an office building, house, hydroelectric plant, or bridge—does not move. A company using a fixed-position layout may be called a **project organization** because it is typically involved in large, complex projects such as construction or exploration. Project organizations generally make a unique product, rely on highly skilled labor, produce very few units, and have high production costs per unit.

Firms that use a **process layout** organize the transformation process into departments that group related processes. A metal fabrication plant, for example, may have a cutting department, a drilling department, and a polishing department. A hospital

project organization
a company using a fixed-position layout because it is typically involved in large, complex projects such as construction or exploration.

process layout a layout that organizes the transformation process into departments that group related processes.

may have an X-ray unit, an obstetrics unit, and so on. These types of organizations are sometimes called **intermittent organizations**, which deal with products of a lesser magnitude than do project organizations, and their products are not necessarily unique but possess a significant number of differences. Doctors, makers of custom-made cabinets, commercial printers, and advertising agencies are intermittent organizations because they tend to create products to customers' specifications and produce relatively few units of each product. Because of the low level of output, the cost per unit of product is generally high.

The **product layout** requires that production be broken down into relatively simple tasks assigned to workers, who are usually positioned along an assembly line. Workers remain in one location, and the product moves from one worker to another. Each person in turn performs his or her required tasks or activities. Companies that use assembly lines are usually known as **continuous manufacturing organizations**, so named because once they are set up, they run continuously, creating products with many similar characteristics. Examples of products produced on assembly lines are automobiles, television sets, vacuum cleaners, toothpaste, and meals from a cafeteria. Continuous manufacturing organizations using a product layout are characterized by the standardized product they produce, the large number of units produced, and the relatively low unit cost of production.

> " Every industry has a basic, underlying technology that dictates the nature of its transformation process. "

Many companies actually use a combination of layout designs. For example, an automobile manufacturer may rely on an assembly line (product layout) but may also use a process layout to manufacture parts.

Technology Every industry has a basic, underlying technology that dictates the nature of its transformation process. The steel industry continually tries to improve steelmaking techniques. The health care industry performs research into medical technologies and pharmaceuticals to improve the quality of health care service. Two developments that have strongly influenced the operations of many businesses are computers and robotics.

Computers have been used for decades and on a relatively large scale since IBM introduced its 650 series in the late 1950s. The operations function makes great use of computers in all phases of the transformation process. **Computer-assisted design (CAD)**, for example, helps engineers design components, products, and processes on the computer instead of on paper. CAD is used in 3D printing. CAD software is used to develop a 3D image. Then, the CAD file is sent to the printer. The printer is able to use layers of liquid, powder, paper, or metal to construct a 3D model.[13] **Computer-assisted manufacturing (CAM)** goes a step further, employing specialized computer systems to actually guide and control the transformation processes. Such systems

IROBOT: ROBOTS FOR THE REAL WORLD

The story of iRobot begins with three smart people who loved building robots. Rodney Brooks, an MIT professor, and Colin Angle and Helen Greiner, both MIT students, founded the company in 1990. Their vision was to build robots for the real world, not just for scientists in labs, and take the first step toward fulfilling the dream of useful household automation sparked by shows like *The Jetsons*. However, this did not happen overnight; the company spent its first decade on contract work, building specialized robots for research labs and large companies, and barely remaining solvent in the process.

Everything changed in 2002 when iRobot released the Roomba—the smash hit autonomous vacuum cleaner. The product took iRobot from $15 million in 2002 to $94 million in 2004 (as of 2014, the company's sales were over $500 million). Although the Roomba is iRobot's best-known invention, the company has also developed innovative robots to assist search-and-rescue teams, military operations, and remote business collaboration and medical care. Thanks to iRobot, we are one step closer to living in the future.[12]

can monitor the transformation process, gathering information about the equipment used to produce the products and about the product itself as it goes from one stage of the transformation process to the next. The computer provides information to an operator who may, if necessary, take corrective action. In some highly automated systems, the computer itself can take corrective action. At Dell's OptiPlex Plant, electronic instructions are sent to double-decker conveyor belts that speed computer components to assembly stations. Two-member teams are told by computers which PC or server to build, with initial assembly taking only three to four minutes. Then more electronic commands move the products to a finishing area to be customized, boxed, and sent to waiting delivery trucks.

Using **flexible manufacturing**, computers can direct machinery to adapt to different versions of similar operations. For example, with instructions from a computer, one machine can be programmed to carry out its function for several different versions of an engine without shutting down the production line for refitting.

The use of drones in business operations would vastly change the technology landscape. Drones refer to unmanned aerial vehicles and have long been used in military operations. Amazon generated excitement when CEO Jeff Bezos announced the company's future intention to use drone aircraft to deliver packages to customers in as little as 30 minutes. It is estimated that drones could save Amazon $2 per delivery. Despite its promise, use of drone technology for operations such as delivery services is uncertain due to regulatory concerns. The Federal Aviation Administration released regulations that would require drones to remain in visual site of their operators. While this represents an obstacle for companies in using drones for long-distance delivery, they continue to work toward more favorable legislation. Drones are estimated to generate $10 billion in new spending within the next 10 years.[14]

Robots are also becoming increasingly useful in the transformation process. These "steel-collar" workers have become particularly important in industries such as nuclear power, hazardous-waste disposal, ocean research, and space construction and maintenance, in which human lives would otherwise be at risk. Robots are used in numerous applications by companies around the world. Many assembly operations—cars, television sets, telephones, stereo equipment, and numerous other products—depend on industrial robots. As the field of robotics becomes more sophisticated, costs for robots are becoming more affordable for smaller factories. One toy manufacturer in Pennsylvania paid $25,000 for a robot that it uses to move parts and perform assembly functions. Researchers continue to make more sophisticated robots, extending their use beyond manufacturing and space programs to various industries, including laboratory research, education, medicine, and household activities.[15] There are many advantages in using robotics, such as more successful surgeries, reshoring manufacturing activities back to America, energy conservation, and safer work practices.[16]

When all these technologies—CAD/CAM, flexible manufacturing, robotics, computer systems, and more—are integrated, the result is **computer-integrated manufacturing (CIM)**, a complete system that designs products, manages machines and materials, and controls the operations function. Companies adopt CIM to boost productivity and quality and reduce costs. Such technology, and computers in particular, will continue to make strong inroads into operations on two fronts—one dealing with the technology involved in manufacturing and one dealing with the administrative functions and processes used by operations managers. The operations manager must be willing to work with computers and other forms of technology and to develop a high degree of computer literacy.

Sustainability and Manufacturing

Manufacturing and operations systems are moving quickly to establish environmental sustainability and minimize negative impact on the natural environment. Sustainability deals with conducting activities in such a way as to provide for the long-term well-being of the natural environment, including all biological entities. Sustainability issues are becoming increasingly important to stakeholders and consumers, as they pertain to the future health of the planet. Some sustainability issues include pollution of the land, air, and water, climate change, waste management, deforestation, urban sprawl, protection of biodiversity, and genetically modified foods.

For example, Biogen Idec, the world's oldest biotechnology company, set a goal to increase sustainability of operations in water, energy, and materials usage by 15 percent in 2015. The company reached this goal in 2012 by using an internally developed tool called Risk-Weighted Environmental Index to measure the impact of its operations on the environment. As a result, the company was awarded a spot on the Dow Jones Sustainability World Index. Biogen Idec is the first American biotechnology company to be awarded this honor.[17]

New Belgium Brewing is another company that illustrates green initiatives in operations and manufacturing. New Belgium was the first brewery to adopt 100 percent wind-powered electricity, reducing carbon emissions by 1,800 metric tons a year. It uses a steam condenser to capture hot water to be reused for boiling the next batch of barley and hops. Then the steam is redirected to heat the floor tiles and de-ice the loading docks in cold Colorado weather. Used barley and hops are given to local farmers to feed cattle. The company is moving to aluminum cans because they can be recycled an infinite number of times, and recycling one can

FOOD GIANTS INVESTING IN SUSTAINABILITY

When most people think of companies' sustainability efforts, they consider activities such as powering their businesses with renewable energy or reducing waste. However, one major way of increasing sustainability that is often overlooked involves developing a greener supply chain. A number of the biggest packaged and processed food companies are taking significant steps toward more sustainable shipping practices. Three of these companies include General Mills, Smithfield Foods, and Mars.

With $18 billion in annual sales, General Mills's operation and supply chain practices have a major influence on the environment. In five years it reduced solid-waste generation by 33 percent, energy consumption by 6 percent, and greenhouse gas emission rates by 6 percent. The company has also committed to a 2020 goal of sustainably sourcing its top 10 ingredients, which represent 50 percent of its total raw material purchases.

As the world's largest pork producer and processor, Smithfield earns $13 billion in revenue. Although it has been fined in the past for environmental violations, the company hired a chief sustainability officer, plans to reduce water and energy consumption by 10 percent, and intends to create a zero-waste-to-landfill facility for each independent subsidiary it owns. In terms of shipping, Smithfield is undertaking packaging reduction projects to reduce waste.

The $33 billion Mars company promised that by 2040, its offices and factories will use no fossil fuels and emit no greenhouse gases. It also has goals for the immediate future, including sending zero waste to landfill in 2015. It also seeks to reduce negative environmental effects of its supply chain through packaging reduction projects and plans to source all seafood products 100 percent sustainably by 2020.[18]

🔵 Discussion Questions

1. Why might these companies be focusing on improving their sustainability practices?

2. Describe some of the ways that these companies are increasing sustainability in their supply chains?

3. Why is it important not to overlook the supply chain when considering a company's sustainability efforts?

The outdoor clothing company Patagonia is always looking for a greener way to design, produce, and recycle its products. The company's mission statement: Build the best product, cause no unnecessary harm, and use business to inspire and implement solutions to the environmental crisis.
© Jonathan Alcorn/ZUMA Press, Inc/Alamy

save enough electricity to run a television for three hours or save a half gallon of gasoline.

Biogen Idec and New Belgium Brewing demonstrate that reducing waste, recycling, conserving, and using renewable energy not only protect the environment, but can also gain the support of stakeholders. Green operations and manufacturing can improve a firm's reputation along with customer and employee loyalty, leading to improved profits.

Much of the movement to green manufacturing and operations is the belief that global warming and climate change must decline. The McKinsey Global Institute (MGI) says that just by investing in existing technologies, the world's energy use could be reduced by 50 percent by the year 2020. Creating green buildings and higher mileage cars could yield $900 billion in savings per year by 2020.[19] Companies like General Motors and Ford are adapting to stakeholder demands for greater sustainability by producing smaller and more fuel-efficient cars. Tesla has taken sustainability even further by making a purely electric vehicle that also ranks at the top in safety. The company also makes sure that its manufacturing facilities operate sustainably by installing solar panels and using other renewable sources of energy. Green products produced through green operations and manufacturing are our future. A report authored by the Center for American Progress cites ways that cities and local governments can play a role. For example, Los Angeles plans to save the city utility costs by retrofitting hundreds of city buildings while creating a green careers training program for low-income residents. Newark, New Jersey, and Richmond, California, also have green jobs training programs.[20] Government initiatives provide space for businesses to innovate their green operations and manufacturing.

LO 8-4 Specify some techniques managers may use to manage the logistics of transforming inputs into finished products.

MANAGING THE SUPPLY CHAIN

A major function of operations is **supply chain management**, which refers to connecting and integrating all parties or members of the distribution system in order to satisfy customers.[21] Also called logistics, supply chain management includes all the activities involved in obtaining and managing raw materials and component parts, managing finished products, packaging them, and getting them to customers. UPS implemented a cloud-based supply chain management system to better control international operations. This allowed for more accuracy and on-time delivery of shipments, better management and coordination of suppliers, and real-time shipment status of packages.[22] The supply chain integrates firms such as raw material suppliers, manufacturers, retailers, and ultimate consumers into a seamless flow of information and products.[23] Some aspects of logistics (warehousing, packaging, distributing) are so closely linked with marketing that we will discuss them in Chapter 12. In this section, we look at purchasing, managing inventory, outsourcing, and scheduling, which are vital tasks in the transformation of raw materials into finished goods. To illustrate logistics, consider a hypothetical small business—we'll call it Rushing Water Canoes Inc.—that manufactures aluminum canoes, which it sells primarily to sporting goods stores and river-rafting expeditions. Our company also makes paddles and helmets, but the focus of the following discussion is the manufacture of the company's quality canoes as they proceed through the logistics process.

Purchasing

Purchasing, also known as procurement, is the buying of all the materials needed by the organization. The purchasing department aims to obtain items of the desired quality in the right quantities at the lowest possible cost. Rushing Water Canoes, for example, must procure not only aluminum and other raw materials, and various canoe parts and components, but also machines and equipment, manufacturing supplies (oil, electricity, and so on), and office supplies in order to make its canoes. People in the purchasing department locate and evaluate suppliers of these items. They must constantly be on the lookout for new materials or parts that will do a better job or cost less than those currently being used. The purchasing function can be quite complex and is one area made much easier and more efficient by technological advances.

Not all companies purchase all of the materials needed to create their products. Oftentimes, they can make some components more economically and efficiently than can an outside supplier. Zara, a Spanish fast fashion retailer, manufactures the majority of the clothes it sells.[24] On the other hand, firms sometimes find that it is uneconomical to make or purchase an item, and instead arrange to lease it from another organization. Some airlines lease airplanes rather than buy them. Whether to purchase, make, or lease a needed item generally depends on cost, as well as on product availability and supplier reliability.

Managing Inventory

Once the items needed to create a product have been procured, some provision has to be made for storing them until they are needed. Every raw material, component, completed or partially completed product, and piece of equipment a firm uses—its **inventory**—must be accounted for, or controlled. There are three basic types of inventory. *Finished-goods inventory* includes those products that are ready for sale, such as a fully assembled automobile ready to ship to a dealer. *Work-in-process inventory* consists of those products that are partly completed or are in some stage of the transformation process. At McDonald's, a cooking hamburger represents work-in-process inventory because it must go through several more stages before it can be sold to a customer. *Raw materials inventory* includes all the materials that have been purchased to be used as inputs for making other products. Nuts and bolts are raw materials for an automobile manufacturer, while hamburger patties, vegetables, and buns are raw materials for the fast-food restaurant. Our fictional Rushing Water Canoes has an inventory of materials for making canoes, paddles, and helmets, as well as its inventory of finished products for sale to consumers.

supply chain management connecting and integrating all parties or members of the distribution system in order to satisfy customers.

purchasing the buying of all the materials needed by the organization; also called procurement.

inventory all raw materials, components, completed or partially completed products, and pieces of equipment a firm uses.

inventory control the process of determining how many supplies and goods are needed and keeping track of quantities on hand, where each item is, and who is responsible for it.

economic order quantity (EOQ) model a model that identifies the optimum number of items to order to minimize the costs of managing (ordering, storing, and using) them.

just-in-time (JIT) inventory management a technique using smaller quantities of materials that arrive "just in time" for use in the transformation process and therefore require less storage space and other inventory management expense.

purchase of insurance to cover any losses that might occur due to fire or other unforeseen events.

Inventory managers spend a great deal of time trying to determine the proper inventory level for each item. The answer to the question of how many units to hold in inventory depends on variables such as the usage rate of the item, the cost of maintaining the item in inventory, future costs of inventory and other procedures associated with ordering or making the item, and the cost of the item itself. For example, the price of copper has fluctuated between $2.00 and $4.50 a pound over the past five years.[25] Firms using copper wiring for construction, copper pipes for plumbing, and other industries requiring copper have to analyze the trade-offs between inventory costs and expected changes in the price of copper. Several approaches may be used to determine how many units of a given item should be procured at one time and when that procurement should take place.

The Economic Order Quantity Model To control the number of items maintained in inventory, managers need to determine how much of any given item they should order. One popular approach is the **economic order quantity (EOQ) model**, which identifies the optimum number of items to order to minimize the costs of managing (ordering, storing, and using) them.

Just-in-Time Inventory Management An increasingly popular technique is **just-in-time (JIT) inventory management**, which eliminates waste by using smaller quantities of materials that arrive "just in time" for use in the transformation process and therefore require less storage space and other inventory management expense. JIT minimizes inventory by providing an almost continuous flow of items from suppliers to the production facility. Many U.S. companies, including Hewlett-Packard, IBM, and Harley-Davidson, have adopted JIT to reduce costs and boost efficiency.

Let's say that Rushing Water Canoes uses 20 units of aluminum from a supplier per day. Traditionally, its inventory manager might order enough for one month at a time: 440 units per order (20 units per day times 22 workdays per month). The expense of such a large inventory could be considerable because of the cost of insurance coverage, recordkeeping, rented storage space, and so on. The just-in-time approach would reduce these costs because aluminum would be purchased in smaller quantities, perhaps in lot sizes of 20, which the supplier would deliver once a day. Of course, for such an approach to be effective, the supplier must be extremely reliable and relatively close to the production facility.

On the other hand, there are some downsides to just-in-time inventory management that marketers must take into account. When the earthquake and tsunami hit Japan, resulting in a nuclear reactor crisis, several Japanese companies halted their

Operations managers are concerned with managing inventory to ensure that there is enough inventory in stock to meet demand.
© Andersen Ross/Digital Vision/Jupiter Images, RF

Inventory control is the process of determining how many supplies and goods are needed and keeping track of quantities on hand, where each item is, and who is responsible for it.

Operations management must be closely coordinated with inventory control. The production of televisions, for example, cannot be planned without some knowledge of the availability of all the necessary materials—the chassis, picture tubes, color guns, and so forth. Also, each item held in inventory—any type of inventory—carries with it a cost. For example, storing fully assembled televisions in a warehouse to sell to a dealer at a future date requires not only the use of space, but also the

The American icon Levi Strauss & Co. has outsourced many of its jobs overseas.
© *Helen Sessions / Alamy*

operations. Some multinationals relied so much upon their Japanese suppliers that their supply chains were also affected. In the case of natural disasters, having only enough inventory to meet current needs could create delays in production and hurt the company's bottom line. For this reason, many economists suggest that businesses store components that are essential for production and diversify their supply chains. That way, if a natural disaster knocks out a major supplier, the company can continue to operate.[26]

Material-requirements Planning Another inventory management technique is **material-requirements planning (MRP)**, a planning system that schedules the precise quantity of materials needed to make the product. The basic components of MRP are a master production schedule, a bill of materials, and an inventory status file. At Rushing Water Canoes, for example, the inventory-control manager will look at the production schedule to determine how many canoes the company plans to make. He or she will then prepare a bill of materials—a list of all

the materials needed to make that quantity of canoes. Next, the manager will determine the quantity of these items that RWC already holds in inventory (to avoid ordering excess materials) and then develop a schedule for ordering and accepting delivery of the right quantity of materials to satisfy the firm's needs. Because of the large number of parts and materials that go into a typical production process, MRP must be done on a computer. It can be, and often is, used in conjunction with just-in-time inventory management.

Outsourcing

Increasingly, outsourcing has become a component of supply chain management in operations. As we mentioned in Chapter 3, outsourcing refers to the contracting of manufacturing or other tasks to independent companies, often overseas. Many companies elect to outsource some aspects of their operations to companies that can provide these products more efficiently, at a lower cost, and with greater customer satisfaction. Globalization has put pressure on supply chain managers to improve speed and balance resources against competitive pressures. Companies outsourcing to China, in particular, face heavy regulation, high transportation costs, inadequate facilities, and unpredictable supply chain execution. Therefore, suppliers need to provide useful, timely, and accurate information about every aspect of the quality requirements, schedules, and solutions to dealing with problems. Companies that hire suppliers must also make certain that their suppliers are following company standards; failure to do so could lead to criticism of the parent company. For example, Tesco, a British grocery chain, had to reevaluate its supply chain after some meat sold in its stores was found to have traces of horse meat. Some changes included sourcing meat from closer locations and conducting DNA testing on meat.[27]

Many high-tech firms have outsourced the production of chips, computers, and telecom equipment to Asian companies. The hourly labor costs in countries such as China, India, and Vietnam are far less than in the United States, Europe, or even Mexico. These developing countries have improved their manufacturing capabilities, infrastructure, and technical and business skills, making them more attractive regions for global sourcing. For instance, Nike outsources almost all of its production to Asian countries such as China and Vietnam. On the other hand, the cost of outsourcing halfway around the world must be considered in decisions. While information technology is often outsourced today, transportation, human resources, services, and even marketing functions can also be outsourced. Our hypothetical Rushing Water Canoes might contract with a local janitorial service to clean its offices and with a local accountant to handle routine bookkeeping and tax-preparation functions.

Outsourcing, once used primarily as a cost-cutting tactic, has increasingly been linked with the development of competitive

routing the sequence of operations through which the product must pass.

scheduling the assignment of required tasks to departments or even specific machines, workers, or teams.

advantage through improved product quality, speeding up the time it takes products to get to the customer, and overall supply-chain efficiencies. Table 8.2 provides the world's top five outsourcing providers that assist mainly in information technology.

Outsourcing allows companies to free up time and resources to focus on what they do best and to create better opportunities to focus on customer satisfaction. Many executives view outsourcing as an innovative way to boost productivity and remain competitive against low-wage offshore factories. However, outsourcing may create conflict with labor and negative public opinion when it results in U.S. workers being replaced by lower-cost workers in other countries.

Routing and Scheduling

After all materials have been procured and their use determined, managers must then consider the **routing**, or sequence of operations through which the product must pass. For example, before employees at Rushing Water Canoes can form aluminum sheets into a canoe, the aluminum must be cut to size. Likewise, the canoe's flotation material must be installed before workers can secure the wood seats. The sequence depends on the product specifications developed by the engineering department of the company.

Once management knows the routing, the actual work can be scheduled. **Scheduling** assigns the tasks to be done to departments or even specific machines, workers, or teams. At Rushing Water, cutting aluminum for the company's canoes might be scheduled to be done by the "cutting and finishing" department on machines designed especially for that purpose.

Many approaches to scheduling have been developed, ranging from simple trial and error to highly sophisticated computer

> "Many executives view outsourcing as an innovative way to boost productivity and remain competitive against low-wage offshore factories."

programs. One popular method is the *Program Evaluation and Review Technique (PERT),* which identifies all the major activities or events required to complete a project, arranges them in a sequence or path, determines the critical path, and estimates the time required for each event. Producing a McDonald's Big Mac, for example, involves removing meat, cheese, sauce, and vegetables from the refrigerator; grilling the hamburger patties; assembling the ingredients; placing the completed Big Mac in its package; and serving it to the customer (Figure 8.3). The cheese, pickles, onions, and sauce cannot be put on before the hamburger patty is completely grilled and placed on the bun. The path that requires the longest time from start to finish is called the *critical path* because it determines the minimum amount of time in which the process can be completed. If any of the activities on the critical path for production of the Big Mac fall behind schedule, the sandwich will not be completed on time, causing customers to wait longer than they usually would.

LO 8-5 Assess the importance of quality in operations management.

MANAGING QUALITY

Quality, like cost and efficiency, is a critical element of operations management, for defective products can quickly ruin a firm. Quality reflects the degree to which a good or service meets the demands and requirements of customers. Customers are increasingly dissatisfied with the quality of service provided by many airlines. Table 8.3 gives the rankings of U.S. airlines in certain operational areas. Determining quality can be difficult because it depends on customers' perceptions of how well the product meets or exceeds their expectations. For example, customer satisfaction on airlines can vary wildly depending on individual customers' perspectives. However, the airline industry is notorious for its dissatisfied customers. Flight delays are a common complaint from airline passengers; 30 percent of all flights arrive late. But most passengers do not select an airline based on how often flights arrive on time.[28]

The fuel economy of an automobile or its reliability (defined in terms of frequency of repairs) can be measured with some degree of precision. Although automakers rely on their own measures of vehicle

▼ **TABLE 8.2** The World's Top Five Outsourcing Providers

Company	Services
ISS	Facility services
Accenture	Management consulting, technology, and outsourcing
CBRE	Commercial real estate services
Kelly Outsourcing and Consulting Group	Business services and solutions
Colliers International	Commercial real estate services

Source: International Association of Outsourcing, "The 2014 Global Outsourcing 100," www.iaop .org/Content/19/165/3879 (accessed March 11, 2015).

quality, they also look to independent sources such as the J.D. Power & Associates annual initial quality survey for confirmation of their quality assessment as well as consumer perceptions of quality for the industry, as indicated in Figure 8.4.

It is especially difficult to measure quality characteristics when the product is a service. A company has to decide exactly which quality characteristics it considers important and then define those characteristics in terms that can be measured. The inseparability of production and consumption and the level of customer contact influence the selection of characteristics of the service that are most important. Employees in high-contact services such as hairstyling, education, legal

services, and even the barista at Starbucks are an important part of the product.

The Malcolm Baldrige National Quality Award is given each year to companies that meet rigorous standards of quality. The Baldrige criteria are (1) leadership, (2) information and analysis, (3) strategic planning, (4) human resources development and management, (5) process management, (6) business results, and (7) customer focus and satisfaction. The criteria have become a worldwide framework for driving business improvement. Four organizations won the award in 2014 representing three different categories: PricewaterhouseCoopers Public Sector Practice (service); Hill Country Memorial and St. David's HealthCare (health care); and Elevations Credit Union (nonprofit).[29]

▼FIGURE 8.3
A Hypothetical PERT Diagram for a McDonald's Big Mac

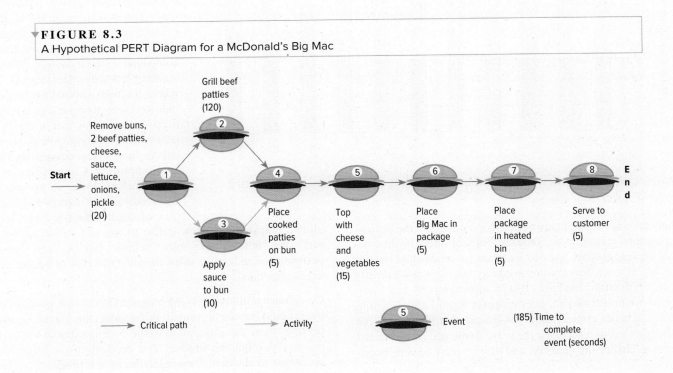

▼ **TABLE 8.3** Airline Scorecard (Best to Worst)

Rank	Overall Rank	On-Time Arrival	Canceled Flights	Extreme Delays	Mishandled Baggage	Involuntary Bumping	Complaints
1	Alaska	Alaska	Virgin American	Alaska	Virgin American	Virgin American	Alaska
2	Virgin American	Delta	Frontier	Delta	Frontier	jetBlue	Southwest
3	Delta	Virgin American	Alaska	Virgin American	jetBlue	Alaska	Delta
4	jetBlue	jetBlue	Southwest	Southwest	Delta	Delta	Virgin American
5	Southwest	American	Delta	jetBlue	Alaska	American	jetBlue
6	Frontier	Frontier	jetBlue	Frontier	American	Southwest	American
7	American	Southwest	American	American	United	Frontier	United
8	United	United	United	United	Southwest	United	Frontier

Sources: On-time and canceled flights data for full year 2014 from masFlight. Includes regional affiliated flights. Extreme delays of 45 minutes or longer were compiled from FlightStats Inc. Mishandled baggage and consumer complaints from U.S. Department of Transportation based on 12 months ended in November. Department of Transportation involuntary-bumping data 12 months through September.

FIGURE 8.4
J.D. Power and Associates Initial Automobile Quality Study

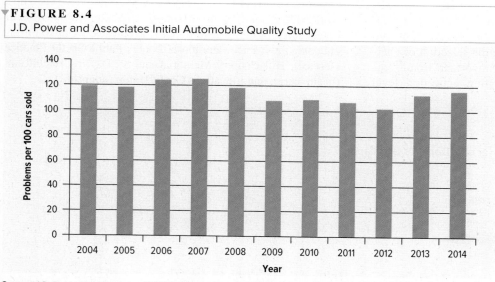

Source: J.D. Power and Associates, "2014 U.S. Initial Quality Study," June 18, 2014, www.jdpower.com/es/node/15646 (accessed March 11, 2015).

Quality is so important that we need to examine it in the context of operations management. **Quality control** refers to the processes an organization uses to maintain its established quality standards. It was a desire to create quality injection-molded parts for printers at affordable prices that prompted entrepreneur Larry Lukis to found Protomold, later renamed Proto Labs. Wanting to design a better printer, Lukis got frustrated at how expensive and long it took to receive the parts. He developed an automated process to change the industry, and the company became popular among engineers who needed quality products quickly or in small batches. Today Proto Labs has become the world's fastest provider of machined and molded parts.[30] Quality has become a major concern in many organizations, particularly in light of intense foreign competition and increasingly demanding customers. To regain a competitive edge, a number of firms have adopted a total quality management approach. **Total quality management (TQM)** is a philosophy that uniform commitment to quality in all areas of the organization will promote a culture that meets customers' perceptions of quality. It involves coordinating efforts to improve customer satisfaction, increasing employee participation, forming and strengthening supplier partnerships, and facilitating an organizational culture of continuous quality improvement. TQM requires constant improvements in all areas of the company as well as employee empowerment.

Continuous improvement of an organization's goods and services is built around the notion that quality is free; by contrast, *not* having high-quality goods and services can be very expensive, especially in terms of dissatisfied customers.[31] A primary tool of the continuous improvement process is *benchmarking,* the measuring and evaluating of the quality of the organization's goods, services, or processes as compared with the quality produced by the best-performing companies in the industry.[32] Benchmarking lets the organization know where it stands competitively in its industry, thus giving it a goal to aim for over time. Now that online digital media are becoming more important in businesses, companies such as Compuware Corporation offer benchmarking tools so companies can monitor and compare the success of their websites. Such tools allow companies to track traffic to the site versus competitors' sites. Studies have shown a direct link between website performance and online sales, meaning this type of benchmarking is important.[33]

Companies employing TQM programs know that quality control should be incorporated throughout the transformation process, from the initial plans to the development of a specific product through the product and production-facility design processes to the actual manufacture of the product. In other words, they view quality control as an element of the product itself, rather than as simply a function of the operations process. When a company makes the product correctly from the outset, it eliminates the need to rework defective products, expedites the transformation process itself, and allows employees to make better use of their time and materials. One method through which many companies have tried to improve quality is **statistical process control**, a system in which management collects and analyzes information about the production process to pinpoint quality problems in the production system.

International Organization for Standardization (ISO)

Regardless of whether a company has a TQM program for quality control, it must first determine what standard of quality it desires and then assess whether its products meet that standard. Product specifications and quality standards must be set so the company can create a product that will compete in the marketplace. Rushing Water Canoes, for example, may specify that each of its canoes has aluminum walls of a specified uniform thickness, that the front and back be reinforced with a specified level of steel, and that each contain a specified amount of flotation material for safety. Production facilities must be designed that can produce products with the desired specifications.

Quality standards can be incorporated into service businesses as well. A hamburger chain, for example, may establish standards relating to how long it takes to cook an order and serve it to customers, how many fries are in each order, how thick the burgers are, or how many customer complaints might be acceptable. Once the desired quality characteristics, specifications, and standards have been stated in measurable terms, the next step is inspection.

The International Organization for Standardization (ISO) has created a series of quality management standards—**ISO 9000**—designed to ensure the customer's quality standards are met. The standards provide a framework for documenting how a certified business keeps records, trains employees,

Intel has adopted ISO 9000 quality standards to ensure consistent quality throughout its global operations.
© Kimberly White/Bloomberg/Getty Images

A MANUFACTURER WITH HUMAN-FOCUSED LEADERSHIP

Even at an international manufacturing company, leadership should be more about people than the supply chain. That's the message of Bob Chapman, longtime CEO of Barry-Wehmiller. The company has annual revenues of $1.7 billion from a variety of manufacturing, technology, and consulting industries. After taking a hard look at the company's culture in 1997, Chapman began to integrate this principle deeply into his firm; now, the company and CEO are known for it. Barry-Wehmiller's Guiding Principles of Leadership describe how it is a people-centered organization: "We measure success by the way we touch the lives of people."

Calling his approach Truly Human Leadership, Chapman believes leaders and companies need to learn how to care about the people who work for them, and not see them merely as "functions" to a corporate goal. This principle finds practical application in various aspects of the firm. For example, the company discontinued the use of timecards after discovering factory workers felt mistrusted because, unlike office workers, they could not make phone calls, get coffee, or perform other normal daily nonwork tasks without punching in and out. The company also has its own school, Barry-Wehmiller University, to teach its principles and values to employees.

The approach seems to have made a real difference. Whereas studies generally find that about 80 percent of employees feel their organizations do not care about them, an independent survey of Barry-Wehmiller employees found the exact opposite: 79 percent believed the company did care. Not only that, but the firm's continued success—15 percent compounded annual growth since 1988—backs up Chapman's claim that human-focused leadership is good for the company as well.[34]

Discussion Questions

1. Why has Barry-Wehmiller's Truly Human Leadership approach been successful?

2. Do you feel that this type of approach is suitable for a manufacturing company?

3. How do you think this approach contributes to the company's success?

tests products, and fixes defects. To obtain ISO 9000 certification, an independent auditor must verify that a business's factory, laboratory, or office meets the quality standards spelled out by the International Organization for Standardization. The certification process can require significant investment, but for many companies, the process is essential to being able to compete. Thousands of companies have been certified, including General Electric Analytical Instruments, which has applied ISO standards to everything from the design to the manufacturing practices of its global facilities.[35] Certification has become a virtual necessity for doing business in Europe in some high-technology businesses. ISO 9002 certification was established for service providers. **ISO 14000** is a comprehensive set of environmental standards that encourages a cleaner and safer world. ISO 14000 is a valuable standard because currently considerable variation exists between the regulations in different nations, and even regions within a nation. These variations make it difficult for organizations committed to sustainability to find acceptable global solutions to problems. The goal of the ISO 14000 standards is to promote a more uniform approach to environmental management and to help companies attain and measure improvements in their environmental performance. **ISO 19600** provides guidelines for compliance management that address risks, legal requirements, and stakeholder needs. This standard deals with both mandatory requirements such as laws and voluntary standards such as principles. Since these are guidelines rather than requirements, companies that comply with ISO 19600 cannot be certified. However, organizations that adopt this standard demonstrate they are committed toward stakeholders and continual improvement in compliance management.[36]

Inspection

Inspection reveals whether a product meets quality standards. Some product characteristics may be discerned by fairly simple inspection techniques—weighing the contents of cereal boxes or measuring the time it takes for a customer to receive his or her hamburger. As part of the ongoing quality assurance program at Hershey Foods, all wrapped Hershey Kisses are checked, and all imperfectly wrapped kisses are rejected. Other inspection techniques are more elaborate. Automobile manufacturers use automated machines to open and close car doors to test the durability of latches and hinges. The food-processing and pharmaceutical industries use various chemical tests to determine the quality of their output. Rushing Water Canoes might use a special device that can precisely measure the thickness of each canoe wall to ensure that it meets the company's specifications.

Organizations normally inspect purchased items, work-in-process, and finished items. The inspection of purchased items and finished items takes place after the fact; the inspection of work-in-process is preventive. In other words, the purpose of inspection of purchased items and finished items is to determine what the quality level is. For items that are being worked on—an automobile moving down the assembly line or a canoe being assembled—the purpose of the inspection is to find defects before the product is completed so that necessary corrections can be made.

Sampling

An important question relating to inspection is how many items should be inspected. Should all canoes produced by Rushing Water be inspected or just some of them? Whether to inspect 100 percent of the output or only part of it is related to the cost of the inspection process, the destructiveness of the inspection process (some tests last until the product fails), and the potential cost of product flaws in terms of human lives and safety.

Some inspection procedures are quite expensive, use elaborate testing equipment, destroy products, and/or require a significant number of hours to complete. In such cases, it is usually desirable to test only a sample of the output. If the sample passes inspection, the inspector may assume that all the items in the lot from which the sample was drawn would also pass inspection. By using principles of statistical inference, management can employ sampling techniques that ensure a relatively high probability of reaching the right conclusion—that is, rejecting a lot that does not meet standards and accepting a lot that does. Nevertheless, there will always be a risk of making an incorrect conclusion—accepting a population that *does not* meet standards (because the sample was satisfactory) or rejecting a population that *does* meet standards (because the sample contained too many defective items).

Sampling is likely to be used when inspection tests are destructive. Determining the life expectancy of lightbulbs by turning them on and recording how long they last would be foolish: There is no market for burned-out lightbulbs. Instead, a generalization based on the quality of a sample would be applied to the entire population of lightbulbs from which the sample was drawn. However, human life and safety often depend on the proper functioning of specific items, such as the navigational systems installed in commercial airliners. For such items, even though the inspection process is costly, the potential cost of flawed systems—in human lives and safety—is too great not to inspect 100 percent of the output.

INTEGRATING OPERATIONS AND SUPPLY CHAIN MANAGEMENT

Managing operations and supply chains can be complex and challenging due to the number of independent organizations that must perform their responsibilities in creating product quality. Managing supply chains requires constant vigilance and the ability to make quick tactical changes. Even Apple Inc., the most admired company in the world, has had supply chain problems. Reports of forced overtime, underage workers, and dangerous conditions at its Chinese supplier factories have resulted in negative publicity for the company.[37] Therefore, managing the various partners involved in supply chains and operations is important because many stakeholders hold the firm responsible for appropriate conduct related to product quality. This requires that the company exercise oversight over all suppliers involved in producing a product. Encouraging suppliers to report problems, issues, or concerns requires excellent communication systems to obtain feedback. Ideally, suppliers will report potential problems before they reach the next level of the supply chain, which reduces damage.

TEAM EXERCISE

Form groups and assign the responsibility of finding companies that outsource their production to other countries. What are the key advantages of this outsourcing decision? Do you see any drawbacks or weaknesses in this approach? Why would a company not outsource when such a tactic can be undertaken to cut manufacturing costs? Report your findings to the class.

Despite the challenges of monitoring global operations and supply chains, there are steps businesses can take to manage these risks. All companies who work with global suppliers should adopt a Global Supplier Code of Conduct and ensure that it is effectively communicated. Additionally, companies should encourage compliance and procurement employees to work together to find ethical suppliers at reasonable costs. Those in procurement are concerned with the costs of obtaining materials for the company. As a result, supply chain and procurement managers must work together to make operational decisions to ensure the selection of the best suppliers from an ethical and cost-effective standpoint. Businesses must also work to make certain that their supply chains are diverse. Having only a few suppliers in one area can disrupt operations should a disaster strike. Finally, companies must perform regular audits on its suppliers and take action against those found to be in violation of company standards.[38] ■

SO YOU WANT A JOB // in Operations Management /

While you might not have been familiar with terms such as *supply chain* or *logistics* or *total quality management* before taking this course, careers abound in the operations management field. You will find these careers in a wide variety of organizations—manufacturers, retailers, transportation companies, third-party logistics firms, government agencies, and service firms. Approximately $1.3 trillion is spent on transportation, inventory, and related logistics activities, and logistics alone accounts for more than 9.5 percent of U.S. gross domestic product.[39] Closely managing how a company's inputs and outputs flow from raw materials to the end consumer is vital to a firm's success. Successful companies also need to ensure that quality is measured and actively managed at each step.

Supply chain managers have a tremendous impact on the success of an organization. These managers are engaged in every facet of the business process, including planning, purchasing, production, transportation, storage and distribution, customer service, and more. Their performance helps organizations control expenses, boost sales, and maximize profits.

Warehouse managers are a vital part of manufacturing operations. A typical warehouse manager's duties include overseeing and recording deliveries and pickups, maintaining inventory records and the product tracking system, and adjusting inventory levels to reflect receipts and disbursements. Warehouse managers also have to keep in mind customer service and employee issues. Warehouse managers can earn up to $60,000 in some cases.

Operations management is also required in service businesses. With more than 80 percent of the U.S. economy in services, jobs exist for services operations. Many service contact operations require standardized processes that often use technology to provide an interface that provides an automatic quality performance. Consider jobs in health care, the travel industry, fast food, and entertainment. Think of any job or task that is a part of the final product in these industries. Even an online retailer such as Amazon.com has a transformation process that includes information technology and human activities that facilitate a transaction. These services have a standardized process and can be evaluated based on their level of achieved service quality.

Total quality management is becoming a key attribute for companies to ensure that quality pervades all aspects of the organization. Quality-assurance managers make median annual pay of $95,681. These managers monitor and advise on how a company's quality management system is performing and publish data and reports regarding company performance in both manufacturing and service industries.[40]

motivating the
workforce

© Hero/Corbis/ Fancy /Glow Images, RF

LEARNING OBJECTIVES

After reading this chapter, you will be able to:

LO 9-1 Define human relations, and determine why its study is important.

LO 9-2 Summarize early studies that laid the groundwork for understanding employee motivation.

LO 9-3 Compare and contrast the human relations theories of Abraham Maslow and Frederick Herzberg.

LO 9-4 Investigate various theories of motivation, including Theories X, Y, and Z; equity theory; and expectancy theory.

LO 9-5 Describe some of the strategies that managers use to motivate employees.

Because employees do the actual work of the business and influence whether the firm achieves its objectives, most top managers agree that employees are an organization's most valuable resource. To achieve organizational objectives, employees must have the motivation, ability (appropriate knowledge and skills), and tools (proper training and equipment) to perform their jobs. Chapter 10 covers topics related to managing human resources, such as those listed earlier. This chapter focuses on how to motivate employees.

We examine employees' needs and motivation, managers' views of workers, and several strategies for motivating employees. Managers who understand the needs of their employees can help them reach higher levels of productivity and thus contribute to the achievement of organizational goals. ■

LO 9-1   Define human relations, and determine why its study is important.

NATURE OF HUMAN RELATIONS

What motivates employees to perform on the job is the focus of **human relations**, the study of the behavior of individuals and groups in organizational settings. In business, human relations involves motivating employees to achieve organizational objectives efficiently and effectively. The field of human relations has become increasingly important over the years as businesses strive to understand how to boost workplace morale, maximize employees' productivity and creativity, and motivate their ever more diverse employees to be more effective.

Motivation is an inner drive that directs a person's behavior toward goals. A goal is the satisfaction of some need, and a need is the difference between a desired state and an actual state. Both needs and goals can be motivating. Motivation explains why people behave as they do; similarly, a lack of motivation explains, at times, why people avoid doing what they should do. Motivating employees to do the wrong things or for the wrong reasons can be problematic, however. Encouraging employees to take excessive risks through high compensation, for example, led to the downfall of AIG and most major U.S. banks. Also, encouraging employees to lie to customers or to create false documentation is unethical and could even have legal ramifications. A person who recognizes or feels a need is motivated to take action to satisfy the need and achieve a goal (Figure 9.1). Consider a person who takes a job as a salesperson. If his or her performance is far below other salespeople's, he or she will likely recognize a need to increase sales. To satisfy that need and achieve success, the person may try to acquire new insights from successful salespeople or obtain additional training to improve sales skills. In

human relations the study of the behavior of individuals and groups in organizational settings.

motivation an inner drive that directs a person's behavior toward goals.

Many companies offer onsite day care as a benefit for employees who have children. Company benefits such as these tend to increase employee satisfaction and motivation.
© BananaStock/PunchStock, RF

FIGURE 9.1
The Motivation Process

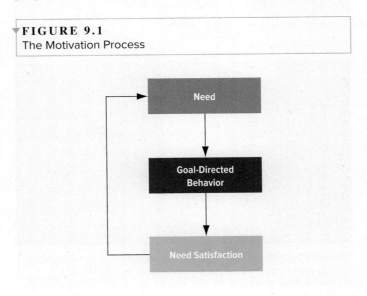

addition, a sales manager might try different means to motivate the salesperson to work harder and to improve his or her skills. Human relations is concerned with the needs of employees, their goals and how they try to achieve them, and the impact of those needs and goals on job performance.

Effectively motivating employees helps keep them engaged in their work. Engagement involves emotional involvement and commitment. Being engaged results in carrying out the expectations and obligations of employment. Many employees are actively engaged in their jobs, while others are not. Some employees do the minimum amount of work required to get by, and some employees are completely disengaged. Motivating employees to stay engaged is a key responsibility of management. For example, to test if his onsite production managers were fully engaged in their jobs, former Van Halen lead singer David Lee Roth placed a line in the band's rider asking for a bowl of M&M's with the brown ones removed. It was a means for the band to test local stage production crews' attention to detail. Because their shows were highly technical, David Lee Roth would demand a complete recheck of everything if he found brown M&M's in the bowl.[1]

One prominent aspect of human relations is **morale**—an employee's attitude toward his or her job, employer, and colleagues. High morale contributes to high levels of productivity, high returns to stakeholders, and employee loyalty. Conversely, low morale may cause high rates of absenteeism and turnover (when employees quit or are fired and must be replaced by new employees). Wegmans Food Markets recognizes the value of happy, committed employees and strives to engage in practices that will create a satisfying workplace. Wegmans offers flexible scheduling, employee scholarship programs (nearly half of employees are 25 years or younger), and strong internal promoting. The CEO of Wegmans stresses that employee growth and satisfaction are key goals of the organization.[2]

DID YOU KNOW?

Absenteeism costs about 20 percent of payroll.[3]

Employees are motivated by their perceptions of extrinsic and intrinsic rewards. An **intrinsic reward** is the personal satisfaction and enjoyment that you feel from attaining a goal. For example, in this class you may feel personal enjoyment in learning how business works and aspire to have a career in business or to operate your own business one day. **Extrinsic rewards** are benefits and/or recognition that you receive from someone else. In this class, your grade is extrinsic recognition of your efforts and success in the class. In business, praise and recognition, pay increases, and bonuses are extrinsic rewards. If you believe that your job provides an opportunity to contribute to society or the environment, then that aspect would represent an intrinsic reward. Both intrinsic and extrinsic rewards contribute to motivation that stimulates employees to do their best in contributing to business goals.

Respect, involvement, appreciation, adequate compensation, promotions, a pleasant work environment, and a positive organizational culture are all morale boosters. Table 9.1 lists some ways to retain good employees. Costco Wholesale, the second largest retailer in America, knows how to retain happy employees. The company pays an average annual rate of $21 per hour plus overtime, gives five weeks of vacation per year, and matches 401(k) contributions; in addition, almost 90 percent of employees are covered by company-sponsored health insurance. The retail industry is peppered with unhappy employees and dwindling profits, but Costco's efforts result in happy workers. The company has not experienced any major labor disputes in its more than 30 years of existence.[4] Many companies offer a diverse array of benefits designed to improve the quality of employees' lives and increase their morale and satisfaction.

Even small symbols of recognition, such as an "Employee of the Month" parking space, can serve as strong motivators for employees.
© *Jason Smith/Getty Images, RF*

▼ **TABLE 9.1** How to Retain Good Employees

1. Challenge your employees.
2. Provide adequate incentives.
3. Don't micromanage.
4. Create a work-friendly environment.
5. Provide opportunities for employee growth.

Source: Adapted from Geoff Williams, "Retaining Employees: 5 Things You Need to Know," *The Huffington Post,* February 2, 2012, www.huffingtonpost.com/2012/02/01/retaining-employees-5-things-you-need-to-know_n_976767.html (accessed March 18, 2015).

▼ **TABLE 9.2** How to Motivate Employees

1. Interact with employees in a friendly and open manner.
2. Equitably dispense rewards and other incentives.
3. Create a culture of collaboration.
4. Provide both positive and negative feedback and constructive criticism.
5. Make employees feel as if they are partners rather than workers.
6. Handle conflicts in an open and professional manner.
7. Provide continuous opportunities for improvement and employee growth.
8. Encourage creativity in problem solving.
9. Recognize employees for jobs well done.
10. Allow employees to make mistakes, as these become learning opportunities.

Some of the "best companies to work for" offer onsite day care, concierge services (e.g., dry cleaning, shoe repair, prescription renewal), domestic partner benefits to same-sex couples, and fully paid sabbaticals. Table 9.2 offers suggestions as to how leaders can motivate employees on a daily basis.

LO 9-2 Summarize early studies that laid the groundwork for understanding employee motivation.

HISTORICAL PERSPECTIVES ON EMPLOYEE MOTIVATION

Throughout the 20th century, researchers have conducted numerous studies to try to identify ways to motivate workers and increase productivity. From these studies have come theories that have been applied to workers with varying degrees of success. A brief discussion of two of these theories—the classical theory of motivation and the Hawthorne studies—provides a background for understanding the present state of human relations.

Classical Theory of Motivation

The birth of the study of human relations can be traced to time and motion studies conducted at the turn of the century by Frederick W. Taylor and Frank and Lillian Gilbreth. Their studies analyzed how workers perform specific work tasks in an effort to improve employees' productivity. These efforts led to the application of scientific principles to management.

According to the **classical theory of motivation**, money is the sole motivator for workers. Taylor suggested that workers who were paid more would produce more, an idea that would benefit both companies and workers. To improve productivity, Taylor thought that managers should break down each job into its component tasks (specialization), determine the best way to perform each task, and specify the output to be achieved by a worker performing the task. Taylor also believed that incentives would motivate employees to be more productive. Thus, he suggested that managers link workers' pay directly to their output. He developed the piece-rate system, under which employees were paid a certain amount for each unit they produced; those who exceeded their quota were paid a higher rate per unit for all the units they produced.

We can still see Taylor's ideas in practice today in the use of financial incentives for productivity. Moreover, companies are increasingly striving to relate pay to performance at both the hourly and managerial level. Incentive planners choose an individual incentive to motivate and reward their employees. In contrast, team incentives are used to generate partnership and collaboration to accomplish organizational goals. Boeing develops sales teams for most of its products, including commercial airplanes. The team dedicated to each product shares in the sales incentive program.

More and more corporations are tying pay to performance in order to motivate—even up to the CEO level. The topic of executive pay has become controversial in recent years, and many corporate boards of directors have taken steps to link executive compensation more closely to corporate performance. Despite these changes, many top executives still receive large compensation packages. John Hammergren, CEO of McKesson, earns $131.2 million in annual compensation.[5]

Like most managers of the early 20th century, Taylor believed that satisfactory pay and job security would motivate employees

Kim Jordan was in high school the first time she heard the quote "Let your life speak"—attributed to George Fox, a founder of American Quakerism. She took the quote to heart, and when she and her husband later co-founded New Belgium Brewing, they decided to "let our business life speak for us as well." From this ideal has developed a company that is not only the third largest craft brewer in the United States (producer of such favorites as Fat Tire and Ranger IPA) but has also received numerous accolades for sustainability, environmental stewardship, and an exceptional workplace environment and employee incentive system.

New Belgium's shares are 100 percent employee-owned through an employee stock ownership plan, and new employees become owners after only one year with the company. Employees are also given financial literacy education and complete access to the company's financial data and performance indicators. By being both invested in the company's success and informed about its current strengths, challenges, and financial position, New Belgium employees can see themselves as actual business owners. Therefore, like all business owners, they have a personal incentive to give their best.

Employment at New Belgium comes with other perks as well. After one year, employees get a free bicycle to encourage sustainable commuting (or alternatively the option to lease a Toyota Prius if they cannot commute by bike). After 5 years, employees enjoy an all-expenses-paid trip to Belgium to learn about the company's history and culture. After 10 years, employees are permitted a four-week paid sabbatical. New Belgium's methods are clearly working as the company boasts an impressive 97 percent employee retention rate.[6]

Discussion Questions

1. Why has New Belgium's employee incentive system been so successful?

2. What types or theories of employee motivation is New Belgium trying to promote with its system?

3. How do you think New Belgium's exceptional workplace contributed to its current success as the third largest craft brewer?

to work hard. However, later studies showed that other factors are also important in motivating workers.

The Hawthorne Studies

Elton Mayo and a team of researchers from Harvard University wanted to determine what physical conditions in the workplace—such as light and noise levels—would stimulate employees to be most productive. From 1924 to 1932, they studied a group of workers at the Hawthorne Works Plant of the Western Electric Company and measured their productivity under various physical conditions.

Some companies let people bring their pets to work as an added incentive to make the workplace seem friendlier.
© Dean Mitchell/Getty Images, RF

What the researchers discovered was quite unexpected and very puzzling: Productivity increased regardless of the physical conditions. This phenomenon has been labeled the Hawthorne effect. When questioned about their behavior, the employees expressed satisfaction because their co-workers in the experiments were friendly and, more importantly, because their supervisors had asked for their help and cooperation in the study. In other words, they were responding to the attention they received, not the changing physical work conditions. The researchers concluded that social and psychological factors could significantly affect productivity and morale. The United Services Automobile Association (USAA) has a built-in psychological factor that influences employee morale. The work of the financial services company serves military and veteran families, which enlivens employees. Genentech, a biotechnology company, also knows how to inspire employees through the development of medications that better the lives of patients. Patients have been known to share their stories with employees, and in one instance, employees put in extra hours to ship breast cancer medication to a hospital when they discovered three patients were awaiting treatment. This shows how important it is for employees to feel like their work matters.[7] Figure 9.2 indicates aspects of the job that appear to be most important for job satisfaction.

The Hawthorne experiments marked the beginning of a concern for human relations in the workplace. They revealed that human factors do influence workers' behavior and that managers who understand the needs, beliefs, and expectations of people have the greatest success in motivating their workers.

FIGURE 9.2
Job Aspects Important to Employee Satisfaction

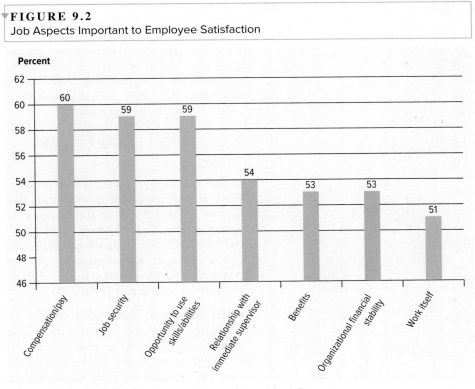

Percent

Note: Represents those who answered "very important."
Source: *Employee Job Satisfaction and Engagement* (SHRM, 2014).

LO 9-3 Compare and contrast the human relations theories of Abraham Maslow and Frederick Herzberg.

THEORIES OF EMPLOYEE MOTIVATION

The research of Taylor, Mayo, and many others has led to the development of a number of theories that attempt to describe what motivates employees to perform. In this section, we will discuss some of the most important of these theories. The successful implementation of ideas based on these theories will vary, of course, depending on the company, its management, and its employees. It should be noted, too, that what worked in the past may no longer work today. Good managers must have the ability to adapt their ideas to an ever-changing, diverse group of employees.

Maslow's Hierarchy of Needs

Psychologist Abraham Maslow theorized that people have five basic needs: physiological, security, social, esteem, and self-actualization. **Maslow's hierarchy** arranges these needs into the order in which people strive to satisfy them (Figure 9.3).

Physiological needs, the most basic and first needs to be satisfied, are the essentials for living—water, food, shelter, and clothing. According to Maslow, humans devote all their efforts to satisfying physiological needs until they are met. Only when these needs are met can people focus their attention on satisfying the next level of needs—security.

Security needs relate to protecting yourself from physical and economic harm. Actions that may be taken to achieve security include reporting a dangerous workplace condition to management, maintaining safety equipment, and purchasing insurance with income protection in the event you become unable to work. Once security needs have been satisfied, people may strive for social goals.

Social needs are the need for love, companionship, and friendship—the desire for acceptance by others. To fulfill social needs, a person may try many things: making friends with a coworker, joining a group, volunteering at a hospital, throwing a party, and so on. Once their social needs have been satisfied, people attempt to satisfy their need for esteem.

Esteem needs relate to respect—both self-respect and respect from others. One aspect of esteem needs is competition—the need to feel that you can do something better than anyone else. Competition often motivates people to increase their productivity. Esteem needs are not as easily satisfied as the needs at lower levels in Maslow's hierarchy because they do not always provide tangible evidence of success. However, these needs can be realized through rewards and increased involvement in organizational activities. Until esteem needs are met, people focus their attention on achieving respect. When they feel they have

FIGURE 9.3
Maslow's Hierarchy of Needs

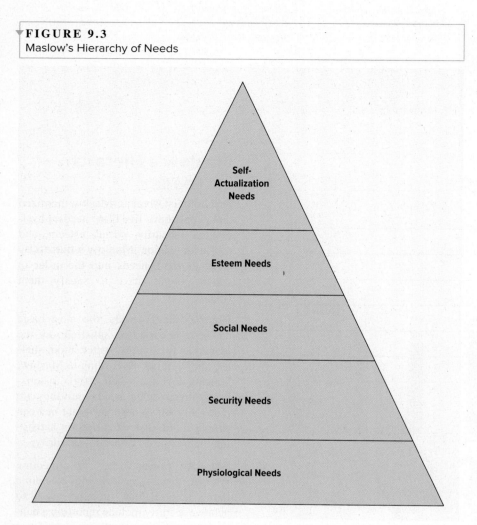

Source: Adapted from Abraham H. Maslow, "A Theory of Human Motivation," *Psychology Review* 50 (1943), pp. 370–396. American Psychology Association.

can be pursued. Thus, people who are hungry and homeless are not concerned with obtaining respect from their colleagues. Only when physiological, security, and social needs have been more or less satisfied do people seek esteem. Maslow's theory also suggests that if a low-level need is suddenly reactivated, the individual will try to satisfy that need rather than higher-level needs. Many laid-off workers probably shift their focus from high-level esteem needs to the need for security. Managers should learn from Maslow's hierarchy that employees will be motivated to contribute to organizational goals only if they are able to first satisfy their physiological, security, and social needs through their work.

Herzberg's Two-Factor Theory

In the 1950s, psychologist Frederick Herzberg proposed a theory of motivation that focuses on the job and on the environment where work is done. Herzberg studied various factors relating to the job and their relation to employee motivation and concluded that they can be divided into hygiene factors and motivational factors (Table 9.3).

Hygiene factors, which relate to the work setting and not to the content of the work, include adequate wages, comfortable and safe working conditions, fair company policies, and job security. These factors do not necessarily motivate employees to excel,

> ## "Maslow's theory maintains that the more basic needs at the bottom of the hierarchy must be satisfied before higher-level goals can be pursued."

achieved some measure of respect, self-actualization becomes the major goal of life.

Self-actualization needs, at the top of Maslow's hierarchy, mean being the best you can be. Self-actualization involves maximizing your potential. A self-actualized person feels that she or he is living life to its fullest in every way. For Stephen King, self-actualization might mean being praised as the best fiction writer in the world; for actress Halle Berry, it might mean winning an Oscar.

Maslow's theory maintains that the more basic needs at the bottom of the hierarchy must be satisfied before higher-level goals

▼ **TABLE 9.3** Herzberg's Hygiene and Motivational Factors

Hygiene Factors	Motivational Factors
Company policies	Achievement
Supervision	Recognition
Working conditions	Work itself
Relationships with peers, supervisors, and subordinates	Responsibility
Salary	Advancement
Security	Personal growth

but their absence may be a potential source of dissatisfaction and high turnover. Employee safety and comfort are clearly hygiene factors.

Many people feel that a good salary is one of the most important job factors, even more important than job security and the chance to use one's mind and abilities. Salary and security, two of the hygiene factors identified by Herzberg, make it possible for employees to satisfy the physiological and security needs identified by Maslow. However, the presence of hygiene factors is unlikely to motivate employees to work harder. For example, many people do not feel motivated to pursue a career as a gastroenterologist (doctors who specialize in the digestive system). Although the job is important and pays more than $250,000 on average, the tasks are routine and most patients are not looking forward to their appointments.[8]

Motivational factors, which relate to the content of the work itself, include achievement, recognition, involvement, responsibility, and advancement. The absence of motivational factors may not result in dissatisfaction, but their presence is likely to motivate employees to excel. Many companies are beginning to employ methods to give employees more responsibility and control and to involve them more in their work, which serves to motivate them to higher levels of productivity and quality.

Hotels are adopting more customer-centric processes in order to better their experiences. Doubletree, a franchise owned by Hilton Hotels and Resorts, has created a CARE committee for each of its locations. The committee is composed of employees from all departments so that they can ensure maximum operational performance and customer satisfaction. Marriott International employees leave personal notes for guests, and their loyalty program is above comparison.[9]

Herzberg's motivational factors and Maslow's esteem and self-actualization needs are similar. Workers' low-level needs (physiological and security) have largely been satisfied by minimum-wage laws and occupational-safety standards set by various government agencies and are therefore not motivators. Consequently, to improve productivity, management should focus on satisfying workers' higher-level needs (motivational factors) by providing opportunities for achievement, involvement, and advancement and by recognizing good performance.

LO 9-4 Investigate various theories of motivation, including Theories X, Y, and Z; equity theory; and expectancy theory.

McGregor's Theory X and Theory Y

In *The Human Side of Enterprise,* Douglas McGregor related Maslow's ideas about personal needs to management. McGregor contrasted two views of management—the traditional view, which he called Theory X, and a humanistic view, which he called Theory Y.

According to McGregor, managers adopting **Theory X** assume that workers generally dislike work and must be forced to do their jobs. They believe that the following statements are true of workers:

1. The average person naturally dislikes work and will avoid it when possible.

2. Most workers must be coerced, controlled, directed, or threatened with punishment to get them to work toward the achievement of organizational objectives.

3. The average worker prefers to be directed and to avoid responsibility, has relatively little ambition, and wants security.[10]

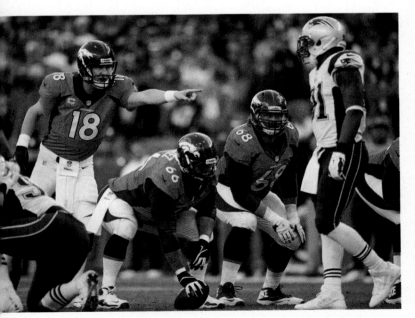

Peyton Manning is known as a team motivator and leader for the Denver Broncos.
© *John Biever/Getty Images*

Managers who subscribe to the Theory X view maintain tight control over workers, provide almost constant supervision, try to motivate through fear, and make decisions in an autocratic fashion, eliciting little or no input from their subordinates. The Theory X style of management focuses on physiological and security needs and virtually ignores the higher needs discussed by Maslow. Foxconn, a manufacturing company that creates components for tech products such as the Apple iPad, is a company that had adopted the Theory X perspective. In China, Foxconn workers lived in crowded dorms and often worked more than 60 hours per week.

The Theory X view of management does not take into account people's needs for companionship, esteem, and personal growth, whereas Theory Y, the contrasting view of management, does. Managers subscribing to the **Theory Y** view assume that workers like to work and that under proper conditions employees will seek out responsibility in an attempt to satisfy their social, esteem, and self-actualization needs.

McGregor describes the assumptions behind Theory Y in the following way:

1. The expenditure of physical and mental effort in work is as natural as play or rest.

2. People will exercise self-direction and self-control to achieve objectives to which they are committed.

3. People will commit to objectives when they realize that the achievement of those goals will bring them personal reward.

4. The average person will accept and seek responsibility.

5. Imagination, ingenuity, and creativity can help solve organizational problems, but most organizations do not make adequate use of these characteristics in their employees.

6. Organizations today do not make full use of workers' intellectual potential.[12]

Obviously, managers subscribing to the Theory Y philosophy have a management style very different from managers subscribing to the Theory X philosophy. Theory Y managers maintain less control and supervision, do not use fear as the primary motivator, and are more democratic in decision making, allowing subordinates to participate in the process. Theory Y managers address the high-level needs in Maslow's hierarchy

> " **Theory Y managers maintain less control and supervision, do not use fear as the primary motivator, and are more democratic in decision making, allowing subordinates to participate in the process.** "

RADIO FLYER CARTS IN A NEW COMPANY CULTURE

In 1917 entrepreneur Antonio Pasin founded Radio Flyer, a toy company that would become well known for its iconic "little red wagon" toy. However, by the time grandson Robert Pasin took over as CEO, the company was losing its relevance in the modern era. Therefore, when Robert Pasin took over, he set about making the firm up-to-date, including revamping the company culture and workplace environment. Radio Flyer has since become famous for its employee satisfaction, including repeated listings on *Fortune* magazine's "Best Small Companies to Work For" list.

Pasin redesigned Radio Flyer's culture to fit its brand as a toy company that has enabled children to find joy, wonder, and adventure in play. He is no longer the CEO but the "Chief Wagon Officer." Such labels permeate the firm, from the "Little Red Rule Award" to the "Smile Squad." The hiring process is also key: Every new addition to the firm must pass a 10-step selection process, including a personal conversation with Pasin himself. This deep focus on cultural fit provides Radio Flyer with the employees it needs to continue making children happy.[11]

as well as physiological and security needs. For instance, the Virgin Group, which is a conglomerate of various businesses in many industries, allows CEOs and managers to run their locations as they see fit. This also applies to complicated expansion measures such as opening foreign locations, which can become very complex. The company has achieved success by empowering employees to make their own decisions and follow their passions.[13] Today, Theory Y enjoys widespread support and may have displaced Theory X.

Theory Z

Theory Z is a management philosophy that stresses employee participation in all aspects of company decision making. It was first described by William Ouchi in his book *Theory Z—How American Business Can Meet the Japanese Challenge*. Theory Z incorporates many elements associated with the Japanese approach to management, such as trust and intimacy, but Japanese ideas have been adapted for use in the United States. In a Theory Z organization, managers and workers share responsibilities; the management style is participative; and employment is long term and often lifelong. Japan has faced a significant period of slowing economic progress and competition from China and other Asian nations. This has led to experts questioning Theory Z, particularly at firms such as Sony and Toyota. Theory Z results in employees feeling organizational ownership. Research has found that such feelings of ownership may produce positive attitudinal and behavioral effects for employees.[14] In a Theory Y organization, managers focus on assumptions about the nature of the worker. The two theories can be seen as complementary. Table 9.4 compares Theory X, Theory Y, and Theory Z.

Equity Theory

According to **equity theory**, how much people are willing to contribute to an organization depends on their assessment of the fairness, or equity, of the rewards they will receive in exchange. In a fair situation, a person receives rewards proportional to the contribution he or she makes to the organization. However, in practice, equity is a subjective notion. Each worker regularly develops a personal input-output ratio by taking stock of his or her contribution (inputs) to the organization in time, effort, skills, and experience and assessing the rewards (outputs) offered by the organization in pay, benefits, recognition, and promotions. The worker compares his or her ratio to the input-output ratio of some other person—a "comparison other," who may be a co-worker, a friend working in another organization, or an "average" of several people working in the organization. If the two ratios are close, the individual will feel that he or she is being treated equitably.

Let's say you have a high school education and earn $25,000 a year. When you compare your input–output ratio with that of a co-worker who has a college degree and makes $35,000 a year, you will probably feel that you are being paid fairly. However, if you perceive that your personal input–output ratio is lower than that of your college-educated co-worker, you may feel that you are being treated unfairly and be motivated to seek change. Or if you learn that your co-worker who makes $35,000 has only a high school diploma, you may feel cheated by your employer. To achieve equity, you could try to increase your outputs by asking for a raise or promotion. You could also try to have your co-worker's inputs increased or his or her outputs decreased. Failing to achieve equity, you may be motivated to look for a job at a different company.

Equity theory might explain why many consumers are upset about CEO compensation. Although the job of the CEO can be incredibly stressful, the fact that they take home millions in compensation, bonuses, and stock options has been questioned. The high unemployment rate coupled with the misconduct that occurred at some large corporations prior to the recession contributed largely to consumers' frustration with executive compensation packages. To counter this perception of pay inequality, several corporations have now begun to tie CEO compensation with company performance. If the company performs poorly for the year, then firms such as

Theory Z a management philosophy that stresses employee participation in all aspects of company decision making.

equity theory an assumption that how much people are willing to contribute to an organization depends on their assessment of the fairness, or equity, of the rewards they will receive in exchange.

▼ **TABLE 9.4** Comparison of theories X, Y, and Z

	Theory X	Theory Y	Theory Z
Countries that Use this Style	China	United States	Japan
Philosophy	Tight control over workers	Assume workers will seek out responsibility and satisfy social needs	Employee participation in all aspects of company decision making
Job Description	Considerable specialization	Less control and supervision; address higher levels of Maslow's hierarchy	Trust and intimacy with workers sharing responsibilities
Control	Tight control	Commitment to objectives with self-direction	Relaxed but required expectations
Worker Welfare	Limited concern	Democratic	Commitment to workers' total lives
Responsibility	Managerial	Collaborative	Participative

Goldman Sachs will cut bonuses and other compensation.[15] While lower compensation rates might appease the general public, some companies are worried that lower pay might deter talented individuals from wanting to assume the position of CEO at their firms.

Because almost all the issues involved in equity theory are subjective, they can be problematic. Author David Callahan has argued that feelings of inequity may underlie some unethical or illegal behavior in business. For example, due to employee theft and shoplifting, Walmart experiences billions in inventory losses every year. Some employees may take company resources to restore what they perceive to be equity. Theft of company resources is a major ethical issue, based on a survey by the Ethics Resource Center.[16] Callahan believes that employees who do not feel they are being treated equitably may be motivated to equalize the situation by lying, cheating, or otherwise "improving" their pay, perhaps by stealing.[17] Managers should try to avoid equity problems by ensuring that rewards are distributed on the basis of performance and that all employees clearly understand the basis for their pay and benefits.

Expectancy Theory

Psychologist Victor Vroom described **expectancy theory**, which states that motivation depends not only on how much a person wants something but also on the person's perception of how likely he or she is to get it. A person who wants something and has reason to be optimistic will be strongly motivated. For example, say you really want a promotion. And let's say

Your motivation depends not only on how much you want something, but also on how likely you are to get it.
© Nyul/Getty Images, RF

because you have taken some night classes to improve your skills, and moreover, have just made a large, significant sale, you feel confident that you are qualified and able to handle the new position. Therefore, you are motivated to try to get the promotion. In contrast, if you do not believe you are likely to get what you want, you may not be motivated to try to get it, even though you really want it.

Goal-Setting Theory

Goal-setting theory refers to the impact that setting goals has on performance. According to this philosophy, goals act as motivators to focus employee efforts on achieving certain performance outcomes. Setting goals can positively impact performance because goals help employees direct their efforts and attention toward the outcome, mobilize their efforts, develop consistent behavior patterns, and create strategies to obtain desired outcomes.[18] For instance, if a marketer at McDonald's has the goal to increase awareness about its McCafé drinks by a specific percentage, he could investigate what types of promotion would be most effective at reaching the target market and invest his efforts in the types that would most likely obtain the company's goal.

In 1954 Peter Drucker introduced the term *management by objectives (MBO)* that has since become important to goal-setting theory. MBO refers to the need to develop goals that both managers and employees can understand and agree upon.[19] This requires managers to work with employees to set personal objectives that will be used to further organizational objectives. By linking managerial objectives with personal objectives, employees often feel a greater sense of commitment toward achieving organizational goals. Hewlett-Packard was an early adopter of MBO as a management style.[20]

STRATEGIES FOR MOTIVATING EMPLOYEES

Based on the various theories that attempt to explain what motivates employees, businesses have developed several strategies for motivating their employees and boosting morale and productivity. Some of these techniques include behavior modification and job design, as well as the already described employee involvement programs and work teams.

LO 9-5 Describe some of the strategies that managers use to motivate employees.

Behavior Modification

Behavior modification involves changing behavior and encouraging appropriate actions by relating the consequences of behavior to the behavior itself. Behavior modification is the most widely discussed application of *reinforcement theory,* the theory that behavior can be strengthened or weakened through

▼ TABLE 9.5 Types of Reinforcement

Reinforcement Type	Example
Positive reinforcement	A car salesperson gets a bonus for exceeding her quota of cars sold.
Avoidance	A graphic designer works late to avoid getting reprimanded for missing a project deadline.
Punishment	A city worker is demoted after receiving a drunk-driving conviction.
Extinction	An ethics officer eliminates bonuses for employees who exceed work objectives in an unethical manner.

the use of rewards and punishments. Table 9.5 describes the four types of reinforcement. The concept of behavior modification was developed by psychologist B. F. Skinner, who showed that there are two types of consequences that can modify behavior—reward and punishment. Skinner found that behavior that is rewarded will tend to be repeated, while behavior that is punished will tend to be eliminated. For example, employees who know that they will receive a bonus such as an expensive restaurant meal for making a sale over $2,000 may be more motivated to make sales. Workers who know they will be punished for being tardy are likely to make a greater effort to get to work on time.

However, the two strategies may not be equally effective. Punishing unacceptable behavior may provide quick results but may lead to undesirable long-term side effects, such as employee dissatisfaction and increased turnover. In general, rewarding appropriate behavior is a more effective way to modify behavior.

Job Design

Herzberg identified the job itself as a motivational factor. Managers have several strategies that they can use to design jobs to help improve employee motivation. These include job rotation, job enlargement, job enrichment, and flexible scheduling strategies.

Job Rotation

Job rotation allows employees to move from one job to another in an effort to relieve the boredom that is often associated with job specialization. Businesses often turn to specialization in hopes of increasing productivity, but there is a negative side effect to this type of job design: Employees become bored and dissatisfied, and productivity declines. Job rotation reduces this boredom by allowing workers to undertake a greater variety of tasks and by giving them the opportunity to learn new skills. With job rotation, an employee spends a specified amount of time performing one job and then moves on to another, different job. The worker eventually returns to the initial job and begins the cycle again.

Job rotation is a good idea, but it has one major drawback. Because employees may eventually become bored with all the jobs in the cycle, job rotation does not totally eliminate the problem of boredom. Job rotation is extremely useful, however, in

situations where a person is being trained for a position that requires an understanding of various units in an organization. Accounting firm PricewaterhouseCoopers believes in the benefits of job rotation. Sometimes this rotation involves rotating an employee to a different job across the world for a short period. This gives employees the chance to see new places as well as learn new skills.[21] Many executive training programs require trainees to spend time learning a variety of specialized jobs. Job rotation is also used to cross-train today's self-directed work teams.

Job Enlargement

Job enlargement adds more tasks to a job instead of treating each task as separate. Like job rotation, job enlargement was developed to overcome the boredom associated with specialization. The rationale behind this strategy is that jobs are more satisfying as the number of tasks performed by an individual increases. Employees sometimes enlarge, or craft, their jobs by noticing what needs to be done and then changing tasks and relationship boundaries to adjust. Individual orientation and motivation shape opportunities to craft new jobs and job relationships. Job enlargement strategies have been more successful in increasing job satisfaction than have job rotation strategies. IBM, AT&T, and Maytag are among the many companies that have used job enlargement to motivate employees.

Job Enrichment

Job enrichment incorporates motivational factors such as opportunity for achievement, recognition, responsibility, and advancement into a job. It gives workers not only more tasks within the job, but more control and authority over the job. Job enrichment programs enhance a worker's feeling of responsibility and provide opportunities for growth and advancement when the worker is able to take on the more challenging tasks. Hyatt Hotels Corporation and Clif Bar use job enrichment to improve the quality of work life for their employees. The potential benefits of job enrichment are great, but it requires careful planning and execution.

Flexible Scheduling Strategies

Many U.S. workers work a traditional 40-hour workweek consisting of five 8-hour days with fixed starting and ending times. Facing problems of poor morale and high absenteeism as well as a diverse workforce with changing needs, many managers have turned to flexible scheduling strategies such as flextime, compressed workweeks, job sharing, part-time work, and telecommuting. A Staples survey revealed that 71 percent of respondents classified telecommuting options as an important benefit when considering a new

job rotation movement of employees from one job to another in an effort to relieve the boredom often associated with job specialization.

job enlargement the addition of more tasks to a job instead of treating each task as separate.

job enrichment the incorporation of motivational factors, such as opportunity for achievement, recognition, responsibility, and advancement, into a job.

flextime a program that allows employees to choose their starting and ending times, provided that they are at work during a specified core period.

compressed workweek a four-day (or shorter) period during which an employee works 40 hours.

job sharing performance of one full-time job by two people on part-time hours.

job. Top benefits of telecommuting for employees include a better work–life balance, reduced stress, and transportation savings.[22]

Flextime is a program that allows employees to choose their starting and ending times, as long as they are at work during a specified core period (Figure 9.4). It does not reduce the total number of hours that employees work; instead, it gives employees more flexibility in choosing which hours they work. A firm may specify that employees must be present from 10:00 a.m. to 3:00 p.m. One employee may choose to come in at 7:00 a.m. and leave at the end of the core time, perhaps to attend classes at a nearby college after work. Another employee, a mother who lives in the suburbs, may come in at 9:00 a.m. in order to have time to drop off her children at a day-care center and commute by public transportation to her job. Flextime provides many benefits, including improved ability to recruit and retain workers who wish to balance work and home life. Customers can be better served by allowing more coverage of customers over longer hours, workstations and facilities can be better utilized by staggering employee use, and rush hour traffic may be reduced. In addition, flexible schedules have been associated with an increase in healthy behaviors on the part of employees. More flexible schedules are associated with healthier lifestyle choices such as increased physical activity and healthier sleep habits.[23]

Related to flextime are the scheduling strategies of the compressed workweek and job sharing. The **compressed workweek** is a four-day (or shorter) period in which an employee works 40 hours. Under such a plan, employees typically work 10 hours per day for four days and have a three-day weekend. The compressed workweek reduces the company's operating expenses because its actual hours of operation are reduced. It is also sometimes used by parents who want to have more days off to spend with their families. The U.S. Bureau of Labor Statistics notes that the following career options provide greater flexibility in scheduling: medical transcriptionist, financial manager, nurse, database administrator, accountant, software developer, physical therapist assistant, paralegal, graphic designer, and private investigator.[24]

Job sharing occurs when two people do one job. One person may work from 8:00 a.m. to 12:30 p.m.; the second person comes in at 12:30 p.m. and works until 5:00 p.m. Job sharing gives both people the opportunity to work as well as time to fulfill other obligations, such as parenting or school. With job sharing, the company has the benefit of the skills of two people for one job, often at a lower total cost for salaries and benefits than one person working eight hours a day would be paid.

Two other flexible scheduling strategies attaining wider use include allowing full-time workers to work part time for a certain period and allowing workers to work at home either full or part time. Employees at some firms may be permitted to work part time for several months in order to care for a new baby or an elderly parent or just to slow down for a little while to "recharge their batteries." When the employees return to full-time work, they are usually given

> **Flextime provides many benefits, including improved ability to recruit and retain workers who wish to balance work and home life.**

FIGURE 9.4
Flextime, Showing Core and Flexible Hours

(Clock diagram showing hours 1–12, with inner ring labeled "Core Time," "Start Time," and "End Time.")

Working from home is becoming increasingly common. Telecommuting, job sharing, and flextime can be beneficial for employees who cannot work normal work hours.
© Jetta Productions/Getty Images

Clif Bar is well known for its highly successful sports snack products, including its Clif Bar line, its Luna Bar line, and others. However, Clif Bar was also recognized for how well it treats its employees, ranking 12th on *Fortune* magazine's "25 Best Medium-Size Companies to Work For." Since the firms that have made *Fortune*'s more general "100 Best Companies to Work For" list have also performed above average in the stock market over the past 15 years, it is worth looking into how these firms have made themselves so worker-friendly.

Clif Bar's workplace reflects its active-lifestyle product line. For example, the gym at its headquarters includes a rock-climbing wall, a variety of free weekly classes from yoga to boot camp, and certified trainers and nutritionists. Employees are allowed 2.5 hours of paid gym time a week. Clif Bar also builds its focus on sustainability into its employee perks, such as a $6,500 reimbursement for buying a company-approved hybrid, biodiesel, or electric-powered vehicle. Finally, Clif Bar extends its commitment to organic and natural ingredients to its employees by providing an on-site cafeteria that serves subsidized meals made with locally sourced and organic food.

These decisions to deeply integrate the company's values into its workplace environment—as well as to offer a variety of other worker benefits such as employee stock ownership plans and a generous amount of paid vacation time—have resulted in both an extremely low turnover rate and an extremely high application rate for open positions. This puts Clif Bar in an ideal position to find and retain the talented and motivated people it needs to be successful.[25]

Discussion Questions

1. Why has Clif Bar's workplace model been so effective?

2. Does it make sense for Clif Bar, whose products target active-lifestyle and health-conscious consumers, to focus on these values in designing its workplace? Why might people prefer working for a company whose workplace closely reflects its customers and products?

3. Why do you think companies that have been nominated among *Fortune*'s "100 Best Companies to Work For" have generally outperformed other companies in the stock market?

---

a position comparable to their original full-time position. Other firms are allowing employees to telecommute or telework (work at home a few days of the week), staying connected via computers, modems, and telephones. Most telecommuters tend to combine going into the office with working from home. In fact, three out of five workers say they do not need to be in the office to be productive.[26]

Although many employees ask for the option of working at home to ease the responsibilities of caring for family members, some have discovered that they are more productive at home without the distractions of the workplace. PGi conducted a survey on telecommuting and found that telecommuters experienced a decrease in stress and absenteeism and an increase in morale and productivity. Perhaps due to the positive morale that telecommuting can create, many Fortune 500 companies—including Apple, Google, and JPMorgan Chase—offer several types of telecommuting positions.[27] Other employees, however, have discovered that they are not suited for working at home. For telecommuting to work, it must be a feasible alternative and must not create significant costs for the company.[28] Bank of America, Yahoo!, and Best Buy are all eliminating their work-from-home programs as they feel that being present in the workplace increases collaboration and productivity. Still, work-at-home programs can help reduce overhead costs for businesses. For example, some companies used to maintain a surplus of office space but have reduced the surplus through employee telecommuting, "hoteling" (being assigned to a desk through a reservation system), and "hot-desking" (several people using the same desk but at different times).

Companies are turning to flexible work schedules to provide more options to employees who are trying to juggle their work duties with other responsibilities and needs. Preliminary results indicate that flexible scheduling plans increase job satisfaction, which, in turn, leads to increases in productivity. Some recent research, however, has indicated there are potential problems with telecommuting. Some managers are reluctant to adopt the practice because the pace of change in today's workplace is faster than ever, and telecommuters may be left behind or actually cause managers more work in helping them stay abreast of changes. Some employers also worry that telecommuting

Businesses have come up with different ways to motivate employees, including rewards such as trophies and plaques to show the company's appreciation.
© *Blend Images/ColorBlind Images/Getty images*

workers create a security risk by creating more opportunities for computer hackers or equipment thieves. Some employees have found that working outside the office may hurt career advancement opportunities, and some report that instead of helping them balance work and family responsibilities, telecommuting increases the strain by blurring the barriers between the office and home. Co-workers call at all hours, and telecommuters are apt to continue to work when they are not supposed to (after regular business hours or during vacation time).

Importance of Motivational Strategies

Motivation is more than a tool that managers can use to foster employee loyalty and boost productivity. It is a process that affects all the relationships within an organization and influences many areas such as pay, promotion, job design, training opportunities, and reporting relationships. Employees are motivated by the nature of the relationships they have with their supervisors, by the nature of their jobs, and by characteristics

TEAM EXERCISE

Form groups and outline a compensation package that you would consider ideal in motivating an employee, recognizing performance, and assisting the company in attaining its cost-to-performance objectives. Think about the impact of intrinsic and extrinsic motivation and recognition. How can flexible scheduling strategies be used effectively to motivate employees? Report your compensation package to the class.

of the organization. Table 9.6 shows companies with excellent motivational strategies, along with the types of strategies they use to motivate employees. Even the economic environment can change an employee's motivation. In a slow growth or recession economy, sales can flatten or decrease and morale can drop because of the need to cut jobs. In the most recent recession, many workers feared losing their jobs and increased the amount they were saving. The firm may have to work harder to keep good employees and to motivate all employees to work to overcome obstacles. In good economic times, employees may be more demanding and be on the lookout for better opportunities. New rewards or incentives may help motivate workers in such economies. Motivation tools, then, must be varied as well. Managers can further nurture motivation by being honest, supportive, empathic, accessible, fair, and open. Motivating employees to increase satisfaction and productivity is an important concern for organizations seeking to remain competitive in the global marketplace. ◼

▼ **TABLE 9.6** Companies with Excellent Motivational Strategies

Company	Motivational Strategies
3M	Gives employees 15–20 percent of their time to pursue on projects
Google	Perks include a massage every other week, free gourmet lunches, tuition reimbursement, a volleyball court, and time to work on own projects
Whole Foods	Employees receive 20 percent discounts on company products, the opportunity to gain stock options, and the ability to make major decisions in small teams
Patagonia	Provides areas for yoga and aerobics, in-house child care services, organic food in its café, and opportunities to go surfing during the day
The Container Store	Provides more than 260 hours of employee training and hosts "We Love Our Employees" Day
Southwest Airlines	Gives employees permission to interact with passengers as they see fit, provides free or discounted flights, and hosts the "Adopt-a-Pilot" program to connect pilots with students across the nation
Nike	Offers tuition assistance, product discounts, onsite fitness centers, and the ability for employees to give insights on how to improve the firm
Apple	Creates a fast-paced, innovative work environment where employees are encouraged to debate ideas
Marriott	Offers discounts at hotels across the world as well as free hotel stays and travel opportunities for employees with exceptional service
Zappos	Creates a fun, zany work environment for employees and empowers them to take as much times as needed to answer customer concerns

SO YOU THINK // You May Be Good at Motivating a Workforce /

If you are good at mediation, smoothing conflict, and have a good understanding of motivation and human relations theories, then you might be a good leader, human resources manager, or training expert. Most organizations, especially as they grow, will need to implement human relations programs. These are necessary to teach employees about sensitivity to other cultures, religions, and beliefs, as well as for teaching the workforce about the organization so that they understand how they fit in the larger picture. Employees need to appreciate the benefits of working together to make the firm run smoothly, and they also need to understand how their contributions help the firm. To stay motivated, most employees need to feel like what they do each day contributes something of value to the firm. Disclosing information and including employees in decision-making processes will also help employees feel valuable and wanted within the firm.

There are many different ways employers can reward and encourage employees. However, employers must be careful when considering what kinds of incentives to use. Different cultures value different kinds of incentives more highly than others. For example, a Japanese worker would probably not like it if she were singled out from the group and given a large cash bonus as reward for her work. Japanese workers tend to be more group oriented, and therefore anything that singles out individuals would not be an effective way of rewarding and motivating. American workers, on the other hand, are very individualistic, and a raise and public praise might be more effective. However, what might motivate a younger employee (bonuses, raises, and perks) may not be the same as what motivates a more seasoned, experienced, and financially successful employee (recognition, opportunity for greater influence, and increased training). Motivation is not an easy thing to understand, especially as firms become more global and more diverse.

Another important part of motivation is enjoying where you work and your career opportunities. Here is a list of the best places to do business and start careers in the United States, according to *Forbes* magazine. Chances are, workers who live in these places have encountered fewer frustrations than those places at the bottom of the list and, therefore, would probably be more content with where they work.[29]

▼ Best Places for Businesses and Careers[30]

Rank	Metro Area	Gross Metro Product*	Metro Population
1	Raleigh, North Carolina	$ 61 billion	1,233,700
2	Des Moines, Iowa	38 billion	594,900
3	Provo, Utah	19 billion	567,000
4	Denver, Colorado	157 billion	2,687,300
5	Fort Collins, Colorado	15 billion	317,500
6	Lincoln, Nebraska	17 billion	313,900
7	Oklahoma City, Oklahoma	61 billion	1,313,200
8	Salt Lake City, Utah	74 billion	1,181,300
9	Seattle, Washington	212 billion	2,779,000
10	Nashville, Tennessee	87 billion	1,670,200

*Gross metro product is the market value of all products produced within a metropolitan area in a given time period; similar to GDP but in a metropolitan area.

chapter ten

managing
human resources

© Zefa RF/Corbis, RF

LEARNING OBJECTIVES

After reading this chapter, you will be able to:

LO 10-1 Define human resources management, and explain its significance.

LO 10-2 Summarize the processes of recruiting and selecting human resources for a company.

LO 10-3 Discuss how workers are trained and their performance appraised.

LO 10-4 Identify the types of turnover companies may experience, and explain why turnover is an important issue.

LO 10-5 Specify the various ways a worker may be compensated.

LO 10-6 Discuss some of the issues associated with unionized employees, including collective bargaining and dispute resolution.

LO 10-7 Describe the importance of diversity in the workforce.

If a business is to achieve success, it must have sufficient numbers of employees who are qualified and motivated to perform the required duties. Thus, managing the quantity (from hiring to firing) and quality (through training, compensating, and so on) of employees is an important business function. Meeting the challenge of managing increasingly diverse human resources effectively can give a company a competitive edge in a global marketplace.

This chapter focuses on the quantity and quality of human resources. First we look at how human resources managers plan for, recruit, and select qualified employees. Next we look at training, appraising, and compensating employees, aspects of human resources management designed to retain valued employees. Along the way, we'll also consider the challenges of managing unionized employees and workplace diversity. ■

LO 10-1 Define human resources management, and explain its significance.

THE NATURE OF HUMAN RESOURCES MANAGEMENT

Chapter 1 defined human resources as labor, the physical and mental abilities that people use to produce goods and services. **Human resources management (HRM)** refers to all the activities involved in determining an organization's human resources needs, as well as acquiring, training, and compensating people to fill those needs. Human resources managers are concerned with maximizing the satisfaction of employees and motivating them to meet organizational objectives productively. In some companies, this function is called personnel management.

HRM has increased in importance over the past few decades, in part because managers have developed a better understanding of human relations through the work of Maslow, Herzberg, and others. How employees are treated is also important to consumers. Approximately 85 percent of consumers say that a company's corporate social responsibility (CSR) practices, *including their treatment of employees,* play a significant role in deciding where to take their business.[1] Moreover, the human resources themselves are changing. Employees today are concerned not only about how much a job pays; they are concerned also with job satisfaction, personal performance, recreation, benefits, the work environment, and their opportunities for advancement. Once dominated by white men, today's workforce includes significantly more women, African Americans, Hispanics, and other minorities, as well as workers who are older and those with disabilities. Human resources managers must be aware of these changes and leverage them to increase the productivity of their employees. Every manager practices some of the functions of human resources management at all times.

> **human resources management (HRM)** all the activities involved in determining an organization's human resources needs, as well as acquiring, training, and compensating people to fill those needs.

Today's organizations are more diverse, with a greater range of women, minorities, and older workers.
© *Digital Vision/Getty Images, RF*

PLANNING FOR HUMAN RESOURCES NEEDS

When planning and developing strategies for reaching the organization's overall objectives, a company must consider whether it will have the human resources necessary to carry out its plans. After determining how many employees and what skills are needed to satisfy the overall plans, the human resources department (which may range from the owner in a small business to

job analysis the determination, through observation and study, of pertinent information about a job—including specific tasks and necessary abilities, knowledge, and skills.

job description a formal, written explanation of a specific job, usually including job title, tasks, relationship with other jobs, physical and mental skills required, duties, responsibilities, and working conditions.

job specification a description of the qualifications necessary for a specific job, in terms of education, experience, and personal and physical characteristics.

recruiting forming a pool of qualified applicants from which management can select employees.

hundreds of people in a large corporation) ascertains how many employees the company currently has and how many will be retiring or otherwise leaving the organization during the planning period. With this information, the human resources manager can then forecast how many more employees the company will need to hire and what qualifications they must have, or determine if layoffs are required to meet demand more efficiently. HRM planning also requires forecasting the availability of people in the workforce who will have the necessary qualifications to meet the organization's future needs. The human resources manager then develops a strategy for satisfying the organization's human resources needs. As organizations strive to increase efficiency through outsourcing, automation, or learning to effectively use temporary workers, hiring needs can change dramatically.

necessary for a specific job, in terms of education (some jobs require a college degree), experience, personal characteristics (ads frequently request outgoing, hardworking persons), and physical characteristics. Both the job description and job specification are used to develop recruiting materials such as newspapers, trade publications, and online advertisements.

> **LO 10-2** Summarize the processes of recruiting and selecting human resources for a company.

RECRUITING AND SELECTING NEW EMPLOYEES

After forecasting the firm's human resources needs and comparing them to existing human resources, the human resources manager should have a general idea of how many new employees the firm needs to hire. With the aid of job analyses, management can then recruit and select employees who are qualified to fill specific job openings.

Recruiting

Recruiting means forming a pool of qualified applicants from which management can select employees. There are two sources from which to develop this pool of applicants—internal and external.

> ## "Managers use the information obtained through a job analysis to develop job descriptions and job specifications."

Next, managers analyze the jobs within the organization so that they can match the human resources to the available assignments. **Job analysis** determines, through observation and study, pertinent information about a job—the specific tasks that comprise it; the knowledge, skills, and abilities necessary to perform it; and the environment in which it will be performed. Managers use the information obtained through a job analysis to develop job descriptions and job specifications.

A **job description** is a formal, written explanation of a specific job that usually includes job title, tasks to be performed (for instance, waiting on customers), relationship with other jobs, physical and mental skills required (such as lifting heavy boxes or calculating data), duties, responsibilities, and working conditions. Job seekers might turn to online websites or databases to help find job descriptions for specific occupations. For instance, the Occupational Information Network has an online database with hundreds of occupational descriptors. These descriptors describe the skills, knowledge, and education needed to fulfill a particular occupation (e.g., human resources).[2] A **job specification** describes the qualifications

Internal sources of applicants include the organization's current employees. Many firms have a policy of giving first consideration to their own employees—or promoting from within. The cost of hiring current employees to fill job openings is inexpensive when compared with the cost of hiring from external sources, and it is good for employee morale. However, hiring from within creates another job vacancy to be filled.

External sources of applicants consist of advertisements in newspapers and professional journals, employment agencies, colleges, vocational schools, recommendations from current employees, competing firms, unsolicited applications, online websites, and social networking sites such as LinkedIn. Internships are also a good way to solicit for potential employees. Many companies hire college students or recent graduates to low-paying internships that give them the opportunity to get hands-on experience on the job. If the intern proves to be a good fit, an organization may then hire the intern as a full-time worker. There are also hundreds of websites where employers can post job openings and job seekers can post their résumés, including Monster.com, USAJobs, Simply Hired, SnagaJob, and CareerBuilder.com.

TheLadders.com is a website that targets career-driven professionals.
© Studio Works/Alamy

TheLadders.com is a website that focuses on career-driven professionals who make salaries of $40,000 or more. Employers looking for employees for specialized jobs can use more focused sites such as computerwork.com. Increasingly, companies can turn to their own websites for potential candidates: Nearly all of the *Fortune* 500 firms provide career websites where they recruit, provide employment information, and take applications. Using these sources of applicants is generally more expensive than hiring from within, but it may be necessary if there are no current employees who meet the job specifications or there are better-qualified people outside the organization. Recruiting for entry-level managerial and professional positions is often carried out on college and university campuses. For managerial or professional positions above the entry level, companies sometimes depend on employment agencies or executive search firms, sometimes called *headhunters*, which specialize in luring qualified people away from other companies. Employers are also increasingly using professional social networking sites such as LinkedIn and Viadeo as recruitment tools. Virtual college job fairs are also becoming common.[3] Figure 10.1 compares the social media sites employers use for recruitment compared to the sites on which job seekers are active.

selection the process of collecting information about applicants and using that information to make hiring decisions.

Selection

Selection is the process of collecting information about applicants and using that information to decide which ones to hire. It includes the application itself, as well as interviewing, testing, and reference checking. This process can be quite lengthy and expensive. Procter & Gamble, for example, offers online applications for jobs in approximately 100 countries. The first round of evaluation involves assessment, and if this stage goes well, the candidate interviews in the region or country to which the applicant applied.[4] Such rigorous scrutiny is necessary to find those applicants who can do the work expected and fit into the firm's structure and culture. If an organization finds the "right" employees through its recruiting and selection process, it will not have to spend as much money later in recruiting, selecting, and training replacement employees.

The Application In the first stage of the selection process, the individual fills out an application form and perhaps has a brief interview. The application form asks for the applicant's name, address, telephone number, education, and previous work experience. The goal of this stage of the selection process is to get acquainted with the applicants and to weed out those who are obviously not qualified for the job. For employees with work experience, most companies

▼**FIGURE 10.1**
Recruiting through Social Media

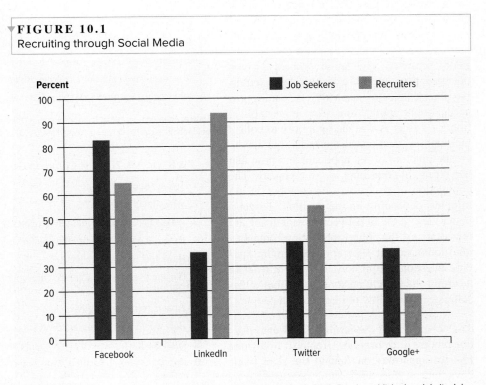

Source: Jobvite survey of 2,135 adults (aged +18), fielded December 12–19, 2013. Results published as *Jobvite Job Seeker Nation Study,* 2014.

The job search is never one-sided. Not only are individuals competing for good jobs, but companies are also seeking to entice top candidates to work for them and not someone else. To this end, firms must keep a close eye on what their desired employees value and adapt themselves accordingly. For the millennial generation, an essential recruiting tool is turning out to be strong and integrated charity and social responsibility programs.

According to recruiters and CFOs, members of the current generation want their work to relate directly to causes they care about. This is drawing many millennials toward founding or joining entrepreneurial ventures with high-tech and/or socially minded goals (the lucrative stock options that often come with getting involved in a startup are beneficial as well). For larger, more traditional companies to compete, they must show a link between themselves and similar causes. Furthermore, research has shown that simply writing big checks to charity doesn't work; employees want to see and participate in active engagement toward philanthropy and social responsibility.

For example, Microsoft matches employee charitable contributions up to $12,000 per employee per year, and will also pay employees $17 per hour for charity volunteer work. Ralph Lauren published its first corporate sustainability report in 2014 and has since reported a significant increase in talent recruitment. Some startups are even capitalizing on the trend: Crowdfunding donation service Givelocity, launched in 2013, is actively soliciting partnerships with corporations that want to increase their philanthropic presence and involvement. As more millennials reach working age and begin seeking jobs, companies should continue building philanthropic components into their businesses to reach them.[5]

Discussion Questions

1. How do companies show commitment to philanthropy beyond simply donating money?

2. Why are company charity and social responsibility programs becoming important factors in the job search for millennials?

3. What makes you believe that a company is truly dedicated to a cause, rather than simply giving what seems to be required to stay competitive?

---

ask for the following information before contacting a potential candidate: current salary, reason for seeking a new job, years of experience, availability, and level of interest in the position. In addition to identifying obvious qualifications, the application can provide subtle clues about whether a person is appropriate for a particular job. For instance, an applicant who gives unusually creative answers may be perfect for a position at an advertising agency; a person who turns in a sloppy, hurriedly scrawled application probably would not be appropriate for a technical job requiring precise adjustments. Most companies now accept online applications. The online application for Target is designed not only to collect biographical data on the applicant, but also to create a picture of the applicant and how that person might contribute to the company. The completion of the survey takes about 15–45 minutes, depending on the position. To get a better view of the fit between the applicant and the company, the online application contains a questionnaire that asks applicants more specific questions, from how they might react in a certain situation to personality attributes like self-esteem or ability to interact with people.

The Interview The next phase of the selection process is the interview. Table 10.1 provides tips for applicants on finding the right work environment. Interviews allow management to obtain detailed information about the applicant's experience and skills, reasons for changing jobs, attitudes toward the job, and an idea of whether the person would fit in with the company. Table 10.2 lists some of the most common questions asked by interviewers, while Table 10.3 reveals some common mistakes candidates make in interviewing. The interviewer can answer the applicant's questions about the requirements

▼ **TABLE 10.1** Interviewing Tips

1. Evaluate the work environment. Do employees seem to get along and work well in teams?
2. Evaluate the attitude of employees. Are employees happy, tense, or overworked?
3. Are employees enthusiastic and excited about their work?
4. What is the organizational culture, and would you feel comfortable working there?

Source: Adapted from "What to Look for during Office Visits," https://careercenter.tamu.edu/guides/interviews/lookforinoffice.cfm?sn=faculty (accessed March 24, 2015).

▼ **TABLE 10.2** Most Common Questions Asked during the Interview

1. Tell me about yourself.
2. Why should I hire you?
3. Please tell me about your future objectives.
4. Has your education prepared you for your career?
5. Have you been a team player?
6. Did you encounter any conflict with your previous professors or employer? What are the steps that you have taken to resolve this issue?
7. What is your biggest weakness?
8. How would your professors describe you?
9. What are the qualities that a manager should possess?
10. If you could turn back time, what would you change?

Source: "Job Interview Skills Training: Top Ten Interview Questions for College Graduates," February 17, 2010, www.articlesbase.com/business-articles/job-interview-skills-training-top-ten-interview-questions-for-college-graduates-1871741.html (accessed March 24, 2015).

▼ **TABLE 10.3** Mistakes Made in Interviewing

1. Not taking the interview seriously.
2. Not dressing appropriately (dressing down).
3. Not appropriately discussing experience, abilities, and education.
4. Being too modest about your accomplishments.
5. Talking too much.
6. Having too much concern about compensation.
7. Speaking negatively of a former employer.
8. Not asking enough or appropriate questions.
9. Not showing the proper enthusiasm level.
10. Not engaging in appropriate follow-up to the interview.

Source: "Avoid the Top 10 Job Interview Mistakes," *All Business*, www.allbusiness.com/slideshow/avoid-the-job-interview-mistakes-16568835-1.html (accessed March 24, 2015).

for the job, compensation, working conditions, company policies, organizational culture, and so on. A potential employee's questions may be just as revealing as his or her answers. Today's students might be surprised to have an interviewer ask them "What's on your Facebook account?" or ask them to show the interviewer their Facebook accounts. Currently, these are legal questions for an interviewer to ask. Approximately 39 percent of employers review job candidates through social media sites.[6] (It is also legal and common for companies to monitor employee work habits and e-mails. While this can be important for monitoring outside threats such as hacking or information leaks, employees might view this as the company's way of saying it does not trust them.[7])

> ❝ Ability and performance tests are used to determine whether an applicant has the skills necessary for the job. ❞

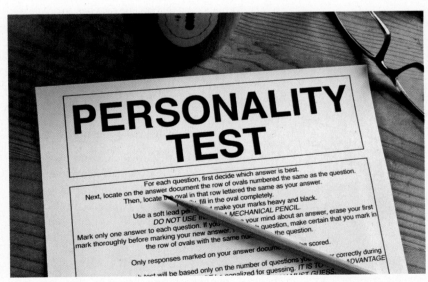

Personality tests such as Myers-Briggs are used to assess an applicant's potential for a certain kind of job. For instance, extroversion and a love of people would be good qualities for a retail job.
© *Kirby Hamilton/Getty Images, RF*

Testing

Another step in the selection process is testing. Ability and performance tests are used to determine whether an applicant has the skills necessary for the job. Aptitude, IQ, or personality tests may be used to assess an applicant's potential for a certain kind of work and his or her ability to fit into the organization's culture. One of the most commonly used tests is the Myers-Briggs Type Indicator. The Myers-Briggs Type Indicator Test is used worldwide by millions of people each year. Although polygraph ("lie detector") tests were once a common technique for evaluating the honesty of applicants, in 1988 their use was restricted to specific government jobs and those involving security or access to drugs. Applicants may also undergo physical examinations to determine their suitability for some jobs, and many companies require applicants to be screened for illegal drug use. Illegal drug use and alcoholism can be particularly damaging to businesses. It has been estimated that 9.1 percent of full-time employees engage in illicit drug use, while 30.5 percent engage in binge drinking.[8] Small businesses may have a higher percentage of these employees because they do not engage in systematic drug testing. If you employ a drug or alcohol abuser, you can expect a 33 percent loss in productivity from this employee. Loss in productivity from alcohol abuse alone costs companies $185 billion each year. Health care costs are also more expensive for those who abuse alcohol—twice as much as those for employees who do not abuse alcohol.[9] E-cigarettes are another growing concern. Many organizations have restrictions on cigarette use but these policies do not necessarily apply to e-cigarettes. As e-cigarette use grows among employees, many of them do not know where they stand regarding their corporate policies.[10]

Because computer knowledge is a requirement for many jobs today, certain companies also require an applicant to take a typing test or tests to determine their knowledge of MS Word, Excel, PowerPoint, and/or other necessary programs. Like the application form and the interview, testing serves to eliminate those who do not meet the job specifications.

Reference Checking Before making a job offer, the company should always check an applicant's references. Reference checking usually involves verifying educational background and previous work experience. An Internet search is often done to determine social media activities or other public activities. While public Internet searches are usually deemed acceptable, asking for private information—while legal—is deemed to be intrusive by many job seekers.[11] Many states are already taking legislative action to ban this practice.[12] Public companies are likely to do more extensive background searches to make sure applicants are not misrepresenting themselves.

Background checking is important because applicants may misrepresent themselves on their applications or résumés. Matthew Martoma, a trader for SAC Capital Advisors, was convicted of conspiracy and securities fraud. Court testimony revealed that he had been expelled from Harvard after forging a transcript for an application and creating an elaborate cover-up. Research has shown that those who are willing to exaggerate or lie on their résumés are more likely to engage in unethical behaviors.[13] As Table 10.4 illustrates, some of the most common types of résumé lies include the faking of credentials, overstatements of skills or accomplishments, lies concerning education/degrees, omissions of past employment, and the falsification of references.[14]

Reference checking is a vital, albeit often overlooked, stage in the selection process. Managers charged with hiring should be aware, however, that many organizations will confirm only that an applicant is a former employee, perhaps with beginning and ending work dates, and will not release details about the quality of the employee's work.

Legal Issues in Recruiting and Selecting

Legal constraints and regulations are present in almost every phase of the recruitment and selection process, and a violation of these regulations can result in lawsuits and fines. Therefore, managers should be aware of these restrictions to avoid legal problems. Some of the laws affecting human resources management are discussed here.

▼ **TABLE 10.4** Top 10 Résumé Lies

1. Stretching dates of employment
2. Inflating past accomplishments and skills
3. Enhancing job titles and responsibilities
4. Exaggerating education and fabricating degrees
5. Having unexplained gaps and periods of "self-employment"
6. Omitting past employment
7. Faking credentials
8. Fabricating reasons for leaving previous job
9. Providing fraudulent references
10. Misrepresenting military record

Source: Adapted from Christopher T. Marquet and Lisa J. B. Peterson, "Résumé Fraud: The Top 10 Lies," www.marquetinternational.com/pdf/Resume%20Fraud-Top%20Ten%20Lies.pdf (accessed March 24, 2015).

Because one law pervades all areas of human resources management, we'll take a quick look at it now. **Title VII of the Civil Rights Act** of 1964 prohibits discrimination in employment. It also created the Equal Employment Opportunity Commission (EEOC), a federal agency dedicated to increasing job opportunities for women and minorities and eliminating job discrimination based on race, religion, color, sex, national origin, or handicap. As a result of Title VII, employers must not impose sex distinctions in job specifications, job descriptions, or newspaper advertisements. In 2014, workplace discrimination charges filed with the EEOC were 88,778. The EEOC received more than 26,027 charges of sexual harassment and pregnancy discrimination. Sexual harassment often makes up the largest number of claims the EEOC encounters each day.[15] The Civil Rights Act of 1964 also outlaws the use of discriminatory tests for applicants. Aptitude tests and other indirect tests must be validated; in other words, employers must be able to demonstrate that scores on such tests are related to job performance, so that no one race has an advantage in taking the tests or is alternatively discriminated against. Although many hope for improvements in organizational diversity, only about 4 percent of Fortune 500 companies are run by people of color. Despite the low number, this is an improvement from the mid-1990s when no Fortune 500 company had a person of color as a CEO. Additionally, 13.3 percent of board seats are now held by racial minorities.[16]

Other laws affecting HRM include the Americans with Disabilities Act (ADA), which prevents discrimination against persons with disabilities. It also classifies people with AIDS as disabled and, consequently, prohibits using a positive AIDS test as reason to deny an applicant employment. The Age Discrimination in Employment Act specifically outlaws discrimination based on age. Its focus is banning hiring practices that discriminate against people 40 years and older. Generally, when companies need employees, recruiters head to college campuses, and when downsizing

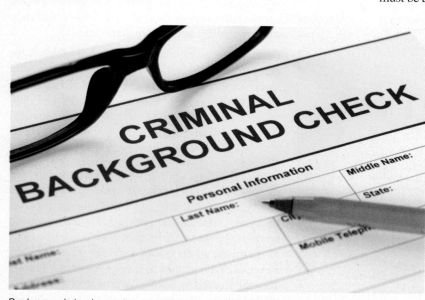

Background checks are important in determining whether employees are accurately describing their work experience and background.
© Ekaterina Minaeva/Getty Images, RF

Title VII of the Civil Rights Act prohibits discrimination in employment. People who feel they have been discriminated against can file a formal complaint with the Equal Employment Opportunity Commission.
© CREATISTA/Getty Images, RF

is necessary, many older workers are offered early retirement. Forced retirement based on age, however, is generally considered to be illegal in the United States, although claims of forced retirement still abound. Until recently, employees in the United Kingdom could be forced to retire at age 65. However, a new law abolished the default retirement age.[17] Indeed there are many benefits that companies are realizing in hiring older workers. Some of these benefits include the fact that they are

orientation
familiarizing newly hired employees with fellow workers, company procedures, and the physical properties of the company.

more dedicated, punctual, honest, and detail oriented; are good listeners; take pride in their work; exhibit good organizational skills; are efficient and confident; are mature; can be seen as role models; have good communication skills; and offer an opportunity for a reduced labor cost because of already having insurance plans.[18] Figure 10.2 shows the age ranges of employed workers in the United States.

The Equal Pay Act mandates that men and women who do equal work must receive the same wage. Wage differences are acceptable only if they are attributed to seniority, performance, or qualifications. In the United States, the typical full-time female employee earns 21.7 percent less than the average full-time employee.[19] In a study by PayScale, gender pay gaps can be found in positions such as chief executive (women earn 87 percent of what men earn), software architect (women earn 88 percent of what men earn), and executive chef (women earn 91 percent of what men earn).[20] Performance quality in these jobs is relatively subjective. Jobs like engineers, actuaries, or electricians, where the performance evaluation is more objective, result in greater salary parity between men and women.[21] However, despite the wage inequalities that still exist, women in the workplace are becoming increasingly accepted among both genders. The working mother is no longer a novelty; in fact, many working mothers seek the same amount of achievement as working men and women who are not mothers.

FIGURE 10.2
U.S. Population Employed by Age Group (in thousands)

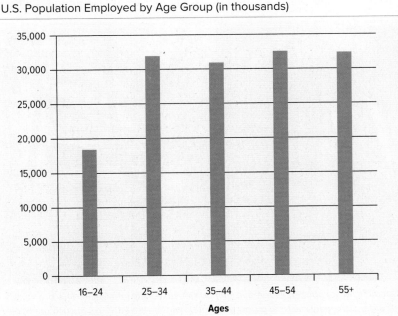

Source: Bureau of Labor Statistics, labor force statistics from the *Current Population Survey,* www.bls.gov/cps/cpsaat03.htm (accessed March 24, 2015).

DEVELOPING THE WORKFORCE

Once the most qualified applicants have been selected, have been offered positions, and have accepted their offers, they must be formally introduced to the organization and trained so they can begin to be productive members of the workforce. **Orientation** familiarizes the newly hired employees with fellow workers, company procedures, and the physical properties of the company. It generally includes a tour of the building; introductions to supervisors, co-workers, and subordinates; and the distribution of organizational manuals describing the organization's policy on vacations, absenteeism, lunch breaks, company benefits, and so on. Orientation also involves socializing the new employee into the ethics and culture of the new company. Many larger companies now show videotapes of procedures, facilities, and key personnel in the organization to help speed the adjustment process.

training teaching employees to do specific job tasks through either classroom development or on-the-job experience.

mentoring supporting, training, and guiding an employee in his or her professional development.

development training that augments the skills and knowledge of managers and professionals.

LO 10-3 Discuss how workers are trained and their performance appraised.

Training and Development

Although recruiting and selection are designed to find employees who have the knowledge, skills, and abilities the company needs, new employees still must undergo **training** to learn how to do their specific job tasks. *On-the-job training* allows workers to learn by actually performing the tasks of the job, while *classroom training* teaches employees with lectures, conferences, videotapes, case studies, and web-based training. For instance, McDonald's trains those interested in company operations and leadership development at the Fred L. Turner

underrepresented areas. For instance, mentoring has been suggested as a way to attract more women to the gas and oil industry.[25]

Development is training that augments the skills and knowledge of managers and professionals. Training and development are also used to improve the skills of employees in their present positions and to prepare them for increased responsibility and job promotions. Training is therefore a vital function of human resources management. At the Container Store, for example, first-year sales personnel receive 263 hours of training about the company's products.[26] Companies are engaging in more experiential and involvement-oriented training exercises for employees. Use of role-plays, simulations, and online training methods are becoming increasingly popular in employee training.

Assessing Performance

Assessing an employee's performance—his or her strengths and weaknesses on the job—is one of the most difficult tasks

> ❝ Mentoring provides employees with more of a one-on-one interaction with somebody in the organization that not only teaches them but also acts as their supporter as they progress in their jobs. ❞

Training Center, otherwise known as Hamburger University. Hamburger University employs full-time professors to train students in a variety of topics, including crew development, restaurant management, middle management, and executive development. Training includes classroom instruction, hands-on instruction, and computer e-learning.[22]

Some companies will go even further and ask a more experienced individual in the organization to mentor a new employee. **Mentoring** involves supporting, training, and guiding an employee in his or her professional development. Mentoring provides employees with more of a one-on-one interaction with somebody in the organization that not only teaches them but also acts as their supporter as they progress in their jobs. It is estimated that 71 percent of Fortune 500 firms offer mentoring programs, including Deloitte and Sun Microsystems.[23] Even small and medium-sized firms agree on the importance of mentoring—93 percent of these organizations claim that mentoring is important to helping them succeed.[24] Another benefit of mentoring is that companies can use this process to attract talent from

for managers. However, performance appraisal is crucial because it gives employees feedback on how they are doing and what they need to do to improve. It also provides a basis

McDonald's has expanded its famous Hamburger University into China. This branch of Hamburger University will train a new generation of Chinese students in such areas as restaurant management, leadership development, and other skills.
© Tannen Maury/Bloomberg /Getty Images

▼ TABLE 10.5 Performance Characteristics

- **Productivity**—rate at which work is regularly produced
- **Quality**—accuracy, professionalism, and deliverability of produced work
- **Job knowledge**—understanding of the objectives, practices, and standards of work
- **Problem solving**—ability to identify and correct problems effectively
- **Communication**—effectiveness in written and verbal exchanges
- **Initiative**—willingness to identify and address opportunities for improvement
- **Adaptability**—ability to become comfortable with change
- **Planning and organization skills**—reflected through the ability to schedule projects, set goals, and maintain organizational systems
- **Teamwork and cooperation**—effectiveness of collaborations with co-workers
- **Ethical judgment**—ability to determine appropriate actions
- **Dependability**—responsiveness, reliability, and conscientiousness demonstrated on the job
- **Creativity**—extent to which resourceful ideas, solutions, and methods for task completion are proposed
- **Sales**—demonstrated through success in selling products, services, yourself, and your company
- **Customer service**—ability to communicate effectively with customers, address problems, and offer solutions that meet or exceed their expectations
- **Leadership**—tendency and ability to serve as a doer, guide, decision maker, and role model
- **Financial management**—appropriateness of cost controls and financial planning within the scope defined by the position

Performance appraisals are important because they provide employees with feedback on how well they are doing as well as areas for improvement.
© *Eric Audras/Onoky/Getty Images, RF*

for determining how to compensate and reward employees, and it generates information about the quality of the firm's selection, training, and development activities. Table 10.5 identifies 16 characteristics that may be assessed in a performance review.

Performance appraisals may be objective or subjective. An objective assessment is quantifiable. For example, a Westinghouse employee might be judged by how many circuit boards he typically produces in one day or by how many of his boards have defects. A Century 21 real estate agent might be judged by the number of houses she has shown or the number of sales she has closed. A company can also use tests as an objective method of assessment. Whatever method they use, managers must take into account the work environment when they appraise performance objectively.

When jobs do not lend themselves to objective appraisal, the manager must relate the employee's performance to some other standard. One popular tool used in subjective assessment is the ranking system, which lists various performance factors on which the manager ranks employees against each other. Although used by many large companies, ranking systems are unpopular with many employees. Qualitative criteria, such as teamwork and communication skills, used to evaluate employees are generally hard to gauge. Such grading systems have triggered employee lawsuits that allege discrimination in grade/ranking assignments. For example, one manager may grade a company's employees one way, while another manager grades a group more harshly depending on the managers' grading style. If layoffs occur, then employees graded by the second manager may be more likely to lose their jobs. Other criticisms of grading systems include unclear wording or inappropriate words that a manager may unintentionally write in a performance evaluation, like *young* or *pretty* to describe an

turnover occurs when employees quit or are fired and must be replaced by new employees.

employee's appearance. These liabilities can all be fodder for lawsuits should employees allege that they were treated unfairly. It is therefore crucial that managers use clear language in performance evaluations and be consistent with all employees. Several employee grading computer packages have been developed to make performance evaluations easier for managers and clearer for employees.[27] Figure 10.3 shows that the majority of HR professionals view their organizations' performance appraisals as average. This suggests that many companies' performance appraisals could be improved to evaluate employee performance better.

Another performance appraisal method used by many companies is the 360-degree feedback system, which provides feedback from a panel that typically includes superiors, peers, and subordinates. Because of the tensions it may cause, peer appraisal appears to be difficult for many. However, companies that have success with 360-degree feedback tend to be open to learning and willing to experiment and are led by executives who are direct about the expected benefits as well as the challenges.[28] Managers and leaders with a high emotional intelligence (sensitivity to their own as well as others' emotions) assess and reflect upon their interactions with colleagues on a daily basis. In addition, they conduct follow-up analysis on their projects, asking the right questions and listening carefully to responses without getting defensive of their actions.[29]

Another trend occurring at some companies is the decrease of negative employee feedback. Executives have begun to recognize that hard tactics can harm employee confidence. Negative feedback tends to overshadow positive feedback, so employees may get discouraged if performance reviews are phrased too negatively. At the same time, it is important for managers to provide constructive criticism on employee weaknesses in addition to their strengths so workers know what to expect and how they are viewed.[30]

Whether the assessment is objective or subjective, it is vital that the manager discuss the results with the employee, so that the employee knows how well he or she is doing the job. The

> ## "The results of a performance appraisal become useful only when they are communicated, tactfully, to the employee and presented as a tool to allow the employee to grow and improve in his or her position and beyond. "

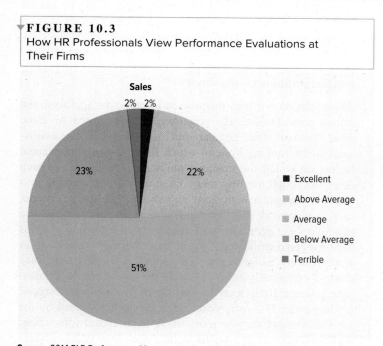

FIGURE 10.3
How HR Professionals View Performance Evaluations at Their Firms

Sales

- 2% Excellent
- 2% Above Average
- 22% Average
- 51% Below Average
- 23% Terrible

■ Excellent
■ Above Average
■ Average
■ Below Average
■ Terrible

Source: 2014 BLR Performance Management Survey of 1,481 HR professionals, http://hr.blr.com/HRnews/Performance-Termination/Performance-Employee-Appraisal/Infographic-2014-employeeperformance-appraisal-pr#s (accessed March 24, 2015).

results of a performance appraisal become useful only when they are communicated, tactfully, to the employee and presented as a tool to allow the employee to grow and improve in his or her position and beyond. Performance appraisals are also used to determine whether an employee should be promoted, transferred, or terminated from the organization.

> **LO 10-4** Identify the types of turnover companies may experience, and explain why turnover is an important issue.

Turnover

Turnover, which occurs when employees quit or are fired and must be replaced by new employees, results in lost productivity from the vacancy, costs to recruit replacement employees, management time devoted to interviewing, training, and socialization expenses for new employees. However, some companies have created innovative solutions for reducing turnover. Accenture, a global management consulting firm, has 275,000 employees around the world who travel frequently. Because of the hectic pace of the job and constant traveling, the company has instituted a unique wellness program offered to its on-the-go employees to encourage them to take care of their health while getting their jobs done. This program is personalized to the lifestyles of the employees and offers health tips and exercises that are effective but not time-consuming. Accenture employees have rated this program as fun and relevant to their lives, resulting in higher job satisfaction. Job satisfaction is one of the best ways of reducing turnover.[31] Part of the reason for turnover may be overworked employees as a result of downsizing and a lack of training and advancement opportunities.[32] Of course, turnover is not always an unhappy occasion when it takes the form of a promotion or transfer.

A **promotion** is an advancement to a higher-level job with increased authority, responsibility, and pay. In some companies and most labor unions, seniority—the length of time a person has been with the company or at a particular job classification—is the key issue in determining who should be promoted. Most managers base promotions on seniority only when they have candidates with equal qualifications: Managers prefer to base promotions on merit.

A **transfer** is a move to another job within the company at essentially the same level and wage. Transfers allow workers to obtain new skills or to find a new position within an organization when their old position has been eliminated because of automation or downsizing.

Separations occur when employees resign, retire, are terminated, or are laid off. Employees may be terminated, or fired, for poor performance, violation of work rules, absenteeism, and so on. Businesses have traditionally been able to fire employees *at will*, that is, for any reason other than for race, religion, sex, or age, or because an employee is a union organizer. However, recent legislation and court decisions now require that companies fire employees fairly, for just cause only. Managers must take care, then, to warn employees when their performance is unacceptable and may lead to dismissal, elevating the importance of performance evaluations. They should also document all problems and warnings in employees' work records. To avoid the possibility of lawsuits from individuals who may feel they have been fired unfairly, employers should provide clear, business-related reasons for any firing, supported by written documentation if possible. Employee disciplinary procedures should be carefully explained to all employees and should be set forth in employee handbooks. Table 10.6 illustrates what *not* to do when you are terminated.

Many companies have downsized in recent years, laying off tens of thousands of employees in their effort to become more productive and competitive. For example, Intel reduced its workforce by 5 percent due to lower-than-expected sales growth.[33] Layoffs are sometimes temporary; employees may be brought back when business conditions improve. When layoffs are to be permanent, employers often help employees find other jobs and may extend benefits while the employees search for new employment. Such actions help lessen the trauma of the layoffs. Fortunately, there are several business areas that are choosing not to downsize.

A well-organized human resources department strives to minimize losses due to separations and transfers because recruiting and training new employees is very expensive. Note that a high turnover rate in a company may signal problems with the selection and training process, the compensation program, or even the type of company. To help reduce turnover, companies have tried a number of strategies, including giving employees more interesting job responsibilities (job enrichment), allowing for increased job flexibility, and providing more employee benefits. When employees do choose to leave

Many companies in recent years are choosing to downsize by eliminating jobs. Reasons for downsizing might be due to financial constraints or the need to become more productive and competitive.
© Jamie Grill/JGI/ Blend Images/Getty Images, RF

promotion an advancement to a higher-level job with increased authority, responsibility, and pay.

transfer a move to another job within the company at essentially the same level and wage.

separations employment changes involving resignation, retirement, termination, or layoff.

▼ **TABLE 10.6** Actions You Should and Shouldn't Do When You Are Terminated

1. Do not criticize your boss who terminated you.
2. Do not take files or property that is not yours.
3. Do try to get a reference letter.
4. Do not criticize your former employer in job interviews.
5. Look to the future and be positive about new job opportunities.

the organization, the company will often ask them to conduct an *exit interview*. An exit interview is a survey used to determine why the employee is leaving the organization. The feedback hopefully will alert the company to processes it can improve upon to dissuade valuable employees from leaving in the future.

> **LO 10-5** Specify the various ways a worker may be compensated.

COMPENSATING THE WORKFORCE

People generally don't work for free, and how much they are paid for their work is a complicated issue. Also, designing a fair compensation plan is an important task because pay and benefits represent a substantial portion of an organization's expenses. Wages that are too high may result in the company's products being priced too high, making them uncompetitive in the market. Wages that are too low may damage employee morale and result in costly turnover. Remember that compensation is one of the hygiene factors identified by Herzberg.

Designing a fair compensation plan is a difficult task because it involves evaluating the relative worth of all jobs within the business while allowing for individual efforts. Compensation for a specific job is typically determined through a **wage/salary survey**, which tells the company how much compensation comparable firms are paying for specific jobs that the firms have in common. Compensation for individuals within a specific job category depends on both the compensation for that job and the individual's productivity. Therefore, two employees with identical jobs may not receive exactly the same pay because of individual differences in performance.

Financial Compensation

Financial compensation falls into two general categories—wages and salaries. **Wages** are financial rewards based on the number of hours the employee works or the level of output achieved. Wages based on the number of hours worked are called time wages. The federal minimum wage increased to $7.25 per hour for covered nonexempt workers.[34] However, Congress is expected to vote on whether to increase the minimum wage to $10.10. If passed, the minimum wage would increase over the next few years. Many members of Congress want to increase the minimum wage to $15.00 per hour.[35] Tipped wages must be $2.13 per hour as long as tips plus the wage of $2.13 per hour equal the minimum

wage of $7.25 per hour.[36] Many states also mandate minimum wages; in the case where the two wages are in conflict, the higher of the two wages prevails. There may even be differences between city and state minimum wages. In New Mexico, the minimum wage is $7.50, whereas in the state capitol of Santa Fe, the minimum wage is $10.66, due to a higher cost of living. When Santa Fe went to $10.66 per hour on March 1, 2014, it became one of the highest minimum-wage cities in the United States.[37] Table 10.7 compares wages and other information for Costco and Walmart, two well-known discount chains. Time wages are appropriate when employees are continually interrupted and when quality is more important than quantity. Assembly-line workers, clerks, and maintenance personnel are commonly paid on a time-wage basis. The advantage of time wages is the ease of computation. The disadvantage is that time wages provide no incentive to increase productivity. In fact, time wages may encourage employees to be less productive.

To overcome these disadvantages, many companies pay on an incentive system, using piece wages or commissions. Piece wages are based on the level of output achieved. A major advantage of piece wages is that they motivate employees to supervise their own activities and to increase output. Skilled craftworkers are often paid on a piece-wage basis.

The other incentive system, **commission**, pays a fixed amount or a percentage of the employee's sales. Kele & Co Jewelers in Plainfield, Illinois, makes sterling silver jewelry and offers semiprecious stones and gemstones at affordable prices. Its handcrafted jewelry is sold through the Internet (www .keleonline.com) and through independent sales representatives (ISRs) all over the country. The unique aspect of Kele's sales process is its innovative sales and commission structure. ISRs have no minimum sales quotas, sales are shared among team members during training and after being promoted, and there is no requirement to purchase inventory as jewelry is shipped from Kele headquarters. ISRs receive a 30 to 50 percent commission on sales. The goal is to increase the profit margin and earning potential of the salespeople. The company's goal is to

▼ **TABLE 10.7** Costco versus Walmart

	Costco	Walmart
Number of employees	189,000	2.2 million
Revenue	$112.6 billion	$485.65 billion
Average pay per hour	$21	$12.94
World's most admired ranking	16	30
Strengths	Management quality; financial soundness; people management	Use of corporate assets; financial soundness; global competitiveness

Sources: Costco Wholesale, "Corporate Profile," http://phx.corporateir.net/phoenix.zhtml?c=83830&p= irol-homeprofile (accessed March 24, 2015); "Costco Wholesale: Most Admired 2015," *Fortune,* http:// fortune.com/worlds-most-admired-companies/costco-wholesale-16/ (accessed March 24, 2015); Walmart, "Our Locations," http://corporate.walmart.com/ourstory/locations/united-states (accessed March 24, 2015); "Wal-Mart Stores: Most Admired 2015," http://fortune.com/worlds-most-admired-companies/wal-mart-stores-38/ (accessed March 24, 2015).

become the largest direct sales company in the industry.[38] This method motivates employees to sell as much as they can. Some companies also combine payment based on commission with time wages or salaries.

A **salary** is a financial reward calculated on a weekly, monthly, or annual basis. Salaries are associated with white-collar workers such as office personnel, executives, and professional employees. Although a salary provides a stable stream of income, salaried workers may be required to work beyond usual hours without additional financial compensation.

In addition to the basic wages or salaries paid to employees, a company may offer **bonuses** for exceptional performance as an incentive to increase productivity further. Many workers receive a bonus as a "thank you" for good work and an incentive to continue working hard. Many owners and managers are recognizing that simple bonuses and perks foster happier employees and reduce turnover. Bonuses are especially popular among Wall Street firms. In 2014, Wall Street disbursed more than $28.5 billion in bonuses to more than 167,800 employees.[39]

Another form of compensation is **profit sharing**, which distributes a percentage of company profits to the employees whose work helped to generate those profits. Some profit-sharing plans involve distributing shares of company stock to employees. Usually referred to as *ESOPs*—employee stock ownership plans—they have been gaining popularity in recent years. One reason for the popularity of ESOPs is the sense of partnership that they create between the organization and employees. Profit sharing can also motivate employees to work hard, because increased productivity and sales mean that the profits or the stock dividends will increase. Many organizations offer employees a stake in the company through stock purchase plans, ESOPs, or stock investments through 401(k) plans. Employees below senior management levels rarely received stock options until recently. Companies are adopting broad-based stock option plans to build a stronger link between employees' interests and the organization's interests. ESOPs have met with enormous success over the years, and employee-owned stock has even outperformed the stock market during certain periods. Many businesses have found employee stock options a great way to boost productivity and increase morale. As of 2014, there were nearly 7,000 ESOPs covering about 13.5 million employees in the United States.[40]

Benefits

Benefits are nonfinancial forms of compensation provided to employees, such as pension plans for retirement; health, disability, and life insurance; holidays and paid days off for vacation or illness; credit union membership; health programs; child care; elder care; assistance with adoption; and more. According to the Bureau of Labor Statistics, employer costs for employee compensation for civilian workers in the United States average $31.32 per hour worked. Wages and salaries account for approximately 70 percent of those costs, while benefits account for 30 percent of the cost. Legally required benefits (Social Security, Medicare, federal and state employment insurance, and workers' compensation) account for 7.6 percent of total compensation.[41] Such benefits increase employee security and, to a certain extent, their morale and motivation.

Table 10.8 lists some of the benefits Internet search engine Google offers its employees. Although health insurance is a common benefit for full-time employees, rising health care costs have forced a growing number of employers to trim this benefit. Even government workers, whose wages and benefits used to be virtually guaranteed safe, have seen reductions in health care and other benefits. Surveys have revealed that with the decrease in benefits comes a decrease in employee loyalty. Walmart, Home Depot, and Walgreens have discontinued health care coverage for employees who work fewer than 30 hours a week.[42]

Benefits are particularly important to younger generations of employees. Starbucks recognizes the importance of how benefits can significantly impact an employee's health and well-being. As a result, it is one of only a few fast-food companies to offer its part-time employees health insurance. Additionally, Starbucks began offering employees a benefit called College Achievement Plan in which it pays full tuition for employees to finish a bachelor's degree at Arizona State University. Costco is also known for its significant benefits. Eighty-eight percent of employees at Costco have health insurance, and its

An onsite fitness center is just one of the benefits that large companies have begun to offer employees. Such onsite benefits like fitness centers and child care are particularly important for employees who work long hours or who struggle to maintain a healthy work–life balance.
© *monkeybusinessimages/Getty Images, RF*

THE MOST COMMON COUNSELING SERVICES OFFERED INCLUDE DRUG- AND ALCOHOL-ABUSE TREATMENT PROGRAMS, FITNESS PROGRAMS, SMOKING CESSATION CLINICS, STRESS-MANAGEMENT CLINICS, FINANCIAL COUNSELING, FAMILY COUNSELING, AND CAREER COUNSELING.

▼ **TABLE 10.8** Google's Employees' Benefits

- Health insurance:
- Vacation (15 days per year for one–three years' employment; 20 days off for four–five years' employment; 25 days for more than six years' employment)
- Twelve paid holidays/year
- Savings plans
  - 401(k) retirement plan, matched by Google
  - Flexible spending accounts
- Disability and life insurance
- Employee assistance program
- Free lunches and snacks
- Massages, gym membership, hair stylist, fitness class, and bike repair
- Weekly activities
- Maternity leave
- Legal advice
- Tuition reimbursement
- Employee referral plan
- Onsite doctor
- Backup child care
- Holiday parties, health fair, credit union, roller hockey, outdoor volleyball court, discounts for local attractions

Source: Google, "Benefits," https://www.google.com/about/careers/lifeatgoogle/benefits/ (accessed March 24, 2015).

employee turnover rate is 10 percent versus 74.9 percent for part-time workers in the retail industry.[43]

A benefit increasingly offered is the employee assistance program (EAP). Each company's EAP is different, but most offer counseling for and assistance with those employees' personal problems that might hurt their job performance if not addressed. The most common counseling services offered include drug- and alcohol-abuse treatment programs, fitness programs, smoking cessation clinics, stress-management clinics, financial counseling, family counseling, and career counseling. Lowe's, for example, offers work–life seminars, smoking cessation clinics, and other assistance programs for its employees.[44] EAPs help reduce costs associated with poor productivity, absenteeism, and other workplace issues by helping employees deal with personal problems that contribute to these issues. For example, exercise and fitness programs reduce health insurance costs by helping employees stay healthy. Family counseling may help workers trying to cope with a divorce or other personal problems to better focus on their jobs.

Companies try to provide the benefits they believe their employees want, but diverse people may want different things. In recent years, some single workers have felt that co-workers with spouses and children seem to get "special breaks" and extra time off to deal with family issues. Some companies use flexible benefit programs to allow employees to choose the benefits they would like, up to a specified amount.

URBAN LENDING SOLUTIONS HIRES OUTSIDE THE BOX

In 2002 former professional athlete Charles Sanders and his wife, Elisa, founded Urban Lending Solutions (ULS), a real estate company in Pittsburgh, Pennsylvania. The real estate industry is highly competitive and especially vulnerable to changes in the market. Because of this volatility in the market, Charles Sanders, who serves as CEO, takes a different approach to hiring employees. While other real estate companies focus on hiring seasoned professionals, Sanders looks for intellect and ambition in potential hires regardless of their experience. He has hired people ranging from managers at fast-food restaurants to the newly graduated. As a result, ULS has grown to over 1,773 employees, a more than 257 percent increase since 2009.

ULS believes in the importance of employee training. It established its training program, called Urban University, to offer 15 courses meant to teach new hires everything they need to know, while preparing them to become adaptable when market conditions change. ULS's training and hiring approach has allowed the company to expand its services across the nation, retain valuable employees, and successfully respond to the difficulties of the latest housing market crash.[45]

Fringe benefits include sick leave, vacation pay, pension plans, health plans, and any other extra compensation. Many states and cities are adopting new policies on sick leave that mandate a certain number of paid sick days a worker can take. It is often lower-wage employees who do not receive paid sick leave, yet they are the ones who usually cannot afford to take a day off if it is unpaid.[46] Soft benefits include perks that help balance life and work. They include onsite child care, spas, food service, and even laundry services and hair salons. These soft benefits motivate employees and give them more time to focus on their job. About 95 percent of millennials view a healthy work–life balance as important.[47]

Cafeteria benefit plans provide a financial amount to employees so that they can select the specific benefits that fit their needs. The key is making benefits flexible, rather than giving employees identical benefits. As firms go global, the need for cafeteria or flexible benefit plans becomes even more important. For some employees, benefits are a greater motivator and differentiator in jobs than wages. For many Starbucks

employees who receive health insurance when working part time, this benefit could be the most important compensation.

Over the past two decades, the list of fringe benefits has grown dramatically, and new benefits are being added every year.

LO 10-6   Discuss some of the issues associated with unionized employees, including collective bargaining and dispute resolution.

MANAGING UNIONIZED EMPLOYEES

Employees who are dissatisfied with their working conditions or compensation have to negotiate with management to bring about change. Dealing with management on an individual basis is not always effective, however, so employees may organize themselves into **labor unions** to deal with employers and to achieve better pay, hours, and working conditions. Organized employees are backed by the power of a large group that can hire specialists to represent the entire union in its dealings with management. Union workers make significantly more than nonunion employees. The United States has a roughly 11.1 percent unionization rate. Figure 10.4 displays unionization rates by state. On average, the median usual weekly earnings of unionized full-time and salary workers are about $200 more than their non-union counterparts.[48]

However, union growth has slowed in recent years, and prospects for growth do not look good. One reason is that most blue-collar workers, the traditional members of unions, have already been organized. Factories have become more automated and need fewer blue-collar workers. The United States has shifted from a manufacturing to a service economy, further reducing the

FIGURE 10.4
Union Membership Rates by State

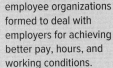

(U.S. rate = 11.3 percent)

Legend:
- 20.0% or more
- 15.0%–19.9%
- 10.0%–14.9%
- 5.0%–9.9%
- 4.9% or less

Source: Bureau of Labor Statistics, "Union Members—2014," January 23, 2015, www.bls.gov/news.release/pdf/union2.pdf (accessed March 24, 2015).

demand for blue-collar workers. Moreover, in response to foreign competition, U.S. companies are scrambling to find ways to become more productive and cost efficient. Job enrichment programs and participative management have blurred the line between management and workers. Because workers' say in the way plants are run is increasing, their need for union protection is decreasing. Many workers fail to see the benefits of union membership if they do not have complaints or grievances against their employers.[49]

Nonetheless, labor unions have been successful in organizing blue-collar manufacturing, government, and health care workers, as well as smaller percentages of employees in other industries. Consequently, significant aspects of HRM, particularly compensation, are dictated to a large degree by union contracts at many companies. Therefore, we'll take a brief look at collective bargaining and dispute resolution in this section.

Collective Bargaining

Collective bargaining is the negotiation process through which management and unions reach an agreement about compensation, working hours, and working conditions for the bargaining unit (Figure 10.5). The objective of negotiations is to reach agreement about a **labor contract**, the formal, written document that spells out the relationship between the union and management for a specified period of time, usually two or three years.

In collective bargaining, each side tries to negotiate an agreement that meets its demands; compromise is frequently necessary. Management tries to negotiate a labor contract that permits the company to retain control over things like work schedules; the hiring and firing of workers; production standards; promotions, transfers, and separations; the span of management in each department; and discipline. Unions tend to focus on contract issues such as magnitude of wages;

better pay rates for overtime, holidays, and undesirable shifts; scheduling of pay increases; and benefits. These issues will be spelled out in the labor contract, which union members will vote to either accept (and abide by) or reject.

Many labor contracts contain a *cost-of-living escalator* (or *adjustment*) *(COLA) clause*, which calls for automatic wage increases during periods of inflation to protect the "real"

▼FIGURE 10.5
The Collective Bargaining Process

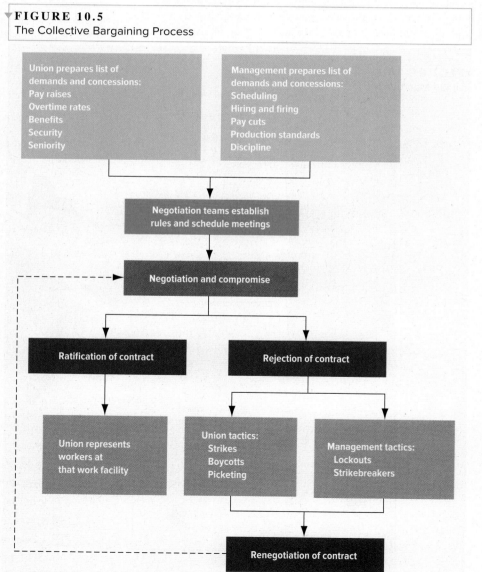

income of the employees. During tough economic times, unions may be forced to accept *givebacks*—wage and benefit concessions made to employers to allow them to remain competitive or, in some cases, to survive and continue to provide jobs for union workers.

Resolving Disputes

Sometimes, management and labor simply cannot agree on a contract. Most labor disputes are handled through collective bargaining or through grievance procedures. When these processes break down, however, either side may resort to more drastic measures to achieve its objectives.

Labor Tactics **Picketing** is a public protest against management practices and involves union members marching (often waving antimanagement signs and placards) at the employer's plant or work site. Picketing workers hope that their signs will arouse sympathy for their demands from the public and from other unions. Picketing may occur as a protest or in conjunction with a strike.

Strikes (employee walkouts) are one of the most effective weapons labor has. By striking, a union makes carrying out the normal operations of a business difficult at best and impossible at worst. Strikes receive widespread publicity, but they remain a weapon of last resort. However, in extreme cases, workers may organize a strike with the help of unions and coalitions to which they do not yet belong. Hundreds of truck workers went on strike in British Columbia over disagreements on pay rates. The strikes created a massive backlog of lumber and pulp cargo that would normally be transported to Port Metro Vancouver. It is estimated that the port strike stopped up to 90 percent of container traffic.[50] Strikes over wages have also occurred at well-known companies including McDonald's, Dollar Tree, Dollar General, BP, and Sunoco.[51] While it is mostly the case that the mere threat of a strike is enough to make management back down, there are times when the issues are heatedly debated and regulatory agencies become involved.

A **boycott** is an attempt to keep people from purchasing the products of a company. In a boycott, union members are asked not to do business with the boycotted organization. Some unions may even impose fines on members who ignore the boycott. To gain further support for their objectives, a union involved in a boycott may also ask the public—through picketing and advertising—not to purchase the products of the picketed firm.

Management Tactics Management's version of a strike is the **lockout;** management actually closes a work site so that employees cannot go to work. Lockouts are used, as a general rule, only when a union strike has partially shut down a plant and it seems less expensive for the plant to close completely. Kellogg locked out workers from its Memphis cereal plant for three months due to failure to reach a negotiating agreement on employees' wages and benefits. The situation escalated, with the company deciding to cut off the employees' health insurance for the duration of the strike.[52]

Strikebreakers, called "scabs" by striking union members, are people hired by management to replace striking employees. Managers hire strikebreakers to continue operations and reduce the losses associated with strikes—and to show the unions that they will not bow to their demands. Strikebreaking is generally a last-resort measure for management because it does great damage to the relationship between management and labor.

Outside Resolution Management and union members normally reach mutually agreeable decisions without outside assistance. Sometimes though, even after lengthy negotiations, strikes, lockouts, and other tactics, management and labor still cannot resolve a contract dispute. In such cases, they have three choices: conciliation, mediation, and arbitration. **Conciliation** brings in a neutral third party to keep labor and management talking. The conciliator has no formal power over union representatives or over management. The conciliator's goal is to get both parties to focus on the issues and to prevent negotiations from breaking down. Like conciliation, **mediation** involves bringing in a neutral third party, but the mediator's role is to suggest or propose a solution to the problem. The Association of Mineworkers and Construction Union (AMCU) and platinum workers had to meet with South African state mediators in order to resolve a dispute that was costing the country $36 million per day.[53] Mediators have no formal power over either labor or management. With **arbitration**, a neutral third party is brought in to settle the dispute, but the arbitrator's solution is legally binding and enforceable. Chevron won an arbitration case against the country of Ecuador regarding an ongoing 20-year dispute over pollution. The international arbitration panel ruled that the original case did not consider the fact that Ecuador had released the company from liability in the 1990s. Chevron was able to avoid a $19 billion penalty as a result.[54] Generally, arbitration takes place on a voluntary basis—management and labor must agree to it, and they usually split the cost (the arbitrator's fee and expenses) between them. Occasionally, management and labor

diversity the participation of different ages, genders, races, ethnicities, nationalities, and abilities in the workplace.

submit to *compulsory arbitration*, in which an outside party (usually the federal government) requests arbitration as a means of eliminating a prolonged strike that threatens to disrupt the economy.

THE IMPORTANCE OF WORKFORCE DIVERSITY

Customers, employees, suppliers—all the participants in the world of business—come in different ages, genders, races, ethnicities, nationalities, and abilities, a truth that business has come to label **diversity**. Understanding this diversity means recognizing and accepting differences as well as valuing the unique perspectives such differences can bring to the workplace.

The Characteristics of Diversity

When managers speak of diverse workforces, they typically mean differences in gender and race. While gender and race are important characteristics of diversity, others are also important. We can divide these differences into primary and secondary characteristics of diversity. In the lower segment of Figure 10.6, age, gender, race, ethnicity, abilities, and sexual orientation represent *primary characteristics* of diversity that are inborn and cannot be changed. In the upper section of Figure 10.6 are eight *secondary characteristics* of diversity—work background, income, marital status, military experience, religious beliefs, geographic location, parental status, and education—which *can* be changed. We acquire, change, and discard them as we progress through our lives.

> "Once dominated by white men, today's workforce includes significantly more women, African Americans, Hispanics, and other minorities, as well as disabled and older workers."

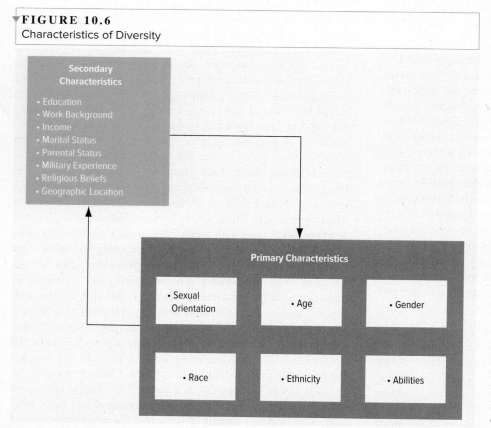

FIGURE 10.6
Characteristics of Diversity

Secondary Characteristics
- Education
- Work Background
- Income
- Marital Status
- Parental Status
- Military Experience
- Religious Beliefs
- Geographic Location

Primary Characteristics
- Sexual Orientation
- Age
- Gender
- Race
- Ethnicity
- Abilities

Defining characteristics of diversity as either primary or secondary enhances our understanding, but we must remember that each person is defined by the interrelation of all characteristics. In dealing with diversity in the workforce, managers must consider the complete person—not one or a few of a person's differences.

Why Is Diversity Important?

The U.S. workforce is becoming increasingly diverse. Once dominated by white men, today's workforce includes significantly more women, African Americans, Hispanics, and other minorities, as well as disabled and older workers. The census bureau has predicted that by 2043, minorities will make up more than 50 percent of the U.S. population.[55] These groups have traditionally faced discrimination and higher unemployment rates and have been denied opportunities to assume leadership roles in corporate America. Consequently, more and more companies are trying to improve HRM programs to recruit, develop, and retain more diverse

Some of the major benefits of diversity include a wider range of employee perspectives, greater innovation and creativity, and the ability to target a diverse customer base more effectively.
© Beathan/Corbis, RF

employees to better serve their diverse customers. Some firms are providing special programs such as sponsored affinity groups, mentoring programs, and special career development opportunities. Kaiser Permanente has incorporated diversity into its goals and corporate strategies. More than half of the company's board of directors consists of minorities, while 60 percent are women. This level of diversity has earned Kaiser Permanente fourth place on DiversityInc.'s Top 50 Companies for Diversity list.[56] Diversity and equal rights is so important to Kaiser Permanente that it has established the Institute for Culturally Competent Care and the nine Centers of Excellence to pave the way for equal health care for all, including minorities, immigrants, and those with disabilities.[57] On the other hand, Silicon Valley has been criticized for its lack of diversity. Among leading technology companies in Silicon Valley, 5 percent of their workers are African American and Hispanic versus 14 percent of college-educated workers. Women are also underrepresented. Top companies in Silicon Valley admit that 20 percent or less of their technical staff are women, and they are highly underrepresented in nontechnical jobs.[58] Table 10.9 shows the top companies for minorities according to a study by DiversityInc. Effectively managing diversity in the workforce involves cultivating and valuing its benefits and minimizing its problems.

The Benefits of Workforce Diversity

There are a number of benefits to fostering and valuing workforce diversity, including the following:

1. More productive use of a company's human resources.

2. Reduced conflict among employees of different ethnicities, races, religions, and sexual orientations as they learn to respect each other's differences.

3. More productive working relationships among diverse employees as they learn more about and accept each other.

4. Increased commitment to and sharing of organizational goals among diverse employees at all organizational levels.

5. Increased innovation and creativity as diverse employees bring new, unique perspectives to decision-making and problem-solving tasks.

6. Increased ability to serve the needs of an increasingly diverse customer base.[59]

Companies that do not value their diverse employees are likely to experience greater conflict, as well as prejudice and discrimination. Among individual employees, for example, racial slurs and gestures, sexist comments, and other behaviors by co-workers harm the individuals at whom such behavior is directed. The victims of such behavior may feel hurt, depressed, or even threatened and suffer from lowered self-esteem, all of which harm their productivity and morale. In such cases, women and minority employees may simply leave the firm, wasting the time, money, and other resources spent on hiring and training them. When discrimination comes from a supervisor, employees may also fear for their jobs. A discriminatory atmosphere can not only harm productivity and increase turnover, but it may also subject a firm to costly lawsuits and negative publicity.

▼ **TABLE 10.9** Top 50 Companies For Diversity

1. Novartis Pharmaceuticals Corporation	26. BASF
2. Sodexo	27. Eli Lilly and Company
3. Ernst & Young	28. Northrop Grumman
4. Kaiser Permanente	29. WellPoint
5. PricewaterhouseCoopers	30. Colgate-Palmolive
6. MasterCard Worldwide	31. Kellogg Company
7. Procter & Gamble	32. Dell
8. Prudential Financial	33. The Coca-Cola Company
9. Johnson & Johnson	34. The Walt Disney Company
10. AT&T	35. Kraft Foods Group
11. Deloitte	36. TIAA-CREF
12. Accenture	37. Allstate Insurance Company
13. Abbott	38. Toyota Motor North America
14. Merck & Co	39. Wyndham Worldwide
15. Cummins	40. Rockwell Collins
16. Marriott International	41. Medtronic
17. Wells Fargo	42. Time Warner
18. Cox Communications	43. Verizon Communications
19. Aetna	44. Comcast
20. General Mills	45. TD Bank
21. KPMG	46. Monsanto
22. Target	47. KeyCorp
23. IBM	48. JCPenney
24. ADP	49. AbbVie
25. New York Life	50. Nielsen

Source: "The 2014 DiversityInc Top 50 Companies for Diversity," *DiversityInc,* 2014, www.diversityinc.com/the-diversityinc-top-50-companies-for-diversity-2014/ (accessed May 12, 2014).

affirmative action programs legally mandated plans that try to increase job opportunities for minority groups by analyzing the current pool of workers, identifying areas where women and minorities are underrepresented, and establishing specific hiring and promotion goals, with target dates, for addressing the discrepancy.

Astute businesses recognize that they need to modify their human resources management programs to target the needs of *all* their diverse employees as well as the needs of the firm itself. They realize that the benefits of diversity are long term in nature and come only to those organizations willing to make the commitment. Most importantly, as workforce diversity becomes a valued organizational asset, companies spend less time managing conflict and more time accomplishing tasks and satisfying customers, which is, after all, the purpose of business.

Affirmative Action

Many companies strive to improve their working environment through **affirmative action programs**, legally mandated plans that try to increase job opportunities for minority groups by analyzing the current pool of workers, identifying areas where women and minorities are underrepresented, and establishing specific hiring and promotion goals along with target dates for meeting those goals to resolve the discrepancy. Affirmative action began in 1965 as Lyndon B. Johnson issued the first of a series of presidential directives. It was designed to make up for past hiring and promotion prejudices, to overcome workplace discrimination, and to provide equal employment opportunities for blacks and whites. Since then, minorities have made solid gains.

Legislation passed in 1991 reinforces affirmative action but prohibits organizations from setting hiring quotas that might result in reverse discrimination. Reverse discrimination occurs when a company's policies force it to consider only minorities or women instead of concentrating on hiring the person who is best qualified. More companies are arguing that affirmative action stifles their ability to hire the best employees, regardless of their minority status. Because of these problems, affirmative action became politically questionable.

TRENDS IN MANAGEMENT OF THE WORKFORCE

As unemployment reached 10 percent during the last recession, businesses laid off almost 9 million employees. Even after the recession and financial crisis, many firms reduced hiring and pushed workers to spend more time on the job for the same or less pay. Because of the economic uncertainty, this postrecession austerity has pervaded the workplace and inflated U.S. productivity. While companies are squeezing workers to cut costs, they are also drawing clear lines between workers and managers and are reducing privileges and benefits.

Many employees are developing grievances, claiming that they are being overworked. The number of lawsuits filed by

USING EMPOWERED EMPLOYEES TO HELP MANAGE A CHANGING WORK ENVIRONMENT

A key aspect in managing the workforce is to be aware of how employees can contribute toward organizational change and decisions. HR professionals recognize that while managers may act as role models for employees, employees who are empowered can exert a significant influence over other employees in the workplace. Those employees within the organization who seem respected and highly influential are termed influencers. A growing trend in workforce management is to recognize the power of these empowered employees and use them to make new organizational decisions, processes, and plans more acceptable to employees.

One major way of getting these "informal influencers" on board is by using participative management to make them a part of the organizational decision-making process. Before this can be done, however, companies must first identify which of their employees are held in high esteem by their co-workers. A variety of companies, including giants such as Procter & Gamble and Cisco Systems, use surveys, analysis of internal e-mail and social media interaction data, and other methods to construct "influence ranks" of employees. They then invite these top influencers to join in on management meetings or participate in special training and advancement programs. When changes or new programs are announced and the influencers are naturally sought out to hear concerns and give advice, they can help co-workers better handle and/or buy into the transition. This nonhierarchal structure and an emphasis on encouraging employees to work out problems on their own has been highly successful for Google, known for its more participative management structure.[60]

Discussion Questions

1. Is it a good idea for businesses to try to use informal influencers to more smoothly implement business decisions and reduce employee resistance?

2. How would you feel if you were recognized as an influencer in your company and invited to management meetings and training programs as a result? How would you respond?

3. Describe some ways that Cisco, Procter & Gamble, and Google have used empowered employees as major contributors toward organizational change and decision making.

employees against their employers continues to rise. Many of the claims include working overtime without being appropriately compensated, being overworked to the point of physical injury, and not being compensated for time waiting for company mandated security checks.[61]

The nature of the workplace is changing as well. The increasing use of smartphones and tablet computers is blurring the line between leisure and work time, with some employers calling employees after hours.[62] Employees themselves are mixing work and personal time by using social media in the office. In fact, theft of time is a major form of misconduct in the workplace. This is requiring companies to come up with new policies that limit how employees can use social media in the workplace. Clearly, technology is changing the dynamics of the workplace in both positive and negative ways.

It is important for human resources managers to be aware of legal issues regarding worker rights. Strict criteria—such as having management responsibilities, having advanced degrees, or making more than $455 a week—determine whether an

employee is exempt from overtime pay.[63] Interestingly, although it might currently be legal for employers to request an applicant's Facebook password, employees who "rant" about their employers on Facebook can receive some form of legal protection. Under the National Labor Relations Act of 1935, certain private-sector employees are allowed to complain about working conditions and pay—which seems to apply to social media sites as well. Threats, on the other hand, are not protected.[64] Hence, human resources managers should understand these issues to ensure that an employee is not wrongfully terminated.

Despite the grim outlook of the past few years, hiring trends appear to be on the rise. Companies are finding that as consumer demands rise, their current employees are hitting the limits of productivity, requiring firms to hire more workers.[65] This will require firms not only to know about relevant employee laws, but also to understand how benefits and employee morale can contribute to overall productivity. Many of the most successful firms have discovered ways to balance costs with the well-being of their employees. ■

SO YOU WANT TO WORK // in Human Resources /

Managing human resources is a challenging and creative facet of a business. It is the department that handles the recruiting, hiring, training, and firing of employees. Because of the diligence and detail required in hiring and the sensitivity required in firing, human resources managers have a broad skill set. Human resources, therefore, is vital to the overall functioning of the business because without the right staff a firm will not be able to effectively carry out its plans. Like in basketball, a team is only as strong as its individual players, and those players must be able to work together and to enhance strengths and downplay weaknesses. In addition, a good human resources manager can anticipate upcoming needs and changes in the business, hiring in line with the dynamics of the market and organization.

Once a good workforce is in place, human resources managers must ensure that employees are properly trained and oriented and that they clearly understand some elements of what the organization expects. Hiring new people is expensive, time-consuming, and turbulent; thus,

it is imperative that all employees are carefully selected, trained, and motivated so that they will remain committed and loyal to the company. This is not an easy task, but it is one of the responsibilities of the human resources manager. Because even with references, a résumé, background checks, and an interview, it can be hard to tell how a person will fit in the organization, the HR manager needs to have skills to be able to anticipate how every individual will "fit in." Human resources jobs include compensation, labor relations, benefits, training, ethics, and compliance managers. All of the tasks associated with the interface of hiring, developing, and maintaining employee motivation come into play in human resources management. Jobs are diverse and salaries will depend on responsibilities, education, and experience.

One of the major considerations for an HR manager is workforce diversity. A multicultural, multiethnic workforce consisting of men and women will help bring a variety of viewpoints and improve the quality and creativity of organizational decision making. Diversity is an asset

and can help a company avoid blind spots or too much harmony in thought, background, and perspective, which stifles good team decisions. However, a diverse workforce can present management challenges. Human resources management is often responsible for managing diversity training and compliance to make sure employees do not violate the ethical culture of the organization or break the law. Different people have different goals, motivations, and ways of thinking about issues that are informed by their culture, religion, and the people closest to them. No one way of thinking is necessarily more right or wrong than others, and all are valuable. A human resources manager's job can become very complicated because of diversity. To be good at it you should be aware of the value of differences, strive to be culturally sensitive, and ideally have a strong understanding and appreciation of different cultures and religions. Human resources managers' ability to manage diversity and differences will affect their overall career success.

customer-driven
Marketing

© NuStock/ E-plus/Getty Images, RF

LEARNING OBJECTIVES

After reading this chapter, you will be able to:

LO 11-1 Define marketing, and describe the exchange process.

LO 11-2 Specify the functions of marketing.

LO 11-3 Explain the marketing concept and its implications for developing marketing strategies.

LO 11-4 Examine the development of a marketing strategy, including market segmentation and marketing mix.

LO 11-5 Investigate how marketers conduct marketing research and study buying behavior.

LO 11-6 Summarize the environmental forces that influence marketing decisions.

Marketing involves planning and executing the development, pricing, promotion, and distribution of ideas, goods, and services to create exchanges that satisfy individual and organizational goals. These activities ensure that the products consumers want to buy are available at a price they are willing to pay and that consumers are provided with information about product features and availability. Organizations of all sizes and objectives engage in these activities.

In this chapter, we focus on the basic principles of marketing. First we define and examine the nature of marketing. Then we look at how marketers develop marketing strategies to satisfy the needs and wants of their customers. Next we discuss buying behavior and how marketers use research to determine what consumers want to buy and why. Finally, we explore the impact of the environment on marketing activities. ■

LO 11-1   Define marketing, and describe the exchange process.

THE NATURE OF MARKETING

A vital part of any business undertaking, **marketing** is a group of activities designed to expedite transactions by creating, distributing, pricing, and promoting goods, services, and ideas. These activities create value by allowing individuals and organizations to obtain what they need and want. A business cannot achieve its objectives unless it provides something that customers value. But just creating an innovative product that meets many users' needs is not sufficient in today's volatile global marketplace. Products must be conveniently available, competitively priced, and uniquely promoted.

Marketing is an important part of a firm's overall strategy. Other functional areas of the business—such as operations, finance, and all areas of management—must be coordinated with marketing decisions. Marketing has the important function of providing revenue to sustain a firm. Only by creating trust and effective relationships with customers can a firm succeed in the long run. Businesses try to respond to consumer wants and needs and to anticipate changes in the environment. Unfortunately, it is difficult to understand and predict what consumers want: Motives are often unclear; few principles can be applied consistently; and markets tend to fragment, each desiring customized products, new value, or better service.

It is important to note what marketing is not: It is not manipulating consumers to get them to buy products they do not want. It is not just selling and advertising; it is a systematic approach to satisfying consumers. Marketing focuses on the many activities—planning, pricing, distributing, and promoting products—that foster exchanges. Unfortunately, the mass media and movies sometimes portray marketing as unethical or as not adding value to business. In this chapter, we point out that marketing is essential and provides important benefits in making products available to consumers.

The Exchange Relationship

At the heart of all business is the **exchange**, the act of giving up one thing (money, credit, labor, goods) in return for something else (goods, services, or ideas). Businesses exchange their goods, services, or ideas for money or credit supplied by customers in a voluntary *exchange relationship,* illustrated in Figure 11.1. The buyer must feel good about the purchase, or the exchange will not continue. If your cell phone service works everywhere, you will probably feel good about using its services. But if you have a lot of dropped calls, you will probably use another phone service next time.

For an exchange to occur, certain conditions are required. As indicated by the arrows in Figure 11.1, buyers and sellers must be able to communicate about the "something of value" available to each. An exchange does not necessarily take place just because buyers and sellers have something of value to exchange. Each participant must be willing to give up his or her respective "something of value" to receive the "something" held by the other. You are willing to exchange your "something of value"—your money or credit—for soft drinks, football tickets,

> **marketing** a group of activities designed to expedite transactions by creating, distributing, pricing, and promoting goods, services, and ideas.

> **exchange** the act of giving up one thing (money, credit, labor, goods) in return for something else (goods, services, or ideas).

> "A business cannot achieve its objectives unless it provides something that customers value."

FIGURE 11.1
The Exchange Process: Giving Up One Thing in Return for Another

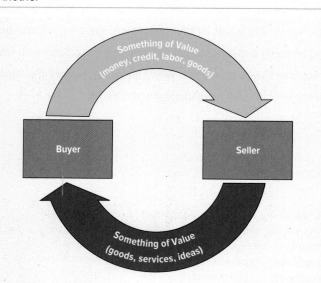

Something of Value
(money, credit, labor, goods)

Buyer

Seller

Something of Value
(goods, services, ideas)

or new shoes because you consider those products more valuable or more important than holding on to your cash or credit potential.

When you think of marketing products, you may think of tangible things—cars, smartphones, or books, for example. What most consumers want, however, is a way to get a job done, solve a problem, or gain some enjoyment. You may purchase a Hoover vacuum cleaner not because you want a vacuum cleaner but because you want clean carpets. Starbucks serves coffee drinks at a premium price, providing convenience, quality, and an inviting environment. Starbucks serves people who drink coffee or tea. Therefore, the tangible product itself may not be as important as the image or the benefits associated with the product. This intangible "something of value" may be capability gained from using a product or the image evoked by it, or even the brand name. Good examples of brand names that are easy to remember include Avon's Skin So Soft, Tide detergent, and the Ford Mustang. The label or brand name may also offer the added bonus of being a conversation piece in a social environment, such as Dancing Bull or Smoking Loon wine.

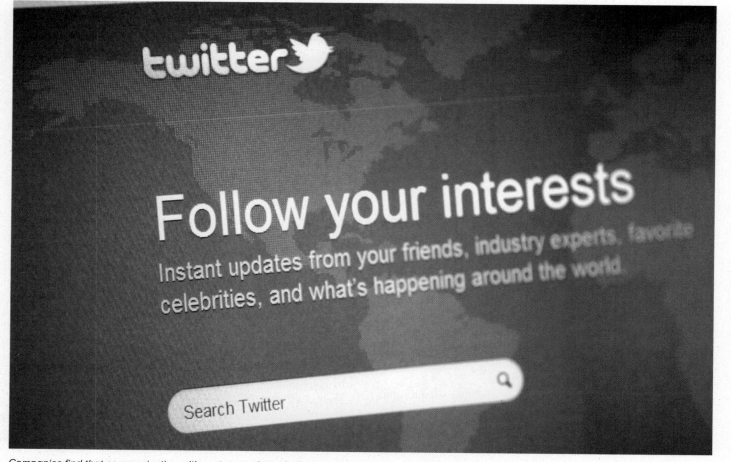

Companies find that communicating with customers through digital media sites can enhance customer relationships and create value for their brands.
© *Desislava Vasileva/Zoonar/Alamy, RF*

Functions of Marketing

Marketing focuses on a complex set of activities that must be performed to accomplish objectives and generate exchanges. These activities include buying, selling, transporting, storing, grading, financing, marketing research, and risk taking.

Buying   Everyone who shops for products (consumers, stores, businesses, governments) decides whether and what to buy. A marketer must understand buyers' needs and desires to determine what products to make available.

Selling   The exchange process is expedited through selling. Marketers usually view selling as a persuasive activity that is accomplished through promotion (advertising, personal selling, sales promotion, publicity, and packaging).

Transporting   Transporting is the process of moving products from the seller to the buyer. Marketers focus on transportation costs and services.

Storing   Like transporting, storing is part of the physical distribution of products and includes warehousing goods. Warehouses hold some products for lengthy periods in order to create time utility. Time utility has to do with being able to satisfy demand in a timely manner. This especially pertains to a seasonal good such as orange juice. Fresh oranges are only available for a few months annually, but consumers demand juice throughout the entire year. Sellers must arrange for cold storage of orange juice concentrate so that they can maintain a steady supply all of the time.

Grading   Grading refers to standardizing products by dividing them into subgroups and displaying and labeling them so that consumers clearly understand their nature and quality. Many products, such as meat, steel, and fruit, are graded according to a set of standards that often are established by the state or federal government.

Financing   For many products, especially large items such as automobiles, refrigerators, and new homes, the marketer arranges credit to expedite the purchase.

Marketing Research   Through research, marketers ascertain the need for new goods and services. By gathering information regularly, marketers can detect new trends and changes in consumer tastes.

Risk Taking   Risk is the chance of loss associated with marketing decisions. Developing a new product creates a chance of loss if consumers do not like it enough to buy it. Spending money to hire a sales force or to conduct marketing research also involves risk. The implication of risk is that most marketing decisions result in either success or failure.

Creating Value with Marketing[1]

Value is an important element of managing long-term customer relationships and implementing the marking concept. We view **value** as a customer's subjective assessment of benefits relative to costs in determining the worth of a product (Customer value = Customer benefits − Customer costs).

Customer benefits include anything a buyer receives in an exchange. Hotels and motels, for example, basically provide a room with a bed and bathroom, but each firm provides a different level of service, amenities, and atmosphere to satisfy its guests. Hampton Inn offers the minimum services necessary to maintain a quality, efficient, low-price overnight accommodation. In contrast, the Ritz-Carlton provides every imaginable service a guest might desire and strives to ensure that all service is of the highest quality. Customers judge which type of accommodation offers them the best value according to the benefits they desire and their willingness and ability to pay the costs associated with the benefits.

Customer costs include anything a buyer must give up to obtain the benefits the product provides. The most obvious cost is the monetary price of the product, but nonmonetary costs can be equally important in a customer's determination of value. Two nonmonetary costs are the time and effort customers expend to find and purchase desired products. To reduce time and effort, a company can increase product availability, thereby making it more convenient for buyers to purchase the firm's products. Another nonmonetary cost is risk, which can be reduced by offering good basic warranties for an additional charge. Another risk-reduction strategy is increasingly popular in today's catalog/telephone/Internet shopping environment. L.L.Bean, for example, uses a guarantee to reduce the risk involved in ordering merchandise from its catalogs.

In developing marketing activities, it is important to recognize that customers receive benefits based on their experiences. For example, many computer buyers consider services such as fast delivery, ease of installation, technical advice, and training assistance to be important elements of the product. Customers also derive benefits from the act of shopping and selecting products. These benefits can be affected by the atmosphere or environment of a store, such as Red Lobster's nautical/seafood theme.

The Marketing Concept

A basic philosophy that guides all marketing activities is the **marketing concept**, the idea that an organization should try to satisfy customers' needs through coordinated activities

value a customer's subjective assessment of benefits relative to costs in determining the worth of a product.

marketing concept the idea that an organization should try to satisfy customers' needs through coordinated activities that also allow it to achieve its own goals.

that also allow it to achieve its own goals. According to the marketing concept, a business must find out what consumers desire and then develop the good, service, or idea that fulfills their needs or wants. The business must then get the product to the customer. In addition, the business must continually alter, adapt, and develop products to keep pace with changing consumer needs and wants. For instance, Burger King is following McDonald's lead by dropping soda as an option in Happy Meals. Although parents can still order soft drinks for their children, they are not listed on the Happy Meal menu. This is a response to continued concerns over childhood obesity and stakeholder demands to improve the quality of food targeted toward children.[2] To remain competitive, companies must be prepared to add to or adapt their product lines to satisfy customers' desires for new fads or changes in eating habits. Each business must determine how best to implement the marketing concept, given its own goals and resources.

Trying to determine customers' true needs is increasingly difficult because no one fully understands what motivates

Trader Joe's, which sells many lines of organic and natural food products, is often thought to have better deals than some of its competitors. The grocery chain attempts to meet consumer demands for high-quality food at reasonable prices.
© ZUMA Press, Inc/Alamy

> **"According to the marketing concept, a business must find out what consumers desire and then develop the good, service, or idea that fulfills their needs or wants."**

people to buy things. However, Estée Lauder, founder of her namesake cosmetics company, had a pretty good idea. When a prestigious store in Paris rejected her perfume in the 1960s, she "accidentally" dropped a bottle on the floor where nearby customers could get a whiff of it. So many asked about the scent that Galeries Lafayette was obliged to place an order. Lauder ultimately built an empire using then-unheard-of tactics like free samples and gifts with purchases to market her "jars of hope."[4]

Although customer satisfaction is the goal of the marketing concept, a business must also achieve its own objectives, such as boosting productivity, reducing costs, or achieving a percentage of a specific market. If it does not, it will not survive. For example, Lenovo could sell computers for $50 and give customers a lifetime guarantee, which would be great for customers but not so great for Lenovo. Obviously, the company must strike a balance between achieving organizational objectives and satisfying customers.

BLUE BOTTLE COFFEE PROVIDES A QUALITY EXPERIENCE

At John Freeman's Blue Bottle Coffee Company headquartered in Oakland, California, coffee is more than a commodity. Blue Bottle embraces the third-wave movement, a movement that makes premium coffee into an exquisite experience of purity, flavor, and artisanship, similar to wine and cigars. To show that this experience is worth

paying for, Blue Bottle has adopted a different pricing and marketing style than that of traditional coffee shops or even Starbucks.

For example, the shops of Blue Bottle emphasize the coffee experience above all else. Beverages come in only one size and cannot be ordered "to go." There are no plugs or Wi-Fi to allow distraction, and the

beans for each order are freshly ground and brewed from scratch right in front of the customer. The price: between $4 and $7 per cup.

While this may be too expensive for the average consumer often targeted by coffee shops, Blue Bottle clearly shows that its niche target market are those who appreciate the quality and experience of coffee.[3]

To implement the marketing concept, a firm must have good information about what consumers want, adopt a consumer orientation, and coordinate its efforts throughout the entire organization; otherwise, it may be awash with goods, services, and ideas that consumers do not want or need. Successfully implementing the marketing concept requires that a business view the customer's perception of value as the ultimate measure of work performance and improving value, and the rate at which this is done, as the measure of success.[5] Everyone in the organization who interacts with customers—*all* customer-contact employees—must know what customers want. They are selling ideas, benefits, philosophies, and experiences—not just goods and services.

Someone once said that if you build a better mousetrap, the world will beat a path to your door. Suppose you do build a better mousetrap. What will happen? Actually, consumers are not likely to beat a path to your door because the market is so competitive. A coordinated effort by everyone involved with the mousetrap is needed to sell the product. Your company must reach out to customers and tell them about your mousetrap, especially how your mousetrap works better than those offered by competitors. If you do not make the benefits of your product widely known, in most cases, it will not be successful. One reason that Apple is so successful is because of its stores. Apple's more than 450 national and international retail stores market computers and electronics in a way unlike any other computer manufacturer or retail establishment. The upscale stores, located in high-rent shopping districts, show off Apple's products in modern, spacious settings to encourage consumers to try new things—like making a movie on a computer. Not only are consumers allowed to try out or "test drive" Apple's tech products, but the company has iPad stations in its stores equipped with a customer service app to answer customer questions.[6] So for some companies, like Apple Inc., you need to create stores to sell your product to consumers. You could also find stores that are willing to sell your product to consumers for you. In either situation, you must implement the marketing concept by making a product with satisfying benefits and making it available and visible.

Orville Wright said that an airplane is "a group of separate parts flying in close formation." This is what most companies are trying to accomplish: They are striving for a team effort to deliver the right good or service to customers. A breakdown at any point in the organization—whether it be in production, purchasing, sales, distribution, or advertising—can result in lost sales, lost revenue, and dissatisfied customers.

Evolution of the Marketing Concept

The marketing concept may seem like the obvious approach to running a business and building relationships with customers. However, businesspeople are not always focused on customers when they create and operate businesses. Many companies fail to grasp the importance of customer relationships and fail to

implement customer strategies. A firm's marketing department needs to share information about customers and their desires with the entire organization. Our society and economic system have changed over time, and marketing has become more important as markets have become more competitive.

The Production Orientation

During the second half of the 19th century, the Industrial Revolution was well under way in the United States. New technologies, such as electricity, railroads, internal combustion engines, and mass-production techniques, made it possible to manufacture goods with ever increasing efficiency. Together with new management ideas and ways of using labor, products poured into the marketplace, where demand for manufactured goods was strong.

The Sales Orientation

By the early part of the 20th century, supply caught up with and then exceeded demand, and businesspeople began to realize they would have to "sell" products to buyers. During the first half of the 20th century, businesspeople viewed sales as the primary means of increasing profits in what has become known as a sales orientation. Those who adopted the sales orientation perspective believed the most important marketing activities were personal selling and advertising. Today some people still inaccurately equate marketing with a sales orientation.

The Market Orientation

By the 1950s, some businesspeople began to recognize that even efficient production and extensive promotion did not guarantee sales. These businesses, and many others since, found that they must first determine what customers want and then produce it, rather than making the products first and then trying to persuade customers that they need them. Managers at General Electric first suggested that the marketing concept was a companywide philosophy of doing business. As more organizations realized the importance of satisfying customers' needs, U.S. businesses entered the marketing era, one of market orientation.

A **market orientation** requires organizations to gather information about customer needs, share that information throughout the entire firm, and use it to help build long-term relationships with customers. Top executives, marketing managers, nonmarketing managers (those in production, finance, human resources, and so on), and customers all become mutually dependent and cooperate in developing and carrying out a market orientation. Nonmarketing managers must communicate with marketing managers to share information important to understanding the customer. Consider the 125-year history of Wrigley's gum. In 1891, the gum was given away to promote sales of baking powder (the company's original product). The gum was launched as its own

In 2006, the extra-thick, high-protein "Greek yogurt" style made up 0.7 percent of the U.S. yogurt market and was considered a specialty item—more often stocked in the ethnic sections of grocery stores than next to other yogurt. Entrepreneur Hamdi Ulukaya saw this as an opportunity and founded Chobani to popularize Greek yogurt in the United States. Today Greek yogurt accounts for 52 percent of U.S. yogurt sales, and Chobani—a $1 billion company—was unquestionably the driving force behind its explosion in popularity.

In addition to seizing a prime opportunity at the right moment, Chobani's success can be attributed to savvy marketing and pricing decisions. First, Chobani insisted its Greek yogurt be stocked in dairy sections next to other yogurt, rather than in specialty areas. This was a serious risk—there was no guarantee that regular yogurt shoppers would take any interest in a new, unfamiliar variety. However, it paid off by immediately positioning Chobani's yogurt as a serious competitor in the general yogurt market rather than as a niche item.

Second, Chobani spent $250,000 designing a unique cup design that was wider and more colorful than the tall and thin yogurt cup standard at the time. This allowed its product to stand out immediately from the crowd, attracting customer notice.

Finally, rather than the common practice of selling a new product at a low price and then raising it after gaining market share, Chobani started its yogurt at a premium price. The risk again paid off by allowing Chobani to start making money and reinvest its earnings much more quickly, as well as not having to raise prices later and lose goodwill and price-conscious customers.[7]

Discussion Questions

1. Describe the risks Chobani took in adopting its marketing strategy.

2. Why do you think Chobani's marketing decisions were so successful?

3. Describe how Chobani helped promote not only its own brand, but the entire Greek yogurt industry in the United States.

---

product in 1893, and after four generations of Wrigley family CEOs, the company continues to reinvent itself and focus on consumers. Eventually, the family made the decision to sell the company to Mars. Wrigley now functions as a standalone subsidiary of Mars. The deal combined such popular brands as Wrigley's gums and Life Savers with Mars's M&M's, Snickers, and Skittles to form the world's largest confectionary company.

Trying to assess what customers want, which is difficult to begin with, is further complicated by the rate at which trends, fashions, and tastes can change. Businesses today want to satisfy customers and build meaningful long-term relationships

Tesla meets the needs of customers who care about the environment and wish to improve their environmental footprint by driving an electric vehicle.

© *Jessica Brandi Lifland/Polaris/Newscom*

with them. It is more efficient and less expensive for the company to retain existing customers and even increase the amount of business each customer provides the organization than to find new customers. Most companies' success depends on increasing the amount of repeat business; therefore, relationship building between company and customer is key. Many companies are turning to technologies associated with customer relationship management to help build relationships and boost business with existing customers.

Although it might be easy to dismiss customer relationship management as time-consuming and expensive, this mistake could destroy a company. Customer relationship management (CRM) is important in a market orientation because it can result in loyal and profitable customers. Without loyal customers, businesses would not survive; therefore, achieving the full profit potential of each customer relationship should be the goal of every marketing strategy. At the most basic level, profits can be obtained through relationships by acquiring new customers, enhancing the profitability of existing customers, and extending the duration of customer relationships. The profitability of loyal customers throughout their relationship with the company (their lifetime customer value) should not be underestimated. For instance, Pizza Hut has a lifetime customer value of approximately $8,000, whereas Cadillac's lifetime customer value is approximately $332,000.[8]

Communication remains a major element of any strategy to develop and manage long-term customer relationships. By providing multiple points of interactions with customers—that is, websites, telephone, fax, e-mail, and personal contact—companies can personalize customer relationships.[9] Like many online retailers, Amazon.com stores and analyzes purchase data in an attempt to understand each customer's interests. This information helps the online retailer improve its ability to satisfy individual customers and thereby increase sales of books, music, movies, and other products to each customer. The ability to identify individual customers allows marketers to shift their focus from targeting groups of similar customers to increasing their share of an individual customer's purchases. Regardless of the medium through which communication occurs, customers should ultimately be the drivers of marketing strategy because they understand what they want. Customer relationship management systems should ensure that marketers listen to customers in order to respond to their needs and concerns and build long-term relationships.

marketing strategy a plan of action for developing, pricing, distributing, and promoting products that meet the needs of specific customers.	**market** a group of people who have a need, purchasing power, and the desire and authority to spend money on goods, services, and ideas.	**target market** a specific group of consumers on whose needs and wants a company focuses its marketing efforts.

LO 11-4 Examine the development of a marketing strategy, including market segmentation and marketing mix.

DEVELOPING A MARKETING STRATEGY

To implement the marketing concept and customer relationship management, a business needs to develop and maintain a **marketing strategy**, a plan of action for developing, pricing, distributing, and promoting products that meet the needs of specific customers. This definition has two major components: selecting a target market and developing an appropriate marketing mix to satisfy that target market.

Selecting a Target Market

A **market** is a group of people who have a need, purchasing power, and the desire and authority to spend money on goods, services, and ideas. A **target market** is a more specific group of consumers on whose needs and wants a company focuses its marketing efforts. Target markets can be further segmented into business markets and consumer markets.

Business-to-business (B2B) marketing involves marketing products to customers who will use the product for resale, direct use in daily operations, or direct use in making other products. John Deere, for instance, sells earth-moving equipment to construction firms and tractors to farmers. Most people, however, tend to think of *business-to-consumer*

marketing (B2C), or marketing directly to the end consumer. Sometimes products are used by both types of markets. Cleaning supplies such as Windex are consumer products when sold to households but business products when sold for janitorial purposes. Consumer products are purchased to satisfy personal and family needs.

Marketing managers may define a target market as a relatively small number of people within a larger market, or they may define it as the total market (Figure 11.2). Rolls-Royce, for example, targets its products at a very exclusive, high-income market—people who want the ultimate in prestige in an automobile. On the other hand, Ford Motor Company manufactures a variety of vehicles including Lincolns, Mercurys, and Ford Trucks in order to appeal to varied tastes, needs, and desires.

▼**FIGURE 11.2**
Target Market Strategies

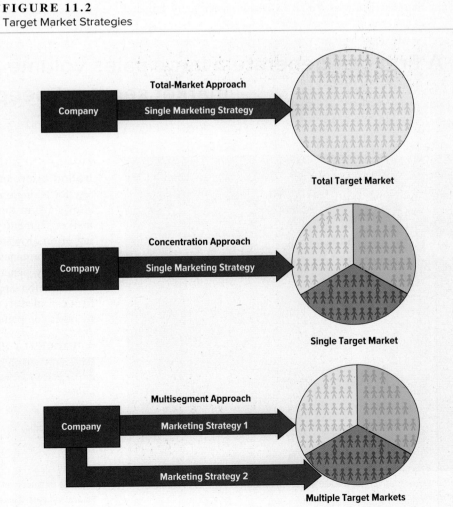

total-market approach an approach whereby a firm tries to appeal to everyone and assumes that all buyers have similar needs.

market segmentation a strategy whereby a firm divides the total market into groups of people who have relatively similar product needs.

market segment a collection of individuals, groups, or organizations who share one or more characteristics and thus have relatively similar product needs and desires.

Some firms use a **total-market approach**, in which they try to appeal to everyone and assume that all buyers have similar needs and wants. Sellers of salt, sugar, and many agricultural products use a total-market approach because everyone is a potential consumer of these products. This approach is also referred to as *mass marketing*. Most firms, though, use **market segmentation** and divide the total market into groups of people. A **market segment** is a collection of individuals, groups, or organizations who share one or more characteristics and thus have relatively similar product needs and desires. Women are the largest market segment, with 51 percent of the U.S. population. At the household level, segmentation can identify each woman's social attributes, culture, and stages in life to determine preferences and needs.

Another market segment on which many marketers are focusing is the growing Hispanic population. MillerCoors launched Coors Light Summer Brew as a line extension specifically targeted toward the Hispanic consumer market. The beer has a citrus flavor because research shows the Hispanic market prefers flavored drinks. Its fruit-flavored Redd's Apple Ale has already captured 10 percent of the markets in certain areas with heavy Latino population.[10] Despite these possibilities, however, businesses are finding it challenging to target the Hispanic market due to the varied interests and backgrounds of Latino consumers.[11] The companies hope to create relationships with Hispanic consumers in order to gain their loyalty. One of the challenges for marketers in the future will be to effectively address an increasingly racially diverse United States. The minority population of the United States is about 116 million (37 percent of the total population).[12] In future decades, the purchasing power of minority market segments is set to grow by leaps and bounds. Table 11.1 shows the buying power of minority groups in the United States. Companies will have to learn how to most effectively reach these growing segments. Companies use market segmentation to focus their efforts and resources on specific target markets so that they can develop a productive marketing strategy. Two common approaches to segmenting markets are the concentration approach and the multisegment approach.

> ## A firm can generate a large sales volume by penetrating a single market segment deeply.

Dollar Shave Club targets a niche market of men who desire fresh blades at cost-effective prices.
© Sean P. Aune

Market Segmentation Approaches In the **concentration approach**, a company develops one marketing strategy for a single market segment. The concentration approach allows a firm to specialize, focusing all its efforts on the one market segment. Porsche, for example, directs all its marketing efforts toward high-income individuals who want to own high-performance vehicles. A firm can generate a large sales volume by penetrating a single market segment deeply. The concentration approach may be especially effective when a firm can identify and develop products for a segment ignored by other companies in the industry.

▼ **TABLE 11.1** Buying Power of U.S. Minorities by Race (billions)

	1990	2000	2010	2012	2015
Total	$4,200	$7,300	$11,200	$12,200	$15,100
Black	316	600	947	1,000	1,300
Native American	20	40	87	103	148
Asian	115	272	609	718	1,000
Hispanic*	210	488	1,000	1,200	1,700

*Because Hispanic is an ethnic group, they may belong to any of the other races.
Source: Jeffrey M. Humphreys, *The Multicultural Economy 2012* (Athens, GA: The University of Georgia Terry College of Business Selig Center for Economic Growth, 2013).

In the **multisegment approach**, the marketer aims its marketing efforts at two or more segments, developing a marketing strategy for each. Many firms use a multisegment approach that includes different advertising messages for different segments. Companies also develop product variations to appeal to different market segments. The U.S. Post Office, for example, offers personalized stamps, while Mars Inc. sells personalized M&M's through mymms.com. Many other firms also attempt to use a multisegment approach to market segmentation, such as the manufacturer of Raleigh bicycles, which has designed separate marketing strategies for racers, tourers, commuters, and children.

Niche marketing is a narrow market segment focus when efforts are on one small, well-defined group that has a unique, specific set of needs. Niche segments are usually very small compared to the total market for the products. Many airlines cater to first-class flyers, who comprise only 10 percent of international air travelers. To meet the needs of these elite customers, airlines include special perks along with the spacious seats. To take advantage of the growing niche market of wearable technologies, Apple is developing a smart watch called iWatch.[13]

For a firm to successfully use a concentration or multisegment approach to market segmentation, several requirements must be met:

1. Consumers' needs for the product must be heterogeneous.

2. The segments must be identifiable and divisible.

3. The total market must be divided in a way that allows estimated sales potential, cost, and profits of the segments to be compared.

4. At least one segment must have enough profit potential to justify developing and maintaining a special marketing strategy.

5. The firm must be able to reach the chosen market segment with a particular market strategy.

Bases for Segmenting Markets Companies segment markets on the basis of several variables:

1. *Demographic*—age, sex, race, ethnicity, income, education, occupation, family size, religion, social class. These characteristics are often closely related to customers' product needs and purchasing behavior, and they can be readily measured. For example, deodorants are often segmented by sex: Secret and Soft & Dri for women; Old Spice and Mennen for men.

2. *Geographic*—climate, terrain, natural resources, population density, subcultural values. These influence consumers' needs and product usage. Climate, for example, influences consumers' purchases of clothing, automobiles, heating and air conditioning equipment, and leisure activity equipment.

3. *Psychographic*—personality characteristics, motives, lifestyles. Soft-drink marketers provide their products in several types of packaging, including two-liter bottles and cases of cans, to satisfy different lifestyles and motives.

4. *Behavioristic*—some characteristic of the consumer's behavior toward the product. These characteristics commonly involve some aspect of product use. Benefit segmentation is also a type of behavioristic segmentation. For instance, low-fat, low-carb food products would target those who desire the benefits of a healthier diet.

Developing a Marketing Mix

The second step in developing a marketing strategy is to create and maintain a satisfying marketing mix. The **marketing mix** refers to four marketing activities—product, price, distribution (place), and promotion—that the firm can control to achieve specific goals within a dynamic marketing environment (Figure 11.3). The buyer or the target market is the central focus of all marketing activities.

Product A product—whether a good, a service, an idea, or some combination—is a complex mix of tangible and intangible attributes that provide satisfaction and benefits. A *good* is a physical entity you can touch. A Porsche Cayenne, a Hewlett-Packard printer, and a kitten available for adoption at an animal shelter are examples of goods. A *service* is the application of human and mechanical efforts to people or objects to provide intangible benefits to customers. Air travel, dry cleaning, haircuts, banking, insurance, medical care, and day care are examples of services. *Ideas* include concepts, philosophies, images, and issues. For instance, an attorney, for a fee, may advise you about what rights you have in the event that the IRS decides to audit your tax return. Other marketers of ideas include political parties, churches, and schools.

▼**FIGURE 11.3**
The Marketing Mix: Product, Price, Distribution (Place), and Promotion

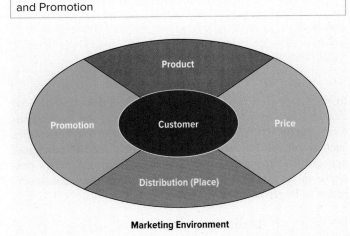

Marketing Environment

A product has emotional and psychological, as well as physical characteristics, that include everything that the buyer receives from an exchange. This definition includes supporting services such as installation, guarantees, product information, and promises of repair. Products usually have both favorable and unfavorable attributes; therefore, almost every purchase or exchange involves trade-offs as consumers try to maximize their benefits and satisfaction and minimize unfavorable attributes.

Products are among a firm's most visible contacts with consumers. If they do not meet consumer needs and expectations, sales will be difficult, and product life spans will be brief. The product is an important variable—often the central focus— of the marketing mix; the other variables (price, distribution, and promotion) must be coordinated with product decisions.

Price Almost anything can be assessed by a **price**, a value placed on an object exchanged between a buyer and a seller. Although the seller usually establishes the price, it may be negotiated between the buyer and the seller. The buyer usually exchanges purchasing power—income, credit, wealth—for the satisfaction or utility associated with a product. Because financial price is the measure of value commonly used in an exchange, it quantifies value and is the basis of most market exchanges.

Marketers view price as much more than a way of assessing value, however. It is a key element of the marketing mix because it relates directly

DID YOU KNOW?

During its first year of operation, sales of Coca-Cola averaged just nine drinks per day for total first-year sales of $50. Today, Coca-Cola products are consumed at the rate of 1.7 billion drinks per day.[14]

the "4 Ps") is making products available to customers in the quantities desired. For example, consumers can rent DVDs and videogames from a physical store, a vending machine, or an online service. Intermediaries, usually wholesalers and retailers, perform many of the activities required to move products efficiently from producers to consumers or industrial buyers. These activities involve transporting, warehousing, materials handling, and inventory control, as well as packaging and communication.

Critics who suggest that eliminating wholesalers and other middlemen would result in lower prices for consumers do not recognize that eliminating intermediaries would not do away with the need for their services. Other institutions would have to perform those services, and consumers would still have to pay for them. In addition, in the absence of wholesalers, all producers would have to deal directly with retailers or customers, keeping voluminous records and hiring extra people to deal with customers.

Promotion **Promotion** is a persuasive form of communication that attempts to expedite a marketing exchange by influencing individuals, groups, and organizations to accept goods, services, and ideas. Promotion includes advertising, personal selling, publicity, and sales promotion, all of which we will look at more closely in Chapter 12.

The aim of promotion is to communicate directly or indirectly with individuals, groups,

> **"The aim of promotion is to communicate directly or indirectly with individuals, groups, and organizations to facilitate exchanges."**

to the generation of revenue and profits. Prices can also be changed quickly to stimulate demand or respond to competitors' actions. The sudden increase in the cost of commodities such as oil can create price increases or a drop in consumer demand for a product. When gas prices rise, consumers purchase more fuel-efficient cars; when prices fall, consumers return to larger vehicles.[15]

Distribution **Distribution** (sometimes referred to as "place" because it helps to remember the marketing mix as

and organizations to facilitate exchanges. When marketers use advertising and other forms of promotion, they must effectively manage their promotional resources and understand product and target market characteristics to ensure that these promotional activities contribute to the firm's objectives.

Most major companies have set up websites on the Internet to promote themselves and their products. While traditional advertising media such as television, radio, newspapers, and

Redbox departed from the more traditional brick-and-mortar rental stores by choosing to distribute its DVD rentals through vending machines.
© JoeFox/Alamy

MARKETING RESEARCH AND INFORMATION SYSTEMS

Before marketers can develop a marketing mix, they must collect in-depth, up-to-date information about customer needs. **Marketing research** is a systematic, objective process of getting information about potential customers to guide marketing decisions. Such information might include data about the age, income, ethnicity, gender, and educational level of people in the target market, their preferences for product features, their attitudes toward competitors' products, and the frequency with which they use the product. For instance, marketing research has revealed that consumers often make in-store purchase decisions in three seconds or less.[18] Marketing research is vital because the marketing concept cannot be implemented without information about customers.

A marketing information system is a framework for accessing information about customers from sources both inside and outside the organization. Inside the organization, there is a continuous flow of information about prices, sales, and expenses. Outside the organization, data are readily available through private or public reports and census statistics, as well as from many other sources. Computer networking technology provides a framework for companies to connect to useful databases and customers with instantaneous information about product acceptance, sales performance, and buying behavior. This information is important to planning and marketing strategy development.

Two types of data are usually available to decision makers. **Primary data** are observed, recorded, or collected directly from respondents. If you've ever participated in a telephone survey about a product, recorded your TV viewing habits for ACNielsen or Arbitron, or even responded to a political opinion poll, you provided the researcher with primary data. Primary data must be gathered by researchers who develop a method to observe phenomena or research respondents. Many companies use "mystery shoppers" to visit their retail establishments and report on whether the stores were adhering to the companies' standards of service. These undercover customers

magazines remain important, digital advertising on websites and social media sites is growing. Not only can digital advertising be less expensive, but advertising offerings such as Google AdWords allow companies to pay only when users click on the link or advertisement.[16] Additionally, social media sites offer advertising opportunities for both large and small companies. Firms can create a Facebook page and post corporate updates for free. Not to be outdone, Twitter also allows advertisers to purchase Promoted Tweets on the site. Promoted Tweets are just like regular tweets (except for the name), allowing users to respond or re-tweet them to their friends.[17]

Direct Marketing News is a good source for secondary marketing research. The publication contains up-to-date information on market trends and data.
© Courtesy of Haymarket Media, Inc.

document their observations of store appearance, employee effectiveness, and customer treatment. Mystery shoppers provide valuable information that helps companies improve their organizations and refine their marketing strategies.[19] Companies also use surveys and focus groups to gauge customer opinion. Table 11.2 provides the rankings for organizations with the best customer service. A weakness of surveys is that respondents are sometimes untruthful in order to avoid seeming foolish or ignorant. Although focus groups can be more expensive than surveys, they allow marketers to understand how consumers express themselves as well as observe their behavior patterns.[20]

Some methods for marketing research use passive observation of consumer behavior and open-ended questioning techniques. Called ethnographic or observational research, the approach can help marketers determine what consumers really think about their products and how different ethnic or demographic groups react to them.

Secondary data are compiled inside or outside the organization for some purpose other than changing the current situation. Marketers typically use information compiled by the U.S. Census Bureau and other government agencies, databases created by marketing research firms, as well as sales and other internal reports, to gain information about customers.

Online Marketing Research

The marketing of products and collecting of data about buying behavior—information on what people actually buy and how they buy it—represents marketing research of the future.

New information technologies are changing the way businesses learn about their customers and market their products. Interactive multimedia research, or *virtual testing*, combines sight, sound, and animation to facilitate the testing of concepts as well as packaging and design features for consumer products. The evolving development of telecommunications and computer technologies is allowing marketing researchers quick and easy access to a growing number of online services and a vast database of potential respondents.

Marketing research can use digital media and social networking sites to gather useful information for marketing decisions. Sites such as Twitter, Facebook, and LinkedIn can be good substitutes for focus groups. Online surveys can serve as an alternative to mail, telephone, or personal interviews.

Social networks are a great way to obtain information from consumers who are willing to share their experiences about products and companies. In a way, this process identifies those consumers who develop an identity or passion for certain products, as well as those consumers who have concerns about quality or performance. It is possible for firms to tap into existing online social networks and simply "listen" to what consumers have on their mind. Firms can also encourage consumers to join a community or group so that they can share their opinions with the business.

A good outcome from using social networks is the opportunity to reach new voices and gain varied perspectives on the creative process of developing new products and promotions. For instance, Kickstarter gives aspiring entrepreneurs the ability to market their ideas online. Funders can then choose whether to fund those ideas in return for a finished product or a steep discount.[21] To some extent, social networking is democratizing design by welcoming consumers to join in the development process for new products.[22]

Online surveys are becoming an important part of marketing research. Traditionally, the process of conducting surveys

▼ **TABLE 11.2** Companies with the Best Customer Service

Rank	Company	Excellence Rating (%)
1	Amazon.com	57.5%
2	Hilton Worldwide	41.4
3	Marriott International	39.9
4	Chick-fil-A	38.6
5	American Express	37.7
6	Trader Joe's	37.2
7	UPS	36.7
8	Sony	36.5
9	Hewlett-Packard	36.2
10	Apple	35.7

Source: Douglas A. McIntyre et al., "Customer Service Hall of Fame," *Wall St. 24/7,* July 18, 2014, http://247wallst.com/special-report/2014/07/18/customer-service-hall-of-fame/ (accessed April 2, 2015).

Starbucks attempts to influence consumers' buying behavior by offering free Wi-Fi and a comfortable retail environment.
© *Jill Braaten/McGraw-Hill Education*

online involved sending questionnaires to respondents either through e-mail or through a website. However, digital communication has increased the ability of marketers to conduct polls on blogs and social networking sites. The benefits of online market research include lower costs and quicker feedback. For example, Julep Beauty, which sells skin care products, nail polish, and makeup, frequently uses social media to test and sell new products. Julep uses feedback from customers in the development of new products. Based on this feedback, the company was able to introduce 300 products within a one-year period.[23] By monitoring consumers' feedback, companies can understand customer needs and adapt their goods or services.

BUYING BEHAVIOR

Carrying out the marketing concept is impossible unless marketers know what, where, when, and how consumers buy; conducting marketing research into the factors that influence

- **Motivation**, as we said in Chapter 9, is an inner drive that directs a person's behavior toward goals. A customer's behavior is influenced by a set of motives rather than by a single motive. A buyer of a tablet computer, for example, may be motivated by ease of use, ability to communicate with the office, and price.

- **Learning** brings about changes in a person's behavior based on information and experience. For instance, a smartphone app that provides digital news or magazine content could eliminate the need for print copies. If a person's actions result in a reward, he or she is likely to behave the same way in similar situations. If a person's actions bring about a negative result, however—such as feeling ill after eating at a certain restaurant—he or she will probably not repeat that action.

- **Attitude** is knowledge and positive or negative feelings about something. For example, a person who feels strongly about protecting the environment may refuse to buy products that harm the earth and its inhabitants.

> **Marketers analyze buying behavior because a firm's marketing strategy should be guided by an understanding of buyers.**

buying behavior helps marketers develop effective marketing strategies. **Buying behavior** refers to the decision processes and actions of people who purchase and use products. It includes the behavior of both consumers purchasing products for personal or household use and organizations buying products for business use. Marketers analyze buying behavior because a firm's marketing strategy should be guided by an understanding of buyers. People view pets as part of their families, and they want their pets to have the best of everything. Iams, which markets the Iams and Eukanuba pet food brands, recognized this trend and shifted its focus. Today, it markets high-quality pet food, fancy pet treats, sauces, and other items. Both psychological and social variables are important to an understanding of buying behavior.

Psychological Variables of Buying Behavior

Psychological factors include the following:

- **Perception** is the process by which a person selects, organizes, and interprets information received from his or her senses, as when experiencing an advertisement or touching a product to better understand it.

- **Personality** refers to the organization of an individual's distinguishing character traits, attitudes, or habits. Although market research on the relationship between personality and buying behavior has been inconclusive, some marketers believe that the type of car or clothing a person buys reflects his or her personality.

Social Variables of Buying Behavior

Social factors include **social roles**, which are a set of expectations for individuals based on some position they occupy. A person may have many roles: mother, wife, student, executive. Each of these roles can influence buying behavior. Consider a woman choosing an automobile. As a mother, she might prefer to purchase a safe, gasoline-efficient car such as a Volvo. Her environmentally supportive colleagues at work might urge her to forgo buying a car and instead use public transportation and Uber. Because millennials (those between the ages of 18 and 34) tend to prefer vehicles that represent how they see themselves,[24] the woman's ourdoorsy 18-year-old son may want her to purchase a Ford Explorer to take on camping trips, while her 20-year-old daughter thinks she should buy a cool, classy car such as a Ford Mustang. Thus, in choosing which car to buy, the woman's buying behavior may be affected by the opinions

reference groups groups with whom buyers identify and whose values or attitudes they adopt.

social classes a ranking of people into higher or lower positions of respect.

culture the integrated, accepted pattern of human behavior, including thought, speech, beliefs, actions, and artifacts.

and experiences of her family and friends and by her roles as mother, daughter, and employee.

Other social factors include reference groups, social classes, and culture.

- **Reference groups** include families, professional groups, civic organizations, and other groups with whom buyers identify and whose values or attitudes they adopt. A person may use a reference group as a point of comparison or a source of information. A person new to a community may ask other group members to recommend a family doctor, for example.

- **Social classes** are determined by ranking people into higher or lower positions of respect. Criteria vary from one society to another. People within a particular social class may develop common patterns of behavior. People in the upper-middle class, for example, might buy a Lexus or a BMW as a symbol of their social class.

- **Culture** is the integrated, accepted pattern of human behavior, including thought, speech, beliefs, actions, and artifacts. Culture determines what people wear and eat and where they live and travel. Many Hispanic Texans and New Mexicans, for example, buy *masa trigo,* the dough used to prepare flour tortillas, which are basic to southwestern and Mexican cuisine.

Understanding Buying Behavior

Although marketers try to understand buying behavior, it is extremely difficult to explain exactly why a buyer purchases a particular product. The tools and techniques for analyzing consumers are not exact. Marketers may not be able to determine accurately what is highly satisfying to buyers, but they know that trying to understand consumer wants and needs is the best way to satisfy them. For some time, Hasbro seemed to focus mainly on the toy market for young boys. However, after studying how young girls play and interact with toys, Hasbro was able to introduce many lines that have become popular among female children, including My Little Pony and Nerf Rebelle (an extension of the Nerf product that targets active young girls). Today, Hasbro has gained share from the market for girls and has been better able to compete against major rival Mattel.[26]

> **LO 11-6** Summarize the environmental forces that influence marketing decisions.

THE MARKETING ENVIRONMENT

A number of external forces directly or indirectly influence the development of marketing strategies; the following political, legal, regulatory, social, competitive, economic, and technological forces comprise the marketing environment.

- *Political, legal, and regulatory forces*—laws and regulators' interpretation of laws, law enforcement and regulatory activities, regulatory bodies, legislators and legislation, and political

TESLA'S MARKETING APPROACH SHOCKS THE CAR INDUSTRY

The automotive industry tends to be dominated by huge companies with deep pockets, making it difficult for newcomers to enter. It would be nearly impossible for an intrepid startup to find an unclaimed spot, much less sweep industry award shows and grab widespread media attention with one of its first cars. Yet Tesla Motors did exactly that.

The company is only a decade old, but its luxury-aimed, all-electric vehicles, and specifically the much-praised Model S (priced starting at $64,000, considered inexpensive for the luxury-car market), have found an untapped niche in wealthy customers interested in the unique advantages of electric done well, from fuel savings to structural longevity to exceptional speed and performance.

A market-oriented look at Tesla reveals a variety of strategies to build awareness and develop its brand that are both clever and low cost—necessary to compete with the industry giants (Nissan spent $25 million during a one-year period advertising its electric Nissan Leaf). With an in-house marketing team of only seven employees, the company does no traditional magazine or television advertising, instead focusing on developing buzz through industry contacts, social media, and news coverage. It does not sell its cars through dealerships, but directly through its website, and each car is assembled on demand. To allow potential customers to see the car in person, it opens small, nonselling showrooms in popular malls. Even its service centers send a branding message, with their floors painted white to emphasize that electric cars do not leak oil or other messy fluids. Tesla will need all the technological and strategic innovation it can muster to achieve its long-term goal of producing the world's first truly practical electric car for the average consumer.[25]

Discussion Questions

1. What is Tesla's target market?
2. Why did Tesla succeed in breaking into the automotive industry where so many others have failed?
3. How do each of Tesla's individual marketing choices fit into its overall marketing strategy?

actions of interest groups. Specific laws, for example, require that advertisements be truthful and that all health claims be documented.

- *Social forces*—the public's opinions and attitudes toward issues such as living standards, ethics, the environment, lifestyles, and quality of life. For example, social concerns have led marketers to design and market safer toys for children.

- *Competitive and economic forces*—competitive relationships such as those in the technology industry, unemployment, purchasing power, and general economic conditions (prosperity, recession, depression, recovery, product shortages, and inflation).

- *Technological forces*—computers and other technological advances that improve distribution, promotion, and new-product development.

Marketing requires creativity and consumer focus because environmental forces can change quickly and dramatically. Changes can arise from social concerns and economic forces such as price increases, product shortages, and altering levels of demand for commodities. Recently, climate change, global warming, and the impact of carbon emissions on our environment have become social concerns and are causing businesses to rethink marketing strategies. These environmental issues have persuaded governments to institute stricter limits on greenhouse gas emissions. For instance, in the United States the government has mandated that by 2025 vehicles must be able to reach 54.5 miles per gallon on average.[27] This is causing automobile companies like General Motors to investigate ways to make their cars more fuel efficient without significantly raising the price. At the same time, these laws are also introducing opportunities for new products. Concerns over the environment are encouraging automobile companies to begin releasing electric vehicles, such as the Chevrolet Volt and the Nissan Leaf.

Because such environmental forces are interconnected, changes in one may cause changes in others. Consider that because of evidence linking children's consumption of soft drinks and fast foods to health issues such as obesity, diabetes, and osteoporosis, marketers of such products have experienced negative publicity and calls for legislation regulating the sale of soft drinks in public schools.

Although the forces in the marketing environment are sometimes called uncontrollables, they are not totally so. A marketing manager can influence some environmental variables. For example, businesses can lobby legislators to dissuade them from passing unfavorable legislation. Figure 11.4 shows the variables in the marketing environment that affect the marketing mix and the buyer.

THE IMPORTANCE OF MARKETING TO BUSINESS AND SOCIETY

As this chapter has shown, marketing is a necessary function to reaching consumers, establishing relationships, and creating revenue. While some critics might view marketing as a way to change what consumers want, marketing is essential in

---

FIGURE 11.4
The Marketing Mix and the Marketing Environment

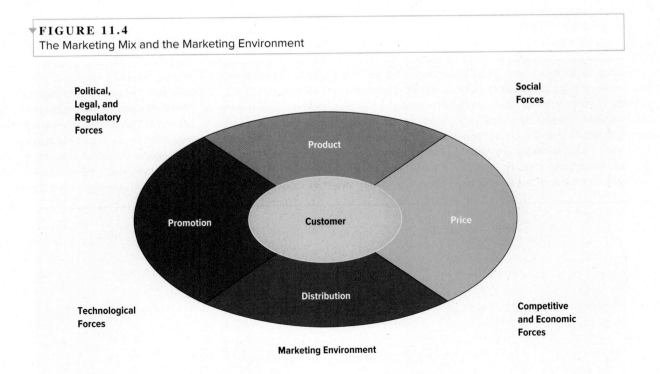

communicating the value of goods and services. For consumers, marketing is necessary to ensure that they get the products they desire at the right places in the right quantities at a reasonable price. From the perspective of businesses, marketing is necessary in order to form valuable relationships with customers to increase profitability and customer support. The importance of the sales function is increasing more than other areas of the business.[28]

It is not just for-profit businesses that engage in marketing activities. Nonprofit organizations, government institutions, and even

people must market themselves to spread awareness and achieve desired outcomes. All organizations must reach their target markets, communicate their offerings, and establish high-quality services. For instance, nonprofit organization The Leukemia and Lymphoma Society uses print, radio, web, and other forms of media to market its Team in Training racing events to recruit participants and solicit support. Without marketing, it would be nearly impossible for organizations to connect with their target audiences. Marketing is therefore an important contributor to business and societal well-being ■

SO YOU WANT A JOB // in Marketing /

You probably did not think as a child how great it would be to grow up and become a marketer. That's because often marketing is associated with sales jobs, but opportunities in marketing, public relations, product management, advertising, e-marketing, and customer relationship management and beyond represent almost one-third of all jobs in today's business world. To enter any job in the marketing field, you must balance an awareness of customer needs with business knowledge while mixing in creativity and the ability to obtain useful information to make smart business decisions.

Marketing starts with understanding the customer. Marketing research is a vital aspect in marketing decision making and presents many job opportunities. Market researchers survey customers to determine their habits, preferences, and aspirations. Activities include concept testing, product testing, package testing, test-market research, and new-product research. Salaries vary, depending on the nature and level of the position as well as the type, size, and location of the firm. An entry-level market analyst may make between $24,000 and $50,000, while a market research director may earn from $75,000 to $200,000 or more.

One of the most dynamic areas in marketing is direct marketing, where a seller solicits a response from a consumer using direct communications methods such as telephone, online communication, direct mail, or catalogs. Jobs in direct marketing include buyers, catalog managers, research/mail-list managers, or order fulfillment managers. Most positions in direct marketing involve planning and market analysis. Some require the use of databases to sort and analyze customer information and sales history.

Use of the Internet for retail sales is growing, and the Internet continues to be very useful for business-to-business sales, so e-marketing offers many career opportunities, including customer relationship management (CRM). CRM helps companies market to customers through relationships, maintaining customer loyalty. Information technology plays a huge role in such marketing jobs, as you need to combine technical skills and marketing knowledge to effectively communicate with customers. Job titles include e-marketing manager, customer relationship manager, and e-services manager. A CRM customer service manager may receive a salary in the $40,000 to $45,000 range, and experienced individuals in charge of online product offerings may earn up to $100,000.

A job in any of these marketing fields will require a strong sense of the current trends in business and marketing. Customer service is vital to many aspects of marketing, so the ability to work with customers and to communicate their needs and wants is important. Marketing is everywhere, from the corner grocery or local nonprofit organization to the largest multinational corporations, making it a shrewd choice for an ambitious and creative person. We will provide additional job opportunities in marketing in Chapter 12.

dimensions of
marketing strategy

© Hisham Ibrahim/Photographer's Choice RF/Getty Images, RF

LEARNING OBJECTIVES

After reading this chapter, you will be able to:

LO 12-1 Describe the role of product in the marketing mix, including how products are developed, classified, and identified.

LO 12-2 Define price, and discuss its importance in the marketing mix, including various pricing strategies a firm might employ.

LO 12-3 Identify factors affecting distribution decisions, such as marketing channels and intensity of market coverage.

LO 12-4 Specify the activities involved in promotion, as well as promotional strategies and promotional positioning.

The key to developing a marketing strategy is selecting a target market and maintaining a marketing mix that creates long-term relationships with customers. Getting just the right mix of product, price, distribution (place), and promotion (the 4 Ps) is critical if a business is to satisfy its target customers and achieve its own objectives (implement the marketing concept).

In Chapter 11, we introduced the marketing concept and the various activities important in developing a marketing strategy. In this chapter, we'll take a closer look at the four dimensions of the marketing mix—product, price, distribution (place), and promotion—used to develop the marketing strategy. The focus of these marketing mix elements is a marketing strategy that builds customer relationships and satisfaction. ■

"Each year, thousands of products are introduced, but few of them succeed."

THE MARKETING MIX

The marketing mix is the part of marketing strategy that involves decisions regarding controllable variables. After selecting a target market, marketers have to develop and manage the dimensions of the marketing mix to give their firm an advantage over competitors. Successful companies offer at least one dimension of value usually associated with a marketing mix element that surpasses all competitors in the marketplace in meeting customer expectations. However, this does not mean that a company can ignore the other dimensions of the marketing mix; it must maintain acceptable, and if possible distinguishable, differences in the other dimensions as well.

Walmart, for example, emphasizes price ("Save money, live better"). Procter & Gamble is well known for its promotion of top consumer brands such as Tide, Cheer, Crest, Ivory, and Head & Shoulders. Xiaomi, a three-year-old Chinese consumer electronics company, has achieved impressive scale by utilizing a low-cost, feature-rich strategy.[2]

> **LO 12-1** Describe the role of product in the marketing mix, including how products are developed, classified, and identified.

PRODUCT STRATEGY

As mentioned previously, the term *product* refers to goods, services, and ideas. Because the product is often the most visible

DID YOU KNOW?

Less than 10 percent of new products succeed in the marketplace, and 90 percent of successes come from a handful of companies.[1]

of the marketing mix dimensions, managing product decisions is crucial. In this section, we'll consider product development, classification, mix, life cycle, and identification.

Developing New Products

Each year, thousands of products are introduced, but few of them succeed. For instance, Honda discontinued its Insight, the first hybrid model introduced into the United States, after lackluster sales.[3] Figure 12.1 shows the different steps in the product-development process. Before introducing a new product, a business must follow a multistep process: idea development, the screening of new ideas, business analysis, product development, test marketing, and commercialization. A firm can take considerable time to get a product ready for the market: It took more than 20 years for the first photocopier, for example. Additionally, sometimes an idea or product prototype might be shelved only to be returned to later. The late Apple CEO Steve Jobs admitted that the iPad actually came before the iPhone in the product-development process. Once it was realized that the scrolling mechanism he was thinking of using could be used to develop a phone, the iPad idea was placed on a shelf for the time being. Apple later returned to develop the product and released the iPad in 2010.[4]

Idea Development New ideas can come from marketing research, engineers, and outside sources such as advertising agencies and management consultants. Nike has a separate division—Nike Sport Research Lab—where scientists, athletes, engineers, and designers work together to develop technology of the future. The teams research ideas in biomechanics,

FIGURE 12.1
Product-Development
Process

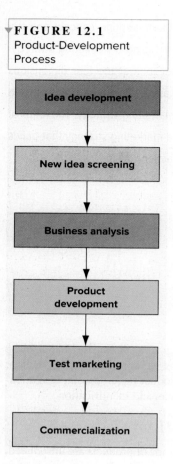

- Idea development
- New idea screening
- Business analysis
- Product development
- Test marketing
- Commercialization

perception, athletic performance, and physiology to create unique, relevant, and innovative products. These final products are tested in environmental chambers with real athletes to ensure functionality and quality before being introduced into the market.[5] As we said in Chapter 11, ideas sometimes come from customers, too. Other sources are brainstorming and intracompany incentives or rewards for good ideas. New ideas can even create a company. When Jeff Bezos came up with the idea to sell books over the Internet in 1992, he had no idea it would evolve into a billion-dollar firm. After failing to convince his boss of the idea, Bezos left to start Amazon.[7]

New Idea Screening
The next step in developing a new product is idea

While attending Yale in 1966, FedEx founder Fred Smith studied a mathematical discipline called topology, which inspired his vision for creating the company. Realizing the potential efficiencies of connecting all points on a network through a central hub, Smith used what he learned to get FedEx off the ground.
© Jill Braaten/McGraw-Hill Education

screening. In this phase, a marketing manager should look at the organization's resources and objectives and assess the firm's ability to produce and market the product. Important aspects to be considered at this stage are consumer desires, the competition, technological changes, social trends, and political, economic, and environmental considerations. Basically, there are two reasons new products succeed: They are able to meet a need or solve a problem better than products already

SEVENTH GENERATION EXPANDS BEYOND HOUSEHOLD GOODS INTO WATER, TEA, AND COFFEE

Household goods and personal care products company Seventh Generation has built a reputation for its environmentally friendly "green" focus. It caters to customers who prefer their everyday items, such as dish soap and paper towels, to be made and packaged with recycled materials and contain natural ingredients. Its success is leading the company to expand beyond household goods into new markets, seeking other product lines that meet customer needs and provide a positive impact. In doing so, it must make careful choices to keep its brand strong and not stretch itself too thin across unrelated industries.

Seventh Generation acquired Bobble, a reusable water bottle with a built-in filter, believing the product fit well with Seventh Generation's vision. The bottle continues to be sold under the Bobble name. Seventh Generation also expanded into coffee and tea by acquiring the startup Gamila. Gamila's two products are the Teastick, an elegantly designed loose-leaf tea infuser that can replace disposable teabags, and the Impress Coffee Brewer, which makes a high-quality cup of coffee using a unique process that does not require disposable filters or pods. Seventh Generation incorporated these products into the Bobble brand.

Can a company known for toilet paper and trash bags find success in beverages by focusing on the unifying themes of good design and environmental stewardship? Keeping the Seventh Generation and Bobble brand names separate may be a conscious strategic choice to facilitate this transition. Seventh Generation must carefully choose its steps to reap the benefits of expansion and diversification while maintaining its reputation and core business.[6]

Discussion Questions

1. From a marketing and branding standpoint, has Seventh Generation made good choices in new-product strategies? Why or why not?

2. How can Seventh Generation maintain a strong and consistent brand image as it grows and diversifies?

3. Into which other types of products or industries might Seventh Generation consider expanding?

available or they add variety to the product selection currently on the market. Bringing together a team of knowledgeable people including designers, engineers, marketers, and customers is a great way to screen ideas. Using the Internet to encourage collaboration represents a rich opportunity for marketers to screen ideas. Most new product ideas are rejected during screening because they seem inappropriate or impractical for the organization.

Business Analysis Business analysis is a basic assessment of a product's compatibility in the marketplace and its potential profitability. Both the size of the market and competing products are often studied at this point. The most important question relates to market demand: How will the product affect the firm's sales, costs, and profits?

Product Development If a product survives the first three steps, it is developed into a prototype that should reveal the intangible attributes it possesses as perceived by the consumer. Product development is often expensive, and few product ideas make it to this stage. New product research and development costs vary. Adding a new color to an existing item may cost $100,000 to $200,000, but launching a completely new product can cost millions of dollars. During product development, various elements of the marketing mix must be developed for testing. Copyrights, tentative advertising copy, packaging, labeling, and descriptions of a target market are integrated to develop an overall marketing strategy.

Test Marketing Test marketing is a trial minilaunch of a product in limited areas that represent the potential market. It allows a complete test of the marketing strategy in a natural environment, giving the organization an opportunity to discover weaknesses and eliminate them before the product is fully launched. SOHM Inc., a generic pharmaceutical manufacturing firm, began test marketing some of its over-the-counter and skin care products in U.S. retailers. Traditionally, SOHM has been more focused on emerging markets in Africa, Southeast Asia, and Latin America.[8] Because test marketing requires significant resources and expertise, market research companies like ACNielsen can assist firms in test marketing their products. Figure 12.2 shows a sample of test markets marketing-research firms often use to test products to predict how successful they might be on a nationwide scale.

Commercialization Commercialization is the full introduction of a complete marketing strategy and the launch of the product for commercial success. During commercialization, the firm gears up for full-scale production, distribution, and promotion. For example, 7-Eleven is developing a healthier, fresher line of foods to appeal to health conscious consumers. Although convenience stores are not usually associated with healthy products, 7-Eleven hopes to change this by offering salads, healthy sandwiches, juices, and wraps along with its more popular Slurpee and Twinkie products. The company is launching this healthier fare in Southern California. If successful in California, 7-Eleven plans to move into full commercialization.[9]

test marketing a trial minilaunch of a product in limited areas that represent the potential market.

commercialization the full introduction of a complete marketing strategy and the launch of the product for commercial success.

consumer products products intended for household or family use.

Classifying Products

Products are usually classified as either consumer products or industrial products. **Consumer products** are for household or family use; they are not intended for any purpose other than daily living. They can be further classified as convenience products, shopping products, and specialty products on the basis of consumers' buying behavior and intentions.

- *Convenience products,* such as eggs, milk, bread, and newspapers, are bought frequently, without a lengthy search, and often for immediate consumption. Consumers spend virtually no time planning where to purchase these products and usually accept whatever brand is available.

▼FIGURE 12.2
Common Test-Market Cities

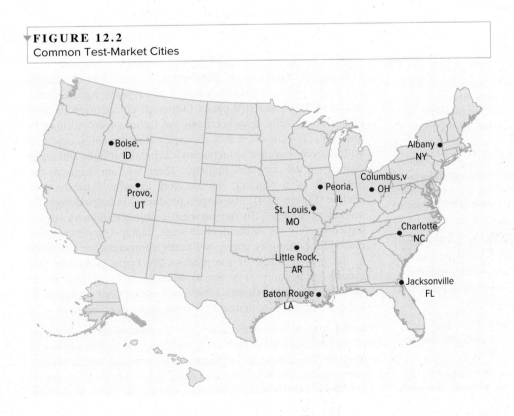

Coca-Cola BlāK is a coffee-flavored soft drink that Coca-Cola introduced in 2006. It is an example of a product that did not survive. Many consumers did not like the taste, and Coca-Cola discontinued the drink in 2008.
© John Flournoy/McGraw-Hill Education

- *Shopping products,* such as furniture, audio equipment, clothing, and sporting goods, are purchased after the consumer has compared competitive products and "shopped around." Price, product features, quality, style, service, and image all influence the decision to buy.

- *Specialty products,* such as ethnic foods, designer clothing and shoes, art, and antiques, require even greater research and shopping effort. Consumers know what they want and go out of their way to find it; they are not willing to accept a substitute.

Business products are used directly or indirectly in the operation or manufacturing processes of businesses. They are usually purchased for the operation of an organization or the production of other products; thus, their purchase is tied to specific goals and objectives. They too can be further classified:

- *Raw materials* are natural products taken from the earth, oceans, and recycled solid waste. Iron ore, bauxite, lumber, cotton, and fruits and vegetables are examples.

- *Major equipment* covers large, expensive items used in production. Examples include earth-moving equipment, stamping machines, and robotic equipment used on auto assembly lines.

- *Accessory equipment* includes items used for production, office, or management purposes, which usually do not become part of the final product. Computers, fax machines, calculators, and hand tools are examples.

- *Component parts* are finished items, ready to be assembled into the company's final products. Tires, window glass, batteries, and spark plugs are component parts of automobiles.

- *Processed materials* are things used directly in production or management operations but are not readily identifiable as component parts. Varnish, for example, is a processed material for a furniture manufacturer.

- *Supplies* include materials that make production, management, and other operations possible, such as paper, pencils, paint, cleaning supplies, and so on.

- *Industrial services* include financial, legal, marketing research, security, janitorial, and exterminating services. Purchasers decide whether to provide these services internally or to acquire them from an outside supplier.

Product Line and Product Mix

Product relationships within an organization are of key importance. A **product line** is a group of closely related products that are treated as a unit because of a similar marketing strategy. At Colgate-Palmolive, for example, the oral care product line includes Colgate toothpaste, toothbrushes, and dental floss. A **product mix** is all the products offered by an organization. Figure 12.3 displays a sampling of the product mix and product lines of the Colgate-Palmolive Company.

Product Life Cycle

Like people, products are born, grow, mature, and eventually die. Some products have very long lives. Ivory Soap was introduced in 1879 and still exists (although competition leading to decreased sales may soon put the future of Ivory Soap in question). In contrast, a new computer chip is usually outdated within a year because of technological breakthroughs and rapid changes in the computer industry. There are four stages in the life cycle of a product: introduction, growth, maturity, and decline (Figure 12.4). The stage a product is in helps determine marketing strategy. In the personal computer industry, desktop computers are in the decline stage, laptop computers have reached the maturity stage, and tablet computers are currently in the growth stage of the product life cycle (although this growth has begun to slow down). Manufacturers of these products are adopting different advertising and pricing strategies to maintain or increase demand for these types of computers.

In the *introductory stage,* consumer awareness and acceptance of the product are limited, sales are zero, and profits are negative. Profits are negative because the firm has spent money on research, development, and marketing to launch the product. During the introductory stage, marketers focus on making

FIGURE 12.3
Colgate-Palmolive's Product Mix and Product Lines

Product Mix

Product Lines

Oral Care	Personal Care	Home Care	Pet Nutrition
Toothpaste	*Deodorant*	*Dishwashing*	Hill's Prescription Diet
Colgate Total	Speed Stick	Palmolive	Hill's Science Diet
Advanced	Lady Speed Stick	AJAX	Hill's Ideal Balance
Colgate Optic	*Liquid Hand Soap*	Dermassage	Hill's Healthy Advantage
White	Softsoap		
Colgate Kids	*Body Wash*	*Fabric Conditioner*	
Colgate Dora the	Softsoap	Suavitel	
Explorer	Irish Spring		
Colgate SpongeBob	Softsoap		
SquarePants	*Bar Soap*		
Colgate 2in1	Irish Spring		
Toothbrushes	*Toiletries for Men*	*Household Cleaner*	
Colgate 360°	Afta	Murphy Oil Soap	
Colgate Max White	Skin Bracer	Fabuloso	
Colgate Total		AJAX	
Professional			

Source: Colgate-Palmolive, "Colgate World of Care," www.colgatepalmolive.com/app/Colgate/US/CompanyHomePage.cvsp (accessed April 9, 2015).

FIGURE 12.4
The Life Cycle of a Product

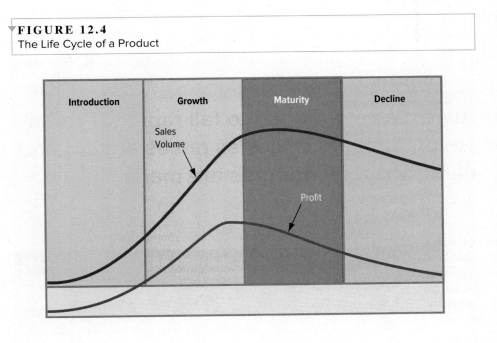

consumers aware of the product and its benefits. Google Glass for businesses is in the introductory stage of the product life cycle. Google Glass is a wearable technology that enables users to take pictures, make phone calls, and reply to e-mails through voice commands. Google's initial release of Glass caused a privacy backlash, prompting Google to pull the product. It has since introduced a new version targeted toward businesses in industries such as healthcare. A consumer version is in the works.[10] Table 12.1 shows some familiar products at different stages of the product life cycle. Sales accelerate as the product enters the growth stage of the life cycle.

In the *growth stage,* sales increase rapidly and profits peak, then start to decline. One reason profits start to decline during the growth stage is that new companies enter the market, driving prices down and increasing marketing expenses. Beats by Dre Studio headphones are currently in the growth stage. Launched in 2008, the premium headphone brand holds 27 percent of the $1.8 billion headphone market and 57 percent of the premium headphone market. Since the brand's debut, the company has added products to include speakers, earphones, proprietary software technology, and a music streaming service.[11]

▼ **TABLE 12.1** Products at Different Stages of the Product Life Cycle

Introduction	Growth	Maturity	Decline
Google Glass	Tablet computer	Laptop computer	Desktop computer
Smart watch	LEGO Friends	Print newspaper	CD player
Electric car	Ford Focus	Chevrolet Corvette	PT Cruiser

During the growth stage, the firm tries to strengthen its position in the market by emphasizing the product's benefits and identifying market segments that want these benefits.

Sales continue to increase at the beginning of the *maturity stage,* but then the sales curve peaks and starts to decline while profits continue to decline. This stage is characterized by severe competition and heavy expenditures. In the United States, soft drinks have hit the maturity stage. Firms such as PepsiCo and Coca-Cola have taken many steps to try to revitalize sales, from introducing soda in smaller package sizes to adopting healthier product lines to expanding their reach internationally in places like Africa.[12]

During the *decline stage,* sales continue to fall rapidly. Profits also decline and may even become losses as prices are cut and necessary marketing expenditures are made. As profits drop, firms may eliminate certain models or items. To reduce expenses and squeeze out any remaining profits, marketing expenditures may be cut back, even though such cutbacks accelerate the sales decline. Finally, plans must be made for phasing out the product and introducing new ones to take its place. Apple iPods have been in decline in recent years as tablets and phones are being designed to serve as music listening devices. The iPod classic is rumored to be phased out of Apple's product line and has not been updated in a few years. Touchscreen iPods and the iPod shuffle, while also included in the decline stage of the product life cycle, are not yet being prepared for exit from the marketplace.[13]

is aiming for the middle of the market positioning to achieve a successful comeback with these new products.[15]

Identifying Products

Branding, packaging, and labeling can be used to identify or distinguish one product from others. As a result, they are key marketing activities that help position a product appropriately for its target market.

Branding **Branding** is the process of naming and identifying products. A *brand* is a name, term, symbol, design, or combination that identifies a product and distinguishes it from other products. Consider that Google, iPod, and TiVo are brand names that are used to identify entire product categories, much like Xerox has become synonymous with photocopying and Kleenex with tissues. Protecting a brand name is important in maintaining a brand identity. The world's 10 most valuable brands are shown in Table 12.2. The brand name is the part of the brand that can be spoken and consists of letters, words, and numbers—such as WD-40 lubricant. A *brand mark* is the part of the brand that is a distinctive design, such as the silver star on the hood of a Mercedes or McDonald's golden arches logo. A **trademark** is a brand that is registered with the U.S. Patent and Trademark Office and is thus legally protected from use by any other firm.

Two major categories of brands are manufacturer brands and private distributor brands. **Manufacturer brands** are brands initiated and owned by the manufacturer to identify products

> **During the *decline stage*, sales continue to fall rapidly. Profits also decline and may even become losses as prices are cut and necessary marketing expenditures are made.**

At the same time, it should be noted that product stages do not always go one way. Some products that have moved to the maturity stage or to the decline stage can still rebound through redesign or new uses for the product. One prime example is baking soda. Originally, baking soda was used only for cooking, which meant it reached the maturity stage very quickly. However, once it was discovered that baking soda could be used as a deodorizer, sales shot up and bumped baking soda back into the growth stage.[14] Similarly, Acer is trying to make a comeback by releasing new lines of tablets and cell phones. The company focuses on value by offering quality products inexpensively. The Iconia One 7, for instance, is a 7-inch tablet that looks and functions just like the competition but costs significantly less. The company has also introduced a hybrid laptop–tablet combination product to appeal to more customers. Acer

▼ **TABLE 12.2** The 10 Most Valuable Brands in the World

Rank	Brand	Brand Value ($ millions)	Brand Value % Change
1	Google	$158,843	40%
2	Apple	147,880	−20
3	IBM	107,541	−4
4	Microsoft	90,185	29
5	McDonald's	85,706	−5
6	Coca-Cola	80,683	3
7	Visa	79,197	41
8	AT&T	77,883	3
9	Marlboro	67,341	−3
10	Amazon.com	64,255	41

Source: Millward Brown Optimer, "Brandz™ Top 100 Most Valuable Global Brands 2014," www.millwardbrown.com/brandz/2014/Top100/Docs/2014_BrandZ_Top100_Chart.pdf (accessed May 27, 2014).

from the point of production to the point of purchase. Kellogg's, Sony, and Texaco are examples. **Private distributor brands**, which may be less expensive than manufacturer brands, are owned and controlled by a wholesaler or retailer, such as Pantry Essentials (Safeway), Great Value (Walmart), and Member's Mark (Sam's Wholesale Club). The names of private brands do not usually identify their manufacturer. While private-label brands were once considered cheaper and of poor quality, such as Walmart's Ol'Roy dog food, many private-label brands are increasing in quality and image and are competing with national brands. For instance, a number of companies are hiring professional designers to design their private-label brands, replacing the traditional two-color packaging schemes often associated with private-label products. JCPenney partnered with Canadian designer Joe Fresh to feature a collection of clothing for under $70.[16] The grocery retailer Tesco has several types of private-label brands, and its branding strategy has performed so effectively that consumers may end up paying more for Tesco's own products than for branded goods.[17] Manufacturer brands are fighting hard against private distributor brands to retain their market share. Private distributor brands have increased more than 18 percent in the past several years as food prices have risen and economic conditions have declined.[18]

Another type of brand that has developed is **generic products**—products with no brand name at all. They often come in plain simple packages that carry only the generic name of the product—peanut butter, tomato juice, aspirin, dog food, and so on. They appeal to consumers who may be willing to sacrifice quality or product consistency to get a lower price. Sales of generic brands have significantly decreased in recent years, although generic pharmaceuticals are commonly purchased due to their lower price.

Companies use two basic approaches to branding multiple products. In one, a company gives each product within its complete product mix its own brand name. Warner-Lambert, which was acquired by Pfizer in 2000, sells many well-known consumer products—Dentyne, Chiclets, Listerine, Halls, Rolaids, and Trident—each individually branded. This branding policy ensures that the name of one product does not affect the names of others, and different brands can be targeted at different segments of the same market, increasing the company's market share (its percentage of the sales for the total market for a product). Another approach to branding is to develop a family of brands with each of the firm's products carrying the same name or at least part of the name. Gillette, Sara Lee, and IBM use this approach. Finally, consumers may react differently to domestic versus foreign brands. Table 12.3 provides a snapshot of the most popular car brands. Note that only three are U.S. brands.

Packaging The **packaging**, or external container that holds and describes the product, influences consumers' attitudes and their buying decisions. Surveys have shown that consumers are willing to pay more for certain packaging attributes. One of the attributes includes clearly stated nutrition and ingredient labeling, especially those characteristics indicating whether a product is organic, gluten free, or environmentally friendly. Recyclable and biodegradable packaging is also popular.[19] It is estimated that consumers' eyes linger only 2.5 seconds on each product on an average shopping trip; therefore, product packaging should be designed to attract and hold consumers' attention.

A package can perform several functions, including protection, economy, convenience, and promotion. Packaging can also be used to appeal to emotions. For example, Chobani yogurt focuses on package design as a means of appealing to customers. The design is meant to express that the product tastes as good as it looks.[20] On the other hand, organizations must also exert

▼ **TABLE 12.3** Best-Selling Car Brands in the World

Ranking	Vehicle Model	Country of Origin
1	Toyota Corolla	Japan
2	Hyundai Elantra	South Korea
3	Wuling Sunshine	China
4	Ford Focus	United States
5	Kia Rio	South Korea
6	Ford Fiesta	United States
7	Volkswagen Jetta	Germany
8	Toyota Camry	Japan
9	Chevrolet Cruze	United States
10	Volkswagen Golf	Germany

Source: "The World's Best-Selling Cars," *Forbes,* www.forbes.com/pictures/mkk45ekfi/ford-fiesta-in-shanghai-by-night/ (accessed April 2, 2015).

Clorox uses a family branding strategy so that consumers will recognize when a product is affiliated with the brand.
© *Bloomberg/Getty Images*

caution before changing the designs of highly popular products. Olive Garden encountered resistance when it changed its logo design to a more modern look. Critics believe the new design relays a cheaper and carefree feeling that was not embodied by the traditional logo.[21]

Labeling

Labeling, the presentation of important information on the package, is closely associated with packaging. The content of labeling, often required by law, may include ingredients or content, nutrition facts (calories, fat, etc.), care instructions, suggestions for use (such as recipes), the manufacturer's address and toll-free number, website, and other useful information. This information can have a strong impact on sales. The labels of many products, particularly food and drugs, must carry warnings, instructions, certifications, or manufacturers' identifications.

Product Quality

Quality reflects the degree to which a good, service, or idea meets the demands and requirements of customers. Quality products are often referred to as reliable, durable, easily maintained, easily used, a good value, or a trusted brand name. The level of quality is the amount of quality that a product possesses, and the consistency of quality depends on the product maintaining the same level of quality over time.

Quality of service is difficult to gauge because it depends on customers' perceptions of how well the service meets or exceeds their expectations. In other words, service quality is judged by consumers, not the service providers. For this reason, it is quite common for perceptions of quality to fluctuate from year to year. For instance, General Motors recalled millions of vehicles due to quality control issues. Problems included faulty ignition switches that prompted General Motors to issue a recall on the Chevy Cobalt. These recalls are having a negative impact on consumers' perceptions of GM's brands. A bank may define service quality as employing friendly and knowledgeable employees, but the bank's customers may be more concerned with waiting time, ATM access, security, and statement accuracy. Similarly, an airline traveler considers on-time arrival, on-board Internet or TV connections, and satisfaction with the ticketing and boarding process. The American Customer Satisfaction Index produces customer satisfaction scores for 10 economic sectors, 43 industries, and more than 300 companies. The latest results show that overall customer satisfaction was 75.2 (out of a possible 100), with increases in some industries balancing out drops in others.[22] Table 12.4 shows the customer satisfaction rankings of some of the most popular personal care and cleaning product companies.

The quality of services provided by businesses on the Internet can be gauged by consumers on such sites as ConsumerReports.org and BBBOnline. The subscription service offered by ConsumerReports.org provides consumers with a view of digital marketing sites' business, security, and privacy policies, while BBBOnline is dedicated to promoting responsibility online. As consumers join in by posting business and product reviews on the Internet on sites such as Yelp, the public can often get a much better idea of the quality of certain goods and services. Quality can also be associated with where the product is made. For example, "Made in U.S.A." labeling can be perceived as having a different value and quality. This includes strict laws on how much of a product can be made outside the United States to still qualify for the "Made in USA" label. There are differences in the perception of quality and value between U.S. consumers and Europeans when comparing products made in the United States, Japan, Korea, and China.[23] Chinese brands are usually perceived as lower quality, while Japanese and Korean products are perceived as being of higher quality. However, China is trying to change consumer perceptions of its low brand quality. The increase in middle and upper classes in China has led to a rise in Chinese-branded luxury goods.[24]

Google is the most valuable brand worldwide. It owns a variety of brands, including the search engine Google, the web browser Chrome, the video sharing site YouTube, and the social networking site Google+.
© Oliver Berg/Picture alliance/Newscom

▼ **TABLE 12.4** Personal Care and Cleaning Products Customer Satisfaction Ratings

Company	Score
Clorox	85
Colgate-Palmolive	83
Procter & Gamble	82
Dial	81
Unilever	80

Source: American Customer Satisfaction Index, "Benchmarks by Industry: Personal Care and Cleaning Products," 2014, www.theacsi.org/index.php?option=com_content&view=article&id=147&catid=&Itemid=212&i=Personal+Care+and+Cleaning+Products (accessed April 2, 2015).

LO 12-2 Define price, and discuss its importance in the marketing mix, including various pricing strategies a firm might employ.

PRICING STRATEGY

Previously, we defined price as the value placed on an object exchanged between a buyer and a seller. Buyers' interest in price stems from their expectations about the usefulness of a product or the satisfaction they may derive from it. Because buyers have limited resources, they must allocate those resources to obtain the products they most desire. They must decide whether the benefits gained in an exchange are worth the buying power sacrificed. Almost anything of value can be assessed by a price. Many factors may influence the evaluation of value, including time constraints, price levels, perceived quality, and motivations to use available information about prices.[25] Figure 12.5 illustrates a method for calculating the value of a product. Indeed, consumers vary in their response to price: Some focus solely on the lowest price, while others consider quality or the prestige associated with a product and its price. Some types of consumers are increasingly "trading up" to more status-conscious products, such as automobiles, home appliances, restaurants, and even pet food, yet remain price-conscious for other products such as cleaning and grocery goods. In setting prices, marketers must consider not just a company's cost to produce a good or service, but the perceived value of that item in the marketplace. Products' perceived value has benefited marketers at Starbucks, Sub-Zero, BMW, and Petco—which can charge premium prices for high-quality, prestige products—as well as Sam's Clubs and Costco—which offer basic household products at everyday low prices.

Price is a key element in the marketing mix because it relates directly to the generation of revenue and profits. In large part, the ability to set a price depends on the supply of and demand for a product. For most products, the quantity demanded goes up as the price goes down, and as the price goes up, the quantity demanded goes down. Changes in buyers' needs, variations in the effectiveness of other marketing mix variables, the presence of substitutes, and dynamic environmental factors can influence demand. The demand and price for coal has decreased as the price for natural gas has decreased due to an increase in supply.

Morton's Steakhouse uses a prestige pricing model to indicate the high quality of its food.
© Raymond Boyd/Getty Images

▼FIGURE 12.5
Calculating the Value of a Product

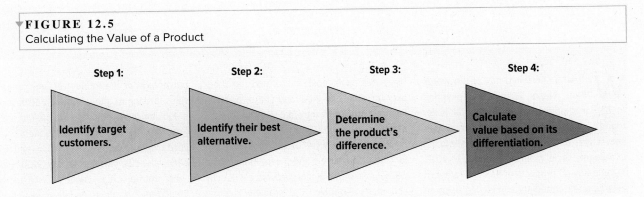

Step 1: Identify target customers.

Step 2: Identify their best alternative.

Step 3: Determine the product's difference.

Step 4: Calculate value based on its differentiation.

Source: Rafi Mohammed, "Use Price to Profit and Grow," *Forbes.com*, March 25, 2010, www.forbes.com/2010/03/25/profit-gain-value-mckinsey-sears-whirlpool-cmo-network-rafi-mohammed.html (accessed April 15, 2012).

Price is probably the most flexible variable in the marketing mix. Although it may take years to develop a product, establish channels of distribution, and design and implement promotion, a product's price may be set and changed in a few minutes. Under certain circumstances, of course, the price may not be so flexible, especially if government regulations prevent dealers from controlling prices. Of course, price also depends on the cost to manufacture a good or provide a service or idea. A firm may temporarily sell products below cost to match competition, to generate cash flow, or even to increase market share, but in the long run, it cannot survive by selling its products below cost.

Pricing Objectives

Pricing objectives specify the role of price in an organization's marketing mix and strategy. They usually are influenced not only by marketing mix decisions but also by finance, accounting, and production factors. Maximizing profits and sales, boosting market share, maintaining the status quo, and survival are four common pricing objectives.

Specific Pricing Strategies

Pricing strategies provide guidelines for achieving the company's pricing objectives and overall marketing strategy. They specify how price will be used as a variable in the marketing mix. Significant pricing strategies relate to the pricing of new products, psychological pricing, and price discounting.

Pricing New Products

Setting the price for a new product is critical: The right price leads to profitability; the wrong price may kill the product. In general, there are two basic strategies to setting the base price for a new product. **Price skimming** is charging the highest possible price that buyers who want the product will pay. Price skimming is used with luxury goods items. Gucci bags, for example, often run into the thousands of dollars. Price skimming is often used to allow the company to generate much-needed revenue to help offset the costs of research and development. Conversely, a **penetration price** is a low price designed to help a product enter the market and gain market share rapidly. When Netflix entered the market, it offered its rentals at prices much lower than the average rental stores and did not charge late fees. Netflix quickly gained market share and eventually drove many rental stores out of business. Penetration pricing is less flexible than price skimming; it is more difficult to raise a penetration price than to lower a skimming price. Penetration pricing is used most often when marketers suspect that competitors will enter the market shortly after the product has been introduced.

Psychological Pricing

Psychological pricing encourages purchases based on emotional rather than rational responses to the price. For example, the assumption behind *even/odd pricing* is that people will buy more of a product for $9.99 than $10.00 because it seems to be a bargain at the odd price. The assumption behind *symbolic/prestige pricing* is that high prices connote high quality. Thus the prices of certain fragrances and cosmetics are set artificially high to give the impression of superior quality. Some over-the-counter drugs are priced high because consumers associate a drug's price with potency.

Reference Pricing

Reference pricing is a type of psychological pricing in which a lower-priced item is compared to a more expensive brand in hopes that the consumer will use the higher price as a comparison price. The main idea is to make the

WANELO: 11 MILLION USERS, $100 MILLION VALUATION, NO PRODUCTS

Wanelo, a shortened mix of the words "Want, Need, Love," is attempting to be for shopping what "Facebook is for friends," according to founder Deena Varshavskaya. It tries to "optimize" shopping in a deeply social manner. Founded in 2012, Wanelo has no products of its own; rather, it acts as an intermediary connecting users to millions of products from stores worldwide.

Users can save, post, share, and tag products for others to view and share, and can instantly buy items they like with the click of a button.

Wanelo relies on its social media platform for connecting buyers and sellers. The product will sell, Varshavskaya argues, once it directly and elegantly solves the problem customers need it to solve. Wanelo earns a certain percentage of the money retailers make on sales through its site, although Varshavskaya is looking for additional revenue-generating opportunities. In one year Wanelo's user base exploded from 1 to 11 million, and it has been valued by investors at over $100 million. Other entrepreneurs could do well to learn from Wanelo's role as an intermediary in the marketing channel.[26]

item appear less expensive compared with other alternatives. For example, Walmart might place its Great Value brand next to a manufacturer's brand such as Bayer or Johnson & Johnson so that the Great Value brand will look like a better deal.

Price Discounting Temporary price reductions, or **discounts**, are often employed to boost sales. Although there are many types, quantity, seasonal, and promotional discounts are among the most widely used. Quantity discounts reflect the economies of purchasing in large volumes. Seasonal discounts to buyers who purchase goods or services out of season help even out production capacity. Promotional discounts attempt to improve sales by advertising price reductions on selected products to increase customer interest. Often promotional pricing is geared toward increased profits. Taco Bell, with its reputation for value, has been labeled the "best-positioned U.S. brand" to do well in a recession economy as consumers look for cheaper fast-food options. Taco Bell's Dollar Cravings Menu offers selections priced at $1.[27] KFC, Wendy's, and McDonald's all offer Value Menus as well, with items priced around $1.

> **LO 12-3** Identify factors affecting distribution decisions, such as marketing channels and intensity of market coverage.

DISTRIBUTION STRATEGY

The best products in the world will not be successful unless companies make them available where and when customers want to buy them. In this section, we will explore dimensions of distribution strategy, including the channels through which products are distributed, the intensity of market coverage, and the physical handling of products during distribution.

Marketing Channels

A **marketing channel**, or channel of distribution, is a group of organizations that move products from producer to customers. Marketing channels make products available to buyers when and where they desire to purchase them. Organizations that bridge the gap between a product's manufacturer and the ultimate consumer are called *middlemen,* or intermediaries. They create time, place, and ownership utility. Two intermediary organizations are retailers and wholesalers.

> **Today, there are too many stores competing for too few customers, and, as a result, competition between similar retailers has never been more intense.**

Retailers buy products from manufacturers (or other intermediaries) and sell them to consumers for home and household use rather than for resale or for use in producing other products. Toys 'Я' Us, for example, buys products from Mattel and other manufacturers and resells them to consumers. By bringing together an assortment of products from competing producers, retailers create utility. Retailers arrange for products to be moved from producers to a convenient retail establishment (place utility). They maintain hours of operation for their retail stores to make merchandise available when consumers want it (time utility). They also assume the risk of ownership of inventories (ownership utility). Table 12.5 describes various types of general merchandise retailers.

Today, there are too many stores competing for too few customers, and, as a result, competition between similar retailers has never been more intense. In addition, retailers face challenges such as shoplifting. Further, competition between different types of stores is changing the nature of retailing. Supermarkets compete with specialty food stores, wholesale clubs, and discount stores. Department stores compete with nearly every other type of store, including specialty stores, off-price chains, category killers, discount stores, and online retailers. For this reason, many businesses have turned to nonstore retailing to sell their products. Some nonstore retailing is performed by traditional retailers to complement their in-store offerings. For instance, Walmart and Macy's have created online shopping sites to retain customers and compete against other businesses. Other companies retail outside of physical stores entirely.

Some companies rely on **direct marketing**, which is the use of nonpersonal media to communicate products, information, and the opportunity to purchase via media such as mail, telephone, or the Internet. For example, Duluth Trading has stores but specializes in catalog marketing, especially with products such as jeans, work boots, and hats. Another form of nonstore retailing is **direct selling**, which involves the marketing of products to ultimate consumers through face-to-face sales presentations at home or in the workplace. The top three global direct selling companies are Amway, Avon, and Herbalife. Most individuals who engage in direct selling work on a part-time basis because they like the product and often sell to their own social networks.

Wholesalers are intermediaries who buy from producers or from other wholesalers

Type of Retailer	Description	Examples
Department store	Large, full-service store organized by departments	Nordstrom, Macy's, Neiman Marcus
Discount store	Offers fewer services than department stores; store atmosphere reflects value pricing	Walmart, Stein Mart, Target
Convenience store	Small self-service store carrying many items for immediate consumption	Circle K, 7-Eleven, Allsups
Supermarket	Large store carrying most food items as well as nonfood items for daily family use	Trader Joe's, Albertsons, Wegmans
Superstore	Very large store that carries most food and nonfood products that are routinely purchased	Super Walmart, Meijer
Hypermarket	The largest retail store that takes the foundation of the discount store and provides even more food and nonfood products	Carrefour, Tesco Extra
Warehouse club	Large membership establishment with food and nonfood products and deep discounts	Costco, BJ's Wholesale Club, Sam's Club
Warehouse showroom	Large facility with products displayed that are often retrieved from a less expensive adjacent warehouse	IKEA, Cost Plus

and sell to retailers. They usually do not sell in significant quantities to ultimate consumers. Wholesalers perform the functions listed in Table 12.6.

Wholesalers are extremely important because of the marketing activities they perform, particularly for consumer products. Although it is true that wholesalers can be eliminated, their functions must be passed on to some other entity, such as the producer, another intermediary, or even the customer. Wholesalers help consumers and retailers by buying in large quantities, then selling to retailers in smaller quantities. By stocking an assortment of products, wholesalers match products to demand. Sysco is a food wholesaler for the food services industry. The company provides food, preparation, and serving products to restaurants, hospitals, and other institutions that provide meals outside the home.[28] *Merchant wholesalers* like Sysco take title to the goods, assume risks, and sell to other wholesalers, business customers, or retailers. *Agents* negotiate sales, do not own products, and perform a limited number of functions in exchange for a commission.

Supply Chain Management

In an effort to improve distribution channel relationships among manufacturers and other channel intermediaries, supply chain management creates alliances between channel members. In Chapter 8, we defined supply chain management as connecting and integrating all parties or members of the distribution system in order to satisfy customers. It involves long-term partnerships among marketing channel members working together to reduce costs, waste, and unnecessary movement in the entire marketing channel in order to satisfy customers. It goes beyond traditional channel members (producers, wholesalers, retailers, customers) to include *all* organizations involved in moving products from the producer to the ultimate customer. In a survey of business managers, a disruption in the supply chain was viewed as the number-one crisis that could decrease revenue.[29]

▼ **TABLE 12.6** Major Wholesaling Functions

Physical distribution	• Inventory management • Transportation • Warehousing • Materials handling
Promotion	• Personal selling • Publicity • Sales promotion • Advertising
Inventory control and data processing	• Information systems management • Inventory control • Transaction monitoring • Financial and accounting data analysis
Risk taking	• Inventory decision making • Product deterioration • Theft control
Financing and budgeting	• Investment capital • Credit management • Cash flow and receivables management
Marketing research and information systems	• Primary market research • Big data analysis • Marketing analytics

The focus shifts from one of selling to the next level in the channel to one of selling products *through* the channel to a satisfied ultimate customer. Information, once provided on a guarded, "as needed" basis, is now open, honest, and ongoing. Perhaps most importantly, the points of contact in the relationship expand from one-on-one at the salesperson–buyer level to multiple interfaces at all levels and in all functional areas of the various organizations.

Channels for Consumer Products

Typical marketing channels for consumer products are shown in Figure 12.6. In Channel A, the product moves from the producer directly to the consumer. Farmers who sell their fruit and vegetables to consumers at roadside stands or farmer's markets use a direct-from-producer-to-consumer marketing channel.

In Channel B, the product goes from producer to retailer to consumer. This type of channel is used for products such as college textbooks, automobiles, and appliances. In Channel C, the product is handled by a wholesaler and a retailer before it reaches the consumer. Producer-to-wholesaler-to-retailer-to-consumer marketing channels distribute a wide range of products including refrigerators, televisions, soft drinks, cigarettes, clocks, watches, and office products. In Channel D, the product goes to an agent, a wholesaler, and a retailer before going to the consumer. This long channel of distribution is especially useful for convenience products. Candy and some produce are often sold by agents who bring buyers and sellers together.

Services are usually distributed through direct marketing channels because they are generally produced *and* consumed simultaneously. For example, you cannot take a haircut home for later use. Many services require the customer's presence and participation: The sick patient must visit the physician to receive treatment; the child must be at the day care center to receive care; the tourist must be present to sightsee and consume tourism services.

Channels for Business Products

In contrast to consumer goods, more than half of all business products, especially expensive equipment or technically complex products, are sold through direct marketing channels. Business customers like to communicate directly with producers of such products to gain the technical assistance and personal assurances that only the producer can offer. For this reason, business buyers prefer to purchase expensive and highly complex mainframe computers directly from IBM, Unisys, and other mainframe producers. Other business products may be distributed through channels employing wholesaling intermediaries such as industrial distributors and/or manufacturer's agents.

Intensity of Market Coverage

A major distribution decision is how widely to distribute a product—that is, how many and what type of outlets should carry it. The intensity of market coverage depends on buyer behavior, as well as the nature of the target market and the competition. Wholesalers and retailers provide various intensities of market coverage and must be selected carefully to ensure success. Market coverage may be intensive, selective, or exclusive.

Intensive distribution makes a product available in as many outlets as possible. Because availability is important to purchasers of convenience products such as bread, milk, gasoline, soft drinks, and chewing gum, a nearby location with a minimum of time spent searching and waiting in line is most important to the consumer. To saturate markets intensively, wholesalers and many varied retailers try to make the product available at every location where a consumer might desire to purchase it. Zoom Systems provides robotic vending machines for products beyond candy and drinks. Zoom has 1,500 machines in airports and hotels across the United States, some selling items such as Apple iPods, Neutrogena hair and skin products, and Sony products. The vending machines accept credit cards and allow sales to occur in places where storefronts would be impossible.[30] Through partnering with different companies, today's ZoomShops sell a variety of brands, including products from Sephora, Best Buy, Macy's, and Rosetta Stone.[31]

Selective distribution uses only a small number of all available outlets to expose products. It is used most often for products that consumers buy only after shopping and comparing price, quality, and style. Many products sold on a selective basis require salesperson assistance, technical advice, warranties, or repair service to maintain consumer satisfaction. Typical products include automobiles, major

FIGURE 12.6
Marketing Channels for Consumer Products

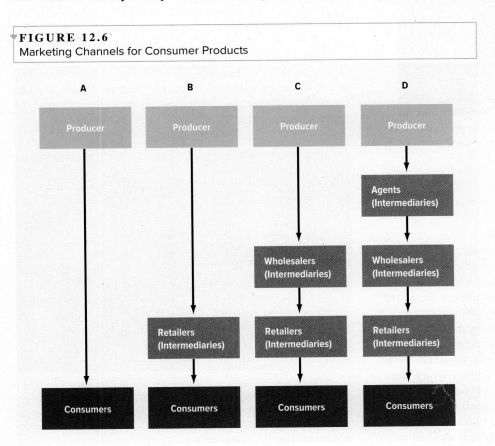

Physical Distribution

Physical distribution includes all the activities necessary to move products from producers to customers—inventory control, transportation, warehousing, and materials handling. Physical distribution creates time and place utility by making products available when they are wanted, with adequate service and at minimum cost. Both goods and services require physical distribution. Many physical distribution activities are part of supply chain management, which we discussed in Chapter 8; we'll take a brief look at a few more now.

Transportation

Transportation, the shipment of products to buyers, creates time and place utility for products, and thus is a key element in the flow of goods and services from producer to consumer. The five major modes of transportation used to move products between cities in the United States are railways, motor vehicles, inland waterways, pipelines, and airways.

Railroads are a cost-effective method of transportation for many products. Heavy commodities, foodstuffs, raw materials, and coal are examples of products carried by railroads. Trucks have greater flexibility than railroads because they can reach more locations. Trucks handle freight quickly and economically, offer door-to-door service, and are more flexible in their packaging requirements than are ships or airplanes. Air transport offers speed and a high degree of dependability but is the most expensive means of transportation; shipping is less expensive and is the slowest form. Pipelines are used to transport petroleum, natural gas, semiliquid coal, wood chips, and certain chemicals. Pipelines have the lowest costs for products that can be transported via this method. Many products can be moved most efficiently by using more than one mode of transportation.

The Jessica Simpson Collection is a line of fashion products for women. The collection is distributed through retailers including Macy's, Dillard's, Nordstrom, and Lord & Taylor.
© Jamie McCarthy/Jessica Simpson Collection/Getty Images Entertainment/ Getty Images

The Burlington/Santa Fe Railroad is the second-largest freight railroad in North America. Although passenger trains have dwindled in favor of other forms of transportation, the railroad continues to be important for carrying freight to other parts of the country.
© Michele Wassell/Age fotostock/Alamy

appliances, clothes, and furniture. Ralph Lauren is a brand that uses selective distribution.

Exclusive distribution exists when a manufacturer gives an intermediary the sole right to sell a product in a defined geographic territory. Such exclusivity provides an incentive for a dealer to handle a product that has a limited market. Exclusive distribution is the opposite of intensive distribution in that products are purchased and consumed over a long period of time, and service or information is required to develop a satisfactory sales relationship. Products distributed on an exclusive basis include high-quality musical instruments, yachts, airplanes, and high-fashion leather goods. Aircraft manufacturer Piper Aircraft uses exclusive distribution by choosing only a few dealers in each region. The company has more than 30 locations in several countries, including the Americas and China.[32]

warehousing the design and operation of facilities to receive, store, and ship products.

materials handling the physical handling and movement of products in warehousing and transportation.

integrated marketing communications coordinating the promotion mix elements and synchronizing promotion as a unified effort.

advertising a paid form of nonpersonal communication transmitted through mass media, such as television commercials or magazine advertisements.

advertising campaign designing a series of advertisements and placing them in various media to reach a particular target market.

Factors affecting the selection of a mode of transportation include cost, capability to handle the product, reliability, and availability, and, as suggested, selecting transportation modes requires trade-offs. Unique characteristics of the product and consumer desires often determine the mode selected.

Warehousing
Warehousing is the design and operation of facilities to receive, store, and ship products. A warehouse facility receives, identifies, sorts, and dispatches goods to storage; stores them; recalls, selects, or picks goods; assembles the shipment; and finally, dispatches the shipment.

Companies often own and operate their own private warehouses that store, handle, and move their own products. Firms might want to own or lease a private warehouse when their goods require special handling and storage or when they have large warehousing needs in a specific geographic area. Private warehouses are beneficial because they provide customers with more control over their goods. However, fixed costs for maintaining these warehouses can be quite high.[33] They can also rent storage and related physical distribution services from public warehouses. While public warehouses store goods for more than one company, providing firms with less control over distribution, they are often less expensive than private warehouses and are useful for seasonal production or low-volume storage.[34] Regardless of whether a private or a public warehouse is used, warehousing is important because it makes products available for shipment to match demand at different geographic locations.

Materials Handling
Materials handling is the physical handling and movement of products in warehousing and transportation. Handling processes may vary significantly due to product characteristics. Efficient materials-handling procedures increase a warehouse's useful capacity and improve customer service. Well-coordinated loading and movement systems increase efficiency and reduce costs.

Importance of Distribution in a Marketing Strategy
Distribution decisions are among the least flexible marketing mix decisions. Products can be changed over time; prices can be changed quickly; and promotion is usually changed regularly. But distribution decisions often commit resources and establish contractual relationships that are difficult if not impossible to change. As a company attempts to expand into new markets, it may require a complete change in distribution. Moreover, if a firm does not manage its marketing channel in the most efficient manner and provide the best service, then a new competitor will evolve to create a more effective distribution system.

> **LO 12-4** Specify the activities involved in promotion, as well as promotional strategies and promotional positioning.

PROMOTION STRATEGY
The role of promotion is to communicate with individuals, groups, and organizations to facilitate an exchange directly or indirectly. It encourages marketing exchanges by attempting to persuade individuals, groups, and organizations to accept goods, services, and ideas. Promotion is used not only to sell products but also to influence opinions and attitudes toward an organization, person, or cause. The state of Texas, for example, has successfully used promotion to educate people about the costs of highway litter and thereby reduce littering. Most people probably equate promotion with advertising, but it also includes personal selling, publicity, and sales promotion. The role that these elements play in a marketing strategy is extremely important.

The Promotion Mix
Advertising, personal selling, publicity, and sales promotion are collectively known as the promotion mix because a strong promotion program results from the careful selection and blending of these elements. The process of coordinating the promotion mix elements and synchronizing promotion as a unified effort is called **integrated marketing communications**. When planning promotional activities, an integrated marketing communications approach results in the desired message for customers. Different elements of the promotion mix are coordinated to play their appropriate roles in delivery of the message on a consistent basis.

Advertising
Perhaps the best-known form of promotion, **advertising** is a paid form of nonpersonal communication transmitted through mass media, such as television commercials, magazine advertisements, or online ads. Even Google, one of the most powerful brands in the world, advertises. Google has turned to outdoor advertising on buses, trains, and ballparks in San Francisco and Chicago to promote its Google Maps feature.[35] Commercials featuring celebrities, customers, or unique creations serve to grab viewers' attention and pique their interest in a product.

An **advertising campaign** involves designing a series of advertisements and placing them in various media to reach a particular target audience. The basic content and form of an advertising campaign are a function of several factors. A product's features, uses, and benefits affect the content of the campaign

ADVERTISING REGULATION CHALLENGES SMALL BUSINESSES

U.S. law requires advertising to be "truthful and non-deceptive." Claims must be based on actual evidence, although puffery, or exaggeration that everyone recognizes as such, is allowed. However, there are no clear boundaries between what constitutes puffery and what represents deceptive advertising. For example, a class-action lawsuit accused Red Bull's slogan of being deceptive. They claimed the slogan promised some sort of physical enhancement at a minimum, such as improved concentration or reaction speed, and that customers had experienced no such boost. Others would likely disagree with this assessment and maintain that the slogan was an example of puffery that in no way guaranteed physical enhancement in and of itself. Red Bull settled the lawsuit for over $13 million.

Small businesses have a hard time complying with advertising law due to lack of legal departments or in-house counsel. This makes them more likely to accidentally cross the legal line between zealous promotion and deception, especially since the Internet makes it easy to develop and publish advertising campaigns. Also, because federal law allows competitors to sue each other for false advertising, some small businesses accuse large companies of using litigation as a weapon to stifle competition. For example, Procter & Gamble sued small toothpaste company Hello Products based on its "99% Natural" labels. Hello Products believed the claim was accurate and in legal compliance, but it changed the labels and settled the lawsuit to avoid paying large legal fees. That same year, Unilever sued a new mayonnaise startup, Hampton Creek, claiming it could not call its product mayonnaise because it does not contain eggs.

Considering there were fewer than 10 false advertising court decisions in 1990, but over 60 two decades later, small businesses must continue to expect close scrutiny of their advertising and adjust their strategies accordingly.[36]

Discussion Questions

1. How can small businesses ensure they do not engage in misleading advertising and protect themselves from false advertising lawsuits?

2. Why do you believe puffery is allowed in advertising? Why is there often a fine line between puffery and deceptive advertising?

3. Is it fair for large companies such as Unilever to target smaller firms for misleading advertising if the intent of the small firms was not to mislead?

["Advertising media are the vehicles or forms of communication used to reach a desired audience."]

---

message and individual ads. Characteristics of the people in the target audience—gender, age, education, race, income, occupation, lifestyle, and other attributes—influence both content and form. When Procter & Gamble promotes Crest toothpaste to children, the company emphasizes daily brushing and cavity control, whereas it promotes tartar control and whiter teeth when marketing to adults. To communicate effectively, advertisers use words, symbols, and illustrations that are meaningful, familiar, and attractive to people in the target audience.

An advertising campaign's objectives and platform also affect the content and form of its messages. If a firm's advertising objectives involve large sales increases, the message may include hard-hitting, high-impact language and symbols. When campaign objectives aim at increasing brand awareness, the message may use much repetition of the brand name and words and illustrations associated with it. Thus, the advertising platform is the foundation on which campaign messages are built.

Advertising media are the vehicles or forms of communication used to reach a desired audience. Print media include newspapers, magazines, direct mail, and billboards, while electronic media include television, radio, and Internet advertising. Choice of media obviously influences the content and form of the message. Effective outdoor displays and short broadcast spot announcements require concise, simple messages. Magazine and newspaper advertisements can include considerable detail and long explanations. Because several kinds of media offer geographic selectivity, a precise message can be tailored

Hot Wheels uses celebrities, like Danica Patrick, colorful packaging, and fun advertisements to appeal to children.
© Tony Ding/Mattel/AP Images

to a particular geographic section of the target audience. For example, a company advertising in *Time* might decide to use one message in the New England region and another in the rest of the nation. A company may also choose to advertise in only one region. Such geographic selectivity lets a firm use the same message in different regions at different times. On the other hand, some companies are willing to pay extensive amounts of money to reach national audiences. Marketers spent approximately $4.5 million for one 30-second advertising slot during the 2015 Super Bowl due to its national reach and popularity.[37]

The use of online advertising is increasing. However, advertisers are demanding more for their ad dollars and proof that they are working, which is why Google AdWords charges companies only when users click on the ad. Certain types of ads are more popular than pop-up ads and banner ads that consumers find annoying. One technique is to blur the lines between television and online advertising. TV commercials may point viewers to a website for more information, where short "advertainment" films continue the marketing message. Marketers might also use the Internet to show advertisements or videos that were not accepted by mainstream television. SodaStream's original Super Bowl commercial featured celebrity Scarlett Johansson criticizing rivals Coca-Cola and Pepsi by ending the ad with "Sorry, Coke and Pepsi." The last line was removed from the advertisement aired during the Super Bowl, but the original ad was featured online in its original uncensored format.[38]

Infomercials—typically 30-minute blocks of radio or television air time featuring a celebrity or upbeat host talking about and demonstrating a product—have evolved as an advertising method. Toll-free numbers and website addresses are usually provided so consumers can conveniently purchase the product or obtain additional information. Although many consumers and companies have negative feelings about infomercials, apparently they get results.

Personal Selling **Personal selling** is direct, two-way communication with buyers and potential buyers. For many

Google used publicity to drive sales before its Google Glass product was launched the first time.
© *Filip Singer/EPA/epa european pressphoto agency b.v./Alamy*

products—especially large, expensive ones with specialized uses, such as cars, appliances, and houses—interaction between a salesperson and the customer is probably the most important promotional tool.

Personal selling is the most flexible of the promotional methods because it gives marketers the greatest opportunity to communicate specific information that might trigger a purchase. Only personal selling can zero in on a prospect and attempt to persuade that person to make a purchase. Although personal selling has a lot of advantages, it is one of the most costly forms of promotion. A sales call on an industrial customer can cost more than $400.

There are three distinct categories of salespersons: order takers (for example, retail sales clerks and route salespeople), creative salespersons (for example, automobile, furniture, and insurance salespeople), and support salespersons (for example, customer educators and goodwill builders who usually do not take orders). For most of these salespeople, personal selling is a six-step process:

1. *Prospecting:* Identifying potential buyers of the product.

2. *Approaching:* Using a referral or calling on a customer without prior notice to determine interest in the product.

3. *Presenting:* Getting the prospect's attention with a product demonstration.

4. *Handling objections:* Countering reasons for not buying the product.

5. *Closing:* Asking the prospect to buy the product.

6. *Following up:* Checking customer satisfaction with the purchased product.

Publicity **Publicity** is nonpersonal communication transmitted through the mass media but not paid for directly by the firm. A firm does not pay the media cost for publicity and is not identified as the originator of the message; instead, the message is presented in news story form. Obviously, a company can benefit from publicity by releasing to news sources newsworthy messages about the firm and its involvement with the public. Many companies have *public relations* departments to try to gain favorable publicity and minimize negative publicity for the firm.

Although advertising and publicity are both carried by the mass media, they differ in several major ways. Advertising messages tend to be informative, persuasive, or both; publicity is mainly informative. Advertising is often designed to have an immediate impact or to provide specific information to persuade a person to act; publicity describes what a firm is doing, what products it is launching, or other newsworthy information, but seldom calls for action. When advertising is used, the

personal selling direct, two-way communication with buyers and potential buyers.

publicity nonpersonal communication transmitted through the mass media but not paid for directly by the firm.

organization must pay for media time and select the media that will best reach target audiences. The mass media willingly carry publicity because they believe it has general public interest. Advertising can be repeated a number of times; most publicity appears in the mass media once and is not repeated.

Advertising, personal selling, and sales promotion are especially useful for influencing an exchange directly. Publicity is extremely important when communication focuses on a company's activities and products and is directed at interest groups, current and potential investors, regulatory agencies, and society in general.

A variation of traditional advertising is buzz marketing, in which marketers attempt to create a trend or acceptance of a product. Companies seek out trendsetters in communities and get them to "talk up" a brand to their friends, family, co-workers, and others. Samsung displayed a piece of its marketing genius during the Oscars when it orchestrated a celebrity "selfie" with its new Galaxy Note III. It went so far as to teach the host of the awards show, Ellen Degeneres, exactly how to use the device and how to take the picture. The photo was quickly shared across various social media platforms, becoming one of the most widely shared images. The stunt caught Apple's attention to the extent that it created a "Buzz Marketing Manager" position in order to compete on this level.[39] Other marketers using the buzz technique include Hebrew National ("mom squads" grilled the company's hot dogs), and Red Bull (its sponsorship of the stratosphere space diving project). The idea behind buzz marketing is that an accepted member of a particular social group will be more credible than any form of paid communication.[40] The concept works best as part of an integrated marketing communication program that also includes traditional advertising, personal selling, sales promotion, and publicity.

A related concept is viral marketing, which describes the concept of getting Internet users to pass on ads and promotions to others. Dove's "Real Beauty Sketches" video compared sketches of women as they described themselves to sketches of themselves as others described them. The video was meant to show how women often do not recognize their outward beauty. The video went viral, reaching 114 million views just one month after its release. It became the most viral video of its time.[41]

Sales Promotion

Sales promotion involves direct inducements offering added value or some other incentive for buyers to enter into an exchange. Sales promotions are generally easier

Companies use a pull strategy by offering coupons in the hopes of convincing customers to visit their stores.
© Jamie Grill/Tetra Images/Getty Images, RF

to measure and less expensive than advertising. The major tools of sales promotion are store displays, premiums, samples and demonstrations, coupons, contests and sweepstakes, refunds, and trade shows. Coupon-clipping in particular has become more common during the recent recession. While coupons in the past decade traditionally had a fairly low redemption rate, with about 2 percent being redeemed, the recent recession caused an upsurge in coupon usage. There has also been a major upsurge in the use of mobile coupons, or coupons sent to consumers over mobile devices. The redemption rate for mobile coupons is 10 times higher than that of traditional coupons, with a 10 percent rate versus a 1 percent redemption rate.[42] While coupons can be a valuable tool in sales promotion, they cannot be relied upon to stand by themselves, but should be part of an overall promotion mix. Sales promotion stimulates customer purchasing and increases dealer effectiveness in selling products. It is used to enhance and supplement other forms of promotion. Sampling a product may also encourage consumers to buy. This is why many grocery stores provide free samples in the hopes of influencing consumers' purchasing decisions. In a given year, almost three-fourths of consumer product companies may use sampling.

Promotion Strategies: To Push or to Pull

In developing a promotion mix, organizations must decide whether to fashion a mix that pushes or pulls the product (Figure 12.7). A **push strategy** attempts to motivate intermediaries to push the product down to their customers. When a push strategy is used, the company attempts to motivate wholesalers and retailers to make the product available to their customers. Sales personnel may be used to persuade intermediaries

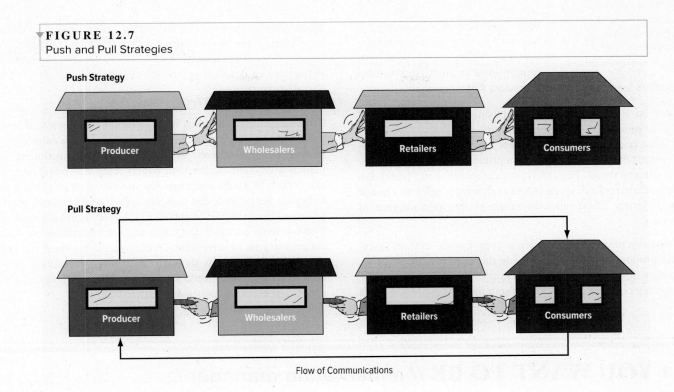

Flow of Communications

to offer the product, distribute promotional materials, and offer special promotional incentives for those who agree to carry the product. For example, salespeople from pharmaceutical companies will often market new products to doctors in the hope that the doctors will recommend their products to their clients. A **pull strategy** uses promotion to create consumer demand for a product so that consumers exert pressure on marketing channel members to make it available. For a while, T-Mobile was the only major carrier that did not have the iPhone. The iPhone was not compatible with T-Mobile's 3G frequencies, so Apple largely sidestepped T-Mobile. However, the popularity of the iPhone and decreasing market share caused T-Mobile to revamp its spectrum to run on the iPhone better. This is an example of how consumer pull caused a company to change its practices.[43] Additionally, offering free samples prior to a product rollout encourages consumers to request the product from their favorite retailer.

A company can use either strategy, or it can use a variation or combination of the two. The exclusive use of advertising indicates a pull strategy. Personal selling to marketing channel members indicates a push strategy. The allocation of promotional resources to various marketing mix elements probably determines which strategy a marketer uses.

Objectives of Promotion

The marketing mix a company uses depends on its objectives. It is important to recognize that promotion is only one element of the marketing strategy and must be tied carefully to the goals of the firm, its overall marketing objectives, and the other elements of the marketing strategy. Firms use promotion for many reasons, but typical objectives are to stimulate demand, to stabilize sales, and to inform, remind, and reinforce customers.

Increasing demand for a product is probably the most typical promotional objective. Stimulating demand, often through advertising and sales promotion, is particularly important when a firm is using a pull strategy.

Another goal of promotion is to stabilize sales by maintaining the status quo—that is, the current sales level of the product. During periods of slack or decreasing sales, contests, prizes, vacations, and other sales promotions are sometimes offered to customers to maintain sales goals. Advertising is often used to stabilize sales by making customers aware of slack use periods. For example, auto manufacturers often provide rebates, free options, or lower-than-market interest rates to stabilize sales and thereby keep production lines moving during temporary slowdowns. A stable sales pattern allows the firm to run efficiently by maintaining a consistent level of production and storage and utilizing all its functions so that it is ready when sales increase.

An important role of any promotional program is to inform potential buyers about the organization and its products. A major portion of advertising in the United States, particularly in daily newspapers, is informational. Providing information about the availability, price, technology, and features of a product is

promotional positioning the use of promotion to create and maintain an image of a product in buyers' minds.

very important in encouraging a buyer to move toward a purchase decision. Nearly all forms of promotion involve an attempt to help consumers learn more about a product and a company.

Promotion is also used to remind consumers that an established organization is still around and sells certain products that have uses and benefits. Often advertising reminds customers that they may need to use a product more frequently or in certain situations. Pennzoil, for example, has run television commercials reminding car owners that they need to change their oil every 3,000 miles to ensure proper performance of their cars.

Reinforcement promotion attempts to assure current users of the product that they have made the right choice and tells them how to get the most satisfaction from the product. Also, a company could release publicity statements through the news media about a new use for a product. Additionally, firms can have salespeople communicate with current and potential customers about the proper use and maintenance of a product—all in the hope of developing a repeat customer.

Promotional Positioning

Promotional positioning uses promotion to create and maintain an image of a product in buyers' minds. It is a natural result of market segmentation. In both promotional positioning and market segmentation, the firm targets a given product or brand at a portion of the total market. A promotional strategy helps differentiate the product and makes it appeal to a particular market segment. For example, to appeal to safety-conscious consumers, Volvo heavily promotes the safety and crashworthiness of Volvo automobiles in its advertising. Volkswagen has done the same thing with its edgy ads showing car crashes. Promotion can be used to change or reinforce an image. Effective promotion influences customers and persuades them to buy.

SO YOU WANT TO BE // a marketing manager /

Many jobs in marketing are closely tied to the marketing mix functions: product, price, distribution (place), and promotion. Often the job titles could be sales manager, distribution or supply chain manager, advertising account executive, or store manager.

A distribution manager arranges for transportation of goods within firms and through marketing channels. Transportation can be costly, and time is always an important factor, so minimizing their effects is vital to the success of a firm. Distribution managers must choose one or a combination of transportation modes from a vast array of options, taking into account local, federal, and international regulations for different freight classifications; the weight, size, and fragility of products to be shipped; time schedules; and loss and damage ratios. Manufacturing firms are the largest employers of distribution managers.

A product manager is responsible for the success or failure of a product line. This requires a general knowledge of advertising, transportation modes, inventory control, selling and sales management, promotion, marketing research, packaging, and pricing. Frequently, several years of selling and sales management experience are prerequisites for such a position as well as college training in business administration. Being a

product manager can be rewarding both financially and psychologically.

Some of the most creative roles in the business world are in the area of advertising. Advertising pervades our daily lives, as businesses and other organizations try to grab our attention and tell us about what they have to offer. Copywriters, artists, and account executives in advertising must have creativity, imagination, artistic talent, and expertise in expression and persuasion. Advertising is an area of business in which a wide variety of educational backgrounds may be useful, from degrees in advertising itself, to journalism or liberal arts degrees. Common entry-level positions in an advertising agency are found in the traffic department, account service (account coordinator), or the media department (media assistant). Advertising jobs are also available in many manufacturing or retail firms, nonprofit organizations, banks, professional associations, utility companies, and other arenas outside of an advertising agency.

Although a career in retailing may begin in sales, there is much more to retailing than simply selling. Many retail personnel occupy management positions, focusing on selecting and ordering merchandise, promotional activities, inventory control, customer credit operations, accounting, personnel, and store security. Many

specific examples of retailing jobs can be found in large department stores. A section manager coordinates inventory and promotions and interacts with buyers, salespeople, and consumers. The buyer's job is fast-paced, often involving much travel and pressure. Buyers must be open-minded and foresighted in their hunt for new, potentially successful items. Regional managers coordinate the activities of several retail stores within a specific geographic area, usually monitoring and supporting sales, promotions, and general procedures. Retail management can be exciting and challenging. Growth in retailing is expected to accompany the growth in population and is likely to create substantial opportunities in the coming years.

While a career in marketing can be very rewarding, marketers today agree that the job is getting tougher. Many advertising and marketing executives say the job has gotten much more demanding in the past 10 years, viewing their number-one challenge as balancing work and personal obligations. Other challenges include staying current on industry trends or technologies, keeping motivated/inspired on the job, and measuring success. If you are up to the challenge, you may find that a career in marketing is just right for you to utilize your business knowledge while exercising your creative side as well.

THE IMPORTANCE OF MARKETING STRATEGY

Marketing creates value through the marketing mix. For customers, value means receiving a product in which the benefit of the product outweighs the cost, or price paid for it. For marketers, value means that the benefits (usually monetary) received from selling the product outweigh the costs it takes to develop and sell it. This requires carefully integrating the marketing mix into an effective marketing strategy. One misstep could mean a loss in profits, whether it be from a failed product idea, shortages or oversupply of a product, a failure to effectively promote the product, or prices that are too high or too low. And while some of these marketing mix elements can be easily fixed, other marketing mix elements such as distribution can be harder to adapt.

TEAM EXERCISE

Form groups and search for examples of convenience products, shopping products, specialty products, and business products. How are these products marketed? Provide examples of any ads that you can find to show examples of the promotional strategies for these products. Report your findings to the class.

On the other hand, firms that develop an effective marketing mix to meet customer needs will gain competitive advantages over those that do not. Often, these advantages occur when the firm excels at one or more elements of the marketing mix. Walmart has a reputation for its everyday low prices, while Tiffany's is known for its high-quality jewelry. However, excelling at one element of the marketing mix does not mean that a company can neglect the others. The best product cannot succeed if consumers do not know about it or if they cannot find it in stores. Additionally, firms must constantly monitor the market environment to understand how demand is changing and whether adaptations in the marketing mix are needed. It is therefore essential that every element of the marketing mix be carefully evaluated and synchronized with the marketing strategy. Only then will firms be able to achieve the marketing concept of providing products that satisfy customers' needs while allowing the organization to achieve its goals. ■

digital marketing and
social networking

© Dolphfyn/Alamy, RF

LEARNING OBJECTIVES

After reading this chapter, you will be able to:

LO 13-1 Define digital media and digital marketing, and recognize their increasing value in strategic planning.

LO 13-2 Demonstrate the role of digital marketing, and define social networking in today's business environment.

LO 13-3 Show how digital media affect the marketing mix.

LO 13-4 Illustrate how businesses can use different types of social networking media.

LO 13-5 Identify legal and ethical considerations in digital media.

The Internet and information technology have dramatically changed the environment for business.[1] Marketers' new ability to convert all types of communications into digital media has created efficient, inexpensive ways of connecting businesses and consumers and has improved the flow and the usefulness of information. Businesses have the information they need to make more informed decisions, and consumers have access to a greater variety of products and more information about choices and quality. This has resulted in a shift in the balance of power between consumer and marketer.[2]

The defining characteristic of information technology in the 21st century is accelerating change. New systems and applications advance so rapidly that it is almost impossible to keep up with the latest developments. Startup companies emerge that quickly overtake existing approaches to digital media. When Google first arrived on the scene, a number of search engines were fighting for dominance. With its fast, easy-to-use search engine, Google became number one and is now challenging many industries, including advertising, newspapers, mobile phones, and book publishing. Google has up to 90 percent of the market share in the European Union, raising questions about whether it might have too much power. EU antitrust regulators have charged Google with abusing its dominance in the web search market. However, despite its success in certain regions, Google faces challenges from search engines in other parts of the world, including China's Baidu.[3] Social networking continues to advance as the channel most observers believe will dominate digital communication in the near future. Today, people spend more time on social networking sites, such as Facebook, than they spend on e-mail.

In this chapter, we first provide some key definitions related to digital marketing and social networking. Next, we discuss using digital media in business and digital marketing. We look at marketing mix considerations when using digital media and pay special attention to social networking. Then we focus on digital marketing strategies—particularly new communication channels

Amazon's mobile applications make it easier for users to shop and purchase items on the go.
© *LearningStockImages/Alamy*

like social networks—and consider how consumers are changing their information searches and consumption behavior to fit emerging technologies and trends. Finally, we examine the legal and social issues associated with information technology, digital media, and e-business. ■

e-business carrying out the goals of business through utilization of the Internet.

digital media electronic media that function using digital codes via computers, cellular phones, smartphones, and other digital devices that have been released in recent years.

digital marketing uses all digital media, including the Internet and mobile and interactive channels, to develop communication and exchanges with customers.

facilitates business transactions, allowing companies to network with manufacturers, wholesalers, retailers, suppliers, and outsource firms to serve customers more quickly and more efficiently. The telecommunication opportunities created by the Internet have set the stage for digital marketing's development and growth.

Digital communication offers a completely new dimension in connecting with others. Some of the characteristics that distinguish digital from traditional communication are addressability, interactivity, accessibility, connectivity, and control. These terms are discussed in Table 13.1.

> **LO 13-1** Define digital media and digital marketing, and recognize their increasing value in strategic planning.

GROWTH AND BENEFITS OF DIGITAL COMMUNICATION

Let's start with a clear understanding of our focus in this chapter. First, we can distinguish **e-business** from traditional business by noting that conducting e-business means carrying out the goals of business through the use of the Internet. **Digital media** are electronic media that function using digital codes—when we refer to digital media, we mean media available via computers and other digital devices, including mobile and wireless ones like smartphones.

Digital marketing uses all digital media, including the Internet and mobile and interactive channels, to develop communication and exchanges with customers. *Digital marketing* is a term we will use often, because we are interested in all types of digital communications, regardless of the electronic channel that transmits the data. Digital marketing goes beyond the Internet and includes mobile phones, banner ads, digital outdoor marketing, and social networks.

The Internet has created tremendous opportunities for businesses to forge relationships with consumers and business customers, target markets more precisely, and even reach previously inaccessible markets at home and around the world. The Internet also

> **LO 13-2** Demonstrate the role of digital marketing, and define social networking in today's business environment.

USING DIGITAL MEDIA IN BUSINESS

The phenomenal growth of digital media has provided new ways of conducting business. Given almost instant communication with precisely defined consumer groups, firms can use real-time exchanges to create and stimulate interactive communication, forge closer relationships, and learn more accurately about consumer and supplier needs. Consider that Amazon.com, one of the most successful electronic businesses, ranked number 35 on the *Fortune* 500 list of America's largest corporations. Amazon is a true digital marketer, getting much of its revenue from international sales.[4] Many of you may not remember a world before Amazon because it has completely transformed how many people shop.

Because it is fast and inexpensive, digital communication is making it easier for businesses to conduct marketing research,

> "Digital communication offers a completely new dimension in connecting with others."

▼ **TABLE 13.1** Characteristics of Digital Marketing

Characteristic	Definition	Example
Addressability	The ability of the marketer to identify customers before they make a purchase	Amazon installs cookies on a user's computer that allows it to identify the owner when he or she returns to the website.
Interactivity	The ability of customers to express their needs and wants directly to the firm in response to its marketing communications	Texas Instruments interacts with its customers on its Facebook page by answering concerns and posting updates.
Accessibility	The ability for marketers to obtain digital information	Google can use web searches done through its search engine to learn about customer interests.
Connectivity	The ability for consumers to be connected with marketers along with other consumers	Mary Kay offers users the opportunity to sign up for My MK, a system that connects customers with beauty consultants and allows them to develop their own personalized space.
Control	The customers' ability to regulate the information they view as well as the rate and exposure to that information	Consumers use Kayak to discover the best travel deals.

provide and obtain price and product information, and advertise, as well as to fulfill their business goals by selling goods and services online. Even the U.S. government engages in digital marketing activities—marketing everything from Treasury bonds and other financial instruments to oil-drilling leases and wild horses. Procter & Gamble uses the Internet as a fast, cost-effective means for marketing research, judging consumer demand for potential new products by inviting online consumers to sample new-product prototypes and provide feedback. If a product gets rave reviews from the samplers, the company might decide to introduce it.

New businesses and even industries are evolving that would not exist without digital media. Vimeo is a video website founded by filmmakers to share creative videos. The site lets users post or view videos from around the world. It has become one of the most popular video websites after YouTube and Netflix.[5]

The reality, however, is that Internet markets are more similar to traditional markets than they are different. Thus, successful digital marketing strategies, like traditional business strategies, focus on creating products that customers need or want, not merely developing a brand name or reducing the costs associated with online transactions. Instead of changing all industries, digital technology has had much more impact in certain industries where the cost of business and customer transactions has been very high. For example, investment trading is less expensive online because customers can buy and sell investments, such as stocks and mutual funds, on their own. Firms such as Charles Schwab Corp., the biggest online brokerage firm, have been innovators in promoting online trading. Traditional brokers such as Merrill Lynch have had to follow with online trading for their customers.

Because the Internet lowers the cost of communication, it can contribute significantly to any industry or activity that depends on the flow of digital information such as entertainment, health care, government services, education, and computer services like software development. The publishing industry is transitioning away from print newspapers, magazines, and books as more consumers purchase e-readers, like the Kindle Fire or iPad, or read the news online. Even your textbook is available electronically. Because publishers save money on paper, ink, and shipping, many times electronic versions of books are cheaper than their paper counterparts.

Digital media can also improve communication within and between businesses. In the future, most significant gains will come from productivity improvements within businesses. Communication is a key business function, and improving the speed and clarity of communication can help businesses save time and improve employee problem-solving abilities. Digital media can be a communications backbone that helps to store knowledge, information, and records in management information systems so co-workers can access it when faced with a problem to solve. A well-designed management information system that utilizes digital technology can, therefore, help reduce confusion, improve organization and efficiency, and facilitate clear communications. Given the crucial role of communication and information in business, the long-term impact of digital media on economic growth is substantial, and it will inevitably grow over time.

Firms also need to control access to their digital communication systems to ensure worker productivity. This can be a challenge. For example, in companies across the United States, employees are surfing the Internet for as much as an hour during each workday. Many firms are trying to curb this practice by limiting employees' access to instant messaging services, streaming music, and websites with adult content.[6]

Home Depot has an application that connects mobile users to its website to search and shop for products.
© *Studio Works/Alamy*

DIGITAL MEDIA AND THE MARKETING MIX

While digital marketing shares some similarities with conventional marketing techniques, a few valuable differences stand out. First, digital media make customer communications faster and interactive. Second, digital media help companies reach new target markets more easily, affordably, and quickly than ever before. Finally, digital media help marketers utilize new resources in seeking out and communicating with customers. One of the most important benefits of digital marketing is the ability of marketers and customers to easily share information. Through websites, social networks, and other digital media, consumers can learn about everything they consume and use in their lives, ask questions, voice complaints, indicate preferences, and otherwise communicate about their needs and desires. Many marketers use e-mail, mobile phones, social networking, wikis, media sharing, blogs, videoconferencing, and other technologies to coordinate activities and communicate with employees, customers, and suppliers. Twitter, considered both a social network and a microblog, illustrates how these digital technologies can combine to create new communication opportunities.

Nielsen Marketing Research revealed that consumers now spend more time on social networking sites than they do on e-mail, and social network use is still growing. With digital media, even small businesses can reach new markets through these inexpensive communication channels. Brick-and-mortar companies like Walmart utilize online catalogs and company websites and blogs to supplement their retail stores. Internet companies like Amazon and Zappos that lack physical stores let customers post reviews of their purchases on their websites, creating company-sponsored communities.

One aspect of marketing that has not changed with digital media is the importance of achieving the right marketing mix. Product, distribution, promotion, and pricing are as important as ever for successful online marketing strategies. It is essential for businesses large and small to use digital media effectively, not only to grab or maintain market share but also to streamline their organizations and offer customers entirely new benefits and convenience. Let's look at how businesses are using digital media to create effective marketing strategies on the web.

Product Considerations
Like traditional marketers, digital marketers must anticipate consumer needs and preferences, tailor their goods and services to meet these needs, and continually upgrade them to remain competitive. The connectivity created by digital media provides the opportunity for adding services and can enhance product benefits. Some products, such as online games, applications, and virtual worlds, are only available via digital media. The more than 1 million applications available on the iPad, for instance, provide examples of products that are only available in the digital world.[7] Businesses can often offer more items online than they could in a retail store.

The ability to access information for any product can have a major impact on buyer decision making. However, with larger companies now launching their own extensive marketing campaigns, and with the constant sophistication of digital technology, many businesses are finding it necessary to upgrade their product offerings to meet consumer needs. As we mentioned in a previous chapter, companies such as Julep Beauty use feedback from social media to test new products.[8] The Internet provides a major resource for learning more about consumer wants and needs.

Distribution Considerations
The Internet is a new distribution channel for making products available at the right time, at the right place, and in the right quantities. Marketers' ability to process orders electronically and increase the speed of communications via the Internet reduces inefficiencies, costs, and redundancies while increasing speed throughout the marketing channel. Shipping times and costs have become an important consideration in attracting customers, prompting many companies to offer consumers low shipping costs or next-day delivery. Although consumers still flock to brick-and-mortar stores to purchase items, they tend to spend less time shopping because they have already determined what they want online. Approximately 73 percent of U.S. consumers research shoes, toys, clothing, and other items on the Internet before going to the store. Online shopping is also significantly increasing, with 201 million U.S. consumers finding and purchasing items online. Convenience and constant availability are two major reasons why consumers prefer to shop online.[9]

These changes in distribution are not limited to the Western world. In a revolutionary shift in China, where online shopping had not been widely adopted by consumers, businesses are now realizing the benefits of marketing online. One of the first adopters of Internet selling was the Chinese company Taobao, a consumer auction site that also features sections for Chinese brands and retailers. Today parent company Alibaba is expanding into new markets. At the same time, there are concerns that many of the items sold on Taobao are counterfeit, and Alibaba is challenging the idea that it tolerates knockoff goods on its website.[10] Consumer trends demonstrate that the shift of distributing through digital networks is well under way worldwide.

Promotion Considerations
Perhaps one of the best ways businesses can utilize digital media is for promotion purposes—whether they are increasing brand awareness, connecting with consumers, or taking advantage of social networks or virtual worlds (discussed later) to form relationships and generate positive publicity or "buzz" about their products. Thanks to online promotion, consumers can be more informed than ever, including reading customer-generated content before making purchase decisions. Consumer consumption patterns are radically changing, and marketers must adapt their promotional efforts to meet them.

If marketers find it difficult to adapt their promotional strategies to online marketing, many social networks offer tools to help. For instance, Facebook has its "Facebook Exchange" and "Facebook Offers" to help businesses target their promotions to the right audiences. "Facebook Exchange" is a tool that provides marketers with the ability to target their advertisements to people based upon other activities they have done on the Internet. "Facebook Offers" allows businesses to provide customers with discounts on their Facebook pages. MGM Resorts International used both these tools in a campaign to acquire new customers, promote loyalty, and increase current customer activity. It is estimated that MGM received a 5-fold return on its advertising investment using "Facebook Offers" and a 15-fold return using "Facebook Exchange."[11] Marketers that choose to capitalize on these opportunities have the chance to significantly boost their firms' brand exposure.

Pricing Considerations Price is the most flexible element of the marketing mix. Digital marketing can enhance the value of products by providing extra benefits such as service, information, and convenience. Through digital media, discounts and other promotions can be quickly communicated. As consumers have become better informed about their options, the demand for low-priced products has grown, leading to the creation of deal sites

way consumers communicate with each other and with firms. Sites such as Facebook and Twitter have emerged as opportunities for marketers to build communities, provide product information, and learn about consumer needs. By the time you read this, it is possible there will be new social network sites that continue to advance digital communication and opportunities for marketers.

You might be surprised to know that social networks have existed in some form or other for 40 years. The precursors of today's social networks began in the 1970s as online bulletin boards that allowed users with common interests to interact with one another. The first modern social network was Six Degrees.com, launched in 1997. This system permitted users to create a profile and connect with friends—the core attributes of today's networks.[13] Although SixDegrees eventually shut down for lack of interest, the seed of networking had been planted.[14] Other social networks followed, with each new generation becoming increasingly sophisticated. Today's sites offer a multitude of consumer benefits, including the ability to download music, games, and applications; upload photos and videos; join groups; find and chat with friends; comment on friends' posts; and post and update status messages.

> **"Social networks are a valued part of marketing because they are changing the way consumers communicate with each other and with firms."**

where consumers can directly compare prices. Expedia.com, for instance, provides consumers with a wealth of travel information about everything from flights to hotels that lets them compare benefits and prices. Many marketers offer buying incentives like online coupons or free samples to generate consumer demand for their products. Polkadot Alley actually sells products through Facebook twice a week. Photos of items are posted to its Facebook wall, and shoppers who want to purchase the items write posts on Facebook. An auction determines the price through an application called Soldsie, which also helps process the Facebook transactions.[12] For the business that wants to compete on price, digital marketing provides unlimited opportunities.

> **LO 13-4** Illustrate how businesses can use different types of social networking media.

Social Networking

A **social network** is a website where users can create a profile and interact with other users, post information, and engage in other forms of web-based communication. Social networks are a valued part of marketing because they are changing the

As the number of social network users increases, interactive marketers are finding opportunities to reach out to consumers in new target markets. Snapchat is a mobile photo messaging application popular among teenagers. Users can send photos, messages, or videos to their friends for a certain amount of time. Afterward the post is deleted from the recipient's phone and Snapchat servers. McDonald's, General Electric, and Taco Bell

Marketers can use the popular microblogging site Twitter to connect with customers and answer questions.
© Denise McCullough RF/Denise McCullough, RF

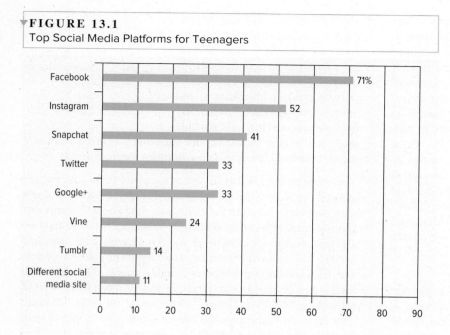

Source: Pew Research Center's Teens Relationships Survey, September 25–October 9, 2014, and February 10–March 16, 2015. $n = 1,060$ teens aged 13 to 17.

have all marketed through this site.[15] Figure 13.1 shows the top social media platforms for teenagers. We'll have more to say about how marketers utilize social networks later in this chapter.

An important question relates to how social media sites are adding value to the economy. Marketers at companies like Ford and Zappos, for instance, are using social media to promote products and build consumer relationships. Many companies are adopting the digital forum Memo, an internal social network where employees can vent anonymously and managers can respond. The forum is intended to inform managers of employee concerns without placing pressure on the employee to confront his or her supervisors.[16] Professionals such as professors, doctors, and engineers also share ideas on a regular basis. Even staffing organizations use social media, bypassing traditional e-mail and telephone channels. While billions of dollars in investments are being funneled into social media, it may be too early to assess the exact economic contribution of social media to the entire economy.[17]

TYPES OF CONSUMER-GENERATED MARKETING AND DIGITAL MEDIA

Although digital marketing has generated exciting opportunities for companies to interact with their customers, digital media are also more consumer-driven than traditional media. Internet users are creating and reading consumer-generated content as never before and are having a profound effect on marketing in the process.

Two factors have sparked the rise of consumer-generated information:

1. The increased tendency of consumers to publish their own thoughts, opinions, reviews, and product discussions through blogs or digital media.

2. Consumers' tendencies to trust other consumers over corporations. Consumers often rely on the recommendations of friends, family, and fellow consumers when making purchasing decisions.

Marketers who know where online users are likely to express their thoughts and opinions can use these forums to interact with them, address problems, and promote their companies. Table 13.2 describes some of the most popular social and digital networking sites among global consumers. Types of digital media in which Internet users are likely to participate include social networks, blogs, wikis, video sharing sites, podcasts, virtual reality sites, and mobile applications. Let's look a little more closely at each.

Social Networks

The increase in social networking across the world is exponential. It is estimated that today's adults spend approximately 42.1 minutes per day on Facebook alone.[18] As social networks evolve, both marketers and the owners of social networking sites are realizing the opportunities such networks offer—an influx of advertising dollars for site owners and a large reach for the advertiser. As a result, marketers have begun investigating and experimenting with promotion on social networks. Two popular social networking sites are Facebook and Twitter.

Facebook In April 2008, the social networking site Facebook became the most popular social networking site in the world.

Many companies have Facebook pages to promote products and stay connected to consumers.
© *Consumer Trends/Alamy*

TABLE 13.2 Popular Social and Digital Networks among Users

Digital Network	Purpose	Description
Facebook	Social networking	The most popular social networking site in the world at 1.2 billion users. Facebook users create profiles and search the network for people with whom to connect.
Twitter	Social networking	Members can post their own content under 140 characters or follow other posts.
LinkedIn	Professional networking	The top professional social network used for recruiting, following companies, and connecting with other professionals.
YouTube	Video sharing	The third most popular site on the web globally. YouTube allows users to watch, upload, and tag videos.
Instagram	Photo sharing	A mobile application that allows users to give their photos a dreamy or retrospective look and easily share them with others.
Pinterest	Bookmarking and photo sharing	Users share photos or images and create online bulletin boards in which they can "pin" or "repin" those they like and share with others.
Google+	Social networking	A social media site allowing users to create profiles and connect with one another, enabling Google to identify users across its various services.
Buzzfeed	Social news sharing	A social news website with articles, quizzes, and other content appealing to users.
Tumblr	Blogging	A blogging site in which anyone can post text, hyperlinks, photos, and more.
Reddit	Bookmarking and social sharing	A bookmarking social media website in which users can post interesting personal photos and global news reports and then vote on them to determine where these postings appear on the page.

Facebook users create profiles, which they can make public or private, and then search the network for people with whom to connect. The site has 1.2 billion users worldwide. Facebook also has a video feature that enables the sharing and tagging of videos.[19]

For this reason, many marketers are turning to Facebook to market products, interact with consumers, and gain free publicity. It is possible for a consumer to become a "fan" of a major company like Starbucks by clicking on the "Like" icon on the coffee retailer's Facebook page. Promoted posts, one of the features Facebook has to offer businesses, allow companies to develop advertisements that show up in the News Feeds of those who have "liked" the organization and in the News Feeds of their friends.[21]

Additionally, social networking sites are useful for relationship marketing, or the creation of relationships that mutually benefit the business and customer. Approximately 30 percent of consumers claim social media have some influence on their purchasing decisions. As a result, firms are spending more time on the quality of their Facebook interactions. Ritz-Carlton, for instance, spends a significant amount of time analyzing its social media conversations and reaching out to noncustomers. Businesses are shifting their emphasis from selling a product or promoting a brand to developing beneficial relationships in which brands are used to generate a positive outcome for the consumer.[22]

Twitter Twitter is a hybrid of a social networking site and a microblogging site that asks users one simple question: "What's

LOLLY WOLLY DOODLE COMPANY GOES VIRAL USING FACEBOOK

Brandi Temple began her children's clothing business, Lolly Wolly Doodle, on eBay, posting designs which she then made to order. Demand grew steadily, but slowly, until the day she tried selling some extra merchandise on Facebook. When she sold more that day on Facebook than she had in a month on eBay, she realized she was on to something.

By 2013, Lolly Wolly Doodle was bringing in $11 million in revenue. It claims to do more sales through Facebook than any other company in the world. Lolly's unique model works like this: Every day, the company posts new clothing designs on its Facebook page. Customers order by commenting with their e-mail address and size/customization requests. The company manufactures the amount ordered,

then reviews the amount of sales; if the design was popular enough, it is added to the company's permanent collection.

Analysts are hailing the model as revolutionary not only for social sales but also for fashion in general. Its use of "test runs" and just-in-time manufacturing avoids the usual problems of overproduction and next season markdowns experienced by traditional clothing companies.[20]

happening?" Members can post answers of up to 140 characters, which are then available for their registered "followers" to read. It sounds simple enough, but Twitter's effect on digital media has been immense. The site quickly progressed from a novelty to a social networking staple, attracting millions of viewers each month.[23] Nearly half of these users visit the site on a daily basis, while approximately 30 percent visit the site multiple times per day.[24]

Twitter followers of Dunkin' Donuts and the Sports Channel.[30] Marketers are clearly taking notice of the various marketing opportunities Twitter has to offer.

Blogs and Wikis

Today's marketers must recognize that the impact of consumer-generated material like blogs and wikis and their significance to online consumers have increased a great deal. **Blogs** (short for web logs) are web-based journals in which writers can editorialize and interact with other Internet users. More than three-fourths of Internet users read blogs.[31] In fact, the blogging site Tumblr, which allows anyone to post text, hyperlinks,

> **Although 140 characters may not seem like enough for companies to send an effective message, shorter social media messages appear to be more effective.**

Although 140 characters may not seem like enough for companies to send an effective message, shorter social media messages appear to be more effective. Tweets with words shorter than 100 characters are found to have a 17 percent higher engagement rate with users, and Facebook has shown similar data.[25] The National Football League uses Twitter to provide football highlights for sports followers.[26] These efforts are having an impact; more than half of Twitter's active and monthly users follow companies or brands. This indicates three times more the exposure for businesses on Twitter than on Facebook.[27]

Like other social networking sites, Twitter is being used to enhance customer service and create publicity about company products. Progressive Corp. purchases advertisements in the form of tweets from its television spokesperson Flo, who provides updates for her more than 33,000 Twitter followers.[28] Twitter offers companies the ability to target different users based on information it collects about apps installed on users' mobile devices.[29]

Twitter also expanded into video with its acquisition of the mobile application Vine. In keeping with Twitter's reputation for short, concise postings, Vine allows users to display up to six seconds of video and share them with other users. Vine has become highly popular among celebrities and teenagers. Dunkin' Donuts became the first company to create a television commercial on Vine during ESPN's Monday Night pregame show. It later developed three videos themed after the Super Bowl to share with

pictures, and other media for free, became one of the top 10 online destinations. The site has 232 million blogs and more than 108 million posts. In 2013, Yahoo! purchased Tumblr for $1.1 billion.[32]

Blogs give consumers power, sometimes more than companies would like. Bloggers can post whatever they like about a company or its products, whether their opinions are positive or negative, true or false. For instance, although companies sometimes force bloggers to remove blogs, readers often create copies of the blog post and spread it across the Internet after the original's removal. In other cases, a positive review of a good or service posted on a popular blog can result in large increases in sales. Thus, blogs can represent a potent threat or opportunity to marketers.

Rather than trying to eliminate blogs that cast their companies in a negative light, some firms are using their own blogs, or employee blogs, to answer consumer concerns or defend their corporate reputations. Direct selling firm Tastefully Simple operates a blog of easy recipes. Users can look for recipes based on the main ingredient used, type of course, or cooking method.[34] As blogging changes the face of media, smart companies are using it to build enthusiasm for their products and create relationships with consumers.

Wikis are websites where users can add to or edit the content of posted articles. One of the best known is Wikipedia, an online encyclopedia with more than 34 million entries in more than 285 languages on nearly every subject imaginable.[35]

DID YOU KNOW?

Searching is the most popular online activity.[33]

Wikipedia is one of the 10 most popular sites on the web, and because much of its content can be edited by anyone, it is easy for online consumers to add detail and supporting evidence and to correct inaccuracies in content. Wikipedia used to be completely open to editing, but in order to stop vandalism, the site had to make some topics off-limits that are now editable only by a small group of experts.

Like all digital media, wikis have advantages and disadvantages for companies. Wikis about controversial companies like Walmart and Nike often contain negative publicity, such as about workers' rights violations. However, monitoring relevant wikis can provide companies with a better idea of how consumers feel about the company or brand. Some companies also use wikis as internal tools for teams working on projects that require a great deal of documentation.[36]

There is too much at stake financially for marketers to ignore wikis and blogs. Despite this fact, statistics show that less than one-fourth of Fortune 500 companies have a corporate blog.[37] Marketers who want to form better customer relationships and promote their company's products must not underestimate the power of these two media outlets.

Media Sharing

Businesses can also share their corporate messages in more visual ways through media sharing sites. Media sharing sites allow marketers to share photos, videos, and podcasts. Media sharing sites are more limited in scope in how companies interact with consumers. They tend to be more promotional than reactive. This means that while firms can promote their products through videos or photos, they usually do not interact with consumers through personal messages or responses. At the same time, the popularity of these sites provides the potential to reach a global audience of consumers.

Video sharing sites allow virtually anybody to upload videos, from professional marketers at Fortune 500 corporations to the average Internet user. Some of the most popular video sharing sites include YouTube, Vimeo, and Daily*motion*. Video sharing sites give companies the opportunity to upload ads and informational videos about their products. A few videos become viral at any given time, and although many of these gain popularity because they embarrass the subject in some way, others reach viral status because people find them entertaining. **Viral marketing** occurs when a message gets sent from person to person to person. It can be an extremely effective tool for marketers—particularly on the Internet, where one click can send a message to dozens or hundreds of people simultaneously. Marketers are taking advantage of the viral nature of video sharing sites like YouTube, either by creating their own unique videos or advertising on videos that have already reached viral status. For example, Subway developed a web-based sitcom series it released on its YouTube channel and Hulu. The first part of the series follows a young Subway employee as he encounters the trials of being a teenager. The second part focuses on characters in college working

at Subway as their part-time jobs. The videos were watched more than 30 million times on YouTube and Hulu, winning an Effie Award for best marketing content for a restaurant.[38]

Businesses do not always have to develop their own videos from scratch, but can utilize the skills and services of others. For instance, consumer-generated videos can be used to convey an authentic message without spending large amounts of money on advertising firms. GoPro was transformed from a small camera firm into a successful company due to the videos consumers took of themselves using GoPro cameras.[39] Social media sites are also providing resources to help smaller businesses develop low-cost video campaigns. For instance, YouTube purchased the video startup Directr to provide tools that small businesses can use to create and upload videos about their companies. YouTube wants to help small companies realize the benefits of promoting corporate videos through its site.[40]

Photo sharing sites allow users to upload and share their photos and short videos with the world. Well-known photo sharing sites include Instagram, Imgur, Shutterfly, Photobucket, and Flickr. Owned by Yahoo! Flickr is one of the most popular photo sharing sites on the Internet. A Flickr user can upload images, edit them, classify the images, create photo albums, and share photos with friends without having to e-mail bulky image files or send photos through the mail. However, Instagram has surpassed Flickr as the most popular photo sharing site. Instagram is a mobile application that allows users to make their photos look dreamy or retrospective with different tints and then share them with their friends.[41] The Eddie Bauer

Flickr is a popular photo sharing site. Marketers can use Flickr to post photos of products or company activities.
© *TomBham/Alamy*

viral marketing
a marketing tool that uses a networking effect to spread a message and create brand awareness. The purpose of this marketing technique is to encourage the consumer to share the message with friends, family, co-workers, and peers.

Since its Facebook acquisition, Instagram has doubled its user base to about 200 million active users per month, with a third of those living outside the United States. To generate revenue Instagram has begun to slowly incorporate paid ads into its platform despite objections from many of its users. Instagram had already previously been forced to roll back an updated user policy when users complained about the fact that it would have allowed the company to use privately uploaded photos in advertising. Instagram realized that it needed to reach a delicate balance between user privacy, profit, and functionality. Although there is a huge potential to increase profits through ad revenue, showing too many ads poses the risk of losing customers and degrading the image and usability of the service.

Instagram is one of many online tech companies that are prioritizing company growth over profits. Pinterest, Snapchat, and Tumblr are following a similar strategy as Instagram—focus on growing a larger user base and worry about profits later. Amazon.com has also maintained very low profits to continue to grow rapidly in its markets.

Facebook expects that Instagram's massive user base will translate into future revenue, but choosing the correct time to aggressively promote monetization of the services is critical. The highly personalized nature of social media, privacy expectations from users, and profit obligations to shareholders is a balance that Instagram needs to continually maintain. The company's current strategy is slanted toward platform growth, but this is likely to change as more ways to monetize the service are discovered.[42]

● Discussion Questions

1. Should Facebook continue following its strategy of using Instagram to amass a larger user base rather than working to make the service more profitable?

2. How can tech companies increase goodwill and indirectly affect profits for parent companies?

3. What is the best way to incorporate advertising into Instagram feeds while limiting the amount of resentment among current and future Instagram users?

---

website has an icon on its main website that will take users to its Instagram stream.[43] To compete against Twitter's short-form video service Vine, Facebook has added 13 filters for video to the Instagram app. With more and more people using mobile apps or accessing the Internet through their smartphones, the use of photo sharing through mobile devices is likely to increase.

Other sites are emerging that take photo sharing to a new level. Pinterest is a photo sharing bulletin board site that combines photo sharing with elements of bookmarking and social networking. Users can share photos and images among other Internet users, communicating mostly through images that they "pin" to their boards. Other users can "repin" these images to their boards, follow each other, "like" images, and make comments. Marketers have found that an effective way of marketing through Pinterest is to post images conveying a certain emotion that represents their brand.[44] Because Pinterest users create boards that deal with their interests, marketers have the opportunity to develop messages encouraging users to purchase the product that interests them. Pinterest plans to learn how to influence a customer to go from showing interest in a product to purchasing it. This knowledge will help companies market through Pinterest's website.[45]

Photo sharing represents an opportunity for companies to market themselves visually by displaying snapshots of company events, company staff, and/or company products. Nike, Audi, and MTV have all used Instagram in digital marketing

> **Podcasting offers the benefit of convenience, giving users the ability to listen to or view content when and where they choose.**

campaigns. Whole Foods has topic boards on Pinterest featuring recipes, farm scenes, and more to reinforce its brand image.[46] Zales Jewelers has topic boards on Pinterest featuring rings as well as other themes of love, including songs, wedding cake, and wedding dresses. Digital marketing companies are also scanning photos and images on photo sharing sites to gather insights about how brands are being displayed or used. They hope to offer these insights to big-name companies such as Kraft. The opportunities for marketers to use photo sharing sites to gather information and promote brands appear limitless.[47]

Podcasts are audio or video files that can be downloaded from the Internet via a subscription that automatically delivers new content to listening devices or personal computers. Podcasting offers the benefit of convenience, giving users the ability to listen to or view content when and where they choose. The markets podcasts reach are ideal for marketers, especially the 18–34 demographic, which includes the young and the affluent.[48] They also impact consumer buying habits. For instance, listening to nutrition podcasts while in the grocery store increases the likelihood that shoppers will purchase healthier items.[49]

As podcasting continues to catch on, radio stations and television networks like CBC Radio, NPR, MSNBC, and PBS are creating podcasts of their shows to profit from this growing trend. Many companies hope to use podcasts to create brand awareness, promote their products, and encourage customer loyalty.

Virtual Gaming

Games and programs allowing viewers to develop avatars that exist in an online virtual world have exploded in popularity in the 21st century. Virtual games and realities include Second Life, Everquest, Angry Birds, and the role-playing game World of Warcraft. These sites can be described as social networks with a twist. Virtual realities are three-dimensional, user-created worlds that have their own currencies, lands, and residents that come in every shape and size. Internet users who participate in virtual realities such as Second Life choose a fictional persona, called an *avatar*. Farmville provides a similar virtual world experience, except it is limited to life on a farm.

Real-world marketers and organizations have been eager to capitalize on the popularity of virtual gaming sites. MediaSpike specializes in placing brands into mobile games. Geico Powersports and Mountain Dew are two brands that have worked with MediaSpike to appear in mobile games.[50] It is estimated that consumers spend 32 percent of their time with mobile apps on gaming activities. Lexus has taken advantage of this opportunity by placing a virtual Lexus in the game Real Racing 3. McDonald's, Ford, and Wheat Thins plan on having in-game campaigns for their brands.[51] Even Facebook is looking into opportunities associated with virtual reality. Its purchase of Oculus Rift—a virtual reality startup—signals its interest in exploring live chatting and social virtual tours.[52]

Mobile Marketing

As digital marketing becomes increasingly sophisticated, consumers are beginning to utilize mobile devices like smartphones as a highly functional communication method. The iPhone and iPad have changed the way consumers communicate, and a growing number of travelers are using their smartphones to find online maps, travel guides, and taxis. In industries such as hotels, airlines, and car rental agencies, mobile phones have become a primary method for booking reservations and communicating about services. Other marketing uses of mobile phones include sending shoppers timely messages related to discounts and shopping opportunities.[53] For these reasons, mobile marketing has exploded in recent years—mobile phones have become an important part of our everyday lives and can even affect how we shop. For instance, it is estimated that shoppers who are distracted by their phones in-store increased their unplanned purchases by 12 percent over those who are not.[54] Marketers are estimated to spend $64.25 billion on mobile marketing.[55] To avoid being left behind, brands must recognize the importance of mobile marketing.

E-commerce sales on smartphones is also rapidly growing. Sales are estimated to reach $638 billion by 2018.[56] This makes it essential for companies to understand how to use mobile tools to create effective campaigns. Some of the more common mobile marketing tools include the following:

- *SMS messages:* SMS messages are text messages of 160 words or less. SMS messages have been an effective way to send coupons to prospective customers.[57]

- *Multimedia messages:* Multimedia messaging takes SMS messaging a step further by allowing companies to send video, audio, photos, and other types of media over mobile devices. Gap used Instagram Direct as the outlet for their "What I Wore Today (#WIWT)" campaign, allowing users to win a Gap denim tablet case.[58]

- *Mobile advertisements:* Mobile advertisements are visual advertisements that appear on mobile devices. Companies might choose to advertise through search engines, websites, or even games accessed on mobile devices. Consumers tend to pay more attention to advertisements on their mobile devices than on their televisions, carrying important implications for online marketers.[59]

- *Mobile websites:* Mobile websites are websites designed for mobile devices. Approximately 60 percent of all online traffic comes from mobile devices.[60]

- *Location-based networks:* Location-based networks are built for mobile devices. Some popular location-based networks include Google Waze and Foursquare, which lets users check in and share their location with others. Dunkin' Donuts, Phillips 66, and Panera have all released campaigns through Google Waze. Dunkin' Donuts uses the Google Waze mapping app to offer advertisements to consumers driving toward its stores based on location and time of day.[61]

- *Mobile applications:* Mobile applications (known as *apps*) are software programs that run on mobile devices and give users access to certain content.[62] Businesses release apps to help consumers access more information about their company or to provide incentives. Apps are discussed in further detail in the next section. Figure 13.2 shows the percentage of time users in the United States spend on different smartphone apps.

FIGURE 13.2
Percentage of Time Spent Using Different Smartphone Apps
Note: Respondents in the United States

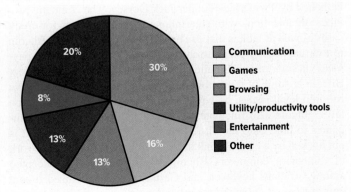

- Communication — 30%
- Games — 16%
- Browsing — 13%
- Utility/productivity tools — 13%
- Entertainment — 8%
- Other — 20%

Source: Adapted from Ericsson ConsumerLab, *Communication in the World of Apps*, June 2015, p. 4, http://www.ericsson.com/res/docs/2015/consumerlab/ericsson-consumerlab-communication-in-the-world-of-apps.pdf (accessed September 23, 2015).

Applications and Widgets

Applications are adding an entirely new layer to the marketing environment, as approximately half of all American adult cell phone users have applications on their mobile devices.[63] The most important feature of apps is the convenience and cost savings they offer to the consumer. Certain apps allow consumers to scan a product's barcode and then compare it with the prices of identical products in other stores. Mobile apps also enable customers to download in-store discounts. As of 2014, an estimated 58 percent of American adults have smartphones, so businesses cannot afford to miss out on the chance to profit from these new trends.[64]

To remain competitive, companies are beginning to use mobile marketing to offer additional incentives to consumers. Marriott used Apple's iBeacon technology to launch its LocalPerks initiative. The technology located the mobile devices of Marriott guests to determine their location and send them daily deals and other marketing messages.[65] Another application that marketers are finding useful is the QR scanning app. QR codes are black-and-white squares that sometimes appear in magazines, posters, and storefront displays. Smartphone users who have downloaded the QR scanning application can open their smartphones and scan the code, which contains a hidden message accessible with the app. The QR scanning app recognizes the code and opens the link, video, or image on the phone's screen. Marketers are using QR codes to promote their companies and offer consumer discounts.[66]

Mobile payments are also gaining traction, and companies like Google, Apple, and Square are working to capitalize on this opportunity.[67] Google Wallet and Apple Pay are mobile apps that store credit card information on the smartphone. When the shopper is ready to check out, he or she can tap the phone at the point of sale for the transaction to be registered.[68] Square is a company launched by Twitter co-founder Jack Dorsey. The company provides organizations with smartphone swiping devices for credit cards as well as tablets that can be used to tally purchases. Bitcoin is a virtual peer-to-peer currency that can be used to make a payment via smartphone. Smaller organizations have begun to accept Bitcoin at some of their stores. Virtual currency exchanges have run into legal issues, however, due to state money-transmission laws. Bitcoin also fluctuates in value, making it risky for companies to hold onto the virtual currency for long periods.[69] It is not backed by a central bank and its software is run on a network of volunteers' computers. Bitcoin is being increasingly accepted among officials, however, and Germany has recognized it as a unit of account.[70] On the other hand, a major scandal has caused some to question Bitcoin's use. Mt. Gox, a Bitcoin exchange, reportedly lost 650,000 Bitcoins. A lawsuit was filed, and Mt. Gox declared bankruptcy.[71] The success of mobile payments in revolutionizing the shopping experience will largely depend upon retailers to adopt this payment system, but companies such as Starbucks are already jumping at the opportunity.

Widgets are small bits of software on a website, desktop, or mobile device that perform a simple purpose, such as providing stock quotes or blog updates. Marketers might use widgets to display news headlines, clocks, or games on their web pages.[72] For example, CNBC uses widgets to send alerts and financial news to subscribers. Widgets have been used by companies as a form of viral marketing—users can download the widget and send it to their friends with a click of a button.[73] Widgets downloaded to a user's desktop can update the user on the latest company or product information, enhancing relationship marketing between companies and their fans. Hotels, restaurants, and other tourist locations can download TripAdvisor widgets to their websites. These widgets display the latest company reviews, rewards, and other TripAdvisor content directly to the company's website.[74] Widgets are an innovative digital marketing tool to personalize web pages, alert users to the latest company information, and spread awareness of the company's products.

USING DIGITAL MEDIA TO REACH CONSUMERS

We've seen that customer-generated communications and digital media connect consumers as never before. These connections let consumers share information and experiences without company interference so they get more of the "real story" on a product or company feature. In many ways, these media take some of the professional marketer's power to control and dispense information and place it in the hands of the consumer.

However, this shift does not have to spell doom for marketers, who can choose to utilize the power of the consumer and Internet technology to their advantage. While consumers use digital media to access more product information, marketers can use the same sites to get better and more targeted information about the consumer—often more than they could gather through traditional marketing venues. Marketers increasingly use consumer-generated content to aid their own marketing efforts, even going so far as to incorporate Internet bloggers in their publicity campaigns. Finally, marketers are also beginning to use the Internet to track the success of their online marketing campaigns, creating an entirely new way of gathering marketing research.

The challenge for digital media marketers is to constantly adapt to new technologies and changing consumer patterns. Unfortunately, the attrition rate for digital media channels is very high,

The use of mobile coupons is increasing. Consumers appreciate these types of coupons for their convenience. Retailers like mobile coupons because they save money from having to print and distribute them.
© Mark Dierker/McGraw-Hill Education

▼ **TABLE 13.3** Social Technographics

Creators	Publish a blog Publish personal web pages Upload original video Upload original audio/music Write articles or stories and post them
Conversationalists	Update status on social networking sites Post updates on Twitter
Critics	Post ratings/reviews of products Comment on someone else's blog Contribute to online forums Contribute to/edit articles in a wiki
Collectors	Use RSS feeds Add tags to web pages or photos "Vote" for websites online
Joiners	Maintain profile on a social networking site Visit social networking sites
Spectators	Read blogs Watch video from other users Listen to podcasts Read online forums Read customer ratings/reviews
Inactives	None of the activities

Sources: Charlene Li and Josh Bernoff, *Groundswell* (Boston: Harvard Business Press, 2008), p. 43; "Forrester Unveils New Segment of Social Technographics—The Conversationalists," *360 Digital Connections,* January 21, 2010, http://blog.360i.com/social-media/forrester-new-segment-social-technographics-conversationalists (accessed May 19, 2014).

with some dying off each year as new ones emerge. As time passes, digital media are becoming more sophisticated so as to reach consumers in more effective ways. Those that are not able to adapt and change eventually fail.

Charlene Li and Josh Bernoff of Forrester Research, a technology and market research company, emphasize the need for marketers to understand these changing relationships in the online media world. By grouping consumers into different segments based on how they utilize digital media, marketers can gain a better understanding of the online market and how best to proceed.[75]

Table 13.3 shows seven ways that Forrester Research groups consumers based on their Internet activity (or lack thereof). The categories are not mutually exclusive; online consumers can participate in more than one at a time.

Creators are consumers who create their own media outlets, such as blogs, podcasts, consumer-generated videos, and wikis.[76] Consumer-generated media are increasingly important to online marketers as a conduit for addressing consumers directly. The second group of Internet users is *conversationalists.* Conversationalists regularly update their Twitter feeds or status updates on social networking sites. Although they are less involved than creators, conversationalists spend time at least once a week (and often more) on digital media sites posting updates.[77] The third category, *critics,* consists of people who comment on blogs or post ratings and reviews on review websites such as Yelp. Because many online shoppers read ratings and reviews to aid their

purchasing decisions, critics should be a primary component in a company's digital marketing strategy. The next category is *collectors.* They collect information and organize content generated by critics and creators.[78] Reddit and Delicious are some popular sites for collectors. Because collectors are active members of the online community, a company story or site that catches the eye of a collector is likely to be posted, discussed on collector sites, and made available to other online users looking for information.

Joiners include all who become users of Twitter, Facebook, or other social networking sites. It is not unusual for consumers to be members of several social networking sites at once. Joiners use these sites to connect and network with other users, but as we've seen, marketers too can take significant advantage of these sites to connect with consumers and form customer relationships.[79] The last two segments are Spectators and Inactives. *Spectators,* who read online information but do not join groups or post anywhere, are the largest group in most countries. *Inactives* are online users who do not participate in any digital online media, but their numbers are dwindling.

Marketers need to consider what proportion of online consumers are creating, conversing, rating, collecting, joining, or simply reading online materials. As in traditional marketing efforts, they need to know their target market. For instance, where spectators make up the majority of the online population, companies should post their own corporate messages through blogs and websites promoting their organizations.

About three-quarters of online shoppers read ratings and reviews before making a decision.
© webpics/Alamy

Retailers such as Amazon, Netflix, and Priceline allow consumers to post comments on their sites about the books, movies, and travel arrangements they sell. Today, most online shoppers search the Internet for ratings and reviews before making major purchase decisions.

While consumer-generated content about a firm can be either positive or negative, digital media forums do allow businesses to closely monitor what their customers are saying. In the case of negative feedback, businesses can communicate with consumers to address problems or complaints much more easily than through traditional communication channels. Yet despite the ease and obvious importance of online feedback, many companies do not yet take full advantage of the digital tools at their disposal.

> **LO 13-5** Identify legal and ethical considerations in digital media.

USING DIGITAL MEDIA TO LEARN ABOUT CONSUMERS

Marketing research and information systems can use digital media and social networking sites to gather useful information about consumers and their preferences. Sites such as Twitter and Facebook can be good substitutes for focus groups. Online surveys can serve as an alternative to mail, telephone, or personal interviews.

Crowdsourcing describes how marketers use digital media to find out the opinions or needs of the crowd (or potential markets). Communities of interested consumers join sites like threadless.com, which designs T-shirts, or crowdspring.com, which creates logos and print and web designs. These companies give interested consumers opportunities to contribute and give feedback on product ideas. Crowdsourcing lets companies gather and utilize consumers' ideas in an interactive way when creating new products.

Consumer feedback is an important part of the digital media equation. Ratings and reviews have become exceptionally popular. Online reviews are estimated to influence the buying decisions of approximately 90 percent of U.S. consumers.[80]

LEGAL AND SOCIAL ISSUES IN INTERNET MARKETING

The extraordinary growth of information technology, the Internet, and social networks has generated many legal and social issues for consumers and businesses. These issues include privacy concerns, the risk of identity theft and online fraud, and the need to protect intellectual property. The U.S. Federal Trade Commission (FTC) compiles an annual list of consumer complaints related to the Internet and digital media. We discuss these in this section, as well as steps that individuals, companies, and the government have taken to address them. Table 13.4 describes industry best practices for digital marketers to consider before launching digital marketing campaigns.

Privacy

Businesses have long tracked consumers' shopping habits with little controversy. However, observing the contents of a consumer's shopping cart or the process a consumer goes through when choosing a box of cereal generally does not result in the collection of specific, personally identifying data. Although using credit cards, shopping cards, and coupons forces consumers to

▼ **TABLE 13.4** Best Practices for Digital Marketing Campaigns

1. Implement privacy during the conceptualization phase of the marketing campaign.
2. Disclose all passive tracking systems used to collect information.
3. For data collection involving third parties, disclose clear guidelines regarding how the data will be used and who owns it. Provide ways for users to opt-out of tracking or e-mail marketing through visible notices.
4. Screen age of users if appropriate for the campaign. Collecting personal information of children under 13 requires parental consent. If marketing to children is allowed, ensure that the content and language is appropriate for the age range targeted.
5. Ensure that all tracking or data collection activities that occur do not conflict with the company's online privacy policy.
6. Adopt security measures for any data collected from users. User information must be protected, particularly if it is identifiable.
7. Be aware of all legal requirements and industry codes of ethics on digital marketing.

Sources: Adapted from Jesse Brody, "Terms and Conditions," *Marketing News,* November 2014, pp. 34–41; Direct Marketing Association, *Direct Marketing Association's Guidelines for Ethical Business Practice,* January 2014, http://thedma.org/wpcontent/uploads/DMA_Guidelines_January_2014.pdf (accessed January 7, 2015).

give up a certain degree of anonymity in the traditional shopping process, they can still choose to remain anonymous by paying cash. Shopping on the Internet, however, allows businesses to track them on a far more personal level, from the contents of their online purchases to the websites they favor. Current technology has made it possible for marketers to amass vast quantities of personal information, often without consumers' knowledge, and to share and sell this information to interested third parties. Governments have issued subpoenas to companies like Google and Microsoft for user information when pursuing legal action. For example, the U.S. Justice Departments gets some of its most effective evidence from e-mails in processing cases.

How is personal information collected on the web? Many sites follow users online by storing a "cookie," or an identifying string of text, on users' computers. Cookies permit website operators to track how often a user visits the site, what he or she looks at while there, and in what sequence. They also allow website visitors to customize services, such as virtual shopping carts, as well as the particular content they see when they log onto a web page. Users have the option of turning off cookies on their machines, but nevertheless the potential for misuse has left many consumers uncomfortable with this technology.

Due to consumer concerns over privacy, the FTC is considering developing regulations that would better protect consumer privacy by limiting the amount of consumer information that businesses can gather online. Other countries are pursuing similar actions. The European Union passed a law requiring companies to get users' consent before using cookies to track their information. In the United States, one proposed solution for consumer Internet privacy is a "do not track" bill, similar to the "do not call" bill for telephones, to allow users to opt out of having their information tracked.[82] While consumers may welcome such added protections, web advertisers, who use consumer information to better target advertisements to online consumers, see it as a threat. In response to impending legislation, many web advertisers are attempting self-regulation in order to stay ahead of the game. For instance, the Digital Advertising Alliance (DAA) adopted privacy guidelines for online advertisers and created a "trusted mark" icon that websites adhering to their guidelines can display. However, because it is self-regulatory, not all digital advertisers may choose to participate in its programs.[83]

Identity Theft

Identity theft occurs when criminals obtain personal information that allows them to impersonate someone else in order to use the person's credit to access financial accounts and make purchases. This requires organizations to implement increased security measures to prevent database theft. The most common complaints relate to government documents/benefits fraud, followed by credit card fraud, utility fraud, bank fraud, employment fraud, and loan fraud.

The Internet's relative anonymity and speed make possible both legal and illegal access to databases storing Social Security numbers, drivers' license numbers, dates of birth, mothers' maiden names, and other information that can be used to establish a credit card or bank account in another person's name in

THE ETHICS OF INTERNET TRACKING AND BEHAVIORAL ADVERTISING

It is no secret that online advertisers are trying to track consumer Internet activity and use the information to target ads toward each person's interests and preferences. These efforts used to be largely limited to individual websites tracking their own visitors. Now, however, technology enables the tracking of Internet users across sites. For example, every site with Facebook's ubiquitous "Like" button—as well as every smartphone with the Facebook app installed—sends Facebook information, which it then uses to target ads to its users.

Advertisers argue that this method, known as targeted or behavioral advertising, is a win–win for both businesses and consumers. When ads are targeted to fit each user's behavior, users are more likely to see offerings in which they have an interest, improving their online experience. Targeted ads are also more efficient for businesses, meaning companies can spend less on advertising—and, presumably, pass on the cost savings to customers. Finally, as most of the currently free-to-use websites on the Internet survive on advertising revenue, online advertisers warn that restricting or limiting advertising could lead to a much less open and free Internet.

Critics, on the other hand, point out the serious privacy concerns raised by tracking people's every online move, often without their knowledge or consent. Furthermore, this information is not necessarily secure—as evidenced by the continuing reports of large companies suffering data breaches—and can be used by criminals to commit fraud, identity theft, and other crimes. Privacy advocates want the behavioral advertising industry to be strictly regulated. In the meantime, they are encouraging consumers to learn about how to control and restrict the collection and use of their information.[81]

Discussion Questions

1. What ethical considerations and concerns are implicated by behavioral advertising?

2. Discuss some of the benefits to the consumer that may occur with behavioral advertising.

3. As a consumer, are you concerned about behavioral advertising? Will you change your online behavior in response?

order to make fraudulent transactions. One growing scam used to initiate identity theft fraud is the practice of *phishing,* whereby con artists counterfeit a well-known website and send out e-mails directing victims to it. There visitors find instructions to reveal sensitive information such as their credit card numbers. Phishing scams have faked websites for PayPal, AOL, and the Federal Deposit Insurance Corporation.

Some identity theft problems are resolved quickly, while other cases take weeks and hundreds of dollars before a victim's bank balances and credit standings are restored. To deter identity theft, the National Fraud Center wants financial institutions to implement new technologies such as digital certificates, digital signatures, and biometrics—the use of fingerprinting or retina scanning.

Online Fraud

Online fraud includes any attempt to purposely deceive online. Many cybercriminals use hacking to commit online fraud. Hackers break into websites and steal users' personal information. Home Depot, Target, and JPMorgan Chase are some notable cases where cybercriminals hacked into these companies' systems and stole information. Sony experienced a devastating attack that shut down its entire computer network and resulted in the theft of 27 gigabytes of files.[84]

Privacy advocates advise that the best way to stay out of trouble is to avoid giving out personal information, such as Social Security numbers or credit card information, unless the site is definitely legitimate. Using a different password for each website users visit is another important way to avoid becoming the victim of online fraud. Passwords should be complex enough that a cybercriminal cannot easily guess it. However, many consumers do not do this because of the hassle it takes in remembering complex passwords for multiple sites.[85]

Credit card fraud is a major type of fraud that occurs online. One way to tackle online fraud for credit cards is to use a pin number when doing online transactions. Banks are releasing credit cards with embedded chips rather than magnetic tape to make it harder for fraud to occur. In Europe this type of credit card combined with the use of a pin number has deterred credit card fraud. This is because the consumers use their pin numbers as well as the embedded chip in their credit cards to make purchases. However, U.S. banks are not requiring Americans to input their pin numbers, which might limit their effectiveness in preventing online fraud within the United States.[86]

Intellectual Property and Other Illegal Activity

In addition to protecting personal privacy, Internet users and others want to protect their rights to property they may create, including songs, movies, books, and software. Such intellectual property consists of the ideas and creative materials developed to solve problems, carry out applications, and educate and entertain others.

The file-sharing protocol BitTorrent allows users to share and download files. The U.S. Copyright Group obtained the IP addresses of users who downloaded specific movies using BitTorrent technology and are taking action against thousands of BitTorrent users for illegally downloading protected content.
© Adam Berry/Bloomberg/Getty Images

Although intellectual property is generally protected by patents and copyrights, each year losses from the illegal copying of computer programs, music, movies, compact discs, and books reach billions of dollars in the United States alone. This has become a particular problem with digital media sites. YouTube has often faced lawsuits on intellectual property infringement. With millions of users uploading content to YouTube, it can be hard for Google to monitor and remove all the videos that may contain copyrighted materials.

Illegal sharing of content is another major intellectual property problem. Consumers rationalize the pirating of software, videogames, movies, and music for a number of reasons. First, many feel they just don't have the money to pay for what they want. Second, because their friends engage in piracy and swap digital content, some users feel influenced to engage in this activity. Others enjoy the thrill of getting away with something with a low risk of consequences. And finally, some people feel being tech-savvy allows them to take advantage of the opportunity to pirate content.[87]

Illicit online marketing is becoming a serious issue for law enforcement across the globe. The ease of the Internet and the difficulty in pinpointing perpetrators are leading drug buyers to deal in illegal drugs over the Internet. Websites that deal in illegal drugs are looking increasingly legitimate, even employing marketing strategies and customer service.[88] Sales of counterfeit goods are another problem. Knockoffs of popular products seized by federal officials annually are valued at over $1 billion. Counterfeit products, particularly from overseas, are thriving on the Internet because they can be shipped directly to customers without having to be examined by Customs officials when shipped through ports. Some firms, including UGG Boots, are creating online services allowing users to type in the address to verify whether the electronic retailer is a legitimate seller.[89]

DIGITAL MEDIA'S IMPACT ON MARKETING

To be successful in business, you need to know much more than how to use a social networking site to communicate with friends. Developing a strategic understanding of how digital marketing can make business more efficient and productive is increasingly necessary. If you are thinking of becoming an entrepreneur, then the digital world can open doors to new resources and customers. Smartphones, mobile broadband, and webcams are among the tools that can make the most of an online business world, creating greater efficiency at less cost. For example, rather than using traditional phone lines, Skype helps people make and receive calls via the Internet and provides free video calling and text messaging for about 10 percent of the cost of a land line.[90] It is up to businesses and entrepreneurs to develop strategies that achieve business success using existing and future technology, software, and networking opportunities.

Traditional businesses accustomed to using print media can find the transition to digital challenging. New media may require employees with new skills or additional training for current employees. There is often a gap between technical knowledge of how to develop sites and how to develop effective digital marketing strategies to enhance business success. Determining the correct blend of traditional and new media requires careful consideration; the mix will vary depending on the business, its size, and its target market. Future career opportunities will require skills in both traditional and digital media areas so that marketers properly understand and implement marketing strategies that help businesses achieve a competitive advantage. ∎

> ### TEAM EXERCISE
>
> Develop a digital marketing promotion for a local sports team. Use Twitter, Facebook, and other social networking media to promote ticket sales for next season's schedule. In your plan, provide specific details and ideas for the content you would use on the sites. Also, describe how you would encourage fans and potential fans to go to your site. How would you use digital media to motivate sports fans to purchase tickets and merchandise and attend games?

["Developing a strategic understanding of how digital marketing can make business more efficient and productive is increasingly necessary."]

SO YOU WANT TO BE // a Digital Marketer /

The business world has grown increasingly dependent on digital marketing to maintain communication with stakeholders. Reaching customers is often a major concern, but digital marketing can also be used to communicate with suppliers, concerned community members, and special interest groups about issues related to sustainability, safety practices, and philanthropic activities. Many types of jobs exist: account executive directors of social media and director of marketing for digital products, as well as digital advertisers, online marketers, global digital marketers, and brand managers are prominently listed on career opportunity websites.

Entrepreneurs are taking advantage of the low cost of digital marketing, building social networking sites to help market their products. In fact, some small businesses such as specialty publishing, personal health and beauty, and other specialty products can use digital marketing as the primary channel for reaching consumers. Many small businesses are posting signs outside their stores with statements such as "Follow us on Twitter" or "Check out our Facebook page."

To utilize digital marketing, especially social networking, requires more than information technology skills related to constructing websites, graphics, videos, podcasts, etc. Most importantly, one must be able to determine how digital media can be used in implementing a marketing strategy. All marketing starts with identifying a target market and developing a marketing mix to satisfy customers. Digital marketing is just another way to reach customers, provide information, and develop relationships. Therefore, your opportunity for a career in this field is greatly based on understanding the messages, desired level of interactivity, and connectivity that helps achieve marketing objectives.

As social media use skyrockets, digital marketing professionals will be in demand. The experience of many businesses and research indicate digital marketing is a powerful way to increase brand exposure and generate traffic. In fact, a study conducted on Social Media Examiner found that 85 percent of marketers surveyed believe generating exposure for their business is their number-one advantage in Internet marketing. As consumers use social networking for their personal communication, they will be more open to obtaining information about products through this channel. Digital marketing could be the fastest-growing opportunity in business.

To prepare yourself for a digital marketing career, learn not only the technical aspects, but also how social media can be used to maximize marketing performance. A glance at careerbuilder.com indicates that management positions such as account manager, digital marketing manager, and digital product manager can pay from $60,000 to $170,000 or more per year.

chapter fourteen

accounting and
financial statements

© BananaStock/PictureQuest, RF

A ccounting, the financial "language" that organizations use to record, measure, and interpret all of their financial transactions and records, is very important in business. All businesses—from a small family farm to a giant corporation—use the language of accounting to make sure they use their money wisely and to plan for the future. Nonbusiness organizations such as charities and governments also use accounting to demonstrate to donors and taxpayers how well they are using their funds and meeting their stated objectives.

This chapter explores the role of accounting in business and its importance in making business decisions. First, we discuss the uses of accounting information and the accounting process. Then, we briefly look at some simple financial statements and accounting tools that are useful in analyzing organizations worldwide. ■

THE NATURE OF ACCOUNTING

Simply stated, **accounting** is the recording, measurement, and interpretation of financial information. Large numbers of people and institutions, both within and outside businesses, use accounting tools to evaluate organizational operations. The Financial Accounting Standards Board has been setting the principles and standards of financial accounting and reporting in the private sector since 1973. Its mission is to establish and improve standards of financial accounting and reporting for the guidance and education of the public, including issuers, auditors, and users of financial information. However, the accounting scandals at the turn of the last century resulted when many accounting firms and businesses failed to abide by generally accepted accounting principles, or GAAP. Consequently, the federal government has taken a greater role in making rules, requirements, and policies for accounting firms and businesses through the Securities and Exchange Commission's (SEC) Public Company Accounting Oversight Board. For example, the Public Company Accounting Oversight Board filed a disciplinary order against Deloitte & Touche for permitting a suspended auditor to participate in auditing activities. This violated the Sarbanes-Oxley Act (SOX). The Public Company Accounting Oversight Board imposed a $2 million fine against Deloitte for the violation.[1]

To better understand the importance of accounting, we must first understand who prepares accounting information and how it is used.

Accountants

Many of the functions of accounting are carried out by public or private accountants.

Public Accountants Individuals and businesses can hire a **certified public accountant (CPA)**, an individual who has been certified by the state in which he or she practices to provide accounting services ranging from the preparation of financial records and the filing of tax returns to complex audits of corporate financial records. Certification gives a public accountant the right to express, officially, an unbiased opinion regarding the accuracy of the client's financial statements. Most public accountants are either self-employed or members of large public accounting firms such as Ernst & Young, KPMG, Deloitte, and PricewaterhouseCoopers, together referred to as "the Big Four." In addition, many CPAs work for one of the second-tier accounting firms that are much smaller than the Big Four firms. Table 14.1 lists the top-ranked accounting firms based on prestige and issues important to the accounting profession.

While there will always be companies and individual money managers who can successfully hide illegal or misleading accounting practices for a while, eventually they are exposed. After the accounting scandals of Enron and Worldcom in the early 2000s, Congress passed the Sarbanes-Oxley Act, which required firms to be more rigorous in their accounting and reporting practices. Sarbanes-Oxley made accounting firms separate their consulting and auditing businesses and punished corporate executives with potential jail sentences for inaccurate, misleading, or illegal accounting statements. This seemed to reduce the accounting errors among nonfinancial companies, but declining housing prices exposed some of the questionable practices by banks and mortgage companies. Only five years after the passage of the Sarbanes-Oxley Act, the world experienced a financial crisis starting in 2008—part of which

accounting the recording, measurement, and interpretation of financial information.

certified public accountant (CPA) an individual who has been state certified to provide accounting services ranging from the preparation of financial records and the filing of tax returns to complex audits of corporate financial records.

▼ **TABLE 14.1** Prestige Rankings of Accounting Firms

2015 Rank	2014 Rank	Change	Company	Score	Location
1	1	–	PwC (PricewaterhouseCoopers) LLP	8.354	New York, NY
2	4	▲	Ernst & Young LLP	8.220	New York, NY
3	2	▼	Deloitte LLP	8.080	New York, NY
4	6	▲	KPMG LLP	7.710	New York, NY
5	3	▼	Grant Thornton LLP	7.572	Chicago, IL
6	5	▼	BDO USA LLP	7.238	Chicago, IL
7	7	–	McGladrey LLP	7.030	Chicago, IL
8	10	▲	Plante Moran	6.821	Southfield, MI
9	11	▲	Baker Tilly Virchow Krause, LLP	6.675	Chicago, IL
10	27	▲	Crowe Horwath LLP	6.462	Chicago, IL

Source: "The Best Accounting Firms," www.vault.com/company-rankings/accounting/ (accessed April 8, 2015).

was due to excessive risk taking and inappropriate accounting practices. Many banks failed to understand the true state of their financial health. Banks also developed questionable lending practices and investments based on subprime mortgages made to individuals who had poor credit. When housing prices declined and people suddenly found that they owed more on their mortgages than their homes were worth, they began to default. To prevent a depression, the government intervened and bailed out some of the United States' largest banks. Congress passed the Dodd-Frank Act in 2010 to strengthen the oversight of financial institutions. This act gave the Federal Reserve Board the task of implementing the legislation. It is expected that financial institutions will have at least one year to implement the requirements. This legislation limits the types of assets commercial banks can buy; the amount of capital they must maintain; and the use of derivative instruments such as options, futures, and structured investment products.

A growing area for public accountants is *forensic accounting*, which is accounting that is fit for legal review. It involves analyzing financial documents in search of fraudulent entries or financial misconduct. Functioning as much like detectives as accountants, forensic accountants have been used since the 1930s. In the wake of the accounting scandals of the early 2000s, many auditing firms are rapidly adding or expanding forensic or fraud-detection services. Additionally, many forensic accountants root out evidence of "cooked books" for federal agencies like the Federal Bureau

Ernst & Young is a part of the "Big Four," or the four largest international accounting firms. The other three are PricewaterhouseCoopers, KPMG, and Deloitte Touche Tohmatsu.
© Kristoffer Tripplaar/Alamy

private accountants accountants employed by large corporations, government agencies, and other organizations to prepare and analyze their financial statements.

certified management accountants (CMAs) private accountants who, after rigorous examination, are certified by the National Association of Accountants and who have some managerial responsibility.

managerial accounting the internal use of accounting statements by managers in planning and directing the organization's activities.

cash flow the movement of money through an organization over a daily, weekly, monthly, or yearly basis.

of Investigation or the Internal Revenue Service. The Association of Certified Fraud Examiners, which certifies accounting professionals as *certified fraud examiners (CFEs),* has grown to more than 75,000 members.[3]

Private Accountants Large corporations, government agencies, and other organizations may employ their own **private accountants** to prepare and analyze their financial statements. With titles such as controller, tax accountant, or internal auditor, private accountants are deeply involved in many of the most important financial decisions of the organizations for which they work. Private accountants can be CPAs and may become **certified management accountants (CMAs)** by passing a rigorous examination by the Institute of Management Accountants.

Accounting or Bookkeeping?

The terms *accounting* and *bookkeeping* are often mistakenly used interchangeably. Much narrower and far more mechanical than accounting, bookkeeping is typically limited to the routine, day-to-day recording of business transactions. Bookkeepers are responsible for obtaining and recording the information that accountants require to analyze a firm's financial position. They generally require less training than accountants. Accountants, on the other hand, usually complete course work beyond their basic four- or five-year college accounting degrees. This additional training allows accountants not only to record financial information, but to understand, interpret, and even develop the sophisticated accounting systems necessary to classify and analyze complex financial information.

The Uses of Accounting Information

Accountants summarize the information from a firm's business transactions in various financial statements (which we'll look at in a later section of this chapter) for a variety of stakeholders, including managers, investors, creditors, and government agencies. Many business failures may be directly linked to ignorance of the information

DID YOU KNOW?

Corporate fraud costs are estimated at $3.7 trillion annually.[2]

"hidden" inside these financial statements. Likewise, most business successes can be traced to informed managers who understand the consequences of their decisions. While maintaining and even increasing short-run profits is desirable, the failure to plan sufficiently for the future can easily lead an otherwise successful company to insolvency and bankruptcy court.

Basically, managers and owners use financial statements (1) to aid in internal planning and control and (2) for external purposes such as reporting to the Internal Revenue Service, stockholders, creditors, customers, employees, and other interested parties. Figure 14.1 shows some of the users of the accounting information generated by organizations and other stakeholders.

Internal Uses **Managerial accounting** refers to the internal use of accounting statements by managers in planning and directing the organization's activities. Perhaps management's greatest single concern is **cash flow**, the movement of money through an organization over a daily, weekly, monthly, or yearly basis. Obviously, for any business to succeed, it needs to generate enough cash to pay its bills as they fall due. However, it is not at all unusual for highly successful and rapidly growing

FIGURE 14.1
The Users of Accounting Information

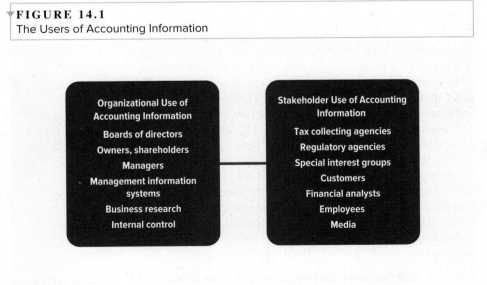

Source: Adapted from *Principles of Accounting,* 4th edition. Houghton Mifflin Company, 1990. Authors: Belverd E. Needles, Henry R. Anderson, and James C. Caldwell.

companies to struggle to make payments to employees, suppliers, and lenders because of an inadequate cash flow. One common reason for a so-called cash crunch, or shortfall, is poor managerial planning.

Managerial accountants also help prepare an organization's **budget**, an internal financial plan that forecasts expenses and income over a set period of time. It is not unusual for an organization to prepare separate daily, weekly, monthly, and yearly budgets. Think of a budget as a financial map, showing how the company expects to move from Point A to Point B over a specific period of time. While most companies prepare *master budgets* for the entire firm, many also prepare budgets for smaller segments of the organization such as divisions, departments, product lines, or projects. "Top-down" master budgets begin at the upper management level and filter down to the individual department level, while "bottom-up" budgets start at the department or project level and are combined at the chief executive's office. Generally, the larger and more rapidly growing an organization, the greater will be the likelihood that it will build its master budget from the ground up.

Regardless of focus, the principal value of a budget lies in its breakdown of cash inflows and outflows. Expected operating expenses (cash outflows such as wages, materials costs, and taxes) and operating revenues (cash inflows in the form of payments from customers) over a set period of time are carefully forecast and subsequently compared with actual results. Deviations between the two serve as a "trip wire" or "feedback loop" to launch more detailed financial analyses in an effort to pinpoint trouble spots and opportunities.

External Uses

Managers also use accounting statements to report the business's financial performance to outsiders. Such statements are used for filing income taxes, obtaining credit from lenders, and reporting results to the firm's stockholders. They become the basis for the information provided in the official corporate **annual report**, a summary of the firm's financial information, products, and growth plans for owners and potential investors. While frequently presented between slick, glossy covers prepared by major advertising firms, the single most important component of an annual report is the signature of a certified public accountant attesting that the required financial statements are an accurate reflection of the underlying financial condition of the firm. Financial statements meeting these conditions are termed *audited*. The primary external users of audited accounting information are government agencies, stockholders and potential investors, and lenders, suppliers, and employees.

During the global financial crisis, it turns out that Greece had been engaging in deceptive accounting practices, with the help of U.S. investment banks. Greece used financial techniques to hide massive amounts of debt from its public balance sheets. Eventually, the markets figured out the country might not be able to pay off its creditors. The European Union and the International Monetary Fund came up with a plan to give Greece some credit relief, but tied to this was the message to "get your financial house in order." The European problem was often referred to as the PIGS. This referred to Portugal, Italy, Ireland, Greece, and Spain—all of which were having debt problems. The PIGS caused cracks in the European Monetary Union. While Germany demanded austerity, others wanted more growth-oriented strategies. By the middle of 2015, Europe was pursuing more growth strategies but the PIGS were still stuck in the mud, except for Ireland, which was making better progress than the others. For its part, Greece elected a new left-wing government that promised to renegotiate its loans tied to austerity as it claimed the restrictions placed on it were keeping it from growing its economy and generating the revenue to pay off the loans. In many ways Greece's new aggressive approach alienated many of its lenders, and there was talk of the country exiting the Eurozone. Time will tell what will be the end result.

To top this off, the *New York Times* reported that many states, such as Illinois and California, have the same problems as the PIGS—debt overload. These states have "budgets that will not balance, accounting that masks debt, the use of derivatives to plug holes, and armies of retired public workers who are counting on pension benefits that are proving harder and harder to pay." Fortunately for California, by the middle of 2015, it was making better progress than Illinois. Clearly, the financial crisis will have some lasting effects that need clear accounting solutions.[4]

Financial statements evaluate the return on stockholders' investment and the overall quality of the firm's management team. As a result, poor performance, as documented in the

The annual report is a summary of the firm's financial information, products, and growth plans for owners and potential investors. Many investors look at a firm's annual report to determine how well the company is doing financially.
© pandpstock001/Getty Images, RF

Sustainability measurements might soon become part of annual reports. Investors are demanding information from companies about their sustainability efforts and how environmental regulations will affect costs of operations. As sustainability concerns and the threat of climate change increase, some predict that environmental metrics will become part of generally accepted accounting principles.

ExxonMobil Corp. made headlines with its decision to publish a report explaining to investors how environmental regulation will affect the costs of drilling oil and gas. These costs are considered risks by the organization because they will likely increase the price of oil and gas, which impacts shareholders. ExxonMobil estimates that by 2040 the costs of environmental regulation in developed nations such as the United States and the European Union will cost the company $80 per ton of oil and gas.

ExxonMobil's decision to disclose the costs of environmental risks is a breakthrough for the industry. Although the Securities and Exchange Commission requires standardized annual reports to include some data of how climate change can affect earnings, this information is often minimal. More than one-third of insurance companies, for instance, do not disclose climate-change risk in their reports. However, as investors demand more disclosure, global firms are beginning to comply. More than 80 percent of firms on the London Stock Exchange and Deutsche Börse release this information.

Organizational initiatives have been developed to provide guidance for organizations in sustainability reporting. The Global Reporting Initiative, for instance, provides measurements for standalone reports. The Climate Disclosures Standards Board collaborates with business professionals and accountants to develop a global framework for sustainability disclosure in mainstream reports.[5]

Discussion Questions

1. Why are investors demanding more environmental information from companies?

2. How does regulation affect ExxonMobil's operational risk?

3. How might environmental metrics be incorporated into generally accepted accounting principles?

> ## Many view accounting as a primary business language.

---

financial statements, often results in changes in top management. Potential investors study the financial statements in a firm's annual report to determine whether the company meets their investment requirements and whether the returns from a given firm are likely to compare favorably with other similar companies.

As one of the biggest banks in the United States, Wells Fargo specializes in banking, mortgage, and financial services. The data it provides can be used in financial statements.
© Kim White/Bloomberg/Getty Images

Banks and other lenders look at financial statements to determine a company's ability to meet current and future debt obligations if a loan or credit is granted. To determine this ability, a short-term lender examines a firm's cash flow to assess its ability to repay a loan quickly with cash generated from sales. A long-term lender is more interested in the company's profitability and indebtedness to other lenders.

Labor unions and employees use financial statements to establish reasonable expectations for salary and other benefit requests. Just as firms experiencing record profits are likely to face added pressure to increase employee wages, so too are employees unlikely to grant employers wage and benefit concessions without considerable evidence of financial distress.

LO 14-2 Demonstrate the accounting process.

THE ACCOUNTING PROCESS

Many view accounting as a primary business language. It is of little use, however, unless you know how to "speak" it. Fortunately, the fundamentals—the accounting equation and the

assets a firm's economic resources, or items of value that it owns, such as cash, inventory, land, equipment, buildings, and other tangible and intangible things.

liabilities debts that a firm owes to others.

owners' equity equals assets minus liabilities and reflects historical values.

accounting equation assets equal liabilities plus owners' equity.

double-entry bookkeeping a system of recording and classifying business transactions that maintains the balance of the accounting equation.

double-entry bookkeeping system—are not difficult to learn. These two concepts serve as the starting point for all currently accepted accounting principles.

The Accounting Equation

Accountants are concerned with reporting an organization's assets, liabilities, and owners' equity. To help illustrate these concepts, consider a hypothetical floral shop called Anna's Flowers, owned by Anna Rodriguez. A firm's economic resources, or items of value that it owns, represent its **assets**—cash, inventory, land, equipment, buildings, and other tangible and intangible things. The assets of Anna's Flowers include counters, refrigerated display cases, flowers, decorations, vases, cards, and other gifts, as well as something known as "goodwill," which in this case is Anna's reputation for preparing and delivering beautiful floral arrangements on a timely basis. **Liabilities**, on the other hand, are debts the firm owes to others. Among the liabilities of Anna's Flowers are a loan from the Small Business Administration and money owed to flower suppliers and other creditors for items purchased. The **owners' equity** category contains all of the money that has ever been contributed to the company that never has to be paid back. The funds can come from investors who have given money or assets to the company, or it can come from past profitable operations. In the case of Anna's Flowers, if Anna were to sell off, or liquidate, her business, any money left over after selling all the shop's assets and paying off its liabilities would comprise her owners' equity. The relationship among assets, liabilities, and owners' equity is a fundamental concept in accounting and is known as the **accounting equation:**

$$\text{Assets} = \text{Liabilities} + \text{Owners' equity}$$

Double-Entry Bookkeeping

Double-entry bookkeeping is a system of recording and classifying business transactions in separate accounts in order to maintain the balance of the accounting equation. Returning to Anna's Flowers, suppose Anna buys $325 worth of roses on credit from the Antique Rose Emporium to fill a wedding order. When she records this transaction, she will list the $325 as a liability or a debt to a supplier. At the same time, however, she will also record $325 worth of roses as an asset in an account known as "inventory." Because the assets and liabilities are on different sides of the accounting equation, Anna's accounts increase in total size (by $325) but remain in balance:

$$\text{Assets} = \text{Liabilities} + \text{Owners' equity}$$
$$\$325 = \$325$$

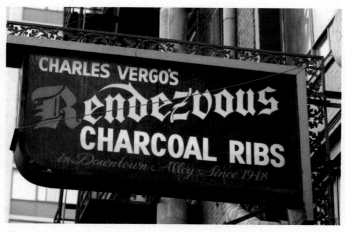

The owners' equity portion of a company's balance sheet, such as that of Rendezvous Barbecue in Memphis, Tennessee, includes the money the company's owners have put into the firm.
© Bob Fila/MCT/Newscom

Thus, to keep the accounting equation in balance, each business transaction must be recorded in two separate accounts.

In the final analysis, all business transactions are classified as assets, liabilities, or owners' equity. However, most organizations further break down these three accounts to provide more specific information about a transaction. For example, assets may be broken down into specific categories such as cash, inventory, and equipment, while liabilities may include bank loans, supplier credit, and other debts.

Figure 14.2 shows how Anna used the double-entry bookkeeping system to account for all of the transactions that took place in her first month of business. These transactions include her initial investment of $2,500, the loan from the Small Business Administration, purchases of equipment and inventory, and the purchase of roses on credit. In her first month of business, Anna generated revenues of $2,000 by selling $1,500 worth of inventory. Thus, she deducts, or (in accounting notation that is appropriate for assets) *credits,* $1,500 from inventory and adds, or *debits,* $2,000 to the cash account. The difference between Anna's $2,000 cash inflow and her $1,500 outflow is represented by a credit to owners' equity, because it is money that belongs to her as the owner of the flower shop.

The Accounting Cycle

In any accounting system, financial data typically pass through a four-step procedure sometimes called the **accounting cycle**. The steps include examining source documents, recording transactions in an accounting journal, posting recorded transactions, and preparing financial statements. Figure 14.3 shows how Anna works through them. Traditionally, all of these steps were performed using paper, pencils, and erasers (lots of erasers!), but today the process is often fully computerized.

Step One: Examine Source Documents

Like all good managers, Anna Rodriguez begins the accounting cycle by gathering and examining source documents—checks, credit card receipts, sales slips, and other related evidence concerning specific transactions.

Step Two: Record Transactions

Next, Anna records each financial transaction in a **journal**, which is basically just a time-ordered list of account transactions. While most businesses keep a general journal in which all transactions are recorded, some classify transactions into specialized journals for specific types of transaction accounts.

Step Three: Post Transactions

Anna next transfers the information from her journal into a **ledger**, a book or computer program with separate files for each account. This process is known as *posting*. At the end of the accounting period (usually yearly, but occasionally quarterly or monthly), Anna prepares a *trial balance*, a summary of the balances of all the accounts in the general ledger. If, upon totalling, the trial balance doesn't balance (that is, the accounting equation is not in balance), Anna or her accountant must look for mistakes (typically an error in one or more of the ledger entries) and correct them. If the trial balance is correct, the accountant can then begin to prepare the financial statements.

Step Four: Prepare Financial Statements

The information from the trial balance is also used to prepare the company's financial statements. In the case of public corporations and certain other organizations, a CPA must *attest,* or certify, that the organization followed generally accepted accounting principles in preparing the financial statements. When these statements have been completed, the organization's books are "closed," and the accounting cycle begins anew for the next accounting period.

FINANCIAL STATEMENTS

The end result of the accounting process is a series of financial statements. The income statement, the balance sheet, and the statement of cash flows are the best-known examples of financial statements. They are provided to stockholders and potential investors in a firm's annual report as well as to other relevant outsiders such as creditors, government agencies, and the Internal Revenue Service.

It is important to recognize that not all financial statements follow precisely the same format. The fact that different organizations generate income in different ways suggests that when it comes to financial statements, one size definitely does not fit all. Manufacturing firms, service providers, and nonprofit

accounting cycle the four-step procedure of an accounting system: examining source documents, recording transactions in an accounting journal, posting recorded transactions, and preparing financial statements.

journal a time-ordered list of account transactions.

ledger a book or computer file with separate sections for each account.

FIGURE 14.2
The Accounting Equation and Double-Entry Bookkeeping for Anna's Flowers

	Assets			=	Liabilities	+	Owners' Equity
	Cash	Equipment	Inventory		Debts to suppliers	Loans	Equity
Cash invested by Anna	$2,500.00						$2,500.00
Loan from SBA	$5,000.00					$5,000.00	
Purchase of furnishings	−$3,000.00	$3,000.00					
Purchase of inventory	−$2,000.00		$2,000.00				
Purchase of roses			$3,325.00		$3,325.00		
First month sales	$2,000.00		−$1,500.00				$500.00
Totals	$4,500.00	$3,000.00	$8,325.00		$3,325.00	$5,000.00	$3,000.00
	$8,325			=	$5,325	+	$3,000
	$8,325 Assets			=	$8,325 (Liabilities + Owners' Equity)		

FIGURE 14.3
The Accounting Process for Anna's Flowers

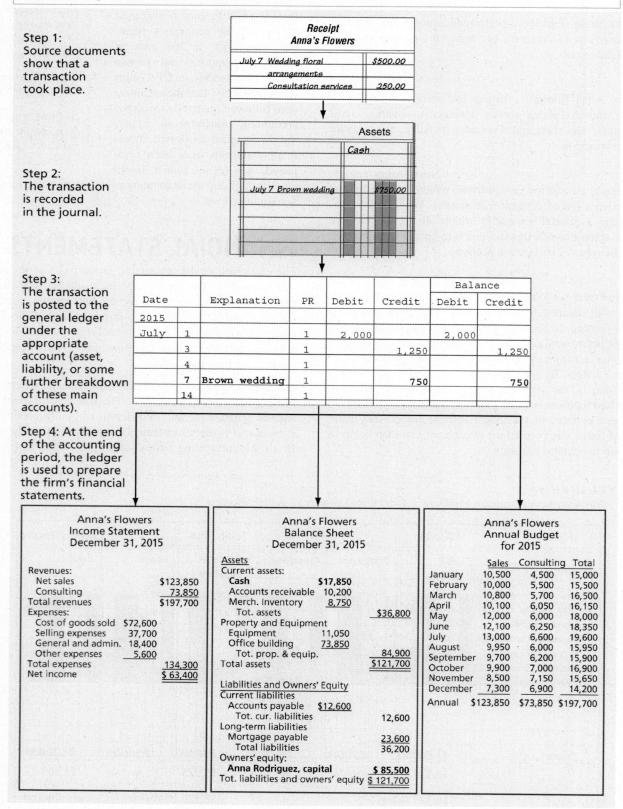

Step 1:
Source documents show that a transaction took place.

Receipt
Anna's Flowers

July 7 Wedding floral arrangements	$500.00
Consultation services	250.00

Step 2:
The transaction is recorded in the journal.

Assets

Cash

July 7 Brown wedding $750.00

Step 3:
The transaction is posted to the general ledger under the appropriate account (asset, liability, or some further breakdown of these main accounts).

	Date		Explanation	PR	Debit	Credit	Balance Debit	Balance Credit
	2015							
	July	1		1	2,000		2,000	
		3		1		1,250		1,250
		4		1				
		7	Brown wedding	1		750		750
		14		1				

Step 4: At the end of the accounting period, the ledger is used to prepare the firm's financial statements.

Anna's Flowers
Income Statement
December 31, 2015

Revenues:		
Net sales		$123,850
Consulting		73,850
Total revenues		$197,700
Expenses:		
Cost of goods sold	$72,600	
Selling expenses	37,700	
General and admin.	18,400	
Other expenses	5,600	
Total expenses		134,300
Net income		$ 63,400

Anna's Flowers
Balance Sheet
December 31, 2015

Assets
Current assets:

Cash	**$17,850**	
Accounts receivable	10,200	
Merch. Inventory	8,750	
Tot. assets		$36,800

Property and Equipment

Equipment	11,050	
Office building	73,850	
Tot. prop. & equip.		84,900
Total assets		$121,700

Liabilities and Owners' Equity
Current liabilities

Accounts payable	$12,600	
Tot. cur. liabilities		12,600
Long-term liabilities		
Mortgage payable		23,600
Total liabilities		36,200

Owners' equity:

Anna Rodriguez, capital		**$ 85,500**
Tot. liabilities and owners' equity		$ 121,700

Anna's Flowers
Annual Budget
for 2015

	Sales	Consulting	Total
January	10,500	4,500	15,000
February	10,000	5,500	15,500
March	10,800	5,700	16,500
April	10,100	6,050	16,150
May	12,000	6,000	18,000
June	12,100	6,250	18,350
July	13,000	6,600	19,600
August	9,950	6,000	15,950
September	9,700	6,200	15,900
October	9,900	7,000	16,900
November	8,500	7,150	15,650
December	7,300	6,900	14,200
Annual	$123,850	$73,850	$197,700

organizations each use a different set of accounting principles or rules upon which the public accounting profession has agreed. As we have already mentioned, these are sometimes referred to as *generally accepted accounting principles (GAAP)*. Each country has a different set of rules that the businesses within that country are required to use for their accounting process and financial statements. However, a number of countries have adopted a standard set of accounting principles known as International Financial Reporting Standards. The United States has discussed adopting these standards to create a more standardized system of reporting for global investors. Moreover, as is the case in many other disciplines, certain concepts have more than one name. For example, *sales* and *revenues* are often interchanged, as are *profits, income,* and *earnings.* Table 14.2 lists a few common equivalent terms that should help you decipher their meaning in accounting statements.

> **LO 14-3** Examine the various components of an income statement in order to evaluate a firm's "bottom line."

The Income Statement

The question "What's the bottom line?" derives from the income statement, where the bottom line shows the overall profit or loss of the company after taxes. Thus, the **income statement** is a financial report that shows an organization's profitability over a period of time, be that a month, quarter, or year. By its very design, the income statement offers one of the clearest possible pictures of the company's overall revenues and the costs incurred in generating those revenues. Other names

for the income statement include profit and loss (P&L) statement or operating statement. A sample income statement with line-by-line explanations is presented in Table 14.3, while Table 14.4 presents the income statement of Microsoft. The income statement indicates the firm's profitability or income (the bottom line), which is derived by subtracting the firm's expenses from its revenues.

Revenue **Revenue** is the total amount of money received (or promised) from the sale of goods or services, as well as from other business activities such as the rental of property and investments. Nonbusiness entities typically obtain revenues through donations from individuals and/or grants from governments and private foundations. One of the controversies in accounting has been when a business should recognize revenue. For instance, should an organization book revenue during a project or after the project is completed? Differences in revenue recognition have caused similar organizations to book different accounting results. A proposed rule states that firms should book revenue when "it satisfie[s] a performance obligation by transferring a promised good or service to a customer."[6]

For most manufacturing and retail concerns, the next major item included in the income statement is the **cost of goods sold**, the amount of money the firm spent (or promised to spend) to buy and/or produce the products it sold during the accounting period. This figure may be calculated as follows:

$$\text{Cost of goods sold} = \text{Beginning inventory} + \text{Interim purchases} - \text{Ending inventory}$$

Let's say that Anna's Flowers began an accounting period with an inventory of goods for which it paid $5,000. During the period, Anna bought another $4,000 worth of goods, giving the shop a total inventory available for sale of $9,000. If, at the end of the accounting period, Anna's inventory was worth $5,500, the cost of goods sold during the period would have been $3,500 ($5,000 + $4,000 − $5,500 = $3,500). If Anna had total revenues of $10,000 over the same period of time, subtracting the cost of goods sold ($3,500) from the total revenues of $10,000 yields the store's **gross income** or **profit** (revenues minus the cost of goods sold required to generate the revenues): $6,500. The same process occurs at Microsoft. As indicated in Table 14.4, the cost of goods sold was more than $20.25 billion in 2013. Notice that Microsoft calls it cost of revenue, rather than cost of goods sold.

▼ **TABLE 14.2** Equivalent Terms in Accounting

Term	Equivalent Term
Revenues	Sales
	Goods or services sold
Gross profit	Gross income
	Gross earnings
Operating income	Operating profit
	Earnings before interest and taxes (EBIT)
	Income before interest and taxes (IBIT)
Income before taxes (IBT)	Earnings before taxes (EBT)
	Profit before taxes (PBT)
Net income (NI)	Earnings after taxes (EAT)
	Profit after taxes (PAT)
Income available to common stockholders	Earnings available to common stockholders

▼ **TABLE 14.3** Sample Income Statement

The following exhibit presents a sample income statement with all the terms defined and explained.

Company Name for the Year Ended December 31	
Revenues (sales)	Total dollar amount of products sold (includes income from other business services such as rental-lease income and interest income).
Less: Cost of goods sold	The cost of producing the goods and services, including the cost of labor and raw materials as well as other expenses associated with production.
Gross profit	The income available after paying all expenses of production.
Less: Selling and administrative expense	The cost of promoting, advertising, and selling products as well as the overhead costs of managing the company. This includes the cost of management and corporate staff. One non-cash expense included in this category is depreciation, which approximates the decline in the value of plant and equipment assets due to use over time. In most accounting statements, depreciation is not separated from selling and administrative expenses. However, financial analysts usually create statements that include this expense.
Income before interest and taxes (operating income or EBIT)	This line represents all income left over after operating expenses have been deducted. This is sometimes referred to as operating income since it represents all income after the expenses of operations have been accounted for. Occasionally, this is referred to as EBIT, or earnings before interest and taxes.
Less: Interest expense	Interest expense arises as a cost of borrowing money. This is a financial expense rather than an operating expense and is listed separately. As the amount of debt and the cost of debt increase, so will the interest expense. This covers the cost of both short-term and long-term borrowing.
Income before taxes (earnings before taxes—EBT)	The firm will pay a tax on this amount. This is what is left of revenues after subtracting all operating costs, depreciation costs, and interest costs.
Less: Taxes	The tax rate is specified in the federal tax code.
Net income	This is the amount of income left after taxes. The firm may decide to retain all or a portion of the income for reinvestment in new assets. Whatever it decides not to keep it will usually pay out in dividends to its stockholders.
Less: Preferred dividends	If the company has preferred stockholders, they are first in line for dividends. That is one reason why their stock is called "preferred."
Income to common stockholders	This is the income left for the common stockholders. If the company has a good year, there may be a lot of income available for dividends. If the company has a bad year, income could be negative. The common stockholders are the ultimate owners' and risk takers. They have the potential for very high or very poor returns since they get whatever is left after all other expenses.
Earnings per share	Earnings per share is found by taking the income available to the common stockholders and dividing by the number of shares of common stock outstanding. This is income generated by the company for each share of common stock.

Expenses **Expenses** are the costs incurred in the day-to-day operations of an organization. Three common expense accounts shown on income statements are (1) selling, general, and administrative expenses; (2) research, development, and engineering expenses; and (3) interest expenses (remember that the costs directly attributable to selling goods or services are included in the cost of goods sold). Selling expenses include advertising and sales salaries. General and administrative expenses include salaries of executives and their staff and the costs of owning and maintaining the general office. Research and development costs include scientific, engineering, and

▼ **TABLE 14.4** Microsoft Corporation Consolidated Statement of Earnings (in millions, except share per data)

Year Ended June 30	2013	2012	2011
Revenue	$77,849	$73,723	$69,943
Cost of revenue	20,249	17,530	15,577
Gross profit	57,600	56,193	54,366
Operating expenses:			
Research and development	10,411	9,811	9,043
Sales and marketing	15,276	13,857	13,940
General and administrative	5,149	4,569	4,222
Goodwill impairment	0	6,193	0
Total operating expenses	30,836	34,430	27,205

(Continued)

Year Ended June 30	2013	2012	2011
Operating income	26,764	21,763	27,161
Other income	288	504	910
Income before income taxes	27,052	22,267	28,071
Provision for income taxes	5,189	5,289	4,921
Net income	$21,863	$16,978	$23,150
Earnings per share:			
Basic	$ 2.61	$ 2.02	$ 2.73
Diluted	$ 2.58	$ 2.00	$ 2.69
Weighted average shares outstanding:			
Basic	8,375	8,396	8,490
Diluted	8,470	8,506	8,593
Cash dividends declared per common share	$ 0.92	$ 0.80	$ 0.64

Source: Microsoft Corporation 2013 Annual Report.

marketing personnel and the equipment and information used to design and build prototypes and samples. Interest expenses include the direct costs of borrowing money.

The number and type of expense accounts vary from organization to organization. Included in the general and administrative category is a special type of expense known as **depreciation**, the process of spreading the costs of long-lived assets such as buildings and equipment over the total number of accounting periods in which they are expected to be used. Consider a manufacturer that purchases a $100,000 machine expected to last about 10 years. Rather than showing an expense of $100,000 in the first year and no expense for that equipment over the next nine years, the manufacturer is allowed to report depreciation expenses of $10,000 per year in each of the next 10 years because that better matches the cost of the machine to the years the machine is used. Each time this depreciation is "written off" as an expense, the book value of the machine is also reduced by $10,000. The fact that the equipment has a zero value on the firm's balance sheet when it is fully depreciated (in this case, after 10 years) does not necessarily mean that it can no longer be used or is economically worthless. Indeed, in some industries, machines used every day have been reported as having no book value whatsoever for more than 30 years.

Net Income **Net income** (or net earnings) is the total profit (or loss) after all expenses including taxes have been deducted from revenue. Generally, accountants divide profits into individual sections such as operating income and earnings before interest and taxes. Microsoft, for example, lists earnings before income taxes, net earnings, and earnings per share of outstanding stock (see Table 14.4). Like most companies, Microsoft presents not only the current year's results but also the previous two years' income statements to permit comparison of performance from one period to another.

Temporary Nature of the Income Statement Accounts Companies record their operational activities in the revenue and expense accounts during an accounting period. Gross profit, earnings before interest and taxes, and net income are the results of calculations made from the revenues and expenses accounts; they are not actual accounts. At the end of each accounting period, the dollar amounts in all the revenue and expense accounts are moved into an account called "Retained Earnings," one of the owners' equity accounts. Revenues increase owners' equity, while expenses decrease it. The resulting change in the owners' equity account is exactly equal to the net income. This shifting of dollar values from the revenue and expense accounts allows the firm to begin the next accounting period with zero balances in those accounts. Zeroing out the balances enables a company to count how much it has sold and how many expenses have been incurred during a period of time. The basic accounting equation (Assets = Liabilities + Owners' equity) will not balance until the revenue and expense account balances have been moved or "closed out" to the owners' equity account.

One final note about income statements: You may remember that corporations may choose to make cash payments called dividends to shareholders out of their net earnings. When a corporation elects to pay dividends, it decreases the cash account (in the assets category of the balance sheet) as well as a capital account (in the owners' equity category of the balance sheet). During any period of time, the owners' equity account may change because of the sale of stock (or contributions/withdrawals by owners), the net income or loss, or the dividends paid.

Royal Dutch Shell is the world's second largest company with approximately $460 billion in revenue.
© *Agencja Fotograficzna Caro/Alamy*

ACCOUNTING FIRM KEEPS EMPLOYEES MOVING

During tax season, certified public accountants (CPAs) work 12- to 13-hour days. This leaves little time for exercise. However, Indiana-based CPA firm Dauby O'Connor & Zaleski LLC (DOZ) has joined a wellness program to ensure its busy CPAs get the movement they need to stay healthy. The improvement in health and mental alertness can also pay dividends in productivity and accounting. DOZ has adopted the MOVband wristband so employees can track their physical activity. Employees are also encouraged to adopt the MOVABLE challenge of trying to move five miles each day. Rather than measuring just steps, the wristband clocks all of the wearer's movements to provide a holistic picture of how much activity the wearer is exerting. The purpose is to keep moving and inspire the CPAs to engage in activities collectively, even during the busiest of times—such as taking group walks during lunch. Those who are able to meet goals are rewarded with prizes. Employees at DOZ are so motivated that the company has been listed on the *Indianapolis Star* Top Work Places 2014.[7]

LO 14-4 Interpret a company's balance sheet to determine its current financial position.

The Balance Sheet

The second basic financial statement is the **balance sheet**, which presents a "snapshot" of an organization's financial position at a given moment. As such, the balance sheet indicates what the organization owns or controls and the various sources of the funds used to pay for these assets, such as bank debt or owners' equity.

The balance sheet takes its name from its reliance on the accounting equation: Assets *must* equal liabilities plus owners' equity. Table 14.5 provides a sample balance sheet with line-by-line explanations. Unlike the income statement, the balance sheet does not represent the result of transactions completed over a specified accounting period. Instead, the balance sheet

> ["The balance sheet takes its name from its reliance on the accounting equation: Assets *must* equal liabilities plus owners' equity."]

▼ **TABLE 14.5** Sample Balance Sheet

The following exhibit presents a balance sheet in word form with each item defined or explained.

Typical Company	December 31
Assets	This is the major category for all physical, monetary, or intangible goods that have some dollar value.
Current assets	Assets that are either cash or are expected to be turned into cash within the next 12 months.
Cash	Cash or checking accounts.
Marketable securities	Short-term investments in securities that can be converted to cash quickly (liquid assets).
Accounts receivable	Cash due from customers in payment for goods received. These arise from sales made on credit.
Inventory	Finished goods ready for sale, goods in the process of being finished, or raw materials used in the production of goods.
Prepaid expense	A future expense item that has already been paid, such as insurance premiums or rent.
Total current assets	The sum of the above accounts.
Fixed assets	Assets that are long term in nature and have a minimum life expectancy that exceeds one year.
Investments	Assets held as investments rather than assets owned for the production process. Most often the assets include small ownership interests in other companies.
Gross property, plant, and equipment	Land, buildings, and other fixed assets listed at original cost.
Less: Accumulated depreciation	The accumulated expense deductions applied to all plant and equipment over their life. Land may not be depreciated. The total amount represents in general the decline in value as equipment gets older and wears out. The maximum amount that can be deducted is set by the U.S. Federal Tax Code and varies by type of asset.
Net property, plant, and equipment	Gross property, plant, and equipment minus the accumulated depreciation. This amount reflects the book value of the fixed assets and not their value if sold.

(Continued)

▼ **TABLE 14.5** Sample Balance Sheet *(continued)*

Typical Company	December 31
Other assets	Any other asset that is long term and does not fit into the above categories. It could be patents or trademarks.
Total assets	The sum of all the asset values.
Liabilities and Stockholders' Equity	This is the major category. Liabilities refer to all indebtedness and loans of both a long-term and short-term nature. Stockholders' equity refers to all money that has been contributed to the company over the life of the firm by the owners'.
Current liabilities	Short-term debt expected to be paid off within the next 12 months.
Accounts payable	Money owed to suppliers for goods ordered. Firms usually have between 30 and 90 days to pay this account, depending on industry norms.
Wages payable	Money owned to employees for hours worked or salary. If workers receive checks every two weeks, the amount owed should be no more than two weeks' pay.
Taxes payable	Firms are required to pay corporate taxes quarterly. This refers to taxes owed based on earnings estimates for the quarter.
Notes payable	Short-term loans from banks or other lenders.
Other current liabilities	The other short-term debts that do not fit into the above categories.
Total current liabilities	The sum of the above accounts.
Long-term liabilities	All long-term debt that will not be paid off in the next 12 months.
Long-term debt	Loans of more than one year from banks, pension funds, insurance companies, or other lenders. These loans often take the form of bonds, which are securities that may be bought and sold in bond markets.
Deferred income taxes	This is a liability owed to the government but not due within one year.
Other liabilities	Any other long-term debt that does not fit the above two categories.
Stockholders' equity	The following three categories are the owners' investment in the company.
Common stock	The tangible evidence of ownership is a security called common stock. The par value is stated value and does not indicate the company's worth.
Capital in excess of par (a.k.a. contributed capital)	When shares of stock were sold to the owners, they were recorded at the price at the time of the original sale. If the price paid was $10 per share, the extra $9 per share would show up in this account at 100,000 shares times $9 per share, or $900,000.
Retained earnings	The total amount of earnings the company has made during its life and not paid out to its stockholders as dividends. This account represents the owners' reinvestment of earnings into company assets rather than payments of cash dividends. This account does not represent cash.
Total stockholders' equity	This is the sum of the above equity accounts representing the owners' total investment in the company.
Total liabilities and stockholders' equity	The total short-term and long-term debt of the company plus the owners' total investment. This combined amount *must* equal total assets.

is, by definition, an accumulation of all financial transactions conducted by an organization since its founding. Following long-established traditions, items on the balance sheet are listed on the basis of their original cost less accumulated depreciation, rather than their present values.

Balance sheets are often presented in two different formats. The traditional balance sheet format placed the organization's assets on the left side and its liabilities and owners' equity on the right. More recently, a vertical format, with assets on top followed by liabilities and owners' equity, has gained wide acceptance. Microsoft's balance sheet for 2012 and 2013 is presented in Table 14.6. In the sections that follow, we'll briefly describe the basic items found on the balance sheet; we'll take a closer look at a number of these in Chapter 16.

Assets All asset accounts are listed in descending order of *liquidity*—that is, how quickly each could be turned into cash. **Current assets**, also called short-term assets, are those that are used or converted into cash within the course of a calendar year. Cash is followed by temporary investments, accounts receivable, and inventory, in that order. **Accounts receivable** refers to money owed the company by its clients or customers who have promised to pay for the products at a later date. Accounts receivable usually includes an allowance for bad debts that management does not expect to collect. The bad-debts adjustment is

These machines from Caterpillar would be considered long-term assets on the balance sheet.
© surveyorphoto/Alamy

normally based on historical collections experience and is deducted from the accounts receivable balance to present a more realistic view of the payments likely to be received in the future, called net receivables. Inventory may be held in the form of raw materials, work-in-progress, or finished goods ready for delivery.

Long-term or fixed assets represent a commitment of organizational funds of at least one year. Items classified as fixed include long-term investments, plant and equipment, and intangible assets, such as corporate "goodwill," or reputation, as well as patents and trademarks.

Liabilities As seen in the accounting equation, total assets must be financed either through borrowing (liabilities) or through owner investments (owners' equity). **Current liabilities** include a firm's financial obligations to short-term creditors, which must be repaid within one year, while long-term liabilities have longer repayment terms. **Accounts payable** represents amounts owed to suppliers for goods and services purchased with credit. For example, if you buy gas with a BP credit card, the purchase represents an account payable for you (and an account receivable for BP). Other liabilities include wages earned by employees but not yet paid and taxes owed to the government. Occasionally, these accounts are consolidated into an **accrued expenses** account, representing all unpaid financial obligations incurred by the organization.

Owners' Equity Owners' equity includes the owners' contributions to the organization along with income earned by the organization and retained to finance continued growth and development. If the organization were to sell off all of its assets and pay off all of its liabilities, any remaining funds would belong to the owners. Not surprisingly, the accounts listed as owners' equity on a balance sheet may differ dramatically from company to company. Corporations sell stock to investors, who then become the owners of the firm. Many corporations issue two, three, or even more different classes of common and preferred stock, each with different dividend payments and/ or voting rights. Google has three

▼ **TABLE 14.6** Microsoft Corporation Consolidated Balance Sheets (in millions, except per share data)

June 30	2013	2012
Assets		
Current assets:		
Cash and cash equivalents	$ 3,804	$ 6,938
Short-term investments (including securities loaned of $579 and $785)	73,218	56,102
Total cash, cash equivalents, and short-term investments	77,022	63,040
Accounts receivable, net of allowance for doubtful accounts of $336 and $389	17,486	15,780
Inventories	1,938	1,137
Deferred income taxes	1,632	2,035
Other	3,388	3,092
Total current assets	101,466	85,084
Property and equipment, net of accumulated depreciation of $12,513 and $10,962	9,991	8,269
Equity and other investments	10,844	9,776
Goodwill	14,655	13,452
Intangible assets, net	3,083	3,170
Other long-term assets	2,392	1,520
Total assets	$142,431	$121,271
Liabilities and stockholders' equity		
Current liabilities:		
Accounts payable	$ 4,828	$ 4,175
Current portion of long-term debt	2,999	1,231
Accrued compensation	4,117	3,875
Income taxes	592	789

(Continued)

June 30	2013	2012
Liabilities and stockholders' equity		
Short-term unearned revenue	20,639	18,653
Securities lending payable	645	814
Other	3,597	3,151
Total current liabilities	37,417	32,688
Long-term debt	12,601	10,713
Long-term unearned revenue	1,760	1,406
Deferred income taxes	1,709	1,893
Other long-term liabilities	10,000	8,208
Total liabilities	63,487	54,908
Commitments and contingencies		
Stockholders' equity:		
Common stock and paid-in capital—shares authorized 24,000; outstanding 8,328 and 8,381	67,306	65,797
Retained earnings (deficit)	9,895	(856)
Accumulated other comprehensive Income	1,743	1,422
Total stockholders' equity	78,944	66,363
Total liabilities and stockholders' equity	$142,431	$121,271

▼ **TABLE 14.7** Consolidated Statements of Cash Flows (in millions)

Year Ended June 30	2013	2012	2011
Operations			
Net income	$ 21,863	$ 16,978	$ 23,150
Adjustments to reconcile net income to net cash from operations:			
Goodwill impairment	0	6,193	0
Depreciation, amortization, and other	3,755	2,967	2,766
Stock-based compensation expense	2,406	2,244	2,166
Net recognized losses (gains) on investments and derivatives	80	(200)	(362)
Excess tax benefits from stock-based compensation	(209)	(93)	(17)
Deferred income taxes	(19)	954	2
Deferral of unearned revenue	44,253	36,104	31,227
Recognition of unearned revenue	(41,921)	(33,347)	(28,935)
Changes in operating assets and liabilities:			
Accounts receivable	(1,807)	(1,156)	(1,451)
Inventories	(802)	184	(561)
Other current assets	(129)	493	(1,259)
Other long-term assets	(478)	(248)	62
Accounts payable	537	(31)	58
Other current liabilities	146	410	(1,146)
Other long-term liabilities	1,158	174	1,294
Net cash from operations	28,833	31,626	26,994

(Continued)

classes of stock, with the class B stock having more voting rights than class A shares. These are sometimes called founder's shares and allow the founders to maintain control over the company even though they do not own the majority of the shares. Ford Motor has the same type of voting structure. Because each type of stock issued represents a different claim on the organization, each must be represented by a separate owners' equity account, called contributed capital.

LO 14-5 Analyze the statement of cash flows to evaluate the increase and decrease in a company's cash balance.

The Statement of Cash Flows

The third primary financial statement is called the **statement of cash flows**, which explains how the company's cash changed from the beginning of the accounting period to the end. Cash, of course, is an asset shown on the balance sheet, which provides a snapshot of the firm's financial position at one point in time. However, many investors and other users of financial statements want more information about the cash flowing into and out of the firm than is provided on the balance sheet in order to better understand the company's financial health. The statement of cash flows takes the cash balance from one year's balance sheet and compares it with the next while providing detail about how the firm used the cash. Table 14.7 presents Microsoft's statements of cash flows.

The change in cash is explained through details in three categories: cash from (used for) operating activities, cash from (used for) investing activities, and cash from (used for) financing activities. *Cash from operating activities* is calculated by combining the changes in the revenue accounts, expense accounts, current

▼ **TABLE 14.7** Consolidated Statements of Cash Flows (in millions) *(Continued)*

Year Ended June 30	2013	2012	2011
Financing			
Short-term debt repayments, maturities of 90 days or less, net	0	0	(186)
Proceeds from issuance of debt	4,883	0	6,960
Repayments of debt	(1,346)	0	(814)
Common stock issued	931	1,913	2,422
Common stock repurchased	(5,360)	(5,029)	(11,555)
Common stock cash dividends paid	(7,455)	(6,385)	(5,180)
Excess tax benefits from stock-based compensation	209	93	17
Other	(10)	0	(40)
Net cash used in financing	(8,148)	(9,408)	(8,376)
Investing			
Additions to property and equipment	(4,257)	(2,305)	(2,355)
Acquisition of companies, net of cash acquired, and purchases of intangible and other assets	(1,584)	(10,112)	(71)
Purchases of investments	(75,396)	(57,250)	(35,993)
Maturities of investments	5,130	15,575	6,897
Sales of investments	52,464	29,700	15,880
Securities lending payable	(168)	(394)	1,026
Net cash used in investing	(23,811)	(24,786)	(14,616)
Effect of exchange rates on cash and cash equivalents	(8)	(104)	103
Net change in cash and cash equivalents	(3,134)	(2,672)	4,105
Cash and cash equivalents, beginning of period	6,938	9,610	5,505
Cash and cash equivalents, end of period	$ 3,804	$ 6,938	$ 9,610

asset accounts, and current liability accounts. This category of cash flows includes all the accounts on the balance sheet that relate to computing revenues and expenses for the accounting period. If this amount is a positive number, as it is for Microsoft, then the business is making extra cash that it can use to invest in increased long-term capacity or to pay off debts such as loans or bonds. A negative number may indicate a business that is in a declining position with regards to operations. Negative cash flow is not always a bad thing, however. Negative cash flow might indicate a company is in the rapid growth phase but not yet making a profit. This is often true of small-growth companies in technology and biotech.

Cash from investing activities is calculated from changes in the long-term or fixed asset accounts. If this amount is negative, as is the case with Microsoft, we can see that the company bought $4.3 billion of property and equipment. It also purchased $75 billion of investments and sold $52 billion of investments

for a total negative cash flow of $23.8 billion. A positive figure usually indicates a business that is selling off existing long-term assets and reducing its capacity for the future.

Finally, *cash from financing activities* is calculated from changes in the long-term liability accounts and the contributed capital accounts in owners' equity. If this amount is negative, the company is likely paying off long-term debt or returning contributed capital to investors. In the case of Microsoft, it sold some debt for an increase in cash of $4.88 billion, but repurchased stock and paid a dividend, which resulted in negative cash flow from financing.

RATIO ANALYSIS: ANALYZING FINANCIAL STATEMENTS

The income statement shows a company's profit or loss, while the balance sheet itemizes the value of its assets, liabilities, and owners' equity. Together, the two statements provide the means to answer two critical questions: (1) How much did the firm make or lose? and (2) How much is the firm presently worth based on historical values found on the balance sheet? **Ratio analysis**, calculations that measure an organization's financial health, brings the complex information from the income statement and balance sheet into sharper focus so that managers, lenders, owners, and other interested parties can measure and compare the organization's productivity, profitability, and financing mix with other similar entities.

As you know, a ratio is simply one number divided by another, with the result showing the relationship between the two numbers. For example, we measure fuel efficiency with miles per gallon. This is how we know that 55 mpg in a Toyota Prius is much better than the average car. Financial ratios are used to weigh and evaluate a firm's performance. An absolute value such as earnings of $70,000 or accounts receivable of

$200,000 almost never provides as much useful information as a well-constructed ratio. Whether those numbers are good or bad depends on their relation to other numbers. If a company earned $70,000 on $700,000 in sales (a 10 percent return), such an earnings level might be quite satisfactory. The president of a company earning this same $70,000 on sales of $7 million (a 1 percent return), however, should probably start looking for another job!

Ratios by themselves are not very useful. It is the relationship of the calculated ratios to both prior organizational performance and the performance of the organization's "peers," as well as its stated goals, that really matters. Remember, while the profitability, asset utilization, liquidity, debt ratios, and per share data we'll look at here can be very useful, you will never see the forest by looking only at the trees.

Profitability Ratios

Profitability ratios measure how much operating income or net income an organization is able to generate relative to its assets,

assets very productively—a key managerial failing. For its construction, the return on assets calculation requires data from both the income statement and the balance sheet.

$$\text{Return on assets} = \frac{\text{Net income (Net earnings)}}{\text{Total assets}}$$

$$= \frac{\$21,863}{\$142,431} = 15.35\%$$

In the case of Microsoft, every $1 of assets generated a return of close to 15 percent, or profits of 15.35 cents per dollar.

Stockholders are always concerned with how much money they will make on their investment, and they frequently use the return on equity ratio as one of their key performance yardsticks. **Return on equity** (also called return on investment [ROI]),

> ## Profitability ratios measure how much operating income or net income an organization is able to generate relative to its assets, owners' equity, and sales.

owners' equity, and sales. The numerator (top number) used in these examples is always the net income after taxes. Common profitability ratios include profit margin, return on assets, and return on equity. The following examples are based on the 2013 income statement and balance sheet for Microsoft, as shown in Tables 14.4 and 14.6. Except where specified, all data are expressed in millions of dollars.

The **profit margin**, computed by dividing net income by sales, shows the overall percentage of profits earned by the company. It is based solely upon data obtained from the income statement. The higher the profit margin, the better the cost controls within the company and the higher the return on every dollar of revenue. Microsoft's profit margin is calculated as follows:

$$\text{Profit margin} = \frac{\text{Net income (Net earnings)}}{\text{Sales (Total net revenues)}}$$

$$= \frac{\$21,863}{\$77,849} = 28.08\%$$

Thus, for every $1 in sales, Microsoft generated profits after taxes of 28 cents.

Return on assets, net income divided by assets, shows how much income the firm produces for every dollar invested in assets. A company with a low return on assets is probably not using its

calculated by dividing net income by owners' equity, shows how much income is generated by each $1 the owners have invested in the firm. Obviously, a low return on equity means low stockholder returns and may indicate a need for immediate managerial attention. Because some assets may have been financed with debt not contributed by the owners, the value of the owners' equity is usually considerably lower than the total value of the firm's assets. Microsoft's return on equity is calculated as follows:

$$\text{Return on equity} = \frac{\text{Net income}}{\text{Stockholders' equity}}$$

$$= \frac{\$21,863}{\$78,944} = 27.69\%$$

For every dollar invested by Microsoft stockholders, the company earned a 27.69 percent return, or 27.69 cents per dollar invested.

Asset Utilization Ratios

Asset utilization ratios measure how well a firm uses its assets to generate each $1 of sales. Obviously, companies using their assets more productively will have higher returns on assets than their less efficient competitors. Similarly, managers can use asset utilization ratios to pinpoint areas of inefficiency in their operations. These ratios (receivables turnover, inventory turnover, and total asset turnover) relate balance sheet assets to sales, which are found on the income statement.

DO "BEAR-RAID" FIRMS HELP KEEP COMPANIES HONEST?

Short selling is an investment practice that makes money off a company's decline. It involves borrowing shares of a company's stock from a broker, selling that stock, then later re-buying the same amount of stock and returning it to the broker. If the company's share price has declined in the meantime, the investor pockets the difference.

Some investors are attempting to build short selling into a business model. They look for companies engaging in misleading financial practices and prepare reports detailing their findings. They then short sell the company's stock, publish the report, and profit from the resulting drop in share price. The practice of actively trying to push down a company's stock to profit from a short sell is known as "bear-raiding." If accomplished through false accusations, bear-raiding is a form of fraud. However, bear-raid firms argue that what they are doing is different and beneficial to society because they are exposing dishonest companies that are lying to investors; the short sell profit they gain is merely payment for their socially responsible work.

For example, a Spanish Wi-Fi hotspot provider called Gowex was a rising star, with market capitalization of over $1.9 billion. A bear-raid firm called Gotham City Research published a report claiming that 90 percent of Gowex's sales were fake. Gowex declared bankruptcy, and the CEO admitted the company had been severely falsifying its financials. Bear-raid firms point to such success stories as proof of their benefit. Critics, however, argue they are corporate predators who make money at the expense of legitimate investors, citing examples where bear-raid firms have profited from accusations that were later proven false.[8]

Discussion Questions

1. Are bear-raid firms performing a socially beneficial service, or are they completely self-serving?

2. Does the threat of scrutiny from bear-raid firms provide an incentive for companies to manage and represent their finances honestly?

3. Do you believe bear-raid firms are encroaching on the territory of governmental regulators, audits, and other established methods of financial oversight? Why or why not?

The **receivables turnover**, sales divided by accounts receivable, indicates how many times a firm collects its accounts receivable in one year. It also demonstrates how quickly a firm is able to collect payments on its credit sales. Obviously, no payments means no profits. Microsoft collected its receivables 4.45 times per year, which translates to about 80 days that receivables are outstanding. This is most likely due to the trade terms they give their corporate customers.

$$\frac{\text{Receivables}}{\text{turnover}} = \frac{\text{Sales (Total net revenues)}}{\text{Receivables}}$$

$$= \frac{\$77,849}{\$17,486} = 4.45 \times$$

Inventory turnover, sales divided by total inventory, indicates how many times a firm sells and replaces its inventory over the course of a year. A high inventory turnover ratio may indicate great efficiency but may also suggest the possibility of lost sales due to insufficient stock levels. Microsoft's inventory turnover indicates that it replaced its inventory 40.17 times last year, or about every 9 days. This high inventory turnover is a reflection that Microsoft has very little physical inventory and instead downloads its Windows programs over the Internet.

$$\frac{\text{Inventory}}{\text{turnover}} = \frac{\text{Sales (Total net revenues)}}{\text{Inventory}}$$

$$= \frac{\$77,849}{\$1,938} = 40.17 \times$$

Total asset turnover, sales divided by total assets, measures how well an organization uses all of its assets in creating sales. It indicates whether a company is using its assets productively. Microsoft generated $0.55 in sales for every $1 in total corporate assets. The cause of this low total asset turnover is the $77 billion of cash that Micosoft has on its balance sheet. Cash does not produce sales dollars.

$$\frac{\text{Total asset}}{\text{turnover}} = \frac{\text{Sales (Total net revenues)}}{\text{Total assets}}$$

$$= \frac{\$77,849}{\$142,431} = 0.55 \times$$

Liquidity Ratios

Liquidity ratios compare current (short-term) assets to current liabilities to indicate the speed with which a company can turn its assets into cash to meet debts as they fall due. High liquidity ratios may satisfy a creditor's need for safety, but ratios that are too high may indicate that the organization is not using its current assets efficiently. Liquidity ratios are generally best examined in conjunction with asset utilization ratios because high turnover ratios imply that cash is flowing through an organization very quickly—a situation that dramatically reduces the need for the type of reserves measured by liquidity ratios.

The **current ratio** is calculated by dividing current assets by current liabilities. Microsoft's current ratio indicates that for every $1 of current liabilities, the firm had $2.71 of current assets on hand. The relatively high current ratio is also due to the $77 billion of cash on hand, which is part of the current asset total. If we take cash out of current assets, the numerator drops to $24,444, and the current ratio drops to 0.65.

$$\text{Current ratio} = \frac{\text{Current assets}}{\text{Current liabilities}}$$

$$= \frac{\$101,466}{\$37,417} = 2.71 \times$$

The **quick ratio** (also known as the **acid test**) is a far more stringent measure of liquidity because it eliminates inventory, the least liquid current asset. It measures how well an organization can meet its current obligations without resorting to the sale of its inventory. Because Microsoft has so little inventory ($1.9 billion out of $101.4 billion of current assets), the quick ratio is almost exactly the same as the current ratio.

$$\text{Quick ratio} = \frac{\text{Current assets} - \text{Inventory}}{\text{Current liabilities}}$$

$$= \frac{\$99,528}{\$37,417} = 2.66 \times$$

Debt Utilization Ratios

Debt utilization ratios provide information about how much debt an organization is using relative to other sources of capital, such as owners' equity. Because the use of debt carries an interest charge that must be paid regularly regardless of profitability, debt financing is much riskier than equity.

Unforeseen negative events such as recessions affect heavily indebted firms to a far greater extent than those financed exclusively with owners' equity. Because of this and other factors, the managers of most firms tend to keep debt-to-asset levels below 50 percent. However, firms in very stable and/or regulated industries, such as electric utilities, often are able to carry debt ratios well in excess of 50 percent with no ill effects.

The **debt to total assets ratio** indicates how much of the firm is financed by debt and how much by owners' equity. To find the value of Microsoft's total debt, you must add current liabilities to long-term debt and other liabilities.

$$\text{Debt to total assets} = \frac{\text{Debt (Total liabilities)}}{\text{Total assets}}$$

$$= \frac{\$63,487}{\$142,431} = 45\%$$

Thus, for every $1 of Microsoft's total assets, 45 percent is financed with debt. The remaining 65 percent is provided by owners' equity.

The **times interest earned ratio**, operating income divided by interest expense, is a measure of the safety margin a company has with respect to the interest payments it must make to its creditors. A low times interest earned ratio indicates that even a small decrease in earnings may lead the company into financial straits. Microsoft had so little interest expense that it did not list it as a separate item on the income statement. In this case, the analyst has to go searching through the footnotes to the financial statements. In note 3, we find that interest expense was $429 million. Putting this into the calculation, we find that interest expense is covered 62.39 times by operating income. A lender would have no worries about receiving interest payments from Microsoft.

$$\text{Times interest earned} = \frac{\text{EBIT (Operating income)}}{\text{Interest (from note 3)}}$$

$$= \frac{\$26,764}{\$429} = 62.39 \times$$

Per Share Data

Investors may use **per share data** to compare the performance of one company with another on an equal, or per share, basis. Generally, the more shares of stock a company issues, the less income is available for each share.

earnings per share net income or profit divided by the number of stock shares outstanding.

dividends per share the actual cash received for each share owned.

Earnings per share is calculated by dividing net income or profit by the number of shares of stock outstanding. This ratio is important because yearly changes in earnings per share, in combination with other economy-wide factors, determine a company's overall stock price. When earnings go up, so does a company's stock price—and so does the wealth of its stockholders.

$$\text{Diluted earnings per share} = \frac{\text{Net income}}{\text{Number of shares outstanding (diluted)}}$$
$$= \frac{\$21,863}{8,470} = \$2.58$$

We can see from the income statement that Microsoft's basic earnings per share declined from $2.73 per share to $2.61, and this decline also shows up in diluted earnings per share. This drop in earnings can be attributed to Microsoft's new Windows software, which the market did not embrace. You can see from the income statement that diluted earnings per share include more shares than the basic calculation; this is because diluted shares include potential shares that could be issued due to the exercise of stock options or the conversion of certain types of debt into common stock. Investors generally pay more attention to diluted earnings per share than basic earnings per share.

Dividends per share are paid by the corporation to the stockholders for each share owned. The payment is made from earnings after taxes by the corporation but is taxable income to the stockholder. Thus, dividends result in double taxation: The corporation pays tax once on its earnings, and the stockholder pays tax a second time on his or her dividend income. Since 2004, Microsoft has raised its dividend every year, from $0.16 per share to $0.92 per share. A note of clarification is needed on the number of shares outstanding of 8,375 million versus the 8,103 million listed in the denominator. Share count for earnings per share are weighted average shares over the year. However, as the share count goes up, the weighted average can be higher than the actual shares on which dividends were paid. The 8,103 shares were found by dividing $0.92 into the dividends paid on the statement of cash flow.

$$\text{Dividends per share} = \frac{\text{Dividends paid}}{\text{Number of shares outstanding}}$$
$$= \frac{\$7,456}{8,103} = \$0.92$$

Industry Analysis

We have used Microsoft as a comparison to Google because they are competitive in many technology areas, including software and the Internet. They both have a lot of intellectual property and cash balances, and they do not produce hardware like Apple and Hewlett-Packard do. Google has revenues of $59.8 billion. Many investors view Microsoft as an old technology company and Google as a new technology company with more growth opportunities. In fact, between 2011 and 2013, Microsoft's revenues grew only 11 percent while Google's revenues grew almost 58 percent. Reflecting this growth is that investors are willing to pay more for one dollar of Google's earnings per share than one dollar of Microsoft's EPS. In fact, in June of 2014, Google had a price to earnings per share ratio (PE) of 30.7 times and Microsoft had a PE of 15.5 times.

Microsoft dominates Google on the profitability ratios generating a higher profit margin, return on assets, and return on equity ratios. Both companies have very little accounts receivable or inventory, so they show very high receivables and inventory turnover ratios. However, because they each have large cash balances, their total asset turnover ratios are very low, which is not what you would expect with low receivables and inventory investment. At the end of 2013, Microsoft had $77 billion and Google had $58.7 billion of cash, cash equivalents, and short-term investments on their balance sheets. Because of their high cash balances, both companies show high current and quick ratios and, because of very little inventory, their quick ratios are almost equal to their current ratios.

Microsoft has more debt than Google, which is indicated by the debt to total assets ratio. While Microsoft has more debt than Google, the times interest earned ratio indicates that Microsoft's earnings before interest and taxes cover its interest expense at a higher level than does Google.

Table 14.8 doesn't show earnings per share growth, but it is important in forecasting dividend growth. As you can see from the table, Google does not pay a dividend even though it has cash and its earnings per share grew 28 percent between 2011

Increased profit margins allow companies such as New Belgium to invest in new production facilities in Asheville, North Carolina.
© SeanPavonePhoto/Getty Images, RF

TABLE 14.8 Industry Analysis Year Ending 2013

	Google	Microsoft
Profit margin	21.60%	28.08%
Return on assets	11.65%	15.35%
Return on equity	14.80%	27.69%
Receivables turnover	6.74×	4.45×
Inventory turnover	140.43×	40.17×
Total asset turnover	0.54×	0.55×
Current ratio	4.58×	2.71×
Quick ratio	4.55×	2.66×
Debt to total assets	21.00%	45.00%
Times interest earned	26.35×	62.39×
Diluted earnings per share	$38.13	$2.58
Dividends per share	$0.00	$0.92

Source: Data calculated from 2013 annual reports.

As another member of the "Big Four" accounting firms, Deloitte must maintain high standards of accounting ethics to secure its reputation for integrity.
© Alex Segre/Alamy

and 2013. Microsoft pays $0.92 per share even though its earnings per share had negative growth of 4 percent. Despite the negative earnings per share growth, Microsoft raised its dividends 43 percent over the same time period. That is easy to do when you have $77 billion of cash on hand and dividends only cost $7.5 billion. The moral of the story is that the faster a company grows, the more funds the company retains for future growth or, in the case of both companies, acquisitions of new technology created by smaller companies.

THE IMPORTANCE OF INTEGRITY IN ACCOUNTING

The financial crisis and the recession that followed provided another example of a failure in accounting reporting. Many firms attempted to exploit loopholes and manipulate accounting processes and statements. Banks and other financial institutions often held assets off their books by manipulating their accounts. In 2010, the examiner for the Lehman Brothers' bankruptcy found that the most common example of removing assets or liabilities from the books was entering into what is called a "repurchase agreement." In a repurchase agreement, assets are transferred to another entity with the contractual promise of buying them back at a set price. In the case of Lehman Brothers and other

companies, repurchase agreements were used as a method of "cooking the books" that allowed them to manipulate accounting statements so that their ratios looked better than they actually were. If the accountants, the SEC, and the bank regulators had been more careful, these types of transactions would have been discovered and corrected.

On the other hand, strong compliance to accounting principles creates trust among stakeholders. Accounting and financial planning is important for all organizational entities, even cities. The City of Maricopa in Arizona received the Government Finance Officers Association of the United States and Canada (GFOA) Distinguished Budget Presentation Award for its governmental budgeting. The city scored proficient in its policy, financial plan, operations guide, and communications device. Integrity in accounting is crucial to creating trust, understanding the financial position of an organization or entity, and making financial decisions that will benefit the organization.[9]

It is most important to remember that integrity in accounting processes requires ethical principles and compliance with both the spirit of the law and professional standards in the accounting profession. Most states require accountants preparing to take the CPA exam to take accounting ethics courses. Transparency and accuracy in reporting revenue, income, and assets develops trust from investors and other stakeholders. ■

SO YOU WANT TO BE // an Accountant /

Do you like numbers and finances? Are you detail oriented, a perfectionist, and highly accountable for your decisions? If so, accounting may be a good field for you. If you are interested in accounting, there are always job opportunities available no matter the state of the economy. Accounting is one of the most secure job options in business. Of course, becoming an accountant is not easy. You will need at least a bachelor's degree in accounting to get a job, and many positions require additional training. Many states demand coursework beyond the 120 to 150 credit hours collegiate programs require for an accounting degree. If you are really serious about getting into the accounting field, you will probably want to consider getting your master's in accounting and taking the CPA exam. The field of accounting can be complicated, and the extra training provided through a master's in accounting program will prove invaluable when you go out looking for a good job. Accounting is a volatile discipline affected by changes in legislative initiatives.

With corporate accounting policies changing constantly and becoming more complex, accountants are needed to help keep a business running smoothly and within the bounds of the law. In fact, the number of jobs in the accounting and auditing field are expected to increase 16 percent between 2010 and 2020, with more than 1.4 million jobs in the United States alone by 2020. Jobs in accounting tend to pay quite well, with the median salary standing at $61,690. If you go on to get your master's degree in accounting, expect to see an even higher starting wage. Of course, your earnings could be higher or lower than these averages, depending on where you work, your level of experience, the firm, and your particular position.

Accountants are needed in the public and the private sectors, in large and small firms, in for-profit and not-for-profit organizations. Accountants in firms are generally in charge of preparing and filing tax forms and financial reports. Public-sector accountants are responsible for checking the veracity of corporate and personal records in order to prepare tax filings. Basically, any organization that has to deal with money and/or taxes in some way or another will be in need of an accountant, either for in-house service or occasional contract work. Requirements for audits under the Sarbanes-Oxley Act and rules from the Public Company Accounting Oversight Board are creating more jobs and increased responsibility to maintain internal controls and accounting ethics. The fact that accounting rules and tax filings tend to be complex virtually ensures that the demand for accountants will never decrease.[10]

fifteen

money and the
financial system

© Ingram Publishing , RF

LEARNING OBJECTIVES

After reading this chapter, you will be able to:

LO 15-1 Define money, its functions, and its characteristics.

LO 15-2 Describe various types of money.

LO 15-3 Specify how the Federal Reserve Board manages the money supply and regulates the American banking system.

LO 15-4 Compare and contrast commercial banks, savings and loan associations, credit unions, and mutual savings banks.

LO 15-5 Distinguish among nonbanking institutions such as insurance companies, pension funds, mutual funds, and finance companies.

LO 15-6 Investigate the challenges ahead for the banking industry.

From Wall Street to Main Street, both overseas and at home, money is the one tool used to measure personal and business income and wealth. **Finance** is the study of money: how it's made, how it's lost, and how it's managed. This chapter introduces you to the role of money and the financial system in the economy. Of course, if you have a checking account, automobile insurance, a college loan, or a credit card, you already have personal experience with some key players in the financial world.

We begin our discussion with a definition of money and then explore some of the many forms money may take. Next, we examine the roles of the Federal Reserve Board and other major institutions in the financial system. Finally, we explore the future of the finance industry and some of the changes likely to occur over the course of the next several years. ∎

MONEY IN THE FINANCIAL SYSTEM

Strictly defined, **money**, or *currency,* is anything generally accepted in exchange for goods and services. Materials as diverse as salt, cattle, fish, rocks, shells, cloth, as well as precious metals such as gold, silver, and copper have long been used by various cultures as money. Most of these materials were limited-supply commodities that had their own value to society (for example, salt can be used as a preservative and shells and metals as jewelry). The supply of these commodities therefore determined the supply of "money" in that society. The next step was the development of "IOUs," or slips of paper that could be exchanged for a specified supply of the underlying commodity. "Gold" notes, for instance, could be exchanged for gold, and the money supply was tied to the amount of gold available. While paper money was first used in North America in 1685 (and even earlier in Europe), the concept of *fiat money*—a paper money not readily convertible to a precious metal such as gold—did not gain full acceptance until the Great Depression in the 1930s. The United States abandoned its gold-backed currency standard largely in response to the Great Depression and converted to a fiduciary, or fiat, monetary system. In the United States, paper money is really a government "note" or promise, worth the value specified on the note.

Functions of Money

No matter what a particular society uses for money, its primary purpose is to enable a person or organization to transform a desire into an action. The desire may be for entertainment actions, such as party expenses; operating actions, such as paying for rent, utilities, or employees; investing actions, such as buying property or equipment; or financing actions, such as for starting or growing a business. Money serves three important functions: as a medium of exchange, a measure of value, and a store of value.

finance the study of money; how it's made, how it's lost, and how it's managed.

money anything generally accepted in exchange for goods and services.

> "No matter what a particular society uses for money, its primary purpose is to enable a person or organization to transform a desire into an action."

Medium of Exchange   Before fiat money, the trade of goods and services was accomplished through *bartering*—trading one good or service for another of similar value. As any school-age child knows, bartering can become quite inefficient—particularly in the case of complex, three-party transactions involving peanut butter sandwiches, baseball cards, and hair barrettes. There had to be a simpler way, and that was to decide on a single item—money—that can be freely converted to any other good upon agreement between parties.

Measure of Value

As a measure of value, money serves as a common standard or yardstick of the value of goods and services. For example, $2 will buy a dozen large eggs and $25,000 will buy a nice car in the United States. In Japan, where the currency is known as the yen, these same transactions would cost about 185 yen and 2.3 million yen, respectively. Money, then, is a common denominator that allows people to compare the different goods and services that can be consumed on a particular income level. While a star athlete and a "burger-flipper" are paid vastly different wages, each uses money as a measure of the value of their yearly earnings and purchases.

Store of Value

As a store of value, money serves as a way to accumulate wealth (buying power) until it is needed. For example, a person making $1,000 per week who wants to buy a $500 computer could save $50 per week for each of the next 10 weeks. Unfortunately, the value of stored money is directly dependent on the health of the economy. If, due to rapid inflation, all prices double in one year, then the purchasing power value of the money "stuffed in the mattress" would fall by half. On the other hand, deflation occurs when prices of goods fall. Deflation might seem like a good thing for consumers, but in many ways it can be just as problematic as inflation. Periods of major deflation often lead to decreases in wages and increases in debt burdens.[1] Deflation also tends to be an indicator of problems in the economy. Deflation indicates a very slow growth or shrinking economy with high unemployment and falling prices. Over the past 25 years, we have seen deflation in Japan and more recently Ireland in 2009. Given a choice, central banks like the Federal Reserve would rather have a small amount of inflation than deflation.

Characteristics of Money

To be used as a medium of exchange, money must be acceptable, divisible, portable, stable in value, durable, and difficult to counterfeit.

Acceptability

To be effective, money must be readily acceptable for the purchase of goods and services and for the settlement of debts. Acceptability is probably the most important characteristic of money: If people do not trust the value of money, businesses will not accept it as a payment for goods and services, and consumers will have to find some other means of paying for their purchases.

Divisibility

Given the widespread use of quarters, dimes, nickels, and pennies in the United States, it is no surprise that the principle of divisibility is an important one. With barter, the lack of divisibility often makes otherwise preferable trades impossible, as would be an attempt to trade a steer for a loaf of bread. For money to serve effectively as a measure of value, all items must be valued in terms of comparable units—dimes for a piece of bubble gum, quarters for laundry machines, and dollars (or dollars and coins) for everything else.

Portability

Clearly, for money to function as a medium of exchange, it must be easily moved from one location to the next. Large colored rocks could be used as money, but you couldn't carry them around in your wallet. Paper currency and metal coins, on the other hand, are capable of transferring vast purchasing power into small, easily carried (and hidden!) bundles. Few Americans realize it, but more U.S. currency is in circulation outside the United States than within. Currently, about $1.358 trillion of U.S. currency is in circulation, and the majority is held outside the United States.[2] Some countries, such as Panama, even use the U.S. dollar as their currency. Retailers in other countries often state prices in dollars and in their local currency.

For centuries, people on the Micronesian island of Yap have used giant round stones, like the ones shown here, for money. The stones aren't moved, but their ownership can change.
© Michael Runkel/Robert Harding World Imagery / Alamy

Stability Money must be stable and maintain its declared face value. A $10 bill should purchase the same amount of goods or services from one day to the next. The principle of stability allows people who wish to postpone purchases and save their money to do so without fear that it will decline in value. As mentioned earlier, money declines in value during periods of inflation, when economic conditions cause prices to rise. Thus, the same amount of money buys fewer and fewer goods and services. In some countries, people spend their money as fast as they can in order to keep it from losing any more of its value. Instability destroys confidence in a nation's money and its ability to store value and serve as an effective medium of exchange. It also has an impact on other countries. When Switzerland decided no longer to hold its Swiss franc at a fixed exchange rate with the euro, other countries were concerned because they tended to view the Swiss franc as relatively "safe" for investments. This change will make Swiss exports more expensive and imports less expensive. The investment community is wary of changes in the stability of a currency, and the change caused massive losses for investors and the plunging of the Swiss stock market.[3] Ultimately, people faced with spiraling price increases avoid the increasingly worthless paper money at all costs, storing all of their savings in the form of real assets such as gold and land.

Durability Money must be durable. The crisp new dollar bills you trade at the music store for the hottest new Blu-ray movie will make their way all around town for about six years before being replaced (see Table 15.1). Were the value of an old, faded bill to fall in line with the deterioration of its appearance, the principles of stability and universal acceptability would fail (but, no doubt, fewer bills would pass through the washer!). Although metal coins, due to their much longer useful life, would appear to be an ideal form of money, paper currency is far more portable than metal because of its light weight. Today, coins are used primarily to provide divisibility.

Difficulty to Counterfeit Finally, to remain stable and enjoy universal acceptance, it almost goes without saying that money must be very difficult to counterfeit—that is, to duplicate illegally. Every country takes steps to make counterfeiting difficult. Most use multicolored money, and many use specially watermarked papers that are virtually impossible to duplicate. Counterfeit bills represent less than 0.03 percent of the currency in circulation in the United States,[5] but it is becoming increasingly easy for counterfeiters to print money. This illegal printing of money is fueled by hundreds of people who often circulate only small amounts of counterfeit bills. On the other hand, even rogue governments such as North Korea are known to

▼ **TABLE 15.1** Life Expectancy of Money

How long is the life span of U.S. paper money?

When currency is deposited with a Federal Reserve Bank, the quality of each note is evaluated by sophisticated processing equipment. Notes that meet our strict quality criteria—that is, they are still in good condition—continue to circulate, while those that do not are taken out of circulation and destroyed. This process determines the life span of a Federal Reserve note.

Life span varies by denomination. One factor that influences the life span of each denomination is how the denomination is used by the public. For example, $100 notes are often used as a store of value. This means that they pass between users less frequently than lower denominations that are more often used for transactions, such as $5 notes. Thus, $100 notes typically last longer than $5 notes.

Denomination	Estimated Life Span*
$ 1	5.9 years
$ 5	4.9 years
$ 10	4.2 years
$ 20	7.7 years
$ 50	3.7 years
$100	15.0 years

*Estimated life spans as of December 2012. Because the $2 does not widely circulate, we do not publish its estimated life span.

Source: Board of Governors of the Federal Reserve System, "How Long Is the Life Span of U.S. Paper Money?" www.federalreserve.gov/faqs/how-long-is-the-life-span-of-us-paper-money.htm (accessed April 6, 2015).

DID YOU KNOW?

Around 75 percent of counterfeit currency is found and destroyed before it ever reaches the public.[4]

make counterfeit U.S. currency. To thwart the problem of counterfeiting, the U.S. Treasury Department redesigned the U.S. currency, starting with the $20 bill in 2003, the $50 bill in 2004, the $10 bill in 2006, the $5 bill in 2008, and the $100 bill in 2010. For the first time, U.S. money includes subtle colors in addition to the traditional green, as well as enhanced security features, such as a watermark, security thread, and color-shifting ink.[6] Although counterfeiting is not as much of an issue with coins, U.S. metal coins are usually worth more for the metal than their face value. It has begun to cost more to manufacture coins than what they are worth monetarily.

As Table 15.2 indicates, it costs more than a penny to manufacture a penny, resulting in a call to discontinue it. Because it costs more to produce pennies and nickels than what they are worth, these coins have generated losses of $664.0 million in an eight-year period.[7] The redeeming feature of printing money is that the U.S. mint makes money on dimes, quarters, and dollars. Also, it costs only 5.4 cents to make a $1 bill and 10.2 cents to make a $20 or $50 bill. So what the U.S. Mint loses on pennies and nickels, the Treasury makes up on paper money.

The U.S. government redesigns currency to stay ahead of counterfeiters and protect the public.
© Ahlapot/Getty Images, RF

▼ **TABLE 15.2** Costs to Produce Pennies and Nickels

Fiscal Year	Cent Unit Cost (¢)	Nickel Unit Cost (¢)	Revenue from Coins ($ millions)
2014	1.70¢	8.10¢	$ (90.5)
2013	1.83	9.40	(104.5)
2012	1.99	10.10	(109.2)
2011	2.41	11.18	(116.7)
2010	1.79	9.22	(42.6)
2009	1.62	6.03	(22.0)
2008	1.42	8.83	(47.0)
2007	1.67	9.53	(98.6)
2006	1.21	5.97	(32.9)
Total			($664.0)

Source: Various annual reports of the U.S. Mint.

LO 15-2 Describe various types of money.

Types of Money

While paper money and coins are the most visible types of money, the combined value of all the printed bills and all the minted coins is actually rather insignificant when compared with the value of money kept in checking accounts, savings accounts, and other monetary forms.

You probably have a **checking account** (also called a *demand deposit*), money stored in an account at a bank or other financial institution that can be withdrawn without advance notice. One way to withdraw funds from your account is by writing a *check*, a written order to a bank to pay the indicated individual or business the amount specified on the check from money already on deposit. Figure 15.1 explains the significance of the numbers found on a typical U.S. check. As legal instruments, checks serve as a substitute for currency and coins and are preferred for many transactions due to their lower risk of loss. If you lose a $100 bill, anyone who finds or steals it can spend it. If you lose a blank check, however, the risk of catastrophic loss is quite low. Not only does your bank have a sample of your signature on file to compare with a suspected forged signature, but you can render the check immediately worthless by means of a stop-payment order at your bank.

There are several types of checking accounts, with different features available for different monthly fee levels or specific minimum account balances. Some checking accounts earn interest (a small percentage of the amount deposited in the account that the bank pays to the depositor). One such interest-bearing checking account is the *NOW (Negotiable Order of Withdrawal) account* offered by most financial institutions. The interest rate paid on such accounts varies with the interest rates available in the economy but is typically quite low (more recently less than 1 percent but in the past between 2 and 5 percent).

Savings accounts (also known as *time deposits*) are accounts with funds that usually cannot be withdrawn without advance notice and/or have limits on the number of withdrawals per period. While seldom enforced, the "fine print" governing most savings accounts prohibits withdrawals without two or three days' notice. Savings accounts are not generally used for transactions or as a medium of exchange, but their funds can be moved to a checking account or turned into cash.

Money market accounts are similar to interest-bearing checking accounts, but with more restrictions. Generally, in exchange for slightly higher interest rates, the owner of a money market account can write only a limited number of

FIGURE 15.1
A Check

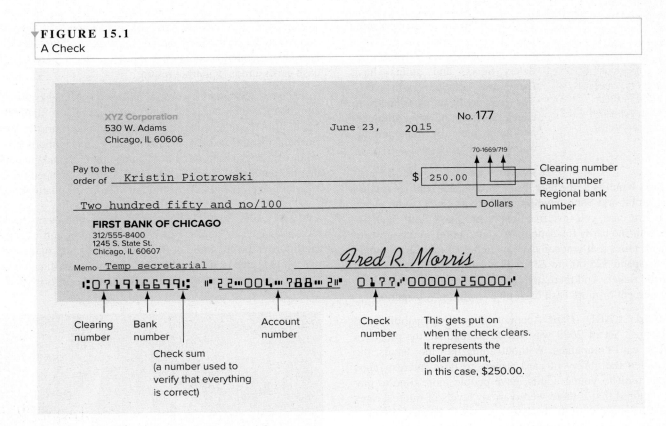

checks each month, and there may be a restriction on the minimum amount of each check.

Certificates of deposit (CDs) are savings accounts that guarantee a depositor a set interest rate over a specified interval of time as long as the funds are not withdrawn before the end of the interval—six months, one year, or seven years, for example. Money may be withdrawn from these accounts prematurely only after paying a substantial penalty. In general, the longer the term of the CD, the higher is the interest rate it earns. As with all interest rates, the rate offered and fixed at the time the account is opened fluctuates according to economic conditions.

Credit cards allow you to promise to pay at a later date by using preapproved lines of credit granted by a bank or finance company. They are a popular substitute for cash payments because of their convenience, easy access to credit, and acceptance by merchants around the world. The institution that issues

Credit cards have many advantages, including being able to buy expensive items and pay them off a little at a time. However, this can easily lead an individual to incur spiraling credit card debt that is hard to pay off.
© Comstock Images, RF

the credit card guarantees payment of a credit charge to merchants and assumes responsibility for collecting the money from the cardholders. Card issuers charge a transaction fee to the merchants for performing the credit check, guaranteeing the payment, and collecting the payment. The fee is typically between 2 and 5 percent, depending on the type of card. American Express fees are usually higher than Visa and MasterCard.

The original American Express cards require full payment at the end of each month, but American Express now offers credit cards similar to Visa, MasterCard, and Discover that allow cardholders to make installment payments and carry a maximum balance. There is a minimum monthly payment with interest charged on the remaining balance. Some people pay off their credit cards monthly, while other make monthly payments. Charges for unpaid balances can run 18 percent or higher at an annual rate, making credit card debt one of the most expensive ways to borrow money.

Besides the major credit card companies, many stores—Target, Saks Fifth Avenue, Macy's, Bloomingdales, Sears, and others—have their own branded credit cards. They use credit rating agencies to check the credit of the cardholders and they generally make money on the finance charges.

Reward cards are credit cards that carry benefits to the user. For example, gas stations such as ExxonMobil and Shell have branded credit cards so that when you use the card, you save five or six cents per gallon. Others—such as airline cards for American, Delta, and United—reward you with miles that you can use for flights. Of course, you may have to spend $25,000 to $35,000 to earn enough miles for a domestic ticket. And there are cash-back credit cards that give you 1 percent or more cash back on everything you spend.

The Credit CARD (Card Accountability Responsibility and Disclosure) Act of 2009 was passed to regulate the practices of credit card companies. Without going into the details, the law limited the ability of card issuers to raise interest rates, limited credit to young adults, gave people more time to pay bills, required that if there were various levels of interest rates that the balances with the highest rate would be paid off first, and made clearer due dates on billing cycles, along with several other provisions. For college students, the most important part of the law is that young adults under the age of 21 will have to have an adult co-signer or show proof that they have enough income to handle the debt limit on the card.

This act is important to all companies and cardholders. Research indicates that approximately 40 percent of lower- and middle-income households use credit cards to pay for basic necessities. Yet there is also good news. The average credit card debt for lower- and middle-income households has decreased in recent years. On the other hand, studies also show that college students tend to lack the financial literacy needed to understand credit cards and their requirements. Approximately 90 percent of college students with credit cards have credit card debt. Therefore, vulnerable segments of the population such as college students should be careful about which credit cards to choose and how often they use them.[8]

A **debit card** looks like a credit card but works like a check. The use of a debit card results in a direct, immediate, electronic payment from the cardholder's checking account to a merchant or other party. While they are convenient to carry and profitable for banks, they lack credit features, offer no purchase "grace period," and provide no hard "paper trail." Debit cards are gaining more acceptance with merchants, and consumers like debit cards because of the ease of getting cash from an increasing number of ATMs. Financial institutions also want consumers to use debit cards because they reduce the number of teller transactions and check processing costs. Some cash management accounts at retail brokers like Merrill Lynch offer deferred debit cards. These act like a credit card but debit to the cash management account once a month. During that time, the cash earns a money market return.

Traveler's checks, money orders, and cashier's checks are other common forms of "near money." Although each is slightly different from the others, they all share a common characteristic: A financial institution, bank, credit company, or neighborhood currency exchange issues them in exchange for cash and guarantees that the purchased note will be honored and exchanged for cash when it is presented to the institution making the guarantee.

Credit Card Fraud More and more computer hackers have managed to steal credit card information and either use the information for Internet purchases or actually make a card exactly the same as the stolen card. The most significant breach was at Target, where the retail giant lost the information for

One of the roles of the Federal Reserve is to use its policies to keep money flowing. Money is the lifeblood of the economy. If banks become too protective of their funds and stop lending money, the economy can grind to a halt.
© Skyhobo/Getty Images, RF

more than 40 million credit cards to hackers. Losses on credit card theft run into the billions, but consumers are usually not liable for the losses. However, consumers should be careful with debit cards because once the money is out of the account, the bank and credit card companies cannot get it back. Debit cards do not have the same level of protection as credit cards.

THE AMERICAN FINANCIAL SYSTEM

The U.S. financial system fuels our economy by storing money, fostering investment opportunities, and making loans for new businesses and business expansion as well as for homes, cars, and college educations. This amazingly complex system includes banking institutions, nonbanking financial institutions such as finance companies, and systems that provide for the electronic transfer of funds throughout the world. Over the past 20 years, the rate at which money turns over, or changes hands, has increased exponentially. Different cultures place unique values on saving, spending, borrowing, and investing. The combination of this increased turnover rate and increasing

interactions with people and organizations from other countries has created a complex money system. First, we need to meet the guardian of this complex system.

LO 15-3 Specify how the Federal Reserve Board manages the money supply and regulates the American banking system.

The Federal Reserve System

The guardian of the American financial system is the **Federal Reserve Board**, or "the Fed," as it is commonly called, an independent agency of the federal government established in 1913 to regulate the nation's banking and financial industry. The Federal Reserve System is organized into 12 regions, each with a Federal Reserve Bank that serves its defined area (Figure 15.2). All the Federal Reserve banks except those in Boston and Philadelphia have regional branches. The Cleveland

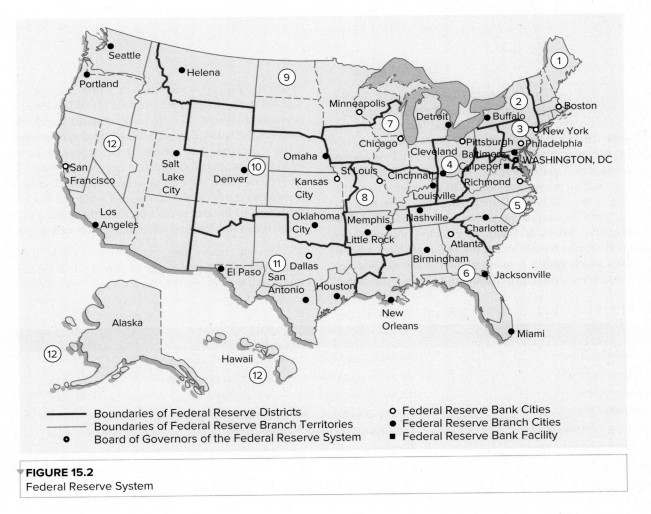

FIGURE 15.2
Federal Reserve System

Federal Reserve Bank, for example, is responsible for branch offices in Pittsburgh and Cincinnati.

The Federal Reserve Board is the chief economic policy arm of the United States. Working with Congress and the president, the Fed tries to create a positive economic environment capable of sustaining low inflation, high levels of employment, a balance in international payments, and long-term economic growth. To this end, the Federal Reserve Board has four major responsibilities: (1) to control the supply of money, or monetary policy; (2) to regulate banks and other financial institutions; (3) to manage regional and national checking account procedures, or check clearing; and (4) to supervise the federal deposit insurance programs of banks belonging to the Federal Reserve System.

nature of our economy means that more and more U.S. dollars are circulating overseas. Using several different measures of the money supply, the Fed establishes specific growth targets which, presumably, ensure a close balance between money supply and money demand. The Fed fine-tunes money growth by using four basic tools: open market operations, reserve requirements, the discount rate, and credit controls (see Table 15.3). There is generally a lag of 6 to 18 months before the effect of these changes shows up in economic activity.

Open market operations refer to decisions to buy or sell U.S. Treasury bills (short-term debt issued by the U.S. government; also called T-bills) and other investments in the open market. The actual purchase or sale of the investments is performed by the New York Federal Reserve Bank. This monetary tool, the most commonly employed of all Fed operations, is performed almost daily in an effort to control the money supply.

"The Fed controls the amount of money available in the economy through monetary policy."

Monetary Policy The Fed controls the amount of money available in the economy through **monetary policy**. Without this intervention, the supply of and demand for money might not balance. This could result in either rapid price increases (inflation) because of too little money or economic recession and a slowdown of price increases (disinflation) because of too little growth in the money supply. In very rare cases (the Depression of the 1930s) the United States has suffered from deflation, when the actual purchasing power of the dollar has increased as prices declined. To effectively control the supply of money in the economy, the Fed must have a good idea of how much money is in circulation at any given time. This has become increasingly challenging because the global

When the Fed buys securities, it writes a check on its own account to the seller of the investments. When the seller of the investments (usually a large bank) deposits the check, the Fed transfers the balance from the Federal Reserve account into the seller's account, thus increasing the supply of money in the economy and, hopefully, fueling economic growth. The opposite occurs when the Fed sells investments. The buyer writes a check to the Federal Reserve, and when the funds are transferred out of the purchaser's account, the amount of money in circulation falls, slowing economic growth to a desired level.

The second major monetary policy tool is the **reserve requirement**, the percentage of deposits that banking institutions must hold in reserve ("in the vault," as it were). Funds so

▼ **TABLE 15.3** Fed Tools for Regulating the Money Supply

Activity	Effect on the Money Supply and the Economy
Buy government securities	The money supply increases; economic activity increases.
Sell government securities	The money supply decreases; economic activity slows down.
Raise discount rate	Interest rates increase; the money supply decreases; economic activity slows down.
Lower discount rate	Interest rates decrease; the money supply increases; economic activity increases.
Increase reserve requirements	Banks make fewer loans; the money supply declines; economic activity slows down.
Decrease reserve requirements	Banks make more loans; the money supply increases; economic activity increases.
Relax credit controls	More people are encouraged to make major purchases, increasing economic activity.
Restrict credit controls	People are discouraged from making major purchases, decreasing economic activity.

held are not available for lending to businesses and consumers. For example, a bank holding $10 million in deposits, with a 10 percent reserve requirement, must have reserves of $1 million. If the Fed were to reduce the reserve requirement to, say, 5 percent, the bank would need to keep only $500,000 in reserves. The bank could then lend to customers the $500,000 difference between the old reserve level and the new lower reserve level, thus increasing the supply of money. Because the reserve requirement has such a powerful effect on the money supply, the Fed does not change it very often, relying instead on open market operations most of the time.

The third monetary policy tool, the **discount rate**, is the rate of interest the Fed charges to loan money to any banking institution to meet reserve requirements. The Fed is the lender of last resort for these banks. When a bank borrows from the Fed, it is said to have borrowed at the "discount window," and the interest rates charged there are often higher than those charged on loans of comparable risk elsewhere in the economy. This added interest expense, when it exists, serves to discourage banks from borrowing from the Fed.

When the Fed wants to expand the money supply, it lowers the discount rate to encourage borrowing. Conversely, when the Fed wants to decrease the money supply, it raises the discount rate. The increases in interest rates that occurred in the United States from 2003 through 2006 were the result of more than 16 quarter-point (0.25 percent) increases in the Fed discount rate. The purpose was to keep inflation under control and to raise rates to a more normal level as the economy recovered from the recession of 2001. During the most recent recession, which started in 2007, the Fed lowered interest rates to nearly zero in order to encourage borrowing. In an environment where credit markets were nearly frozen, the Fed utilized monetary policy to stimulate spending. Not surprisingly, economists watch changes in this sensitive interest rate as an indicator of the Fed's monetary policy.

The final tool in the Fed's arsenal of weapons is **credit controls**—the authority to establish and enforce credit rules for financial institutions and some private investors. For example, the Fed can determine how large a down payment individuals and businesses must make on credit purchases of expensive items such as automobiles, and how much time they have to finish paying for the purchases. By raising and lowering minimum down payment amounts and payment periods, the Fed can stimulate or discourage credit purchases of "big ticket" items. The Fed also has the authority to set the minimum down payment investors must use for the credit purchases of stock. Buying stock with credit—"buying on margin"—is a popular investment strategy among individual speculators. By altering the margin requirement (currently set at 50 percent of the price of the purchased stocks), the Fed can effectively control the total amount of credit borrowing in the stock market.

Regulatory Functions The second major responsibility of the Fed is to regulate banking institutions that are members of the Federal Reserve System. Accordingly, the Fed establishes and enforces banking rules that affect monetary policy and the overall level of the competition between different banks. It determines which nonbanking activities, such as brokerage services, leasing, and insurance, are appropriate for banks and which should be prohibited. The Fed also has the authority to approve or disapprove mergers between banks and the formation of bank holding companies. In an effort to ensure that all rules are enforced and that correct accounting procedures are being followed at member banks, surprise bank examinations are conducted by bank examiners each year.

Check Clearing The Federal Reserve provides national check processing on a huge scale. Divisions of the Fed known as check clearinghouses handle almost all the checks written against a bank in one city and presented for deposit to a bank in a second city. Any banking institution can present the checks it has received from others around the country to its regional Federal Reserve Bank. The Fed passes the checks to the appropriate regional Federal Reserve Bank, which then sends the checks to the issuing bank for payment. With the advance of electronic payment systems and the passage of the Check Clearing for the 21st Century Act (Check 21 Act), checks can now be processed in a day. The Check 21 Act allows banks to clear checks electronically by presenting an electronic image of the check. This eliminates mail delays and time-consuming paper processing.

Depository Insurance The Fed is also responsible for supervising the federal insurance funds that protect the deposits of member institutions. These insurance funds will be discussed in greater detail in the following section.

> **LO 15-4** Compare and contrast commercial banks, savings and loan associations, credit unions, and mutual savings banks.

Banking Institutions

Banking institutions accept money deposits from and make loans to individual consumers and businesses. Some of the most important banking institutions include commercial banks, savings and loan associations, credit unions, and mutual savings banks. Historically, these have all been separate institutions. However, new hybrid forms of banking institutions that perform two or more of these functions have emerged over the past two decades. The following all have one thing in common: They are businesses whose objective is to earn money by managing, safeguarding, and lending money to others. Their sales revenues come from the fees and interest that they charge for providing these financial services.

discount rate the rate of interest the Fed charges to loan money to any banking institution to meet reserve requirements.

credit controls the authority to establish and enforce credit rules for financial institutions and some private investors.

JPMorgan Chase is the second largest commercial bank in the United States behind Bank of America.
© Bebeto Matthews/AP Images

level playing field for global banking competition. As commercial banks and investment banks have merged, the financial landscape has changed. Consolidation remains the norm in the U.S. banking industry. The financial crisis and the economic recession that began in 2007 and lasted into 2012 only accelerated the consolidation as large, healthy banks ended up buying weak banks that were in trouble. JPMorgan Chase bought Wachovia and the investment bank Bear Stearns; Wells Fargo bought Washington Mutual; PNC bought National City Bank; and Bank of America bought Countrywide Credit and Merrill Lynch. Most of these purchases were made with financial help from the U.S. Treasury and Federal Reserve. By 2012, the banks had paid back their loans, but the financial meltdown exposed some high-risk activities in the banking industry that Congress wanted to curtail. The result was the passage of the Dodd-Frank Act. This act added many new regulations, but the two most important changes raised the required capital banks had to hold on their balance sheet and limited certain types of high-risk trading activities.

Commercial Banks

The largest and oldest of all financial institutions are **commercial banks**, which perform a variety of financial services. They rely mainly on checking and savings accounts as their major source of funds and use only a portion of these deposits to make loans to businesses and individuals. Because it is unlikely that all the depositors of any one bank will want to withdraw all of their funds at the same time, a bank can safely loan out a large percentage of its deposits.

Today, banks are quite diversified and offer a number of services. Commercial banks make loans for virtually any conceivable legal purpose, from vacations to cars, from homes to college educations. Banks in many states offer *home equity loans,* by which home owners can borrow against the appraised value of their already purchased homes. Banks also issue Visa and MasterCard credit cards and offer CDs and trusts (legal entities set up to hold and manage assets for a beneficiary). Many banks rent safe deposit boxes in bank vaults to customers who want to store jewelry, legal documents, artwork, and other valuables. In 1999, Congress passed the Financial Services Modernization Act, also known as the Gramm-Leach-Bliley Bill. This act repealed the Glass Steagall Act, which was enacted in 1929 after the stock market crash and prohibited commercial banks from being in the insurance and investment banking business. This puts U.S. commercial banks on the same competitive footing as European banks and provides a more

Savings and Loan Associations

Savings and loan associations (S&Ls), often called "thrifts," are financial institutions that primarily offer savings accounts and make long-term loans for residential mortgages. A mortgage is a loan made so that a business or individual can purchase real estate, typically a home; the real estate itself is pledged as a guarantee (called *collateral*) that the buyer will repay the loan. If the loan is not repaid, the savings and loan has the right to repossess the property. Prior to the 1970s, S&Ls focused almost exclusively on real estate lending and accepted only savings accounts. Today, following years of regulatory changes, S&Ls compete directly with commercial banks by offering many types of services.

Savings and loans have gone through a metamorphosis since the early 1990s, after having almost collapsed in the 1980s. Today, many of the largest savings and loans have merged with commercial banks. This segment of the financial services industry plays a diminished role in the mortgage lending market.

Credit Unions

A **credit union** is a financial institution owned and controlled by its depositors, who usually have a common employer, profession, trade group, or religion. The Aggieland Credit Union in College Station, Texas, for example, provides banking services for faculty, employees, and current and former students of Texas A&M University. A savings account at a credit

The Dodd-Frank Act of 2010, enacted in response to the financial crisis, imposed many new regulations on large financial institutions in the United States. For major banks, these include strict capital retention requirements, many new regulatory charges, and a complex and involved yearly "stress test" by the Federal Reserve. These regulations are meant to provide oversight and tighter control over companies so "systemically important" that their failure would have a significant impact on the financial system as a whole. Under the law, all banks with assets over $50 billion are considered systemically important and subject to the tighter regulations.

Although $50 billion sounds like a large amount, it is relatively unremarkable by large banking standards. Consider that the four biggest banking institutions are at well over $1.5 trillion in assets each. This has led some policymakers to argue that the law's threshold is far too low, encompassing banks whose failure would have little to no systemic impact. This is problematic for both the banks, who have to spend significant amounts to comply with the regulations, and the regulators, whose attention is diverted to less important companies rather than the ones they should be focusing on.

The law is also having unexpected practical effects. Banks whose assets are approaching $50 billion are restraining their own growth to avoid going over, preferring to wait for a very large deal or set of deals—say $30 million or more—that would make "crossing the line" worth it. Congress is expected to soon revisit the $50 billion threshold and consider whether it should be raised or even replaced with a different standard, such as guidelines for a case-by-case analysis of whether an institution is systemically important.[9]

Discussion Questions

1. What are the advantages and disadvantages of the $50 billion threshold?

2. Why are banks waiting for big deals before crossing the $50 billion threshold?

3. What does this situation tell you about the effect of legal changes on business decisions and strategies?

---

union is commonly referred to as a share account, while a checking account is termed a share draft account. Because the credit union is tied to a common organization, the members (depositors) are allowed to vote for directors and share in the credit union's profits in the form of higher interest rates on accounts and/or lower loan rates.

While credit unions were originally created to provide depositors with a short-term source of funds for low-interest consumer loans for items such as cars, home appliances, vacations, and college, today they offer a wide range of financial services. Generally, the larger the credit union, the more sophisticated its financial service offerings will be.

Mutual Savings Banks
Mutual savings banks are similar to savings and loan associations, but, like credit unions, they are owned by their depositors. Among the oldest financial institutions in the United States, they were originally established to provide a safe place for savings of particular groups of people, such as fishermen. Found mostly in New England, they are becoming more popular in the rest of the country as some S&Ls have converted to mutual savings banks to escape the stigma created by the widespread S&L failures in the 1980s.

Insurance for Banking Institutions
The **Federal Deposit Insurance Corporation (FDIC)**, which insures individual bank accounts, was established in 1933 to help stop bank failures throughout the country during the Great Depression. Today, the FDIC insures personal accounts up to a maximum of $250,000 at nearly 8,000 FDIC member institutions.[10] While most major banks are insured by the FDIC, small institutions in some states may be insured by state insurance funds or private insurance companies. Should a member bank fail, its depositors can recover all of their funds, up to $250,000. Amounts over $250,000, while not legally covered by the insurance, are in fact usually covered because the Fed understands very well the enormous damage that would result to the financial system should these large depositors withdraw their money. When the financial crisis occurred, the FDIC increased the deposit insurance amount from $100,000 to $250,000 on a temporary basis to increase consumer confidence in the banking system. The Dodd-Frank Act passed on July 21, 2010, made the $250,000 insurance per account permanent. The *Federal Savings and Loan Insurance Corporation (FSLIC)* insured thrift deposits prior to its insolvency and failure during the S&L crisis of the 1980s. Now, the insurance functions once overseen by the FSLIC are handled directly by the FDIC through

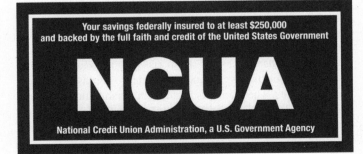

The National Credit Union Administration has the important job of regulating and chartering credit unions and insuring their deposits through its National Credit Union Insurance Fund.
© Courtesy of National Credit Union Administration

its Savings Association Insurance Fund. The **National Credit Union Administration (NCUA)** regulates and charters credit unions and insures their deposits through its National Credit Union Insurance Fund.

When they were originally established, Congress hoped that these insurance funds would make people feel secure about their savings so that they would not panic and withdraw their money when news of a bank failure was announced. The "bank run" scene in the perennial Christmas movie *It's a Wonderful Life,* when dozens of Bailey Building and Loan depositors attempted to withdraw their money (only to have the reassuring figure of Jimmy Stewart calm their fears), was not based on mere fiction. During the Great Depression, hundreds of banks failed and their depositors lost everything. The fact that large numbers of major financial institutions failed in the 1980s and 1990s—without a single major banking panic—underscores the effectiveness of the current insurance system. Large bank failures occurred once again during the most recent recession. According to the FDIC, 474 banks failed between January 2009 and May 31, 2014. Compare this to 52 failures between January 2000 and December 31, 2008, and you can grasp the impact of the financial crisis and long-lasting recession. For the March 2014 ending quarter, the FDIC reported that the number of problem banks had declined for 12 quarters in a row. This reflects an improving economy and a healthier financial system. It is safe to say that most depositors go to sleep every night without worrying about the safety of their savings.

LO 15-5 Distinguish among nonbanking institutions such as insurance companies, pension funds, mutual funds, and finance companies.

Nonbanking Institutions

Nonbank financial institutions offer some financial services, such as short-term loans or investment products, but do not accept deposits. These include insurance companies, pension funds, mutual funds, brokerage firms, nonfinancial firms, and finance companies. Table 15.4 lists the assets of some diversified financial services firms. You can see that banks dominate.

Diversified Firms There are many nonfinancial firms that help finance their customers' purchases of expensive equipment. For example, Caterpillar (construction equipment), Boeing

▼ **TABLE 15.4** Leading Diversified Financial Services Firms

	2014 Assets (in millions)
JPMorgan Chase	$2,573,128
Citigroup Inc.	1,842,530
American Express	159,103
Ameriprise	148,810
Visa	38,569
AON	29,772
Apollo Global Management	23,179
Invesco	20,463
Marsh & McLennan	17,840

Source: S&P Capital IQ reports.

(airplanes), and General Electric (jet engines and locomotives) help their customers finance these large-scale expensive purchases through their finance subsidiaries. At one time, General Electric's credit subsidiary accounted for 40 percent of the company's revenues, but this is slowly falling as the company divests itself of consumer credit operations. Automobile companies such as Ford and General Motors have also traditionally had credit subsidiaries to help customers finance their cars.

Insurance Companies **Insurance companies** are businesses that protect their clients against financial losses from certain specified risks (death, injury, disability, accident, fire, theft, and natural disasters, for example) in exchange for a fee, called a premium. Because insurance premiums flow into the companies regularly, but major insurance losses cannot be timed with great accuracy (though expected risks can be assessed with considerable precision), insurance companies generally have large amounts of excess funds. They typically invest these or make long-term loans, particularly to businesses in the form of commercial real estate loans.

Pension Funds **Pension funds** are managed investment pools set aside by individuals, corporations, unions, and some nonprofit organizations to provide retirement income for members. One type of pension fund is the *individual retirement account (IRA),* which is established by individuals to provide for their personal retirement needs. IRAs can be invested in a variety of financial assets, from risky commodities such as oil or cocoa to low-risk financial "staples" such as U.S. Treasury securities. The choice is up to each person and is dictated solely by individual objectives and tolerance for risk. The interest earned by all of these investments may be deferred tax-free until retirement.

In 1997, Congress revised the IRA laws and created a Roth IRA. Although similar to a traditional IRA in that investors may contribute $5,500 per year, the money in a Roth IRA is considered an after-tax contribution. Workers over 50 can add an extra $1,000, but in all cases, if you make too much money, you cannot fund a Roth. When the money is withdrawn at retirement, no tax is paid on the distribution. The Roth IRA is beneficial to young people who can allow a long time for their money to compound and who may be able to have their parents or grandparents fund the Roth IRA with gift money.

Most major corporations provide some kind of pension plan for their employees. Many of these are established with bank trust departments or life insurance companies. Money is deposited in a separate account in the name of each individual employee, and when the employee retires, the total amount in the account can be either withdrawn in one lump sum or taken as monthly cash payments over some defined time period (usually for the remaining life of the retiree).

Social Security, the largest pension fund, is publicly financed. The federal government collects Social Security funds from payroll taxes paid by both employers and employees. The Social Security Administration then takes these monies and makes payments to those eligible to receive Social Security benefits—individuals who are retired or disabled and the young children of deceased parents.

Mutual Funds

A **mutual fund** pools individual investor dollars and invests them in large numbers of well-diversified securities. Individual investors buy shares in a mutual fund in the hope of earning a high rate of return and in much the same way as people buy shares of stock. Because of the large numbers of people investing in any one mutual fund, the funds can afford to invest in hundreds (if not thousands) of securities at any one time, minimizing the risks of any single security that does not do well. Mutual funds provide professional financial management for people who lack the time and/or expertise to invest in particular securities, such as government bonds. While there are no hard-and-fast rules, investments in one or more mutual funds are one way for people to plan for financial independence at the time of retirement.

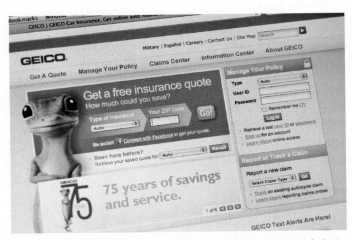

Geico Insurance allows users to input their information on its website to receive an auto insurance quote quickly and conveniently.
© NetPhotos/Alamy

A special type of mutual fund called a *money market fund* invests specifically in short-term debt securities issued by governments and large corporations. Although they offer services such as check-writing privileges and reinvestment of interest income, money market funds differ from the money market accounts offered by banks primarily in that the former represent a pool of funds, while the latter are basically specialized, individual checking accounts. Money market funds usually offer slightly higher rates of interest than bank money market accounts.

Brokerage Firms and Investment Banks

Brokerage firms buy and sell stocks, bonds, and other securities for their customers and provide other financial services. Larger brokerage firms like Merrill Lynch, Charles Schwab, and Edward Jones offer financial services unavailable at their smaller competitors. Merrill Lynch, for example, offers the Merrill Lynch Cash Management Account (CMA), which pays interest on deposits and allows clients to write checks, borrow money, and withdraw cash much like a commercial bank. The largest of the brokerage firms (including Merrill Lynch) have developed so many specialized services that they may be considered financial networks—organizations capable of offering virtually all of the services traditionally associated with commercial banks. The rise of online brokerage firms has helped investors who want to do it themselves at low costs. Firms like E-Trade, TDAmeritrade, and Scottrade offer investors the ability to buy and sell securities for $7 to $10 per trade, while the same trade at Morgan Stanley might cost $125. E-Trade offers banking services, debit cards, wire transfers, and many of the same services that the traditional brokerage firms offer.

Most brokerage firms are really part financial conglomerates that provide many different kinds of services besides buying and selling securities for clients. For example, Merrill Lynch also is an investment banker, as are Morgan Stanley and Goldman Sachs. The **investment banker** underwrites new issues of securities for corporations, states, and municipalities needed to raise money in the capital markets. The new issue market is called a *primary market* because the sale of the securities is for the first time. After the first sale, the securities trade in the *secondary markets* by brokers. The investment banker advises on the price of the new securities and generally guarantees the sale while overseeing the distribution of the securities through the selling brokerage houses. Investment bankers also act as dealers who make markets in securities. They do this by offering to sell the securities at an asked price (which is a higher rate) and buy the securities at a bid price (which is a lower rate)—the difference in the two prices represents the profit for the dealer.

Finance Companies Finance companies are businesses that offer short-term loans at substantially higher rates of interest than banks. Commercial finance companies make loans to businesses, requiring their borrowers to pledge assets such as equipment, inventories, or unpaid accounts as collateral for the loans. Consumer finance companies make loans to individuals. Like commercial finance companies, these firms require some sort of personal collateral as security against the borrower's possible inability to repay their loans. Because of the high interest rates they charge and other factors, finance companies typically are the lender of last resort for individuals and businesses whose credit limits have been exhausted and/or those with poor credit ratings.

Electronic Banking

Since the advent of the computer age, a wide range of technological innovations has made it possible to move money all across the world electronically. Such "paperless" transactions have allowed financial institutions to reduce costs in what has been, and continues to be, a virtual competitive battlefield. **Electronic funds transfer (EFT)** is any movement of funds by means of an electronic terminal, telephone, computer, or magnetic tape. Such transactions order a particular financial institution to subtract money from one account and add it to another. The most commonly used forms of EFT are automated teller machines, automated clearinghouses, and home banking systems.

> Since the advent of the computer age, a wide range of technological innovations has made it possible to move money all across the world electronically.

Automated Teller Machines Probably the most familiar form of electronic banking is the **automated teller machine (ATM)**, which dispenses cash, accepts deposits, and allows balance inquiries and cash transfers from one account to another. ATMs provide 24-hour banking services—both at home (through a local bank) and far away (via worldwide ATM networks such as Cirrus and Plus). Rapid growth, driven by both strong consumer acceptance and lower transaction costs for banks (about half the cost of teller transactions), has led to the installation of hundreds of thousands of ATMs worldwide. Table 15.5 presents some interesting statistics about ATMs.

Automated Clearinghouses **Automated clearinghouses (ACHs)** permit payments such as deposits or withdrawals to be

▼ **TABLE 15.5** Facts about ATM Use

There are 2.2 million ATMs currently in use.
The average cash withdrawal from ATMs is $60.
The typical ATM consumer will visit an ATM 7.4 times per month.
The total ratio of people per ATM is 3,000:1.
ATM users spend approximately 23 percent more than non-ATM users.
The top ATM owners are Cardtronics, Payment Alliance, Bank of America, JPMorgan Chase, and Wells Fargo.

Source: Lenpenzo, Trends Today, "ATM Machines Statistics," March 2, 2012, www.statisticbrain.com/atm-machine-statistics/ (accessed April 6, 2015).

finance companies businesses that offer short-term loans at substantially higher rates of interest than banks.

electronic funds transfer (EFT) any movement of funds by means of an electronic terminal, telephone, computer, or magnetic tape.

automated teller machine (ATM) the most familiar form of electronic banking, which dispenses cash, accepts deposits, and allows balance inquiries and cash transfers from one account to another.

automated clearinghouses (ACHs) a system that permits payments such as deposits or withdrawals to be made to and from a bank account by magnetic computer tape.

made to and from a bank account by magnetic computer tape. Most large U.S. employers, and many others worldwide, use ACHs to deposit their employees' paychecks directly to the employees' bank accounts. While direct deposit is used by only 50 percent of U.S. workers, nearly 100 percent of Japanese workers and more than 90 percent of European workers utilize it. The largest user of automated clearinghouses in the United States is the federal government, with 99 percent of federal government employees and 65 percent of the private workforce receiving their pay via direct deposit. More than 82 percent of all Social Security payments are made through an ACH system. The Social Security Administration is trying to reduce costs, theft, and fraud, so if you apply for Social Security benefits, you must receive your payments electronically.

The advantages of direct deposits to consumers include convenience, safety, and potential interest earnings. It is estimated that more than 4 million paychecks are lost or stolen annually, and FBI studies show that 2,000 fraudulent checks are cashed every day in the United States. Checks can never be lost or stolen with direct deposit. The benefits to businesses include decreased check-processing expenses and increased employee productivity. Research shows that businesses that use direct deposit can save more than $1.25 on each payroll check processed. Productivity could increase by $3 to $5 billion annually if all employees were to use direct deposit rather than taking time away from work to deposit their payroll checks.

Some companies also use ACHs for dividend and interest payments. Consumers can also use ACHs to make periodic (usually monthly) fixed payments to specific creditors without ever having to write a check or buy stamps. The estimated number of bills paid annually by consumers is 20 billion, and the total number paid through ACHs is estimated at only 8.5 billion. The average consumer who writes 10 to 15 checks each month would save $41 to $62 annually in postage alone.[12]

Online Banking Many banking activities are now conducted on a computer at home or at work, or through wireless devices such as cell phones and PDAs anywhere there is a wireless "hot point." Consumers and small businesses can now make a bewildering array of financial transactions at home or on the go 24 hours a day. Functioning much like a vast network of personal ATMs, companies like Google and Apple provide online banking services through mobile phones, allowing subscribers to make sophisticated banking transactions, buy and sell stocks and bonds, and purchase products and airline tickets without ever leaving home or speaking to another human being. Many banks allow customers to log directly into their accounts to check balances, transfer money between accounts, view their

Computers and handheld devices have made online banking extremely convenient. However, hackers have stolen millions from banking customers by tricking them into visiting websites and downloading malicious software that gives hackers access to their passwords.
© Carl Court/Getty Images

account statements, and pay bills via home computer or other Internet-enabled devices. Computer and advanced telecommunications technology have revolutionized world commerce; 62 percent of adults list Internet banking as their preferred banking method, making it the most popular banking method in the United States.[13]

LO 15-6 Investigate the challenges ahead for the banking industry.

Future of Banking

Rapid advances and innovations in technology are challenging the banking industry and requiring it to change. As we said earlier, more and more banks, both large and small, are offering electronic access to their financial services. ATM technology is rapidly changing, with machines now dispensing more than just cash. Online financial services, ATM technology, and bill presentation are just a few of the areas where rapidly changing technology is causing the banking industry to change as well.

Impact of Financial Crisis The premise that banks will get bigger over the next 10 years is uncertain. During 2007–2008, the financial markets collapsed under the weight of declining housing prices, subprime mortgages (mortgages with low-qualifying borrowers), and risky securities backed by these subprime mortgages. Because the value of bank assets declined dramatically, most large banks like CitiBank, Bank of America, and Wachovia had a shrinking capital base. That is, the amount of debt in relation to their equity was so high that they were below the minimum required capital requirements.

During this period, the Federal Reserve took unprecedented actions that included buying up troubled assets from the banks and lending money at the discount window to nonbanks such as investment banks and brokers. The Fed also entered

maturing bonds in new securities and maintaining a high level of assets on its balance sheet. A major issue involves the impact this will have on the economy once the Fed begins to sell these securities.

Lastly, the future of the structure of the banking system is in the hands of the U.S. Congress. In reaction to the financial meltdown and severe recession, Congress passed the Dodd-Frank Wall Street Reform and Consumer Protection Act. The full name implies that the intent of the act is to eliminate the ability of banks to create this type of problem in the future.

> **In broad general terms, shadow banking refers to companies performing banking functions of some sort that are not regulated by banking regulators.**

into the financial markets by making markets in commercial paper and other securities where the markets had ceased to function in an orderly fashion. Additionally, the Fed began to pay interest on reserves banks kept at the Fed and finally, it kept interest rates low to stimulate the economy and to help the banks regain their health. Because banks make money by the spread between their borrowing and lending rates, the Fed managed the spread between long- and short-term rates to generate a fairly large spread for the banks.

Additionally, to keep interest rates low and stimulate the economy, the Fed bought $85 billion of mortgages and other financial assets on a monthly basis. By December 2014, it had accumulated over $4 trillion of securities on its balance sheet. By 2015, the Fed was no longer adding new securities to its portfolio but was reinvesting its interest and principal from

Shadow Banking In broad general terms, shadow banking refers to companies performing banking functions of some sort that are not regulated by banking regulators. All the types of financial institutions listed earlier in the Nonbanking Institutions section can be considered shadow banks under this definition. Shadow banking activities are increasing. In a letter to shareholders in the 2013 annual report, Jamie Dimon, CEO and chair of JPMorgan Chase, was quoted as saying to his shareholders that the bank will face tough competitors, including shadow banking. He may have said it best in the following quote:

> Many of these institutions are smart and sophisticated and will benefit as banks move out of certain products and services. Nonbank financial competitors will look at every product we price, and if they can do it cheaper with their set of capital providers, they will. There is nothing inherently wrong with this—it is a natural state of affairs and, in some cases, may benefit the

clients who get the better price. But regulators should—and will—be looking at how all financial companies (including non-bank competitors) need to be regulated and will be evaluating what is better to be done by banks vs. non-banks and vice versa.[15]

In addition to shadow banks mentioned by Dimon, there are the peer-to-peer lenders like Prosper, a company that matches investors and borrowers with loans of between $2,000 and $35,000. There are other sources of funding by Internet websites such as GoFundMe, which helps people enhance their life skills, raise money for health care

issues, and more. Another similar website is Kickstarter, which funds creative projects in the worlds of art, film, games, music, publishing, and so on. In many cases, funds provided for these projects replace loans that might have been used to develop the project. These forms of funding are growing rapidly. Kickstarter was formed in October 2009 and has already received a total of $1.6 billion to fund 82,000 projects.[16] There is also the budding use of virtual money and other futuristic ideas, so only time will tell how the world of banking changes over time and how bank regulators will deal with these nonbank institutions. ▪

SO YOU'RE INTERESTED // in Financial Systems or Banking /

You think you might be interested in going into finance or banking, but it is so hard to tell when you are a full-time student. Classes that seem interesting when you take them might not translate in an interesting work experience after you graduate. A great way to see if you would excel at a career in finance is to get some experience in the industry. Internships, whether they are paid or unpaid, not only help you figure out what you might really want to do after you graduate but they are also a great way to build up your résumé, put your learning to use, and start generating connections within the field.

For example, Pennsylvania's Delaware County District Attorney's Office has been accepting business students from Villanova University for a six-month internship. The student works in the economic-crime division, analyzing documents of people under investigation for financial

crimes ranging from fraud to money laundering. The students get actual experience in forensic accounting and have the chance to see whether this is the right career path. On top of that, the program has saved the county an average of $20,000 annually on consulting and accounting fees, not to mention that detectives now have more time to take on larger caseloads. One student who completed the program spent his six months investigating a case in which the owner of a sewage treatment company had embezzled a total of $1 million over the course of nine years. The student noted that the experience helped him gain an understanding about how different companies handle their financial statements, as well as how accounting can be applied in forensics and law enforcement.

Internship opportunities are plentiful all over the country, although you may need to do some

research to find them. To start, talk to your program advisor and your professors about opportunities. Also, you can check company websites where you think you might like to work to see if they have any opportunities available. City, state, or federal government offices often provide student internships as well. No matter where you end up interning, the real-life skills you pick up, as well as the résumé boost you get, will be helpful in finding a job after you graduate. When you graduate, commercial banks and other financial institutions offer major employment opportunities. In 2008–2009, a major downturn in the financial industry resulted in mergers, acquisitions, and financial restructuring for many companies. While the immediate result was a decrease in job opportunities, as the industry recovers, there will be many challenging job opportunities available.[17]

chapter SIXteen

financial management and securities markets

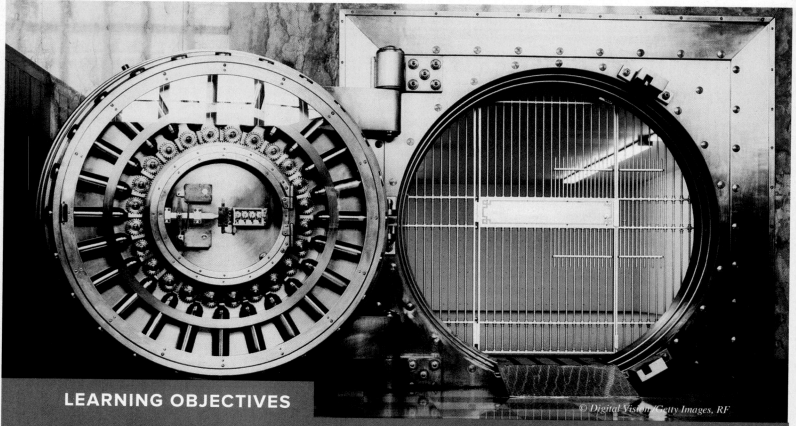

© Digital Vision/Getty Images, RF

LEARNING OBJECTIVES

After reading this chapter, you will be able to:

LO 16-1 Describe some common methods of managing current assets.

LO 16-2 Identify some sources of short-term financing (current liabilities).

LO 16-3 Summarize the importance of long-term assets and capital budgeting.

LO 16-4 Specify how companies finance their operations and manage fixed assets with long-term liabilities, particularly bonds.

LO 16-5 Discuss how corporations can use equity financing by issuing stock through an investment banker.

LO 16-6 Describe the various securities markets in the United States.

While it's certainly true that money makes the world go around, financial management is the discipline that makes the world turn more smoothly. Indeed, without effective management of assets, liabilities, and owners' equity, all business organizations are doomed to fail—regardless of the quality and innovativeness of their products. Financial management is the field that addresses the issues of obtaining and managing the funds and resources necessary to run a business successfully. It is not limited to business organizations: All organizations, from the corner store to the local nonprofit art museum, from giant corporations to county governments, must manage their resources effectively and efficiently if they are to achieve their objectives.

In this chapter, we look at both short- and long-term financial management. First, we discuss the management of short-term assets, which companies use to generate sales and conduct ordinary day-to-day business operations. Next we turn our attention to the management of short-term liabilities, the sources of short-term funds used to finance the business. Then, we discuss the management of long-term assets such as plants, equipment, and the use of common stock (equity) and bonds (long-term liability) to finance these long-term corporate assets. Finally, we look at the securities markets, where stocks and bonds are traded. ∎

MANAGING CURRENT ASSETS AND LIABILITIES

Managing short-term assets and liabilities involves managing the current assets and liabilities on the balance sheet (discussed in Chapter 14). Current assets are short-term resources such as cash, investments, accounts receivable, and inventory. Current liabilities are short-term debts such as accounts payable, accrued salaries, accrued taxes, and short-term bank loans. We use the terms current and short term interchangeably because short-term assets and liabilities are usually replaced by new assets and liabilities within three or four months, and always within a year. Managing short-term assets and liabilities is sometimes called **working capital management** because short-term assets and liabilities continually flow through an organization and are thus said to be "working."

> **LO 16-1** Describe some common methods of managing current assets.

Managing Current Assets

The chief goal of financial managers who focus on current assets and liabilities is to maximize the return to the business on cash, temporary investments of idle cash, accounts receivable, and inventory.

Managing Cash A crucial element facing any financial manager is effectively managing the firm's cash flow. Remember that cash flow is the movement of money through an organization on a daily, weekly, monthly, or yearly basis. Ensuring

that sufficient (but not excessive) funds are on hand to meet the company's obligations is one of the single most important facets of financial management.

Idle cash does not make money, and corporate checking accounts typically do not earn interest. As a result, astute money managers try to keep just enough cash on hand, called **transaction balances**, to pay bills—such as employee wages, supplies, and utilities—as they fall due. To manage the firm's cash and ensure that enough cash flows through the organization quickly and efficiently, companies try to speed up cash collections from customers.

To facilitate collection, some companies have customers send their payments to a **lockbox**, which is simply an address for receiving payments, instead of directly to the company's main address. The manager of the lockbox, usually a commercial bank, collects payments directly from the lockbox several times a day and deposits them into the company's bank account. The bank can then start clearing the checks and get the money into the company's checking account much more quickly than if the payments had been submitted directly to the company. However, there is no free lunch: The costs associated with lockbox systems make them worthwhile only for those companies that receive thousands of checks from customers each business day.

working capital management the managing of short-term assets and liabilities.

transaction balances cash kept on hand by a firm to pay normal daily expenses, such as employee wages and bills for supplies and utilities.

lockbox an address, usually a commercial bank, at which a company receives payments in order to speed collections from customers.

Large firms with many stores or offices around the country, such as HSBC Finance Corporation, frequently use electronic funds transfer to speed up collections. HSBC Finance Corporation's local offices deposit checks received each business day into their local banks and, at the end of the day, HSBC Finance Corporation's corporate office initiates the transfer of all collected funds to its central bank for overnight investment. This technique is especially attractive for major international companies, which face slow and sometimes uncertain physical delivery of payments and/or less-than-efficient check-clearing procedures.

More and more companies are now using electronic funds transfer systems to pay and collect bills online. Companies generally want to collect cash quickly but pay out cash slowly. When companies use electronic funds transfers between buyers and suppliers, the speed of collections and disbursements increases to one day. Only with the use of checks can companies delay the payment of cash by three or four days until the check is presented to their bank and the cash leaves their account.

Investing Idle Cash As companies sell products, they generate cash on a daily basis, and sometimes cash comes in faster than it is needed to pay bills. Organizations often invest this "extra" cash, for periods as short as one day (overnight) or for as long as one year, until it is needed. Such temporary investments of cash are known as **marketable securities**. Examples include U.S. Treasury bills, certificates of deposit, commercial paper, and eurodollar deposits. Table 16.1 summarizes a number of different marketable securities used by businesses and some sample interest rates on these investments as of June 23, 2006, and April 2, 2015. The safety rankings are relative. While all of the listed securities are very low risk, the U.S. government securities are the safest. You can see from the table that interest rates have declined during the two periods presented.

You may never see interest rates this low in your lifetime. The Fed used monetary policy to lower interest rates to stimulate borrowing and investment during the severe recession of 2007–2009 and continued to maintain low rates into 2015 to stimulate employment and economic growth. The Fed has stated that it expects to continue with low interest rates into 2015 or even 2016, which would be unprecedented. Although many economists expect the Fed to raise interest rates in late 2015, the

▼ **TABLE 16.1** Short-Term Investment Possibilities for Idle Cash

Type of Security	Maturity	Seller of Security	Interest Rate 6/23/2006	4/2/2015	Safety Level
U.S. Treasury bills	90 days	U.S. government	4.80%	0.03%	Excellent
U.S. Treasury bills	180 days	U.S. government	5.05	0.13	Excellent
Commercial paper	30 days	Major corporations	5.14	0.08	Very good
Certificates of deposit	90 days	U.S. commercial banks	5.40	0.25	Very good
Certificates of deposit	180 days	U.S. commercial banks	5.43	0.30	Very good
Eurodollars	90 days	European commercial banks	5.48	0.19	Very good

Sources: Board of Governors of the Federal Reserve System, "Selected Interest Rates (Weekly)—H.15," April 7, 2015, www.federalreserve.gov/releases/H15/current/default.htm (accessed April 7, 2015); Fidelity, "Certificates of Deposit," www.fidelity.com/fixed-income-bonds/cds (accessed April 7, 2015).

increase may be only 0.25 percent. This would still leave rates at a historic low.

Many large companies invest idle cash in U.S. **Treasury bills (T-bills)**, which are short-term debt obligations the U.S. government sells to raise money. Issued weekly by the U.S. Treasury, T-bills carry maturities of between one week and one year. U.S. T-bills are generally considered to be the safest of all investments and are called risk free because the U.S. government will not default on its debt.

Commercial certificates of deposit (CDs) are issued by commercial banks and brokerage companies. They are available in minimum amounts of $100,000 but are typically in units of $1 million for large corporations investing excess cash. Unlike consumer CDs (discussed in Chapter 15), which must be held until maturity, commercial CDs may be traded prior to maturity. Should a cash shortage occur, the organization can simply sell the CD on the open market and obtain needed funds.

One of the most popular short-term investments for the largest business organizations is **commercial paper**—a written promise from one company to another to pay a specific amount of money. Because commercial paper is backed only by the name and reputation of the issuing company, sales of commercial paper are restricted to only the largest and most financially stable companies. As commercial paper is frequently bought and sold for durations of as short as one business day, many "players" in the market find themselves buying commercial paper with excess cash on one day and selling it to gain extra money the following day.

During 2007 and 2008, the commercial paper market simply stopped functioning. Investors no longer trusted the IOUs of even the best companies. Companies that had relied on commercial paper to fund short-term cash needs had to turn to the banks for borrowing. Those companies who had existing lines of credit at their bank were able to draw on their line of credit. Others were in a tight spot. Eventually, the Federal Reserve entered the market to buy and sell commercial paper for its own portfolio. This is something the Fed was not in the habit of doing. But it rescued the market, and the market has functioned well in the past few years.

Some companies invest idle cash in international markets such as the **eurodollar market**, a market for trading U.S. dollars in foreign countries. Because the eurodollar market was originally developed by London banks, any dollar-denominated deposit in a non-U.S. bank is called a eurodollar deposit, regardless of whether the issuing bank is actually located in Europe, South America, or anyplace else. For example, if you travel overseas and deposit $1,000 in a German bank, you will have "created" a eurodollar deposit in the amount of $1,000. Because the U.S. dollar is accepted by most countries for international trade, these dollar deposits can be used by international companies to settle their accounts. The market created for trading such investments offers firms with extra dollars a chance to earn a slightly higher rate of return with just a little more risk than they would face by investing in U.S. Treasury bills.

Individuals and companies can invest their idle cash in marketable securities such as U.S. Treasury bills, commercial paper, and eurodollar deposits.
© Tetra Images/Getty Images, RF

Maximizing Accounts Receivable After cash and marketable securities, the balance sheet lists accounts receivable and inventory. Remember that accounts receivable is money owed to a business by credit customers. For example, if you charge your Shell gasoline purchases, until you actually pay for them with cash or a check, they represent an account receivable to Shell. Many businesses make the vast majority of their sales on credit, so managing accounts receivable is an important task.

Each credit sale represents an account receivable for the company, the terms of which typically require customers to pay the full amount due within 30, 60, or even 90 days from the date of the sale. To encourage quick payment, some businesses offer some of their customers discounts of between 1 and 2 percent if they pay off their balance within a specified period of time (usually between 10 and 30 days). On the other hand, late payment charges of between 1 and 1.5 percent serve to discourage slow payers from sitting on their bills forever. The larger the early payment discount offered, the faster customers will tend to pay their accounts. Unfortunately, while discounts increase cash flow, they also reduce profitability. Finding the right balance between the added advantages of early cash receipt and the disadvantages of reduced profits is no simple matter. Similarly, determining the optimal balance between the higher sales likely to result from extending credit to customers with less than sterling credit ratings and the higher bad-debt losses likely to result from a more lenient credit policy is also challenging. Information on company credit ratings is provided by local credit bureaus, national credit-rating agencies such as Dun and Bradstreet, and industry trade groups.

Optimizing Inventory While the inventory that a firm holds is controlled by both production needs and marketing considerations, the financial manager has to coordinate inventory purchases to manage cash flows. The object is to minimize the firm's investment in inventory without experiencing production cutbacks as a result of critical materials shortfalls or lost sales due to insufficient finished goods inventories. Every dollar invested in inventory is a dollar unavailable for investment in some other area of the organization. Optimal inventory levels are determined in large part by the method of production. If a firm attempts to produce its goods just in time to meet sales demand, the level of inventory will be relatively low. If, on the other hand, the firm produces materials in a constant, level pattern, inventory increases when sales decrease and decreases when sales increase. One way that companies are optimizing inventory is through the use of radio frequency identification (RFID) technology. Companies such as Walmart better manage their inventories by using RFID tags. An RFID tag, which contains a silicon chip and an antenna, allows a company to use radio waves to track and identify the products to which the tags are attached. These tags are primarily used to track inventory shipments from the manufacturer to the buyer's warehouses and then to the individual stores and also cut down on trucking theft because the delivery truck and its contents can be tracked.

The automobile industry is an excellent example of an industry driven almost solely by inventory levels. Because it is inefficient to continually lay off workers in slow times and call them back in better times, Ford, General Motors, and Toyota try to set and stick to quarterly production quotas. Automakers typically try to keep a 60-day supply of unsold cars. During particularly slow periods, however, it is not unusual for inventories to exceed 100 days of sales.

Although less publicized, inventory shortages can be as much of a drag on potential profits as too much inventory. Not having an item on hand may send the customer to a competitor—forever. Complex computer inventory models are frequently employed to determine the optimum level of inventory a firm should hold to support a given level of sales. Such models can indicate how and when parts inventories should be ordered so that they are available exactly when required—and not a day before. Developing and maintaining such an intricate production and inventory system is difficult, but it can often prove to be the difference between experiencing average profits and spectacular ones.

Loans are important for most consumers purchasing a home or business. Interest rates have been at historic lows over the past few years but are expected to increase in the long run.
© Andy Dean Photography/Alamy, RF

LO 16-2 Identify some sources of short-term financing (current liabilities).

Managing Current Liabilities

While having extra cash on hand is a delightful surprise, the opposite situation—a temporary cash shortfall—can be a crisis. The good news is that there are several potential sources of short-term funds. Suppliers often serve as an important source through credit sales practices. Also, banks, finance companies, and other organizations offer short-term funds through loans and other business operations.

Accounts Payable Remember from Chapter 14 that accounts payable is money an organization owes to suppliers for goods and services. Just as accounts receivable must be actively managed to ensure proper cash collections, so too must accounts payable be managed to make the best use of this important liability.

The most widely used source of short-term financing, and therefore the most important account payable, is **trade credit**—credit extended by suppliers for the purchase of their goods and services. While varying in formality, depending on both the organizations involved and the value of the items purchased, most trade credit agreements offer discounts to organizations that pay their bills early. A supplier, for example, may offer trade terms of "1/10 net 30," meaning that the purchasing organization may take a 1 percent discount from the invoice amount if it makes payment by the 10th day after receiving the bill. Otherwise, the entire amount is due within 30 days. For example, pretend that you are the financial manager in charge of payables. You owe Ajax Company $10,000, and it offers trade terms of 2/10 net 30. By paying the amount due within 10 days, you can save 2 percent of $10,000, or $200. Assume you place orders with Ajax once per month and have 12 bills of $10,000 each per year. By taking the discount every time, you will save 12 times $200, or $2,400, per year. Now assume you are the financial manager of Gigantic Corp., and it has monthly payables of $100 million per month. Two percent of $100 million is $2 million per month. Failure to take advantage of such trade discounts can add up to large opportunity losses over the span of a year.

Bank Loans Virtually all organizations—large and small—obtain short-term funds for operations from banks. In most instances, the credit services granted these firms take the form of a line of credit or fixed dollar loan. A **line of credit** is an arrangement by which a bank agrees to lend a specified amount of money to the organization upon request—provided that the bank has the required funds to make the loan. In general, a business line of credit is very similar to a consumer credit card, with the exception that the preset credit limit can amount to millions of dollars.

In addition to credit lines, banks also make **secured loans**—loans backed by collateral that the bank can claim if the borrowers do not repay the loans—and **unsecured loans**—loans backed only by the borrowers' good reputation and previous credit rating. Both individuals and businesses build their credit rating from their history of borrowing and repaying borrowed funds on time and in full. The three national credit-rating services are Equifax, TransUnion, and Experian. A lack of credit history or a poor credit history can make it difficult to get loans from financial institutions. The *principal* is the amount of money borrowed; *interest* is a percentage of the principal that the bank charges for use of its money. As we mentioned in Chapter 15, banks also pay depositors interest on savings accounts and some checking accounts. Thus, banks charge borrowers interest for loans and pay interest to depositors for the use of their money. In addition, these loans may include origination fees.

One of the complaints from borrowers during the financial meltdown and recession was that banks weren't willing to lend. There were several causes. Banks were trying to rebuild their capital, and they didn't want to take the extra risk that lending offers in an economic recession. They were drowning in bad debts and were not sure how future loan losses would affect their capital. The banks' lack of lending caused problems for small businesses. Smaller regional banks did a better job of maintaining small business loans than the major money center banks who suffered most in the recession.

The **prime rate** is the interest rate commercial banks charge their best customers for short-term loans. For many years, loans at the prime rate represented funds at the lowest possible cost. For some companies other alternatives may be cheaper, such as borrowing at the London Interbank Offer Rate (LIBOR) or using commercial paper.

The interest rates on commercial loans may be either fixed or variable. A variable or floating-rate loan offers an advantage when interest rates are falling but represents a distinct disadvantage when interest rates are rising. Between 1999 and 2004, interest rates plummeted, and borrowers refinanced their loans with low-cost fixed-rate loans. Nowhere was this more visible than in the U.S. mortgage markets, where homeowners lined up to refinance their high-percentage home mortgages with lower-cost loans, in some cases as low as 5 percent on a 30-year loan. These mortgage interest rates had returned to 6.5 percent by mid-2006, but by April 2015 had declined to less than 4.0 percent. Individuals and corporations have the same motivation: to minimize their borrowing costs. During this period

factor a finance company to which businesses sell their accounts receivable—usually for a percentage of the total face value.

long-term (fixed) assets production facilities (plants), offices, and equipment—all of which are expected to last for many years.

capital budgeting the process of analyzing the needs of the business and selecting the assets that will maximize its value.

of historically low interest rates, companies ramped up their borrowing, bought back stock, and locked in large amounts of debt at low rates. Think back to Chapter 14 and imagine what impact this behavior will have on the interest coverage ratio.

Nonbank Liabilities Banks are not the only source of short-term funds for businesses. Indeed, virtually all financial institutions, from insurance companies to pension funds, from money market funds to finance companies, make short-term loans to many organizations. The largest U.S. companies also actively engage in borrowing money from the eurodollar and commercial paper markets. As noted earlier, both of these funds' sources are typically slightly less expensive than bank loans.

In some instances, businesses actually sell their accounts receivable to a finance company known as a **factor**, which gives the selling organizations cash and assumes responsibility for collecting the accounts. For example, a factor might pay $60,000 for receivables with a total face value of $100,000 (60 percent of the total). The factor profits if it can collect more than what it paid for the accounts. Because the selling organization's customers send their payments to a lockbox, they may have no idea that a factor has bought their receivables.

Additional nonbank liabilities that must be efficiently managed to ensure maximum profitability are taxes owed to the government and wages owed to employees. Clearly, businesses are responsible for many different types of taxes, including federal, state, and local income taxes, property taxes, mineral rights taxes, unemployment taxes, Social Security taxes, workers' compensation taxes, excise taxes, and more. While the public tends to think that the only relevant taxes are on income and sales, many industries must pay other taxes that far exceed those levied against their income. Taxes and employees' wages represent debt obligations of the firm, which the financial manager must plan to meet as they fall due.

> **"** All assets and projects must be continually reevaluated to ensure their compatibility with the organization's needs. **"**

LO 16-3 Summarize the importance of long-term assets and capital budgeting.

MANAGING FIXED ASSETS

Up to this point, we have focused on the short-term aspects of financial management. While most business failures are the result of poor short-term planning, successful ventures must

also consider the long-term financial consequences of their actions. Managing the long-term assets and liabilities and the owners' equity portion of the balance sheet is important for the long-term health of the business.

Long-term (fixed) assets are expected to last for many years—production facilities (plants), offices, equipment, heavy machinery, furniture, automobiles, and so on. In today's fast-paced world, companies need the most technologically advanced, modern facilities and equipment they can afford. Automobile, oil refining, and transportation companies are dependent on fixed assets.

Modern and high-tech equipment carry high price tags, and the financial arrangements required to support these investments are by no means trivial. Leasing is just one approach to financing. Obtaining major long-term financing can be challenging for even the most profitable organizations. For less successful firms, such challenges can prove nearly impossible. One approach is leasing assets such as equipment, machines, and buildings. Leasing involves paying a fee for usage rather than owning the asset. There are two kinds of leases: capital leases and operating leases. A capital lease is a long-term contract and shows up on the balance sheet as an asset and liability. The operating lease is a short-term cancelable lease and does not show up on the balance sheet. We'll take a closer look at long-term financing in a moment, but first let's address some issues associated with fixed assets, including capital budgeting, risk assessment, and the costs of financing fixed assets.

Capital Budgeting and Project Selection

One of the most important jobs performed by the financial manager is to decide what fixed assets, projects, and investments will earn profits for the firm beyond the costs necessary to fund them. The process of analyzing the needs of the business and selecting the assets that will maximize its value is called **capital budgeting**, and the capital budget is the amount of money budgeted for investment in such long-term assets. But capital budgeting does not end with the selection and purchase of a particular piece of land, equipment, or major investment. All assets and projects must be continually reevaluated to ensure their compatibility with the organization's needs. Financial executives believe most budgeting activities are occasionally or frequently unrealistic or irrelevant. If a particular asset does not live up to expectations, then management must determine why and take necessary corrective action. Budgeting is not an exact process, and managers must be flexible when new information is available.

Assessing Risk

Every investment carries some risk. Figure 16.1 ranks potential investment projects according to estimated risk. When

Capital budgeting involves determining the amount of financial resources that will be needed to purchase long-term assets such as an office building.
© Corbis/Glow images, RF

FIGURE 16.1
Qualitative Assessment of Capital Budgeting Risk

considering investments overseas, risk assessments must include the political climate and economic stability of a region. The decision to introduce a product or build a manufacturing facility in England would be much less risky than a decision to build one in the Middle East, for example.

The longer a project or asset is expected to last, the greater its potential risk because it is hard to predict whether a piece of equipment will wear out or become obsolete in 5 or 10 years. Predicting cash flows one year down the road is difficult, but projecting them over the span of a 10-year project is a gamble.

The level of a project's risk is also affected by the stability and competitive nature of the marketplace and the world economy as a whole. IBM's latest high-technology computer product is far more likely to become obsolete overnight than is a similar $10 million investment in a manufacturing plant. Dramatic changes in the marketplace are not uncommon. Indeed, uncertainty created by the rapid devaluation of Asian currencies in the late 1990s wrecked a host of assumptions in literally hundreds of projects worldwide. Financial managers must constantly consider such issues when making long-term decisions about the purchase of fixed assets.

Pricing Long-Term Money

The ultimate profitability of any project depends not only on accurate assumptions of how much cash it will generate, but also on its financing costs. Because a business must pay interest on money it borrows, the returns from any project must cover not only the costs of operating the project but also the interest expenses for the debt used to finance its construction. Unless an organization can effectively cover all of its costs—both financial and operating—it will eventually fail.

Clearly, only a limited supply of funds is available for investment in any given enterprise. The most efficient and profitable companies can attract the lowest-cost funds because they typically offer reasonable financial returns at very low relative risks. Newer and less prosperous firms must pay higher costs to attract capital because these companies tend to be quite risky. One of the strongest motivations for companies to manage their financial resources wisely is that they will, over time, be able to reduce the costs of their funds and in so doing increase their overall profitability.

In our free-enterprise economy, new firms tend to enter industries that offer the greatest potential rewards for success. However, as more and more companies enter an industry, competition intensifies, eventually driving profits down to average levels. The digital music player market of the early 2000s provides an excellent example of the changes in profitability that typically accompany increasing competition. The sign of a successful capital budgeting program is that the new products create higher than normal profits and drive sales and the stock price up. This has certainly been true for Apple when it made the decision to enter the consumer electronics industry. In 2001, Apple introduced the first iPod. Since then, the iPod has undergone many enhancements in size, style, and different versions such as the small Nano. Sales of iPods have declined over time as iPhones took their place as music players. It was the iPod that made the iTunes Store possible, which has continued to grow at rates of 38 percent from 2011 to 2012 and 25 percent from 2012 to 2013. It now accounts for $16 billion in revenues. The iPhone, introduced in 2007, has now gone through many annual updates with the latest being the iPhone 6. Apple set a new record by selling 74.5 million iPhone 6s during the quarter ending December 31, 2014. Finally, the iPad tablet was introduced in 2010 and is now the second best product after the iPhone. Interestingly, Apple did not appear to be negatively affected by the recession. In fact, its sales grew from $42.9 billion in 2009 to $182.8 billion in 2014. It is on track to keep up its growth as it expands into China, India, and other emerging markets. An interesting development was that the ease of synchronization with all Apple computers caused an increase in the sale of iMacs and MacBooks. The Apple watch will continue to synchronize with other Apple products. The jury is still out as to the impact the Apple watch will have on Apple sales.

Even with a well-planned capital budgeting program, it may be difficult for Apple to stay ahead of the competition because the Google Android platform is being used by Apple's competitors.

Apple stock trades at approximately 100 times what it did nearly 10 years ago.
© Bloomberg/Getty Images

This intense competition may make it difficult to continue market dominance for any extended period. However, Apple is now the most valuable company in the world, valued at $734 billion on April 2, 2015. On June 9, 2014, Apple split its stock seven for one, meaning that for every share you owned, you would get six more for a total of seven shares. There is no real gain involved because the stock price is divided by 7, so stockholders still have the same value, just more shares at a lower price. An investor who bought $1,000 of Apple stock in 2003 for $0.91 would have 1,100 shares of Apple stock worth $138,611 on April 7, 2015. The problem is having the patience to continue to hold such a winner without taking some profits along the way.[2]

Maintaining market dominance is also difficult in the personal computer industry, particularly because tablet computers are taking away market share. With increasing competition, prices have fallen dramatically since the 1990s. Weaker companies have failed, leaving the most efficient producers/marketers scrambling for market share. The expanded market for personal computers dramatically reduced the financial returns generated by each dollar invested in productive assets. The "glory days" of the personal computer industry—the time in which fortunes could be won and lost in the space of an average-sized garage—have long since passed into history. Personal computers have essentially become commodity items, and profit margins for companies in this industry have shrunk as the market matures.

LO 16-4 Specify how companies finance their operations and manage fixed assets with long-term liabilities, particularly bonds.

FINANCING WITH LONG-TERM LIABILITIES

As we said earlier, long-term assets do not come cheaply, and few companies have the cash on hand to open a new store across town, build a new manufacturing facility, research and develop a new life-saving drug, or launch a new product worldwide. To develop such fixed assets, companies need to raise low-cost long-term funds to finance them. Two common choices for raising these funds are attracting new owners *(equity financing)*, which we'll look at in a moment, and taking on long-term liabilities *(debt financing)*, which we'll look at now.

Long-term liabilities are debts that will be repaid over a number of years, such as long-term bank loans and bond issues. These take many different forms, but in the end, the key word is *debt*. Companies may raise money by borrowing it from commercial banks or other financial institutions in the form of lines of credit, short-term loans, or long-term loans. Many corporations acquire debt by borrowing money from pension funds, mutual funds, or life-insurance funds.

Companies that rely too heavily on debt can get into serious trouble should the economy falter; during these times, they may not earn enough operating income to make the required interest payments (remember the times interest earned ratio in Chapter 14). In severe cases when the problem persists too long, creditors will not restructure loans but will instead sue for the interest and principal owed and force the company into bankruptcy.

Bonds: Corporate IOUs

Much long-term debt takes the form of **bonds**, which are debt instruments that larger companies sell to raise long-term funds. In essence, the buyers of bonds (bondholders) loan the issuer of the bonds cash in exchange for regular interest payments until the loan is repaid on or before the specified maturity date. The bond itself is a certificate, much like an IOU, that represents the company's debt to the bondholder. Bonds are issued by a wide variety of entities, including corporations; national, state, and local governments; public utilities; and nonprofit corporations. Most bondholders need not hold their bonds until maturity; rather, the existence of active secondary markets of brokers and dealers allows for the quick and efficient transfer of bonds from owner to owner.

The bond contract, or *indenture*, specifies all of the terms of the agreement between the bondholders and the issuing organization. The indenture, which can run more than 100 pages, specifies the basic terms of the bond, such as its face value, maturity date, and the annual interest rate. Table 16.2 briefly explains how to determine these and more things about a bond from a bond quote, as it might appear in *Barron's* magazine.

The face value of the bond, its initial sales price, is typically $1,000. After this, however, the price of the bond on the open market will fluctuate along with changes in the economy (particularly, changes in interest rates) and in the creditworthiness of the issuer. Bondholders receive the face value of the bond along with the final interest payment on the maturity date. The annual interest rate (often called the *coupon rate*) is the guaranteed percentage of face value that the company will pay to the bond owner every year. For example, a $1,000 bond with a coupon rate of 7 percent would pay $70 per year in interest. In most cases, bond indentures specify that interest payments be made every six months. In the example above, the $70 annual payment would be divided into two semiannual payments of $35.

In addition to the terms of interest payments and maturity date, the bond indenture typically covers other important topics, such as repayment methods, interest payment dates, procedures to be followed in case the organization fails to make the interest payments, conditions for the early repayment of the bonds, and any conditions requiring the pledging of assets as collateral.

Types of Bonds

Not surprisingly, there are a great many different types of bonds. Most are **unsecured bonds**, meaning that they are not backed by collateral; such bonds are termed *debentures*. **Secured bonds**, on the other hand, are backed by specific collateral that must be forfeited in the event that the issuing firm defaults. Whether secured or unsecured, bonds may be repaid in one lump sum or with many payments spread out over a period of time. **Serial bonds**, which are different from secured bonds, are actually a sequence of small bond issues of progressively longer maturity. The firm pays off each of the serial bonds as they mature. **Floating-rate bonds** do not have fixed interest payments; instead, the interest rate changes with current interest rates otherwise available in the economy.

In recent years, a special type of high-interest-rate bond has attracted considerable attention (usually negative) in the financial press. High-interest bonds, or **junk bonds** as they are popularly known, offer relatively high rates of interest because they have higher inherent risks. Historically, junk bonds have been associated with companies in poor financial health and/or startup firms with limited track records. In the mid-1980s, however, junk bonds became a very attractive method of financing corporate

▼ **TABLE 16.2** Bonds—Global Investment Grade Quoted in U.S. Dollars

13-June-14	Coupon	Maturity	Last Price	Last Yield	Est. Spread*	UST**	Est $ Vol (000s)
GE Capital	3.450	May 15, 2024	100.172	3.429	83	10	147,634
AT&T	4.800	June 15, 2044	100.787	4.750	135	30	260,529
Goldman Sachs	6.750	October 1, 2037	120.425	5.223	182	30	173,795

*Estimated spreads, in basis points (100 basis points is one percentage point), over the 2-, 5-, 10-, or 30-year hot run Treasury note/bond.

**Comparable U.S. Treasury issue. Coupon—the percentage in interest payment that the bond pays based on a $1,000 bond

Maturity—the day on which the issuer will reissue the principal

Last Price—last price at which the security is traded

Last Yield—yield-to-maturity for the investor that buys the bond today and holds it until it matures

Est. Spread—amount of additional yield the investor will earn each year compared to a U.S. Treasury bond or note of the same maturity

UST—U.S. Treasury bond

Est $ Vol (000s)—number of individual bonds that were bought and sold on the date indicated

Sources: MarketAxess Corporate BondTicker, www.bondticker.com; *Barron's,* "Corporate Bonds," June 16, 2014, http://online.barrons.com/public/page/9_0210-corpbonds.html (accessed June 16, 2014).

mergers; they remain popular today with many investors as a result of their very high relative interest rates. But higher risks are associated with those higher returns (upward of 12 percent per year in some cases) and the average investor would be well advised to heed those famous words: Look before you leap!

website. You should be familiar with EPS from Chapter 14. However, *beta* is a new term, and Nike's beta of 0.67 indicates that its stock price is 67 percent as volatile as the Standard & Poor's 500 Index. The market cap represents the total value of Nike's common stock, or the value of the company. The target price is the analysts' consensus of the potential stock price.

Preferred stock was defined in Chapter 14 as corporate ownership that gives the stockholder preference in the distribution of the company's profits but not the voting and control rights accorded

> ## "A second means of long-term financing is through equity."

LO 16-5 Discuss how corporations can use equity financing by issuing stock through an investment banker.

FINANCING WITH OWNERS' EQUITY

A second means of long-term financing is through equity. Remember from Chapter 14 that owners' equity refers to the owners' investment in an organization. Sole proprietors and partners own all or a part of their businesses outright, and their equity includes the money and assets they have brought into their ventures. Corporate owners, on the other hand, own stock or shares of their companies, which they hope will provide them with a return on their investment. Stockholders' equity includes common stock, preferred stock, and retained earnings.

Common stock (introduced in Chapter 4) is the single most important source of capital for most new companies. On the balance sheet, the common stock account is separated into two basic parts—common stock at par and capital in excess of par. The *par value* of a stock is simply the dollar amount printed on the stock certificate and has no relation to actual *market value*—the price at which the common stock is currently trading. The difference between a stock's par value and its offering price is called *capital in excess of par*. Except in the case of some very low-priced stocks, the capital in excess of par account is significantly larger than the par value account. Table 16.3 briefly explains how to gather important information from a stock quote, as it appears on Yahoo!'s

to common stockholders. Thus, the primary advantage of owning preferred stock is that it is a safer investment than common stock.

All businesses exist to earn profits for their owners. Without the possibility of profit, there can be no incentive to risk investors' capital and succeed. When a corporation has profits left over after

▼ **TABLE 16.3** A Basic Stock Quote

Nike, Inc. (NKE) - NYSE ★ Follow

76.31 ↓0.36(0.47%) Jun 10, 4:00PM EDT

After Hours: **76.39** ↑ 0.08 (0.10%) Jun 10, 7:16PM EDT

Prev Close:	76.67	Day's Range:	76.24–76.92
Open:	76.34	52wk Range:	59.11–80.26
Bid:	75.88 x 100	Volume:	2,576,422
Ask:	77.00 x 300	Avg Vol (3m):	3,608,820
1y Target Est:	82.54	Market Cap:	67.01B
Beta:	0.67	P/E (ttm):	26.05
Next Earnings Date:	26-Jun-14📅	EPS (ttm):	2.93
		Div & Yield:	0.96 (1.30%)

1. The **52-week high and low**—the highest and lowest prices, respectively, paid for the stock in the last year; for Nike stock, the highest was $80.26 and the lowest price, $59.11 .
2. **Stock**—the name of the issuing company. When followed by the letters "pf," the stock is a preferred stock .
3. **Symbol**—the ticker tape symbol for the stock; NKE .
4. **Dividend**—the annual cash dividend paid to stockholders; Nike paid a dividend of $0.96 per share of stock outstanding.
5. **Dividend yield**—the dividend return on one share of common stock; 1.30 percent .
6. **Volume**—the number of shares traded on this day; Nike, 2,576,422 .
7. **Close**—Nike's last sale of the day was for $76.31 .
8. **Net change**—the difference between the previous day's close and the close on the day being reported; Nike was down $0.36 .

Source: Yahoo! Finance, http://finance.yahoo.com/q?s (accessed June 16, 2014).

paying all of its expenses and taxes, it has the choice of retaining all or a portion of its earnings and/or paying them out to its shareholders in the form of dividends. **Retained earnings** are reinvested in the assets of the firm and belong to the owners in the form of equity. Retained earnings are an important source of funds and are, in fact, the only long-term funds that the company can generate internally.

When the board of directors distributes some of a corporation's profits to the owners, it issues them as cash dividend payments. But not all firms pay dividends. Many fast-growing firms like Google retain all of their earnings because they can earn high rates of return on the earnings they reinvest. Companies with fewer growth opportunities like Campbell Soup or Verizon typically pay out large proportions of their earnings in the form of dividends, thereby allowing their stockholders to reinvest their dividend payments in higher-growth companies. Table 16.4 presents a sample of companies and the dividend each paid on a single share of stock. As shown in the table, when the dividend is divided by the price the result is the **dividend yield**. The dividend yield is the cash return as a percentage of the price but does not reflect the total return an investor earns on the individual stock. If the dividend yield is 2.76 percent on Campbell Soup and the stock price increases by 10 percent from $45.26 to $49.79 then the total return would be 12.76 percent. It is not clear that stocks with high dividend yields will be preferred by investors to those with little or no dividends. Most large companies pay their stockholders dividends on a quarterly basis.

▼ **TABLE 16.4** Estimated Common Stock Price-Earnings Ratios and Dividends for Selected Companies

Ticker Symbol	Company Name	Price per Share	Dividend per Share	Dividend Yield	Earnings per Share*	Price-Earnings Ratio
AEO	American Eagle	$ 11.06	$0.50	4.52%	$ 0.31	35.68
AXP	American Express	94.76	1.04	1.10	5.06	18.73
AAPL	Apple	92.29	1.88	2.04	5.96	15.48
CPB	Campbell Soup	45.26	1.25	2.76	1.66	27.27
DIS	Disney	84.31	0.86	1.02	3.89	21.67
F	Ford	16.52	0.50	3.03	1.61	10.26
GOOG	Google	551.35	0.00	0.00	19.09	28.88
HOG	Harley Davidson	69.79	1.10	1.58	3.49	20.00
HD	Home Depot	78.43	1.88	2.40	3.93	19.96
MCD	McDonald's	99.76	3.24	3.25	5.50	18.14
MSFT	Microsoft	40.58	1.12	2.76	2.67	15.20
PG	Procter & Gamble	79.76	2.57	3.22	3.75	21.27
LUV	Southwest Airlines	25.72	0.24	0.93	1.20	21.43
VZ	Verizon	49.04	2.12	4.32	4.48	10.95

* Earnings per share are for the latest 12-month period and do not necessarily match year-end numbers.

Source: Yahoo! Finance, http://finance.yahoo.com/ (June 12, 2014).

INVESTMENT BANKING

A company that needs more money to expand or take advantage of opportunities may be able to obtain financing by issuing stock. The first-time sale of stocks and bonds directly to the public is called a *new issue.* Companies that already have stocks or bonds outstanding may offer a new issue of stock to raise additional funds for specific projects. When a company offers its stock to the public for the very first time, it is said to be "going public," and the sale is called an *initial public offering (IPO).*

New issues of stocks and bonds are sold directly to the public and to institutions in what is known as the **primary market**—the market where firms raise financial capital. The primary market differs from **secondary markets**, which are stock exchanges and over-the-counter markets where investors can trade their securities with other investors rather than the company that issued the stock or bonds. Primary market transactions actually raise cash for the issuing corporations, while secondary market transactions do not. For example, when Facebook went public on May 18, 2012, its IPO raised $16 billion for the company and stockholders, who were cashing in on their success. Once the investment bankers distributed the stock to retail brokers, the brokers sold it to clients in the secondary market for $38 per share. The stock got off to a rocky start and hit a low of $17.73 in September 2012. However, by April 7, 2015, it was at $82.32. You might want to check out its current price for fun.

Investment banking, the sale of stocks and bonds for corporations, helps such companies raise funds by matching people and institutions who have money to invest with corporations in need of resources to exploit new opportunities. Corporations usually employ an investment banking firm to help sell their securities in the primary market. An investment banker helps firms establish appropriate offering prices for their securities. In addition, the investment banker takes care of the myriad details and securities regulations involved in any sale of securities to the public.

Just as large corporations such as IBM and Microsoft have a client relationship with a law firm and an accounting firm, they also have a client relationship with an investment banking firm. An investment banking firm such as Merrill Lynch, Goldman Sachs, or Morgan Stanley can provide advice about financing plans, dividend policy, or stock repurchases, as well as advice on mergers and acquisitions. Many now offer additional banking services, making them "one-stop shopping" banking centers. When Pixar merged with Disney, both companies used investment bankers to help them value the transaction. Each firm wanted an outside opinion about what it was worth to the other. Sometimes mergers fall apart because the companies cannot agree on the price each company is worth or the structure of management after the merger. The advising investment banker, working with management, often irons out these details. Of course, investment bankers do not provide these services for free. They usually charge a fee of between 1 and 1.5 percent of the transaction. A $20 billion merger can generate between $200 and $300 million in investment banking fees. The merger mania of the late 1990s allowed top investment bankers to earn huge sums. Unfortunately, this type of fee income is dependent on healthy stock markets, which seem to stimulate the merger fever among corporate executives.

LO 16-6 Describe the various securities markets in the United States.

THE SECURITIES MARKETS

Securities markets provide a mechanism for buying and selling securities. They make it possible for owners to sell their stocks and bonds to other investors. Thus, in the broadest sense, stocks and bonds markets may be thought of as providers of liquidity—the ability to turn security holdings into cash quickly and at minimal expense and effort. Without liquid securities markets, many potential investors would sit on the sidelines rather than invest their hard-earned savings in securities. Indeed, the ability to sell securities at well-established market prices is one of the very pillars of the capitalistic society that has developed over the years in the United States.

Unlike the primary market, in which corporations sell stocks directly to the public, secondary markets permit the trading of previously issued securities. There are many different secondary markets for both stocks and bonds. If you want to purchase 100 shares of Google common stock, for example, you must purchase this stock from another investor or institution. It is the active buying and selling by many thousands of investors that establishes the prices of all financial securities. Secondary market trades may take place on organized exchanges or in what is known as the over-the-counter market. Many brokerage houses exist to help investors with financial decisions, and many offer their services through the Internet. One such broker is Charles Schwab. Its site offers a wealth of information and provides educational material to individual investors.

?

DID YOU KNOW?

A single share of Coca-Cola stock purchased during its original 1919 IPO would be worth more than $5 million today.[4]

The New York Stock Exchange is the world's largest stock exchange in terms of market capitalization.
© Steve Allen/Brand X Pictures/PunchStock, RF

Stock Markets

Stock markets exist around the world in New York, Tokyo, London, Frankfort, Paris, and other world locations. The two biggest stock markets in the United States are the New York Stock Exchange (NYSE) and the NASDAQ market.

Exchanges used to be divided into organized exchanges and over-the-counter markets, but during the past several years, dramatic changes have occurred in the markets. Both the NYSE and NASDAQ became publicly traded companies. They were previously not-for-profit organizations but are now for-profit companies. Additionally, both exchanges bought or merged with electronic exchanges. In an attempt to expand their markets, NASDAQ acquired the OMX, a Nordic stock exchange headquartered in Sweden, and the New York Stock Exchange merged with Euronext, a large European electronic exchange that trades options and futures contracts as well as common stock.

Traditionally, the NASDAQ market has been an electronic market, and many of the large technology companies such as Microsoft, Google, Apple, and Facebook trade on the NASDAQ market. The NASDAQ operates through dealers who buy and sell common stock (inventory) for their own accounts. The NYSE used to be primarily a floor-traded market, where brokers meet at trading posts on the floor of the New York Stock Exchange to buy and sell common stock. The brokers act as agents for their clients and do not own their own inventory. Today, more than 50 percent of NYSE trading is electronic. This traditional division between the two markets is becoming less significant as the exchanges become electronic.

Electronic markets have grown quickly because of the speed, low cost, and efficiency of trading that they offer over floor trading. One of the fastest-growing electronic markets has been the Intercontinental Exchange (referred to as ICE). ICE, based in Atlanta, Georgia, primarily trades financial and commodity futures products. It started out as an energy futures exchange, and in its 15 years of existence, it has broadened its futures contracts into an

array of commodities and derivative products. In December 2012, ICE made an offer to buy the New York Stock Exchange. When the NYSE became a public company and had common stock trading in the secondary market, rather than the hunter, it became the prey. On November 13, 2013, ICE completed its takeover of the NYSE. One condition of the takeover was that ICE had to divest itself of Euronext because international regulators thought the company would have a monopoly on European derivative markets. Also acquired as part of the NYSE family of exchanges was the London International Financial Futures Exchange (LIFFE). Many analysts thought that LIFFE was the major reason ICE bought the NYSE—not for its equity markets trading common stocks. So, ICE sold Euronext to a group of European investors, many of whom were institutional investors such as banks, mutual funds, and investment banks. What we are seeing is the globalization of securities markets and the increasing reliance on electronic trading.

over-the-counter (OTC) market
a network of dealers all over the country linked by computers, telephones, and Teletype machines.

The Over-the-Counter Market

Unlike the organized exchanges, the **over-the-counter (OTC) market** is a network of dealers all over the country linked by computers, telephones, and Teletype machines. It has no central location. Today, the OTC market consists of small stocks, illiquid bank stocks, penny stocks, and companies whose stocks trade on the "pink sheets." Once NASDAQ was classified as an exchange by the SEC, it was no longer part of the OTC market. Further, because most corporate bonds and all U.S. securities are traded over the counter, the OTC market regularly accounts for the largest total dollar value of all of the secondary markets.

Measuring Market Performance

Investors, especially professional money managers, want to know how well their investments are performing relative to the market as a whole. Financial managers also need to know how their companies' securities are performing when compared with their competitors'. Thus, performance measures—averages and indexes—are very important to many different people. They not only indicate the performance of a particular securities market but also provide a measure of the overall health of the economy.

Indexes and averages are used to measure stock prices. An *index* compares current stock prices with those in a specified base period, such as 1944, 1967, or 1977. An *average* is the average of certain stock prices. The averages used are usually not simple calculations, however. Some stock market averages (such as the Standard & Poor's Composite Index) are weighted averages, where the weights employed are the total market values of each stock in the index (in this case 500). The Dow Jones Industrial Average (DJIA) is a price-weighted average. Regardless of how they are constructed, all market averages of stocks move together closely over time. See Figure 16.2, which graphs the Dow Jones Industrial Average. Notice the sharp downturn in

FIGURE 16.2
Recent Performance of Stock Market and Dow Jones Industrial Average

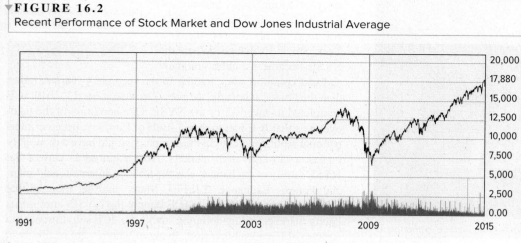

Source: "Dow Jones Industrial Average," Yahoo! Finance, http://finance.yahoo.com/ (accessed April 6, 2015).

the market during the 2008–2009 time period and the recovery that started in 2010. Investors perform better by keeping an eye on the long-term trend line and not the short-term fluctuations. Contrarian investors buy when everyone else is panicked and prices are low because they play the long-term trends. However, for many, this is psychologically a tough way to play the market.

companies are just a small fraction of the total number of companies listed on the New York Stock Exchange, because of their size they account for about 25 percent of the total value of the NYSE.

The numbers listed in an index or average that tracks the performance of a stock market are expressed not as dollars but as a number on a fixed scale. If you know, for example, that the Dow Jones Industrial Average climbed from 860 in August 1982 to a high of 11,497 at the beginning of 2000, you can see clearly that the value of the Dow Jones Average increased more than 10 times in this 19-year period, making it one of the highest rate of return periods in the history of the stock market.

Unfortunately, prosperity did not last long once the Internet bubble burst. Technology stocks and new Internet companies were responsible for the huge increase in stock prices. Even

[**"Many investors follow the activity of the DJIA to see whether the stock market has gone up or down."**]

Many investors follow the activity of the DJIA to see whether the stock market has gone up or down. Table 16.5 lists the 30 companies that currently make up the Dow. In March 2015 Apple replaced AT&T in the DJIA, which makes sense since it is the most valuable company in the world. Although these

▼ TABLE 16.5 The 30 Stocks in the Dow Jones Industrial Average

3M Co	General Electric	Nike
American Express Co	Goldman Sachs	Pfizer
Apple Inc.	Home Depot	Procter & Gamble
Boeing	Intel	Travelers Companies
Caterpiller	IBM	United Health Group
Chevron	Johnson & Johnson	United Technologies
Cisco Systems	JPMorgan Chase	Verizon
Coca-Cola	McDonald's	Visa
DuPont	Merck	Walmart
ExxonMobil	Microsoft	Walt Disney

Source: "Dow Jones Industrial Average," http://finance.yahoo.com (accessed April 6, 2015).

companies with few sales and no earnings were selling at prices that were totally unreasonable. It is always easier to realize that a bubble existed after it has popped. By September 2002, the Dow Jones Industrial Average hit 7,461. The markets stabilized and the economy kept growing; investors were euphoric when the Dow Jones Industrial Average hit an all-time high of 14,198 in October 2007. However, once the housing bubble burst, the economy and the stock market went into a free fall. The DJIA bottomed out at 6,470 in March 2009. The market entered a period of recovery, and by April 2010, it hit a new high for the year of 10,975. On March 1, 2015, the DJIA hit an all-time record high of 18,288. The good news is that even when the market has been rather flat, an investor would have collected dividends, which are not reflected in the index. Perhaps this roller-coaster ride indicates why some people are afraid to enter the market and buy common stocks. If you look at the long-term trend and long-term returns in common stocks, they far outdistance bonds and government securities.

Recognizing financial bubbles can be difficult. It is too easy to get caught up in the enthusiasm that accompanies rising markets. Knowing what something is worth in economic terms is the test of true value. During the housing bubble, banks made

INCREASED DISCLOSURE, BUT DOES ANYONE ACTUALLY READ IT?

Print out the Apple iTunes terms and conditions, and you will find they are 32 pages long. This is at least partly the result of a continuing congressional trend toward requiring companies to disclose information—from the number of calories in packaged food, to the interest rates and term details of mortgage agreements, to accounting practices and financial metrics in corporate financial reports. The idea is that disclosure of important information will allow the public to make more informed decisions, reduce questionable business practices, and improve marketplace efficiency.

However, some analysts are arguing that required disclosure has gone overboard to the point of being counterproductive. Rather than inform the public, the ballooning length and amount of documents to read and sign means fewer people read them at all. Not only that, but companies are able to bury inflammatory or negative information deep within pages of legalese and unimportant data.

This is a problem in quarterly and yearly corporate financial reports as well. For large companies, these documents can reach 200 pages, making it difficult for even dedicated investors to fully understand a firm's financial position—and easy for firms to hide negative information. Enron, in fact, did exactly that; after its collapse, investors realized the footnotes to its financial reports were filled with warning signs. The issue has even given rise to a new business model—so-called bear-raid firms, who make money by deeply analyzing these reports in the hopes of uncovering fraudulent practices. Instead of requiring further disclosure of company actions, concerned analysts argue Congress could better protect consumers by focusing on closer regulation of those company actions themselves.[5]

Discussion Questions

1. What advantages are there for company disclosure of financial information?

2. Have financial disclosure requirements gone too far and become counterproductive?

3. How could disclosure rules be changed to get useful information out to consumers without the information overload problem?

---

loans to subprime borrowers to buy houses. (Remember that the prime rate is the rate for the highest quality borrowers and subprime loans are generally made to those who do not qualify for regular ones.) As more money poured into the housing market, the obvious supply and demand relationship from economics would indicate that housing prices would rise. As prices rose, speculators entered the real estate market trying to make a fast buck. States such as Florida, Arizona, Nevada, and California were the favorite speculative spots and the states with the largest decline in house prices. To make matters worse, banks had created the home equity loan years ago so that borrowers could take out a second mortgage against their house and deduct the interest payment for tax purposes. Many homeowners no longer thought about paying off their mortgages but instead used the increase in the price of their houses to borrow more money. This behavior was unsustainable.

The bankers engaged in risky financial behavior packaged up billions of dollars of mortgages into securitized assets. In other words, an investor could buy a pool of assets and collect the interest income and eventually get a payment at the end of the life of the product. This technique allowed banks to make a mortgage, collect a fee, package the mortgage, and collect another fee. These securitized mortgages were sold to the market as asset-backed securities with a AAA credit rating off their books and replaced with cash to make more loans. In this case, when the bubble burst, it had extremely severe consequences for the economy, workers, and investors.

People defaulted on loans when they could no longer afford to pay the mortgage. Many of these people shouldn't have been able to borrow in the first place. The defaults caused housing prices to fall, and some people who had home equity loans no longer had any equity left in their house. Some homeowners owed the bank more than the house was worth, and they started walking away from their mortgage. At the same time, investors realized that the mortgage-backed securities they owned were probably not worth what they thought they were worth, and prices of these assets plummeted. Banks and other financial service firms that had these assets on their books suffered a double whammy. They had loan losses and losses on mortgage-backed securities that another division of the bank had bought for investment purposes. Soon, many banks were close to violating their capital requirement, and the U.S. Treasury and Federal Reserve stepped in—with the help of funding from Congress—to make bank loans, buy securities that were illiquid, and invest in the capital of the banks by buying preferred stocks.

Home Depot is a member of the Dow Jones Industrial Average and has excelled in financial performance with increases in dividends and escalating stock prices.
© *Deposit Photos/Glow Images, RF*

The consensus of most economists is that through the actions of the U.S. Treasury and the Federal Reserve, the U.S. economy escaped what might have been another depression equal to or worse than the depression of the 1930s. The recession of 2007–2009 lasted 18 months and was the longest recession since the 1930s. Some worry that as the Federal Reserve becomes less accommodating and lets interest rates rise, the rising interest rates will have a negative effect on stock prices. This is always possible if corporate earnings do not increase enough to outweigh the impact of higher required returns motivated by higher rates and higher inflation.

For investors to make sound financial decisions, it is important that they stay in touch with business news, markets, and indexes. Of course, business and investment magazines, such as *Bloomberg Businessweek, Fortune,* and *Money,* offer this type of information. Many Internet sites, including CNN/*Money, Business Wire, USA Today,* other online newspapers, and *PR Newswire,* offer this information, as well. Many sites offer searchable databases of information by topic, company, or keyword. However investors choose to receive and review business news, doing so is a necessity in today's market. ∎

SO YOU WANT TO WORK // in Financial Management or Securities /

Taking classes in financial and securities management can provide many career options, from managing a small firm's accounts receivable to handling charitable giving for a multinational to investment banking to stock brokerage. We have entered into a less certain period for finance and securities jobs, however. In the world of investment banking, the past few years have been especially challenging. Tens of thousands of employees from Wall Street firms have lost their jobs. This phenomenon is not confined to New York City either, leaving the industry with a lot fewer jobs around the country. This type of phenomenon is not isolated to the finance sector either. In the early 2000s, the tech sector experienced a similar downturn, from which it has subsequently largely recovered. Undoubtedly, markets will bounce back and job creation in finance and securities will increase again—but until that happens the

atmosphere across finance and securities will be more competitive than it has been in the past. However, this does not mean that there are no jobs. All firms need financial analysts to determine whether a project should be implemented, when to issue stocks or bonds, or when to initiate loans. These and other forward-looking questions such as how to invest excess cash must be addressed by financial managers. Economic uncertainty in the financial and securities market has made for more difficulty in finding the most desirable jobs.

Why this sudden downturn in financial industry prospects? A lot of these job cuts came in response to the subprime lending fallout and subsequent bank failures such as Bear Stearns. All of these people had to look for new jobs in new organizations, increasing the competitive level in a lot of different employment areas. For young job-seekers with relatively little experience, this

may result in a great deal of frustration. On the other hand, by the time you graduate, the job market for finance majors could be in recovery and rebuilding with new employees. Uncertainty results in hiring freezes and layoffs but leaves firms lean and ready to grow when the cycle turns around, resulting in hiring from the bottom up.

Many different industries require people with finance skills. So do not despair if you have a difficult time finding a job in exactly the right firm. Most students switch companies a number of times over the course of their careers. Many organizations require individuals trained in forecasting, statistics, economics, and finance. Even unlikely places like museums, aquariums, and zoos need people who are good at numbers. It may require some creativity, but if you are committed to a career in finance, look to less obvious sources—not just the large financial firms.[6]

notes

Chapter 1

1. Josh Mitchell, "Americans Are Buying Less-Efficient Cars as Gasoline Prices Dive," *The Wall Street Journal,* January 6, 2015, http://blogs.wsj.com/economics/2015/01/06/americans-are-buying-less-efficient-cars-as-gasoline-prices-dive/ (accessed January 21, 2015).

2. Association for Women in Science, "Who We Are," http://www.awis.org/?WhoWeAre (accessed January 13, 2015).

3. Serena Ng, "Soap Opera: Amazon Moves In with P&G," *The Wall Street Journal,* October 15, 2013, pp. A1 and A2.

4. "Got Milk?" www.gotmilk.com/ (accessed January 27, 2015).

5. "About Bill Daniels," www.danielsfund.org/About-Us/About-Bill-Daniels.asp (accessed January 27, 2015).

6. Victoria Burnett, "The Latest on Travel to Cuba," *The New York Times,* January 20, 2014, http://www.nytimes.com/2015/01/21/travel/the-latest-on-travel-to-cuba.html?_r=0 (accessed January 21, 2015).

7. "Special Report: The Visible Hand," *The Economist,* January 21, 2012, pp. 3–5.

8. James T. Areddy and Craig Karmin, "China Stocks Once Frothy, Fall by Half in Six Months," *The Wall Street Journal,* April 16, 2008, pp. 1, 7.

9. "Special Report: The Visible Hand."

10. "Special Report: The World in Their Hands," *The Economist,* January 21, 2012, pp. 15–17.

11. Ian Bremmer, "The New Rules of Globalization," *Harvard Business Review,* January 2014, https://hbr.org/2014/01/the-new-rules-of-globalization (accessed January 16, 2015).

12. "The Shark Tank," *ABC,* http://abc.go.com/shows/shark-tank/bios (accessed January 27, 2015).

13. Gabi Thesing and Whitney McFerron, with Benjamin Katz, "This Apple Was Once Headed to Russia. Not Anymore," *Bloomberg Businessweek,* September 15–21, 2014, pp. 13–15; Council of the European Union, "Council Examines Impact of Russian Ban on Imports of Agricultural Products," May 9, 2014, http://www.consilium.europa.eu/homepage/showfocus?focusName=council-examines-impact-of-russian-ban-on-imports-of-eu-agricultural-products&lang=en (accessed September 22, 2014); Ashifa Kassam, Kim Wilsher, Philip Oltermann, Remi Adekoya, and Libby Brooks, "Russian Food Embargo Leaves Europe with Glut of Fruit, Pork and Mackerel," *The Guardian,* August 15, 2014, http://www.theguardian.com/world/2014/aug/15/ukraine-europe-news (accessed September 22, 2014).

14. U.S. Energy Information Administration, "Crude Oil Prices Peaked Early in 2012," August 21, 2012, http://www.eia.gov/todayinenergy/detail.cfm?id=7630 (accessed January 21, 2015); "5 Year Crude Oil Prices and Price Charts," InvestmentMine, http://www.infomine.com/investment/metal-prices/crude-oil/5-year/ (accessed January 21, 2015).

15. Douglas MacMillan, "The Fiercest Rivalry in Tech: Uber vs. Lyft," *The Wall Street Journal,* August 12, 2014, p. B1; Trevor Hughes, "Passengers Flock to Upstart Car Services," *USA Today,* July 10, 2014, p. 5B; James Nash, "The Company Cities Love to Hate," *Bloomberg Businessweek,* July 3, 2014, pp. 31–33; Sam Schechner, "Uber Tries to Thwart Ban in French Court," *The Wall Street Journal,* November 29–30, 2014, p. B4; Joanna Sugden, Aditi Malhotra, and Douglas MacMillan, "Uber under Attack around Globe," *The Wall Street Journal,* December 10, 2014, pp. B1, B4.

16. World International Property Organization, "International Patent Filings Set New Record in 2011," March 5, 2012, www.wipo.int/pressroom/en/articles/2012/article_0001.html (accessed February 20, 2014).

17. Paul Toscano, "The Worst Hyperinflation Situations of All Time," *CNBC,* February 14, 2011, http://www.cnbc.com/id/41532451 (accessed January 27, 2015).

18. "Zimbabwe," *CIA—The World Factbook,* https://www.cia.gov/library/publications/the-world-factbook/geos/zi.html (accessed January 27, 2015).

19. Ambrose Evans-Pritchard, "France Is 'Sliding into a Deflationary Vortex,'" *Business Insider,* December 12, 2014, http://www.businessinsider.com/france-is-sliding-into-a-deflationary-vortex-2014-12 (accessed January 21, 2015).

20. Mark Gongloff, "China's Economy Just Overtook the U.S. in One Key Measure," *The Huffington Post,* October 8, 2014, http://www.huffingtonpost.com/2014/10/08/china-gdp-tops-us_n_5951374.html (accessed January 13, 2015).

21. Mike Patton, "The U.S. Debt: Why It Will Continue to Rise," *Forbes,* September 18, 2014, http://www.forbes.com/sites/mikepatton/2014/09/18/the-u-s-debt-why-it-will-continue-to-rise/ (accessed January 21, 2015).

22. Neil Shah, "Baby Bust Threatens Growth," *The Wall Street Journal,* December 4, 2014, p. A3.

23. U.S. Census Bureau, "State & County Quick Facts," http://quickfacts.census.gov/qfd/states/00000.html (accessed January 27, 2015); Haya El Nasser, Gregory Korte, and Paul Overberg, "308.7 Million," *USA Today,* December 22, 2010, p. 1A.

24. U.S. Bureau of Labor Statistics, *Women in the Labor Force: A Databook,* Report 1049, May 2014, www.bls.gov.

25. Dinah Eng and Stephen Gordon, "The Nuts and Bolts of Restoration Hardware," *Fortune,* January 1, 2015, pp. 23–24.

26. Eli Lilly, "Heritage," www.lilly.com/about/heritage/Pages/heritage.aspx (accessed January 27, 2015).

27. Walmart, "Corporate & Financial Facts," http://news.walmart.com/walmart-facts/corporate-financial-fact-sheet (accessed January 27, 2015).

28. Matthew Boyle, "Ben & Jerry's GMO Food Fight," *Bloomberg Businessweek,* August 4–10, 2014, pp. 18–20; Terri Hallenbeck, "How Ben & Jerry's Says Goodbye to GMOs," *Burlington Free Press,* June 16, 2014, http://www.burlingtonfreepress.com/story/news/local/2014/06/15/ben-jerrys-non-gmo/10380407/ (accessed September 15, 2014); Dale Buss, "In Vermont, Unilever Fights—and Ben & Jerry's Fund—Anti-GMO Activism," *Brand Channel,* June 16, 2014, http://www.brandchannel.com/home/post/140616-Unilever-Ben-Jerrys-GMO.aspx (accessed September 15, 2014); Paul Courson, "Oil-drilling Protestors Bring Dessert," *CNN,* April 22, 2005, http://www.cnn.com/2005/TECH/science/04/22/anwr.protests/ (accessed September 15, 2014); Ben & Jerry's, "Our History," http://www.benjerry.com/about-us (accessed September 15, 2014); Unilever, "Introduction to Unilever," http://www.unilever.com/aboutus/introductiontounilever/ (accessed September 15, 2014).

29. Joann S. Lublin, "New Report Finds a "Diversity Dividend' at Work," *The Wall Street Journal,* January 20, 2015, http://blogs.wsj.com/atwork/2015/01/20/new-report-finds-a-diversity-dividend-at-work/ (accessed January 27, 2015).

30. "The 2011 World's Most Ethical Companies," *Ethisphere,* 2011, Q1, pp. 37–43.

31. Isabelle Maignon, Tracy L. Gonzalez-Padron, G. Tomas, M. Hult, and O. C. Ferrell, "Stakeholder Orientation: Development and Testing of a Framework for Socially Responsible Marketing," *Journal of Strategic Marketing,* 19, no. 4 (July 2011), pp. 313–338.

32. Small Business Administration Office of Advocacy, *Frequently Asked Questions,* 2012, www.sba.gov/sites/default/files/FAQ_Sept_2012.pdf (accessed January 27, 2015); Joel Holland, "Save the World, Make a Million," *Entrepreneur,* April 2010, www.entrepreneur.com/magazine/entrepreneur/2010/april/205556.html (accessed January 27, 2015); iContact, www.icontact.com (accessed January 27, 2015).

Chapter 2

1. Jacquelyn Smith, "The World's Most Ethical Companies," *Forbes,* March 6, 2013, http://www.forbes.com/sites/jacquelynsmith/2013/03/06/the-worlds-most-ethical-companies-in-2013/(accessed February 5, 2015).

2. Kimberly Blanton, "Creating a Culture of Compliance," *CFO,* July/August 2011, pp. 19–21.

3. John Carreyrou and Christopher S. Stewart, "Task Force Accuses 90 of Bilking Medicare," *The Wall Street Journal,* May 14, 2014, A4.

4. Ronald Alsop, "Corporate Scandals Hit Home," *The Wall Street Journal,* February 19, 2004, http://online.wsj.com/news/articles/SB107715182807433462 (accessed February 6, 2015).

5. Betsy Morris, "Truck-Stop Operator Settles U.S. Probe," *The Wall Street Journal,* July 15, 2014, B1.

6. O. C. Ferrell, John Fraedrich, and Linda Ferrell, *Business Ethics: Ethical Decision Making and Cases,* 8th ed. (Mason, OH: South-Western Cengage Learning, 2011), p. 7.

7. Kathryn Dill, "Report: CEOs Earn 331 Times As Much As Average Workers, 774 Times As Much As Minimum Wage Earners," *Forbes,* April 15, 2014, http://www.forbes.com/sites/kathryndill/2014/04/15/report-ceos-earn-331-times-as-much-as-average-workers-774-times-as-much-as-minimum-wage-earners/ (accessed January 15, 2015).

8. Peter Burrows, "Cisco Cuts CEO's Pay After Missing Sales, Profit Targets," *Bloomberg,* September 30, 2014, http://www.bloomberg.com/news/2014-10-01/cisco-cuts-ceo-s-pay-after-missing-sales-profit-targets.html (accessed January 15, 2015).

9. Valerie Bauerlein, "Former Governor Gets Two Years," *The Wall Street Journal,* January 7, 2015, p. A3.

10. Ken Belson, "N.F.L. Domestic Violence Policy Toughened in Wake of Ray Rice Case," *The New York Times,* August 28, 2014, http://www.nytimes.com/2014/08/29/sports/football/roger-goodell-admits-he-was-wrong-and-alters-nfl-policy-on-domestic-violence.html?_r=0 (accessed January 15, 2015).

11. Ferrell, Fraedrich, and Ferrell, *Business Ethics.*

12. Sharon Terlep and Ben Cohen, "Ruling on Pay Has NCAA Weighing Its Next Steps," *The Wall Street Journal,* August 11, 2014, p. A3; Tim Dahlberg, "Court Ruling on Paying College Athletes Will Fundamentally Change the NCAA," *Business Insider,* August 10, 2014, http://www.businessinsider.com/court-ruling-on-paying-college-athletes-2014-8 (accessed February 6, 2015); Ben Strauss and Marc Tracy, "N.C.A.A. Must Allow Colleges to Pay Athletes, Judge Rules," August 8, 2014, *New York Times,* http://www.nytimes.com/2014/08/09/sports/federal-judge-rules-against-ncaa-in-obannon-case.html (accessed February 6, 2015); The New York Times Company, "O'Bannon Case Decision," *New York Times,* August 9, 2014, http://www.nytimes.com/interactive/2014/08/09/sports/09obannondoc.html (accessed February 6, 2015).

13. Jef Feeley, "U.S. Judge Says Wal-Mart Must Face Mexican-Bribe Claims," *Bloomberg Businessweek,* October 1, 2014, http://www.businessweek.com/news/2014-09-30/wal-mart-judge-finds-retailer-must-face-mexican-bribe-claims (accessed January 15, 2015).

14. Ethics Resource Center, *2011 National Business Ethics Survey®: Ethics in Transition* (Arlington, VA: Ethics Resource Center, 2012).

15. Bobby White, "The New Workplace Rules: No Video Watching," *The New York Times,* March 3, 2008, p. B1.

16. Shana Lebowitz, "What's Behind a Rise in Workplace Bullying?" *USA Today,* October 8, 2013, www.usatoday.com/story/news/health/2013/10/08/hostileworkplace-less-productive/2945833/ (accessed February 6, 2015).

17. Carolyn Kinsey Goman, "Is Your Boss a Bully?" *Forbes,* April 6, 2014, http://www.forbes.com/sites/carolkinseygoman/2014/04/06/is-your-boss-a-bully/ (accessed January 15, 2015).

18. Theodore V. Wells Jr., Brad S. Karp, Bruce Birenboim, and David W. Brown, *Report to the National Football League Concerning Issues of Workplace Conduct at the Miami Dolphins,* February 14, 2014, http://63bba9dfdf9675bf3f10-68be460ce43dd2a60d-d64ca5eca4ae1d.r37.cf1.rackcdn.com/PaulWeissReport.pdf (accessed February 6, 2015).

19. Elizabeth A. Harris, "American Apparel Ousts Its Founder, Dov Charney, Over Nude Photos," *The New York Times,* June 21, 2014, http://www.nytimes.com/2014/06/22/business/in-firing-dov-charney-american-apparel-cites-posting-of-naked-pictures.html (accessed January 15, 2015).

20. National Railroad Passenger Corporation Office of Inspector General, "Employee Pads Expense Reports with False Meal Checks," September 30, 2014, Case OIG-I-2014-514.

21. Coca-Cola Company, *Code of Business Conduct: Acting Around the Globe,* p. 13.

22. Barbara Kiviat, "A Bolder Approach to Credit-Agency Rating Reform," *Time,* September 18, 2009, http://business.time.com/2009/09/18/a-bolder-approach-to-credit-rating-agency-reform/ (accessed February 6, 2015).

23. Matthew Goldstein, "Martoma, SAC Capital Ex-Trader, Gets 9 Years in Prison," *The New York Times,* September 8, 2014, http://dealbook.nytimes.com/2014/09/08/hours-before-sentencing-u-s-judge-says-cohen-trades-should-count-against-martoma/ (accessed January 15, 2015).

24. Christopher M. Matthews, "Ruling Puts Dent In Insider Probes," *The Wall Street Journal,* December 11, 2014, p. A1.

25. *Corruption Perceptions Index 2014.* Copyright Transparency information, http://www.transparency.org/cpi2014/results/ (accessed February 6, 2015).

26. Holly Ellyatt, "EU Lawmakers Vote to Break Up Google," *CNBC,* November 27, 2014, http://www.cnbc.com/id/102222045# (accessed February 5, 2015).

27. Matthew Garrett, "Your Best Employee Stinks and May Be Stealing from You," *Forbes,* October 1, 2013, http://www.forbes.com/sites/matthewgarrett/2013/10/01/your-best-employee-sucks-and-may-be-stealing-from-you/ (accessed February 27, 2014).

28. Bruce Horovitz, "Newest Menu Items: Calories," *USA Today,* November 25, 2014, p. 1B

29. Matt Rocheleau, "64 Dartmouth College Students Face Discipline over Cheating," *Boston Globe,* January 8, 2015, http://www.bostonglobe.com/metro/2015/01/08/dartmouth/GN8oLJcg-Kj7R1nOoPNiLdL/story.html (accessed February 5, 2015).

30. Tom Vanden Hook, "Kickback Scandal Rocks Army," *USA Today,* February 4, 2014, p. 1A; Helene Cooper, "92 Air Force Officers Suspended for Cheating on Their Missile Exam," *The New York Times,* January 30, 2014, http://www.nytimes.com/2014/01/31/us/politics/92-air-force-officers-suspended-for-cheating-on-their-missile-exam.html (accessed February 6, 2015); Kevin Liptak, "U.S. Navy Discloses Nuclear Exam Cheating," *CNN,* February 4, 2014, http://www.cnn.com/2014/02/04/us/navy-cheating-investigation/index.html (accessed February 6, 2015); Julian E. Barnes, "Military Makes Ethics a Priority," *The Wall Street Journal,* February 3, 2014, p. A4.

31. "Campaign Warns about Drugs from Canada," *CNN,* February 5, 2004, www.cnn.com; Gardiner Harris and Monica Davey, "FDA Begins Push to End Drug Imports," *The New York Times,* January 23, 2004, p. C1.

32. European Commission, "Questions & Answers: New Rules for Tobacco Products," February 26, 2014, http://europa.eu/rapid/press-release_MEMO-14-134_en.htm (accessed February 5, 2015).

33. Peter Evans, "U.K. Plans to Outlaw Branding on Cigarette Packs," *The Wall Street Journal,* January 22, 2015, http://www.wsj.com/articles/u-k-plans-to-outlaw-branding-on-cigarette-packs-1421947530 (accessed February 5, 2015).

34. Ethics Resource Center, *2005 National Business Ethics Survey* (Washington, DC: Ethics Resource Center, 2005), p. 43.

35. Thomas M. Jones, "Ethical Decision Making by Individuals in Organizations: An Issue-Contingent Model," *Academy of Management Review* 2 (April 1991), pp. 371–73.

36. Sir Adrian Cadbury, "Ethical Managers Make Their Own Rules," *Harvard Business Review* 65 (September–October 1987), p. 72.

37. Ferrell, Fraedrich, and Ferrell, *Business Ethics,* pp. 174–75.

38. Ethics Resource Center, *2009 National Business Ethics Survey* (Washington, DC: Ethics Resource Center, 2009), p. 41.

39. Texas Instruments, "Texas Instruments Rated One of the 'World's Most Ethical Companies' by Ethisphere Institute," March 6, 2013, http://newscenter.ti.com/2013-03-06-Texas-Instruments-rated-one-of-the-Worlds-Most-Ethical-Companies-by-Ethisphere-Institute (accessed February 6, 2015).

40. Ethics Resource Center, *2013 National Business Ethics Survey®* *of the U.S. Workforce* (Arlington, VA: Ethics Resource Center, 2014).

41. Alan Katz, "SEC Pays $30 Million to Whistle-Blower in Largest Reward," *Bloomberg,* September 22, 2014, http://www.bloomberg.com/news/articles/2014-09-22/sec-pays-30-million-to-whistleblower-in-largest-award (accessed February 5, 2015).

42. Ferrell, Fraedrich, and Ferrell, *Business Ethics,* p. 13.

43. Deloitte LLP, "Trust in the Workplace: 2010 Ethics & Workplace Survey," (n.d.), http://www.bentley.edu/centers/sites/www.bentley.edu.centers/files/centers/cbe/cbe-external-surveys/deloitte-2010-ethics-and-workplace-survey.pdf (accessed February 6, 2015).

44. Archie B. Carroll, "The Pyramid of Corporate Social Responsibility: Toward the Moral Management of Organizational Stakeholders," *Business Horizons* 34 (July/August 1991), p. 42.

45. "Organizational Stakeholders," *Business Horizons* 34 (July/August 1991), p. 42; Kelly Kennedy, "Pharmacies Look to Snuff Tobacco Sales," *USA Today,* February 6, 2014, p. 1A.

46. Bryan Walsh, "Why Green Is the New Red, White and Blue," *Time,* April 28, 2008, p. 46.

47. Adam Shriver, "Not Grass-Fed, But at Least Pain-Free," *The New York Times,* February 18, 2010, www.nytimes.com/2010/02/19/opinion/19shriver.html (accessed February 6, 2015).

48. Alan Beattie, "Countries Rush to Restrict Trade in Basic Foods," *Financial Times,* April 2, 2008, p. 1.

49. Merrill Douglas and Bud Snodgrass, "Bud Snodgrass: Oils Well That Ends Well," *Inbound Logistics,* May 2014, pp. 10–11; Universal Lubricants website, http://www.universallubes.com/ (accessed January 15, 2015).

50. Cone Communications, "Cone Releases 2013 Cone Communications Green Gap Trend Tracker," April 2, 2013, http://www.cone-comm.com/2013-green-gap-trend-tracker-1 (accessed February 6, 2015).

51. "2014 World's Most Ethical Companies—Honorees," *Ethisphere,* http://ethisphere.com/worlds-mostethical/wme-honorees/ (accessed April 7, 2014).

52. Ucilia Wang, "Campbell Soup CEO: 'You Can Lead the Change or Be a Victim of Change,'" *The Guardian,* October 25, 2013, http://www.theguardian.com/sustainable-business/campbell-soup-ceo-business-social-responsibility (accessed November 14, 2014).

53. Ferrell, Fraedrich, and Ferrell, *Business Ethics,* pp. 13–19.

54. Anupreeta Das, "NetJets Puts Buffett in Rare Pinch," *The Wall Street Journal,* January 6, 2015, pp. C1–C2.

55. Joann S. Lublin, "Study Links Diverse Leadership with Firms' Financial Gains," *The Wall Street Journal,* January 20, 2015, http://www.wsj.com/articles/study-links-diverse-leadership-with-firms-financial-gains-1421792018 (accessed February 5, 2015).

56. U.S. Equal Employment Opportunity Commission, "Popeye's Chicken Franchisee to Pay $25,000 to Settle EEOC Disability Discrimination Lawsuit," September 4, 2014, http://www.eeoc.gov/eeoc/newsroom/release/9-4-14.cfm (accessed January 15, 2015).

57. Hannah Karp, "Ticketmaster to Pay for Cryptic Fees," *The Wall Street Journal,* June 3, 2014, B3.

58. Joshua Green, "Tankchair: A Love Story," *Bloomberg Businessweek,* June 5, 2014, pp. 93–96; Tankchair website, http://www.tankchair.com/ (accessed December 2, 2014); Scott Stump, "After Seeing His Paralyzed Wife Cry, Veteran Invents Incredible 'Tankchair,'" *Today,* June 19, 2014, http://www.today.com/money/after-seeing-his-paralyzed-wife-cry-veteran-invents-incredible-tankchair-1D79823493 (accessed December 2, 2014).

59. Todd Littman, "Win-Win Emissions Reductions Strategies," Victoria Transport Policy Institute, www.vtpi.org/wwclimate.pdf (accessed February 5, 2015).

60. Katherine Noyes, "Can 'Urban Mining' Solve the World's E-waste Problem?" *Fortune,* June 26, 2014, http://fortune.com/2014/06/26/blueoak-urban-mining-ewaste/ (accessed January 15, 2015).

61. Cornelia Dean, "Drugs Are in the Water, Does It Matter?" The New York Times, April 3, 2007, http://www.nytimes.com/2007/04/03/science/earth/03water.html?pagewanted=print&_r=0 (accessed September 30, 2015).

62. "Amazon Rainforest Deforestation at Lowest in 23 Years, Brazil Government Says," *Reuters,* December 5, 2011, www.reuters.com/article/2011/12/06/us-brazilamazon-idUSTRE7B42OE20111206 (accessed August 11, 2014); Brian Clark Howard, "Brazil Leads World in Reducing Carbon Emissions by Slashing Deforestation," *National Geographic,* June 5, 2014, http://news.nationalgeographic.com/

news/2014/06/140605-brazil-deforestation-carbon-emissions-environment/ (accessed January 15, 2015).

63. Janet Larsen and Savina Venkova, "Plan B Updates," April 22, 2014, http://www.earth-policy.org/plan_b_updates/2014/update122 (accessed January 15, 2015).

64. "Few State Laws Restrict Plastic Bags," *New York Times,* May 18, 2013, http://www.nytimes.com/interactive/2013/05/19/sunday-review/few-state-laws-restrict-plastic-bags.html (accessed February 6, 2015).

65. Josie Huang, "LA to Become Biggest City to Ban Plastic Bags on Jan. 1," *Southern California Public Radio,* December 24, 2013, www.scpr.org/news/2013/12/24/41147/plastic-bag-ban-los-angeles-la/ (accessed February 6, 2015).

66. "San Diego Hotel Makes Smart Sustainable Changes to Save Energy & Money," SDGE, September 5, 2013, www.sdge.com/newsroom/2013-09-05/san-diegohotel-makes-smart-sustaina-blechanges-save-energy-money (accessed February 25, 2014).

67. Bryan Walsh, "Power Surge," *Time,* October 7, 2013, pp. 34–39; Adam Lashinsky, "First Solar Rises Again," *Fortune,* February 3, 2014, pp. 76–84; Lou Kilzer, "Solar Panel Prices Finally Rebound," *Trib Live,* November 14, 2013, http://triblive.com/business/headlines/5070584-74/solar-prices-chinese#axzz3DnCxyrnB (accessed September 22, 2014); Angel Publishing LLC, "Solar Industry Rebound," Energy & Capital Special Report, 2014, http://www.energyandcapital.com/report/solar-industry-rebound/866 (accessed September 22, 2014).

68. "GreenChoice Program Details," Austin Energy (n.d.), http://austinenergy.com/wps/wcm/connect/d6b29f5f-052c-4aeb-b52d-73e4dd0265b7/updatedProgramDetails.pdf?MOD$AJPERES (accessed February 6, 2015).

69. "Certification," Home Depot, https://corporate.homedepot.com/CorporateResponsibility/Environment/WoodPurchasing/Pages/Certification.aspx (accessed February 6, 2015).

70. Chiquita, Bananalink, www.bananalink.org.uk/ (accessed February 6, 2015).

71. GE Foundation, "United Way," www.gefoundation.com/employeeprograms/united-way/ (accessed February 6, 2015).

72. Blue Smoke Coffee website, www.bluesmokecoffee.com/Soul.html (accessed February 6, 2015).

73. Bureau of Labor Statistics, "Labor Force Statistics from the Current Population Survey, http://data.bls.gov/timeseries/LNS14000000 (accessed February 6, 2015).

74. "Protests as E.U. Leaders Talk Unemployment," *The Washington Post,* October 8, 2014, http://www.washingtonpost.com/posttv/world/protests-as-eu-leaders-talk-unemployment/2014/10/08/dbcabcd4-4f0b-11e4-877c-335b53ffe736_video.html (accessed January 15, 2015).

75. Andrea Hsu, "Iowa Town Braces for New Reality in Factory Closure's Wake," *NPR,* April 8, 2013, www.npr.org/2013/04/08/176596732/iowa-town-braces-for-new-realityin-factory-closures-wake (accessed February 6, 2015).

76. Peter Cappelli, "Why Companies Aren't Getting the Employees They Need," *The Wall Street Journal,* October 24, 2011, pp. R1, R6.

77. Fifth Third Bank, "Fifth Third Bank Launches 'Reemployment' Campaign; Dedicates Marketing Effort to Help Job Seekers Get Back to Work Sooner," May 29, 2014, https://www.53.com/mkg/press-releases/press-release-2014-05-29.html (accessed January 15, 2015).

78. "Who Really Pays for CSR Initiatives," *Environmental Leader,* February 15, 2008, http://www.environmentalleader.com/2008/02/15/who-really-pays-for-csr-initiatives/ (accessed

February 6, 2015); "Global Fund," www.joinred.com/globalfund (accessed April 7, 2014); Reena Jana, "The Business of Going Green," *BusinessWeek Online,* June 22, 2007, http://www.bloomberg.com/bw/stories/2007-06-22/the-business-benefits-of-going-greenbusinessweek-business-news-stock-market-and-financial-advice (accessed February 6, 2015).

79. Bart Jansen, "Justice Settles Merger Lawsuit with AA, US Airways," *USA Today,* November 12, 2013, www.usatoday.com/story/travel/flights/2013/11/12/justice-mergeramerican-us-airways/3506367/ (accessed February 6, 2015).

80. Maureen Dorney, "Congress Passes Federal Anti-Spam Law: Preempts Most State Anti-Spam Laws," *DLA Piper,* December 3, 2003, http://franchiseagreements.com/global/publications/detail.aspx?pub$622 (accessed April 7, 2014).

81. Matthias Rieker, "Cybercriminals Target Brokers," *The Wall Street Journal,* February 4, 2015, p. C3.

82. Christine Birkner, "Know Your Rights," *Marketing News,* August 2014, pp. 4–5; Sirius XM Satellite Radio website, http://www.siriusxm.com/corporate (accessed October 16, 2014); Shirley Halperin, "Major Labels Unite in Lawsuit Against SiriusXM," *The Hollywood Reporter,* September 11, 2013, http://www.hollywoodreporter.com/thr-esq/major-labels-unite-lawsuit-siriusxm-627554 (accessed October 16, 2014); Ben Sisario, "Sirius XM Loses Lawsuit on Royalties for Oldies," *The New York Times,* September 23, 2014, http://www.nytimes.com/2014/09/24/business/media/sirius-xm-loses-suit-on-royalties-for-oldies.html?_r$0 (accessed October 16, 2014).

83. Edward Wyatt, "F.T.C. Fines Yelp and TinyCo for Violating Children's Privacy Rules" *The New York Times,* September 17, 2014, http://bits.blogs.nytimes.com/2014/09/17/f-t-c-fines-yelp-and-tinyco-for-violating-childrens-privacy-rules/?_r$0 (accessed January 15, 2015).

84. Ashby Jones, "Nation's In-House Counsel Are Worried about Ethics, Data and 'Trolls,'" *The Wall Street Journal,* February 2, 2015, http://blogs.wsj.com/law/2015/02/02/nations-in-house-counsel-are-worried-about-ethics-data-and-trolls/ (accessed February 5, 2015).

85. Jean Eaglesham and Ashby Jones, "Whistle-blower Bounties Pose Challenges," *The Wall Street Journal,* December 13, 2010, pp. C1, C3.

86. "Office of Financial Research," U.S. Department of Treasury, www.treasury.gov/initiatives/Pages/ofr.aspx (accessed February 6, 2015); "Financial Stability Oversight Council," U.S. Department of Treasury, http://www.treasury.gov/initiatives/fsoc/Pages/home.aspx (accessed February 6, 2015).

Chapter 3

1. Nick Parker, "BMW's Billion-Dollar Bet on Mexico," *CNN Money,* July 8, 2014, http://money.cnn.com/2014/07/08/news/companies/bmw-mexico/ (accessed January 15, 2015).

2. Subway, "Explore Our World," http://www.subway.com/subway-root/ExploreOurWorld.aspx (accessed January 16, 2015).

3. Deloitte, "2013 Global Manufacturing Competitiveness Index," 2013, http://www2.deloitte.com/content/dam/Deloitte/global/Documents/Manufacturing/gx_2013%20Global%20Manufacturing%20Competitiveness%20Index_11_15_12.pdf (accessed February 9, 2015).

4. "Starbucks Coffee International," Starbucks, http://www.starbucks.com/business/international-stores (accessed January 16, 2015).

5. Elisabeth Sullivan, "Choose Your Words Wisely," *Marketing News,* February 15, 2008, p. 22.

6. UPI, "Apple Store in 2013 Hit $10 Billion Mark in App Sales," January 7, 2014, www.upi.com/Science_News/Technology/2014/01/07/Apple-Store-in-2013-hit-10-billion-markin-app-sales/UPI-89931389121203/ (accessed February 9, 2015); Alex Williams, "Apple Reports Q4 Retail Sales of $4.5 Billion with $50 Million in Sales per Apple Store," *Tech Crunch,* October 28, 2013, http://techcrunch.com/2013/10/28/apple-reports-q4-retail-sales-of-4-5-billion-with-50-million-in-sales-per-apple-store/ (accessed February 9, 2015).

7. "Global Footprint," Caterpillar.com, http://www.caterpillar.com/en/company/corp-overview/global-footprint.html (accessed February 9, 2015).

8. Santanu Choudhury, "Tata Motors Thinks 'Aspirational,'" *The Wall Street Journal,* August 13, 2014, p. B5; Trefis Team, "Riding On China Growth, Jaguar Land Rover Could Reach One Million Annual Sales By 2020," *Forbes,* July 10, 2014, http://www.forbes.com/sites/greatspeculations/2014/07/10/riding-on-china-growth-jaguar-land-rover-could-reach-one-million-annual-sales-by-2020/ (accessed September 19, 2014); "Tata Motors Slips over 1% as Global Sales Decline 10% in August," *The Economic Times,* September 16, 2014, http://articles.economictimes.indiatimes.com/2014-09-16/news/53983585_1_passenger-vehicles-category-global-sales-jaguar-land-rover (accessed September 19, 2014); N. Greeshma, "Tata Bolt Continues Testing in India, Launch Next Year, Expected Price, Feature Details," *International Business Times,* September 18, 2014, http://www.ibtimes.co.in/tata-bolt-continues-testing-india-launch-next-year-expected-price-feature-details-609377 (accessed September 19, 2014); "India's Ratan Tata Sees Brighter Future for Upmarket Nano," *Arab News,* November 30, 2013, http://www.arabnews.com/news/485446?quicktabs_stat2=0 (accessed September 19, 2014); Vikas Yogi, "Tata Bolt and Zest—What to Expect," *NDTV AUT,* July 24, 2014, http://auto.ndtv.com/news/tata-bolt-and-zest-what-to-expect-530845 (accessed October 13, 2014).

9. Statista, "Total Population in the United States from 2003 to 2013 (in millions)," 2013, www.statista.com/statistics/263762/total-population-of-the-united-states/ (accessed February 9, 2015).

10. Sullivan, "Choose Your Words Wisely."

11. Stephan Faris, "How Poland Became Europe's Most Dynamic Economy," *Bloomberg Businessweek,* November 27, 2013, http://www.bloomberg.com/bw/articles/2013-11-27/how-poland-became-europes-most-dynamic-economy (accessed February 9, 2015).

12. Economist staff, "Europe's Unlikely Star," *The Economist,* June 28, 2014, p. 13.

13. Paul Davidson, "We Produce More at Home with New Drilling Methods," *USA Today,* February 11, 2014, p. 1B.

14. Frank Witsil, "Call Center Jobs Increase as More Return from Overseas," *USA Today,* August 4, 2014, http://www.usatoday.com/story/money/business/2014/08/04/call-center-jobs-overseas/13560107/ (accessed January 15, 2015).

15. U.S. Bureau of the Census, Foreign Trade Division, "U.S. Trade in Goods and Services—Balance of Payments (BOP) Basis," February 6, 2014, www.census.gov/foreign-trade/statistics/historical/gands.pdf (accessed February 9, 2015).

16. Colum Murphy and Mike Ramsey, "Tesla Plans to Add Charging Network in China," *The Wall Street Journal,* January 15, 2014, p. B6; Daisuke Wakabayashi, Lorraine Luk, Ian Sherr, and Paul Mozur, "Apple Nears Major Expansion," *The Wall Street Journal,* September 7–8, 2014, p. B1.

17. U.S. Bureau of the Census, Foreign Trade Division, "U.S. Trade in Goods and Services—Balance of Payments (BOP) Basis," February 6, 2014, www.census.gov/foreign-trade/statistics/historical/gands.pdf (accessed February 9, 2015).

18. Ibid.

19. Ian Bremmer, "Sea of Troubles," *Time* 185, no. 1 (2015), p. 18.

20. Economist staff, "Shaken, Not Stirred," *The Economist,* January 24, 2015, p. 48.

21. Stephan Fairs, "Drill Sergeant: For Greenland Prime Minister Aleqa Hammond, Global Warming Means Mining Riches, Economic Independence—and Freedom," *Bloomberg Businessweek,* May 3–7, 2014, pp. 62–67; Steve Almasy, "With environmental Spotlight on Greenland, More Tourists Want Closer Look," *CNN,* April 24, 2012, http://www.cnn.com/2012/04/22/travel/greenland-tourism-climate-change/ (accessed September 15, 2014); James Owen, "Global Warming Good for Greenland?" *National Geographic,* October 17, 2007, http://news.nationalgeographic.com/news/2007/10/071017-greenland-warming.html (accessed September 15, 2014).

22. "India Likely to Ease Restrictions for Foreign Online Retailers in July," *ABC News,* June 5, 2014, http://www.abc.net.au/news/2014-06-05/india-online-retail/5503980 (accessed January 16, 2015); Chris Devonshire, "Expert Commentary: Joint Ventures for Market Entry in India," *India Briefing,* August 22, 2014, http://www.india-briefing.com/news/expert-commentary-joint-ventures-market-entry-india-8932.html/ (accessed January 16, 2015).

23. Eli Sugarman, "How Brazil and the EU Are Breaking the Internet," *Forbes,* May 19, 2014, http://www.forbes.com/sites/elisugarman/2014/05/19/how-brazil-and-the-eu-are-breaking-the-internet/ (accessed February 9, 2015).

24. Joe Harpaz, "Will Irish Tax Law Change Stop Corporate Inversions?" *Forbes,* October 15, 2014, http://www.forbes.com/sites/joeharpaz/2014/10/15/will-irish-tax-law-change-stop-corporate-inversions/ (accessed January 16, 2015); Robert W. Wood, "Whopper? Microsoft Skirts Billions In Taxes, Google, HP & Apple Have It Their Way Too," *Forbes,* August 26, 2014, http://www.forbes.com/sites/robertwood/2014/08/26/whopper-microsoft-skirts-billions-in-taxes-google-hp-apple-have-it-their-way-too/ (accessed February 9, 2015).

25. "The Restricted Zone in Mexico," Penner & Associates—Mexico Law Firm and Business Consulting for Mexico, www.mexicolaw.com/LawInfo17.htm (accessed February 9, 2015).

26. The Software Alliance, "Security Threats Rank as Top Reason Not to Use Unlicensed Software," *BSA Compliance Survey,* http://globalstudy.bsa.org/2013/ (accessed January 16, 2015).

27. John W. Miller, "Cliffs Natural Resources Cries Foul over Steel Imports," *The Wall Street Journal,* February 3, 2015, http://www.wsj.com/articles/cliffs-natural-resources-cries-foul-over-steel-imports-1423003627 (accessed February 9, 2015).

28. CNBC staff, "Here's What $100 Gets you in Cuban Rum and Cigars," *CNBC,* January 22, 2015, http://www.cnbc.com/id/102361188 (accessed February 9, 2015).

29. Kitty Bean Yancey and Laura Bly, "Door May Be Inching Open for Tourism," *USA Today,* February 20, 2008, p. A5; Sue Kirchhoff and Chris Woodyard, "Cuba Trade Gets 'New Opportunity,'" *USA Today,* February 20, 2008, p. B1.

30. Reuters, "Indonesia Challenges EU over Anti-dumping on Biodiesel Imports—WTO," June 11, 2014, http://www.reuters.com/article/2014/06/11/us-trade-biodiesel-idUSKBN0EM14X20140611 (accessed November 26, 2014); European Commission, "EU to Impose Definitive Anti-dumping Duties on Biodiesel from Argentina and Indonesia," November 21, 2013, http://europa.eu/rapid/press-release_IP-13-1140_en.htm (accessed November 26, 2014).

31. Julie Jargon, "Burger King Heads to India—Finally," *The Wall Street Journal,* November 20, 2013, p. B9; Preetika Rana, "Burger King Brings Beef-Free Whoppers to India," *The Wall Street Journal,* October 30, 2014, http://blogs.wsj.com/indiarealtime/2014/10/30/burger-king-brings-beef-free-whoppers-to-india-2/ (accessed November 16, 2015).

32. Laurie Burkitt, "Tiffany Finds Sparkle in Overseas Markets," *The Wall Street Journal,* December 26, 2013, p. B4.

33. Julie Jargon, "Starbucks Shifts in Europe," *The Wall Street Journal,* November 30–December 1, 2013, p. B3.

34. "Slogans Gone Bad," Joe-ks, www.joe-ks.com/archives_apr2004/slogans_gone_bad.htm (accessed February 9, 2015).

35. Preetika Rana, "Ad Confronts Taboos for Women in India," *The Wall Street Journal,* November 20, 2013, p. A8.

36. J. Bonasia, "For Web, Global Reach Is Beauty—and Challenge," *Investor's Business Daily,* June 13, 2001, p. A6.

37. Quentin Hardy, "Decline in PC Sales Starts to Slow; Largest Makers See Growth," *The New York Times,* October 8, 2014, http://bits.blogs.nytimes.com/2014/10/08/decline-in-pc-sales-starts-to-slow-largest-makers-see-growth/ (accessed November 16, 2015).

38. "What Is the WTO," World Trade Organization (n.d.), www.wto.org/english/thewto_e/whatis_e/whatis_e.htm (accessed April 9, 2014).

39. Reuters, "Indonesia Challenges EU over Anti-dumping on Biodiesel Import—WTO," June 11, 2014, http://www.reuters.com/article/2014/06/11/us-trade-biodiesel-idUSKBN0EM14X20140611 (accessed November 26, 2014); European Commission, "EU to Impose Definitive Anti-dumping Duties on Biodiesel from Argentina and Indonesia," November 21, 2013, http://europa.eu/rapid/press-release_IP-13-1140_en.htm (accessed November 26, 2014).

40. The CIA, *The World Fact Book,* https://www.cia.gov/library/publications/the-world-factbook/rankorder/rankorderguide.html (accessed November 10, 2014); Office of the United States Trade Representative, "U.S.-Canada Trade Facts," http://www.ustr.gov/countries-regions/americas/canada (accessed November 21, 2014).

41. Office of the United States Trade Representative, "U.S.-Canada Trade Facts," http://www.ustr.gov/countries-regions/americas/canada (accessed November 19, 2015).

42. "America's Biggest Partners," *CNBC.com,* www.cnbc.com/id/31064179?slide=11 (accessed February 9, 2015).

43. The CIA, *The World Fact Book,* https://www.cia.gov/library/publications/the-world-factbook/rankorder/rankorderguide.html (accessed November 10, 2014).

44. Executive Office of the United States Trade Representative, "Mexico," http://www.ustr.gov/countries-regions/americas/mexico (accessed January 16, 2015).

45. Jen Wieczner, "Why 2014 Could Be Mexico's Year," *Fortune,* January 13, 2014, pp. 37–38; Adam Williams and Eric Martin, "Mexico Opens New Era as Pena Nieto Signs Energy Law," *Bloomberg,* August 11, 2014, http://www.bloomberg.com/news/articles/2014-08-11/mexico-opens-new-era-as-pena-nieto-signs-energy-law (accessed February 9, 2015).

46. "A Tale of Two Mexicos: North and South," *The Economist,* April 26, 2008, pp. 53–54.

47. United States Census Bureau, "Top Trading Partners—December 2013: Year-to-Date Total Trade," www.census.gov/foreign-trade/statistics/highlights/top/top1312yr.html (accessed February 9, 2015).

48. Pete Engardio and Geri Smith, "Business Is Standing Its Ground," *BusinessWeek,* April 20, 2009, pp. 34–39.

49. "Europe in 12 Lessons," http://europa.eu/abc/12lessons/lesson_2/index_en.htm (accessed February 9, 2015).

50. The CIA, *The World Fact Book,* https://www.cia.gov/library/publications/the-world-factbook/rankorder/rankorderguide.html (accessed November 10, 2014).

51. Stanley Reed, with Ariane Sains, David Fairlamb, and Carol Matlack, "The Euro: How Damaging a Hit?" *BusinessWeek,* September 29, 2003, p. 63; "The Single Currency," *CNN* (n.d.), www.cnn.com/SPECIALS/2000/eurounion/story/currency/ (accessed July 3, 2001).

52. Julia Fioretti, "EU Watchdogs to Apply 'Right to Be Forgotten' Rule on Web Worldwide," *Reuters,* November 26, 2014, http://www.reuters.com/article/2014/11/26/us-google-eu-privacy-idUSKCN0JA1HU20141126 (accessed January 16, 2015); The Economist staff, "Drawing the Line," *The Economist,* October 4, 2014, http://www.economist.com/news/international/21621804-google-grapples-consequences-controversial-ruling-boundary-between (accessed January 16, 2015); Samuel Gibbs, "European Parliament Votes Yes on 'Google Breakup' Motion,'" *The Guardian,* November 27, 2014, http://www.theguardian.com/technology/2014/nov/27/european-parliament-votes-yes-google-breakup-motion (accessed February 9, 2015).

53. Abigail Moses, "Greek Contagion Concern Spurs European Sovereign Default Risk to Record," *Bloomberg,* April 26, 2010, http://www.bloomberg.com/news/articles/2010-04-26/greek-contagion-concern-spurs-european-sovereign-default-risk-to-record (accessed February 9, 2015).

54. James G. Neuger and Joe Brennan, "Ireland Weighs Aid as EU Spars over Debt-Crisis Remedy," *Bloomberg,* http://www.bloomberg.com/news/articles/2010-11-16/ireland-discusses-financial-bailout-as-eu-struggles-to-defuse-debt-crisis (accessed February 9, 2015).

55. Charles Forelle and Marcus Walker, "Dithering at the Top Turned EU Crisis to Global Threat," *The Wall Street Journal,* December 29, 2011, p. A1; Jeff Cox, "US, Europe Face More Ratings Cuts in Coming Years," *CNBC,* January 20, 2012, www.cnbc.com/id/46072354?__source=google%7Ceditorspicks%7C&par=google (accessed February 9, 2015); Charles Forelle, "Greece Defaults and Tries to Move On," *The Wall Street Journal,* March 10, 2012, http://www.wsj.com/articles/SB10001424052970204603004577270542625035960 (accessed February 9, 2015).

56. Economist staff, "Go Ahead, Angela, Make My Day," *The Economist,* January 31, 2015, p. 9.

57. "Powerhouse Deutschland," *Bloomberg Businessweek,* January 3, 2011, p. 93; Alan S. Blinder, "The Euro Zone's German Crisis," *The Wall Street Journal,* December 13, 2011, http://online.wsj.com/article/SB10001424052970203430404577094313707190708.html (accessed February 9, 2015).

58. Bremmer, "Sea of Troubles."

59. "About APEC," www.apec.org/about-us/about-apec.aspx (accessed February 9, 2015).

60. Jake Spring and Xiaoyi Shao, "China's Growth Slowest Since Global Crisis, Annual Target at Risk," *Reuters,* October 21, 2014, http://www.reuters.com/article/2014/10/21/us-china-economy-gdp-idUSKCN0IA05W20141021 (accessed January 16, 2015).

61. Charles Riley and Feng Ke, "China to Overtake U.S. as World's Top Trader," *CNN,* January 10, 2014, http://money.cnn.com/2014/01/10/news/economy/china-us-trade/ (accessed February 9, 2015).

62. U.S. Environmental Protection Agency, "Global Greenhouse Gas Emissions Data," www.epa.gov/climatechange/ghgemissions/global.html (accessed February 9, 2015); Joshua Keating, "China Passes U.S. as World's Largest Oil Importer," *Slate,* October 11, 2013, www.slate.com/blogs/the_world_/2013/10/11/china_now_world_s_largest_net_oil_importer_surpassing_united_states.html (accessed February 9, 2015).

63. Dinny McMahon, "In Tasmania, Teddy Bears Bring Whiff of Success," *The Wall Street Journal,* April 10, 2014, p. A1, A10; Dinny McMahon and Yang Jie, "All of Australia's Lavender Not Enough to Satisfy China's 'Bobbie Bear' Appetite," *The Wall Street Journal,* April 17, 2014, http://blogs.wsj.com/chinarealtime/2014/04/17/all-of-australias-lavender-not-enough-to-satisfy-chinas-bobbie-bear-appetite/ (accessed September 22, 2014); Wolfgang Georg Arlt, "How Did Tasmanian Lavender Bears Turn into a Social Media Sensation In China—Third Update June 2014," *Forbes,* December 16, 2013, http://www.forbes.com/sites/profdrwolfganggarlt/2013/12/16/social-media-bring-tasmanian-lavender-bear-into-chinese-bedrooms-china-outbound-tourism-best-practice-example/ (accessed February 9, 2015); Peter Cai, "Why China Went Bullish on Bobbie the Bear," *Business Spectator,* January 22, 2014, http://www.businessspectator.com.au/article/2014/1/22/china/why-china-went-bullish-bobbie-bear (accessed September 22, 2014).

64. "The Rise of Capitalism," *The Economist,* January 21, 2012, p. 11.

65. Dexter Roberts, "Corporate China's Black Hole of Debt," *Bloomberg Businessweek,* November 19–22, 2012, pp. 15–16.

66. Charles Riley, "Starbucks to Open First Store in Vietnam," *CNN,* January 3, 2013, http://www.wsj.com/articles/SB10001424127887323374504578218111829498652 (accessed February 9, 2015).

67. "Overview," Association of Southeast Asian Nations, http://www.asean.org/asean/about-asean/overview (accessed February 9, 2015).

68. Parag Khanna, "ASEAN Is Key to 'Asian Century,'" *CNN,* August 15, 2013, http://www.cnn.com/2013/08/14/opinion/asean-dream-khanna/ (accessed November 21, 2014).

69. ASEAN website, http://www.asean.org/ (accessed February 9, 2015).

70. "Agreement on the Common Effective Preferential Tariff (CEPT) Scheme for the ASEAN Free Trade Area (AFTA)," Association of Southeast Asian Nations, http://www.asean.org/communities/asean-economic-community/item/agreement-on-the-common-effective-preferential-tariff-cept-scheme-for-the-asean-free-trade-area-afta (accessed February 9, 2015).

71. R.C., "No Brussels Sprouts in Bali," *The Economist,* November 18, 2011, www.economist.com/blogs/banyan/2011/11/asean-summits (accessed February 9, 2015).

72. Economist staff, "Thaksin Times," *The Economist,* January 31, 2015, p. 31.

73. Eric Bellman, "Asia Seeks Integration Despite EU's Woes," *The Wall Street Journal,* July 22, 2011, p. A9.

74. David J. Lynch, "The IMF Is . . . Tired Fund Struggles to Reinvent itself," *USA Today,* April 19, 2006, p. B1.

75. WTSC Industrial Group, http://www.wtsc.eu/index.shtml (accessed February 9, 2015).

76. Walter B. Wriston, "Ever Heard of Insourcing?" Commentary, *The Wall Street Journal,* March 24, 2004, p. A20.

77. "Here, There and Everywhere," a Special Report, *The Economist,* January 19, 2013, pp. 1–20.

78. Nick Heath, "Banks: Offshoring, Not Outsourcing," *Bloomberg BusinessWeek,* March 10, 2009, www.businessweek.com/ globalbiz/content/mar2009/gb20090310_619247.htm (accessed February 9, 2015).

79. Panos Mourdoukoutas, "How GM Wins in China," *Forbes,* February 19, 2013, www.forbes.com/sites/panosmourdoukoutas/2013/02/19/how-gm-wins-in-china/ (accessed March 9, 2015); General Motors, "About GM China," http://media.gm.com/media/cn/en/gm/company.html (accessed January 16, 2015).

80. PR Newswire, "Avon and KORRES Enter into a Strategic Alliance in Latin America," Avon website, February 10, 2014, http://media.avoncompany.com/index.php?s=10922&item=126262 (accessed January 16, 2015).

81. Cynthia Koons and Makiko Kitamura, "Walgreen Stays in U.S. as It Buys Rest of Alliance Boots," *Bloomberg,* August 6, 2014, http://www.bloomberg.com/news/2014-08-05/walgreen-said-not-to-exit-u-s-in-deal-to-buy-boots.html (accessed January 16, 2015).

82. Guo Changdong and Ren Ruqin, "Nestle CEO visits Tianjin," *China Daily,* August 12, 2010, www.chinadaily.com.cn/m/tianjin/e/2010-08/12/content_11146560.htm (accessed February 9, 2015); "Our People," Nestlé, http://www.nestle.com/csv/our-people (accessed February 9, 2015); Nestle, "How Many Factories Do You Have?" http://www.nestle.com/aboutus/ask-nestle/answers/how-many-factories-do-you-have (accessed January 16, 2015).

83. O. C. Ferrell, John Fraedrich, and Linda Ferrell, *Business Ethics,* 6th ed. (Boston: Houghton Mifflin, 2005), pp. 227–30.

84. Saritha Rai, "How Domino's Won India," *Fast Company,* February 2015, pp. 54–58.

85. Export.gov, www.export.gov/about/index.asp (accessed February 9, 2015); CIBER Web, http://CIBERWEB.msu.edu (accessed February 9, 2015).

Chapter 4

1. "Where Are All the Women Entrepreneurs: Q&A with Sangeeta Badal," *Gallup Business Journal,* October 30, 2014, http://www.gallup.com/businessjournal/179024/women-entrepreneurs.aspx (accessed January 30, 2015)

2. Maggie Overfelt, "Start-Me-Up: How the Garage Became a Legendary Place to Rev Up Ideas," *Fortune Small Business,* September 1, 2003, http://money.cnn.com/magazines/fsb/fsb_archive/2003/09/01/350784/index.htm (accessed February 23, 2015).

3. Network Solutions LLC, "Hosting Options," 2015, http://www.networksolutions.com/web-hosting/index-v5.jsp (accessed February 23, 2015); Network Solutions LLC, Network Solutions website, http://www.networksolutions.com/web-hosting/index-v5.jsp (accessed February 23, 2015).

4. Webco, "Webco's General Partnership," ww2.webcogp.com/webcos-approach.html (accessed February 23, 2015).

5. "Master Limited Partnership—MLP," *Investopedia,* http://www.investopedia.com/terms/m/mlp.asp (accessed February 23, 2015).

6. Mike Esterl, "Judge Pores Over Case of Tea," *The Wall Street Journal,* September 4, 2014, p. B8; Nate Raymond, "Judge rules AriZona Iced Tea Co-founder, Son Owed $1 Billion for Buyout," *Reuters,* October 14, 2014, http://www.reuters.com/article/2014/10/14/us-arizonaicedtea-trial-idUSKCN0I31TS20141014 (accessed December 4, 2014); BevNet.com staff, "A Brief History of Arizona," July-August 2009, BevNet, http://www.bevnet.com/magazine/issue/2009/a_brief_history_of_arizona (accessed December 4, 2014); Claire Zillman, "Unpaid Taxes, Guns, and Potential Bankruptcy: The bitter battle for AriZona Iced Tea," *Fortune,* July 10, 2014, http://fortune.com/2014/07/10/arizona-iced-tea/ (accessed December 4, 2014);

Peter Mahler, "50% Owner of AriZona Iced Tea, Claiming Shareholder Oppression, Files for Involuntary Dissolution of Multi-Billion Dollar Enterprise," *New York Business Divorce,* October 11, 2010, http://www.nybusinessdivorce.com/2010/10/articles/grounds-for-dissolution/50-owner-of-arizona-iced-tea-claiming-shareholder-oppression-files-for-involuntary-dissolution-of-multibillion-dollar-enterprise/ (accessed December 4, 2014).

7. Morgan Lewis website, http://www.morganlewis.com/index.cfm/fuseaction/practiceArea.introduction/nodeID/51fe28f8-210f-442a-b73d-d4255bed92c6/ (accessed January 30, 2015); Ranker, "100 Largest Law Firms in the World," 2015, http://www.ranker.com/list/100-largest-law-firms-in-the-world/business-and-company-info (accessed January 30, 2015).

8. Bill Orben, "uBreakiFix Launches Franchise Unit, Sets Sights on 125 Stores This Year," *Orlando Business Journal,* February 20, 2013, http://www.bizjournals.com/orlando/blog/2013/02/ubreakifix-launches-franchise-unit.html (accessed February 23, 2015); "About uBreakiFix," uBreakiFix Careers website, http://careers.ubreakifix.com/about-ubreakifix/#.VOuVr3nTBVI (accessed February 23, 2015).

9. PwC, "Facts and Figures," 2013, www.pwc.com/gx/en/about-pwc/facts-and-figures.jhtml (accessed February 23, 2015).

10. Sarah Griffiths, "Snapchat Settles Lengthy Lawsuit with Former University Classmate—and Admit the App WAS His Idea," *Daily Mail,* September 10, 2014, http://www.dailymail.co.uk/sciencetech/article-2750807/Snapchat-founders-settle-lengthy-lawsuit-former-classmate-admit-app-WAS-idea.html (accessed February 23, 2015).

11. Alistair Barr, "Google's $100 Billion Cash Pile Prompts Call for Dividend," *The Wall Street Journal,* November 1, 2014, http://blogs.wsj.com/digits/2014/11/01/googles-expected-100-billion-cash-pile-prompts-call-for-dividend/ (accessed January 30, 2015).

12. "America's Largest Private Companies: Publix Super Markets," *Forbes,* October 2014, http://www.forbes.com/companies/publix-super-markets/ (accessed January 30, 2015).

13. "America's Largest Private Companies," *Forbes,* December 31, 2013, www.mars.com/global/about.aspx (accessed February 23, 2015); Carla Zanetos Scully, "2014 Global Top 100: Candy Industry's Exclusive List of the Top 100 Confectionery Companies in the World!" *Candy Industry,* January 31, 2014, www.candyindustry.com/articles/86039-global-top-100-candy-industrys-exclusivelist-of-the-top-100-confectionerycompanies-in-the-world?page=5 (accessed February 23, 2015).

14. Deborah Orr, "The Secret World of Mars," *Forbes,* April 28, 2008, http://www.forbes.com/2008/04/28/billionaires-mars-wrigley-biz-billies-cz_do_0428marsfamily.html (accessed February 23, 2015).

15. "America's Largest Private Companies."

16. Tim Worstall, "The Internal Economics of Amazon's No Profits Growth Model," *Forbes,* September 7, 2014, http://www.forbes.com/sites/timworstall/2014/09/07/the-internal-economics-of-amazons-no-profits-growth-model/ (accessed February 23, 2015).

17. Liz Hoffman, "Moelis Founder to Keep Control after IPO," *The Wall Street Journal,* March 4, 2014, http://blogs.wsj.com/moneybeat/2014/03/04/moelis-founder-to-keep-control-after-ipo/ (accessed February 23, 2015).

18. Liyan Chen, "The World's Largest Companies: China Takes Over the Top Three Spots," *Forbes,* May 7, 2014, http://www.forbes.com/sites/liyanchen/2014/05/07/the-worlds-largest-companies-china-takes-over-the-top-three-spots/ (accessed February 23, 2015).

19. Ibid.

20. Leslie Picker and Lulu Yilun Chen, "Alibaba's Banks Boost IPO Size to Record of $25 Billion," *Bloomberg,* September 22, 2014, http://www.bloomberg.com/news/articles/2014-09-22/alibaba-s-banks-said-to-increase-ipo-size-to-record-25-billion (accessed February 23, 2015).

21. Brendan Marasco, "3 Reasons Dell Went Private," *The Motley Fool,* November 1, 2013, www.fool.com/investing/general/2013/11/01/3-reasons-dell-went-private.aspx (accessed February 23, 2015).

22. Elko & Associates Limited, "Private Operating Foundations," February 23, 2011, http://blog.elkocpa.com/nonprofit-tax-exempt/private-operating-foundations (accessed February 23, 2015); Foundation Group, "What is a 501(c)(3)?" http://www.501c3.org/what-is-a-501c3/ (accessed February 23, 2015).

23. O.C. Ferrell, John Fraedrich, and Linda Ferrell, *Business Ethics: Ethical Decision Making and Cases,* 8th ed. (Mason, OH: South-Western Cengage Learning, 2011), p. 109.

24. P. Nash Jenkins, "American Apparel Fires Controversial Founder and CEO Dov Charney," *Time,* June 19, 2014, http://time.com/2898151/american-apparel-fires-controversial-founder-and-ceo-dov-charney/ (accessed January 30, 2015); Hayley Peterson, "American Apparel Strikes Deal," *Business Insider,* July 9, 2014, http://www.businessinsider.com/american-apparel-gets-25-million-investment-2014-7 (accessed January 30, 2015).

25. Diane Brady, "Cozy Corporate Directors Raise Their Pay to $1,000 an Hour," *Bloomberg Businessweek,* May 30, 2013, http://www.bloomberg.com/bw/articles/2013-05-30/cozy-corporate-boards-vote-to-pay-themselves-1-000-an-hour (accessed February 23, 2015).

26. P&G, "Board Composition," 2014, www.pg.com/en_US/company/global_structure_operations/governance/board_composition.shtml (accessed February 23, 2015).

27. Cordell Eddings, "Apple Plans $5 Billion Bond Sale; Fourth Since 2013," *Bloomberg Business,* February 2, 2015, http://www.bloomberg.com/news/articles/2015-02-02/apple-said-to-plan-5-billion-bond-offering-in-fourth-since-2013 (accessed February 23, 2015); Mike Cherney, "Microsoft's Bond Sale Is Largest of the Year at $10.75 Billion," *The Wall Street Journal,* February 9, 2015, http://www.wsj.com/articles/microsofts-bond-sale-is-largest-of-the-year-at-10-75-billion-1423513035 (accessed February 23, 2015).

28. Richard Rubin, "Bid to Lower Corporate Tax Rate Stirs Backlash From Business," *Bloomberg,* January 13, 2015, http://www.bloomberg.com/news/articles/2015-01-13/bid-to-lower-corporate-tax-rate-stirs-backlash-from-businesses (accessed February 23, 2015).

29. Joseph Nathan Kane, *Famous First Facts,* 4th ed. (New York: The H.W. Wilson Company, 1981), p. 202.

30. PR Newswire, "Raytheon and General Dynamics Joint Venture Awarded U.S. Air Force Launch and Test Range Contract," *Raytheon,* January 9, 2015, http://raytheon.mediaroom.com/2015-01-09-Raytheon-and-General-Dynamics-joint-venture-awarded-U-S-Air-Force-Launch-and-Test-Range-Contract (accessed February 23, 2015).

31. Robert D. Hisrich and Michael P. Peters, *Entrepreneurship,* 5th ed. (Boston: McGraw-Hill, 2002), pp. 315–16.

32. "Company Overview of Mrs. Fields Famous Brands, LLC," *Bloomberg Business,* February 23, 2015, http://www.bloomberg.com/research/stocks/private/snapshot.asp?privcapId=3553769 (accessed February 23, 2015).

33. Coop Directory, "Coop Directory Service Listing," www .coopdirectory.org/directory.htm#Massachusetts (accessed February 23, 2015).

34. "2014 Top Company: OtterBox," *ColoradoBiz Magazine,* September/October 2014, p. 30; April Joyner, "How I Reinvented My Business," *Inc.,* October 14, 2011, http://www.inc.com/inc5000/201109/ otterbox-curt-richardson-how-i-reinvented-my-business.html (accessed September 16, 2014); "OtterBox," *Forbes,* http://www. forbes.com/companies/otterbox/ (accessed September 16, 2014).

35. Aaron Tilley, "Google Acquires Smart Thermostat Maker Nest for $3.2 Billion," *Forbes,* January 13, 2014, http://www.forbes. com/sites/aarontilley/2014/01/13/google-acquires-nest-for-3-2- billion/ (accessed February 23, 2015).

36. Eric Savitz, "Did Google Buy a Lemon? Motorola Mobility Whiffs Q4," *Forbes,* January 8, 2012, http://www.forbes.com/sites/eric- savitz/2012/01/08/did-google-buy-a-lemon-motorola-mobility- whiffs-q4/ (accessed February 23, 2015); Brian Womack, "Google Discloses $151 Million Price Tag for Zagat Service," *Bloomberg Business,* October 26, 2011, http://www.bloomberg. com/news/articles/2011-10-27/google-spent-151-million-on- zagat-review-service-last-quarter (accessed February 23, 2015).

37. "Nasty Medicine," *The Economist,* July 5, 2014, pp. 53–54; John Kell, "Hertz Adopts 'Poison Pill,'" *The Wall Street Journal,* December 31, 2013, p. B2; Liz Hoffman, "'Poison Pill' Gets a Bit More Toxic," *The Wall Street Journal,* May 8, 2014, p. C1; RTT Staff Writer, "Carl Icahn Strikes Deal with Hertz to Appoint His Three Nominees to Board," *RTT News,* September 16, 2014, http://www.rttnews.com/2384588/carl-icahn-strikes-deal-with- hertz-to-appoint-his-three-nominees-to-board.aspx (accessed September 17, 2014).

38. Vidya L. Nathan, "Zoetis Adopts Poison Pill after Ackman Picks Up Stake," *Reuters,* November 14, 2014, http://www.reuters.com/ article/2014/11/14/us-zoetis-poisonpill-idUSKCN0IY2J520141114 (accessed January 30, 2015).

Chapter 5

1. Small Business Administration Department of Advocacy, "Frequently Asked Questions," March 2014, https://www.sba.gov/ sites/default/files/FAQ_March_2014_0.pdf (accessed March 3, 2015).

2. Joshua Yaffa, "Signs of a Russian Thaw (Toward Business)," *The New York Times,* December 28, 2013, http://www.nytimes. com/2013/12/29/business/international/signs-of-a-russian- thaw-toward-business.html (accessed March 3, 2015).

3. Marco della Cava, "USA Today Entrepreneur of the Year," *USA Today,* December 11, 2014, pp. 1B–2B.

4. Scott Gerber, "Blake Mycoskie," *Inc.,* December 2014/January 2015, p. 144.

5. Small Business Administration Department of Advocacy, "Frequently Asked Questions."

6. National Association of Women Business Owners, "About Us," http://nawbo.org/section_2.cfm (accessed February 13, 2015).

7. Silvana Ordoñez, "Minorities: The Force Fueling Small-Business Growth," *CNBC,* May 12, 2014, http://www.cnbc.com/id/101639528 (accessed February 13, 2015).

8. Sam Frizell, "Mercado of America," *Time,* April 28, 2015, pp. 42–45; "About Us," The Legaspi Company website, http://www.thelegaspi. com/jos-de-jes-s-legaspi/ (accessed February 12, 2015).

9. Small Business Administration Department of Advocacy, "Frequently Asked Questions."

10. "Statistics of U.S. Businesses (SUSB)," *Statistics of U.S. Businesses,* www.census.gov/econ/susb/index.html (accessed March 3, 2015).

11. "Bittersweet Synergy: Domestic Outsourcing in India," *The Economist,* October 22, 2009, p. 74.

12. John Tozzi, "Innovation: Tap to Unlock," *Bloomberg Business- week,* June 13, 2013, p. 42.

13. SCORE Association, "Small Biz Stats & Trends," https://www. score.org/node/148155 (accessed February 13, 2015).

14. Michael Wolff, "Uber: Tech Company of the Year," *USA Today,* December 23, 2013, pp. 1B, 3B.

15. Dinah Eng and Patrick Leon Esquerré, "Even Texans Can Love Quiche," *Fortune,* September 2, 2013, pp. 27–30.

16. Suzanne Kapner, "J.C. Penney Resurrects Its Catalog," *The Wall Street Journal,* January 19, 2015, http://www.wsj.com/articles/j- c-penney-resurrects-its-catalog-1421695574 (accessed March 3, 2015).

17. "5 Minutes with Neil Blumenthal," *Delta Sky,* September 2014, p. 30; Warby Parker website, https://www.warbyparker.com/ (accessed October 14, 2014); Jessica Pressler, "20/30 Vision," *New York Magazine,* August 11, 2013, http://nymag.com/news/fea- tures/warby-parker-2013-8/ (accessed October 14, 2014); David Zax, "Fast Talk: How Warby Parker's Cofounders Disrupted the Eyewear Industry and Stayed Friends," *Fast Company,* February 22, 2012, http://www.fastcompany.com/1818215/fast-talk-how- warby-parkers-cofounders-disrupted-eyewear-industry-and- stayed-friends (accessed October 14, 2014); Marcus Wohlsen, "Is Warby Parker Too Good To Last?" *Wired,* June 25, 2015, http:// www.wired.com/2014/06/warby-parkers-quest-to-prove-not- sucking-is-the-ultimate-innovation/ (accessed October 14, 2014).

18. Christine Birkner, "Southern Sweet Spot," *Marketing News,* January 2014, pp. 16–17.

19. Small Business Administration Department of Advocacy, "Frequently Asked Questions."

20. Lev Grossman, "Head Trip," *Time,* April 7, 2014, pp. 36–41.

21. Jefferson Graham, "Start-Up Cooks Up a Future for Food," *USA Today,* December 23, 2013, p. 4B.

22. Small Business Administration Department of Advocacy, "Frequently Asked Questions."

23. Susan Payton, "Attention, Micropreneurs: You're Not Alone in Small Business," *Forbes,* May 12, 2014, http://www.forbes.com/ sites/allbusiness/2014/05/12/attention-micropreneurs-youre- not-alone-in-small-business/ (accessed February 13, 2015).

24. Matt Hickey, "This Is Project Wedge: New, Easy, Indie Portable Projection System," *Forbes,* January 24, 2014, http://www. forbes.com/sites/matthickey/2014/01/24/this-is-project-wedge- new-easy-indie-portable-projection-system/ (accessed Feb- ruary 13, 2015); Nikki McCoy, "Project Wedge: From Tablet to Projection in an Instant," NorthwestMilitary.com, June 12, 2014, http://www.northwestmilitary.com/music-and-culture/arts-fea- tures/2014/06/Project-Wedge-From-tablet-to-projection-in-an- instant/ (accessed February 13, 2015); Rolf Boone, "Olympia Startup Wins PLU Business Plan Competition," *The Olympian,* May 1, 2014, http://www.theolympian.com/2014/05/01/3112036/ olympia-startup-wins-plu-business.html (accessed February 13, 2015).

25. Danielle Kucera, "Stitch Fix Nabs $12 Million from Benchmark to Customize Commerce," *Bloomberg,* October 17, 2013, http:// www.bloomberg.com/news/articles/2013-10-17/stitch-fix-nabs- 12-million-from-benchmark-to-customize-commerce (accessed April 10, 2014); Nicole Laporte, "Getting Their Fix," *Fast Com- pany,* March 2014, pp. 44–46.

26. Sandra Block and Lisa Gerstner, "Strike It Rich!," *Kiplinger's Per- sonal Finance,* May 2014, pp. 62–68; Virginia B. Wood, "Peached Tortilla Competes in Food Truck Challenge Tomorrow," *Austin*

Chronicle, June 13, 2013, http://www.austinchronicle.com/daily/food/2013-06-13/peached-tortilla-competes-in-food-truck-challenge-on-friday-june-14/ (accessed December 4, 2014); Meghan McCarron, "Peached Tortilla is Going Brick & Mortar in Allandale," *Austin Eater,* January 21, 2014, http://austin.eater.com/2014/1/21/6294025/peached-tortilla-is-going-brick-mortar-in-allandale (accessed December 4, 2014); The Peached Tortilla, "About Us," http://thepeachedtortilla.com/about/ (accessed December 4, 2014).

27. Thomas W. Zimmerer and Norman M. Scarborough, *Essentials of Entrepreneurship and Small Business Management,* 6th ed. (Upper Saddle River, NJ: Pearson Prentice Hall, 2005), pp. 118–24.

28. Ibid.

29. "Find a Chapter," SCORE, https://www.score.org/chapters-map (accessed February 13, 2015); SCORE Staten Island website, https://statenisland.score.org/ (accessed February 13, 2015).

30. Entrepreneur Media, Inc., "Getting Started with Business Incubators," *Entrepreneur,* http://www.entrepreneur.com/article/52802 (accessed February 13, 2015).

31. Adapted from "Tomorrow's Entrepreneur," *Inc. State of Small Business,* 23, no. 7 (2001), pp. 80–104.

32. CNN Library, "Baby Boomer Generation Fast Facts," *CNN,* September 1 2014, http://www.cnn.com/2013/11/06/us/baby-boomer-generation-fast-facts/ (accessed February 13, 2015).

33. Molly Smith, "Managing Generation Y as They Change the Workforce," *Reuters,* January 8, 2008, www.reuters.com/article/2008/01/08/idUS129795+08-Jan-2008+BW20080108" (accessed March 3, 2015); Richard Fry, "This Year, Millennials Will Overtake Baby Boomers," *Pew Research,* http://www.pewresearch.org/fact-tank/2015/01/16/this-year-millennials-will-overtake-baby-boomers/ (accessed February 13, 2015).

34. Jeffrey S. Passel and D'Vera Cohn, "U.S. Population Projections: 2005-2050," *Pew Research Center,* February 11, 2008, http://www.pewsocialtrends.org/2008/02/11/us-population-projections-2005-2050/ (accessed February 13, 2015); Hector Cordero-Guzman, "The 'Majority-Minority' America Is Coming, So Why Not Get Ready?" *MSNBC,* July 15, 2014, http://www.msnbc.com/melissa-harris-perry/the-majority-minority-america-coming-so-why-not-get-ready (accessed February 13, 2015); "Changing Patterns in U.S. Immigration and Population," *The Pew Charitable Trusts,* December 18, 2014, http://www.pewtrusts.org/en/research-and-analysis/issue-briefs/2014/12/changing-patterns-in-us-immigration-and-population (accessed February 13, 2015).

35. Amit Chowdhry, "Imgur Pro Is Now Free For Everyone," *Forbes,* February 10, 2015, http://www.forbes.com/sites/amitchowdhry/2015/02/10/imgur-pro-is-now-free-for-everyone/ (accessed February 13, 2015); Brad Stone, "How Imgur Became a Photo-Sharing Hit," *Bloomberg,* January 23, 2014, http://www.bloomberg.com/news/articles/2014-01-23/how-imgur-became-a-photo-sharing-hit (accessed February 13, 2015).

36. Jason Nazar, "16 Surprising Statistics Facts about Small Businesses," *Forbes,* September 9, 2013, http://www.forbes.com/sites/jasonnazar/2013/09/09/16-surprising-statistics-about-small-businesses/ (accessed February 13, 2015); U.S. Small Business Administration, "Home-Based Businesses," https://www.sba.gov/content/home-based-businesses (accessed February 13, 2015).

37. Wendy Koch, "Poof! Two Friends Turn Air Pollution into Plastic Goods," *USA Today,* December 31, 2013, p. 2A; Newlight Technologies website, http://newlight.com/ (accessed September 16, 2014); "Company Overview of Newlight Technologies, LLC," *Bloomberg Businessweek,*" http://investing.businessweek.com/research/stocks/ private/snapshot.asp?privcapId=225749737 (accessed September 16, 2014); Gabrielle Karol, "Newlight Technologies Raises $9.2M to Make Plastic from Greenhouse Gases," *Fox Business,* April 16, 2014, http://smallbusiness.foxbusiness.com/technology-web/2014/04/16/newlight-technologies-raises-2m-to-make-plastic-from-greenhouse-gases/ (accessed September 16, 2014).

38. Gifford Pinchott III, *Intrapreneuring* (New York: Harper & Row, 1985), p. 34.

39. Paul Brown, "How to Cope with Hard Times," *The New York Times,* June 10, 2008, www.nytimes.com/2008/06/10/business/smallbusiness/10toolkit.html?_r%205%201&ref%205%20smallbusiness&orefslogin&gwh=A256B42494736F9E2C604851BF6451DC&gwt=regi" (accessed March 3, 2015).

Chapter 6

1. Pete Pachal, "Samsung Bets Big on Curved TVs," *Mashable,* March 20, 2014, http://mashable.com/2014/03/20/samsung-curved-tvs/ (accessed March 4, 2015); Brian X. Chen, "Television Sales Look Grim Again This Year," *The New York Times,* November 6, 2013, http://bits.blogs.nytimes.com/2013/11/06/television-sales-look-grim-again-this-year/ (accessed March 4, 2015).

2. Suzanne Heyn, "Sorting through Options," *Inbound Logistics,* May 2014, pp. 48–52.

3. "Seventh Generation: Ethosolution Go Green Products and All Natural Cleaners," EthoSolutions, http://www.ethosolutions.org/seventh-generation-ethosolution-go-green/ (accessed March 4, 2015).

4. Stephanie Strom, "CVS Vows to Quit Selling Tobacco Products," *The New York Times,* February 5, 2014, http://www.nytimes.com/2014/02/06/business/cvs-plans-to-end-sales-of-tobacco-products-by-october.html (accessed March 29, 2014); Kyle Stock, "The Strategy Behind CVS's No-Smoking Campaign," *Bloomberg Businessweek,* February 5, 2014, http://www.bloomberg.com/bw/articles/2014-02-05/the-strategy-behind-cvss-no-smoking-campaign (accessed March 4, 2015).

5. Jayson Derrick, "Nike's 2017 Objective: $36 Billion Revenue," *The Motley Fool,* October 20, 2014, www.fool.com/investing/general/2013/10/20/nikes-2017-objectives-36-billion-in-revenue.aspx (accessed March 4, 2015).

6. Eric Pfanner, "After Losses, Yet Another Overhaul for Sony," *The New York Times,* February 6, 2014, http://www.nytimes.com/2014/02/07/technology/sony-to-sell-pc-unit-amid-dwindling-sales.html (accessed March 4, 2015); Jackie Northam, "As Overseas Costs Rise, More U.S. Companies Are 'Reshoring,'" *NPR,* January 27, 2014, www.npr.org/blogs/parallels/2014/01/22/265080779/as-overseas-costs-rise-more-u-scompanies-are-reshoring (accessed March 4, 2015).

7. G. Tomas, M. Hult, David W. Cravens, and Jagdish Sheth, "Competitive Advantage in the Global Marketplace: A Focus on Marketing Strategy," *Journal of Business Research* 51 (January 2001), p. 1.

8. Michigan Department of Natural Resources Fisheries Division, "Tactical Plan," October 24, 2013, www.michigan.gov/documents/dnr/FD-TacticalPlan-Oct2013-FINAL_438248_7.pdf (accessed March 4, 2015).

9. Dennis McCafferty, "The Ten Commandments of Disaster Recovery," May 13, 2013, http://www.cioinsight.com/it-strategy/infrastructure/slideshows/the-ten-commandments-of-disaster-recovery (accessed March 4, 2015).

10. Ed Legge, "Seats Rebounds after Fire," *WiscNews,* February 11, 2015, http://www.wiscnews.com/news/local/article_75d9e84e-7e7a-5db8-8c14-bea1dd85311d.html (accessed February 16, 2015).

11. Suzanne Kapner, "Crocs to Restructure, Cutting Jobs and Stores," *The Wall Street Journal,* July 21, 2014, http://www.wsj.com/articles/crocs-to-restructure-cutting-jobs-and-stores-1405984742 (accessed February 16, 2015).

12. PRWeb, "Collabera Named 2014 'Best Staffing Firm to Work For' by Staffing Industry Analysts for Record Third Consecutive Year," *PRWeb,* March 25, 2014, www.prweb.com/releases/2014/03/prweb11698621.htm (accessed March 4, 2015); Collabera, "Home," www.collabera.com (accessed March 4, 2015).

13. "Labor Force Statistics from the Current Population Survey," Bureau of Labor Statistics, www.bls.gov/cps/ (accessed March 4, 2015).

14. C. O. Trevor, and A. J. Nyberg, "Keeping Your Headcount When All About You Are Losing Theirs: Downsizing, Voluntary Turnover Rates, and the Moderating Role of HR Practices," *Academy of Management Journal,* 51 (2008), pp. 259–76.

15. Jon Kaufman and Rob Markey, "Who Keeps You Jazzed about Your Job?" *Forbes,* February 11, 2014, http://www.forbes.com/sites/baininsights/2014/02/11/who-keeps-you-jazzed-about-your-job/ (accessed March 4, 2015).

16. Brent Snavely and Alissa Priddle, "Fiat Chrysler Maps Out Big 5-Year Plan," *USA Today,* May 7, 2014, p. 2B; Christina Rogers and Gilles Castonguay, "Fiat CEO Outlines Goals in Chrysler Merger," *The Wall Street Journal,* January 14, 2014, p. B5; Agnieszka Flak, "Fiat Chrysler CEO Sticks to 2014 Guidance," *Reuters,* September 11, 2014, http://www.reuters.com/article/2014/09/11/us-fiat-outlook-idUSKBN0H60ZF20140911 (accessed September 17, 2014).

17. "IAPP Hits 20K Members—Meet One from Malaysia," International Association of Privacy Professionals, February 5, 2015, https://privacyassociation.org/news/a/iapp-hits-20k-members-meet-one-from-malaysia/ (accessed February 16, 2015).

18. Catalyst Inc., "Women CEOs of the S&P 500," http://www.catalyst.org/knowledge/women-ceos-sp-500 (accessed February 16, 2015).

19. Ross Kerber, "Growth in Compensation for U.S. CEOs May Have Slowed," *Reuters,* March 17, 2014, www.reuters.com/article/2014/03/17/ us-compensation-ceos-2013-insight-idUSBREA2G05520140317 (accessed March 4, 2015).

20. DiversityInc, "The DiversityInc Top 50 Companies for Diversity," *DiversityInc,* 2014, http://www.diversityinc.com/the-diversity-inc-top-50-companies-for-diversity-2014/ (accessed March 4, 2015); Diversity Best Practices Staff, "Inside Diversity Structure at Sodexo, Johnson & Johnson, and Rockwell Automation," *Diversity Best Practices,* January 29, 2013, http://www.diversitybestpractices.com/news-articles/inside-diversity-structure-sodexo-johnson-johnson-and-rockwell-automation (accessed March 4, 2015).

21. Laura Nichols, "Agencies Called to Step Up the Pace on Diversity Efforts," *PRWeek,* February 7, 2014, http://www.prweek.com/article/1283550/agencies-called-step-pace-diversity-efforts (accessed March 4, 2015).

22. Clay Latimer, "Philip Pillsbury's Treats Turned into Tasty Sales," *Investor's Business Daily,* August 1, 2013, p. A3; Funding Universe, "The Pillsbury Company History," *International Directory of Company Histories,* Vol. 62, St. James Press, 2004, http://www.fundinguniverse.com/company-histories/the-pillsbury-company-history/ (accessed November 25, 2014); Walter Waggoner, "Philip Pillsbury of Minnesota; Led Food Products Concern," *The New York Times,* June 16, 1984, http://www.nytimes.com/1984/06/16/obituaries/philip-pillsbury-of-minnesota-led-food-products-concern.html (accessed November 25, 2014); Constance L. Hays and Andrew Ross Sorkin, "General Mills Is Seen in a $10.5 Billion Deal for Pillsbury," *The New York Times,* July 17, 2000, http://www.nytimes.com/2000/07/17/business/general-mills-is-seen-in-a-10.5-billion-deal-for-pillsbury.html (accessed November 25, 2014).

23. Del Jones, "Autocratic Leadership Works—Until It Fails," *USA Today,* June 5, 2003, http://usatoday30.usatoday.com/news/nation/2003-06-05-raines-usat_x.htm (accessed March 4, 2015).

24. George Manning and Kent Curtis, *The Art of Leadership* (New York: McGraw-Hill, 2003), p. 125.

25. Rachel Feintzeig, "You're Fired! And We Really Mean It," *The Wall Street Journal,* November 5, 2014, pp. B1, B6.

26. Bruce J. Avolio and William L. Gardner, "Authentic Leadership Development: Getting to the Root of Positive Forms of Leadership," *The Leadership Quarterly,* 2005, pp. 315–38.

27. John P. Kotter, "What Leaders Really Do," *Harvard Business Review,* December 2001, http://fs.ncaa.org/Docs/DIII/What%20Leaders%20Really%20Do.pdf (accessed March 4, 2015).

28. Jen Wieczner, "Bristol-Myers Squibb CEO Steps Down, Replaced by COO," *Fortune,* January 20, 2015, http://fortune.com/2015/01/20/bristol-myers-ceo-replaced/ (accessed February 16, 2015).

29. C. L. Pearce and C. C. Manz, "The New Silver Bullets of Leadership: The Importance of Self- and Shared Leadership in Knowledge Work," *Organizational Dynamics,* 34, no. 2 (2005), pp. 130–40.

30. Deborah Harrington-Mackin, *The Team Building Tool Kit* (New York: New Directions Management, 1994); Joseph P. Folger, Marshall Scott Poole, and Randall K. Stutman, *Working through Conflict: Strategies for Relationships, Groups, and Organizations,* 6th ed. (Upper Saddle River, NJ: Pearson Education, 2009).

31. Kerrie Unsworth, "Unpacking Creativity," *Academy of Management Review,* 26 (April 2001), pp. 289–97.

32. Jeff Bennett and Sara Murray, "Insider Is GM's First Female Chief," *The Wall Street Journal,* December 11, 2013, p. A1; "50 Most Powerful Women," *Fortune,* February 24, 2014, pp. 66–71; Patricia Sellers, "With GM's New Chief," *Fortune,* February 24, 2014, pp. 73–75.

33. Pallavi Gogoi, "A Bittersweet Deal for Wrigley," *BusinessWeek,* May 12, 2008, p. 34I Wrigley, "About Us," www.wrigley.com/global/about-us.aspx (accessed March 4, 2015).

34. *Harvard Business Review* 60 (November–December 1982), p. 160.

35. Dan Schwabel, "5 Reasons Why Your Online Presence Will Replace Your Resume in 10 Years," *Forbes,* February 21, 2012, http://www.forbes.com/sites/danschwabel/2011/02/21/5-reasons-why-your-online-presence-will-replace-your-resume-in-10-years/ (accessed March 4, 2015).

36. "Salary After Taxes," *Employment Spot,* www.employmentspot.com/employment-articles/salary-aftertaxes (accessed September 4, 2014).

37. Bureau of Labor Statistics, "Occupational Employment and Wages News Release—May 2013," http://www.bls.gov/news.release/ocwage.htm (accessed May 4, 2015).

Chapter 7

1. Horace Dediu, "Understanding Apple's Organizational Structure," *Asymco,* July 3, 2013, http://www.asymco.com/2013/07/03/understanding-apples-organizational-structure/ (accessed May 17, 2015); Sam Grobart, "How Samsung Became the World's No. 1 Smartphone Maker," *Bloomberg Businessweek,* March 28, 2013, http://www.bloomberg.com/bw/articles/2013-03-28/

how-samsung-became-the-worlds-no-dot-1-smartphone-maker (accessed March 17, 2015); Jay Yarow, "Apple's New Organizational Structure Could Help It Move Faster," *Business Insider,* May 1, 2013, http://www.businessinsider.com/apples-new-organizational-structure-could-help-it-move-faster-2013-5 (accessed March 17, 2015);

2. Reed Hastings, "How to Set Your Employees Free: Reed Hastings," *Bloomberg Businessweek,* April 12, 2012, http://www.bloomberg.com/bw/articles/2012-04-12/how-to-set-your-employees-free-reed-hastings (accessed March 17, 2015); Dan Lyons, "Advice on Corporate Culture From Netflix's Former Chief Talent Officer," *HubSpot,* May 7, 2013, http://blog.hubspot.com/marketing/netflix-hubspot-corporate-culture-advice (accessed March 31, 2014).

3. Robert Hackett, "A Globe of Opportunity," *Fortune,* February 1, 2015, p. 22.

4. "Best Companies to Work For: Happy Campers," *CNNMoney,* http://money.cnn.com/galleries/2011/news/companies/1104/gallery.best_companies_happy_campers.fortune/2.html (accessed March 17, 2015); Christopher Palmeri, "Zappos Retails Its Culture," *Bloomberg Businessweek,* December 30, 2009, www.businessweek.com/magazine/content/10_02/b4162057120453.htm (accessed March 17, 2015).

5. "The 100 Best Companies to Work For," *Fortune,* February 3, 2014, pp. 108–119; W.L. Gore, "A Team-Based Flats Lattice Structure," http://www.gore.com/en_xx/aboutus/culture/index.html (accessed October 15, 2014); Gary Hamel, "W.L. Gore: Lessons from a Management Revolutionary," *The Wall Street Journal,* March 18, 2010, http://blogs.wsj.com/management/2010/03/18/wl-gore-lessons-from-a-management-revolutionary/ (accessed October 15, 2014).

6. Joe Light, "Finance and Tech Signal Bold Attitudes on Ethics," *The Wall Street Journal,* March 7, 2011, http://online.wsj.com/article/SB10001424052748704728004576176711042012064.html (accessed March 17, 2015).

7. Lisa Magloff, "Examples of Transformational Change," *Chron,* http://smallbusiness.chron.com/examples-transformational-change-18261.html (accessed March 31, 2014); Nokia, "Our story," http://company.nokia.com/en/about-us/our-company/our-story (accessed March 17, 2015).

8. Adam Smith, *Wealth of Nations* (New York: Modern Library, 1937; originally published in 1776).

9. Ben Dipietro, "Automakers Face 'Herculean' Task in Implementing Supply Chain Guidelines," *The Wall Street Journal,* May 28, 2014, http://blogs.wsj.com/riskandcompliance/2014/05/28/automakers-face-herculean-task-in-implementing-supply-chain-guidelines/ (accessed March 5, 2015).

10. Unilever, "Annual Report and Accounts 2013," www.unilever.com/images/Unilever_AR13_tcm13-383757.pdf (accessed March 17, 2015).

11. PepsiCo, "Global Divisions," http://www.pepsico.com/Company/Global-Divisions (accessed March 5, 2015).

12. Diageo, "Our Structure," http://www.diageo.com/en-row/ourbusiness/ourregions/Pages/default.aspx (accessed March 5, 2015).

13. Procter & Gamble, "Strength in Structure," http://www.pg.com/en_US/company/global_structure_operations/corporate_structure.shtml (accessed March 5, 2015).

14. Micah Solomon, "Take These Two Steps to Rival Nordstrom's Customer Service Experience," *Forbes,* March 15, 2014, www.forbes.com/sites/micahsolomon/2014/03/15/the-nordstrom-two-partcustomer-experience-formulalessons-for-your-business/ (accessed March 31, 2014).

15. Julie Jargon, "Burger King Joins Crowd in India," *The Wall Street Journal,* November 19, 2014, http://online.wsj.com/news/articles/SB10001424052702303531204579207792423911748 (accessed March 17, 2015); Lily Kuo, "Why Burger King Should Sell Pizza at Its New Restaurants in India," *Quartz,* November 21, 2013, http://qz.com/149434/whyburger-king-should-sell-pizza-at-itsnew-restaurants-in-india/ (accessed March 17, 2015).

16. "Why Work Here?" www.wholefoodsmarket.com/careers/work-here.php (accessed March 17, 2015).

17. PR Newswire, "PepsiCo Unveils New Organizational Structure, Names CEOs of Three Principle Operating Units," November 5, 2007, http://www.prnewswire.com/news-releases/pepsico-unveils-new-organizational-structure-names-ceos-of-three-principal-operating-units-58668152.html (accessed March 17, 2015); "Global Brands," PepsiCo, http://www.pepsico.com/company/global-brands (accessed April 30, 2014).

18. Jon R. Katzenbach and Douglas K. Smith, "The Discipline of Teams," *Harvard Business Review,* 71 (March– April 1993), p. 19.

19. Ibid.

20. John Baldoni, "The Secret to Team Collaboration: Individuality," *Inc.,* January 18, 2012, http://www.inc.com/john-baldoni/the-secret-to-team-collaboration-is-individuality.html (accessed March 17, 2015).

21. Gregory Ciotti, "Why Remote Teams Are the Future (and How to Make Them Work)," *Help Scout,* October 23, 2013, www.helpscout.net/blog/virtual-teams/ (accessed April 1, 2014).

22. Anneke Seley, "Outside In: The Rise of the Inside Sales Team," *Salesforce.com Blog,* February 3, 2015, http://blogs.salesforce.com/company/2015/02/outside-in-rise-inside-sales-team-gp.html (accessed March 5, 2015).

23. Patrick Kiger, "Task Force Training Develops New Leaders, Solves Real Business Issues and Helps Cut Costs," *Workforce,* September 7, 2011, www.workforce.com/article/20070521/NEWS02/305219996/task-force-trainingdevelops-new-leaders-solves-realbusiness-issues-and-helps-cut-costs (accessed March 17, 2015); Duane D. Stanford, "Coca-Cola Woman Board Nominee Bucks Slowing Diversity Trend," *Bloomberg,* February 22, 2013, http://www.bloomberg.com/news/articles/2013-02-22/coca-cola-s-woman-director-nominee-bucks-slowing-diversity-trend (accessed March 17, 2015).

24. Jerry Useem, "What's That Spell? TEAMWORK," *Fortune,* June 12, 2006, p. 66.

25. Jia Lynnyang, "The Power of Number 4.6," *Fortune,* June 12, 2006, p. 122.

26. Geoff Colvin, "Great Job!" *Fortune,* August 12, 2013, pp. 62–66; JP Dolon, "CEO of the Year David Novak: The Recognition Leader," *Chief Executive,* June 27, 2012, http://chiefexecutive.net/ceo-year-david-novak-the-recognition-leader (accessed October 15, 2014); Shani Magosky, "Heed the Oracle of Kentucky (aka YUM! Brands) CEO David Novak," *The Huffington Post,* June 18, 2013, http://www.huffingtonpost.com/shani-magosky/yum-ceo-david-novak_b_3109882.html (accessed October 15, 2014).

27. Natasha Singer, "Intel's Sharp-Eyed Social Scientist," *The New York Times,* February 15, 2014, http://www.nytimes.com/2014/02/16/technology/intels-sharp-eyed-social-scientist.html?_r=0 (accessed March 17, 2015).

28. Richard S. Wellins, William C. Byham, and Jeanne M. Wilson, *Empowered Teams: Creating Self-Directed Work Groups That Improve Quality, Productivity, and Participation* (San Francisco: Jossey-Bass Publishers, 1991), p. 5.

29. TheIRapp, LLC, "theEMPLOYEEappTM Survey: Internal Communications Affects Job Satisfaction and Employee Engagement,"

APPrise Mobile, May 20, 2014, http://www.thecommsapp.com/media-center/press-releases/theemployeeapp-survey-internal-communications-affects-job-satisfaction-and-employee-engagement (accessed March 5, 2015).

30. Peter Mell and Timothy Grance, "The NIST Definition of Cloud Computing," National Institute of Standards and Technology, Special Publication 800-145, September 2011, http://csrc.nist.gov/publications/nistpubs/800-145/SP800-145.pdf (accessed March 17, 2015).

31. Michael Christian, "Top 10 Ideas: Making the Most of Your Corporate Intranet," April 2, 2009, https://www.claromentis.com/blog/top-10-ideas-making-the-most-of-your-corporate-intranet/ (accessed March 17, 2015).

32. Verne Harnish, "Five Ways to Liberate Your Team from Email Overload," *Fortune,* June 16, 2014, p. 52.

33. Sue Shellenbarger, "They're Gossiping about you," *The Wall Street Journal,* October 8, 2014, pp. D1–D2.

34. Merck, *Our Values and Standards: The Basis of Our Success,* https://www.merck.com/abo0ut/code_of_conduct.pdf (accessed March 16, 2015).

35. Laura Baverman, "After Fire, CEO Moved Fast to Save Business," *USA Today,* September 25, 2014, 6B; Ryan O'Connor, "Rustic Crust Employees Back at work after Fire Damaged Pittsfield Pizza Business," *New Hampshire Union Leader,* April 9, 2014, http://www.unionleader.com/article/20140410/NEWS02/140419974 (accessed September 26, 2014); Jean Mackin, "Rustic Crust Pizza to Pay Employees while It Rebuilds after Fire," *WMUR,* March 11, 2014, http://www.wmur.com/news/rustic-crust-pizza-to-pay-employees-while-it-rebuilds-after-fire/24910344 (accessed September 26, 2014).

36. PBSNewsHour, "Apple Supplier Foxconn Pledges Better Working Conditions, but Will It Deliver?" *YouTube,* www.youtube.com/watch?v=ZduorbCkSBQ (accessed March 17, 2015).

37. Susan M. Heathfield, "Top Ten Employee Complaints," *About.com,* http://humanresources.about.com/od/retention/a/emplo_complaint.htm (accessed March 16, 2015).

Chapter 8

1. Rina Rapuano, "Check Please!" *The Washingtonian Blog,* February 18, 2010, www.washingtonian.com/blogarticles/restaurants/bestbites/15008.html (accessed March 18, 2015).

2. Leonard L. Berry, *Discovering the Soul of Service* (New York: The Free Press, 1999), pp. 86–96.

3. Valerie A. Zeithaml and Mary Jo Bitner, *Services Marketing,* 3rd ed. (Boston: McGraw-Hill Irwin, 2003), pp. 3, 22.

4. Chris Mock, "Quality Control in 2014," *Freddie Mac,* February 10, 2014, www.freddiemac.com/news/blog/chris_mock/20140210_quality_control.html (accessed March 18, 2015).

5. Berrnard Wysocki Jr., "To Fix Health Care, Hospitals Take Tips from the Factory Floor," *The Wall Street Journal,* April 9, 2004, via www.chcanys.org/clientuploads/downloads/Clinical_resources/Leadership%20Articles/LeanThinking_ACF28EB.pdf (accessed March 18, 2015).

6. Ryan Chavis, "Survey: Retailers Looking to Expand Social Media, Tech Solutions in Product Planning," *Drug Store News,* November 4, 2014, www.drugstorenews.com/article/survey-retailers-looking-expand-social-media-techsolutions-product-planning (accessed March 11, 2015).

7. Trefis Team, "Here's Why Micron & Intel Can Gain from an Early Entry in the 3D NAND Market," *Forbes,* March 12, 2015, www.forbes.com/sites/greatspeculations/2015/03/12/heres-why-micron-intel-can-gainfrom-an-early-entry-in-the-3d-nand-market/ (accessed March 18, 2015).

8. Christina Cooke, "America's Rebel Band of Custom-Bike Builders," *The Atlantic,* April 3, 2014, www.theatlantic.com/business/archive/2014/04/americasrebel-band-of-custombikebuilders/360058/ (accessed March 18, 2015).

9. Marie Singer, "The Hershey Company—Company Information," *Market Business News,* April 14, 2014, www.marketbusinessnews.com/hershey-companycompanyinformation/18006 (accessed March 18, 2015).

10. Toyota, "ISO 14001 Certification," www.toyotaindustries.com/csr/environment/management/iso.html (accessed March 11, 2015).

11. Alejandro Lazo, "Tesla Receives Nevada Tax Breaks," *The Wall Street Journal,* September 12, 2014, www.wsj.com/articles/tesla-nevada-tax-breaks-incentives-packageapproved-1410507190 (accessed March 18, 2015).

12. Dinah Eng, "From R2-D2 to Practical Robots," *Fortune,* September 1, 2014, pp. 37–40; "iRobot," *Forbes,* October 2014, www.forbes.com/companies/irobot/ (accessed December 10, 2014); iRobot website, www.irobot.com/ (accessed December 10, 2014).

13. Ross Toro, "How 3D Printers Work (Infographic)," *Live Science,* June 18, 2013, www.livescience.com/37513-how-3d-printers-work-infographic.html (accessed November 18, 2013).

14. Matt Schiavenza, "FAA Drone Regulations Deal Blow to Amazon," *The Atlantic,* February 15, 2015, www.theatlantic.com/business/archive/2015/02/faa-droneregulations-deal-blow-to-amazon/385529/ (accessed March 18, 2015); Chris Anderson, "How I Accidentally Kickstarted the Domestic Drone Boom," June 22, 2012, www.wired.com/2012/06/ff_drones/all/ (accessed March 18, 2015).

15. Timothy Aeppel, "Robots Work Their Way into Small Factories," *The Wall Street Journal,* September 18, 2014, p. B1.

16. Robotic Industries Association, "North American Robotics Shipments Grow in 2013 While New Orders Contract," *Robotics Online,* February 4, 2014, www.robotics.org/content-detail.cfm/Industrial-Robotics-News/North-American-Robotics-Shipments-Grow-in-2013-While-New-Orders-Contract/content_id/4648 (accessed April 2, 2014); Sian Harris, "Will Robots Be the Answer to Our Next Manufacturing Revolution?" *E&T,* January 20, 2014, http://eandt.theiet.org/magazine/2014/01/robots-are-coming.cfm (accessed March 18, 2015); Elisabeth Eitel, "Technology Forecast 2014: Robots Priced for the Masses," *Machine Design,* January 8, 2014, http://machinedesign.com/robotics/technologyforecast-2014-robots-priced-masses (accessed March 18, 2015).

17. Biogen Idec, "Corporate Citizenship Report," 2012, www.biogenidec.com/Files/Filer/USA/CC_2013/2012_Biogen_Idec_Corporate_Citizens hip_Report.pdf (accessed March 18, 2015); Business Wire via The Motley Fool, "Biogen Idec Becomes First U.S.-Based Biotech Named to Dow Jones Sustainability World Index," *Daily Finance,* September 24, 2013, www.biogenidec.com/press_release_details.aspx?ID=14712&Action=1&NewsId=2268&M=NewsV2&PID=61997 (accessed March 18, 2015).

18. "Shippers Go Green," *Inbound Logistics,* December 2013, pp. 57–63; General Mills, "General Mills Commits to Sustainably Source 10 Priority Ingredients by 2020," September 25, 2013, www.generalmills.com/Home/ChannelG/NewsReleases/Library/2013/September/sourcing_10 (accessed December 5, 2014); "General Mills Unveils 2015 Sustainability Goals, Reports Progress on 2010 Goals," *Reliable Plant,* www.reliableplant.com/Read/27453/General-Mills-sustainability-goals (accessed December 5, 2014); Smithfield Foods, "Smithfield Food Steps Up Sustainability Accountability and

Transparency," *CSR Wire,* April 15, 2014, www.csrwire. com/press_releases/36848-Smithfield-Foods-Steps-Up-Sustainability-Accountability-and-Transparency (accessed December 5, 2014); Marc Gunther, "Smithfield Foods and the Quest for Large-Scale, Sustainable Pork," *Green Biz,* April 29, 2011, www.greenbiz.com/blog/2011/04/29/smithfield-foods-and-quest-large-scalesustainable-pork (accessed December 5, 2014); Mars, "Sustainable in a Generation," 2014, www.mars. com/global/about-mars/mars-pia/our-operations/sustainable-in-ageneration.aspx (accessed December 5, 2014); Marc Gunther, "Why Mars Is a Sustainability Leader," Marc Gunther website, May 30, 2012, www.marcgunther.com/why-mars-is-a-sustainability-leader/ (accessed December 5, 2014).

19. Bryan Walsh, "Why Green Is the New Red, White and Blue," *Time,* April 28, 2008, p. 53.

20. Megan Kamerick, "How to Go Green," *New Mexico Business Weekly,* May 23–29, 2008, p. 3.

21. O. C. Ferrell and Michael D. Hartline, *Marketing Strategy* (Mason, OH: South Western, 2011), p. 215.

22. Keisha A. Simmons, "UPS Introduces New Cloud-Based Technology Platform to Improve International Supply Chain Management," *UPS,* November 13, 2012, www.pressroom.ups.com/Press+Releases/Archive/2012/Q4/UPS+Introduces+New+Cloud-Based+Technology+Platform+to+Improve+International+Supply+Chain+Management (accessed March 18, 2015).

23. Ferrell and Hartline, *Marketing Strategy,* p. 215.

24. Susan Berfield and Manuel Baigorri, "Zara's Fast-Fashion Edge," *Bloomberg Businessweek,* November 14, 2013, www. bloomberg.com/bw/articles/2013-11-14/2014-outlook-zaras-fashion-supply-chain-edge (accessed March 18, 2015).

25. Investment Mine, "Historical Copper Prices and Price Chart," April 8, 2014, www.infomine.com/investment/metal-prices/copper/all/ (accessed March 18, 2015).

26. "Broken Links," *The Economist,* March 31, 2001, www.economist. com/node/18486015 (accessed May 12, 2014).

27. Jez Fredenburgh, "Horsemeat: Tesco's Pledges, One Year On," *Farmer's Weekly,* February 21, 2014, www.fwi.co.uk/articles/21/02/2014/143348/horsemeat-tesco39spledges-oneyear-on.htm (accessed March 18, 2015).

28. Susan Carey, "Airlines Play Up Improvements in On-Time Performance," *The Wall Street Journal,* February 10, 2010, p. B6; U.S. Department of Transportation, "Air Travel Consumer Report," March 2014, www.dot.gov/sites/dot.gov/files/docs/2014_March_ATCR.pdf (accessed March 18, 2015).

29. "Four U.S. Organizations Honored with 2014 Baldrige National Quality Award," Baldrige Performance Excellence Program, November 12, 2014, www.nist.gov/baldrige/baldrige-award-111214.cfm (accessed March 11, 2015).

30. Hollie Slade, "Factory of the Future," *Forbes,* November 3, 2014, pp. 92–96; Proto Labs, "About," www.protolabs.com/about (accessed March 11, 2015).

31. Philip B. Crosby, *Quality Is Free: The Art of Making Quality Certain* (New York: McGraw-Hill, 1979), pp. 9–10.

32. Nigel F. Piercy, *Market-Led Strategic Change* (Newton, MA: Butterworth-Heinemann, 1992), pp. 374–85.

33. Bloomberg LLP, "Compuware Gomez Introduces Free Web Performance Benchmarking Tool," *Bloomberg,* February 16, 2010, www.bloomberg.com/apps/news?pid=newsarchive&sid=a3bTx6JLIx7I (accessed March 18, 2015).

34. Scott Leibs, "At This Manufacturer, 'Truly Human Leadership' Trumps the Bottom Line," *Inc.,* May 2014, pp. 53–54; "Truly Human

Leadership, Why?" www.trulyhumanleadership.com/?page_id=39 (accessed December 4, 2014); Barry-Wehmiller, *Guiding Principles of Leadership,* www.barrywehmiller.com/docs/defaultsource/barrywehmiller-vision-documents/guiding-principles-of-leadership. pdf (accessed December 4, 2014); " Barry-Wehmiller—Another Great Participation Age Company," *Chuck Blakeman,* http://chuckblakeman.com/2014/7/texts/barry-wehmiller-another-greatparticipation-age-company (accessed December 4, 2014).

35. "ISO 9001 Certification," GE Power & Water, www.geinstruments. com/company/iso-9001-certification.html (accessed March 18, 2015).

36. PPT presentation at 2014 ECOA conference in Atlanta, by Martin Tolar, GRC Institute, entitled "The First ISO Standard in E&C: What You Need to Know," October 2, 2014; Dick Hortensius, "What Is the General Idea Behind the Proposed ISO 19600?" *Ethics Intelligence,* April 2014, www.ethicintelligence.com/experts/4636-general-idea-behind-iso-19600/ (accessed October 14, 2014).

37. Charles Duhigg and David Barboza, "In China, Human Costs Are Built into an iPad," *The New York Times,* January 25, 2012, www .nytimes.com/2012/01/26/business/ieconomy-apples-ipad-and-thehuman-costs-forworkers-in-china.html?pagewanted=all (accessed February 8, 2012).

38. "Monitoring and Auditing Global Supply Chains Is a Must," *Ethisphere,* 2011, Q3, pp. 38–45.

39. "Employment Opportunities," *Careers in Supply Chain Management,* www.careersinsupplychain.org/career-outlook/empopp .asp (accessed May 12, 2014).

40. "Best Jobs in America," *CNN Money,* http://money.cnn.com/magazines/moneymag/bestjobs/2009/snapshots/48.html (accessed April 24, 2014).

Chapter 9

1. Dan Heath and Chip Heath, "Business Advice from Van Halen," *Fast Company,* March 1, 2010, www.fastcompany.com/1550881/business-advice-van-halen (accessed March 19, 2015).

2. Wegmans, "Fortune's 2014 '100 Best Companies to Work For' List Includes Wegmans, Ranked at #12," January 16, 2014, http://www.wegmans.com/webapp/wcs/stores/servlet/PressReleaseDetailView?productId=774706&storeId=10052&catalogId=10002&langId=-1 (accessed March 18, 2015).

3. Society for Human Resource Management, *Total Financial Impact of Employee Absences in the U.S.,* October 2014, http://www.shrm.org/Research/SurveyFindings/Documents/Kronos_US_Executive_Summary_Final.pdf (accessed March 18, 2015).

4. Brad Stone, "Costco CEO Craig Jelinek Leads the Cheapest, Happiest Company in the World," *Bloomberg Businessweek,* June 6, 2013, http://www.bloomberg.com/bw/articles/2013-06-06/costco-ceo-craig-jelinek-leads-the-cheapest-happiest-company-in-the-world (accessed April 24, 2014); Rebecca Hiscott, "7 Companies That Aren't Waiting for congress to Raise the Minimum Wage," *The Huffington Post,* June 26, 2014, http://www.huffingtonpost.com/2014/06/26/companies-minimum-wage_n_5530835.html (accessed March 18, 2015).

5. Forbes LLC, "Ten Highest Paid CEOs," *Forbes,* 2015, http://www.forbes.com/pictures/eggh45jef/john-hammergren-of-mckesson/ (accessed March 18, 2015).

6. Dinah Eng and Kim Jordan, "Tasting Success in Craft Brewing," *Fortune,* June 30, 2014, pp. 26–28; New Belgium Brewing, "History," http://www.newbelgium.com/brewery/company/history. aspx (accessed December 4, 2014); Keith Gribbens, "Outside Magazine Names New Belgium Brewing as One of America's Best Places to Work (Again)," *Craft Brewing Business,* August 5, 2013, http://www.craftbrewingbusiness.com/news/outside-magazine-names-new-belgium-brewing-as-one-of-americas-

best-places-to-work-again/ (accessed December 4, 2014); Jonny Fullpint, "New Belgium Brewing Named Top Small Workplace," *The FullPint.com*, October 15, 2008, http://thefullpint .com/beer-news/new-belgium-brewing-named-top-small-workplace/ (accessed December 4, 2014).

7. Fortune, "100 Best Companies to Work For—USAA," *CNN Money,* 2014, http://fortune.com/best-companies/ (accessed March 19, 2015); Fortune, "100 Best Companies to Work For—Genentech," *CNN Money,* 2014, http://money.cnn. com/magazines/fortune/best-companies/2014/snapshots/6. html?iid=BC14_fl _list (accessed March 19, 2015).

8. "25 Well-Paying Jobs That Most People Overlook (and Why)," *Business Pundit,* http://www.businesspundit.com/25-well-paying-jobs-that-most-people-overlook-and-why/ (accessed March 19, 2015).

9. Christina Couch, "10 Companies with Excellent Customer Service," *The Huffington Post,* August 15, 2013, www.huffingtonpost .com/2013/08/15/best-customer-service_n_3720052.html (accessed March 19, 2015).

10. Douglas McGregor, *The Human Side of Enterprise* (New York: McGraw-Hill, 1960), pp. 33–34.

11. Catherine Dunn, "Flyin' a Family Business," *Fortune,* May 19, 2014, pp. 28; Radio Flyer website, http://www.radioflyer.com/ (accessed December 10, 2014); Amy Lyman, "A Deep Commitment to Ethical Leadership," *The Trustworthy Leader,* March 15, 2012, http://www.trustworthyleader.org/eng/Blog /17_A-Deep-Commitment-to-Ethical-Leadership.html (accessed December 10, 2014); "#13 – Best Small Workplaces: Radio Flyer, Inc.," Great Place to Work, 2013, http://www.greatplace-towork.com/2013-best-small-workplaces/radio-flyer (accessed December 10, 2014); "#11 – Best Small Workplaces: Radio Flyer, Inc.," *Great Place to Work,* 2012, http://www.greatplacetowork. com/2012-best-workplaces/radio-flyer (accessed December 10, 2014).

12. McGregor, *The Human Side of Enterprise,* pp. 33–34 .

13. Richard Branson, "Richard Branson on Giving Your Employees Freedom," *Entrepreneur,* December 31, 2012, www.entrepreneur .com/article/225272 (accessed March 19, 2015).

14. Jon L. Pierce, Tatiana Kostova, and Kurt T. Kirks, "Toward a Theory of Psychological Ownership in Organizations," *Academy of Management Review,* 26, no. 2 (2001), p. 298.

15. Liz Rappaport, "Goldman Cuts Blankfein's Bonus," *The Wall Street Journal,* February 4, 2012, http:// online.wsj.com/article/ SB10001424052970204662204577201483347787346.html (accessed March 19, 2015).

16. Ethics Resource Center, *2011 National Business Ethics Survey: Ethics in Transition* (Arlington, VA: Ethics Resource Center, 2012), p. 16.

17. Archie Carroll, "Carroll: Do We Live in a Cheating Culture?" *Athens Banner-Herald,* February 21, 2004, www.onlineathens.com/ stories/022204/bus_20040222028.shtml (accessed March 19, 2015).

18. Edwin A. Locke, K.M. Shaw, and Gary P. Latham, "Goal Setting and Task Performance: 1969–1980," *Psychological Bulletin* 90, 1981, pp. 125–152.

19. Peter Drucker, *The Practice of Management* (New York: Harper & Row, 1954).

20. Economist staff, "Management by Objectives," *The Economist,* October 21, 2009, http://www.economist.com/node/14299761 (accessed March 19, 2015).

21. Lauren Weber and Leslie Kwoh, "Co-Workers Change Places," *The Wall Street Journal,* February 21, 2012, http://www.wsj.com/

articles/SB100014240529702040598045772291238912554 72 (accessed March 18, 2015); PricewaterhouseCoopers LLP, "Coaching and Professional Development," 2015, http://www. pwc.com/us/en/about-us/pwc-professional-development.jhtml (accessed March 18, 2015).

22. Business Wire, "Staples Survey Shows Telecommuting Offers Edge to Companies Looking to Recruit Talent," *Staples,* June 2, 2014, http://investor.staples.com/phoenix.zhtml?c= 96244&p=irol-newsArticle&ID=1936154 (accessed March 18, 2015).

23. Robert Preidt, "Workplace Flexibility Can Boost Healthy Behaviors," *ABC News,* March 23, 2008, http://abcnews.go.com/ Health/Healthday/story?id=4509753 (accessed March 19, 2015).

24. My Guides USA.com, "Which Jobs Offer Flexible Work Schedules?" http://jobs.myguidesusa.com/answers-to-myquestions/ whichjobs-offer-flexible-workschedules?/ (accessed March 19, 2015).

25. J. P. Mangalindan, "A Healthier, More Rewarding Workplace," *Fortune,* October 6, 2014, pp. 49–50; Clif Bar, "Clif Bar & Company Chosen One of Nation's Best Places to Work," September 19, 2013, http://www.clifbar.com/article/clif-bar-company-chosen-one-of-nations-best-places-to-work (accessed December 10, 2014); Lauren Drell, "6 Companies with Awesome Employee Perks," *Mashable*, August 7, 2011, http://mashable. com/2011/08/07/startup-employee-perks/ (accessed December 10, 2014).

26. Tara Gravel, "Empowering the Mobile Workforce," Special Advertising Section, *Bloomberg Businessweek,* 2014, http:// www.businessweek.com/adsections/2014/pdf/140811_HR2.pdf (accessed March 18, 2015).

27. PGi, "Telecommuting Reduces Stress and Increases Productivity According to PGi Survey," *PR Newswire,* March 3, 2014, http:// pgi.investorroom.com/2014-03-03-Telecommuting-Reduces-Stress-and-Increases-Productivity-According-to-PGi-Survey (accessed March 19, 2015); PR Web, "Fortune 500 Companies Are Looking for People to Work Remotely (Work From Home)," January 26, 2014, www.prweb.com/releases/2014/01/ prweb11520034.htm (accessed March 19, 2015).

28. Dori Meinert, "Make Telecommuting Pay Off," *Society for Human Resource Management,* June 1, 2011, http://www. shrm.org/publications/hrmagazine/editorialcontent/2011/0611/ pages/0611meinert.aspx (accessed March 19, 2015).

29. "Best Places for Business and Careers," *Forbes,* March 25, 2009, www.forbes.com/lists/2009/1/bizplaces09_Best-Places-For-Business-And-Careers_Rank.html (accessed March 19, 2015).

30. Kurt Badenhausen, "The Best Places for Business and Careers," *Forbes,* July 23, 2014, http://www.forbes.com/best-places-for-business/ (accessed March 18, 2015).

Chapter 10

1. Christine Birkner, "Taking Care of Their Own," *Marketing News,* February 2015, pp. 44–49.

2. "About O*NET," O&NET Resource Center, www.onetcenter. org/overview.html (accessed March 30, 2015).

3. Melissa Korn, "College Job Fairs Go Virtual," *The Wall Street Journal,* April 3, 2014, p. B5.

4. Procter & Gamble, "Our Hiring Process," http://pgcareers.com/ apply/our-hiring-process/ (accessed March 30, 2015).

5. Noelle Knox and Maxwell Murphy, "Charity as a Recruiting Tool," *The Wall Street Journal*, September 2, 2014, p. B4; Taylor Soper, "Microsoft Sees Charitable Efforts as Key Recruiting Tool for Young Talent," *Geekwire,* October 19, 2012, http://

www.geekwire.com/2012/microsoft-sees-charitable-efforts-key-recruiting-tool-young-talent/ (accessed December 12, 2014); Lauren Hepler, "PayPal Veteran on New Charity Crowd-funding Startup, Philanthropy as Millennial Recruiting Tool," *Silicon Valley Business Journal,* March 14, 2014, http://www.bizjournals.com/sanjose/news/2014/03/14/paypal-veteran-on-new-charity-crowdfunding-startup.html?page=all (accessed December 12, 2014).

6. "Should Companies Monitor Their Employees' Social Media?" *The Wall Street Journal,* May 12, 2014, R1.

7. Dune Lawrence, "Tracking the Enemy Within," *Bloomberg Businessweek,* March 16–March 22, 2015, pp. 39–41.

8. *Results from the 2013 National Survey on Drug Use and Health: Summary of National Findings,* 2013, http://www.samhsa.gov/data/sites/default/files/NSDUHresultsPDFWHTML2013/Web/NSDUHresults2013.pdf (accessed March 24, 2015).

9. Center for Disease Control and Prevention, "Alcohol and Substance Misuse," http://www.cdc.gov/workplacehealthpromotion/evaluation/topics/substance-abuse.html (accessed March 25, 2015); National Drug-Free Workplace Alliance, "About Us," http://www.ndwa.org/aboutus.php (accessed March 25, 2015).

10. Lauren Weber and Mike Esterl, "E-Cigarette Rise Poses Quandary for Employers," *The Wall Street Journal,* January 16, 2014, p. A2.

11. Manuel Valdes and Shannon McFarland, "Job Seekers' Facebook Password Asked for During U.S. Interviews," *Huffington Post,* March 20, 2012, www.huffingtonpost.com/2012/03/20/facebookpasswordsjob-seekers_n_1366577.html? (accessed March 30, 2015).

12. Jonathan Dame, "Will Employers Still Ask for Facebook Passwords in 2014?" *USA Today,* January 10, 2014, http://www.usatoday.com/story/money/business/2014/01/10/facebook-passwords-employers/4327739/ (accessed April 28, 2014).

13. Allison Linn, "Desperate Measures: Why Some People Fake Their Resumes," *CNBC,* February 7, 2014, www.cnbc.com/id/101397212 (accessed March 30, 2015); "Martoma Trial: Ex-SAC Trader Was Expelled from Harvard Law School," *The New York Times,* January 9, 2014, http://dealbook.nytimes.com/2014/01/09/ex-sac-trader-was-expelled-from-harvard-law-school/ (accessed March 30, 2015).

14. Christopher T. Marquet and Lisa J. B. Peterson, "Résumé Fraud: The Top Ten Lies," Marquet International, Ltd., www.marquetinternational.com/pdf/Resume%20Fraud-Top%20Ten%20Lies.pdf (accessed March 30, 2015).

15. U.S. Equal Employment Opportunity Commission, "EEOC Releases Fiscal Year 2014 Enforcement and Litigation Data," February 4, 2015, http://www1.eeoc.gov/eeoc/newsroom/release/2-4-15.cfm (accessed March 25, 2015).

16. Claire Zillman, "Microsoft's New CEO: One Minority Exec in a Sea of White," *Fortune,* February 4, 2014, http://fortune.com/2014/02/04/microsofts-new-ceo-one-minority-exec-in-a-sea-of-white/ (accessed March 25, 2015).

17. "Compulsory Retirement Age at 65 Fully Abolished," *BBC News,* October 1, 2011, www.bbc.co.uk/news/business-15127835 (accessed April 4, 2012); "Can You Legally Force Someone to Retire or Is It Age Discrimination?" *LawInfo blog,* http://www.bbc.com/news/business-15127835 (accessed March 30, 2015).

18. Stephen Bastien, "12 Benefits of Hiring Older Workers," *Entrepreneur.com,* September 20, 2006, www.entrepreneur.com/article/167500 (accessed March 30, 2015).

19. Institute for Women's Policy Research, "The Gender Wage Gap: 2014 Earnings Differences by Race and Ethnicity," March 2015, www.iwpr.org (accessed March 25, 2015).

20. "Gender and Pay at Work," PayScale, www.payscale.com/data-packages/gender-wage-gap/job-distribution-by-gender (accessed March 30, 2015).

21. Catherine Rampell, "The Gender Wage Gap, Around the World," March 9, 2010, http://economix.blogs.nytimes.com/2010/03/09/the-gender-wage-gap-around-the-world/ (accessed March 30, 2015).

22. "Our Curriculum," Hamburger University, www.aboutmcdonalds.com/mcd/careers/hamburger_university/our_curriculum.html (accessed March 30, 2015).

23. Chronus Corporation, "How to Use Mentoring in Your Workplace," http://chronus.com/how-to-use-mentoring-in-your-workplace (accessed March 24, 2015).

24. The Sage Group PLC, "Mentoring Statistics," 2015, http://www.sage.com/businessnavigators/research (accessed March 24, 2015).

25. Sue Lam, "Why Mentoring is More Important for Women in Workplace Than You Think," *APQC,* March 10, 2015, http://www.apqc.org/blog/why-mentoring-more-important-women-workplace-you-think (accessed March 24, 2015).

26. The Container Store, "Employee-First Culture," http://standfor.containerstore.com/putting-our-employees-first/ (accessed March 30, 2015).

27. Doug Stewart, "Employee-Appraisal Software," *Inc.,* www.inc.com/magazine/19940615/3288_pagen_2.html (accessed March 30, 2015).

28. Maury A. Peiperl, "Getting 360-Degree Feedback Right," *Harvard Business Review,* January 2001, pp. 142–48.

29. Chris Musselwhite, "Self Awareness and the Effective Leader," *Inc.com,* http://www.inc.com/resources/leadership/articles/20071001/musselwhite.html (accessed March 30, 2015).

30. Rachel Feintzeig, "You're Awesome! Firms Scrap Negative Feedback," *The Wall Street Journal,* February 11, 2015, pp. B1, B5.

31. Rebecca Vesely, "Companies Aim to Improve Wellness of Telecommuting, Traveling Employees, Too," *Workforce,* October 30, 2012, http://www.workforce.com/articles/companies-aim-to-improve-wellness-of-telecommuting-traveling-employees-too (accessed March 30, 2015).

32. Marcia Zidle, "Employee Turnover: Seven Reasons Why People Quit Their Jobs," Ezine, http://ezinearticles.com/?Employee-Turnover:-Seven-Reasons-Why-People-Quit-Their-Jobs&id=42531 (accessed March 30, 2015).

33. Don Clark, "Intel to Pare Workforce as Sales Growth Struggles," *The Wall Street Journal,* January 18–19, 2014, p. B3.

34. "Wage and Hour Division (WHD)," U.S. Department of Labor, www.dol.gov/whd/flsa/index.htm (accessed March 30, 2015).

35. Lauren Fox, "Democrats Push to Pass Minimum Wage Hike Ahead of 2014 Elections," *U.S. News,* April 28, 2014, http://www.usnews.com/news/articles/2014/04/28/democrats-push-to-pass-minimum-wage-hike-ahead-of-2014-elections (accessed May 2, 2014).

36. "Fair Labor Standards Act Advisor," U.S. Department of Labor, www.dol.gov/elaws/faq/esa/flsa/002.htm (accessed March 30, 2015).

37. City of Santa Fe, "Santa Fe's Living Wage Rises to $10.66 an Hour on March 1, 2014," January 22, 2014, www.santafenm.gov/news/detail/santa_fes_living_wage_rises_to_1066_an_hour_on_march_1_2014 (accessed March 30, 2015); New Mexico Department of Workforce Solutions, "Minimum Wage Information," www.dws.state.nm.us/LaborRelations/Resources/MinimumWageInformation (accessed March 30, 2015); Daniel

J. Chacón, "Minimum-Wage Workers in City to See Pay Rise to $10.66," *Santa Fe New Mexican*, January 22, 2014, www.santafenewmexican.com/news/local_news/minimumwage-workers-in-city-to-see-payrise-to/article_6ec202d2-862c-50f3-a4eb-5b8587e102b4.html (accessed March 30, 2015).

38. "Kele & Co: First Innovative Jewelry Company in Direct Sales," May 5, 2008, www.pressreleasepoint.com/kele-ampco-first-innovative-jewelrycompanydirect-sales (accessed March 16, 2010); Kele & Co., "About Kele & Co," 2010, www.keleonline.com/pages/about.html (accessed March 30, 2015).

39. Justin Wolfers, "All You Need to Know about Income Inequality, in One Comparison," *The New York Times,* March 13, 2015, http://www.nytimes.com/2015/03/14/upshot/wall-street-bonuses-vs-total-earnings-of-full-time-minimum-wage-workers .html?_r=0&abt=0002&abg=1 (accessed March 25, 2015).

40. The National Center for Employee Ownership, "ESOP (Employee Stock Ownership Plan) Facts," 2015, http://www.esop.org/ (accessed March 25, 2015).

41. Bureau of Labor Statistics U.S. Department of Labor, "Employer Costs for Employee Compensation – December 2014," March 11, 2015, http://www.bls.gov/news.release/archives/ecec_03112015.pdf (accessed March 25, 2015).

42. Christine Birkner, "Taking Care of Their Own," *Marketing News,* February 2015, pp. 44–49.

43. Ibid.

44. "Work/Life," Lowe's, https://careers.lowes.com/benefits_work .aspx (accessed March 30, 2015).

45. Elaine Pofeldt, "Having Trouble Finding Talent? Look Beyond Resumes," *Inc.,* November 2013, http://www.inc.com/magazine/201311/elaine-pofeldt/hire-power-awards-urban-lending-solutions.html (accessed November 25, 2014); Urban Lending Solutions, "About Us," http://www.urban-ls.com/about-us (accessed November 25, 2014); Paul J. Gough, "*Inc.* Honors Urban Lending Solutions as Top Job-Creator," *Pittsburg Business Times*, December 6, 2012, http://www.bizjournals.com/pittsburgh/news/2012/12/06/inc-honors-urban-lending-solutions-as.html (accessed November 25, 2014).

46. Angus Loten and Sarah E. Needleman, "Laws on Paid Sick Leave Divide Businesses," *The Wall Street Journal*, February 6, 2014, p. B5.

47. Scott Leibs, "Perks that Work," *Inc.*, November 2014, pp. 64–65.

48. Bureau of Labor Statistics, "Union Members Summary," January 23, 2015, http://www.bls.gov/news.release/union2.nr0.htm (accessed March 25, 2015).

49. Tom Walsh, "UAW Needs Stronger Message," *USA Today*, February 17, 2014, p. 1B.

50. David George-Cosh and Ben Dummett, "Port Strike Worsens Backlog," *The Wall Street Journal,* March 13, 2014, p. B3; CBC News, "Vancouver Port Strike Stops 90% of Container Truck Traffic," *CBC News,* March 10, 2014, http://www.cbc.ca/news/canada/british-columbia/vancouver-port-strike-stops-90-of-container-truck-traffic-1.2567458 (accessed March 24, 2015).

51. Christine Birkner, "Taking Care of Their Own," *Marketing News,* February 2015, pp. 44–49.

52. Steven Greenhouse, "Labor Battle at Kellogg Plant in Memphis Drags On," *The New York Times*, February 10, 2014, http://www.nytimes.com/2014/02/11/business/kellogg-workers-in-4th-month-of-lockout-in-memphis.html (accessed March 30, 2015).

53. Ed Stoddard and Zandi Shabalala, "Producers, Union to Meet Mediator Separately in Platinum Strike," *Reuters*, February 10, 2014, http://www.reuters.com/article/2014/02/10/us-safrica-strikes-idUSBREA190BW20140210 (accessed March 30, 2015).

54. Paul M. Barrett, "Chevron Inches Closer to Legal Victory over Ecuador Pollution," *Bloomberg Businessweek*, September 19, 2013, http://www.bloomberg.com/bw/articles/2013-09-19/chevron-inches-closer-to-legal-victory-over-ecuador-pollution (accessed April 29, 2014).

55. Eric Kayne, "Census: White Majority in U.S. Gone by 2043," *NBC News*, June 13, 2013, http://usnews.nbcnews.com/_news/2013/06/13/18934111-census-white-majority-in-us-goneby-2043?lite (accessed March 30, 2015).

56. Press Release, "Kaiser Permanente Named No. 4 on Diversity Inc's Top 50 Companies for Diversity List for 2014," Kaiser Permanente, April 24, 2014, http://share.kaiserpermanente.org/article/kaiser-permanente-named-no-4-on-diversityincs-top-50-companies-for-diversity-list-for-2014/ (accessed March 30, 2015).

57. Melanie Tervalon, "At a Decade: Centers of Excellence in Culturally Competent Care," *The Permanente Journal,* 13, no. 1 (2009), pp. 87–91.

58. Jessica Guynn, Paul Overberg, Marco della Cava, and Jon Swartz, "Silicon Valley Falls Short on Diversity," *USA Today*, December 30, 2014, p. 1A; Jessica Guynn, "Tech's Gender Gap Is Widening," *USA Today*, March 27, 2015, pp. 1B–2B.

59. Taylor H. Cox, Jr., "The Multicultural Organization," *Academy of Management Executives* 5 (May 1991), pp. 34–47; Marilyn Loden and Judy B. Rosener, *Workforce America! Managing Employee Diversity as a Vital Resource* (Homewood, IL: Business One Irwin, 1991).

60. Rachel Feintzeig, "The Boss's Next Demand: Make Lots of Friends," *The Wall Street Journal*, February 12, 2014, pp. B1, B6; Lili Duan and Leigh M. Weiss, "Tapping the Power of Hidden Influencers," McKinsey & Company, March 2014, http://www.mckinsey.com/insights/organization/tapping_the_power_of_hidden_influencers (accessed October 15, 2014); Shel Holtz, "Research Pits Leaders against Internal Influencers to See Who Can Reach More Employees," Holtz Communication, August 6, 2014, http://holtz.com/blog/internal/research-pits-leaders-against-internal-influencers-to-see-who-can-reach-mor/4385/ (accessed October 15, 2014).

61. Kathryn Brenzel, "Taco Hell: Lawsuit against Food Truck Claims Employee Was Overworked without Pay," *NJ.com,* December 9, 2013, www.nj.com/hudson/index.ssf/2013/12/taco_hell_employee_files_lawsuit_against_food_truck_owners_claiming_he_was_overworked_without_pay.html (accessed March 30, 2015); Dave Jamieson, "More Amazon Warehouse Workers Sue Retailer over Unpaid Security Waits," *The Huffington Post,* September 19, 2013, http://www.huffingtonpost.com/2013/09/19/more-amazon-warehouse-workers-sue_n_3950295.html (accessed March 30, 2015); Dave Jamieson, "Join the Booming Dollar Store Economy! Low Pay, Long Hours, May Work While Injured," *Huffington Post*, August 29, 2013, www.huffingtonpost .com/2013/08/29/dollar-storeswork_n_3786781.html (accessed March 30, 2015).

62. Paul Davidson, "Overworked and Underpaid?" *USA Today,* April 16, 2012, pp. 1A–2A.

63. Ibid.

64. Melanie Trottman, "For Angry Employees, Legal Cover for Rants," *The Wall Street Journal,* December 2, 2011, http://online.wsj.com/article/SB1000142405297020371070457704982280971O332.html (accessed March 30, 2015).

65. Martin Crutsinger, "Hiring Grows as Companies Hit Limits with Workers," *MPR News,* March 7, 2012, http://www.mprnews.org/story/2012/03/07/hiring-grows-as-companies-hit-limit (accessed March 30, 2015).

Chapter 11

1. Narendra Rao, "The Keys to New Product Success (Part 1)—Collecting Unarticulated & Invisible Customer Needs," *Product Management & Strategy,* June 19, 2007, https://productstrategy.wordpress.com/2007/06/19/the-keys-to-new-product-succeess-part-1-collecting-unarticulated-invisible-customer-needs/ (accessed April 9, 2015).

2. Bruce Horovitz, "Burger King Drops Soft Drinks Kids' Meals," *USA Today,* http://www.usatoday.com/story/money/2015/03/09/burger-king-fast-food-restaurants-soft-drinks-beverages/24661959/ (accessed April 3, 2015).

3. Danielle Sacks, "Brewing the Perfect Cup," *Fast Company,* September 2014, pp. 86–91; Richard Reynolds, "Coffee's Third Wave," *Imbibe,* http://imbibemagazine.com/Coffee-s-Third-Wave (accessed October 15, 2014); Joel Stein, "Blue Bottle Coffee and the Next Wave of Artisanal Coffee Shops," *Bloomberg Businessweek,* May 1, 2014, http://www.businessweek.com/articles/2014-05-01/blue-bottle-coffee-and-the-next-wave-of-artisanal-coffee-shops (accessed October 15, 2014).

4. "Beauty Queen," *People* 61, no. 18, May 10, 2004, p. 187.

5. Michael Treacy and Fred Wiersema,*The Discipline of Market Leaders* (Reading, MA: Addison Wesley, 1995), p. 176.

6. Jefferson Graham, "At Apple Stores, iPads at Your Service," *USA Today*, May 23, 2011, p. 1B; Apple Inc., "Apple Retail Store," www.apple.com/retail/storelist/ (accessed April 9, 2015).

7. Christine Birkner, "Culturing a Subcategory," *Marketing News*, May 2014, pp. 28–39; Hamdi Ulukaya, "Chobani's Founder on Growing a Start-Up without Outside Investors," *Harvard Business Review,* October 2013, https://hbr.org/2013/10/chobanis-founder-on-growing-a-start-up-without-outside-investors (accessed December 12, 2014); Megan Durisin, "Chobani CEO: Our Success Has Nothing to Do with Yogurt," *Business Insider,* May 3, 2013, http://www.businessinsider.com/the-success-story-of-chobani-yogurt-2013-5 (accessed December 12, 2014).

8. Donna Greiner and Theodore B. Kinni, *1,001 Ways to Keep Customers Coming Back* (New York: Three Rivers Press, 1999).

9. Venky Shankar, "Multiple Touch Point Marketing," American Marketing Association, Faculty Consortium on Electronic Commerce, Texas A&M University, July 14–17, 2001.

10. Beth Kowitt, "Building a Beer for Latinos," *Fortune,* May 1, 2014, http://fortune.com/2014/05/01/building-a-beer-for-latinos/ (accessed April 6, 2015).

11. Alan Gomez, "Voices: Fast-growing Hispanic Market Tough to Tap," *USA Today,* February 28, 2014, http://www.usatoday.com/story/news/nation/2014/02/27/voices-gomez-hispanic-media/5845059/ (accessed April 6, 2015).

12. Eric Kayne, "Census: White Majority in U.S. Gone by 2043," *NBC News,* June 13, 2013, http://usnews.nbcnews.com/_news/2013/06/13/18934111-census-white-majority-in-us-gone-by-2043 (accessed April 6, 2015).

13. Project ENIAC "Apple iWatch Release Date, Specs, Features &Design: WWDC Sneak Peek?" April 2014, http://projecteniac.blogspot.com/2014/04/apple-iwatch-release-date-specs.html (accessed April 9, 2015).

14. Coca-Cola, "The Coca-Cola Company Fact Sheet," http://assets.coca-colacompany.com/90/11/5f21b88444bab46d430b4c578e80/Company_Fact_Sheet.pdf (accessed April 9, 2015); Kim Bhasin, "15 Facts about Coca-Cola That Will Blow Your Mind," *Business Insider,* June 9, 2011, http://www.businessinsider.com/facts-about-coca-cola-2011-6 (accessed April 9, 2015).

15. Hannah Elliott, "Most Fuel-Efficient Cars for the Buck," *Forbes,* March 30, 2009, http://www.forbes.com/2009/03/30/fuel-efficient-cars-lifestyle-vehicles-efficient-cars_slide.html (accessed April 9, 2015).

16. "AdWords," Google, https://adwords.google.com/um/gaiaauth?apt%3DNone%26ltmpl%3Djfk%26ltmpl%3Djfk&error=newacct&sacu=1&sarp=1 (accessed April 9, 2015).

17. Twitter, "What Are Promoted Tweets?" Twitter Help Center, https://support.twitter.com/articles/142101-what-are-promotedtweets# (accessed April 9, 2015).

18. Christine Birkner, "10 Minutes with . . . Raul Murguia Villegas," *Marketing News,* July 30, 2011, pp. 26–27.

19. "MSPA North America," Mystery Shopping Providers Association, http://mysteryshop.org/ (accessed April 9, 2015).

20. Piet Levy, "10 Minutes with . . . Robert J. Morais," *Marketing News,* May 30, 2011, pp. 22–23.

21. Steven Kurutz, "On Kickstarter, Designers' Dream Materialize," *The New York Times,* September 21, 2011, http://www.nytimes.com/2011/09/22/garden/on-kickstarter-designers-dreams-materialize.html (accessed April 9, 2015).

22. Mya Frazier, "Crowd Sourcing," *Delta Sky Mag,* February 2010, p. 73.

23. Carol Tice, "How Social Media Is Fueling the Next $1B Beauty Brand," *Forbes,* January 22, 2014, http://www.forbes.com/sites/caroltice/2014/01/22/girlfriend-power/ (accessed April 6, 2015).

24. Mike Floyd, "Editor's Letter: What Drives Millennials?" *Automobile Magazine,* May 2015, p. 12.

25. "Fully Charged," *The Economist,* March 1, 2014, p. 64; Siimon Reynolds, "You Should Copy Tesla's Way of Marketing," *Forbes,* September 1, 2013, http://www.forbes.com/sites/siimonreynolds/2013/09/01/why-you-should-copy-teslas-way-of-marketing/ (accessed December 10, 2014); Paul J. D'Arcy, "Tesla Model S: The Disruptive Marketing of an Electric Car," *Science of Revenue,* http://scienceofrevenue.com/2013/01/20/tesla-model-s-the-disruptive-marketing-of-an-electric-car/ (accessed December 10, 2014); Nicolas Zart, "The Brilliant Tesla Advertising Strategy, or Lack Thereof," *Teslarati,* September 5, 2014, http://www.teslarati.com/brilliant-tesla-advertising-strategy-lack-thereof/ (accessed December 10, 2014).

26. Matt Townsend, "At Hasbro, Little Girls Become a Big Market," *Bloomberg Businessweek,* March 3–9, 2014, pp. 23–24.

27. Julie Eilperin, "Autos Must Average 54.5 mpg by 2025, New EPA Standards Say," *Washington Post,* August 28, 2012, http://www.washingtonpost.com/national/health-science/autos-must-average-545-mpg-by-2025-new-epa-standards-are-expected-to-say/2012/08/28/2c47924a-f117-11e1-892d-bc92fee603a7_story.html (accessed September 2, 2015).

28. Christian Homburg, Arnd Vomberg, Margit Enke, and Philipp H. Grimm, "The Loss of the Marketing Department's Influence: Is It Really Happening? And Why Worry?" *Journal of the Academy of Marketing Science* 43, no. 1 (2015): pp. 1–13.

Chapter 12

1. Narendra Rao, "The Keys to New Product Success (Part 1)—Collecting Unarticulated & Invisible Customer Needs," *Product Management & Strategy,* June 19, 2007, https://productstrategy.wordpress.com/2007/06/19/the-keys-to-new-product-succeess-part-1-collecting-unarticulated-invisible-customer-needs/ (accessed April 14, 2015).

2. Christina Larson, "Xiaomi," *Fast Company*, 2014, www.fastcompany.com/most-innovativecompanies/2014/xiaomi (accessed April 14, 2015).

3. Ma Jie, "Honda to Halt Production of Insight Hybrid Vehicle," *Bloomberg,* February 26, 2014, http://www.bloomberg.com/

news/2014-02-26/honda-to-end-production-of-insight-hybrid-as-sales-trail-prius.html (accessed April 9, 2015).

4. Associated Press, "Jobs Says iPad Idea Came Before iPhone," June 2, 2010, http://www.foxnews.com/tech/2010/06/02/jobs-says-ipad-idea-came-iphone/ (accessed April 14, 2015).

5. Nike, "Nike Sport Research Lab Incubates Innovation," July 16, 2013, http://news.nike.com/news/nike-sport-research-lab-incubates-innovation (accessed April 14, 2015).

6. Serena Ng, "Seventh Generation Adds Tea and Coffee," *The Wall Street Journal*, July 15, 2014, p. B3; Gamila Company, "Features," http://shop.gamilacompany.com/impress/features/ (accessed October 15, 2014); Aarthi Rayapura, "Seventh Generation Continues Expansion with Gamila Acquisition," *Sustainable Brands,* July 22, 2014, http://www.sustainablebrands.com/news_and_views/startups/aarthi_rayapura/seventh_generation_continues_expansion_gamila_acquisition (accessed October 15, 2014); Alex Rose, "Seventh Generation Expands Their Brand," July 15, 2014, http://www.mychamplainvalley.com/story/d/story/seventh-generation-expands-their-brand/17534/jz_auFkR4EO_KsE_IM4mBQ (accessed October 15, 2014).

7. John A. Byrne, "Greatest Entrepreneurs of Our Time," *Fortune,* April 9, 2012, pp. 68–86; Google Finance, "Amazon.com, Inc.," April 30, 2014, www.google.com/finance?cid=660463 (accessed April 14, 2015).

8. "SHMN:US," *Bloomberg,* May 14, 2014, www.bloomberg.com/quote/SHMN:US/profile (accessed April 14, 2015); "SOHM, Inc. Receives Confirmation for Test Marketing of Its OTC Products from a Retail Chain Store," *YAHOO! Finance*, April 22, 2014, http://finance.yahoo.com/news/sohm-inc-receives-confirmation-test-133000747.html (accessed April 14, 2015).

9. Bruce Horovitz, "7-Eleven Tests 'Healthy' Fresh Food by Fitness Guru," *USA Today*, September 30, 2014, p. 2B.

10. Tony Danova, "BI INTELLIGENCE FORECAST: Google Glass Will Become a Mainstream Product and Sell Millions by 2016," *Business Insider*, December 31, 2013, http://www.businessinsider.com/google-glass-sales-projections-2013-11 (accessed April 14, 2015).

11. Todd Leopold, "How Beats Headphones Changed the Audio World," *CNN*, January 12, 2014, www.cnn.com/2014/01/13/tech/beats-headphones-audio-market/(accessed April 14, 2015); Beats by Dre, "About Us," www.beatsbydre.com/aboutus (accessed April 14, 2015).

12. Duane Stanford, "Africa: Coke's Last Frontier," *Bloomberg Businessweek*, October 28, 2010, www.businessweek.com/magazine/content/10_45/b4202054144294.htm (accessed May 29, 2014); Kim Peterson, "Coke Debuts Smaller Bottles," *MSN Money,* September 19, 2011, http://money.msn.com/topstocks/post.aspx?post=2e4eaa5c-2162-4135-81c6-6d41a02d91b9 (accessed May 29, 2014); Meghra Bahree and Mike Esterl, "PepsiCo's Health Push," *The Wall Street Journal,* July 7, 2011, p. B8.

13. Tom White, "iPod in the Decline Phase of the Product Life Cycle," *tutor2u,* January 29, 2014, http://beta.tutor2u.net/business/blog/ipod-in-the-decline-phase-of-the-product-life-cycle (accessed April 14, 2015); Christina Bonnington, "Say Goodbye to the iPod Classic," *Wired*, September 6, 2013, http://www.wired.com/2013/09/goodbye-ipod-classic/ (accessed April 14, 2015).

14. "Product Life Cycle Stages," April 14, 2015, http://productlifecyclestages.com/ (accessed April 14, 2015).

15. Christina Warren, "Can Acer's New Strategy Help It Make a Comeback?" *Mashable*, April 30, 2014, http://mashable.com/2014/04/30/acer-comeback-strategy/ (accessed May 5, 2014).

16. Megan Durisin, "This Is Joe Fresh, the Brand that May Be JCPenney's Final Lifeline," *Business Insider,* March 14, 2013, http://www.businessinsider.com/joe-fresh-for-jcpenney-launches-2013-3 (accessed April 9, 2015).

17. "Private Label Gets Personal," *Shopper Culture,* October 1, 2009, http://www.shopperculture.com/2009/10/private-label-gets-personal.html (accessed April 14, 2015).

18. James Haggerty, "Shoppers Not Shy on Store Brand Labels," *The Times Tribune,* January 5, 2014, http://thetimes-tribune.com/news/business/shoppers-not-shy-on-store-brandlabels-1.1611508 (accessed April 13, 2015).

19. Mintel, "Beverage Packaging Trends—US—February 2014," February 2014, http://oxygen.mintel.com/sinatra/oxygen/list/id=680559&type=RCItem#0_1___page_RCItem=0 (accessed April 14, 2015).

20. Denise Lee Yohn, "Let Design Do the Talking for Brands," *Forbes*, January 27, 2014, http://www.forbes.com/sites/onmarketing/2014/01/27/let-design-do-the-talking-for-brands/ (accessed April 14, 2015).

21. Lisa Whetstone, "Consumer Feelings on Olive Garden's Logo Change," *Gutcheckit,* March 20, 2014, http://blog.gutcheckit.com/did-olive-garden-do-consumer-research (accessed April 14, 2015).

22. American Customer Satisfaction Index, "ACSI: Drop in Customer Satisfaction Points to Weak Economic Growth," March 24, 2015, http://www.theacsi.org/news-and-resources/press-releases/press-2015/press-release-national-acsi-q4-2014 (accessed April 9, 2015); "About the American Customer Satisfaction Index," http://www.theacsi.org/about-acsi (accessed April 9, 2015).

23. "American Demographics 2006 Consumer Perception Survey," *Advertising Age,* January 2, 2006, p. 9. Data by Synovate.

24. Fast Company staff, "The Top 10 Most Innovative Companies in China," *Fast Company,* 2014, http://www.fastcompany.com/most-innovative-companies/2014/industry/china (accessed April 9, 2015).

25. Rajneesh Suri and Kent B. Monroe, "The Effects of Time Constraints on Consumers' Judgments of Prices and Products," *Journal of Consumer Research,* 30 (June 2003), p. 92.

26. Kurt Soller, "With Enough Customers, You Don't Need a Product," *Bloomberg Businessweek*, April 28–May 4, 2014, p. 70; Tomio Geron, "Inside Wanelo, the Hot Social Shopping Service," *Forbes,* March 27, 2013, http://www.forbes.com/sites/tomiogeron/2013/03/27/inside-wanelo-the-hot-social-shopping-service/ (accessed October 13, 2014); Jessica Stillman, "Wanelo Founder: How I Got 10M Members with No Marketing," *Women 2.0,* August 21, 2013, http://women2.com/2013/08/21/wanelo-founder-how-i-got-10m-members-with-no-marketing/ (accessed October 13, 2014); Natalia Angulo, "Wanelo, Next Verb in Digital Dictionary?" *Fox Business,* July 26, 2013, http://small-business.foxbusiness.com/entrepreneurs/2013/07/26/wanelo-next-verb-in-digital-dictionary/ (accessed December 2, 2014).

27. Ed Lamb, "Taco Bell Quietly Debuts Dollar Cravings Menu," *Ad Week,* August 20, 2014, http://www.adweek.com/news/advertising-branding/taco-bell-debuts-dollar-cravings-menu-159595 (accessed April 9, 2015).

28. Sysco, "The Sysco Story," www.sysco.com/about-sysco.html# (accessed April 14, 2015).

29. "Top Threats to Revenue," *USA Today,* February 1, 2006, p. A1.

30. Zoom Systems, "Company Overview," www.zoomsystems.com/about-us (accessed April 14, 2015); Brad Howarth, "Hear This, iPods from a Vending Machine," *The Sydney Morning Herald,* November 14, 2006, www.smh.com.au

/news/biztech/hearthis-ipods-from-avending-mach
ine/2006/11/13/1163266481869.html (accessed April 14, 2015).

31. Zoom Systems, "Company Overview," www.zoomsystems.com/
about-us (accessed April 14, 2015);

32. Piper, "Piper Expands Its Global Sales Network," March 19, 2013,
http://www.piper.com/piper-expands-global-sales-network-2//
(accessed April 14, 2015); Rick Durden, "Piper Names Dealer
for China," *AV Web*, January 10, 2014, www.avweb.com/
avwebfl ash/news/Piper-Names-Dealer-for-China221250-1.html
(accessed April 14, 2015).

33. William Pride and O. C. Ferrell, *Marketing Foundations,* 5th ed.
(Mason, OH: Cengage Learning, 2013), pp. 415–16.

34. Ibid.

35. Abbey Klaassen, "Even Google Has to Advertise," *Advertising
Age,* June 2, 2008, p. 4.

36. Angus Loten, "For Small Firms, New Perils in Ad Claims," *The
Wall Street Journal,* May 15, 2014, p. B5; Lara O'Reilly, "Red Bull
Will Pay $10 to Customers Disappointed the Drink Didn't Actually
Give Them 'Wings,'" *Business Insider,* October 8, 2014, http://www.
businessinsider.com/red-bull-settles-false-advertising-lawsuit-for-
13-million-2014-10 (accessed December 15, 2014); Stephanie Strom,
"Hellman's Maker Sues Company Over Its Just Mayo Substitute,"
The New York Times, November 10, 2014, http://www.nytimes.
com/2014/11/11/business/unilever-sues-a-start-up-over-mayonnaise-
like-product.html?_r=0 (accessed December 15, 2014).

37. Lindsay Kramer, "Super Bowl 2015: How Much Does a
30-second Television Commercial Cost?" *Syracuse,* January 31,
2015, http://www.syracuse.com/superbowl/index.ssf/2015/01/
super_bowl_2015_how_much_does_commercial_cost_tv_
ad_30_second_spot.html (accessed April 9, 2015).

38. Zayda Rivera, "Scarlett Johansson's Uncensored Soda-
Stream Super Bowl Ad Banned by Fox," *NY Daily News,*
www.nydailynews.com/entertainment/tv-movies/scarlett-
johansson-uncensoredsodastream-super-bowl-ad-
bannedarticle-1.1595712 (accessed April 14, 2015).

39. Don Reisinger, "Apple Follows Samsung in Search for 'Buzz
Marketing Manager,'" *CNET,* May 2, 2014, http://www.cnet.com/
news/apple-to-follow-samsungs-lead-with-search-for-buzz-
marketing-manager/ (accessed April 14, 2015); Jay Yarrow,
"Apple Is Hiring a 'Buzz Marketing Manager' to Get iPhones in
the Hands of More Famous People," *Business Insider,* May 2,
2014, http://www.businessinsider.com/apple-is-hiring-a-buzz-
marketing-manager-2014-5 (accessed May 5, 2014).

40. Gerry Khermouch and Jeff Green, "Buzz Marketing," *Business-
Week,* July 30, 2001, pp. 50–56.

41. Laura Stampler, "How Dove's 'Real Beauty Sketches' Became
the Most Viral Video of All Time," *Business Insider,* May 22,
2013, http://www.businessinsider.com/how-doves-real-beauty-
sketches-became-the-most-viral-ad-video-of-all-time-2013-5
(accessed April 14, 2015).

42. Ajmal Kohgadai, "Why Mobile Coupons Have 10x Higher Redemption Rate Than Traditional Coupons," *Fun Mobility,* October 11,
2013, http://blog.funmobility.com/2013/10/11/why-mobile-coupons-
have-10x-higher-redemption-rate-than-traditional-coupons/
(accessed May 5, 2014); Chuck Martin, "Coupons & the Gradual
Migration to Mobile," *Media Post,* May 2, 2014, www.mediapost.
com/publications/article/199496/coupons-the-gradualmigration-
to-mobile.html (accessed April 14, 2015).

43. Evan Niu, "At Long Last, T-Mobile Is Getting the iPhone," *The
Motley Fool,* December 7, 2012, http://www.fool.com/investing/
general/2012/12/07/at-long-last-t-mobile-is-getting-the-iphone
.aspx (accessed May 15, 2014).

Chapter 13

1. This material in this chapter is reserved for use in the authors'
other textbooks and teaching materials.

2. Lauren I. Labrecque, Jonas vor dem Esche, Charla Mathwick,
Thomas P. Novak, and Charles F. Hofacker, "Consumer Power:
Evolution in the Digital Age," *Journal of Interactive Marketing*
27, no. 4 (November 2013), pp. 257–69.

3. James Kanter and Mark Scott, "Europe Challenges Google,
Seeing Violations of Its Antitrust Law," *The New York Times,*
April 15, 2015, http://www.nytimes.com/2015/04/16/business/
international/european-union-google-antitrust-case.html?_r=0
(accessed April 17, 2015).

4. "Amazon.com: Fortune 500 2014," http://fortune.com/fortune
500/amazon-com-inc-35/ (accessed April 17, 2015).

5. "Top 15 Most Popular Video Websites," *eBiz MBA,* May 2014, http://
www.ebizmba.com/articles/video-websites (accessed April 22,
2015); Vimeo, "About Vimeo," http://vimeo.com/about (accessed
April 22, 2015).

6. Bobby White, "The New Workplace Rules: No Video-Watching,"
The Wall Street Journal, March 4, 2008, p. B1; Ben Bryant,
"Workers Waste an Hour a Day on Facebook, Shopping and
Browsing Holidays, Study Finds," *The Telegraph,* July 22, 2013,
www.telegraph.co.uk/news/uknews/10194322/ Workers-waste-
an-hour-a-day-on-Facebook-shopping-and-browsingholidays-
study-fi nds.html (accessed April 22, 2015).

7. Daniel Nations, "How Many iPad Apps Are in the App Store?"
About Tech, http://ipad.about.com/od/iPad-FAQ/f/How-Many-
iPad-Apps-Are-In-The-App-Store.htm (accessed April 17, 2015).

8. Carol Tice, "How Social Media Is Fueling the Next $1B Beauty
Brand," *Forbes,* January 22, 2014, http://www.forbes.com/sites/
caroltice/2014/01/22/girlfriend-power/ (accessed April 6, 2015).

9. Christine Birkner, "Retail's White Elephants," *Marketing News,*
April 2015, pp. 49–59.

10. Gillian Wong, "Alibaba Disputes U.S. Group's Claim It Tolerates Fake
Goods on Taobao," *The Wall Street Journal,* April 14, 2015, http://
www.wsj.com/articles/alibaba-rebuts-u-s-groups-claim-it-tolerates-
fake-goods-on-taobao-1428981233 (accessed April 17, 2015).

11. Facebook, "MGM Resources International," www.facebook.com/
business/success/mgmresorts-international (accessed May 19, 2014);
Facebook, "Offers," www.facebook.com/help/410451192330456
(accessed April 22, 2015); Facebook, "Facebook Exchange," https://
www.facebook.com/business/a/online-sales/facebook-exchange
(accessed April 22, 2015).

12. Melinda F. Emerson, "How to Run a Facebook Commerce Store,"
The New York Times, August 2, 2013, http://boss.blogs.nytimes.
com/2013/08/02/how-to-run-a-facebook-commerce-store/?_
r=0 (accessed December 12, 2014); "How to Shop—Polkadot
Alley," Facebook, https://www.facebook.com/ThePolkadotAlley/
app_208195102528120 (accessed December 12, 2014).

13. Cameron Chapman, "The History and Evolution of Social
Media," *WebDesigner Depot,* October 7, 2009, http://www.
webdesignerdepot.com/2009/10/the-history-and-evolution-of-
social-media/ (accessed April 22, 2015).

14. Ibid.

15. Adam Kleinberg, "Thinking about Snapchat Advertising? Snap
Out of It," *Advertising Age,* August 22, 2014, http://adage.com/
article/agency-viewpoint/thinking-snapchat-snap/294667/
(accessed December 9, 2014).

16. Erin Griffith, "Snitches' Brew," *Fortune,* April 1, 2015, pp. 46–48.

17. Zachary Karabell, "To Tweet or Not to Tweet," *Time,* April 12,
2011, p. 24.

18. Shea Bennett, "This is How Much Time We Spend on Social Networks Every Day," *Ad Week,* November 18, 2014, http://www.adweek.com/socialtimes/social-media-minutes-day/503160 (accessed April 17, 2015).

19. Wendy Boswell, "Video Websites: The Top Ten," *About Tech,* 2015, http://websearch.about.com/od/imagesearch/tp/popular-videosites.htm (accessed April 17, 2015).

20. Tom Foster, "Along Came Lolly," *Inc.*, June 2014, pp. 24–36; John Koetsier, "Steve Case's $20M investment in Lolly Wolly Doodle Proves the Value of Social Commerce," *Venture Beat,* June 13, 2013, http://venturebeat.com/2013/06/13/steve-case-20m-investment-in-lolly-wolly-doodle-proves-the-value-of-social-commerce/ (accessed December 10, 2014); "Lolly Wolly Doodle," *Facebook,* https://www.facebook.com/LollyWollyDoodle (accessed December 10, 2014).

21. Jefferson Graham, "How to Ride Facebook's Giant Wave," *USA Today,* May 30, 2013, p. 5B.

22. Jeff Elder, "Facing Reality, Companies Alter Social-Media Strategies," *The Wall Street Journal,* June 23, 2014, pp. B1–B2.

23. Jefferson Graham, "Cake Decorator Finds Twitter a Tweet Recipe for Success," *USA Today,* April 1, 2009, p. 5B.

24. Jeff Bullas, "22 Social Media Facts and Statistics You Should Know in 2014," *Jeffbullas.com,* 2014, http://www.jeffbullas.com/2014/01/17/20-social-media-facts-and-statistics-you-should-know-in-2014/ (accessed April 22, 2015); Maeve Duggan and Aaron Smith, "Social Media Update 2013," *Pew Research Internet Project*, December 30, 2013, www.pewinternet.org/2013/12/30/social-media-update-2013/ (accessed April 22, 2015).

25. Christine Birkner, "The Goldfish Conundrum," *Marketing News,* April 2015, pp. 18–19.

26. Amol Sharma, "NFL Throws in with Twitter," *The Wall Street Journal*, September 26, 2013, p. B2.

27. Stephanie Frasco, "100 Facts and Figures about Twitter, and Why They Matter for Your Business," *Social Media Today,* September 26, 2013, http://socialmediatoday.com/stephaniefrasco/1770161/100-facts-figures-about-twitter-business (accessed April 22, 2015).

28. Yoree Koh and Suzanne Vranica, "Advertisers Say Twitter Needs More," *The Wall Street Journal*, October 5-6, 2013, pp. B1, B4; "Flo from Progessive," *Twitter,* https://twitter.com/itsflo (accessed December 11, 2014).

29. Jack Marshall, "Twitter Aims to Target Ads," *The Wall Street Journal*, December 3, 2014, p. B5.

30. Christopher Heine, "Dunkin' Donuts' New Vine Spots Play on Super Bowl Memories," *AdWeek,* January 30, 2014, http://www.adweek.com/news/technology/dunkin-donuts-new-vine-spots-play-super-bowl-memories-155340 (accessed December 11, 2014); Kristin Hodgkinson, "How Brands Are Winning with Vine Videos: 10 Examples," *Social Media Examiner,* September 4, 2014, http://www.socialmediaexaminer.com/vine-videos-10-brand-examples/ (accessed December 11, 2014).

31. "Social Media Summit," Harrisburg University, 2012, www.harrisburgu.edu/academics/professional/socialmedia/index-2012.php (accessed February 16, 2012).

32. Jeff Bercovici, "Tumblr: David Karp's $800 Million Art Project," *Forbes,* January 2, 2013, www.forbes.com/sites/jeffbercovici/2013/01/02/tumblrdavid-karps-800-million-art-project/ (accessed May 6, 2014); "About Tumblr," https://www.tumblr.com/about (accessed April 17, 2015).

33. A.C. Neilson, "Global Faces and Networked Places: A Neilson Report on Social Networking's New Global Footprint," March 2009, http://www.nielsen.com/content/dam/corporate/us/en/newswire/uploads/2009/03/nielsen_globalfaces_mar09.pdf (accessed April 22, 2015).

34. Easy Recipes for Real Life: Tastefully Simple blog, https://www.tastefullysimple.com/ (accessed April 22, 2015); Stacie Schaible, "Dunedin Woman Says 'Mommy' Blogs Hit the Target," *wfla,* December 10, 2013, http://www.wfla.com/story/24184742/mommy-blogs-hit-the-target (accessed April 22, 2015).

35. "Wikipedia: About," *Wikipedia,* April 16, 2015, http://en.wikipedia.org/wiki/Wikipedia:About (accessed April 17, 2015).

36. Charlene Li and Josh Bernoff, *Groundswell* (Boston: Harvard Business Press, 2008), pp. 25–26.

37. Ayaz Nanji, "Blog and Social Media Usage by Fortune 500 Companies," *Marketing Profs,* September 12, 2014, http://www.marketingprofs.com/charts/2014/25998/blog-and-social-media-usage-by-fortune-500-companies (accessed December 11, 2014).

38. Molly Soat, "Teen Dream," *Marketing News,* April 2015, pp. 14–15.

39. Tom Foster, "The GoPro Army," *Inc.,* February 2012, pp. 52–59.

40. Tim Peterson, "YouTube Buys Mobile Video App Directr Because Every Ad Penny Counts," *Advertising Age,* August 6, 2014, http://adage.com/article/digital/youtube-buys-mobile-video-app-ad-penny-counts/294501/ (accessed April 16, 2015).

41. Steven Bertoni, "How Stanford Made Instagram an Instant Success," *Forbes,* August 20, 2012, pp. 56–63; Jefferson Graham, "Instagram Is a Start-Up Magnet," *USA Today,* August 9, 2012, www.usatoday.com/tech/news/story/2012-08-07/instagram-economy/56883474/1 (accessed April 22, 2015); Karen Rosenberg, "Everyone's Lives, in Pictures," *The New York Times,* April 12, 2012, http://www.nytimes.com/2012/04/22/sunday-review/everyones-lives-in-pictures-from-instagram.html?_r=0 (accessed April 22, 2015); K. Ian Crouch, "Instagram's Instant Nostalgia," *The New Yorker,* April 10, 2012, http://www.newyorker.com/culture/culture-desk/instagrams-instant-nostalgia (accessed April 22, 2015); "Top 15 Most Popular Photo Sharing Websites," April 2015, http://www.ebizmba.com/articles/photo-sharing-sites (accessed April 22, 2015).

42. Jessi Hempel, "Instagram is Ready to Take Its Shot," *Fortune,* pp. 72–78; Jim Edwards, "Execs at Instagram Believe They Will Soon Eclipse Twitter as They Head Toward 1 Billion Users," *Business Insider,* May 13, 2014, http://www.businessinsider.com/instagram-and-twitter-user-statistics-2014-5 (accessed October 16, 2014); Trevor Mogg, "Instagram on the Up and Up," *Digital Trends,* March 26, 2014, http://www.digitaltrends.com/social-media/instagram-user-base-crosses-200-million-mark/ (accessed October 16, 2014); Blair Hanley Frank, "Amazon Reports Quarterly Net Losses of $41M, Sales Above $17B, Exceeding Expectations," GeekWire, October 24, 2013, http://www.geekwire.com/2013/amazon-reports-quarterly-loss-41-million/ (accessed October 16, 2014); Victor Luckerson, "These 8 Internet Companies Are Worth over $1 Billion—But They Haven't Made a Dime," *Time,* http://business.time.com/2013/10/29/these-8-internet-companies-are-worth-over-1-billion-but-they-havent-made-a-dime/ (accessed October 16, 2014).

43. Eddie Bauer website, www.eddiebauer.com/home.jsp (accessed April 22, 2015).

44. Laura Schlereth, "Marketers Interest in Pinterest," *Marketing News,* April 30, 2012, pp. 8–9; PR Newswire, "PINTEREST INTEREST: Survey: 17 Percent of Marketers Currently Using or Planning to Join Pinterest," August 22, 2012, http://www.prnewswire.com/news-releases/pinterest-interest-survey-17-percent-of-marketers-currently-using-or-planning-to-join-pinterest-167016325.html (accessed April 22, 2015); Pinterest website, http://pinterest.com/

(accessed May 7, 2014); http://pinterest.com/wholefoods/whole-planetfoundation/ (accessed April 22, 2015).

45. Jeff Bercovici, "Social Media's New Mad Men," *Forbes,* November 2014, pp. 71–82.

46. Kelly Clay, "3 Things You Can Learn about Your Business with Instagram," *Forbes,* August 9, 2012, http://www.forbes.com/sites/kellyclay/2012/08/09/3-things-you-can-learn-about-your-business-with-instagram/ (accessed April 22, 2015).

47. Douglas MacMillan and Elizabeth Dwoskin, "Smile! Marketers Are Mining Selfies," *The Wall Street Journal,* October 10, 2014, pp. B1–B2.

48. Natalie Wires, "The Rising Popularity of Podcasts: Why Listeners Are Rediscovering Podcasts," *Perspective,* March 26, 2014, http://blog.tunheim.com/2014/03/26/rising-popularitypodcasts-listeners-rediscoveringpodcasts/1438#.U2pMWYFdVc8 (accessed April 22, 2015).

49. Ann Lukits, "Podcasts Send Shoppers to Omega-3s," *The Wall Street Journal,* December 9, 2014, p. D2.

50. Dean Takahashi, "MediaSpike Reaches 20M Monthly Users with Product Placement in Social–Mobile Games," *VentureBeat,* October 24, 2013, http://venturebeat.com/2013/10/24/mediaspike-reaches-20m-monthly-users-with-product-placement-in-social-mobile-games/ (accessed April 22, 2015).

51. Mike Shields, "Are Mobile Games the Next Great Ad Medium?" *The Wall Street Journal,* August 18, 2014, http://blogs.wsj.com/cmo/2014/08/18/are-mobile-games-the-next-great-ad-medium/ (accessed April 17, 2015).

52. Austin Carr, "Facebook Everywhere," *Fast Company,* July/August 2014, pp. 56–98.

53. Roger Yu, "Smartphones Help Make Bon Voyages," *USA Today,* March 5, 2010, p. B1.

54. Sean Silverthorpe, "Should Retailers Worry about In-store Mobile Use?" *Insights from Marketing Science Institute,* no. 1 (2015), pp. 1–2.

55. Brian Hongiman, "10 Mobile Marketing Statistics to Help Justify Your Budget," *Digital Lab,* May 5, 2014, http://digitallabblog.com/post/84827360253/10-mobilemarketing-statistics-to-help-justifyyour (accessed April 22, 2015).

56. "Advertisers Will Spend Nearly $600 Billion Worldwide in 2015," *eMarketer,* December 10, 2014, http://www.emarketer.com/Article/Advertisers-Will-Spend-Nearly-600-Billion-World-wide-2015/1011691 (accessed April 17, 2015).

57. Mark Milian, "Why Text Messages Are Limited to 160 Characters," *Los Angeles Times,* May 3, 2009, http://latimesblogs.latimes.com/technology/2009/05/invented-text-messaging.html (accessed April 22, 2015); "Eight Reasons Why Your Business Should Use SMS Marketing," *Mobile Marketing Ratings,* www.mobilemarketingratings.com/eight-reasons-sms-marketing.html (accessed April 22, 2015).

58. Sheldon Ferraro, "Gap the First to Use New Instagram Direct for Their WIWT Campaign," *HashSlush,* December 14, 2013, http://www.hashslush.com/gap-instagram-direct-wwit-campaign/ (accessed April 22, 2015).

59. Thomas Claburn, "Google Tells Businesses 'Fall In Love With Mobile,'" *Information Week,* February 28, 2012, www.information-tionweek.com/news/mobility/business/232601587 (accessed December 12, 2014); Lauren Johnson, "Mobile Video Generates 58pc Brand Recall: Study," *Mobile Marketer,* November 12, 2012, http://www.mobilemarketer.com/cms/news/research/14222.html (accessed December 12, 2014).

60. Shawn Hessinger, "60 Percent of Online Traffic Now Comes from Mobile," *Small Biz Trends,* July 8, 2014, http://smallbiztrends.com/2014/07/online-traffic-report-mobile.html (accessed December 12, 2014).

61. Lauren Johnson, "With Turn-by-Turn Directions, Google's Waze App Wants to Win Mobile Advertising," *Ad Week,* March 24, 2015, http://www.adweek.com/news/technology/turn-turn-directions-google-thinks-it-can-win-mobile-advertising-163642 (accessed April 17, 2015).

62. Anita Campbell, "What the Heck Is an App?" *Small Business Trends,* March 7, 2011, http://smallbiztrends.com/2011/03/what-is-an-app.html (accessed April 22, 2015).

63. "Half of All Adult Cell Phone Owners Have Apps on Their Phones," Pew Internet and American Life Project, November 2, 2011, http://pewinternet.org/~/media/Files/Reports/2011/PIP_Apps-Update-2011.pdf (accessed April 22, 2015).

64. Pew Internet Research, "MobileTechnology Fact Sheet," January 2014, www.pewinternet.org/factsheets/mobile-technology-fact-sheet/ (accessed April 22, 2015).

65. Nancy Trejos, "Marriott App Steers Its Guests to Deals," *USA Today,* July 10, 2014, p. 5B.

66. Umika Pidaparthy, "Marketers Embracing QR Codes, for Better or Worse," *CNN Tech,* March 28, 2011, http://www.cnn.com/2011/TECH/mobile/03/28/qr.codes.marketing/index.html (accessed April 22, 2015).

67. Brad Stone and Olga Kharif, "Pay As You Go," *Bloomberg Businessweek,* July 18–24, 2011, pp. 66–71.

68. "Google Wallet," www.google.com/wallet/what-is-google-wallet.html (accessed April 22, 2015).

69. Sarah E. Needleman, "Banking on Bitcoin's Novelty," *The Wall Street Journal,* June 27, 2013, p. B4; Robin Sidel and Andrew R. Johnson, "States Put Heat on Bitcoin," *The Wall Street Journal,* June 26, 2013, pp. C1–C2.

70. "The Bitcoin Bubble," *The Economist,* November 30, 2013, p.13.

71. "MtGox Bitcoin Exchange Reopens So Users Can Stare Listlessly at Their Loss," *The Guardian,* March 18, 2014, http://www.theguardian.com/technology/2014/mar/18/mtgox-bitcoin-exchange-reopens-so-users-can-stare-listlessly-at-their-loss (accessed April 22, 2015).

72. "All About Widgets," *Webopedia* ™, September 14, 2007, www.webopedia.com/DidYouKnow/Hardware_Software/widgets.asp (accessed April 22, 2015).

73. Rachael King, "Building a Brand with Widgets," *Bloomberg Businessweek*, March 3, 2008, www.businessweek.com/technology/content/feb2008/tc20080303_000743.htm (accessed December 12, 2014).

74. TripAdvisor, "Welcome to TripAdvisor's Widget Center," www.tripadvisor.com/Widgets (accessed April 22, 2015).

75. Li and Bernoff,*Groundswell,* p. 41.

76. Ibid., pp. 41–42.

77. "Forrester Unveils New Segment of Social Technographics—The Conversationalists," *360 Digital Connections*, January 21, 2010, http://blog.360i.com/social-marketing/forrester-new-segment-social-technographics-conversationalists (accessed April 22, 2015).

78. Li and Bernoff,*Groundswell,* p. 44.

79. Ibid., pp. 44–45.

80. Ryan Pinkham, "90% of Consumers Say Online Reviews Impact Buying Decisions . . . And Other Hot Topics," *Constant Contact*, April 12, 2013, http://blogs.constantcontact.com/do-customers-trust-online-reviews/ (accessed April 22, 2015).

81. Geoffrey A. Fowler, "Strategies to Outfox Facebook's Tracking," *The Wall Street Journal*, August 6, 2014, p. D1; AdExchanger, "If a Consumer Asked You, 'Why Is Tracking Good?', What Would You

Say?" *Ad Exchanger*, October 28, 2011, http://www.adexchanger.com/online-advertising/why-is-tracking-good/ (accessed December 15, 2014); Ad Traders, "The Ethical Issues with 3rd Party Behavioral Tracking," *Ad Exchanger*, October 31, 2011, http://www.adexchanger.com/the-debate/3rd-party-behavioral-tracking/ (accessed December 15, 2014); Nicholas Carr, "Tracking Is an Assault on Liberty, with Real Dangers," *The Wall Street Journal*, August 6, 2010, http://online.wsj.com/articles/SB10001424052748703748904575411682714389888 (accessed December 15, 2014).

82. Jon Swartz, "Facebook Changes Its Status in Washington," *USA Today*, January 13, 2011, pp. 1B–2B; John W. Miller, "Yahoo Cookie Plan in Place," *The Wall Street Journal*, March 19, 2011, http://online.wsj.com/news/articles/SB10001424052748703512404576208700813815570 (accessed April 22, 2015).

83. Jesse Brody, "Terms and Conditions," *Marketing News*, November 2014, pp. 34–41.

84. Elizabeth Weise, "Sony Hack Leaves Intriguing Clues," *USA Today*, December 4, 2014, p. 1B.

85. Elizabeth Weise, "Consumers Have to Protect Themselves Online," *USA Today*, May 22, 2014, p. 1B.

86. Jim Zarroli, "U.S. Credit Cards Tackle Fraud with Embedded Chips, But No Pins," *NPR*, January 5, 2015, http://www.npr.org/blogs/alltechconsidered/2015/01/05/375164839/u-s-credit-cards-tackle-fraud-with-embedded-chips-but-no-pins (accessed April 22, 2015).

87. Kevin Shanahan and Mike Hyman "Motivators and Enablers of SCOURing," *Journal of Business Research*, 63 (September–October 2010), pp. 1095–1102.

88. Economist staff, "The Amazons of the Dark Net," *The Economist*, November 1, 2014, pp. 57–58.

89. Erica E. Phillips, "U.S. Officials Chase Counterfeit Goods Online," *The Wall Street Journal*, November 28, 2014, http://www.wsj.com/articles/u-s-officials-chase-counterfeit-goods-online-1417217763 (accessed December 10, 2014).

90. Max Chafkin, "The Case, and the Plan, for the Virtual Company," *Inc.*, April 2010, p. 68.

Chapter 14

1. Public Company Accounting Oversight Board, "PCAOB Announces Settled Disciplinary Order against Deloitte & Touche for Permitting Suspended Auditor to Participate in Firm's Public Company Audit Practice," October 22, 2013, http://pcaobus.org/News/Releases/Pages/10222013_Deloitte.aspx (accessed April 8, 2015).

2. Walter Pavlo, "Association of Certified Fraud Examiners Release 2014 Report on Fraud," *Forbes*, May 21, 2014, http://www.forbes.com/sites/walterpavlo/2014/05/21/association-of-certified-fraud-examiners-release-2014-report-on-fraud/ (accessed April 8, 2015).

3. Association of Certified Fraud Examiners, "About the ACFE," www.acfe.com/about-the-acfe.aspx (accessed April 8, 2015).

4. Mary Williams Walsh, "State Woes Grow Too Big to Camouflage," *CNBC*, March 30, 2010, www.cnbc.com/id/36096491/ (accessed April 8, 2015).

5. Daniel Gilbert, "Exxon to Disclose 'Emissions Risk,'" *The Wall Street Journal*, March 21, 2014, p. B1; Economist staff, "Schumpeter | A green light," *The Economist*, March 29, 2014, p. 74; AICPA, "Sustainability Reporting and Accounting—FAQ," http://www.aicpa.org/InterestAreas/BusinessIndustryAndGovernment/Resources/Sustainability/Pages/Sustainability-FAQs.aspx (accessed September 8, 2014).

6. Sarah Johnson, "Averting Revenue-Recognition Angst," *CFO*, April 2012, p. 21.

7. Deanna White, "Wristbands Get Indiana CPA Firm Moving at Tax Time," *Accounting Web*, February 18, 2014, http://www.accountingweb.com/article/wristbands-get-indiana-cpa-firm-moving-tax-time/223103 (accessed September 19, 2014); MOVABLE website, http://movable.com/our-solutions/the-movement (accessed September 19, 2014); Dauby O'Connor &Zalewski, LLC website, http://www.doz.net/ (accessed September 19, 2014); "Indianapolis Star Top Workplaces," *Indianapolis Star*, http://www.topworkplaces.com/frontend.php/regional-list/list/indystar (accessed September 19, 2014); "Company Overview of Dauby O'Connor & Zalewski, LLC," *Bloomberg Businessweek*, September 19, 2014, http://investing.businessweek.com/research/stocks/private/snapshot.asp?privcapId=46333433 (accessed September 19, 2014).

8. "Got 'em, Gotham," *The Economist*, July 12, 2014, p. 59; Juliet Chung, "Gotham City Research Unmasks Gowex but Stays in Shadows," *The Wall Street Journal*, July 9, 2014, http://online.wsj.com/articles/gotham-city-research-works-in-the-shadows-1404842379 (accessed December 15, 2014); Investopedia Staff, "Short Selling: What Is Short Selling?" *Investopedia*, http://www.investopedia.com/university/shortselling/shortselling1.asp (accessed December 15, 2014); "Bear Raid," *Investopedia*, http://www.investopedia.com/terms/b/bearraid.asp (accessed December 15, 2014).

9. City of Maricopa, "City Finance Department Receives Distinguished Presentation Award for Its Budget," March 25, 2014, http://www.maricopa-az.gov/web/finance-administrativeservice-home/1029-city-s-finance-department-recieves-distinguished-budget-presentation-award-for-its-budget (accessed April 8, 2015).

10. "Accountants and Auditors: Occupational Outlook Handbook," *Bureau of Labor Statistics*, April 6, 2012, www.bls.gov/ooh/Businessand-Financial/Accountants-andauditors.htm (accessed April 8, 2015).

Chapter 15

1. Paul Krugman, "Why Is Deflation Bad?" *The New York Times*, August 2, 2010, http://krugman.blogs.nytimes.com/2010/08/02/why-is-deflation-bad/ (accessed April 8, 2015).

2. Economic Research Federal Reserve Bank of St. Louis, "Currency in Circulation," June 4, 2014, http://research.stlouisfed.org/fred2/series/WCURCIR (accessed April 8, 2015).

3. Economist staff, "Why the Swiss Unpegged the Franc," January 18, 2015, *Economist*, http://www.economist.com/blogs/economist-explains/2015/01/economist-explains-13 (accessed April 8, 2015); "Swiss-made Products Become More Expensive as Franc Rises," *The Sydney Morning Herald*, January 16, 2015, http://www.smh.com.au/national/swissmade-products-become-more-expensive-as-franc-rises-20150116-12riei.html (accessed April 8, 2015).

4. "Weird and Wonderful Money Facts and Trivia," *Happy Worker*, www.happyworker.com/magazine/facts/weird-and-wonderful-money-facts (accessed April 8, 2015).

5. Ibid.

6. The Department of the Treasury Bureau of Engraving and Printing, "Security Features," http://www.moneyfactory.gov/anticounterfeiting/securityfeatures.html (accessed April 8, 2015).

7. Various annual reports of the U.S. Mint.

8. Jessica Dickler, "Americans Still Relying on Credit Cards to Get By," *CNN Money*, May 23, 2012, http://money.cnn.com/2012/05/22/pf/credit-card/index.htm (accessed April 8, 2015); Martin Merzer, "Survey: Students Fail the Credit Card Test," *Fox Business*, April 16,

2012, http://www.foxbusiness.com/personal-finance/2012/04/09/survey-students-fail-credit-card-test/ (accessed April 8, 2015).

9. Saabhira Chaudhuri, "Banks Battle Weight Issues," *The Wall Street Journal*, July 22, 2014, p. C1; Peter Ryan, "Raising the Bank 'SIFI Threshold' Would Make the Financial System Safer," *Bipartisan Policy Center*, April 16, 2014, http://bipartisanpolicy.org/blog/raising-sifi-threshold-would-make-financial-system-safer/ (accessed December 15, 2014); "How the Fight Over the $50B 'Systemic' Cutoff Will Play Out," *bankinvestmentconsultant*, http://www.bankinvestmentconsultant.com/news/regulatory_compliance/how-the-fight-over-the-50-billion-systemic-cutoff-will-play-out-2690861-1.html (accessed December 15, 2014); Economist staff, "Too Small to Torture," May 17, 2014, *The Economist*, May 17, 2014, http://www.economist.com/news/finance-and-economics/21602273-federal-reserve-contemplates-sliding-scale-bureaucracy-banks-too-small (accessed December 15, 2014).

10. "Deposit Insurance Simplification Fact Sheet," FDIC website, www.unitedamericanbank.com/pdfs/FDIC-Insurance-Coverage-Fact-Sheet.pdf (accessed April 8, 2015).

11. Paul Davidson, "Small Firms Seeing More Cash," *USA Today*, January 20, 2014, p. 1B; Karen Mills, "Why Small-Business Lending Has Not Recovered," *Forbes*, August 8, 2014, http://www.forbes.com/sites/hbsworkingknowledge/2014/08/04/why-small-business-lending-has-not-recovered/ (accessed December 15, 2014); Rohit Arora, "Big Banks Are Lending to Bigger Small Businesses," *Small Business Trends*, January 26, 2014, http://smallbiztrends.com/2014/01/big-banks-are-lending-bigger-small-businesses.html (accessed December 15, 2014).

12. "NACHA Reports More Than 18 Billion ACH Payments in 2007," The Free Library, May 19, 2008, www.thefreelibrary.com/NACHA+Reports+More+Than+18+Billion+ACH+Payments+in+2007.-a0179156311 (accessed April 8, 2015).

13. "From the Vault . . ." Ohio Commerce Bank, Winter 2012, http://website-tools.net/google-keyword/site/www.ohiocommerce-bank.com (accessed June 16, 2014).

14. Rhonda Abrams "Strategies: More Small Firms Look at Mobile-Pay Options," *USA Today*, May 15, 2013, http://www.usatoday.com/story/money/columnist/abrams/2013/05/03/small-business-mobile-payments/2131029/ (accessed November 25, 2014); Jon Swartz and Brett Molina, "Take a Stand, and Deliver Digital Cash Register," *USA Today*, May 14, 2013, http://usatoday30.usatoday.com/MONEY/usaedition/2013-05-15-Square-Stand-turns-iPad-into-digital-cash-register_ST_U.htm (accessed November 25, 2014); Christina Chaey, "Square's Stand iPad Register Comes to Apple and Best Buy Retail Stores," *Fast Company*, http://www.fastcompany.com/3014027/fast-feed/squares-stand-ipad-register-comes-to-apple-and-best-buy-retail-stores (accessed

November 25, 2014); "Square Stand," Square website, https://squareup.com/stand (accessed November 25, 2014).

15. JPMorgan 2013 Annual Report, p. 10.

16. Kickstarter, "Seven Things to Know about Kickstarter," https://www.kickstarter.com/hello?ref=footer (accessed April 8, 2015).

17. "CSI Pennsylvania," *CFO Magazine*, March 2008, p. 92.

Chapter 16

1. Sponsored by DuPont and *CR Magazine*, "Good for the Planet and the Bottom Line," *Fortune*, April 29, 2013, advertisement; DuPont, "Expertise That Delivers Business Success," http://www.dupont.com/products-and-services/consulting-services-process-technologies/brands/sustainable-solutions.html (accessed September 8, 2014); DuPont, *2013 Global Sustainability Report*, http://www.dupont.com/content/dam/assets/corporate-functions/our-approach/sustainability/documents/DuPont%202013%20Global%20Reporting%20Initiative%20Report_Final.pdf (accessed September 8, 2014); DuPont, *2013 Global Reporting Initiative*, http://www.dupont.com/content/dam/assets/corporate-functions/our-approach/sustainability/documents/DuPont%202013%20Global%20Reporting%20Initiative%20Report_Final.pdf (accessed September 8, 2014); DuPont, "Market-Facing Goals," http://www.dupont.com/corporate-functions/our-approach/sustainability/commitments/goals-progress/articles/market-facing-goals.html (accessed September 8, 2014).

2. Calculated by Geoff Hirt from Apple's annual reports and website on April 7, 2015.

3. Adam Lashinsky, "Can't Find a Better Man," *Fortune*, February 24, 2014, p. 26; Maveron website, http://www.maveron.com/consumer-only-venture-capital (accessed December 10, 2014); Robert Celashi, "Maveron's Millions and Millions: How Howard Schultz's VC Firm Hits It Big with Consumer Bets," *Upstart Business Journal*, April 26, 2014, http://upstart.bizjournals.com/money/loot/2014/04/26/maveron-zulilly-ipo.html (accessed December 10, 2014).

4. Joshua Kennon, "Should You Invest in an IPO?" About.com, http://beginnersinvest.about.com/od/investmentbanking/a/aa073106a.htm (accessed April 9, 2015).

5. Peter Coy, "Admit It, You Didn't Read a Word of This," *Bloomberg Businessweek*, May 19–25, 2014, pp. 25–27; Arthur J. Radin, "Have We Created Financial Statement Disclosure Overload?" http://www.nysscpa.org/cpajournal/2007/1107/perspectives/p6.htm (accessed December 17, 2014); Ken Tysiac, "Streamlining Disclosures a Tricky Job for FASB," *Journal of Accountancy*, December 12, 2012, http://journalofaccountancy.com/news/2012/dec/20127006.html (November 28, 2014).

6. Vincent Ryan, "From Wall Street to Main Street," *CFO Magazine*, June 2008, pp. 85–86.

name index

subject index

Ford Motor Co., 84, 109, 110, 115, 140, 160, 215, 254, 281, 302, 312
Foreign corporations, 84
Foreign Corrupt Practices Act, 27
Forensic accounting, 268–269
Forest Stewardship Council, 40
Formal communications, 146
Forrester Research, 261
Fortune 500 companies, 183, 189, 192, 194, 250, 257
Fortune magazine, 324
Four Seasons, 131
Foxconn, 147, 178
Franchisee, 106
Franchiser, 106
Franchising, 72, 106–107, 110
Fraud, 46, 296–297
Freddie Mac, 153
Free-enterprise system, 8–9
Free-rein leaders, 124
Fringe benefits, 201
Frito-Lay, 117
Functional departmentalization, 135
Future trends
    for banking institutions, 305–307
    for small businesses, 108–110

G

GEICO Insurance, 303
Genentech, 174
General Agreement on Tariffs and Trade (GATT), 66
General Dynamics, 89
General Electric, 40, 73, 85, 110, 115, 123, 139, 143, 168, 213, 253, 302
General Mills, 84, 160
General Motors, 71, 73, 85, 113, 127, 136, 151, 160, 223, 234, 302, 312
General partnerships, 80–81
Generally accepted accounting principles (GAAP), 267, 275
Generic products, 233
Geographic characteristics, 217
Geographic departmentalization, 135–136
Gillette, 233
Givebacks, 203
Givelocity, 190
Glass Steagall Act (1929), 300
Global strategy, 74, 75
Global warming, 37–38, 62, 223
Globalization, 74, 75
    See also International business
GMO labeling, 18
Goals, 3–4, 114–115, 180
Goal-setting theory, 180
GoFundMe, 307
Gold Violin, 108
Goldman Sachs, 180, 303, 320
Google, 18, 29, 50, 62, 78, 84, 91, 139, 183, 184, 199, 200, 206, 219, 231, 232, 234, 241, 243, 249, 250, 255, 263, 280–281, 286–287, 319
GoPro, 257
Government
    economic role of, 17–19
    top-level management in, 120
Government regulations
    partnerships and, 82
    sole proprietorships and, 79
Gowex, 284
Grading, 211
Grameen Bank, 98

Granite Construction, 32–33
Grapevines, 146
Great Recession, 13
Greece, 68, 270
Green businesses, 41, 160
Green Mountain Coffee, 135
Greenland, 62
Greenwashing, 40
Grocery Manufacturers Association, 18
Gross domestic product (GDP), 13–14
Gross income, 275
Groups in organizations, 142, 143
Growth, managing, 104
Gulf Oil, 17

H

Habitat for Humanity, 3, 18, 152
Hackers, 264
Hamburger University, 194
Hampton Creek, 102, 242
Hampton Inn, 211
Handshake deals, 46
Harley-Davidson, 162
Hasbro, 222
Hawthorne studies, 174
Headhunters, 189
Hebrew National, 244
Hello Products, 242
Herbalife, 100, 115, 237
Hershey Foods, 156, 168
Hertz, 92, 125
Herzberg's two-factor theory, 176–177
Hewlett-Packard, 78, 123, 151, 162, 180, 220
Hierarchy of needs, 175–176
High technology, 101
Hilton Hotels and Resorts, 177, 220
Hiring standards, 41
Hispanic population, 108, 216
HJ Heinz, 85, 116
Holiday Inn, 72
Home Depot, 4, 18, 40, 99, 199, 251, 264, 323
Home equity loans, 300
Home sourcing, 100
Home-based businesses, 109
Honda, 227
Honesty, 29–31
Horizontal communication, 146
Horizontal mergers, 92
Hostess, 48
Hostile takeovers, 92
Hot Wheels, 242
Housing bubble, 322–323
H&R Block, 72
HSBC Finance Corporation, 310
Hulu, 257
Human relations
    management skills in, 123–124
    overview on the nature of, 171–173
Human resources, 6
Human resources management (HRM), 187–207
    compensation plans and, 198–201
    employee empowerment and, 206
    explanation of, 187
    job opportunities in, 207
    legal issues related to, 192–193
    orientation function of, 193
    performance appraisals and, 194–196
    planning process in, 187–188
    recruitment function of, 188–189
    selection function of, 189–192
    team exercise related to, 207
    training and development and, 194

    trends related to, 206–207
    turnover and, 196–198
    unionized employees and, 201–204
    workforce diversity and, 204–206
Human resources managers, 122, 187
Human Side of Enterprise, The (McGregor), 177
Hungary, 12
Hyatt Hotels, 153, 181
Hygiene factors, 176–177
Hyperinflation, 12

I

Iams, 221
IBM, 85, 110, 123, 139, 143, 145, 158, 162, 181, 232, 233, 315
Ideas
    development of, 227–228
    screening of, 228–229
Identity theft, 50, 263–264
IKEA, 155–156
Imgur, 109, 257
Immigrant population, 108
Implied warranty, 46
Import tariffs, 63
Importing, 59, 71
Inactives, 261
Incentive systems, 198
Income statements, 275–277
    definition of, 275
    examples of, 276, 277
    expenses on, 276–277
    net income on, 277
    revenue on, 275
    temporary nature of, 277
Incorporators, 84
Independence, 101–102
Independent sales representatives (ISRs), 198
India, 62, 74, 163
Individual retirement accounts (IRAs), 302–303
Industrial Revolution, 16, 213
Industrialized nations, 61
Industry analysis, 286–287
Inflation, 12, 15
Infomercials, 243
Informal communications, 146
Informal influencers, 206
Informal organization, 146
Information technology (IT) managers, 122
Informational roles, 123
Infrastructure, 61
Initial public offering (IPO), 86, 320
Inn at Little Washington, 152–153
Innovation, 99
Inputs
    definition of, 151
    uniformity of, 154
Inside directors, 87
Insider trading, 29
Insourcing, 73
Inspection process, 168
Instagram, 255, 257, 258
Institute of Management Accountants, 269
Insurance companies, 302
Intangible property, 47
Integrated marketing communications, 241
Intel, 85, 123, 154, 155, 197
Intellectual property, 47, 51, 63, 264
Intensive distribution, 239
Intercontinental Exchange (ICE), 321
Intermittent organizations, 158
International Association of Privacy Professionals, 119

in a nutshell

Goals, activities, and participants make up the fundamentals of business. Understanding the basics of economics and applying them to the United States economy will further your understanding of how business works and provide a framework for learning about business.

The following statements will test your take-away knowledge from this chapter. Do your best to explain each one in the space provided.

LO 1-1 Define basic concepts such as business, product, and profit.

LO 1-2 Identify the main participants and activities of business and explain why studying business is important.

LO 1-3 Define economics and compare the four types of economic systems.

LO 1-4 Describe the role of supply, demand, and competition in a free-enterprise system.

LO 1-5 Specify why and how the health of the economy is measured.

LO 1-6 Trace the evolution of the American economy and discuss the role of the entrepreneur in the economy.

Did your answers include the following important points?

LO 1-1. Define basic concepts such as business, product, and profit.

- A business is individuals or organizations who try to earn a profit by providing products that satisfy people's needs.
- A product is a good, service, or idea that has both tangible and intangible characteristics that provide satisfaction and benefits.
- Profit, the basic goal of business, is the difference between what it costs to make and sell a product and what a customer pays for it.

LO 1-2. Identify the main participants and activities of business and explain why studying business is important.

- The three main participants in business are owners, employees, and customers, but others—government regulators, suppliers, social groups, and so on—are also important.
- Management involves planning, organizing, and controlling the tasks required to carry out the work of the company.
- Marketing refers to those activities—research, product development, promotion, pricing, and distribution—designed to provide goods and services that satisfy customers.
- Finance refers to activities concerned with funding a business and using its funds effectively, and studying business can help you prepare for a career and become a better consumer.

LO 1-3. Define economics and compare the four types of economic systems.

- Economics is the study of how resources are distributed for the production of goods and services within a social system, and an economic system describes how a particular society distributes its resources.
- Communism is an economic system in which the people, without regard to class, own all the nation's resources, whereas in a socialist system, the government owns and operates basic industries, but individuals own most businesses.

- Under capitalism, individuals own and operate the majority of businesses that provide goods and services.
- Mixed economies have elements from more than one economic system; most countries have mixed economies.

LO 1-4. Describe the role of supply, demand, and competition in a free-enterprise system.

- Supply is the number of goods or services that businesses are willing to sell at different prices at a specific time.
- Demand is the number of goods and services that consumers are willing to buy at different prices at a specific time.
- Competition is the rivalry among businesses to persuade consumers to buy goods or services.

LO 1-5. Specify why and how the health of the economy is measured.

- A country measures the state of its economy to determine whether it is expanding or contracting and whether the country needs to take steps to minimize fluctuations.
- One commonly used measure is gross domestic product (GDP), the sum of all goods and services produced in a country during a year.
- A budget deficit occurs when a nation spends more than it takes in from taxes.

LO 1-6. Trace the evolution of the American economy and discuss the role of the entrepreneur in the economy.

- The American economy has evolved through the early economy, the Industrial Revolution, the manufacturing economy, the marketing economy, and the service- and Internet-based economy of today.
- Entrepreneurs play an important role because they risk their time, wealth, and efforts to develop new goods, services, and ideas that fuel the growth of the American economy.

Practical Application

LO 1-1

- When purchasing a product, the consumer is actually buying its anticipated benefits and _____.
- If a business is to be successful in the long run, it must treat its customers, employees, and community with social _____.
- The goal of business is to earn _____.

LO 1-2

- _____ involves activities designed to provide goods and services that fulfill needs and desires of consumers.
- When a business fails or does not make a profit, _____ have the most to lose.
- Advertising, personal selling, coupons, and sweepstakes are forms of _____.

LO 1-3

- Private property, profits, independent business decisions, and choice are rights associated with _____.
- In _____, consumers have a limited choice of goods and services, and prices are usually high.
- Most countries operate as _____, which have elements from more than one economic system.

LO 1-4

- In _____, there are many small businesses selling one standardized product.
- The market structure that exists when there are very few businesses selling a product is called a(n) _____.
- The quantity of products that businesses are willing to sell at different prices at specific times is called _____.

LO 1-5

- During a(n) _____ there is a decline in production, employment, and income.
- _____ is the sum of all goods and services produced in a country during a year.
- A(n) _____ occurs when a nation spends more than it takes in from taxes.

LO 1-6

- The Industrial Revolution changed the United States from an agricultural economy to a(n) _____ one.
- _____ industries account for almost 80 percent of the American economy today.
- A person who risks his or her wealth and time to develop an innovative product or idea for profit is called a(n) _____.

in a nutshell

You must understand the role of ethics and social responsibility in making good business decisions. Learning to recognize business ethics issues, how businesses can improve their ethical behavior, and the impact of how companies respond to these issues is the basis of social responsibility.

The following statements will test your take-away knowledge from this chapter. Do your best to explain each one in the space provided.

LO 2-1 Define business ethics and social responsibility and examine their importance.

LO 2-2 Detect some of the ethical issues that may arise in business.

LO 2-3 Specify how businesses can promote ethical behavior.

LO 2-4 Explain the four dimensions of social responsibility.

LO 2-5 Debate an organization's social responsibilities to owners, employees, consumers, the environment, and the community.

Did your answers include the following important points?

LO 2-1. Define business ethics and social responsibility and examine their importance.

- The principles and standards that determine acceptable conduct in business organizations are defined as business ethics.
- A business's obligation to maximize its positive impact and minimize its negative impact on society illustrates the concept of social responsibility.
- Business ethics relates to an individual's or a work group's decisions that society evaluates as right or wrong, whereas social responsibility is a broader concept that concerns the impact of the entire business's activities on society.
- Socially responsible businesses win the trust and respect of their employees, customers, and society and increase profits.
- Ethics is important in business because it builds trust and confidence in business relationships.

LO 2-2. Detect some of the ethical issues that may arise in business.

- An ethical issue is an identifiable problem, situation, or opportunity requiring a person or organization to choose from among several actions that must be evaluated as right or wrong.
- Ethical issues can be categorized in the context of their relation with conflicts of interest, fairness and honesty, communications, and business associations.

LO 2-3. Specify how businesses can promote ethical behavior.

- Businesses can promote ethical behavior among employees by limiting their opportunity to engage in misconduct.

- Formal codes of ethics, ethical policies, and ethics training programs reduce the incidence of unethical behavior by informing employees what is expected of them and providing punishments for those who fail to comply.

LO 2-4. Explain the four dimensions of social responsibility.

- The four dimensions of social responsibility are economic (being profitable), legal (obeying the law), ethical (doing what is right, just, and fair), and voluntary (being a good corporate citizen).

LO 2-5. Debate an organization's social responsibilities to owners, employees, consumers, the environment, and the community.

- Businesses must maintain proper accounting procedures, provide all relevant information about the performance of the firm to investors, and protect the owners' rights and investments.
- In relations with employees, businesses are expected to provide a safe workplace, pay employees adequately for their work, and treat them fairly.
- Consumerism refers to the activities undertaken by independent individuals, groups, and organizations to protect their rights as consumers.
- Increasingly, society expects businesses to take greater responsibility for the environment, especially with regard to animal rights as well as water, air, land, and noise pollution.
- Many businesses engage in activities to make the communities in which they operate better places for everyone to live and work.

Practical Application

LO 2-1

- If a very successful professional football team has been ignoring the players' use of illegal muscle-building steroids, the owners should begin focusing on improving the organization's _____.
- A company's obligation to increase its positive impact and decrease its negative impact is its _____.
- The _____ criminalized securities fraud and stiffened penalties for corporate fraud.

LO 2-2

- A(n) _____ exists when a person must choose whether to advance his or her own personal interests or those of others.
- Any payment, gift, or special favor intended to influence the outcome of a decision can be considered a(n) _____.
- If a person takes someone's work and presents it as his or her own without mentioning the source, it would be considered an act of _____.

LO 2-3

- _____ occurs when an employee exposes an employer's wrongdoing to outsiders.

- A set of formalized rules and standards that describe what a company expects of its employees is called a(n) _____.
- According to the text, ethical decisions in an organization are influenced by (1) individual moral standards, (2) the influence of managers and co-workers, and (3) _____.

LO 2-4

- Being profitable relates to _____ social responsibility.
- Consumers vote against firms they view as socially irresponsible by not _____.
- Philanthropic contributions made by a business to a charitable organization represent _____ social responsibility.

LO 2-5

- Businesses must first be responsible to their _____.
- Many of the laws regulating safety in the workplace are enforced by _____.
- _____ ensures the fair treatment of consumers who voice complaints about a purchased product.

in a **nutshell**

To learn about business in a global marketplace, you need to understand the nature of international business, including barriers to and promoters of trade across international boundaries. You must also consider the levels of organizational involvement in international business and the strategies used for trading across national borders.

The following statements will test your take-away knowledge from this chapter. Do your best to explain each one in the space provided.

LO 3-1 Explore some of the factors within the international trade environment that influence business.

LO 3-2 Investigate some of the economic, legal, political, social, cultural, and technological barriers to international business.

LO 3-3 Specify some of the agreements, alliances, and organizations that may encourage trade across international boundaries.

LO 3-4 Summarize the different levels of organizational involvement in international trade.

LO 3-5 Contrast two basic strategies used in international business.

Did your answers include the following important points?

LO 3-1. Explore some of the factors within the international trade environment that influence business.

- International business is the buying, selling, and trading of goods and services across national boundaries.
- Importing is the purchase of products and raw materials from another nation; exporting is the sale of domestic goods and materials to another nation.
- A nation's balance of trade is the difference in value between its exports and its imports: a negative balance of trade is a trade deficit.
- An absolute or comparative advantage in trade may determine what products a company from a particular nation will export.

LO 3-2. Investigate some of the economic, legal, political, social, cultural, and technological barriers to international business.

- Companies engaged in international trade must consider the effects of economic, legal, political, social, and cultural differences between nations.
- Wide-ranging legal and political barriers include differing laws (and enforcement), tariffs, exchange controls, quotas, embargoes, political instability, and war.
- Ambiguous cultural and social barriers involve differences in spoken and body language, time, holidays, and other observances and customs.

LO 3-3. Specify some of the agreements, alliances, and organizations that may encourage trade across international boundaries.

- Among the most important promoters of international business are the General Agreement on Tariffs and Trade, the World Trade Organization, the North American Free Trade Agreement, the European Union,

the Asia-Pacific Economic Cooperation, the Association of Southeast Asian Nations, the World Bank, and the International Monetary Fund.

LO 3-4. Summarize the different levels of organizational involvement in international trade.

- Countertrade agreements occur at the import–export level and involve bartering products for other products, and a trading company links buyers and sellers in different countries to foster trade.
- Licensing and franchising occurs when one company allows a foreign company to use its name, products, patents, brands, trademarks, raw materials, and production processes in exchange for a flat fee or royalty.
- Contract manufacturing occurs when a company hires a foreign company to produce a specified volume of the firm's product and allows the final product to carry the domestic firm's name. In a joint venture, companies work as a partnership and share the costs and operation of the business. A strategic alliance is a partnership formed to create competitive advantage on a worldwide basis.
- Direct investment involves purchasing overseas production and marketing facilities, whereas outsourcing involves transferring manufacturing to countries where labor and supplies are cheap. A multinational corporation is one that operates on a worldwide scale, without ties to any one nation or region. Offshoring is the relocation of a business process by a company, or a subsidiary, to another country.

LO 3-5. Contrast two basic strategies used in international business.

- A multinational strategy customizes products, promotion, and distribution according to cultural, technological, regional, and national differences, whereas a global strategy (globalization) standardizes products for the whole world as if it were a single entity.

Practical Application

LO 3-1

- South Africa holds a(n) _____ in diamond deposits in the world.
- The difference between the flow of money into and out of a country is called its _____.
- The transfer of manufacturing and other tasks to places where labor and other supplies are less expensive is called _____.

LO 3-2

- The United States' prohibition of imported Cuban cigars is an example of a(n) _____.
- A group of nations or companies that band together to act as a monopoly is known as a(n) _____.
- A country/business that wants to gain a quick entry into a new market sometimes engages in _____ its products.

LO 3-3

- The _____ makes short-term loans to member countries with trade deficits and provides foreign currencies to member nations.
- The _____ is the largest source of advice and assistance with loans for developing countries.
- Until 1993, each nation of the _____ functioned as a separate market.

LO 3-4

- When a company hires a foreign company to produce a specified volume of the firm's product to specification, it is engaging in _____.
- PepsiCo allows a Canadian firm to use its name, formula, and brands in return for a royalty. This arrangement is known as _____.
- In some industries, _____ allow companies to create competitive advantage on a worldwide basis.

LO 3-5

- Standardizing products for the whole world as if it were a single entity is a characteristic of _____ strategy.
- Most companies doing international business have used the _____ strategy; that is, they have customized their products and distribution to cultural and regional differences.
- The _____ is the global business solutions unit of the U.S. Department of Commerce that offers U.S. firms practical knowledge of international markets and industries, along with a global network.

in a nutshell

Sole proprietorship, partnership, and corporation are three primary forms of business that are used in traditional business, online-only business, or a combination of both. Other forms of business include S corporations, limited liability companies, and cooperatives. In organizing a business, it is helpful to understand the advantages and disadvantages of these forms of business as well as business trends.

The following statements will test your take-away knowledge from this chapter. Do your best to explain each one in the space provided.

LO 4-1 Define and examine the advantages and disadvantages of the sole proprietorship form of organization.

LO 4-2 Identify two types of partnership and evaluate the advantages and disadvantages of the partnership form of organization.

LO 4-3 Describe the corporate form of organization and cite the advantages and disadvantages of corporations.

LO 4-4 Define and debate the advantages and disadvantages of mergers, acquisitions, and leveraged buyouts.

Did your answers include the following important points?

LO 4-1. Define and examine the advantages and disadvantages of the sole proprietorship form of organization.

- The most common form of business is the sole proprietorship. The advantages of this form of business include the fact that it is easy and inexpensive to form, it allows for a high level of secrecy, all profits belong to the owner, the owner has complete control over the business, government regulation is minimal, taxes are paid only once, and the business can be closed easily.
- Disadvantages include the fact that the owner may have to use personal assets to borrow money, sources of external funds are difficult to find, the owner must have many diverse skills, the survival of the business is tied to the life of the owner and his or her ability to work, qualified employees are hard to find, and wealthy sole proprietors pay a higher tax rate than they would under the corporate form of business.

LO 4-2. Identify two types of partnership and evaluate the advantages and disadvantages of the partnership form of organization.

- Partnerships may be general or limited and offer the following advantages: They are easy to organize, they may have higher credit ratings because partners may have more combined wealth, partners can specialize, partnerships can make decisions faster than larger businesses, and government regulations are few.
- Disadvantages include the fact that general partners have unlimited liability for the debts of the partnership, partners are responsible for each other's decisions, the death or termination of one partner requires a new partnership agreement, it is difficult to sell a partnership interest at a fair price, the distribution of profits may not correctly reflect the amount of work done by each partner, and partnerships cannot find external sources of funds as easily as large corporations.

LO 4-3. Describe the corporate form of organization and cite the advantages and disadvantages of corporations.

- A corporation, which is owned by stockholders, is a legal entity created by the state, whose assets and liabilities are separate from those of its owners. They are chartered by a state through articles of incorporation and have a board of directors made up of corporate officers or people from outside the company.
- Advantages include the fact that owners have limited liability, ownership (stock) can be easily transferred, corporations are long-lasting, raising money is easier, and expansion into new businesses is simpler.
- Disadvantages include the fact that the company is taxed on its income and owners pay a second tax on any profits received as dividends, forming a corporation can be expensive, keeping trade secrets is difficult because so much information must be made available to the public and to government agencies, and owners and managers are not always the same and can have different goals.

LO 4-4. Define and debate the advantages and disadvantages of mergers, acquisitions, and leveraged buyouts.

- A merger occurs when two companies (usually corporations) combine to form a new company. An acquisition occurs when one company buys most of another company's stock, whereas in a leveraged buyout, a group of investors borrows money to acquire a company, using the assets of the purchased company to guarantee the loan.
- Advantages include the fact that they can help merging firms gain a larger market share in their industries, acquire valuable assets, and realize lower costs. They can also benefit stockholders by improving companies' market value and stock prices.
- Disadvantages include the fact that they can hurt companies if they force managers to focus on avoiding takeovers at the expense of productivity and profits, they may lead a company to take on too much debt, and they can harm employee morale and productivity.

Practical Application

LO 4-1

- One of the most popular and easiest to establish forms of business in the United States is the _____.
- An individual who is the sole owner of a business faces _____ liability in case of debt.

LO 4-2

- _____ are the least used form of business organization in the United States.
- The decision-making process in a partnership tends to be faster when the partnership is _____.
- In a partnership, owners must share _____, even though a bad decision may have been taken by one of them.

LO 4-3

- Another often-used name for stockholder is _____.
- A(n) _____ is one whose stocks anyone may buy, sell, or trade.
- The organizational form that many consider to be a blend of the best characteristics of corporations, partnerships, and sole proprietorships is the _____.

LO 4-4

- When two companies combine to form a new company, it is called a(n) _____.
- When companies operating at different, but related, levels of an industry merge, it is known as a(n) _____.
- XYZ, Inc. is attempting to avoid a hostile takeover by a corporate raider by allowing stockholders to buy more shares of stock at prices lower than current market value; the _____ method is being used here to avoid the takeover.

in a nutshell

A successful entrepreneur or small-business owner understands the advantages and disadvantages of owning a small business, challenges facing small businesses today, and why small businesses succeed or fail.

The following statements will test your take-away knowledge from this chapter. Do your best to explain each one in the space provided.

LO 5-1 Define entrepreneurship and small business.

LO 5-2 Investigate the importance of small business in the U.S. economy and why certain fields attract small business.

LO 5-3 Specify the advantages of small-business ownership.

LO 5-4 Summarize the disadvantages of small-business ownership, and analyze why many small businesses fail.

LO 5-5 Describe how you go about starting a small business and what resources are needed.

LO 5-6 Evaluate the demographic, technological, and economic trends that are affecting the future of small business.

LO 5-7 Explain why many large businesses are trying to "think small."

Did your answers include the following important points?

LO 5-1. Define entrepreneurship and small business.

- An entrepreneur is a person who creates a business or product and manages his or her resources and takes risks to gain a profit; entrepreneurship is the process of creating and managing a business to achieve desired objectives.
- A small business is one that is not dominant in its competitive area and does not employ more than 500 people.
- Social entrepreneurship is a growing trend among businesses. Social entrepreneurs are individuals who use entrepreneurship to address social problems.

LO 5-2. Investigate the importance of small business in the U.S. economy and why certain fields attract small business.

- Small businesses are vital to the American economy because they provide products, jobs, innovation, and opportunities.
- Retailing, wholesaling, services, manufacturing, and high technology attract small businesses because these industries are relatively easy to enter, require relatively low initial financing, and may experience less heavy competition.

LO 5-3. Specify the advantages of small-business ownership.

- Small-business ownership offers some personal advantages, including independence, freedom of choice, and the option of working at home.
- Business advantages include flexibility, the ability to focus on a few key customers, and the chance to develop a reputation for quality and service.

LO 5-4. Summarize the disadvantages of small-business ownership, and analyze why many small businesses fail.

- Small businesses have many disadvantages for their owners, such as expense, physical and psychological stress, and a high failure rate.
- Small businesses fail for many reasons: undercapitalization, management inexperience or incompetence, neglect, disproportionate burdens imposed by government regulation, and vulnerability to competition from larger companies.

LO 5-5. Describe how you go about starting a small business and what resources are needed.

- Have an idea for developing a small business and devise a business plan to guide the development of the business. Then you must decide what form of business ownership to use and provide funds, either your own or funds provided by friends, families, banks, investors, or other organizations.
- You must also decide whether to start a new business from scratch, buy an existing one, or buy a franchise operation.

LO 5-6. Evaluate the demographic, technological, and economic trends that are affecting the future of small business.

- Changing demographic trends include more older adults as baby boomers age; a large gain in individuals born between the early 1980s and early 2000s known as echo boomers, millennials, or Generation Y; and an increasing number of immigrants to the United States.
- Technological advances and an increase in service exports have created new opportunities for small companies to expand their operations abroad, whereas trade agreements and alliances have created an environment in which small business has fewer regulatory and legal barriers.
- Economic turbulence presents both opportunities for and threats to the survival of small businesses.

LO 5-7. Explain why many large businesses are trying to "think small."

- Large companies are copying small businesses in an effort to make their firms more flexible, resourceful, and innovative, and improve the bottom line.
- This involves downsizing and intrapreneurship, by which an employee takes responsibility for developing innovations within the larger organization.

Practical Application

LO 5-1

- Small businesses provide opportunities for _____ and _____ to succeed in business.
- The Small Business Administration was established to provide _____ assistance to small businesses.
- Small business refers to an owner-managed business that employs not more than _____ people.

LO 5-2

- Small businesses generated nearly _____ of all new jobs created in the United States in recent years.
- _____ attracts entrepreneurs because gaining experience and exposure is relatively easy.
- The fastest growing sector of the U.S. economy is represented by _____.

LO 5-3

- When market conditions change rapidly, a small business usually has fewer layers of management to work through in making decisions; this advantage of a small business is called _____.
- _____ is one of the leading reasons that entrepreneurs choose to go into business for themselves.
- Unlike many large corporations, small businesses can focus on developing products for a defined _____, that is, specific customers.

LO 5-4

- Many people turn a hobby into a business without identifying a(n) _____ for that product; this leads to failure.
- _____ is one of the leading reasons for business failure because most businesses suffer from seasonal variations in sales.
- Initially, the factor that probably affects a company's reputation more than anything else is poorly managed _____.

LO 5-5

- Since Rachel Hollings decided to purchase the rights to own and operate a McDonald's fast-food restaurant rather than start her own operation, she is probably a(n) _____.
- A mortgage is an example of _____.
- _____ are persons or organizations that agree to provide some funds for a new business in exchange for an ownership interest or stock.

LO 5-6

- The _____ segment of the population is probably the wealthiest in the United States.
- The _____ population, the nation's largest minority group, is a vast untapped market for small businesses.
- Deregulation of the _____ market and an interest in fuel conservation has spawned many small businesses.

LO 5-7

- Reducing management layers, corporate staff, and work tasks to make a firm more flexible, resourceful, and innovative is known as _____.
- Individuals who take responsibility for the development of innovations of any kind within larger organizations are called _____.

in a nutshell

A successful manager needs to possess certain skills and follow steps for effective decision making. In doing so, managers accomplish various functions and participate in differing levels and areas of management.

The following statements will test your take-away knowledge from this chapter. Do your best to explain each one in the space provided.

LO 6-1 Define management, and explain its role in the achievement of organizational objectives.

LO 6-2 Describe the major functions of management.

LO 6-3 Distinguish among three levels of management and the concerns of managers at each level.

LO 6-4 Specify the skills managers need in order to be successful.

LO 6-5 Summarize the systematic approach to decision making used by many business managers.

Copyright © 2017 by McGraw-Hill Education ISBN 1259578143 | Ferrell M 5e

Did your answers include the following important points?

LO 6-1. Define management, and explain its role in the achievement of organizational objectives.

- Management is a process designed to achieve an organization's objectives by using its resources effectively and efficiently in a changing environment.
- Managers make decisions about the use of the organization's resources and are concerned with planning, organizing, staffing, directing, and controlling the organization's activities to reach its objectives.

LO 6-2. Describe the major functions of management.

- Planning is the process of determining the organization's objectives and deciding how to accomplish them. Organizing is the structuring of resources and activities to accomplish those objectives efficiently and effectively.
- Staffing is the hiring of people with the necessary skills to carry out the work of the company.
- Directing is motivating and leading employees to achieve organizational objectives and controlling the process of evaluating and correcting activities to keep the organization on course.

LO 6-3. Distinguish among three levels of management and the concerns of managers at each level.

- Top management is responsible for the whole organization and focuses primarily on strategic planning. Middle management develops plans for specific operating areas and carries out the general guidelines set by top management.
- First-line, or supervisory, management supervises the workers and day-to-day operations.
- Managers can also be categorized according to their area of responsibility: finance, production and operations, human resources, marketing, or administration.

LO 6-4. Specify the skills managers need in order to be successful.

- Managers need technical expertise, conceptual skills, analytical skills, human relations skills, and leadership skills.
- Leadership is the ability to influence employees to work toward organizational goals.
- Managers can be classified into three types based on their leadership style. *Autocratic leaders* make all the decisions and then tell employees what must be done and how to do it. *Democratic leaders* involve their employees in decisions. *Free-rein leaders* let their employees work without much interference.
- Another type of leadership gaining in popularity is authentic leadership. Authentic leaders are passionate about the goals and mission of the company, display corporate values in the workplace, and form long-term stakeholder relationships.
- Employee empowerment occurs when employees are provided with the ability to take on responsibilities and make decisions about their jobs. To empower employees, leaders should adopt systems that support their ability to provide input and feedback on company decisions, encourage them to participate in decision making, and train them in leadership skills.

LO 6-5. Summarize the systematic approach to decision making used by many business managers.

- A systematic approach to decision making follows these steps: recognizing and defining the situation, developing options, analyzing options, selecting the best option, implementing the decision, and monitoring the consequences.

Practical Application

LO 6-1

- If a manager is concerned about doing work with the least cost and waste, her primary managerial concern is _____.
- _____ make decisions about the use of an organization's resources and are concerned with planning, organizing, leading, and controlling the organization's activities.
- Managers need to make efficient use of the company's _____ to reach organizational objectives.

LO 6-2

- The type of planning conducted on a long-range basis by top managers is usually called _____.
- Dividing work into small units and assigning it to individuals are tasks related to _____.
- Hiring people to carry out the work of the organization is known as _____.

LO 6-3

- _____ are responsible for tactical planning that will implement the general guidelines established by the top management.
- Decisions regarding adding new products, acquiring companies, and moving into foreign markets would most typically be made by the _____.
- Most people get their first managerial experience as _____ supervising workers and daily operations.

LO 6-4

- Joe met with department heads to listen to their opinions about buying a new machine. Although they all thought it was a good idea, Joe did not buy the machine. Joe's leadership style is _____.
- To train employees, answer questions, and provide guidance in doing a task, managers need _____.
- Those managers who can communicate well, understand the needs of others, and deal effectively with people inside and outside the organization are said to have good _____ skills.
- _____ leaders let their employees work without much interference.
- Authentic leaders are passionate about the goals and mission of the company, display _____ in the workplace, and form long-term _____.
- _____ occurs when employees are provided with the ability to take on responsibilities and make decisions about their jobs.

LO 6-5

- When analyzing options in the decision-making process, managers must consider the appropriateness and _____ of each option.
- Effective implementation of a major decision requires _____.
- Managers need to spend a lot of time in _____ with those who can help in the realization of organizational objectives.

active review card
Organization, Teamwork, and Communication

in a nutshell

An organization's culture affects its operations. It is important in organizing a business to understand the development of structure, including how tasks and responsibilities are organized through specialization and departmentalization, as well as the different forms organizational structure may take.

The following statements will test your take-away knowledge from this chapter. Do your best to explain each one in the space provided.

LO 7-1 Explain the importance of organizational culture.

LO 7-2 Define organizational structure, and relate how organizational structures develop.

LO 7-3 Describe how specialization and departmentalization help an organization achieve its goals.

LO 7-4 Determine how organizations assign responsibility for tasks and delegate authority.

LO 7-5 Compare and contrast some common forms of organizational structure.

LO 7-6 Distinguish between groups and teams, and identify the types of groups that exist in organizations.

LO 7-7 Describe how communication occurs in organizations.

Did your answers include the following important points?

LO 7-1. Explain the importance of organizational culture.

- Organizational culture is the firm's shared values, beliefs, traditions, philosophies, and role models for behavior.
- Organizational culture helps ensure that all members of a company share values and suggests rules for how to behave and deal with problems within the organization.

LO 7-2. Define organizational structure, and relate how organizational structures develop.

- Structure is the arrangement or relationship of positions within an organization; it develops when managers assign work activities to work groups and specific individuals and coordinate the diverse activities required to attain organizational objectives.
- Organizational structure evolves to accommodate growth, which requires people with specialized skills.

LO 7-3. Describe how specialization and departmentalization help an organization achieve its goals.

- Structuring an organization requires that management assign work tasks to specific individuals and groups. Under specialization, managers break labor into small, specialized tasks and assign employees to do a single task, fostering efficiency.
- Departmentalization is the grouping of jobs into working units.
- Businesses may departmentalize by function, product, geographic region, or customer, or they may combine two or more of these.

LO 7-4. Determine how organizations assign responsibility for tasks and delegate authority.

- Delegation of authority means assigning tasks to employees and giving them the power to make commitments, use resources, and take whatever actions are necessary to accomplish the tasks.

- The extent to which authority is delegated throughout an organization determines its degree of centralization.

LO 7-5. Compare and contrast some common forms of organizational structure.

- Line structures have direct lines of authority that extend from the top manager to employees at the lowest level of the organization.
- A multidivisional structure gathers departments into larger groups called divisions. A matrix or project-management structure sets up teams from different departments, thereby creating two or more intersecting lines of authority.

LO 7-6. Distinguish between groups and teams, and identify the types of groups that exist in organizations.

- A group is two or more persons who communicate, have a common identity, and have a common goal, whereas a team is a small group whose members have complementary skills; a common purpose, goals, and approach; and who hold themselves mutually accountable.
- The major distinction is that individual performance is most important in groups, while collective work group performance counts most in teams.
- Special kinds of groups include task forces, committees, project teams, product-development teams, quality-assurance teams, and self-directed work teams.

LO 7-7. Describe how communication occurs in organizations.

- Communication occurs both formally and informally in organizations. Formal communication may be downward, upward, horizontal, and even diagonal.
- Informal communication takes place through friendships and the grapevine.

Practical Application

LO 7-1

- Work philosophies, values, dress codes, work habits, extracurricular activities, and stories make up _____.

LO 7-2

- The arrangement or relationship of positions within an organization is called _____.

LO 7-3

- _____ departmentalization arranges jobs around the needs of various types of customers.
- General Motors is organized into these groups: GMC Trucks, Chevrolet, Buick, and Cadillac. This is called _____ departmentalization.
- Adam Smith illustrated improvements in efficiency through the application of _____.

LO 7-4

- An organization with many layers of managers is considered to be _____.
- An organization operating in a complex and unpredictable environment is likely to be _____.
- When the decisions of a company are very risky and low-level managers lack decision-making skills, the company will tend to _____.

LO 7-5

- The _____ of organization allows managers to specialize in their area of expertise.
- The _____ organizational form is likely to be complex and expensive.
- _____ permit delegation of decision-making authority, and ensure that better decisions are made faster.

LO 7-6

- A temporary group of employees responsible for bringing about a particular change is a(n) _____.
- A special type of project team formed to devise, design, and implement a new product is a(n) _____.
- A(n) _____ is a group of employees responsible for an entire work process or segment that delivers a product to an internal or external customer.

LO 7-7

- When managers recognize that a(n) _____ exists, they should use it to their advantage.
- Progress reports and complaints are part of _____ communication.
- When individuals from different organizational units and levels communicate with each other, it is called _____ communication.

in a nutshell

Production and operations management involves planning and designing the processes that will transform resources into finished products, managing the movement of resources through the transformation process, and ensuring that the products are of the quality expected by customers.

The following statements will test your take-away knowledge from this chapter. Do your best to explain each one in the space provided.

LO 8-1 Define operations management, and differentiate between operations and manufacturing.

LO 8-2 Explain how operations management differs in manufacturing and service firms.

LO 8-3 Describe the elements involved in planning and designing an operations system.

LO 8-4 Specify some techniques managers may use to manage the logistics of transforming inputs into finished products.

LO 8-5 Assess the importance of quality in operations management.

Did your answers include the following important points?

LO 8-1. Define operations management, and differentiate between operations and manufacturing

- Operations management (OM) is the development and administration of the activities involved in transforming resources into goods and services.
- The terms manufacturing and production are used interchangeably to describe the activities and processes used in making tangible products, whereas operations is a broader term used to describe the process of making both tangible and intangible products.

LO 8-2. Explain how operations management differs in manufacturing and service firms.

- Manufacturers and service firms both transform inputs and outputs, but service providers differ from manufacturers in several ways: They have greater customer contact because the service occurs at the point of consumption; their inputs and outputs are more variable than those of manufacturers; because of the human element, service providers are generally more labor intensive; and their productivity measurement is more complex.

LO 8-3. Describe the elements involved in planning and designing an operations system.

- Operations planning relates to decisions about what products to make and for whom and what processes and facilities are needed to produce them.
- Common facility layouts include fixed-position layouts, process layouts, and product layouts.
- Where to locate operations facilities is a crucial decision that depends on proximity to market, availability of raw materials, availability of

transportation, availability of power, climatic influences, availability of labor, and community characteristics.

- Technology is also vital to operations, particularly computer-assisted design, computer-assisted manufacturing, flexible manufacturing, robotics, and computer-integrated manufacturing.

LO 8-4. Specify some techniques managers may use to manage the logistics of transforming inputs into finished products.

- Logistics, or supply chain management, includes all the activities involved in obtaining and managing raw materials and component parts, managing finished products, packaging them, and getting them to customers.
- Common approaches to inventory control include the economic order quantity (EOQ) model, the just-in-time (JIT) inventory concept, and material-requirements planning (MRP).
- Logistics also includes routing and scheduling processes and activities to complete products.

LO 8-5. Assess the importance of quality in operations management.

- Quality is a critical element of operations management because low-quality products can hurt people and harm business.
- Quality control refers to the processes an organization uses to maintain its established quality standards.
- To control quality, a company must establish what standard of quality is desired and determine whether its products meet that standard through inspection.

Practical Application

LO 8-1

- Viewed from the perspective of operations, the money used to purchase a carpenter's tools and the electricity used to run his power saw are _____.
- If an employee is involved with transforming resources into goods and services, then she is in _____ .
- From an operations perspective, food sold at a restaurant and services provided by a plumbing company are _____ .

LO 8-2

- Due to the high degree of automation, products in the manufacturing industry are more _____ than those in the service industry.
- Most goods are manufactured _____ purchase, whereas most services are performed _____ purchase.
- The service industry is _____ intensive, whereas the manufacturing industry is _____ intensive.

LO 8-3

- Television sets, ballpoint pens, and tortilla chips are _____ products because they are produced on an assembly line.

- _____ involves building an item in self-contained units that can be combined or interchanged to create different products.
- When a customer goes to a print shop to order business cards, the manufacturing process used would most likely be _____ .

LO 8-4

- A company that requires all its resources to be brought to a central location is using a(n) _____ .
- Materials that have been purchased to be used as inputs in making other products are included in _____ .
- _____ helps engineers design components, products, and processes on the computer instead of on paper.

LO 8-5

- Determining how many items are to be inspected is called _____ .
- The degree to which a good or service meets the demands and requirements of customers is called _____ .
- _____ is a philosophy that a uniform commitment to quality in all areas of an organization will promote a culture that meets customers' perceptions of quality.

ANSWERS LO8-1 •inputs •operations •outputs LO8-2 •uniform •standardized •before; after •labor-; capital- LO8-3 •standardized •Modular design •customization LO8-4 •fixed-position layout •raw materials inventory •Computer-assisted design (CAD) LO8-5 •sampling •quality •Total quality management (TQM)

> ### in a nutshell
>
> Managers who understand the needs and motivations of workers and strategies for motivating them can help workers reach higher levels of productivity, subsequently contributing to the achievement of organizational goals.

The following statements will test your take-away knowledge from this chapter. Do your best to explain each one in the space provided.

LO 9-1 Define human relations, and determine why its study is important.

LO 9-2 Summarize early studies that laid the groundwork for understanding employee motivation.

LO 9-3 Compare and contrast the human relations theories of Abraham Maslow and Frederick Herzberg.

LO 9-4 Investigate various theories of motivation, including Theories X, Y, and Z; equity theory; and expectancy theory.

LO 9-5 Describe some of the strategies that managers use to motivate employees.

Copyright © 2017 by McGraw-Hill Education ISBN 1259578143 | Ferrell M 5e

Did your answers include the following important points?

LO 9-1. Define human relations, and determine why its study is important.

- Human relations is the study of the behavior of individuals and groups in organizational settings. Its focus is what motivates employees to perform on the job.
- Human relations is important because businesses need to understand how to motivate their employees to be more effective, boost workplace morale, and maximize employees' productivity and creativity.

LO 9-2. Summarize early studies that laid the groundwork for understanding employee motivation.

- Time and motion studies by Frederick Taylor and others helped them analyze how employees perform specific work tasks in an effort to improve their productivity.
- Taylor and the early practitioners of the classical theory of motivation felt that money and job security were the primary motivations of employees; however, the Hawthorne studies revealed that human factors also influence workers' behavior.

LO 9-3. Compare and contrast the human relations theories of Abraham Maslow and Frederick Herzberg.

- Abraham Maslow defined five basic needs of all people and arranged them in the order in which they must be satisfied: physiological, security, social, esteem, and self-actualization.

- Frederick Herzberg divided the characteristics of jobs into hygiene factors and motivational factors.
- Herzberg's hygiene factors can be compared to Maslow's physiological and security needs; motivational factors may include Maslow's social, esteem, and self-actualization needs.

LO 9-4. Investigate various theories of motivation, including Theories X, Y, and Z; equity theory; and expectancy theory.

- Douglas McGregor contrasted two views of management: Theory X suggests workers dislike work, whereas Theory Y suggests that workers not only like work but seek out responsibility to satisfy their higher-order needs.
- Theory Z stresses employee participation in all aspects of company decision making, whereas the equity theory indicates that how much people are willing to contribute to an organization depends on their assessment of the fairness, or equity, of the rewards they will receive in exchange.
- The expectancy theory states that motivation depends not only on how much a person wants something but also on the person's perception of how likely he or she is to get it.

LO 9-5. Describe some of the strategies that managers use to motivate employees.

- Strategies for motivating workers include behavior modification and job design. Among the job design strategies businesses use are job rotations, job enlargement, job enrichment, and flexible scheduling strategies.

Practical Application

LO 9-1

- An inner drive that directs behavior toward objectives is called _____.
- Good morale in an employee is likely to result in _____.
- A(n) _____ is the personal satisfaction that we feel from achieving a goal.

LO 9-2

- Prior to the Hawthorne studies, management theorists believed that the primary motivators of employees were job security and _____ .
- The birth of the study of human relations can be traced to _____ and _____ studies.

LO 9-3

- According to Maslow, living life to the fullest is most closely associated with fulfilling one's _____ need.
- According to Frederick Herzberg, the aspects that relate to the work setting form the _____ factors.

LO 9-4

- Jim has learned that his company is offering a Hawaiian vacation to its best salesperson. He almost won last year and really wants the trip. He is working very hard because he thinks he has a good chance to win. This exemplifies the _____ theory.
- Jack believes that he can get some extra work completed before the deadline by withholding his workers' vacation schedules until the job is completed. Jack is a manager who follows _____.
- The approach that suggests that imagination, ingenuity, and creativity can help solve organizational problems is _____ .

LO 9-5

- A work system that allows employees to choose their starting and ending times as long as they are at work during a specified core period is called _____.
- _____ adds tasks to a job instead of treating each task as a separate job.
- When Kelly reprimands Sarah each time Sarah is late for work, Kelly is applying _____ .

in a nutshell

Human resources managers need to plan for, recruit, and select qualified employees. Yet another aspect of the human resources manager's job is to train, appraise, compensate, and retain valued employees, which can present an added challenge among unionized and diverse employees.

The following statements will test your take-away knowledge from this chapter. Do your best to explain each one in the space provided.

LO 10-1 Define human resources management, and explain its significance.

LO 10-2 Summarize the processes of recruiting and selecting human resources for a company.

LO 10-3 Discuss how workers are trained and their performance appraised.

LO 10-4 Identify the types of turnover companies may experience, and explain why turnover is an important issue.

LO 10-5 Specify the various ways a worker may be compensated.

LO 10-6 Discuss some of the issues associated with unionized employees, including collective bargaining and dispute resolution.

LO 10-7 Describe the importance of diversity in the workforce.

Did your answers include the following important points?

LO 10-1. Define human resources management, and explain its significance.

- Human resources management refers to all the activities involved in determining an organization's human resources needs and acquiring, training, and compensating people to fill those needs.
- It is concerned with maximizing the satisfaction of employees and improving their efficiency to meet organizational objectives.

LO 10-2. Summarize the processes of recruiting and selecting human resources for a company.

- Human resources managers must determine the firm's human resources needs, develop a strategy to meet those needs, and recruit qualified applicants from whom management will select the employees.
- Selection is the process of collecting information about applicants, using that information to decide which to hire, and putting potential hires through the process of application, interview, testing, and reference checking.

LO 10-3. Discuss how workers are trained and their performance appraised.

- Training teaches employees how to do their job tasks, whereas development is training that augments the skills and knowledge of managers and professionals as well as current employees.
- Appraising performance involves identifying an employee's strengths and weaknesses on the job. Performance appraisals may be subjective or objective.

LO 10-4. Identify the types of turnover companies may experience, and explain why turnover is an important issue.

- A promotion is an advancement to a higher-level job with increased authority, responsibility, and pay. A transfer is a move to another job within the company, typically at the same level and wage.
- Separations occur when employees resign, retire, are terminated, or are laid off. Turnovers due to separation are expensive because of the time, money, and effort required to select, train, and manage new employees.

LO 10-5. Specify the various ways a worker may be compensated.

- Wages are financial compensation based on the number of hours worked or the number of units produced, whereas commissions are a fixed amount or percentage of a sale paid as compensation.
- Salaries are compensation calculated on a weekly, monthly, or annual basis, regardless of the number of hours worked or the number of items produced.
- Bonuses and profit sharing are types of financial incentives; benefits are nonfinancial forms of compensation such as vacation, insurance, and sick leave.

LO 10-6. Discuss some of the issues associated with unionized employees, including collective bargaining and dispute resolution.

- Collective bargaining is the negotiation process through which management and unions reach an agreement on a labor contract.
- If labor and management cannot agree on a contract, labor union members may picket, strike, or boycott the firm; management may lock out striking employees, hire strikebreakers, or form employers' associations.
- In a deadlock, labor disputes may be resolved by a third party.

LO 10-7. Describe the importance of diversity in the workforce.

- Companies with diverse workforces experience more productive use of human resources, reduced conflict, better work relationships among workers, increased commitment to and sharing of organizational goals, increased innovation and creativity, and enhanced ability to serve diverse customers.

Practical Application

LO 10-1

- In some companies, the department that handles the human resources management function is still called _____.
- The observation and study of information about a job is called _____.
- The qualifications required for a job are spelled out in a job _____.

LO 10-2

- _____ tests are restricted to specific government jobs and those involving security or access to drugs.
- Professionals who specialize in luring qualified people away from other companies are known as _____.
- Recruiting for entry-level managerial and professional positions is often carried out on _____.

LO 10-3

- The _____ includes a panel consisting of the employee's peers, superiors, and subordinates.
- If Greta received training by watching videotapes and discussing case studies, she received _____ training.
- Joseph has worked at his position for years. He is currently participating in management seminars at company expense. This is an example of _____.

LO 10-4

- Sandy Smith moved to a new job that involved more responsibility and an increase in compensation. She received a(n) _____.
- Susan was terminated from her job by her employer because she was repeatedly late to work. She was _____.
- A(n) _____ rate signifies problems with the selection and training program.

LO 10-5

- To motivate employees such as car salespersons to sell as much as they can, they are paid _____.
- June works at McDonald's part-time as a grill operator. She will probably be paid with the _____ compensation method.
- An employee stock ownership plan is an example of _____.

LO 10-6

- Workers seeking to improve pay and working conditions may join together to form a(n) _____.
- _____ make carrying out normal business operations difficult, if not impossible.
- A(n) _____ might be brought in as a neutral third party to keep union and management representatives talking.

LO 10-7

- Age, gender, and race are _____ characteristics of diversity.
- Secondary characteristics _____.
- Having a diverse workforce has many benefits. One benefit is the _____ use of a company's human resources.

ANSWERS LO10-1 •personnel •job analysis •specification **LO10-2** •Polygraph •headhunters •college and university campuses **LO10-3** •360-degree feedback system •classroom •development **LO10-4** •promotion •fired •high turnover **LO10-5** •commissions •time-wage •profit sharing **LO10-6** •labor union •Strikes •conciliator **LO10-7** •primary •can be changed •more productive

in a nutshell

Marketers develop marketing strategies to satisfy the needs and wants of their customers; they also need to consider buying behavior and use research to determine what consumers want to buy and why. Marketers also need to consider the impact of the environment on marketing activities.

The following statements will test your take-away knowledge from this chapter. Do your best to explain each one in the space provided.

LO 11-1 Define marketing, and describe the exchange process.

LO 11-2 Specify the functions of marketing.

LO 11-3 Explain the marketing concept and its implications for developing marketing strategies.

LO 11-4 Examine the development of a marketing strategy, including market segmentation and marketing mix.

LO 11-5 Investigate how marketers conduct marketing research and study buying behavior.

LO 11-6 Summarize the environmental forces that influence marketing decisions.

Did your answers include the following important points?

LO 11-1. Define marketing, and describe the exchange process.

- Marketing is a group of activities designed to expedite transactions by creating, distributing, pricing, and promoting goods, services, and ideas.
- Marketing facilitates exchange, the act of giving up one thing in return for something else. The central focus is to satisfy needs.

LO 11-2. Specify the functions of marketing.

- Marketing includes many varied and interrelated activities: buying, selling, transporting, storing, grading, financing, marketing research, and risk taking.

LO 11-3. Explain the marketing concept and its implications for developing marketing strategies.

- The marketing concept is the idea that an organization should try to satisfy customers' needs through coordinated activities that also allow it to achieve its goals.
- If a company does not implement the marketing concept by providing products that consumers need and want while achieving its own objectives, it will not survive.

LO 11-4. Examine the development of a marketing strategy, including market segmentation and marketing mix.

- A marketing strategy is a plan of action for creating a marketing mix for a specific target market. Some firms use a total-market approach, designating everyone as the target market.

- Most firms divide the total market into segments of people who have relatively similar product needs.
- A company using a concentration approach develops one marketing strategy for a single market segment, whereas a multisegment approach aims marketing efforts at two or more segments, developing a different marketing strategy for each segment.

LO 11-5. Investigate how marketers conduct marketing research and study buying behavior.

- Carrying out the marketing concept is impossible unless marketers know what, where, when, and how consumers buy; marketing research into the factors that influence buying behavior helps marketers develop effective marketing strategies.
- Marketing research is a systematic, objective process of getting information about potential customers to guide marketing decisions.
- Buying behavior is the decision processes and actions of people who purchase and use products.

LO 11-6. Summarize the environmental forces that influence marketing decisions.

- Several forces influence marketing activities: political, legal, regulatory, social, competitive, economic, and technological.

Practical Application

LO 11-1

- James Johnson has developed a new product, found a store willing to sell it, and agreed to help promote the product's sale. He is engaging in _____.
- When a customer hands the cashier $3 and receives a loaf of bread, a(n) _____ has occurred.

LO 11-2

- When a storeowner spends a lot of money for new products that have yet to be proved sales items, the owner is engaging in the marketing function of _____.
- Richard has acquired a supply of canned fruits and vegetables. He does not yet have a buyer for them, but he's using promotion and other activities to find a buyer. He is performing the marketing function of _____.

LO 11-3

- The goal of the marketing concept is _____.
- _____ remains a major element of any strategy to develop and manage long-term customer relationships.
- During the Industrial Revolution, new technologies fueled strong _____.

LO 11-4

- A plan of action for developing, pricing, distributing, and promoting products that meets the needs of a specific customer is a(n) _____.
- People visiting a ski resort would be viewed by a ski equipment storeowner as the business's _____.
- The aim of _____ is to communicate directly or indirectly with individuals, groups, and organizations to facilitate exchanges.

LO 11-5

- _____ is a systematic and objective process of getting information on potential customers.
- _____ is a psychological variable of buyer behavior.
- _____ are the least expensive data to collect.

LO 11-6

- Purchasing power, recession, and inflation are associated with _____ forces.
- The public's opinions and attitudes toward living standards, ethics, and the environment are considered _____ forces.

in a nutshell

There are four dimensions of marketing—product, price, distribution, and promotion. These elements are used to develop a marketing strategy that builds customer relationships and satisfaction.

The following statements will test your take-away knowledge from this chapter. Do your best to explain each one in the space provided.

LO 12-1 Describe the role of product in the marketing mix, including how products are developed, classified, and identified.

LO 12-2 Define price, and discuss its importance in the marketing mix, including various pricing strategies a firm might employ.

LO 12-3 Identify factors affecting distribution decisions, such as marketing channels and intensity of market coverage.

LO 12-4 Specify the activities involved in promotion, as well as promotional strategies and promotional positioning.

Copyright © 2017 by McGraw-Hill Education ISBN 1259578143 | Ferrell M 5e

Did your answers include the following important points?

LO 12-1. Describe the role of product in the marketing mix, including how products are developed, classified, and identified.

- Products are among a firm's most visible contacts with consumers and must meet consumers' needs to be successful. New-product development is a multistep process including idea development, the screening of new ideas, business analysis, product development, test marketing, and commercialization.
- Products are classified as either consumer or business products. Consumer products can be further classified as convenience, shopping, or specialty products.
- The business product classifications are raw materials, major equipment, component parts, processed materials, supplies, and industrial services.
- Products can also be classified by the stage of the product life cycle. Identifying products includes branding, packaging, and labeling.

LO 12-2. Define price, and discuss its importance in the marketing mix, including various pricing strategies a firm might employ.

- Price is the value placed on an object exchanged between a buyer and a seller. Pricing objectives include survival, maximization of profits and sales volume, and maintenance of the status quo.
- A firm may use price skimming or penetration pricing when introducing a new product. Psychological pricing, reference pricing, and price discounting are other strategies.

LO 12-3. Identify factors affecting distribution decisions, such as marketing channels and intensity of market coverage.

- Making products available to customers is facilitated by middlemen or intermediaries, who bridge the gap between the producer of the product and its ultimate user.
- A marketing channel is a group of marketing organizations that directs the flow of products from producers to consumers.
- Market coverage relates to the number and variety of outlets that make products available to customers; it may be intensive, selective, or exclusive.

LO 12-4. Specify the activities involved in promotion, as well as promotional strategies and promotional positioning.

- Promotion encourages marketing exchanges by persuading individuals, groups, and organizations to accept goods, services, and ideas. The promotion mix includes advertising, personal selling, publicity, and sales promotion.
- A push strategy attempts to motivate intermediaries to push the product down to the customers, whereas a pull strategy tries to create consumer demand for a product so that the consumers exert pressure on marketing channel members to make the product available.
- Typical promotion objectives are to stimulate demand; stabilize sales; and inform, remind, and reinforce customers. Promotional positioning is the use of promotion to create and maintain an image of the product in the mind of the buyer.

Practical Application

LO 12-1

- _____ allows a company to discover the strengths and weaknesses of a product before it is fully launched in the market.
- _____ are less expensive than manufacturer brands and are owned and controlled by a wholesaler or retailer.
- _____ generally appeal to those consumers who are willing to sacrifice quality and product consistency for the sake of lower prices.

LO 12-2

- The pricing policy that allows a company to cover the product's development cost most quickly is _____.
- _____ enables a product to enter the market and rapidly gain market share.
- A cosmetics company believes that it makes more sense to sell its eye shadow at $11.99 rather than $12.00; it is using _____.

LO 12-3

- _____ buy products from manufacturers and sell them to consumers for home and household use.
- When a product is to be made available in as many outlets as possible, wholesalers and retailers engage in _____.

LO 12-4

- When Ford pays a television network to air its commercial, it is using _____.
- When Chiquita uses newspaper ads to introduce its new fruit drink to consumers before introducing it to supermarkets, it is using the _____.
- The mass media willingly carry _____ for a company or product, when believing it has general public interest.

in a nutshell

You must understand the concepts of digital media and digital marketing and how they have become extremely important in strategic planning. The Internet and social networking are becoming increasingly important in people's lives, so you need to understand their impact on business today.

The following statements will test your take-away knowledge from this chapter. Do your best to explain each one in the space provided.

LO 13-1 Define digital media and digital marketing, and recognize their increasing value in strategic planning.

LO 13-2 Demonstrate the role of digital marketing, and define social networking in today's business environment.

LO 13-3 Show how digital media affect the marketing mix.

LO 13-4 Illustrate how businesses can use different types of social networking media.

LO 13-5 Identify legal and ethical considerations in digital media.

Copyright © 2017 by McGraw-Hill Education ISBN 1259578143 | Ferrell M 5e

Did your answers include the following important points?

LO 13-1. Define digital media and digital marketing, and recognize their increasing value in strategic planning.

- Digital media are electronic media that function using digital codes—available via computers and other digital services such as cell phones and smartphones.
- Digital marketing uses digital media to create communications and exchanges with customers.

LO 13-2. Demonstrate the role of digital marketing, and define social networking in today's business environment.

- Firms can use real-time exchanges to stimulate interactive communication, forge closer relationships, and learn more accurately about consumer and supplier needs.
- Digital communication is making it easier for businesses to conduct marketing research, provide price and product information, and advertise.

LO 13-3. Show how digital media affect the marketing mix.

- The Internet is a new distribution channel making products available at the right time, at the right place, and in the right quantities.
- Online promotions are creating well-informed consumers.
- Digital media enhance the value of products by providing extra benefits such as service, information, and convenience.
- The Internet gives consumers access to more information about costs and prices.
- A social network is a web-based meeting place for friends, family, co-workers, and peers that lets users create a profile and connect with other users for different purposes.

LO 13-4. Illustrate how businesses can use different types of social networking media.

- Internet users participate in blogs, wikis, social networks, media-sharing sites, virtual reality sites, mobile marketing, and applications and widgets.
- Marketers have begun investigating and experimenting with promotion on social networks, including Facebook and Twitter.
- Blogs answer consumer concerns and obtain free publicity, whereas wikis give marketers a better understanding of how consumers feel about their companies.
- Photo-sharing sites enable companies to share images of their businesses or products with consumers and often have links that connect users to company-sponsored blogs. Video sharing is allowing many businesses to engage in viral marketing. Podcasts are audio or video files that can be downloaded from the Internet with a subscription that automatically delivers new content to listening devices or personal computers.
- Companies are using the virtual world to gather information about consumer tastes and preferences as well as feedback on products.
- Mobile phones are also being used for communicating with consumers and conducting business, especially in the service industry.
- Apps can help consumers perform services and make purchases more easily; widgets can be used to inform consumers about company updates and can easily go viral.
- Consumers can be classified into one of seven categories depending on how they use digital media: creators, conversationalists, critics, collectors, joiners, spectators, and inactives.

LO 13-5. Identify legal and ethical considerations in digital media.

- The Internet and e-business have raised concerns such as privacy concerns, the risk of identity theft, online fraud, and intellectual property rights.

Practical Application

LO 13-1

- _____ are electronic media that function using digital codes and are available via computers, cell phones, smartphones, and other digital devices.
- _____ uses digital media to develop communication and exchanges with customers.
- _____ means carrying out the goals of business through the use of the Internet.

LO 13-2

- The Internet _____ the cost of communication and is therefore significant in industries such as entertainment, health care, and education.
- Digital media can be a(n) _____ backbone that helps store knowledge, information, and records in management information systems for the employees of a company.

LO 13-3

- The Internet has become a new _____ to make products available for people.
- A recent market research study reveals that people today spend more time on _____ than they do on _____.

- The aspect of marketing that still remains unchanged by the digital media is the importance of achieving the _____.

LO 13-4

- Some companies have started using _____ as internal tools for projects that require a lot of documentation.
- Marketers generally engage in _____ of their products on social networking sites.
- _____ read only online information and are the largest group in most countries.

LO 13-5

- _____ occurs when criminals obtain personal information that allows them to impersonate someone else in order to use the person's credit to access financial accounts and make purchases.
- _____ is a method of initiating identity theft fraud that is growing rapidly.
- _____ of content is a major intellectual property problem especially in the areas of software, music, movies, and videogames.

active review card
Accounting and Financial Statements

in a nutshell

The use of accounting information and the accounting process is important in making business decisions. Understanding simple financial statements and accounting tools is useful in analyzing organizations worldwide.

The following statements will test your take-away knowledge from this chapter. Do your best to explain each one in the space provided.

LO 14-1 Define accounting, and describe the different uses of accounting information.

LO 14-2 Demonstrate the accounting process.

LO 14-3 Examine the various components of an income statement in order to evaluate a firm's "bottom line."

LO 14-4 Interpret a company's balance sheet to determine its current financial position.

LO 14-5 Analyze the statement of cash flows to evaluate the increase and decrease in a company's cash balance.

Copyright © 2017 by McGraw-Hill Education ISBN 1259578143 | Ferrell M 5e

Did your answers include the following important points?

LO 14-1. Define accounting, and describe the different uses of accounting information.

- Accounting is the language businesses and other organizations use to record, measure, and interpret financial transactions.
- Financial statements are used internally to judge and control an organization's performance and to plan and direct its future activities and measure goal attainment.
- External organizations such as lenders, governments, customers, suppliers, and the Internal Revenue Service are major consumers of the information generated by the accounting process.

LO 14-2. Demonstrate the accounting process.

- Assets are an organization's economic resources; liabilities are debts the organization owes to others; owners' equity is the difference between the value of an organization's assets and liabilities.
- This principle can be expressed as the accounting equation: Assets = Liabilities + Owners' equity.
- The double-entry bookkeeping system is a system of recording and classifying business transactions in accounts that maintain the balance of the accounting equation.
- The accounting cycle involves recording transactions in a journal, posting transactions, and preparing financial statements on a continuous basis throughout the life of the organization.

LO 14-3. Examine the various components of an income statement in order to evaluate a firm's "bottom line."

- The income statement indicates a company's profitability over a specific period of time. It shows the bottom line, the total profit (or loss) after all expenses have been deducted from revenue.
- Major components of the income statement include revenue, expenses, and net income.

LO 14-4. Interpret a company's balance sheet to determine its current financial position.

- The balance sheet, which summarizes the firm's assets, liabilities, and owners' equity since its inception, portrays its financial position as of a particular point in time.
- Major classifications included in the balance sheet are current assets, fixed assets, current liabilities, long-term liabilities, and owners' equity.

LO 14-5. Analyze the statement of cash flows to evaluate the increase and decrease in a company's cash balance.

- The statement of cash flows explains how the company's cash changed from the beginning of the accounting period to the end.
- The change in cash is explained through details in three categories: cash from (used for) operating activities, cash from (used for) investing activities, and cash from (used for) financing activities.

Practical Application

LO 14-1

- A(n) _____ is an individual who has been state-certified to provide accounting services ranging from the preparation of financial records and the filing of tax returns to complex audits of corporate financial records.
- An internal financial plan that forecasts expenses and income over a set period of time is known as an organization's _____.
- A(n) _____ is a summary of the firm's financial information, products, and growth plans for owners and potential investors.

LO 14-2

- Trendy, an organization that specializes in hand-stitched clothes, owes money to its suppliers and to the Small Business Administration. The money owed is an example of Trendy's _____ .
- The system of recording and classifying business transactions in separate accounts to maintain the balance of the accounting equation is called _____.
- A(n) _____ is a book or computer program with separate files for each account.

LO 14-3

- The _____ is the amount of money the firm spent to buy and/or produce the products it sold during the accounting period.

- _____ is the process of spreading the costs of long-lived assets such as buildings and equipment over the total number of accounting periods in which they are expected to be used.
- The _____ shows the profit or loss once all taxes and expenses have been deducted from the revenue.

LO 14-4

- Short-term assets that are used or converted into cash within the course of a calendar year are also known as _____.
- _____ represents amounts owed to suppliers for goods and services purchased with credit.
- All unpaid financial obligations of a company are kept in the _____ account.

LO 14-5

- The _____ explains how the company's cash changed from the beginning of the accounting period to the end.
- Cash from _____ is calculated by combining the changes in the revenue accounts, expense accounts, current asset accounts, and current liability accounts.
- Cash from _____ is calculated from changes in the long-term liability accounts and the contributed capital accounts in owners' equity.

in a nutshell

The Federal Reserve Board and other major financial institutions play significant roles in the financial system. In understanding finance, you need to consider the definition of money and the forms money may take. You also need to consider the future of the finance industry and the changes likely to occur over the course of the next several years.

The following statements will test your take-away knowledge from this chapter. Do your best to explain each one in the space provided.

LO 15-1 Define money, its functions, and its characteristics.

LO 15-2 Describe various types of money.

LO 15-3 Specify how the Federal Reserve Board manages the money supply and regulates the American banking system.

LO 15-4 Compare and contrast commercial banks, savings and loan associations, credit unions, and mutual savings banks.

LO 15-5 Distinguish among nonbanking institutions such as insurance companies, pension funds, mutual funds, and finance companies.

LO 15-6 Investigate the challenges ahead for the banking industry.

Copyright © 2017 by McGraw-Hill Education ISBN 1259578143 | Ferrell M 5e

Did your answers include the following important points?

LO 15-1. Define money, its functions, and its characteristics.

- Money is anything generally accepted as a means of payment for goods and services. Money serves as a medium of exchange, a measure of value, and a store of wealth.
- To serve effectively in these functions, money must be acceptable, divisible, portable, durable, stable in value, and difficult to counterfeit.

LO 15-2. Describe various types of money.

- Money may take the form of currency, checking accounts, or other accounts.
- Checking accounts are funds left in an account in a financial institution that can be withdrawn without advance notice.
- Other types of accounts include savings accounts, money market accounts, certificates of deposit, credit cards, and debit cards as well as traveler's checks, money orders, and cashier's checks.

LO 15-3. Specify how the Federal Reserve Board manages the money supply and regulates the American banking system.

- The Federal Reserve Board regulates the U.S. financial system. The Fed manages the money supply by buying and selling government securities, raising or lowering the discount rate, raising or lowering bank reserve requirements, and adjusting down payment and repayment terms for credit purchases.
- It also regulates banking practices, processes checks, and oversees federal depository insurance for institutions.

LO 15-4. Compare and contrast commercial banks, savings and loan associations, credit unions, and mutual savings banks.

- Commercial banks are financial institutions that take and hold deposits in accounts for and make loans to individuals and businesses.

- Savings and loan associations are financial institutions that primarily specialize in offering savings accounts and mortgage loans. Mutual savings banks are similar to S&Ls, except that they are owned by their depositors.
- Credit unions are financial institutions owned and controlled by their depositors.

LO 15-5. Distinguish among nonbanking institutions such as insurance companies, pension funds, mutual funds, and finance companies.

- Insurance companies are businesses that protect their clients against financial losses due to certain circumstances, in exchange for a fee.
- Pension funds are investments set aside by organizations or individuals to meet retirement needs.
- Mutual funds pool investors' money and invest in large numbers of different types of securities, brokerage firms buy and sell stocks and bonds for investors, and finance companies make short-term loans at higher interest rates than banks.

LO 15-6. Investigate the challenges ahead for the banking industry.

- Future changes in financial regulations are likely to result in fewer but larger banks and other financial institutions.
- A growing trend is shadow banking, which refers to companies performing banking functions of some sort that are not regulated by banking regulators.

Practical Application

LO 15-1

- Trading one good or service for another of similar value is known as _____.
- When a dollar bill is handled hundreds of times and is still being used, it has _____.
- When inflation is very high, people no longer believe that money is _____.

LO 15-2

- Another name for a savings account is a(n) _____.
- In general, the longer the term of a certificate of deposit, the higher its _____.
- The acronym NOW, when used in financial circles, stands for _____.

LO 15-3

- To carry out its functions of controlling the supply of money, the Federal Reserve Board uses its _____.
- When the Federal Reserve buys securities, it _____.

LO 15-4

- If employees of a local school district conduct their financial business through the same financial institution that they own

and only they are allowed to join, the institution is probably a(n) _____.
- _____ are the oldest and largest of all financial institutions.
- The _____ was established in 1933 to help stop bank failures throughout the country during the Great Depression and has nearly 8,000 member institutions at present.

LO 15-5

- Insurance companies invest premiums from insured individuals and businesses or make short-term loans, particularly to businesses in the form of _____.
- _____ permits home computer users to conduct banking activities through their personal computers.

LO 15-6

- _____ is an increasing trend that may be concerning because it is not regulated by banking regulators.
- The future of the structure of the American banking system is largely in the hands of the _____.

in a nutshell

Companies use short-term assets to generate sales and conduct ordinary day-to-day business operations and short-term liabilities to finance business. They also use long-term assets such as plant and equipment and long-term liabilities such as stocks and bonds to finance corporate assets. Financial management depends on the management of these assets and liabilities as well as the trade of stocks and bonds.

The following statements will test your take-away knowledge from this chapter. Do your best to explain each one in the space provided.

LO 16-1 Describe some common methods of managing current assets.

LO 16-2 Identify some sources of short-term financing (current liabilities).

LO 16-3 Summarize the importance of long-term assets and capital budgeting.

LO 16-4 Specify how companies finance their operations and manage fixed assets with long-term liabilities, particularly bonds.

LO 16-5 Discuss how corporations can use equity financing by issuing stock through an investment banker.

LO 16-6 Describe the various securities markets in the United States.

Copyright © 2017 by McGraw-Hill Education ISBN 1259578143 | Ferrell M 5e

Did your answers include the following important points?

LO 16-1. Describe some common methods of managing current assets.

- Current assets are short-term resources such as cash, investments, accounts receivable, and inventory.
- Financial managers focus on minimizing the amount of cash kept on hand and increasing the speed of collections through lockboxes and electronic funds transfer and by investing in marketable securities.
- Marketable securities include U.S. Treasury bills, certificates of deposit, commercial paper, and money market funds.
- Managing accounts receivable requires judging customer creditworthiness and creating credit terms that encourage prompt payment.
- Inventory management focuses on determining optimum inventory levels that minimize the cost of storing the ordering inventory without sacrificing too many lost sales due to stockout.

LO 16-2. Identify some sources of short-term financing (current liabilities).

- Current liabilities are short-term debt obligations that must be repaid within one year, such as accounts payable, taxes payable, and notes payable.
- Trade credit is extended by suppliers for the purchase of their goods and services, whereas a line of credit is an arrangement by which a bank agrees to lend a specified amount of money to a business whenever the business needs it.
- Secured loans are backed by collateral; unsecured loans are backed only by the borrower's good reputation.

LO 16-3. Summarize the importance of long-term assets and capital budgeting.

- Long-term or fixed assets are expected to last for many years, such as production facilities, offices, and equipment. Businesses need up-to-date equipment to succeed in today's competitive environment.

- Capital budgeting is the process of analyzing company needs and selecting the assets that will maximize its value; a capital budget is the amount of money budgeted for the purchase of fixed assets.

LO 16-4. Specify how companies finance their operations and manage fixed assets with long-term liabilities, particularly bonds.

- Two common choices for financing are equity financing and debt financing. Long-term liabilities are debts that will be repaid over a number of years, such as long-term bank loans and bond issues.
- A bond is a long-term debt security that an organization sells to raise money. The bond indenture specifies the provisions of the bond contract—maturity date, coupon rate, repayment methods, and others.

LO 16-5. Discuss how corporations can use equity financing by issuing stock through an investment banker.

- Owners' equity represents what owners have contributed to the company and includes common stock, preferred stock, and retained earnings.
- To finance operations, companies can issue new common and preferred stock through an investment banker that sells stocks and bonds to corporations.

LO 16-6. Describe the various securities markets in the United States.

- Securities markets provide the mechanism for buying and selling stocks and bonds. Primary markets allow companies to raise capital by selling new stock directly to investors through investment bankers.
- Secondary markets allow the buyers of previously issued shares of stock to sell them to other owners. Major secondary markets are the New York Stock Exchange, the American Stock Exchange, and the over-the-counter market.
- Investors measure stock market performance by watching stock market averages and indexes.

Practical Application

LO 16-1

- A(n) _____ is an address for receiving payments from customers.
- _____ are short-term debt obligations that the U.S. government sells to raise money.
- Good financial managers minimize the amount of cash available to pay bills in _____.

LO 16-2

- A finance company to which businesses sell their accounts receivable, usually for a percentage of the total face value, is a(n) _____.
- The most widely used source of short-term financing is _____.

LO 16-3

- Plants, offices, and equipment are considered _____ assets.
- The process of analyzing the needs of the business and selecting the assets that will maximize its value is called _____.
- In general, the longer the expected life of a project or asset, the _____ the potential risk.

LO 16-4

- _____ are a sequence of small bond issues of progressively longer maturity.
- Items such as a bond's value, date, and rate are specified in the _____.
- A method of long-term financing that requires repaying funds with interest is _____.

LO 16-5

- The first-time sale of stocks and bonds to the public directly is called _____.
- If a company retains all of its earnings, it will not pay _____.
- Corporations usually employ an investment banking firm to help sell their securities in the _____ .

LO 16-6

- A(n) _____ is a network of dealers rather than an organized exchange.
- A(n) _____ compares current stock prices with those in a specified base period.